Garden of the Sun

Garden of the Sun

A History of
the San Joaquin Valley, 1772-1939

Wallace Smith

Edited and Revised by William B. Secrest, Jr.

Linden Publishing

Fresno CA

GARDEN OF THE SUN
A History of the San Joaquin Valley, 1772-1939
2nd Edition

by
Wallace Smith

Edited and revised, with additions, by
William B. Secrest, Jr.

This edition copyright ©2004 Linden Publishing Inc.

35798642

ISBN: 0-941936-77-5

Cover design by James Goold
Cover Photography by Scott Hayden

Printed in the United States of America

Library of Congress Cataloging-in-Publication Data

Smith, Wallace, 1895-1963
    Garden of the sun : a history of the San Joaquin Valley, 1772-1939/
by Wallace Smith ; edited by William B. Secrest, Jr. -- 2nd ed.
        p. cm.
Includes bibliographical references (p.) and index.
    ISBN 0-941936-77-5 (hardcover : alk. paper)
    1. San Joaquin Valley (Calif.) -- History. I. Secrest, William B., 1930-
II. Title
F868.S173S56 2004
979.4'8--dc22

                                                          2003020898

A Craven Street Book
Linden Publishing Inc.
2006 S. Mary
Fresno, CA 93721 USA
tel 800-345-4447
www.lindenpub.com

To My Parents

who have sowed their youth and strength in helping to develop the San Joaquin Valley in order that their children might reap a more abundant life this book is affectionately dedicated.

Wallace Smith

Contents

Preface

The original inhabitants of the San Joaquin Valley were the Yokuts and the Miwok Indians. An abundance of game, seeds, and roots made existence relatively easy for the aborigines. The first Europeans to enter this region were deserting Spanish soldiers from San Diego. Pedro Fages, who went in search of them, reached this interior valley in 1772 and was the first man of any race or color to make a written report of the San Joaquin.

Although the Spaniards entered the valley at this early date, they failed to make any permanent settlements there. The reasons are many. The ocean served as a highway from Mexico to California and the early settlers naturally located along the coast, where supplies were available. The salubrious climate of the seaboard was preferred to the hot summers of the interior valley. Then, too, the Indian menace retarded development of the San Joaquin for almost a century.

Nevertheless, the San Joaquin Valley soon became well known. During the Spanish period the Franciscan friars and the military forces cooperated in sending more than a score of expeditions into the valley in search of neophytes and suitable mission sites. After Mexico secured control of California, the missions were secularized and the Franciscans perforce ceased their exploration of the interior. But disorders on this Indian frontier resulted in military operations that continued down to the American occupation.

In Mexican days the officials of California were frequently annoyed by foreign intruders into the San Joaquin. Peter Skene Ogden and John McLeod led Hudson's Bay men into the valley; bands of fur traders from the United States, under such men as Smith, Young, and Walker trapped beaver on every stream between Stockton and Grapevine Pass. General John C. Fremont followed afterward with his topographical engineers.

Soon the Mexican soldier was succeeded by the Mexican settler. The first permanent home in the San Joaquin was made by José Noriéga in 1836. The land lying west of the Coast Range had now been occupied, and the increase in population caused men to venture into the Indian-infested region to the east. This penetration from the coast continued steadily for a decade. Paradoxically enough, the white men continued the westward march across the New World by going east. From 1836 to 1846 the Mexican governors of California made thirty land grants in the valley. The ranch homes established by these Spanish-California grantees in the San Joaquin represented much expenditure of labor, disbursement of money, and sacrifice of life.

The coming of the Americans, the discovery of gold, and the growth of coastal cities now sent men surging into the San Joaquin Valley. The demand for beef caused a rapid growth of ranching on the valley floor. The search for gold resulted in a sudden influx of miners into the adjacent foothills. The Indians soon were outnumbered and subdued.

The early trails of the Indians, padres, and Spanish soldiers were replaced by roads. Prairie schooners and stagecoaches, in turn, were soon supplanted by railways. The coming of the Iron Horse stimulated wheat growing. By 1882, the San Joaquin Valley was the famed land of bonanza wheat fields and thirty-six-mule harvesters.

Like other frontiers, the San Joaquin was troubled by outlaws. But brigand chiefs and their followers were finally dispersed, and their glamorous deeds are now but a fading memory. Although permanent settlers were late in arriving in the valley, it was effectively occupied within a half century after the first white man had located there.

War with the Indians engrossed the attention of the American pioneers for a decade after the United States acquired California. During the same years came the organization of the first counties, which were subdivided, from time to time in subsequent years.

A unique feature of expansion in the San Joaquin was the planting of colonies after the fashion of those planted in earlier times along the Atlantic seaboard. The founding of these colonies led to thickly populated centers where intensive farming became the vogue. The light rainfall and the fertility of the soil resulted in extensive irrigation projects, and horticulture either supplanted or augmented cattle raising and wheat growing.

The discovery of oil has been a significant factor in the recent development of the valley. The factory system, with its consequent industrialization of urban centers, created a demand for this commodity. The invention of oil-burning machinery resulted in an active search for oil comparable to the search for gold of an earlier day.

The organization of various forms of cooperative marketing associations has attracted nationwide attention. In spite of the comparative success of many of these ventures, much yet remains to be done in this field of endeavor. Cooperation made possible the early development of the San Joaquin Valley as it passed through, to paraphrase Bancroft, the various stages of game, grazing, gold, grain, and grapes; cooperation alone will make possible its continued growth and prosperity.

The San Joaquin Valley has been the scene of many heroic episodes and stirring deeds. No section of a similar area in the United States can show a greater variety of happenings. The men and the women who have made possible the horticultural paradise known to its residents as the Garden of the Sun are worth remembering. Thoughtful students of life approve Thomas Babington Macaulay's dictum: "A people that take no pride in the noble achievements of remote ancestors will never achieve anything worthy to be remembered with pride by remote descendants."

Personal interviews with men and women of an older generation have convinced me that, while they may never have heard of Jonathan Swift, their philosophy of life has been very similar to that of the caustic English Dean who wrote:

> And he gave it for his opinion, that whoever could make two ears of corn, or two blades of grass, to grow upon a spot of ground where only one grew before, would deserve better of mankind, and do more essential service to his country, than the whole race of politicians put together.

Still dwelling in our midst, but shrinking day by day, is a group of men and women who knew the San Joaquin Valley during primeval years. They have now ceased to harvest in the Garden of the Sun, but they are still able to lead the honest searcher after truth to the far fields of memory, from whence he will come back with his heart full.

W. S.,   1939

Editor's Note

The story behind Garden of the Sun and its author has never appeared in previous editions of the book, and on this occasion—its first reprinting in a generation—a few words on the subject are appropriate, if not overdue.

Wallace Paul Victor Smith was born in Centre City, Minnesota, on May 2, 1895. He was the son of Robert Gustaf and Minnie Smith and the eldest of their five children. In spite of the surname, he was entirely Swedish in ancestry. His maternal grandparents wished to Americanize their surname of Anderson and changed it to Smith, while his father—whose original name was Lofgren—opted for the same change to honor his pater familias, who was a blacksmith.

The Smiths were encouraged to relocate to California by their family minister, Rev. G.E. Kallstedt of the Swedish Methodist Church, who was transferred to Kingsburg sometime around the turn of the century. They reportedly all carried train passes permitting them to return to

Minnesota within a year, if they disliked Kingsburg; but these were never used, and in 1906 the family put down new roots on a farm 3 1/2 miles east of town.

Wallace Smith attended the Kingsburg-area schools, notably Kings River School in Tulare County. In later years, he vividly remembered finishing second in his class (not difficult, as it consisted of only two students) and having to commute to the school by boat for an entire year. The school was located on the side of Kings River opposite from the Smith farm and Kingsburg, and when the easiest access point (a bridge) was washed away in a flood, the easiest way to reach it was by rowboat.

In 1913 Smith graduated from Kingsburg High School. He subsequently attended the University of California (Berkeley), where his studies were interrupted by World War I and service at different domestic U.S. Army facilities. He graduated with a bachelor's degree in 1919 and went on to pursue advanced graduate studies at Cal's history department under the tutelage of noted professors Herbert Eugene Bolton and Herbert Ingram Priestley. By 1927 he had secured a master's degree, with the subject of his thesis being the Spanish exploration of the San Joaquin Valley. The year 1932 saw the awarding of his doctoral degree. The title of his dissertation was "The Development of the San Joaquin Valley, 1772-1882"; in revised and expanded form, this would become the book we know today as Garden of the Sun. (The title, though apt, seems to have been borrowed from a Fresno County Chamber of Commerce slogan of yore.)

At different times Smith served as the vice principal and principal of Kingsburg High School, eventually became a social science instructor at Reedley College and, by the late 1940s, was a professor at Fresno State College (now California State University, Fresno). He was also active in the Kingsburg Chamber of Commerce and American

Legion, and was a sometime fruit grower and fancy chicken raiser. But it is unquestionable that his greatest fame rests on Garden of the Sun. It remains the only history of the San Joaquin Valley ever written, and is thus a basic item of California historical literature. The book also benefits from having been written with a true storyteller's eye for unusual and revealing detail. As his obituary in the Fresno Bee stated, "He wrote as he talked—easily, freely and with grace and charm and understanding." This, as much as the uniqueness of Garden of the Sun's place among Californiana, accounts for the enduring popularity of Smith's writings.

It is of some interest to note that Garden of the Sun acted as the springboard for Smith's only other full-length book. Prodigal Sons, published in 1951, is the best and fullest account of the careers of Chris Evans and John Sontag, who were accused of robbing trains throughout the San Joaquin Valley in the early 1890s. A much-abbreviated account of the men can be found in a Garden of the Sun chapter, also entitled "Prodigal Sons."

While at Fresno State College Smith served as an inspiration to a new generation of local historians; among his students were Cathy Rehart and William Secrest, Sr. They both confirm his considerable powers as a lecturer, and note his tendency toward the sentimental— something that can be seen in Garden of the Sun's frequent snatches of poetry and classical prose. Cathy Rehart recalls that when he gave the final examination for his American history class, he asked all the students to wait in their seats and not leave when the time period was up. When it expired, Smith brought forward a record player and had everyone listen to "Home on the Range." He wept throughout the performance, and when it was over, solemnly shook hands with every student who exited the room.

After teaching for fifteen years at FSC, Smith
unexpectedly died of a heart attack on May 17, 1963.
While he had been a Fresno resident for some years at
that time, in death he returned to the town of his boyhood
and youth, and is interred at the Kingsburg Cemetery.

***

The first edition of Garden of the Sun, published by a
small regional concern in Los Angeles (Lymanhouse),
appeared in 1939. It was bound in a smooth, medium
brown cloth and was apparently limited to 500 copies. A
subsequent printing appeared in the same year, bound in
a white-gray cloth—quantity unknown—with a dust
jacket blurb remarking on the brisk sales of its
predecessor. An egregiously incomplete 3-page index,
absent from the first press run, was tacked onto this
edition; it is sometimes bound in the front of the book, and
sometimes in the back. Subsequent editions feature a
different and more complete index, compiled by unknown
hands and reproduced from a typescript. It would seem
that the first version was compiled hastily, perhaps to
quell complaints that the editio princeps lacked an index
altogether.

No one can be certain of the number of times Garden of
the Sun has been reprinted, but the available evidence
attests to its continued popularity. A statement on the
verso of one title page refers to an "Eighth Edition," but it
is probable those responsible for publication confused the
meaning of "printing" and "edition." The point is
somewhat sticky, in any event; when the book was
reprinted during Smith's lifetime, he periodically added
appendices of new material and revised small sections of
the text. As a consequence, practically all the earlier
printings/editions of the book exhibit variation between
their contents. After his death, the book appears to have

stabilized at a length of 567 pages, with a total of 20 appendices. Given the variations in binding, presswork and paper quality, it seems safe to conclude that the book has undergone at least eight separate printings—and perhaps more. By any reckoning, that is a measure of remarkable success for a regional history work, few of which proceed past a reprinting or two.

After the two Lymanhouse editions, Fresno printer Max Hardison took over as Garden of the Sun's publisher. The last two printings (or thereabouts) of the book were made under the imprint of California History Books, operated by Hardison's friend and sometime business associate, the late Frank Foster. Since his demise, no one has kept the book in print, and its price has ascended to ever-increasing levels. One prominent motivation for this new edition is that quite ordinary Garden of the Sun reprints now command $75 or more on the used book market, with the Lymanhouse editions costing double or more that price.

In preparing this new edition, my first aim has been to keep Wallace Smith's original text and emendations intact, to the greatest extent possible. At the same time, I have felt it necessary to introduce certain changes in the interest of readability, accuracy and adequate documentation.

While Garden of the Sun is largely accurate, the first edition and its progeny all contain a long litany of small errors. Compounding this problem is the fact that Smith was fairly sparse in documenting his text, and the book has far fewer footnotes than it needs. To address these problems I have fact-checked every line of the original, throwing out some dubious or patently false statements, and correcting a legion of small misstatements. By making recourse to Smith's doctoral dissertation, I was able to confirm many sources that went unheralded in Garden of the Sun, and have restored this information via footnotes. The numbering system for these has been changed from the original, with many more passages documented when possible. Un-bracketed footnote texts are Smith's, while bracketed ones are mine.

Along with Garden of the Sun's initial index and footnotes, the abbreviated bibliography presented by Smith was woefully inadequate, especially for those wishing to ascertain additional reading. Fortuitously, there was—and has been—an easy remedy for this defect. The bibliography appended by Smith to his doctoral dissertation describes his sources at considerable length, and features detailed annotations. Consequently, I have placed an amended version of that bibliography in the back of this revised edition, as a far superior substitute to what has hitherto been used. It attempts to list every source Smith is known to have consulted in researching and writing Garden of the Sun.

Much of the material Smith added in appendix form rightfully belongs in the main narrative; unfortunately, he was hindered in making massive textual changes, for they would have disrupted the book's pagination and indexing scheme. Since the present edition has been typographically reset, there was no need to preserve the pre-existing order, and I have integrated all this material into the body of the work. The sole exceptions have been appendix material of obvious supplementary character (such as the lists of Indian tribes and land grants), and appendix material contributed by authors other than Smith himself. These have been retained as discrete units at the end of the book.

I have alluded to the fact that Smith made numerous minor cut-and-paste changes to Garden of the Sun's chapters. Most were of minor character, introduced to rectify or amplify certain statements (and calculated to avoid gross discrepancies in pagination); however, in at least one instance (Chapter 1) the text was substantially rewritten for later editions, and is quite different from the initial version. Since much of this deleted material was factually sound, I have restored it—and so long as the other, later modifications have been accurate, I have allowed them to stand.

Attentive past readers of Garden of the Sun have no doubt noticed that some information is repeated in places, and the book does suffer from lackadaisical copy-editing. I have sought to eliminate these problems by consolidating and reshuffling numerous blocks of text, and moving the position of one chapter (XIV) to better fit in with the book's overall chronological sequence. For the most part these changes have been sequential and not literary; I have tried to leave the words, sentences, and syntax as undisturbed as possible.

It is my hope that readers of the earlier editions of Garden of the Sun will open this book and find a text greatly improved as to accuracy and readability, but with the captivating voice of Wally Smith intact and very much alive. May it also serve to introduce a new generation to one of Californiana's enduring classics.

William B. Secrest, Jr.

September 15, 2003

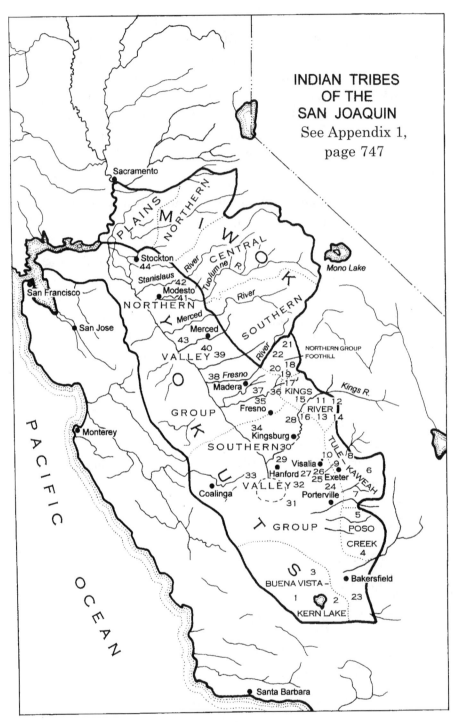

INDIAN TRIBES
OF THE
SAN JOAQUIN
See Appendix 1,
page 747

1

Redskins

Lo, the poor Indian! Whose untutored mind
Sees God in clouds, or hears Him in the wind.
His soul, proud Science never taught to stray
Far as the solar walk, or milky way;
Yet simple Nature to his hope has given,
Behind the cloud-topt hill, an humbler heaven;
Some safer world in depth of woods embraced,
Some happier island in the watery waste,
Where slaves once more their native land behold,
No fiends torment, no Christians thirst for gold.
To be, contents his natural desire,
He asks no Angel's wing, no Seraph's fire;
But thinks, admitted to that equal sky,
His faithful dog shall bear him company.

—Alexander Pope, *An Essay on Man*, Epistle I.

"Who is your dog?" This was the accepted form of
salutation in the San Joaquin Valley in the days when the
world was young and the Yokuts Indians held the valley
floor from Bakersfield to Stockton.[1]

The other tribe to share the valley with the Yokuts

Indians were the Miwok; the latter controlled the foothill area from Fresno River north into the Sacramento Valley and held the northern border lands of the San Joaquin Valley floor.

The word "Yokuts" is both singular and plural in form; hence it is proper to say "one Yokuts" or "several Yokuts." The word Miwok (Mee-walk), to confuse and complicate the terminology, is likewise singular and plural in form; therefore we are obliged to say "one Miwok" and "several Miwok." The Spanish referred to the valley Indians as Tulareños. The bulrushes growing along the streams and the lakes were called tules; the places where the tules grew were therefore the tulares, and the natives became tulareños, or dwellers in the tulares.[2]

Of these two distinct tribes more is known about the Yokuts; the Miwok were nearer the white men's point of entry and the coming of the white man decimated the Miwok, as later it did to the other aborigines. Being the first of the Valley Indians to meet the white man, the Miwok were the first to experience a severe population decline. Their losses were so severe that anthropologists find it difficult to reconstruct their history.[3]

In attempting to determine the population of the Yokuts in their heyday, famed anthropologist A.L. Kroeber of the University of California used 400 as a fair average number for each of the 50 tribes. In the Spanish exploration of the San Joaquin Valley the outstanding figure was Gabriel Moraga. In 1806 he visted many of the tribes in the valley and estimated that each averaged 280 in number. But he did not visit them all. Using 350 as a basis of computation, which makes allowance for the first figure as well as Moraga's estimate, Kroeber placed the Yokuts population at 17,500 souls when the first white man arrived on the scene. The statistics available at the

2

Indian woman splitting acorns at unidentified location, circa 1900.
Owen C. Coy, *Pictorial History of California.*

missions are of no aid as they merely listed the total at
the mission at any one time.[4]

Many of the Indians north of Fresno River were early
removed and missionized; this caused their almost
complete extinction as separate entities. Those south of
Fresno River melted away because their territory was
easily accessible to the white man. The Yokuts held one-
eighth of California and their patrimony was the best part
of the state. The white man wanted the birthright of his
weaker brother and he took it. In return he gave to "Lo,
the poor Indian" a mess of pottage which contained war,
disease, and death.[5]

The Yokuts were not the first human beings to occupy the
San Joaquin Valley. In the autumn of 1949 a rancher,
operating a bulldozer on his land along Kings River a few
hundred yards east of Highway 99, was amazed when he
began to unearth great quantities of human bones. He

3

possessed enough intellectual curiosity and interest to refrain from further operations until Professor Kroeber could be notified. The latter, by then on the retired list, sent some of his younger colleagues to examine the field and make a report. From artifacts, weapons, and skeletal remains, the conclusion was that the people buried there were not Yokuts, but a group which had occupied the Kings River area some ten thousand years ago.[6]

Unlike all other California Indians, the Yokuts were divided into true tribes. By this is meant that each group had a definite name, a distinctive dialect, and a specified territory. However, their tribal dialects were not so differentiated that social intercourse was prevented; neither did they need to resort to the sign language. A Yokuts from Bakersfield could readily converse with one from Stockton. The chief distinction between the foothill and valley Yokuts was linguistic rather than residential or ethnic. But even there the language differences were slight. A Yokuts could visit any one of the 50 tribes and get along without an interpreter.

Topography caused a greater variation in Yokuts foothill speech. The Indians had entered the interior from the mouth of the San Joaquin River. Hence the farther away the tribes settled from this point of radiation, the greater their divergence in speech. Due to this fact and the proximity of the Shoshones, the Yokuts of the southern Sierra had the most distinctive dialect. The foothills along Kings River rise abruptly from the level plains; here the differences in the dialects of plains and hills Indians were sharply marked. North of the San Joaquin River, where it debouches from the foothills into the valley, the transition from plains to hills is more gradual, and so was the difference in speech. Because the hill tribes could do little travelling, and thus met few other Yokuts, and because they were on the Shoshone frontier,

4

where alien words were easily incorporated into their own speech, the greatest differences in Yokuts speech was found among them.

Linguistically and culturally the nearest relatives of the Yokuts were not found among any other California group, but among the Nez Perce Indians of Idaho, the tribe which produced the brilliant strategist and war leader, Chief Joseph, and his brother, Ollicut. How this can be, and why two groups, both relatively small tribes, should be found so far apart, is hard to explain, or even to believe.[7]

The Yokuts derived their name from the word "yokoch" which means "everybody" or "people." In structure the Yokuts language had a simple phonetic system, and did not contain a single prefix. Frank F. Latta, in his valuable biography entitled *Uncle Jeff's Story*, has recorded the following statement by Jefferson Mayfield:

> The language of the valley Indians was always interesting. Many of their words were imitations of the sound made by the things they were to represent. The word for squirrel was skee-til and was spoken sharply much as it is barked by the squirrel. The word for the little ground owl, or billy-owl, as we called it, was peek-ook, and they bobbed their heads like he does when they said it. If you are close to the billy-owl when he bobs his head you will hear him make a little sound like peek-ook. The word for water was il-lik, and always reminded me of the sound made by dripping water. The word for deer was hoey, and was, I believe, an imitation of the blowing snort of a startled deer. The word for snow was pun-pun. The words for ducks and geese were like the gabbling noise they make when feeding, wat-wats and la-la. The word for coyote was ki-yp, and I believe the Spanish got the word coyote from the Indians. Another word that might be confused with the Spanish is cholo. Cholo means white. We call the Spanish, or Mexicans, cholos. I believe we did this because when we came here we heard the Indians calling them cholos, or whites. The word for hawk was swoop. The word for sleep

was wawh-yen, and it almost made me yawn to hear them
say it.[8]

Before the coming of the white men the Yokuts were
composed of approximately 50 tribes; of these, 45 can be
located with reasonable accuracy. For the reader who is
interested in the names and locations of the various so-
called tribes, an accompanying map and Appendix I of this
book will provide the necessary information.

Five groups composed the foothill division of the Yokuts.
The southernmost of these groups consisted of three
tribes. The Tulamni Indians had their village on the west
shore of Buena Vista Lake at the point where the Coast
Range foothills come close to the lake. In their
peregrinations in search of food the Tulamni ranged as far
west as the present site of McKittrick.

The second tribe of this group was the Hometwali, whose
name was derived from a term meaning "southerners."
They resided along the banks of the channel which
connects the two lakes of Kern and Buena Vista, and at
the point where Kern River empties into this channel.
They were also to be encountered along the shores of
Kern Lake.

The now-extinct Tohohai tribesmen spent their time along
the tule sloughs of the lower Kern River where it loses
itself in Tulare Lake. From this point they went on
expeditions as far from home as Goose Lake.[9]

Two tribes composed the Poso Creek group: the Paleuyami
and Komechesi. The Paleuyami tribe had its chief village
at Altau (the salt grass place), just south of Poso Creek.
Other centers of population were in Linn's Valley and at
Poso Flat. These Indians roved over the territory north of
Bakersfield.[10] The Komechesi centered around the White
River. Their habitat lay between Earlimart and California
Hot Springs. Many of the Komechesi Indians were

bilingual due to contact with the Shoshone Indians. The latter occupied all of California east of the Sierra Nevadas; they were the red men encountered in Owens Valley, Death Valley, and the Mojave Desert. From these districts they had swung south and west until they occupied southern California and a part of the coastal plain. Evidence exists to prove that they modified the language of both the Yokuts and the Miwok Indians. A mixture of blood also occurred along the border, especially between the Komechesi, the Bancalache Yokuts, and the various Shoshone sub-tribes.[11]

The Tule-Kaweah group was composed of five tribes. The Yaudenchi held the North and Middle forks of the Tule River and spent their winters around Springville. This region lies due south of Sequoia National Park and north of the Tule River Indian Reservation. In spring and early summer the Yaudenchi went on seed gathering excursions into the Lindsay country and in the autumn they cooperated with their neighbors in hunting elk around Porterville. Cooperation is a live issue among the ranchers of the San Joaquin Valley in the present era and this hunting of elk is one of the earliest recorded instances of organization for mutual aid.[12]

Fishing was another source of income. If there was drought or starvation in the land, and the correlation between these two conditions is apparent, the Yaudenchi travelled as far west as the southern shore of Tulare Lake in search of tule roots. Being observed at work in such a task may have occasioned the contemptuous term "Digger Indians." On these journeys they were outside of their own territory, but all the Yokuts south of the Kaweah River were on friendly terms and they ranged one another's territory freely and without fear. The only exceptions were the Wowol and Chunut tribes of the Tulare Lake area who were inclined to be more than

7

The Chowchilla River, as it appeared to the Pacific Railroad Survey in the 1850s, and much as it would have appeared to the San Joaquin Valley's earliest residents. *Pacific Railroad Surveys*, volume V.

ordinarily combative. The Yuadanchi were also called the Nuchawayi which probably explains why Father Garces referred to them as the Noche Indians when he visited them in 1776. This term meant "easterners" or "uplanders."[13]

The second tribe of the Tule-Kaweah group was the Bokenwadi who visited Garces, also in 1776, and whom he called the Pagninoas. Their tribal custom of never returning "lost and found" articles is the basis for their designation as Bokenwadi. The word "bok" meant "to find" and their theory was "finders keepers, losers weepers." This attitude is not to be confused with theft. Numerically they were a much smaller tribe than the neighboring Yuadanchi. Some of them resided on the southern fork of the Tule River in the region now included within the present Tule River Indian Reservation due east of Pixley and Terra Bella and north of California Hot Springs. Other members of the Bokenwadi tribe had their habitations along Deer Creek as far up this stream as Deer Creek Hot Springs. At this point the Shoshones of the trans-Sierra region were encountered and thus one of the smallest of the Yokuts tribes held the pass against one of the largest of the alien groups. That the aggressive and numerically powerful Shoshones never succeeded in an effective penetration into the valley area proves that the Bokenwadi performed their duty as a "buffer state" not unworthily.

The third tribe of the Tule-Kaweah group was named the Wikchamni which was based on an opprobious term meaning "gluttons." In the summer they hunted in the hills north of the Bokenwadi tribe and in the winter they moved down along the Kaweah River and occupied the foothills east of Visalia.

The Yokod tribe also made the Kaweah River the center of their life but farther down the stream than the Wikchamni Indians. The former usually stayed on the south side of the river and considered the Exeter district their hunting grounds. In their summer expeditions they moved over a greater territory and often went as far south as Lindsay, where they met and fraternized with the Yaudenchi coming up from the Springville country.

The Kaweah River received its name in honor of the Kawia tribe. These people dwelt north of the stream directly across from the Yokod tribe and considered their northern boundary to be Colvin Hill on Rattlesnake Creek. They hunted in the Woodlake region and went as far as Yettem. When Garces visited them in 1776 he named them the Coguifa Indians.[14]

The Indians living north of the Tule-Kaweah group were more pugnacious and distrustful than those to the south. Like the Goths of north Europe, they frequently invaded the more peaceful south for purposes of plunder and glory. The nearest neighbors of the Tule-Kaweah group to the north were the Kings River Yokuts. The largest of these was the Choinimni tribe. Because these Indians occupied

9

a region not easily accessible to the white man the Choinimni still remain the most numerous of their group. Their chief town was at the mouth of the Mill Creek on the south side of Kings River. Its name was Tishechu and means "at the gate." The Choininini held the northern outposts of the Yokuts in the foothills. On the north side of the Middle Fork of Kings River, in that territory where are located Dinkey Creek, Pine Ridge, and Shaver Lake, the natives were the Wobonoch branch of the Mono tribe, Shoshonean Indians who came over the crest of the mountains from Owens Valley. The Choinimni held the eastern outpost a few miles above Mill Creek.[15]

The nearest friends and relatives of the Choinimni were the members of the Michahai tribe who resided on the north side of Mill Creek, at a mountain meadow village called Heshinau at the foot of the pine covered ridge.[16]

A third tribe was the Chukaimina, which ranged the northern and eastern hills of the circular Squaw Valley. Their chief village was about six miles from the mountain meadow of the Michahai Indians; this may seem as if they were close neighbors but six miles is a considerable distance in rugged mountains such as are found there. The Chukaimina hunted and fished along a small affluent of Mill Creek which flowed from the south.

The Indimbich had a village at Chit-atichi (meaning clover); this was on the banks of Mill Creek, near Dunlap. This tribe was numerically weak and relatively unimportant.

The Gashowu tribe occupied the region of Little Dry Creek which empties into the San Joaquin River and also along Big Creek which loses itself in the plains near modern Fresno. They had two important villages: Pohoniu, located on Big Dry Creek below Letcher, and Yokau, on Little Dry Creek in Auberry Valley.

The northern group of the foothill division was composed of five tribes. Those living farthest up the San Joaquin River were called Toltichi, the "stream people." The Mono Indians pushing across the Sierras from the east were their upland neighbors. The Toltichi, now extinct, had their village near what is now the site of the electric power plant beside Kerckhoff Dam. This is situated below the confluence of North Fork with the main channel.

Along the south bank of the San Joaquin River, from a point above Millerton and down toward the valley, was the tribal domain of the Kechayi Indians. Occupying a smaller territory on the opposite side of the river were the Dumna Indians. The Dalinchi tribe occupied the area drained by Coarse Gold Creek and a part of the Fine Gold Creek region.[17]

While the Dalinchi Indians held the drainage area of Coarse Gold, the creek banks were owned by the Chukchansi tribesmen. The latter held not only the banks of Coarse Gold Creek, which was an affluent of the Fresno River, but they also occupied Cottonwood and Picayune creeks, and settlements near what is now Bates. The Chukchansi was the frontier tribe of the Yokuts in the lower foothill region; across Fresno River to the north were a foreign people speaking a different language. They were the Miwok Indians. The latter sometimes penetrated the foothill district south of Fresno River and the Yokuts occasionally crossed, and settled, on the north side. Usually their relations were of a friendly nature.[18]

The southern group of the valley division consisted of thirteen tribes. The one making the farthest southern penetration was the Yauelmani. The members of this tribe had a village on Paso Creek (not to be confused with Poso Creek) below the Tejon ranch house. This village was named Tinliu, meaning "at the hole," and is responsible

11

for the appellation Tinlinin Indians. The Yauelmani tribe was numerous and has more survivors today than any other Yokuts tribe. Thirty miles north of Tinliu the Yauelmani had another village named Woilo, the planting or sowing place. This name is probably evidence of mission influence as the primitive or untrained natives did not cultivate the soil. Another race and another culture have caused a majestic city to rise on the site of the little, squalid Indian village of Woilo; this successor to Woilo is Bakersfield. From Woilo the Yauelmani Indians followed the Kern River up to the hills and often ranged over the plains as far north as White River, and into Bancalache territory. Their southern outposts were along the fringes of Shoshone territory; with the latter tribesmen they frequently intermarried.

The Koyeti tribe, now extinct, held the territory around Porterville and the region from this point toward Woodville and Tipton. They also concentrated in the sloughs of the 16 lower reaches of the Tule River.

When Fathers Garces (1776) and Cabot (1814) visited the tribesmen south of modern Tulare they referred to them as the Choinic Indians. They congregated in the sloughs and deltas of lower Kaweah River, probably along the Outside and the Deep Channels. Their kinsmen, the Wolasi, dwelt along the Cameron Channel, south of Farmersville.

The Visalia and Goshen region was the home of the Telamni tribe; during the Spanish exploration of the San Joaquin Valley these Indians were called Telame Indians and Garces at an earlier date referred to them as Telam, or Torim, Indians.[19]

The Choinok (the Choinic of Garces and Cabot) tribe of Tulare, the Telamni of Visalia and Goshen, and the Wolasi of Farmersville never passed north of Cross Creek without

Unidentified Indian group in Fresno County, circa 1900, with varying dress styles suggesting the extent of their assimilation. M. Theodore Kearney, *Fresno County, California and the Evolution of the Fruit Vale Estate.*

encountering the active hostility of the Nutunutu (or Notonoto) tribe. Cross Creek was considered a fixed tribal boundary and to cross it was an overt act of war. Cross Creek is the first stream encountered south of Kings River; the state highway crosses it between Traver and Goshen; it is one of the off-shoots of the Kaweah River. The warlike Nutunutu lived between Cross Creek and Kings River and most of them congregated in the vicinity of Armona, Hanford, and Kingston; this territory was then a mass of swamps, sloughs, and overflow lands. The white men made of this section of the valley great wheat fields which furnished the setting for *The Octopus*, the famous novel written by Frank Norris. One of the main villages was Chiau, due south of Kingston. Another was located along the south bank of Kings River near Burris Park, about five miles south of Kingsburg. Although they lived downstream from all the other Yokuts except the Tachi, their name Nutunutu was derived from the Yokuts word "not" meaning "up-stream."

The Wimilchi resided on the north bank of the lower part of Kings River where the towns of Lillis, Laton, and Riverdale are located. The Mexican land grant made to Manuel Castro in 1844 was located in their territory. The name of this grant was the Laguna de Tache Rancho and the meaning of this term was "the ranch by the lake of the Tachi Indians." Just why the word for the tribe and the ranch are spelled differently is unknown and perhaps unimportant; it should be noted, however. This land grant extended from Lanare on the west to Kingsburg on the east. The Tachi Indians lived west of Tulare Lake and were frequently encountered by the Spanish soldiers and padres from the coast missions. It was natural to associate their name with the land in the general vicinity of Tulare Lake. The Tachi Indians did not inhabit the Laguna de Tache grant but they nevertheless gave their name to it as they had a greater reputation than the Wimilchi who actually were its original owners.

Farther upstream along Kings River the members of the Wech-i-ket tribe ranged the river bottoms from Reedley to Centerville and out on the plains over present Sanger. Their chief village, Musahau, lay about three miles east of modern Sanger. The name of this rancheria meant "the sweathouse place." It was customary for Indians from many neighboring tribes to gather there once a year for a social time. After the white settlers arrived they also were wont to visit this village during this annual fair. Mono Indians from the Sierras and red men from Tulare Lake were among those present. Horse races were a common form of entertainment at a later date and a game similar to our polo was played. This tribe gradually died out until in 1938 only one woman remained and she was only a halfbreed Wech-i-ket.[20]

A Reedley rancher, Oscar Noren, has had a hobby for years of gathering Indian relics. His private museum, housed in an adobe building erected for that special purpose, contains a remarkable collection of baskets, utensils, weapons, and other equipment. Within a five-mile radius of his home he has picked up Russian, Venetian, and Hudson's Bay beads. The assumption is that the Russian beads were originally distributed at Fort Ross along the Russian River and eventually passed from hand to hand until some were secured by the Wech-i-ket Indians along Kings River. The Venetian beads were the trade beads of the Spanish and came from the coastal missions. The Hudson's Bay beads were carried south from the rendezvous headquarters of the French-Canadian trappers at French Camp, south of Stockton, where as many as four hundred and fifty courieur-du-bois met at their annual rendezvous. From this camp Peter Lebec would carry these trade beads with him as far south as Tejon Pass, where he would be destined to meet his last grizzly bear, and leave his life, his bones, and his name on the map.[21]

The Wowol tribe, the Bubal group referred to by the early explorers sent out by the Spanish, derived its name from the word "wowul" which means "standing." These Indians had a delightful custom of standing in rows and delousing one another when conditions warranted such a process. Their main village was located on an island near the east shore of Tulare Lake. From it they crossed to the mainland on tule rafts and gathered fuel from the willows growing along the outlets of the various streams which fed the lake. This island was later known as Atwells Island and during certain seasons, when the water of the lake receded, it ceased to be an island.

Another village was called Sukwutnu. These villages were located northwest and west of present-day Delano.

The tenth tribe in the southern division of the valley group was named the Chunut. The haunts of this people were in the Kaweah delta along Tulare Lake. They penetrated freely up the sloughs from the lake but refrained from incurring the wrath of the Nutunutu tribe by not going north of Cross Creek. They made excursions into the Corcoran region.

The northernmost of the three Tulare Lake tribes was the Tachi tribe, already referred to in connection with the *Laguna de Tache* land grant. Only a few survive of this tribe, originally among the largest of all the Yokuts tribes. In the *expedientes* issued by the Mexican governors, this tribe was mentioned as inhabitants of the Sanjon de San José. This water channel, known in modern parlance as Fish Slough, connects Tulare Lake with Kings River and in times of flood the water backs up this course into Fresno Slough and thence into the San Joaquin River.[22]

Fish Slough formed a natural barrier between the Tachi Indians and the Wimilchi tribe. The Tachi ranged from Fish Slough west to the Coast Range and hunted over what is now Pleasant Valley. The present sites of Coalinga, Kettleman, and Huron were once in their possession. In the summer they advanced into Nutunutu territory and gathered seeds in the Mussel Slough section and around Lemoore. This powerful tribe was apparently the only one which dared to invade Nutunutu hunting grounds; all others seemed to dread entering the section lying between Kings River and Cross Creek. The Tachi and the Nutunutu were apparently friendly with each other, although not on good terms with their other neighbors.

The Apiachi, not to be confused with the Apaches of the Southwest, lived east of Fish Slough, the outlet of Tulare

Lake during high water, but farther north than the
Wimilchi tribe. Murphy Slough seems to have been the
boundary line between these two tribes. The hunting
grounds of the Apiachi lay to the west of Kingsburg in the
general direction of Elkhorn, Caruthers, and Conejo.[23]
James H. Carson, a relative of Kit Carson, wrote an
article published in the *San Joaquin Republican* of
Stockton in February, 1852, concerning these Indians
whom he had visited some time previously:

> As I remarked before, the Notonotos and Apiachi tribes of
> the Tulares appear to be a distinct race from the Digger
> Indians and the Notonotos declare themselves to be the
> remnant of a great people. These Indians inhabit the shores
> of the lakes and north of Kings River and cultivate corn and
> vegetables. They also catch and dry fish, kill wild horses, and
> jerk their flesh and usually have plenty to eat. The great
> portion of them go into the settlements and towns during the
> summer and work, for which they get well paid. They then
> purchase blankets and clothing and but few of them go
> naked in the winter season. Their habitations also approach
> more toward civilization, being made of mats of woven tule
> and flags which are stretched on poles similar to the lodgings
> of our eastern Indians. Their lodgings also contain many
> mats on which they sleep. I have been several times at the
> rancherias and partaken of the hospitality of the Notonotos,
> which were situated on a point of land at a junction of Kings
> River and Tulare Lake. These Indians are intelligent,
> hospitable, and great friends of the white man, and the only
> Indians in California, perhaps, that have anything like
> recollections or traditions.

The northern group of the valley Indians consisted of ten
tribes. The Pitkachi manufactured salt from alkali and
the product had an unpleasant odor which caused them to
name it "pidik," their term for feces. Thus their tribal
name had an unpleasant connotation. The Pitkachi made
their home south of the San Joaquin River, around
Herndon and Sycamore Point and south over the low-lying

17

plains and swale where Fresno is now situated.

The Wakichi also resided south of the San Joaquin River, but farther up-stream than the Pitkachi. While much of their time was spent in the foothills they were distinctly of the valley group in a linguistic sense. They found their sustenance in the region of Pinedale, Friant, and El Prado.

On the flat plains surrounding Madera and along the banks of Fresno River was found the Hoyima tribe. They controlled the land between Fresno River and the San Joaquin. Their neighbors on the south side of the latter river were the Pitkachi; on the north side of the Fresno River they possessed bitter enemies in the Chauchila tribe, after whom the town of Chowchilla was later named. The Hoyima were unusually combative and frequently engaged the Chauchila and Chukchansi in mortal strife.[24]

The Chauchila tribesmen had a reputation as great warriors, and, on many occasions, they had proved their courage against both red men and white. They were more widely traveled than any of the other Yokuts, and many tribes, ignorant of their nearest neighbors, had heard of the Chauchila. Their tribal name was equated with "murderers," "cruel," and "aggressive," and their neighbors often made the name a bit stronger by defining it as "murderers." The Mojaves despised the Yokuts in general and had a contemptuous term for them; "the tule sleepers." However, they excluded the Chauchila from this category. The foothill occupancy of the Yokuts was sparse north of the Fresno River, and therefore the neighbors of the Chauchila to the east were the Miwok people, who were of another culture and language.[25]

The Chauchila is the last of the Yokuts tribes lying toward the north about whom there is much accurate information. The northern section of the San Joaquin

A highly romanticized view of the early San Joaquin Valley, as delineated by the Pacific Railroad Survey. The scenery is characteristic of the landscape, while the accouterments of the Indian on horseback are not. *Pacific Railroad Surveys*, volume V.

Valley was early the scene of missionary activity. Whole villages were transported to the Franciscan missions. Here was the rendezvous of the renegade neophytes, the scene of raids and battles, the mixing of tribes, and the resultant confusion. Into this region came the first settlers. Yokuts tribes occupied the right bank of the San Joaquin River from its source to its mouth; the west side of the valley from Buena Vista Lake to Mount Diablo was never permanently occupied by any tribe, with the one exception of the Tulamni tribesmen who lived along the west side of Buena Vista Lake and ranged as far as McKittrick and Buttonwillow. The Tachi went west of Tulare Lake during the wet season, but during the dry spell always moved east. Hunting and marauding bands of Yokuts occasionally entered the western half of the valley, a sort of "no-man's-land," but it was never effectively settled.

Today, the population of the San Joaquin is concentrated in the eastern half; the white man has in this respect imitated his red brother. The western half remains arid and the population sparse, although modern engineering skills and irrigation projects are now leading to great changes in the so-called west side. In the early days of the white man's occupation of California, cattle ranches and oil fields were the chief successful ventures. It was on the west side of the valley that Miller & Lux were to acquire a cattle kingdom. The runoff into the San Joaquin Valley of streams from the Coast Range is virtually non-existent; certainly negligible if measured in terms of cubic feet per second. Streams from the Sierra increase in volume of water from south to north. The density of the population in Indian days was closely related to the amount of second feet of water discharged by each stream; the same is true today! [26]

A northern neighbor of the Chauchila was the Noptinte tribe. Its members hunted along the plains and low foothills around Agua Fria, Mariposa, and Raymond.

The Tawalimni tribe received its name from the Yokuts word meaning "stone house" or "cave Indians." They made their home in caves along the banks of a river which is known today as the Tuolumne, the modern way of spelling this tribal name.

After the American occupation Knight's Ferry became one of the most bustling frontier places in the valley. Here were gathered Chinese miners, American gold hunters, gamblers of all nations, Spanish Californians, and Indians. The latter were chiefly of the Lakisamni tribe although neophytes of many tribal derivations fled to this region at an early date and effaced tribal characteristics to a great extent.

The land lying between Turlock and Merced was claimed by the Coconoon (Ausumne) tribe. The tribesmen made their permanent home along the Merced River and ranged along its banks from the foothills to its point of junction with the San Joaquin.

The northernmost of all the Yokuts were the Chulamni tribesmen, who ranged along the Calaveras River, hunted over the present site of Stockton, and made excursions as far west as Mt. Diablo.[27]

Miwok Indians occupied a part of the San Joaquin Valley. They were divided into the Lake, the Coast, and the Interior divisions. The Interior division, the only one coming within the scope of this chapter, was in turn divided into the northern, central, southern, and plains groups. Into the territory occupied by the Interior division entered the Spanish soldier, the friar, and the settler at an early date. Neophytes were secured, many of them absconded, expeditions were sent in search of them, gold miners arrived, and out of this swirl of many races resulted a destruction of tribal lines of demarcation.

In general, we know that the Miwok Indians held the foothill area from Fresno River north into the Sacramento Valley. On the valley floor they were the northern neighbors of the Chulamni tribe of the Yokuts around Stockton. The Miwok Indians penetrated farther into the Sierras than did the Yokuts. The latter disliked cold weather but the Miwok stayed close to the snow line all winter and when spring brought back "blue days and fair," they followed this receding snow line far into the mountains. The Shoshones from the east never succeeded in gaining a foothold in Miwok territory; the latter were supreme to the crest of the Sierras.[28]

The word Miwok, as with the word Yokuts, means people; one of their favorite streams was the Mokelumne. Miwok culture is imperfectly known. Their tribal organization was inferior to the Yokuts but their society was similar in its division into two totemically contrasted halves. Miwok women had more social privileges than Yokuts women and were admitted as spectators to the secret dances of the men. When a woman became a widow she would singe her hair and in other ways express her grief. The formal mourning period lasted for one month. The levirate was observed. Burial was preceded by cremation. Marriage between first cousins was repugnant to them. Business transactions were carried on with a currency of clam shell disks. Dance houses were built with the door always facing the east. The granary was an outside affair and typical of those in general use in California. The development of the San Joaquin Valley is indicated by the change from this Indian granary with a capacity of a few gallons to the white man's warehouse at Traver which held 30,000 tons at one time. The office of Miwok chief was hereditary and the Miwok had a tribal chief, a village chief, and each chief had a herald or messenger.[29]

The Yokuts continued their tribal life to a later date than did the Miwok and hence their organization is better known. Yokuts society was divided into two moieties named the Tohelyuwish and the Nutuwish. Every member in the tribe belonged to one or the other of these lodges. Marriage between persons of the same moiety was absolutely forbidden. Thus a form of religious taboo was introduced which prevented consanguinity. Any, and all other, lines of tribal cleavage were cut through by this social duality.

The Yokuts, like the Miwok, had hereditary chiefs. Since every village was divided into two moieties, each had a chief; thus, the Yokuts system reminds one of the dual kingship of the Spartans. Another official of the Yokuts was the clown with duties similar to that of the medieval court fool. He ridiculed that which was sacred and jeered those in authority. The clown held office for life but his office was not hereditary. A group of transvestite sexual perverts served as tribal morticians and enjoyed certain privileges. Personal inclination naturally determined who were to follow this occupation.[30]

The birth of a child was a great event in the lives of Yokuts parents. In most primitive societies the mother received no special attention, care or favors, and so it is interesting to learn that the Yokuts mother, by tribal law, was placed under certain restrictions for a specified time. She was forbidden to do any work, including cooking. She must not even touch any of her utensils. Truly amazing, and no doubt highly commendable in the estimation of modern men, was the care which was lavished on the husband and father. He, too, was required to rest, and for the same length of time as the mother. He was forbidden to hunt, and must not touch his tools or weapons. Both wife and husband were forbidden by tribal law to eat meat or other solid food. They enjoyed a sort of sabbatical leave with full pay, and their relatives and friends provided them with soup, stew, and mush. This enforced vacation continued in some Yokuts groups until the cord dropped from the child's navel; in other sub-tribes it was dependent upon other conditions, and might continue for months.[31]

Death and burial were solemn affairs. Custom required that the deceased be buried in his home village. If death occurred while absent from home the body was cremated and the ashes sent thither. Many of the Yokuts tribes cremated all their dead, although this rule was not universal among them. Close relatives of the dead abstained from eating meat for one month and professional mourners were employed. At the end of that period a festival of joy was held and the period of sorrow thus formally came to an end.[32]

Marriage was an informal affair. A boy usually presented

to the parents of the girl some beads, which served as an indication of intent to wed. Although descent was reckoned paternally, the new husband always went to reside with his parents-in-law. This arrangement usually was intended to exist for one year. Custom decreed that the son-in-law and mother-in-law exhibit mutual shame whenever they met. Tradition also demanded that neither one ever look at the other, and any conversation between them was absolutely taboo. Thus they solved the age-old mother-in-law problem! No rule forbade marriage within the same village, but usually the mate came from another community.

Polygamy was permissible, but never common since there was never any excess of women. The levirate was responsible for such polygamy as did exist. This institution seems to have been an attempt to face and solve a social problem in the days when there were no orphanages, pensions, or other forms of social security. Many an Indian with several wives and numerous progeny was condemned by misinformed white men as a lustful old billy-goat when actually Lo, the poor Indian, was merely obeying tribal law. This law, unchanging and irrevocable, did not consider a man his brother's keeper, but did hold him responsible for the support and care of that brother's widow and orphans. The man with the many wives may have been very unhappy about it, because it meant much more work in providing food and lodging for the extra dependents. In cases where several brothers died in battle, hunting accidents, or pestilence, the burden placed on the remaining brother must have been almost unbearable. However, someone had to care for the underprivileged. If all the brothers were to die simultaneously, the tribal council would designate other men to serve as Good Samaritans.[33]

Before the white men came, the Yokuts standard of value

was a string of shell disks; this wampum-like currency
came from the coast, and when long enough to wrap
around the hand one and one-half times was called a
"chok." Three choks equaled approximately one yard in
length, and was worth, even at the white man's trading
post, about $5. A bride usually sold for 100 choks, which
would mean a string of sea shell disks about 100 feet long.
Such a rope of shells was worth approximately $165.33 at
the trading post.[34]

The Yokuts enjoyed life and believed in the importance of
recreation and the play life. The game of darts enjoys a
great popularity today, but the Yokuts played it a long
time ago. They enjoyed throwing darts at a mark hidden
by a fence of brush. Foot racing was common in all
villages, and the champion was sent to other villages to
compete with their fastest sprinters. Strangely enough,
only the women played dice. The usual game was for two
women to play on each side, and they threw the dice on a
flat tray. Both sexes played the guessing game, which
involved holding a blanket with hands under it, and turns
were taken to guess in which hand a shell or bone or other
object was held. The skill shown in this game indicated
that the Yokuts were not in any sense sluggish mentally.
Football was played with five men to a team; a ball made
of wood and about five inches in diameter; with four
umpires, two to watch the goals and two in the field. Since
the men played in bare feet it is apparent that there
would be little punting. Instead they dug their toes under
the ball, and managed to toss it from fifty to sixty yards.
The goal consisted of two stakes about four feet high over
which the ball had to pass.

Indian shinny was played with curved sticks and a
wooden ball made from an oak burl. The clubs were cared
for as carefully as a modern golfer cherishes his clubs; in
appearance they resembled hockey sticks. The Yokuts

played this game aggressively, and were much rougher than modern players, but they had such splendid self-control that fights never developed. The goals were about four hundred yards apart and the game ended when one side scored. The game might be short; more likely it might last for five hours.

One Yokuts game, slightly resembling golf, involved two teams taking a ball from a specified point to some object, such as a tree or a rock, located about two hundred yards away, circling this object, and punting the ball back to the starting point, where it would be sunk eventually into a hole much like our modern golf cup. As soon as the ball was sunk, the team would repeat the performance and once again circle the course. When a team was three points ahead it was declared the winner. The umpire worked even harder than the players; he had to run the two hundred yards to the turning place, watch to see that the ball actually went round the specified object, and then run home to see that the ball was properly sunk into the hole.

The pole and hoop game was popular throughout aboriginal California. A slender pole, about ten feet long, was hurled at a disc, about eighteen inches in diameter, made of coiled bark held together with a slender willow shoot, with a hole in the center about three inches wide. This disc, rolled by a bowler past the man holding the pole, was the target. As this disc came spinning by like a wheel, the pole was supposed to be hurled at it; if the thrust went through the three-inch hole in the center, two points were scored. If the disc was hit, but merely knocked over, one point was scored. This game could go on indefinitely.[35]

The weapons of the San Joaquin Valley Indians were fairly good. The chief instrument of warfare and hunting was the bow and arrow. The bows were approximately three feet long and two inches thick and the curvature was reversed to increase the tension. The arrow was long, measuring from the tips of the fingers with one arm outstretched to the opposite shoulder. The Yokuts sometimes secured their bows from the mountain Indians. Little suitable wood for this purpose was to be found in the valley, though laurel was used on occasion. The mountain cedar was the customary material; constant anointing with melted deer marrow kept the bows from drying out in the hot weather. Jefferson Mayfield, a white man who lived with the Yokuts, has been quoted by F. F. Latta as follows:

> Bow making as well as arrow making and bead making, was understood by only a few individuals, even among the Monaches. I know that they used to take their bows to a certain bow maker in the mountains north of Sycamore Creek in order to have him repair or replace the sinew backing on them. The Monaches on Sycamore Creek and on Kings River, at least near us, did not know how to do it. I know too, that the Indians passed down the most of their arts from father to son and guarded their knowledge so closely that I am sure bow making was a trade. The word for bow was chah-lip and for arrow, too-yosh.[36]

Their bows were not as well made as the English long-bow nor were they the equal in skill to the best English archers. The latter used the Mediterranean form of arrow release while the Yokuts used the Mongolian method; in the latter type of archery the string is pulled back with a flexed thumb and the arrow held in the angle between the forefinger and the thumb. Aim was always hastily taken, the arrow drawn back quickly and released in a quick shot.[37]

The buildings of the Yokuts were of different types. The communal kawi had a steep pitch to its roof and was composed of one room with fireplaces arranged for each family residing in this communal hall. Usually ten families occupied one kawi. A shade porch ran along the entire length of the house. A second form was similar to an apartment house with a long series of separate rooms rather than one long hall. Along the lake shores the common type of house was either elliptical or conical and built of tules. The latter type of house was usually erected in rows like houses in a modern city.

A fifth type of Yokuts structure was a large, high-ridged house with two fireplaces and a door placed at each end. Another house, although not a dwelling place, was the shade porch which was merely a flat roof placed on four poles and used as a shelter on hot days. The seventh type was the sweat house, about fifteen feet in length, and comparable to a men's club. Here the men lounged, took the equivalent of Turkish baths, and then rushed pell-mell to the river for a cold shower. Some pioneers assert that the purpose of these baths was to purify their bodies after the bath-less winter months in order to insure successful spring hunting; wild animals have delicate nostrils and might easily be nauseated by vile odors.[38]

The Yokuts and Miwok Indians usually had an abundance and a variety of food; fish, fowl, gophers, rabbits, hares, pine nuts, acorns, lizards, grass seeds, and deer were generally available. Food was bountiful in variety rather than in abundance. If one source failed, they could usually fall back on other kinds of food. In other areas, if the bison, the caribou, or the salmon failed to appear at the proper time, famine was the inevitable result. This was never true in California. Elk, of the tule variety, and pronghorn antelopes were surrounded in long drives called taduwush. Certain men were delegated to shoot them, while other men kept the circle intact. On moonlit nights bears were shot from nests in oak trees while they fed on acorns. At night geese were confused by huge brush fires. Doves were snared by staking a live decoy outside a blind, and then smothered by the hunter's knee to prevent its frightening other possible quarry. Ground buckeye nuts with earth stamped into them were mixed with nademe leaves and thrown into the streams; this poisoned the water and caused the fish to float to the surface. The fish were then scooped up in baskets. This work had to be done rather quickly since the fish were not killed; merely paralyzed temporarily.[39]

Shallow cooking utensils were made of soap stone (steatite) and in these angleworms were stewed in their own fat, and eaten as we eat noodles. The Yokuts were the only Indians in California who would eat dogs; this was a common food among the Sioux Indians. Skunks were smoked to death in their burrows and their odor thus eliminated. All California Indians placed a taboo on coyotes, grizzlies, and all birds of prey or feeders on carrion. Grizzlies were hunted for their pelts rather than for their meat, but during the acorn season they were considered edible.

Pine nuts and acorns, especially the latter, were used to provide flour for bread making. These nuts were ground in mortars, which were usually merely natural pits in an outcropping of granite. Such a pit was used until it became too deep, when another hole in the granite would be selected. The pestle was usually a longish river boulder. Naturally the flour contained a great deal of granite grit, and the old-time Indians often had teeth worn nearly to the gums from chewing on bread which must have tasted slightly like a grindstone. What it did to the stomach is problematical.

On the plains portable mortars were necessary, and usually were made out of wood. Loose mortars of stone were occasionally found, but these were not made by the

Indians; they merely represented a lucky "find." The Indians declared that they were unable to make mortars, and, according to Kroeber, "attribute all stone mortar holes, in situ as well as portable, to the coyote, who employed an agency of manufacture that decency debars from mention."

The Yokuts stored their acorns in a so-called granary, as did the Miwok, which was placed outside their dwellings. This storage box was about the size and shape of the old-time food coolers in use in the San Joaquin Valley during the years immediately preceding World War I. These coolers, covered with wet burlap and placed in a back porch or under an umbrella tree in the backyard, filled a need where ice was not available and prior to the general installation of the modern electric refrigerator. The ordinary home kitchen refrigerator holds about as much food as the old time Yokuts granary.[40]

The Yokuts made boats (balsas) out of tules which resembled rafts. They were used to cross rivers and streams, and for fishing on Tulare Lake. They showed skill in making baskets, and coiled jar-like vessels with flat shoulders. Many of their cradles were so well made and artistic that they have become collectors' items. They used pipes for smoking which were made of wood, and rather short. Their pottery was crude, and blood was used for binding.[41]

The only domestic animal of the Yokuts was the dog. This explains why the term "dog" and "domestic animal" were synonymous. The particular animal in an Indian's totem (eagle or coyote) was considered his domestic animal, and hence literally "my dog." Therefore, when two Yokuts met for the first time the natural greeting was, "Who is your dog?" When Americans meet today they ask questions which are analogous and comparable when they inquire

about one's nationality, church affiliation, lodge membership, or political party alignment. A second form of Yokuts
greeting was, "You—where?" This was brief, concise, and
to the point. Handshaking and public osculation were
unknown. A mother would kiss her child, or two lovers
might exchange kisses, but this was always done in
private. One white man who lived among them for years
stated: "Neither did the Indians naturally shake hands.
They hugged each other about the shoulders like
Frenchmen."[42]

When boys reached the age of puberty they fasted for six
days under the direction of the medicine men. Very thin
acorn soup was the only nourishment permitted. Then
they were given a drink made from Jimson weed roots
(skunk cabbages), which had been crushed and soaked in
water for days. The Jimson weed flower, somewhat
resembling a lily, has an offensive smell, and the extract
made from its roots has a narcotic potency which induced
a drunken stupor with attendant visions. During the
ceremony the boys slept in the open and vomiting was
supposed to presage death. The purpose of this initiation
was to produce longevity, prosperity, and the ability to
dodge arrows.[43]

The tribal shamans, painted with long stripes of white
and red, arranged an annual rattlesnake ceremony
similar to the Hopi snake dance. The snake was teased
and allowed to hang by its fangs from the hand or thumb
of the shaman. After this display of immunity the
shamans were in a position to capitalize on the credulity
of the tribesmen from whom they would extract poison
from wounds which might possibly be inflicted at a later
date. Their logic of causality is hard for us to understand
as it violates our notions of cause and effect.[44]

The climate of the San Joaquin Valley made Indian dress

of less importance than among eastern Indians. The sharply defined seasons of the Atlantic seaboard influenced not only attire but also oratory. Climatic conditions made possible the sententious statement of a great Iroquois chieftain in his eventide of life: "I am an aged hemlock; the winds of an hundred winters have whistled through my branches and I am dead at the top." No California Indian ever said anything as beautiful as that. The Yokuts and Miwok approached the Iroquois or Algonquin Indians neither in striking metaphor nor in ornate apparel. The dandyism of the Sioux who wore his toga-like buffalo robes with the dignity of a Roman senator and the gorgeous head-dresses and artistically decorated leggings of the Iroquois were unknown in California. Along the upper reaches of the San Joaquin the sticky mud of the swamp was often applied to the body in cold weather. One very raw, foggy morning M. G. Vallejo met a naked Miwok Indian and the following conversation ensued:

Vallejo: Why don't you put on some clothes? It is too cold to go naked.

Indian: Is your face cold?

Vallejo: No, but it is used to being bare.

Indian: Well, I am all face.[45]

The Yokuts generally wore rabbit-fur blankets in cold weather. In summer they wore an apron consisting of a buckskin strip a foot wide, and about three and a half feet long. A belt was placed around the waist, the buckskin was inserted between the belt and body in front, then down between the legs and up behind the back and left hanging down over the belt. The larger part of the buckskin apron was left hanging in the rear of the wearer. From a front or rear view it would appear to the casual observer that the Indian thus attired was wearing an ordinary kitchen apron in front and another behind. Moccasins of elk or deer skin were used only on long journeys; occasionally sandals were made of bear skin; but around camp everyone went barefooted.[46]

The coming of the new race caused the sun of the Indian to set while it was still day. New modes of living and new diseases were introduced simultaneously. Soon the Indian was "obliterated into oblivion." Cholera killed hundreds of Tulareño Indians in one season; smallpox was always disastrous; syphilis made frightful inroads; and the Spanish influenza took a heavy toll. Perhaps the latter was aggravated by the Indian mode of dress in cold weather. Add to the foregoing conditions the introduction of liquor, multiply the effect by lack of medical aid, and the answer will explain the subtraction of the Indian from the valley of the San Joaquin:

> They fade as—ay—the April snow,
> In the warm noon, we shrink away;
> And fast they follow, as we go
> Toward the setting day.[47]

Engraving of Father Francisco Garces ministering to the California Indians. Frank Soule et al., *The Annals of San Francisco.*

2   Palefaces

Here roams the wolf, the eagle whets his beak,
Birds, beasts of prey, and wilder men appear.

Lord Byron, *Childe Harold.*

In a little town in the Umbrian hills, forty-two miles north
of Rome, was born in 1182 a boy destined to become
famous. His father, an Italian merchant prince, was a
great admirer of France and named his son Francis.
Plenty of spending money and a charming personality
made Francis the most popular lad in Assisi. Even the
Sons of the nobility cultivated his friendship. Then one
day he was suddenly and overwhelmingly impressed by
the supreme sacrifice paid by Jesus of Nazareth and this
conversion changed not only his own life but the course of
human events. Believing that the opulent medieval
church, busy with its law suits and tax schemes, was not
satisfying the soul hunger of the weak and the heavy
laden, he tried to restore to religion its apostolic
simplicity. The popularity of his mission, which attracted
peasant and peer, attested to the fact that Francis of

Assisi had correctly interpreted the needs of his time.

His followers organized the Franciscan order and went out to save men. An inner urge drove them on and on until one day they stood beside the Golden Gate. Here they founded and named a great city. Only the illness of a woman at Las Llagas Creek and the lameness of a pack-mule prevented José Joaquin Moraga from founding the city of San Francisco on July 4, 1776, and thus properly celebrating the birth of a nation on the Atlantic coast. His party actually arrived at their destination on March 27th, but did not go through the ceremony of founding the city until some days after July 4th.[1]

Soon after their arrival in California the Franciscans were making explorations in the San Joaquin Valley. Although they never founded a mission in the valley, yet by 1800 they had established eighteen missions along the coast of California. Three other missions were established prior to 1823 which marked the close of the Spanish regime. During this Mission period, about sixty-five years in length, more than 80,000 Indians were converted. Contemporary travelers were astounded at the size of the herds and grain fields. All this activity and material welfare existed on the West Coast during the same years that George Washington was busily engaged in developing his estate along the Atlantic Coast.

During the mission period, California consisted of two distinct parts; the coast region and the interior. The latter was but little known. Official documents referred to the valley as a "terra incognita."[2] Almost all Franciscan energy was centered on the coast. The farthest inland penetration was at Soledad, thirty miles from the Pacific. The interior remained a non-Christian area, unexplored and unknown. That portion of interior California now called the San Joaquin Valley was described by a visiting

New England clergyman as "a huge boiler where the sun rises, fixing his hot stare on the world, and stares through the day."[3]

Modern inventions and conveniences have made the valley a comfortable and healthful place in which to live but it is not to be wondered at that the first missions were established on the coast; the climate was salubrious and the ocean served the Spanish as their highway to Mexico. The interior lacked roads and was inaccessible. But gradually new events arose which caused a change in policy and led to a series of explorations and expeditions into the San Joaquin Valley.

The first white men to enter the San Joaquin Valley do not deserve honorable mention. They were renegades. Just why they deserted their posts and who they were is uncertain. The Spanish came to California in 1769 and soldiers began to desert immediately. By 1772 this problem was serious enough to warrant the sending of an expedition in search of them and the commander of this expeditionary force made the first recorded observation of the San Joaquin. His name was Pedro Fages and he is worth remembering.

Fages was in many ways a peculiar personage. He was energetic, industrious, and conscientious in attending to all of those details designated by modern people as "red tape." To the royal service Fages was devoted. His education was fair and so also were his executive abilities. Among the early leaders Fages stands forth as exceptionally original and attractive. He, quick-tempered, stormed over trifles, yet was fond of little children who crowded around him in search of sweets (*dulces*) with which his pockets were usually filled. He would storm and rage over a trifle, ready to quarrel with anyone and yet he was kind hearted and never carried a grudge. Strangely enough,

neither did he excite any deep-seated animosity in others.
He was a brave, skillful hunter, and a dashing horseman.
Much as he esteemed his office, his province, and his
nation, he esteemed perhaps equally as much his horse,
his house, and his garden.[4]

Leaving his native Catalonia, Spain, in May, 1767, as first
lieutenant in the First Battalion, Second Regiment of
Catalan Volunteers of Light Infantry, Fages had served
two years in Mexico. Then he was sent to the California
frontier which he reached on May 1st, 1769. Part of this
first expedition to California went overland and part by
boat. Fages was placed in command of the military forces
aboard the *San Carlos*, which finally cast anchor in San
Diego harbor. Fages remained in chief command until
June 9, 1770, when the arrival of the overland expedition
under the leadership of Gaspar de Portola, governor of
California, relegated him to second place. Thus Fages was
actually the first governor of Alta California. He
accompanied Portola on his expeditions up the coast in
search of Monterey harbor and his work was rewarded on
January 5, 1771, by a commission advancing him to the
rank of captain.[5]

In March, 1772, Fages went on a tour of exploration from
Monterey to San Francisco Bay and thence to the
northern fringes of the San Joaquin Valley. The purpose of
this trip was to reach Point Reyes by land and Fages,
accompanied by Father Juan Crespi, skirted the
southeastern shore along Martinez until they reached the
mouth of the San Joaquin River. This river was followed
southward an indefinite distance beyond Antioch from
where they saw a vast plain stretching beyond the horizon
to the south. Failing to locate a suitable crossing, they
returned to Monterey. Father Crespi kept a diary on this
trip which was the only source of information concerning
it until the one kept by Fages was recently located by

An Idyllic early view of the Kaweah Valley, Tulare County, in its native state, with a band of Indians huddled in the foreground and the Sierra Nevada range as the backdrop. *Pacific Railroad Surveys,* volume V.

Bolton.[6] Fages closed his journal on April 5, 1772, but in a supplement dated November 27, 1773, he mentioned a trip to the southern part of the valley made in the fall of 1772; this expedition will be discussed later.

In May 1772, Fages was in the San Luis Obispo region hunting bears. The soldiers stationed at Monterey needed fresh meat and the few cattle in California at that time were needed for breeding purposes. Therefore Fages supplied the garrison for three months with bear meat. Thus he earned the nickname "The Bear" (El Oso), reminding one of the way in which William Cody secured the sobriquet "Buffalo Bill." Some people were uncharitable enough to say that it was given because of a disposition similar to a bear.

By August, he was back in San Diego quarreling with Father Junipero Serra over the advisability of establishing new missions without additional soldiers as guards, and Serra made a hasty trip to Mexico where his machinations resulted finally in the removal of Fages from office on May 25, 1774. It was during the time that Serra was in Mexico scheming to have Fages removed from office that Fages made his expedition to the southern part of the San Joaquin Valley. In the supplement to the record of his expedition with Father Crespi, Fages made the following entry:

> The San Francisco [Joaquin] which discharges into the estuary of that name, is more than one hundred and twenty leagues in length, in places fifteen to twenty in width, and it winds through a plain which is a labyrinth of lagoons and tulares. The plain is thickly peopled, having many and large rancherias; and it abounds in grain, deer, bears, geese, ducks, cranes; indeed, every kind of animal, terrestrial and aerial. In the rancherias in winter the Indians live in large halls, the families separate from each other; and outside are their houses, spherical in form, where their grains and utensils are kept. The people are good looking, excellently formed, frank and liberal. Theft does not seem to be practiced and they use large stones for grinding. The past year [1772], going in pursuit of deserters, I passed to the eastward of San Diego fifty leagues. Lack of water forced us to the sierras [sic] and we descended to the plain opposite of Mission Gabriel. We then followed the edge of the plain toward the north, about twenty-five leagues, to the pass of Buena Vista [Tejon]. For most of twenty-five leagues we traveled among date palms; and to the east and south the land was more and more a land of palms, but seemed very scarce of water. Over all the plain we saw not a little smoke.

The date palms of Fages were the Joshua trees of the Mojave Desert. He entered the San Joaquin by way of Tejon Pass and proceeded across its southern portion to San Miguel. Thirteen days after this entry by Fages, Father Francisco Palou made a report on the state of the missions. This was written and signed on December 10, 1773, at Carmél. In this report Palóu made the following reference to the Fages expedition of the previous year into the southern San Joaquin:[7]

The captain commander, Don Pedro Fages, tells us that once when he was looking for some deserters behind the sierra he saw a great plain, and in it some immense tule marshes, with many large lakes, from which, judging by their direction, he infers that those rivers (the San Joaquin and its affluents) are formed, and that if the plain were followed above the lakes one would come out at Point Reyes, leaving those rivers on the left, and he adds that the level pass comes to an end opposite the Mission of San Luis.

Bolton traversed the entire route of this expedition by Fages and in the light of his recent investigations, has reversed the conclusions of Bancroft concerning both the direction and route of Fages. Bolton summarized the course taken by Fages as follows:[8]

In the course of his expedition of 1772 he made the first recorded journey through Cajon Canyon, the first exploration of the Mojave Desert, and of Antelope Valley, the first visit to Hughes Lake and Pine Valley, the first march over Tejon Pass and down Grapevine Canyon, thence across the Valley to Buena Vista Lake and to San Luis Obispo.

Following this interior expedition Fages returned to San Diego. Squabbles with his aristocratic young wife, Doña Eulalia, kept the province in an uproar and remain to this day one of the amusing incidents of early California history. She was shocked by the sight of naked Indians and proceeded to give them her husband's clothing as well as her own. Wardrobes were not easily replenished in those days. Disliking the frontier, she prepared to leave for Mexico. Fages called on the assistance of clerical and military forces to aid him in keeping his wife in her proper place which, to Fages, meant California. But she shut herself up for three months and the anathemas of priests and soldiers awed her not a whit. However, a detailed account of the subsequent career of Fages is another story and can not be told here. Suffice to say that he ended his governorship in 1791 and returned to Mexico where he died in late 1794. He had entered the San Joaquin Valley four years before the Declaration of Independence had been signed at Philadelphia, and he closed his political career in California while George Washington was in the midst of his first term as president of the thirteen states on the Atlantic seaboard.[9]

Too often we are prone to consider the early explorers and frontiersmen crude and unlettered. This was seldom true of the Spanish. The greatest Latin scholars in what is now the United States resided, not at Yale or Harvard, but west of the Mississippi among the Spanish soldiers and missionaries. As proof of the fact that Fages possessed a rich vocabulary the following sentence from one of his reports is submitted: "I would indeed have preferred to set forth (either through my own effort or that of some capable persons who might have accompanied me on my wide peregrinations) a purely mathematical cosmography of all this considerable part of our American world."[10]

The first man of any race or color to make scientific observations in the San Joaquin Valley was Father Francisco Garcés. He entered the valley close on the heels of Fages. In fact, he referred in his diary to the camp sites and horse signs left by the Fages expedition of 1772.

Father Garcés carried a quadrant and a mariner's compass and each day in his diary he noted the number of leagues traveled and the points of the compass toward which his course was directed. The average day's journey was six leagues. (A Spanish land league is 2.63 miles long.) Evidently Garcés tried to make his route clear to posterity, but still it is difficult to trace accurately. He gave the latitude at only very distant points. The reports of these early missionaries is often disappointing to us as their primary interest lay not in geography, topography, or in races as such, but rather in the conversion of the

Indians of the San Joaquin Valley's extreme south, in the Tejon vicinity, as they appeared to the Pacific Railroad Survey in the 1850s. *Pacific Railroad Surveys,* volume V.

heathens and in the planting of missions. Nevertheless, Garcés transmitted to later generations valuable information concerning the tribes on the Gila, the Colorado, and in the San Joaquin.[11] What little is known about the natives of that time has come as a result of the work and writings of Spanish friars and soldiers. The only criticism is that they might have given us so much more.

Besides a compass and quadrant, Garcés carried with him on his journey a piece of canvas two feet wide and three feet long. On one side was a painting representing the Virgin Mary, on the other the Devil was pictured reposing in Hell. When Garcés arrived at an Indian village he would unfurl this banner. The Indians invariably exclaimed "Good!" (or its Indian equivalent) when shown the Virgin, and "Bad!" when shown the other side. Garcés would then proceed to question them through his interpreter as to their willingness to become Christian believers and Spanish subjects. The usual answer was the affirmative monosyllable. The journal of Garcés abounds with information of this sort which is of less value to us today than would be an accurate description of the people and the country of his time.

Garcés came to California with Juan Bautista de Anza in 1774; the latter led an overland expedition to California which culminated in the founding of San Francisco. Too active to remain with the column, Garcés scoured the country far and wide. Few modern exponents of physical culture would relish being jerked from hither to yon with such amazing rapidity as was Garcés. He was well nigh perfect physically, being tall in stature, well-formed, of iron frame, and absolutely indefatigable. He dressed well, usually wearing each garment arranged with such care that its wearer would ordinarily have been called dandyish had not the dignity of his manner and the fearless gaze of his cold gray eyes forbidden. Garcés possessed a cold and reasoning fanaticism which is the strongest force yet known in moving the hearts of men.

Six years after the first Franciscan mission had been established in Alta California, Garcés left the missions on the border of Sonora. Finding the group of colonists too slow, he soon left them entirely, followed the Colorado River to the land of the Mojaves, turned west and passed north of the present site of Needles, crossed the Mojave River, and thence to Mission San Gabriel which he reached by passing the sites of modern Cottonwood and Barstow.

Garcés left San Gabriel sometime in April, 1776, and followed a trail lying to the east of the present Ridge Route. In Antelope Valley he camped at Hughes Lake and

44

A stunning display of variously-sized Yokuts baskets, taken circa 1919. Wallace Morgan, *History of Kern County, California.*

near thereto he found "a village where, according to the signs, Señor Capitan Faxes, (Fages) had been."[12] He visited the village of Tinliu in the vicinity of the El Tejon

45

ranch house of a later date and learned that the Spanish were already known and cordially hated by the Indians. In his diary Garcés stated that "those Indians related to me that in their land they had killed two soldiers, who I persuaded myself were deserters, because they were very wicked with the women; adding that the Indians had cut off their hands, laid open their breasts and all the body, torn them asunder, and scattered the remains."[13] Undoubtedly this treatment caused the death of the offending Spanish deserters.

These Indians belonged to the Yauelmani tribe of the Yokuts people. From this point Garcés visited Caliente Creek and then proceeded north to the White River. While in the valley, Garcés learned from the Indians that Juan Bautista de Anza had marched along the coast from Los Angeles to Monterey and was just then exploring the region in the vicinity of Antioch. Apparently the Indians had a well arranged form of underground telegraph, because Garcés verified their reports later and found no discrepancies.[14]

Garcés later learned that in the month of April, 1776, Lieutenant-Colonel Anza, Ensign José Joaquin Moraga, and Padre Pedro Font had entered the northern borders of the valley, and had proceeded twenty miles to the east. The tule swamps and wide rivers discouraged them and they returned to Monterey by way of the Livermore Valley. In their diaries they referred to vast herds of tule elk, animals which are now virtually extinct.[15]

José Joaquin Moraga made a trip into the valley in September, 1776. He left Monterey, crossed the Coast Range, and reached the San Joaquin River about midway between Byron Hot Springs and Bethany. Moraga led his party up the river for three days and probably entered what is now Fresno County. The party forded the river and proceeded a day's journey over the plains toward the east. From this indefinite point the men retraced their steps to the river and followed it downstream to the mouth of the Calaveras and the future site of Stockton.[16]

In November of the same year Captain Rivera and Ensign Moraga repeated the trip made in September. Rivera was the officer who had led one of the two overland forces from Baja California to San Diego in 1769; he had preceded Portolá on that memorable march to settle Alta California. Ensign Sal, one of the younger officers, reported that on this November expedition the following rivers were named: Rio del Pescadero (west channel of the San Joaquin); the Rio San Francisco Javier (middle channel); the Rio San Miguel (west channel); and the Rio de la Pasion (Calaveras).[17]

The first white men to enter the valley arrived in the following order: deserting Spanish soldiers from the coast missions; Captain Pedro Fages, in search of these deserters; Father Francisco Garcés, in search of converts; Colonel Anza, looking for a possible new route back to Mexico; and Ensign Moraga, to determine the nature of the land beyond the ranges.

The exploration of the San Joaquin Valley was to be continued under a politico-religious direction. Instead of the haphazard expeditions of Fages and Garcés, a definite purpose was henceforth to be held in view and not one man, but many men under specific orders, were to be sent out. The time when, the place where, and the conditions under which they went forth form the plot and the setting of another story.

Father Junipero Serra (1717-1784), of the Franciscan order, first president of the California mission system. While the system's reach never extended inland, many of the missions included Yokuts and Miwok neophytes dragged away from their San Joaquin Valley ancestral homes. Owen C. Coy, *Pictorial History of California*

3 Mission Sites

and Neophytes

Though sluggards deem it but a foolish chase,
And marvel men should quit their easy-chair
The weary way and long, long league to trace;—
Oh, there is sweetness in the prairie air,
And life that bloated ease can never hope to share.
Lord Byron, *Childe Harold.*

"What I am sorry for is that many Gentiles are dying from
the many continuous wars, and also from the many
diseases, especially from syphilis!"[1] This sentence from a
letter written by Father Juan Martin in 1804 to his
superior officer, Father José Senán, revealed the condition
of the Indians in the San Joaquin Valley and resulted in a
series of expeditions into that region with the definite
purpose of founding missions. The Franciscans sponsored
the movement, although they were at all times dependent

upon the governor of the department of California for approval of their plans. The latter always appointed the military leaders placed in command of the chief expeditions.

The man who governed California during the period when most of the expeditions were sent into the interior deserves a word in passing. José Joaquin de Arrillaga ruled the department from 1800 to 1814; this uninterrupted fourteen-year term is a record for California governors. Arrillaga was born in Spain, a member of its nobility, in 1750. He served under Juan Bautista de Anza in three fierce Indian campaigns, receiving citation for meritorious conduct under fire.

No one ever found any fault with him but, like most model men, he was not very original. He had a ruddy skin, blue eyes, and was a good example of the tall, red-headed Gothic type often encountered among the Spanish aristocracy. During his administration two things came to disturb the placidity and serenity of an otherwise untroubled existence. First, the Russians came down the coast from Alaska and made a settlement in California; second, the flight of neophytes from the missions to the interior resulted in a serious problem. The second item is the only one which will be discussed here.[2]

The Indians who were at the missions oftentimes failed to appreciate the training which they were receiving. That the friars were oftentimes discouraged is not to be wondered at when the intensity of their own faith is considered. The mission system of which they were the directing part was perhaps an antiquated political system but it endured down to 1834. The mission padres were authorized to call upon the governor for assistance in securing absconding neophytes. This dignitary resided at Monterey and received a salary of 4,000 piastres a year.

He was the general commandant of the troops and
controlled all other persons not directly placed in charge
of the missions. Even the Franciscans recognized his
authority in all matters pertaining to the public welfare
although he did not presume to interfere in strictly
mission affairs. Both political and religious leaders
believed that the best defense against the Indian menace,
which was ever present during the Spanish and Mexican
periods in California, was an active offensive. But they did
not agree on how this was to be carried out.[3]

Father Juan Martin of San Diego wanted to save the
Indians of the tulares from sin and sickness, but Governor
Arrillaga protested, not against the motive but against the
method. The latter believed that the logical place for
missions was not in the tulares, but along the main rivers,
that is, the San Joaquin, the Kings River, and their
tributaries. Father Martin, quiet and unobtrusive, was
likewise determined and persistent, and finally in 1804 he
visited the swamp country with the purpose of locating a
suitable site for a mission. On his journey he went due
east from San Miguel to the present Kern county and
visited the rancheria of Bubal, located east and south of
Tulare Lake; during times of high water the relatively
high land on which this village was located became an
island. This was near Alpaugh, now known as Atwells
Island. During the time when their village was an island
the Indians used tule rafts to reach the mainland. The
chief of Bubal refused to allow the children of his tribe to
be taken to the missions for training and this was a great
disappointment to Martin. The latter visited Sumtache on
the eastern shore of the lake; he made contacts with the
Notonoto, the Tachi, and the Telamni Indians. He found to
his sorrow that they had already had enough contact with
the lower type of white men to suffer from venereal
disease; wherever Father Martin went, the Indians hid

their women. The padre made the following report to his superior officer:

> My venerable Father José Senan: On the fourth of April, this year, the reverend father prefect asked us to inform your reverence about the condition in which the Gentiles near this mission are, and concerning their good disposition to receive holy baptism. In order to comply with your order, I say frankly that the disposition of the Gentiles is wonderful. They have shown good will toward the soldiers who at different times have been there and also toward the neophytes, who have visited the Tulare region on many occasions. Their good will would probably be constant if it were not that runaway Indians from the north make them hostile. Such was the case of the last wanderers who came from one of the Tulare rancherias called Tache. Indians on horseback arrived telling them that the fathers do nothing but kill Indians. Satan does all that is possible to influence more than 4,000 souls who could be placed on the road to salvation if the mission is placed in the Tulare region. I said this to the governor, José Joaquin de Arrillaga, several times, although I know that he is inclined to found one along the river. In fact, in spite of the high opinion I had of the gentleman, I told him when he asked me what I thought of the new foundations in the Tulare region: "Sir, why do you wish to place a mission where they might not want one? What of the rancherias of Bubal, Tache, Chumache, Notonoto, and Telame? Don't they also desire one? Moreover, there is more reason that those who wish and those who ask for one may first of all become the children of God, for those who do not ask for one take up arms against the soldiers that come to their territory. For proof of this truth, I have Father Pedro Munoz, Señor Moran, and myself."
>
> What I am sorry for is that many Gentiles are dying from the many continuous wars, and also from the many diseases, especially from El Mal Gallico [syphilis]. Now if a mission is not given to them soon, and one is not founded, they will not be held in subjection. May God help them and preserve your reverence, with your father companion, Fray Marcos, for many years. This is the wish of your very humble servant.[4]

The "Four Creeks" area of Tulare County, home to many Yokuts tribelets, in its pristine state and as recorded by the Pacific Railroad Survey in the 1850s. *Pacific Railroad Surveys,* volume V.

Martin was one of the outstanding friars in California. He was self-effacing, but his superiors were well aware of his sterling worth. He was one of the few friars who took the oath of republicanism when Mexico broke away from Spain. His journey into the San Joaquin was the first definitely organized expedition made by the Franciscan order. Until that date their progress in California had been exclusively along the coast. When God made California he built a huge Chinese Wall a few miles inland from the Pacific Ocean. This natural wall is called the Coast Range. It guarded the possessions of the mission padres from the barbarians of the interior.

When the Israelites were trying to gain a foothold in the land of Canaan, they sent Joshua and Caleb to spy out the Promised Land. Even so did the Franciscans send their men into the San Joaquin and the reports of the two groups were identically the same. It was a good land but because of its ungodly population, hard to secure and hold without many fighting men.

Conquest to the Franciscans meant spiritual conversion rather than physical bondage. The missions existed for the good of the Indians. Thus far none had been established in the valley. But now, after 1804, two motives impelled the friars to action. One was the dire need of the valley Indians; the other, the necessity of preventing the Indians already at the coast missions from fleeing to the valley where they lost their own religion and instigated the wild Indians to resist the white men. Apparently, the mission system was not popular among the Indians. The neophytes consisted of two groups: those who came because they wanted to come, and those who came because someone else wanted them to come. At first the Indians came to the missions gladly. While they were learning the fundamentals of the Christian religion and acquiring the rudiments of an education, they were called neophytes. But even the slightest discipline was irksome to their untutored souls, and they soon developed a tendency to flee. Father Fernández charged that cruelty to the natives was the cause of their defection; Father Tapis blamed their restiveness to the withdrawal to Mexico in 1803 of the Catalan Volunteers, than whom there had been no greater soldiers in California, and before whom the natives had stood in an awe amounting to terror.[5] Now these soldiers were gone and soon followed the organized exploration of the San Joaquin Valley. Its purpose was to civilize those Indians who were a constant source of worry to the Spanish authorities.

The year following Father Martin's trip into the valley, Mayordomo Higuera and Padre Cueva of Mission San José went on a visit to some sick neophytes in the vicinity of Bethany. While on this pastoral call the padre and his majordomo were attacked by Indians. They escaped, reported the matter, and Sergeant Luis Peralta led an expedition into the valley to chastise the offenders.[6]

Gabriel Moraga, the illustrious son of José Joaquin Moraga, made his first visit to the San Joaquin as an independent commander in 1805. He led a flying column on a scouting trip as far as Kings River. No friar accompanied this expedition and no diary was kept. Moraga and his men reached Kings River on or near January 5th. Since they were devout Christians, they remained quietly in camp during the next day which was the day of Epiphany. This holy day, which commemorates the visit of the Three Wise Men to the infant Jesus at Bethlehem, suggested to Moraga a name for the beautiful river never before seen by white men. He called it the Rio de los Santos Reyes (the River of the Holy Kings).

The next year Moraga again visited Kings River. This time he was accompanied by Father Pedro Muñoz. The latter, well aware of the previous trip and the circumstances of the christening, made this entry in his journal on October 14: "We found, after having traveled five leagues, the Rio de los Santos Reyes, which had been discovered in the previous year, 1805."[7]

The same year, 1805, that Moraga first visited Kings River, he explored the banks of the San Francisco River and re-christened it the San Joaquin. His father José Joaquin Moraga, had given to this river its first name some thirty years earlier. Now his son perpetuated the name of his father, Joaquin, in applying it to this majestic inland stream. The valley took its name after its chief river and so the namesake of the valley was the same man who officially founded San Francisco.[8]

In 1806 Governor Arrillaga adopted a new strategy. Horses, cows, neophytes, and firearms were disappearing together from the missions. Their destination was the San Joaquin Valley and the villains, in this case, were the Indians of the Tulares. This state of affairs was both annoying and serious. The governor planned to carry the war into the enemy's country. The attack was to be made simultaneously on four fronts.

Two of these expeditions went into the Sacramento Valley, and with them we are not concerned. The first of the other two left Santa Barbara on July 19, 1806, for the general direction of the Tulare country. Lieutenant Francisco Ruiz, the commander, was accompanied by a sergeant, a corporal, a platoon of soldiers, and Father Zalvidéa. The latter was the diarist of the expedition. They left in the morning and at nightfall they had reached Mission Santa Inéz. According to Zalvidéa's diary, their line of march led across the southern end of the valley and finally to the south shore of Buena Vista Lake. Indians were observed crossing the water on tule rafts. Sunflowers higher than a man's head were described.

Zalvidéa's route through the valley is hard to trace exactly because he did not travel in a straight line, but made detours to the various Indian villages along the route. He noticed few children; the valley Indians were becoming a decadent race due to the sterility resulting from syphilis. Ruiz and Zalvidea left the valley by way of Tejon Pass.[9]

As a result of observations made on this expedition Zalvidéa reported the Indians friendly and the land arid and alkaline. Naturally an expedition through the valley during the hot summer months was not conducive to creating a favorable impression; everything was parched and dry in that un-irrigated era.[10] The report tended to keep out settlers and this discouragement of colonization made the discovery of gold improbable. This discovery alone could have drawn thither enough people to hold the

Indians standing next to a characteristic elliptical tule hut near Tulare Lake, circa 1900. Owen C. Coy, *Pictorial Hisory of California.*

province against those other Americans of Anglo-Saxon blood and Anglo-Saxon land hunger who were tramp-tramping westward with a mighty tread, firm in the belief that "westward the star of empire takes its way."

The second important expedition of the year was placed under the command of Color-Sergeant Gabriel Moraga, with whom the naming of Kings River is associated. His force of twenty-five men started out from Mission San Juan Bautista, located in what is now San Benito County, approximately thirty miles southwest of the present town of Hollister.

Moraga led his men along San Luis Creek, crossed the San Joaquin River a few miles north of Firebaugh, and explored the region between Dos Palos and Chowchilla. This territory was then largely composed of overflow land and the atmosphere was colored with hordes of yellow

butterflies. This induced Moraga to apply the term
"mariposas" (butterflies) to the region. Today the slough,
the creek, the city, and the county by that name all bear
the Spanish name for butterfly, although the county by
that name lies far to the east of the route taken by
Moraga on this particular occasion. However, the original
Mariposa County included the entire valley floor.[11]

Leaving the slough and its butterflies, Moraga went north
by northwest following closely the route of the present
Highway 99. He crossed and named Mariposa Creek and
Bear (Oso) Creek. The former he followed and explored to
the eastern foothills. The march across the dry plains
parched the throats of the soldiers and when they reached
a large river its cool and refreshing water seemed to them
a veritable river of mercy (Rio de la Merced) and that
name it retains to the present time. The land along this
Merced River was later reported by Munoz as the most
suitable place for a mission site found during the
expedition.[12]

From the Merced River, the explorers continued
northward for a distance of thirty leagues. They crossed
and named the Dolores (Tuolumne) and the Guadalupe
(Stanislaus) and followed the latter into the Sierra
Nevada. Finally they reached the Rio de la Pasion
(Cosumnes), which had been explored and named by
Moraga's father in 1776. In early October the party turned
south. One group followed the foothills of the Sierra, while
the other division marched along the San Joaquin River.
The first group made camp one evening near the later site
of Millerton. The second group reached Kings River near
where Laton was eventually established, at a point later
used as a camp site by Fremont and still later the site of
Kingston. Kings River was followed along its east bank to
the heights within the present Reedley. Here the two
forces were reunited and proceeded southward until they

reached the Kaweah River. For a few days they made camp in the oak forest at Visalia, whose cool shade was a delightful contrast to the arid region through which they had just come. Lieutenant Ruiz and his command had camped at the same place in July; Moraga arrived there in October.[13]

The Kaweah River near Visalia was explored thoroughly for mission sites and its two main branches were named the San Gabriel and the San Miguel. The Tule River was also followed into the hills and named the Rio de San Pedro. After a lengthy examination of the Porterville district, Moraga moved south and spent some time along the Kern River. The latter was followed for several leagues into the eastern foothills. Moraga found no suitable sites there. From this river Moraga led his men to the chief village of the Yauelmani Indians near Tejon Pass. The Spanish passed through this pass on November 1st; two days later they reached San Fernando.[14]

Father Pedro Muñoz was the diarist on this expedition; he affirmed the earlier reports of Zalvidéa and Garcés as to soil, Indians, and mission sites. Both Muñoz and Moraga believed that the Merced region offered the best possibilities for a prospective mission site. The Kings River region was also favorably mentioned but it was farther away and had a larger population of hostile Indians. Therefore a mission along Kings River would also necessitate a presidio and its provision at that time was impossible.

Father Tapis in his general report made in March, 1807, said that as a result of the two expeditions led by Ruiz and Moraga, twenty-four villages had been visited and the acquaintance made of 5,300 Indians. Very few good sites had been located and presidios were deemed a necessity, due to the remoteness and the great population of the interior region.[15]

Scene from the mission rancho days of California, with cattle and Indians (foreground) surveying the tableau. Frank Soule et al., *The Annals of San Francisco.*

During the year 1807 Moraga led twenty-five men to the San Joaquin River and to the Sierra Nevada beyond. This was relatively an unimportant expedition, and nothing worthy of recording happened. The following year Moraga, with his muscles of iron and nerves of steel, made a second remarkable journey into the interior. The motives of Arrillaga were the same in 1808 as they had been in 1806, with the addition that he had now definitely decided to plant missions in the valley at any cost.[16]

Moraga was selected to find suitable sites in the valley directly opposite the missions already located along the coast. Such sites were not available and Moraga verified this assertion by leading another expedition into the San Joaquin. Two years later he was again in the valley. Father José Viader went along on this expedition of 1810. His diary indicates that the party went from Mission Santa Clara to Walnut Creek and thence to the Merced River country. Father Viader reported that the most favorable locality for a mission was along the Merced River, but even this territory was lacking in timber and therefore not ideal for the purpose.[17]

In October of the same year, 1810, Moraga was again in the San Joaquin. This time he went in search of runaway neophytes. He entered the valley by way of Livermore Pass and went east to the present Bethany. He and his men ranged to and fro along the Stanislaus, the Tuolumne, and the Merced. No deserting neophytes were found. Father Viader, who usually accompanied Moraga on his expeditions, was a "large man of fine physique and of more than ordinary ability and merit, both spiritual and temporal. He was reserved, stern in manner, especially to strangers, liked by his friends, frank and courteous to all acquaintances."[18] Robinson, the New England traveler, who saw him on his visit to California, wrote that he was "a good old man, whose heart and soul were in proportion to his immense figure."[19] One evening he was assaulted by disgruntled neophytes. Three burly Indians led by a pugnacious individual named Marcelo jumped on Father Viader from ambush. The latter, built and thewed like James J. Jeffries, bumped their heads together until they were unconscious, then revived them, chided them good-naturedly, forgave them promptly, and with equal promptness made three devoted friends.[20] Men like Father Viader and Gabriel Moraga should correct the erroneous notion that the Spanish-Californians were small and effeminate men.

Moraga, as a result of his 1810 expeditions, reversed his former reports on the Merced country and declared it unsuitable for a mission site. This was the final verdict. The Spanish during 1810 did not reach the limits of previous explorations; however, their work was of value as Father Viader preserved for posterity the Indian names of rancherias and tribes. An interval of quiet followed 1810. No definite move was made into the valley for three years. In other sections of California confusion and fighting took place but in the San Joaquin the big drives were temporarily over. In 1811 Sergeant Sanchez and Padre Abella made a boat trip from Carquinez Strait up the western channel of the San Joaquin and back by way of the eastern channel. In 1812 a soldier named Pico visited the Tachi Indians west of Lemoore and reported that these Indians dug pits from which they ambushed approaching horsemen.[21]

It was not until October, 1813, that Governor Arrillaga felt it incumbent upon himself to again send an expedition into the interior. This was sent for the same reason which had actuated his previous endeavors. Moraga was busy elsewhere, and the command devolved upon Francisco Soto, whose distinction it is to have been the first white child born in San Francisco. This accounts for his given name. He was selected because of his military ability and physical fitness; he was then thirty-seven. This was the first time that Soto had appeared in the valley in the role of an independent commander.[22]

Sergeant Soto took command of his force at Mission San José, which is not to be confused with the present city of San Jose. The latter is located in Santa Clara County, Mission San José lies fifteen miles to the north in Alameda County. The expedition left the morning of October 26th, and reached the mouth of the San Joaquin River where Soto's force of a hundred neophytes were re-enforced by ten soldiers from San Francisco. Here the party embarked in boats and voyaged up the river. In one of the boats was mounted a small cannon. The next day they literally stepped out of their boats into an Indian battle.

It was one of those balmy autumn days which invariably come to bless the San Joaquin Valley after the long hot summers; when the wind delights to fan one's face with its perfumed breath. The sun shone comfortably through broken masses of clouds which were passing rapidly as if intent on getting somewhere in a hurry. It was one of those hours and scenes in which it is easy to get close to the philosophy of the ancient Celts who believed that fairies dwelt happily in the woods and along the streams in the early morning of time.

Perhaps to the Spanish that day the flitting shadows seemed more like elusive brownies. The San Joaquin River at their landing place is broad and shallow. Indian signs were plentiful. As the men, soldiers and neophytes, poured out of the boats in picturesque array they appeared fit for any contest. Noting the freshness of an Indian trail which led into the water the men sent forth a fierce challenging shout. But the woods bordering the river on the other side were silent as the tomb and apparently as unoccupied as a vacuum. Too silent! Nothing moved. In the center of the stream was an island. But evidently no one was there. The quiet and peace made the soldiers anxious.

One said, "We will follow them clear to the Sierras if necessary," to which another replied, "It won't be necessary. Look yonder!" Two Miwok Indians had slipped out of the willows to the water's edge on the island and were thumbing their noses and indulging in other motions indicative of much vileness and contempt. They dared the soldiers to cross and then pretended to go to sleep. It was maddening.

The younger men were near the water's edge. They always are. Young blood is hot blood and only age and experience tempers courage with caution. Soto gave the order to charge. They did. The water of the San Joaquin, waist deep, was splashed into foam and spray. The men reached the island with a rush but the savages had disappeared and the soldiers plunged on to the farther side. They broke ranks and scattered as they beat the underbrush for their quarry. Suddenly there broke forth a hell's chorus of yells which upset the nerves of the stoutest soldiers. They had walked into a trap of a thousand warriors. It scarcely seemed real. Every soldier thought of flight. Though confused and bruised their force remained compact and drove hard at the point between them and the river. The musket smoke served as a smoke screen, yet it also made the men cough and sneeze. The ferocity of the battle increased when they reached the stream. As dead and wounded men fell into the water the river hissed and gurgled in a treacherous fashion. They had rushed to the river for safety and now it threatened to destroy them.

For a time Soto was doubtful of the result. The savages relied on their excessive numbers, were careless of life, and many died. As a last desperate resort, Soto led his men in an assault to dislodge the Indians from the willows along the shore. The natives shrank from the charge, fled across the island, and left the neophytes and Spanish to exult in their triumph. This battle lasted three hours.[23]

Another episode of more interest than importance, and yet worthy of recording, occurred during this same year. A padre accompanied by two soldiers went on a pedestrian tour from Mission San José to the San Ramón Valley and planned to cross the hills into the San Joaquin. While crossing Walnut Creek they were attacked by a horde of

Transportation by oxcart, the precursor of the stagecoach, as used in early-day California. Pen and ink sketch by Frederic Remington. *Fresno County Public Library, California History and Genealogy Room Collection.*

800 Indians. Apolinario Bernal, a gigantic soldier, told the padre and the other soldier to make their escape while he faced the enemy at the narrow crossing of the little stream and then:

> Behind he stayed,
> Not only that, but down the path with bayonet fixed he sped,
> For being ordered to retreat, he just advanced instead,
> And there beside the bridge he stood, broad shouldered and erect,
> Prepared to show to one and all an exercise correct,
> Nor was it long, indeed, before to action he had warmed,
> For that same moment on the bridge the enemy had swarmed,
> They came close following man by man, but each man as he came,
> Received a thrust that laid him low, to every man the same.
> To overthrow this giant then was now their one great aim,
> But ever was the nearest man his shield as others came;
> Yet fiercer still the foe pressed on to desperation wrought

until Bernal was overwhelmed by superior numbers. A demigod could not have done what he had failed to do. And so:

> For him the fight was done,
> Full gallantly he held his post until the day was won;
> Then seemed as if he laid him down to slumber after play,
> Not much more quiet than his wont, but much more pale he lay.[24]

His horse killed, his ammunition gone, he died from the loss of blood. Here is one of those rare examples in history of a man, not losing his life but actually giving it to save others, and yet strangely enough, no official report was ever made of this supreme act of heroism. Alvarado, himself a soldier and resenting the fact that full justice had not been done to Bernal, wrote in his manuscript *History of California*: "The padres never wrote of this brave act, but had it been a priest Rome would have echoed with it."[25]

Search for a suitable mission site having failed in the north around Merced, a fresh attempt was made in the Tulare region to the south. On October 2, 1814, expeditions were made which were not as bloody as those of 1813. Sergeant Ortega, Padre Cabot, and thirty men left San Miguél and explored the Tulare Lake region. They visited Bubal, a village of perhaps 700 inhabitants. Here Father Cabot baptized twenty-six natives. All of these converts were over eighty years of age with one exception; the latter was a man of thirty who was in a dying condition.[26] In the years following this expedition many Tulareños joined the mission at San Miguel because the baptismal records frequently give the home address of "Rancheria de Bubal."

Bubal was located along the southern shore of Tulare

Lake. From this point Ortega led his men north along the east shore a day's march to a village of the same size named Sumtache. The two villages were at war and the Spanish learned that virtue is not always its own reward. In trying to act as peacemakers they were misunderstood and were attacked by the Sumtache warriors. The Spanish lost two horses and the Indians one old woman in the battle.[27]

After the Sumtache fight had ended indecisively and explanations and apologies had taken place, the white men proceeded peacefully to the oak forest near present Visalia where Ruiz and Moraga had camped with their men in 1806. They crossed the San Gabriel River near Visalia and proceeded to the Rancheria de Tache, an Indian village along Kings River with approximately a thousand inhabitants. The villagers hid among the willows and refused to appear. Father Cabot stated that Kings River lacked suitable timber for the erection of big buildings, but he nevertheless recommended that a mission be established along that river. The return journey was perhaps made by taking a route north of the Kings River, circling back by way of Coalinga to Slack Canyon and San Miguel.[28]

Sergeant Ortega, the leader of this expedition, had accompanied Gaspar de Portolá and Junipero Serra in their expedition in search of Monterey Bay. They failed to find it and continued northward. One evening young Ortega left camp to hunt deer and passed over the present site of Daly City. Lying to the east he beheld a great inland body of water. To a soldier and not to a sailor belongs the credit of discovering this great harbor of the Golden Gate. The new mission founded here was dedicated especially to St. Francis. Perhaps for this reason Ortega became a favorite with Serra and later missionaries. Regarding this trip into the San Joaquin and his experiences along Kings River, Father Cabot wrote as follows:

> Finally at two o'clock we arrived at the Rancheria de Tache, which according to information and the number of houses it contains, will probably contain 1,000 inhabitants. We found only thirty-six old men and six old women, because the rest of the people had hidden themselves in the tules, and in spite of being on the banks of the Rio de los Santos Reyes for two days, we could not get to see anyone, aside from the few that have already been seen.
>
> This Kings River carries a great deal of water and of a quality which has no equal. There are good lands and a lot of it fit for cultivation, but in all these lands that I went over there is no timber except a few willows along the banks of the river; neither is there any rock; and they say there is none within twenty leagues distant, which is probably true.
>
> From what I saw and from what they say, there are a great many Indians, and I think there would be none who would not wish to be baptized. May God produce a means that it may be attained—Amen.
>
> From this Rio de Reyes, thanks be to God, we returned happily to this mission on another road about five leagues farther north, but of the same formation as the one at the entrance to the plain. This is as much as I am able to tell you for your guidance, but I have not the least doubt that the time has come to begin a mission in those places, and it would be easy to convert these unfortunate people, for I have known them always to be quiet and docile. Excuse mistakes.[29]

Opera-bouffe battles were common in Spanish-American history. These funny little battles did not mean that the Spanish soldiers were poor fighters. From the time that Cortez landed on the coast of Mexico until José Castro pushed the California military lines up the San Joaquin River to the point where it leaves the foothills, the Spanish people had never paused in their advance against the red men. Even those human gamecocks, the Apaches

Plains between the Kaweah and Kings rivers, in present-day Fresno and Tulare counties, as recorded by the Pacific Railroad Survey in the 1850s. *Pacific Railroad Surveys,* volume V.

of the Southwest, were unable to permanently check these white men who sought land for themselves, converts for heaven, and subjects for the king. In many of their battles the Spanish were not trying to help the "vanishing Americans" make an abrupt exit from this life; they were merely treating them as policemen who try to curb the exuberance of obstreperous college boys on a rampage after a football game. At such times clubs are used to subdue but not to intentionally maim or kill. This explains the series of relatively harmless charges and counter-charges which distinguished some of their battles.

During the following year, 1815, there was comparatively as much stir in California as there was to be exactly a hundred years later during the Panama-Pacific International Exposition. The occasion was the arrival of the new governor, Pablo Vicente Solá, who was destined to be the last of the Spanish governors of California. The erudite and polished recipient of the honors heaped upon him took them all as a matter of course. But as soon as the fiestas and celebrations were over, he began to exhibit great energy in the capture of runaway neophytes.

Governor Solá was a man of medium height, thick set, tremendously strong, florid in complexion, red haired, and a fine example of the Gothic type of Spaniard common among the upper class. His voice was well modulated though inclined to be harsh at times due to the loss of his teeth. He was aristocratic in manner but democratic in his politics. According to Boronda, a private soldier presented his application for retirement from the service to the governor instead of to a lower officer as was customary, and Solá showed his resentment of this breach of official routine by slapping the soldier's face. He required that his subordinates should read Cervantes and this "outside reading course" made him unpopular.[30]

In October, 1815, Solá sent several minor expeditions south into the Tulare region. No journals were kept and little is known about the routes or the results.

On November 4, 1815, Sergeant Juan Ortega, Father Cabot, and thirty soldiers departed from San Miguel for the valley. In order to escape detection they traveled only during the night. The second night out they reached Kings River near the north end of the lake. They attempted to capture two Indian fishermen and their failure in this attempt caused the runaways to give a general alarm.[31]

The Spaniards followed Kings River upstream to the general vicinity of Kingsburg. There they turned east and marched cross country toward the Kaweah River. No deserting neophytes were found and the wild Indians were also in hiding due to the warning given by the fishermen from lower Kings River. Ortega crossed back to Kings River at the point where it leaves the foothills. There he met another party of whites which had been sent out under the command of Sergeant Pico.

Pico had left San Juan Bautista on November 3rd and five days later his force had attacked an Indian village at the junction of the San Joaquin and Kings Rivers in the neighborhood of modern Mendota. Sixty-five captives, of whom fifty were women, had been taken. From this place they marched in an easterly direction across the plains until they reached Kings River near Piedra. A few miles upstream from Piedra they met Ortega and his command.[32]

Thus mutually reinforced, the expedition turned north toward the San Joaquin, recovered a big band of stolen horses, and located one spot where 238 horses had been killed. This wholesale slaughter of horses was not due to wantonness, neither did the Indians steal the horses to ride them; they ate them. The desire to enter the equestrian class came much later. By 1815 the Tulareños had developed a taste for horse meat. This may have been a transmitted aptitude from those days when the little three-toed eohippus skipped from rock to rock in the Sierra Nevada in the days when the world was still young. Present day Californians enjoy "steak bakes," but a barbecue of 238 horses must have been a rare feast.

On the way back to the coast the Ortega and Pico expedition was deliberately misled at Mariposa slough by the Indian guides. As the men floundered in the mud most of the captured Indians escaped. The little army finally reached San Juan Bautista on November 29th.[33]

Governor Solá designated the venture a great success, but the president of the Franciscan Order in Alta California, Father Mariano Payéras, said nothing. He liked the governor because Solá was easily managed. From the point of view of the church, this was an item in the governor's favor. Father Tapis was frank and called the expeditions of 1815 very unsatisfactory. The truth of the matter probably lies between the two expressed views. Results had not justified expectations. The governor's pride and position forbade the admission of defeat; the keen disappointment of men like Father Tapis caused them to discount both the difficulties standing in the way and the things which had actually been accomplished.[34]

No man had more to do with bringing the San Joaquin Valley to the attention of white men than Father Mariano Payéras, the president of all the Franciscan missions in Alta California from 1815 to 1822. In his biennial report for 1815-1816 he urged that missions and presidios should be founded in the valley. He possessed an orderly type of mind and furnished documentary evidence why this was necessary. Nothing was done. Two years later he returned to the subject of missions in the Tulare region. This report for 1817-1818 was a proof that the care of the mission population weighed heavily on the hearts of the friars and revealed a keen appreciation of the need for an advance into the San Joaquin. Payéras was keen and alert; had the government in Spain heeded his suggestions and requests it would have been to its advantage.

Payéras was a great traveler and always showed up at the missions when he was least expected. Like a modern bank examiner, he left no opportunity for "window dressing." His signature is found in every mission register in Alta California. Of all the clergy that ever came to the province, he was the most evenly balanced in ability. He was affable, popular, kind-hearted, and unselfish. No one could quarrel with him. His temper was never ruffled, always serene. He was possessed of wonderful business acumen, with great strength of mind and character, and was a forceful and voluminous letter writer. He never permitted the sanctity of the revenue laws to interfere with the temporal prosperity of the missions. He was faithful and strict in his religious observances, and noted for the size of the gigantic crucifix which always hung with the rosary from his girdle.

Being called to the presidency of the missions at a time when things were in a sorry state, his skillful handling of the situation soon cleared the atmosphere which had been between friars and soldiers rather stormy. The firmness he exercised toward the friars would not have been tolerated from any other prelate. He was suave as Fr. Fermin Lasuén, but more shrewd; zealous as Fr. Sarria, but more broad-minded. In October, 1819, he received official thanks from the king for services rendered in California.[35]

Father Tapis, who had been chagrined at the repeated failures of the soldiers and friars to locate suitable mission sites in the valley, sent Father Luis Martinez into the San Joaquin on a tour of inspection. This party left Mission San Luís Obispo on May 29, 1816, and went directly to Buena Vista Lake. The first village visited was on the plain near the present Taft. Martinez called it Lucluc. The natives there had no desire to become neophytes and declined to espouse Christianity. Martinez finally bought one orphan boy with some beads and fresh meat. Suddenly some misunderstanding caused the Indians to flee precipitately. Messengers sent to reassure the natives were met with a fusillade of arrows and the cries "Kill the coast people." After leaving Lucluc, Martinez led his men nine leagues to the east which brought them to the village of Bubal, which was burned as a reprisal against Indian hostilities. The report made by Martinez was similar to those made by the leaders of former expeditions. He felt that suitable mission sites were not available.[36]

Martinez was one of the most unusual men to lead an expedition into the valley. He was a very capable man and pre-eminently a business manager. To keep his mission prosperous was his great aim and ambition. The horses, mules, and cattle bred at San Luis Obispo were of such quality that a San Lusito was always saleable. Visitors at San Luis Obispo were amazed at the hospitality. No other mission equaled it. Martinez wore the plain habit of the order always, but in other ways he was fond of display. When the mission produce was hauled to Monterey, the finest mules were hitched to the wagons, the Indian drivers were gaily dressed, and Martinez himself rode in a cart at the head of the procession. He was almost too generous to the presidios with mission supplies. In manner he was a popular, jovial man of the world rather than a typical missionary. To inferiors he was kind, to equals haughty, and often affected. With an intimate like Guerra he was jocose at times. He spoke the dialect of the San Luis Obispo Indians fluently and a very plain, blunt Spanish when angry, which never left any one in doubt as to his exact meaning. He was born to command and he did. The Indians both feared and liked him. He could always hold them in check. Unlike Governors Arrillaga and Solá, he was dark complexioned. His big nose had been twisted to one side by a fall from a carriage. At no time did he scandalize the order by his morals.[37]

An unexpected result of this trip which Martinez made was the bitter controversy which developed over the advisability of having soldiers accompany the expeditions. The Martinez party had been led by a friar but soldiers had gone along for protection. Like the two previous expeditions, it was considered a failure. The fight at Lucluc was blamed by the mission authorities on the conduct or presence of soldiers. The latter were always regarded with distrust and suspicion by the Indians. The military authorities insisted that no trips should be made without troops for protection. Soldiers were not always available when wanted and at such times the missionaries were not always willing to wait for a military escort. Then, too, when soldiers were secured they were often the type which tore down what the missionaries had slowly and painfully built up.

Martinez reported to Governor Solá that the soldiers had behaved with honor on his expedition. Father Cabot blamed the Martinez party for getting itself into trouble at Lucluc and claimed that when he went through there in 1815 the Indians were very peaceable. But Father Muñoz in turn disagreed with Cabot because in 1806 he had met with much hostility in the identical region. Thus we find disagreement among contemporary witnesses. Father Sarria wrote this letter to the governor:

> I do not know that any conversion has been effected when the ministers of the gospel have taken troops along. The results have ever been disastrous. Indians begin to look upon them with dread, for the first sight of troops makes them think that subjection and loss of liberty will follow. The consequences will then be either open resistance or flight. Thus the soldiers become an obstacle to missionary efforts. The Indians have no fear nor dread when the missionaries come alone. They will, on the contrary, receive them with many signs of good will.[38]

Yet the Father Prefect must have changed his mind because four months later Friar Juan Cabot visited the Indians to the east and was accompanied by soldiers procured for him by Father Sarria.

As a matter of fact, it was foolish to go without protection. Times had changed since Fages and Garcés had wandered fearlessly and alone. Soldiers and settlers had set bad examples of conduct. Furthermore, soldiers accompanied the friars because the royal and viceroyal regulations expressly ordered them to do so. These orders had been issued because dissatisfied and angry neophytes flocked to the tulares and, like escaped convicts, they feared and hated the law.

In spite of the handicaps caused by a lack of unity in the program affecting the valley, many Tularelios were converted to Christianity. The baptismal records of the missions at San Juan Bautista and San Migñel are a proof of this. The Indians remaining away from the missions disappeared long before the neophytes; this is partially a proof that civilization was good for the red men.

Another factor widening the breach between the Spaniard and the Indian was the type of soldier which appeared in California during the later days of the Spanish regime. The quality of the first soldiers had been fine but the later troops, usually recruited at San Blas, were the dregs of the seaport town. They were usually mixed in blood, short of stature, vile in morals, corrupt in blood, ill-tempered, cowardly, cruel, gamblers, thieves, drunkards, men without discipline and contemptuous of religion. Naturally Father-President Payéras protested against these cholos mingling with the Indians. They were a social menace. According to Bolton, the "soldiers in California, left without their families, chose their companions from among the native women, and thus grievously hampered the work of the friars."[39]

Although the report of Payéras made it clear that the missions were suffering from the influence of the Gentiles and the apostates, he could get no action from the government. A mission in the San Joaquin Valley would have protected the missions on the coast, saved souls for heaven, and gained subjects for the king. Payéras related how the epidemic of 1815 destroyed hundreds of Tulare Indians who pleaded in their extremity for spiritual enlightenment and baptism. Telame, a village of 4,000 inhabitants located near the present site of Dudley in the northwest corner of Kern County, was recommended as a suitable mission location. But the distance and the danger was too great without royal aid and that aid never came.[40]

Familiarity with mission life bred in the absconding neophytes a certain contempt. They learned the evil ways of the vicious white men and often forgot the finer things taught them by the friars. Payéras stated that this disrespect was carried by the apostates to their wild kinsmen in the tulares whom he designated as fickle, unreliable, and thievish. They were rapidly learning to ride and used the missions as their private ranches from which they helped themselves to horses, cattle, and other needed supplies. The lagoons and swamps hampered pursuing soldiers. The Indians laughed at the friars and defied the soldiers. The only salvation for the coast missionaries would be an inland mission supported by a presidio. Lacking such protection, California would eventually become subject to raids similar to those then being made into Sonora by the Apaches.[41]

Providence decreed that no great tragedy occurred in California. But the danger was always present; it dictated policies for a half century. The most common offense of the Indians, both neophytes and Gentiles, was horse stealing. Because of this propensity, the Tulare rancheria of Telame was termed by Payéras "a republic of hell and a diabolical union of apostates."[42] Horse stealing was a serious menace in those early days before horses became numerous. Large bands of the animals were driven into the hills and slaughtered. As late as 1833 an American frontiersman was astonished when he "came to a place in the Sierra Nevadas where there was a great quantity of horse bones. We did not know what it meant; we thought an army must have perished there."[43]

Economically the missions were sufficient unto

themselves. Bolton stated that "the central interest around which the missions were built was the Indian. In respect to the native, the Spanish sovereigns, from the outset, had three fundamental purposes. They desired to convert him, to civilize him, and to exploit him." Provisions were kept in reserve to last two years but if, in spite of this precaution, food became scarce it was customary to send the Indians off to the woods or plains where they were forced to hunt and fish until time to return for the next year's harvest. Besides bringing the gospel to the natives, the Franciscans were required to carry the entire burden of government and military supervision. The load was becoming too heavy and Payéras made this clear in his official report.

The primary object of the Franciscan friars had been the propagation of the faith among the Gentiles; the Indians along the coast had either been civilized or annihilated. The next obvious step led into the interior. These Gentiles had been invited to the missions. Few came. Neophytes, after baptism and a little instruction, frequently returned to their homes without permission. The evil environment of their former haunts caused them to "back-slide." They came to the missions on foot; they often left on horseback. Pursuing soldiers were lost in the tule swamps. Conditions were bad. To bring back the prodigals, to punish the thieves, and to establish a spiritual kingdom in the San Joaquin demanded immediate action.

The plan and the problem of Spain has been stated by Bolton in *The Mission as a Frontier Institution in the Spanish American Colonies*:

> Spain possessed high ideals, but she had peculiar difficulties to contend with. She laid claim to the lion's share of the two Americas but the population was small and little of it could be spared to people the New World. On the other hand, her colonial policy, equaled in humanitarian principles by that of

78

no other country, perhaps, looked to the preservation of the natives and to their elevation to at least a limited citizenship.[44]

In 1818 the missions all along the coast were reporting theft. Father Cabot stated that he feared a general raid from the Colorado River region. Horses were being stolen not only by runaways from the missions, but by the San Joaquin Valley tribesmen who were becoming increasingly bold. They no longer sought meat but mounts. They had become horse Indians, and henceforth the Spanish problem would be more difficult. The Indian disaffection was due partly to abuse by ruffians among the soldiers. Another reason rested with the mission system. In many cases neophytes had been coerced rather than persuaded to come to the missions. Each autumn a launch was sent up the San Joaquin River just after the harvest. The neophytes with the best record at the missions were permitted to go along on this annual outing. This launch was in reality a gunboat armed with a cannon and smaller artillery. Women and children were captured and the husbands and parents then followed along the banks of the river to the mission. Perpetual enmity developed and insatiable was the desire for revenge.[45]

In 1818 the launch party had an unhappy experience. Its members had reached the land of the Cosumnes near Stockton. They landed near a village with the intention of attacking it the next morning. But the Indians forestalled them, captured the cannon and the muskets, and drove the invaders pell-mell to the launch, which left so hurriedly that most of the men were left behind. These latter were soon scattered over the plain and traveled overland toward home. The Indians killed twenty-four of them before they reached the settlements. This fiasco enraged the neophytes and disgusted the padres. Governor Solá determined to destroy the newly created superiority complex of the red men. He arranged for three drives into the Indian country to be made simultaneously. The missions were to furnish money, arms, neophyte soldiers, and horses; the presidios were to provide regular troops under the command of regular army officers.[46]

The advance up the San Joaquin River was led by a cavalry officer, Sergeant José Sanchez. He was a powerful, bandy-legged man, a native of Sinaloa, and a practiced Indian fighter. He was a veteran of twenty campaigns. Brave, ignorant, honest, and unfit for promotion, he saw no need of either government or church and believed a sensible man could get along without either. He quarreled with the friars toward whom he was always hostile. Therefore he was denied the comforts of religion on his death bed and a Christian burial for a time. Sanchez was well acquainted with the country along the San Joaquin. His troops left San Francisco on October 5, 1819, and marched to Mission San José. They carried heavy shields and armor to ward off Indian arrows. The armor consisted of a helmet and jerkin made of leather, which was made of green cowhide. The latter was staked out on the ground and red hot stones placed on the green hide which contracted and thickened until not even a musket ball of that period could penetrate it.

On November 19th this expeditionary force left San José and nothing more was heard from it until the 27th. Then a cloud of smoke was seen mounting toward the eastern sky and it was assumed that a Cosumnes village was burning. The same day Sanchez returned to Mission San José with forty captured women and children. No men were captured as the enraged neophytes had killed all who fell into their clutches. The Spanish lost one white man and the Indians lost forty-one; the cannon stolen during the previous trip was recovered. Thus was the defeat of the launch party avenged.[47]

Sanchez made an official report of his expedition which was lofty in tone. It was this type of writing which the more matter-of-fact Anglo-Americans found ludicrous in the Spanish people. He announced bombastically that his report was "written with gunpowder on the field of battle." Then he related that at "five o'clock Neighbor Ghexbano Chaboya, having been taken ill with a pain in the stomach, the army was halted temporarily; however, it soon set forward again, and arrived at the river with only one accident, occasioned by the horse of Neighbor Leandro Flores again throwing up his heels and giving him a formidable fall."[48]

It is worthy of notice that one of the five soldiers wounded in this battle was a young private, José Maria Amador, a son of the courageous old veteran, Sergeant Pedro Amador, who had come to California in 1769. The same year Daniel Boone had left his home in the Carolinas to seek the "dark and bloody" ground of Kentucky. Amador's name and fame is forever perpetuated in the California county which bears his name.[49]

Sanchez was recommended for promotion because of his work in this campaign and was given a warrant as brevet color sergeant. The same year Sanchez led another expedition into the valley against the Moquelumne Indians. They had a village near the confluence of the Calaveras and the San Joaquin rivers. In this campaign twenty-seven Indians were killed and forty-nine horses regained.[50]

The second of the Sola expeditions in 1819 was composed of forty men led by Lieutenant Jose Maria Estudillo and Sergeant Jose Dolores Pico. Estudillo was the founder of one of the finest of California's old families. He was a skilled accountant and an excellent penman. Although a trifle vain, he was a great social favorite at Monterey, the capital of California and the home of the beautiful women of the province.

Estudillo's army left the capital city of Monterey on October 17 for the Indian in all the pomp and circumstance of war. The route traversed took the Estudillo party through Soledad, San Miguel, and into the tulare country of the present Kern county. All the Indians in the valley apparently had advance information of Solá's proposed drives. There was a leakage somewhere. Estudillo learned that news of his coming had been sent ahead from Soledad. He also learned much from the Indians concerning the operations of the other Spanish forces then in the field.

Estudillo led his men into the eastern foothills of Kern county along the same route explored by Moraga in 1806. The troops then went north to the Visalia region which seems to have been a favorite camping ground. Here they turned west until they reached the slough which they followed to the San Joaquin River. This stream they followed until near Tranquillity. At that point they turned west and crossed the hills, and on November 13th they reached San Juan Bautista. Three days later they were back at Monterey.

The trip had not been successful. No stolen animals were recovered, no runaways regained, and no Gentiles secured for training at the missions. Estudillo agreed with every commander, military and clerical, who had preceded him. A mission could no longer be established in the valley without a presidio of a hundred and fifteen men to support it. The Indians had developed into horse Indians and were able to compete successfully with Spanish cavalry. The natives not only stole horses but they had begun to breed them and regular horse fairs were held along the shores of Tulare Lake for the sale of livestock.

The simple minded natives of the early days had developed but not according to the pattern desired by the Franciscan friars.

In 1820 Sergeant José Sanchez made another trip into the Cosumnes region and recovered seventy stolen horses. The same year Sergeant Soto led an expedition to the village of the Nopochinches in the Mariposa country. Before any constructive action concerning the establishment of missions and presidios in the San Joaquin Valley could be taken, conditions in other parts of the Spanish world led to a series of revolutionary wars which deprived Spain of most of her colonies. Her opportunity in the valley of the San Joaquin was gone forever.[51]

The Mexican period which followed was incomparably romantic and picturesque. It was the period of song and story so delightfully portrayed by Gertrude Atherton in *The Splendid Idle Forties*. In the war with Mexico the United States acquired California and almost immediately the Golden State was admitted into the American Union.

A part of the purpose of this chapter has been to picture the first white men in the San Joaquin Valley in such a way that they will not quite drop out of mind. They are worth remembering. In their fierce passions and in their unconquerable spirit they carried the marks of their West Gothic blood, which long made Spain a dominant power. Long ago when the tribes of the Scandinavian forests sought new homes on distant frontiers they moved from west Gothland (Vastergotland), Sweden, into central and southern Europe. They were the first to break through the walls of the Roman Empire and finally sacked the imperial city itself. They became the ruling class in Spain, and were to be found in isolated groups from the Straits of Gibraltar to the Black Sea. The Vikings were the first to come to the New World; the Dons were the first to stay. They were people of the same blood. The Goths were members of Nature's aristocracy. When the Aztecs first beheld the Spanish Conquistadores they knelt in adoration, thinking their long expected Fair God had come.[52]

These early Spanish feared God and nothing else. Their fearlessness was equaled only by their energy. They claimed the New World and conquered most of it. Fifty years after Columbus reached the West Indies, the Spanish were hunting buffaloes on the plains of Kansas. It took the Anglo-Americans three hundred years to get that far.

And yet the great qualities of the Spaniards were their downfall. They won the world but lost their own future. Their bleaching bones are found in the far-flung outposts of the world, and the few men who returned from the wars, in many cases, married Indian women. This prevented the establishment of homes worthy of the Spanish tradition and decreed that no worthy descendants should remain to honor their memory or perpetuate the inspiration of their handiwork.

They are dead and so is the greatness of Spain. So, today, men from a different clime but of a similar blood are developing the San Joaquin Valley. And to make this clear will be a part of the purpose of subsequent chapters.

> Who now reads clear the roster of that band?
> Alas, time scribbles with a careless hand
> And often pinch-beck doings from that pen
> Bite deep, where deeds and dooms of mighty men
> Are blotted out beneath a sordid scrawl.[53]

4 Buckskin Shirts

and Beaver Traps

I've wandered wide, and wandered far,
But never have I met,
In all this lovely western land,
A spot more lovely yet.

William Cullen Bryant *The Hunter's Serenade.*

The expeditions into the San Joaquin Valley during the
Spanish rule were made under the supervision of the
political authorities, led by military men, and
accompanied by Franciscan friars. The diaries kept by the
friars have furnished an accurate source of information.
In 1823 the Revolutionary War came to a close, and the
Spanish colonies no longer recognized the authority of the
mother country. Mexico became an independent nation,

and California was a part of Mexico from 1823 to 1846.

During the Mexican regime, several expeditionary forces visited the San Joaquin Valley. Many of these were unofficial visits, which were neither sponsored, approved, nor controlled; Russians, French, and Americans entered the valley in violation of national courtesy and international law. Naturally, the records are less accurate and scantier than those of Spanish days.

In 1824, the year Mexico assumed control, the Indian neophytes at the missions of Purisima, Santa Inés, Santa Barbara, and San Fernando revolted. Many of them fled to the San Emidio region in the hills south of McKittrick and Bakersfield. The region south of Buena Vista Lake was one of their favorite haunts. When the Mexican expeditionary force arrived in search of them, it was learned that a Russian officer was teaching the renegade Indians the manual of arms and had improved their marksmanship to such an extent that the Mexican troops were unable to gain a decisive victory. Lieutenant Fabregat fought a battle with them on April 9, 1824, at Buena Vista Lake; it must have been a comic affair, since it lasted for five hours without a single casualty. The Indians shot too close for comfort in the opening volleys and the contestants sparred at long range during the rest of the fight. Sergeant Carlos Carrillo engaged the Indians in a similar contest two days later at San Emidio.[1]

The second expedition of the same year was sent out from Santa Barbara on June 2nd under the command of Captain Portilla. His force of approximately 130 men passed through Ventura, crossed the Santa Clara River, entered Tejon Pass, and finally reached San Emidio where they joined the first party which had left San Miguel in April. By this time the neophytes were penitent, and Portilla succeeded in taking them back to the missions.

86

He led his troops and Indians home by way of Cuyama Valley. Kern Lake was referred to at that time as Lake Misjamin.[2]

Sergeant Sanchez, who had led armies into the valley during Spanish days, was again sent into the San Joaquin. He commanded Mexican troops during some desultory fighting from November 19th to the 27th, 1826. The Cosumnes had killed thirty neophytes at the missions and Sanchez exacted vengeance by killing forty Indians.[3]

The first outstanding Indian chief to appear in the San Joaquin had been a neophyte at Mission San Jose. When he appeared for baptism at the mission, he was given the Christian name of Estanislao; he, in turn, gave his name to a river and a county, which Americans corrupted into the word "Stanislaus." At the mission he had been trained by teachers like Buelna, Labistido, and the one-legged soldier Romero. Estanislao was above the average in intelligence and served for a time as alcalde at Mission San José.

On that momentous occasion when Alcalde Higuera administered to the people of Monterey the oath of allegiance to the Mexican Constitution, Estanislao was a silent but interested spectator. This occurred on May 10, 1825. The three days bull-fighting which followed may have aroused the latent combativeness in his nature. He was living in a period of flux and change and in response to the revolutionary spirit then rampant he fled to the San Joaquin Valley and set up an embryonic republic of his own in the late 1820s. Other neophytes, dissatisfied with mission life, flocked to his standard. Estanislao, possessed of an education superior to his fellow tribesmen, became their leader in the Stanislaus River region whither he had gone. He began openly to defy the Mexican authorities and aided by a great warrior named Cipriano, he stole, looted, burned, and raided the

87

settlements. The depredations of Estanislao finally became so reprehensible that Father Durán of Mission San José appealed to Commandante Martinez for aid. But before any definite action could be taken in this matter another episode occurred which was to prove of great significance.[4]

The first white man to cross the Sierra Nevadas rejoiced in the prosaic name of Smith. He was also the first American, of whom there is record, to enter the San Joaquin Valley. Americans had haunted the coast ever since Pedro Fages had sent his warning to Argüello in 1788 that two ships belonging to George Washington had been sighted near the Farallon Islands outside Golden Gate. But Jedediah Smith was the first man from the United States to make an overland entry into California, and the first known white man to cross the Sierras.

Jedediah Smith differed from most of the other fur trappers of his time. They were illiterate, he was educated; they were a godless set, he was a devout Methodist; they were generally Southerners, he was of New England stock, although born in New York's Susquehanna Valley in 1799. A Yankee in the fur trade was an anomaly. Helen Dwight Fisher described him as follows in the *American Mercury*:

> Somehow in a frontier childhood he picked up a little education—he knew even some Latin— which was to mark him as a superior person in the Rockies, and for it he was actively grateful, even at thirty, to his teacher, a certain Dr. Simons, who must be provided for when Jed had made his pile. In the same childhood he picked up the Methodism which also marked him out. Even the potent religions of the 1820's scarcely penetrated the furmen's haunts, and there were few trappers beside Jed who could at twenty-five make such a powerful prayer on a sudden death out in the wilderness that all hearers were greatly moved, and "persuaded John died in peace."[5]

Some accounts credit this "knight in buckskin" with missionary work among the Indians. Whatever the truth of this assertion may be, the fact remains that:

> We have usually preferred our heroes cut to a pattern, and Jed was hardly the accepted type of Western adventurer. He was a "very mild man and a Christian", who carried a New England sense of sin up and down an incredible number of miles from Montana to Arizona and from the Mississippi to the Pacific, outwitted the Indians, grizzlies, the Hudson Bay Company and the Governor of California with equal zest, sent $200,000 worth of furs and pages of priceless geographical information back to St. Louis in four years, and then sat down in the Wind River valley to consider, not his achievements, but the higher education of his brothers and the state of his soul. "Oh, the perverseness of my wicked heart! I entangle myself too much in the things of time."[6]

In 1825, he became a partner of General William Ashley. Smith was then twenty-six years old and the youngest member of the Rocky Mountain Fur Company. Two years later he led a band of trappers to California by a southern route and finally reached San Gabriel Mission. Here they tarried while Smith tried to explain to Governor Miguel Echeandia, who had moved the capital from Monterey to San Diego, just why he and fourteen other heavily armed Americans were in the province without permission. Finally Smith was allowed to return to the United States and this he did, but by a rather circuitous route. He led his men back through Cajon Pass and into the San Joaquin Valley. His men trapped beavers and otters in the lakes of Kern and Tulare. For a time they lived among the Wimilchi Indians along the north bank of Kings River, and Smith named this river after the tribe. In the journal kept by a member of the party, Smith was quoted as follows: "On my arrival at the river which I named the Wim-mul-che (after the tribe of Indians which reside on it, of that name) I found a few beaver, and elk, deer, and antelope in abundance." He referred to the big lake as the Two Larres.[7] They moved slowly north along the San Joaquin River and reached the Stanislaus in April 1827.

The president of the Franciscan missions in Alta California at that time was Father Narciso Durán, residing at Mission San José. He was aware of the American intrusion into the province but when the party left San Gabriel in January it was taken for granted that they returned directly to the United States. Greatly to his astonishment, Father Durán now learned that these same Americans were on the Stanislaus. On May 15, 1827, four hundred disgruntled neophytes left Mission San José, and Smith was blamed for their defection. As a matter of fact, their unheralded arrival at the American camp caused Smith and his followers to kill several of them before it was learned the true reason for their appearance. In 1827 Mission San José, unpretentious in its buildings, was highly prosperous and its 2,000 neophytes were engaged in producing foodstuffs for the Russians in northern California. Father Durán immediately reported the matter to the authorities and on May 18th Governor Echeandia ordered the arrest of the Americans. In the meantime, Smith wrote the following friendly letter to Father Durán on May 19:

> Reverend Father: I understand through the medium of one of your Christian Indians that you are anxious to know who we are, as some of the Indians have been at the Mission and informed you that there are certain white people in the country. We are Americans, on our journey to the river Columbia. We were at the Mission of San Gabriel, January last. I went to San Diego and saw the General and got a passport from him to pass the mountains, but the snow being so deep, I could not succeed in getting over. I returned to this place, it being the only point to kill meat, to wait a few weeks until the snow melts to go on. The Indians here, also, being friendly, I consider it the most safe point for me to remain until such time as I can cross the Mountains with my horses,

having lost a great many in attempting to cross ten or fifteen days since. I am a long ways from home and anxious to get there as soon as the nature of the case will admit. Our situation is quite unpleasant, being destitute of clothing and most necessaries of life, wild meat being our principal subsistence. I am, Reverend Father, Your strange but real friend and Christian, J. S. Smith. [8]

The beaver and otter pelts of the trappers had assumed huge proportions by this time and many of their supplies were gone. The Spanish along the coast would imprison them rather than feed them or otherwise aid them. Therefore Smith determined to cross the Sierras and report to his associates at their rendezvous near Salt Lake. His first attempt failed. But when Echeandia's messengers arrived to arrest Smith they were too late; Duran's "strange but real friend and Christian" had gone over the mountains. To cross the range required eight days, and he reached Salt Lake safely. Everett Barker Chaffee, who wrote a master's thesis dealing with Smith in California, made a thorough search of documentary evidence and averred that Smith left California by way of the American River. One of Smith's companions on the return trip was Silas Gobel, the blacksmith of the party. [9]

On his return trip, Smith's supplies were stolen by the Mojave Indians and he fled to Mission San Gabriel. There seems to be some basis in fact for the assertion that these Indians had been incited to attack Smith by the California authorities. However, Father Sanchez took pity on him and gave Smith supplies which he transported to his destitute men along the Stanislaus. Smith then visited Father Durán and Governor Echeandía, then at Monterey, where his charming manners and the intercession of a Yankee skipper who went his bond, caused the governor to permit him to proceed unmolested to the Columbia River region. From the Stanislaus the trappers went north and camped along an affluent of the Sacramento River during the winter of 1827 and 1828, known thereafter as the Rio de los Americanos (the American River where James Wilson Marshall was later destined to discover gold).[10]

The following spring they proceeded to Oregon where the hostile Indians destroyed the entire force with the exception of Smith, John Turner, and Arthur Black. The Hudson's Bay factor on the Columbia, Dr. John McLoughlin, sent his men to salvage the remains of this disastrous expedition. Most of the furs, part of the equipment, and the diary of the trip kept by Harrison Rogers, the second in command, were secured. The latter journal has been the chief source of information concerning this expedition. Smith sold the furs to Dr. McLoughlin for $3,000. Such a price indicates that fur-bearing animals in the San Joaquin were abundant at that time; when a thrifty Scotchman representing a reputable firm like Hudson's Bay was willing to pay $3,000 in that day's currency for the pelts gathered during a single season, the quality and the quantity of the goods is self-evident.[11]

Quitting the trapping business, Smith entered the Santa Fe trade in January 1831. In the neighborhood of the Cimarron River the party ran out of water and encountered a severe sandstorm. Jedediah Smith left the main column in search of water. He never came back. His party of twenty-two wagons and seventy-four men could not wait; the men and animals were dying of thirst. They reached Santa Fe on the Fourth of July. Jedediah's pistols were then on sale in the marketplace. It seems that Comanche Indians had killed him just as he located a water hole in the otherwise dry riverbed.

> Other trappers had now found the way to California by Cajon Pass, and soon Joseph Walker was to climb the High Sierras westward. In eleven years John Fremont would be on the

road, and in fifteen years John Sutter would predict from the Sacramento Valley that one thousand souls would cross the mountains in the next year, while the New York Sun shouted something about one hundred thousand emigrants. But the intelligent Christian gentleman who first bucked the Sierra snow was dead at thirty-three, out by the Cimarron River.[12]

While Jedediah Smith and his trappers had been causing the Mexican officials much distress, Estanislao had been free to carry on his racketeering. However, his day of reckoning was drawing nigh. Commandante Martinez gave orders to Sergeant Sanchez to leave the presidio of San Francisco on May 1, 1829, for the San Joaquin Valley front. Sanchez had twenty-eight men and seventy Indian auxiliaries. This little army voyaged up the San Joaquin in a large boat, on which a cannon was present. The Indians had entrenched themselves in a dense thicket of willows and underbrush near the junction of the Stanislaus and San Joaquin rivers.[13]

In the ensuing battle the cannon proved useless and the white men matched their woodcraft and muskets against superior woodcraft and equally good muskets either stolen from the Spaniards or purchased from traders. The Indians glided noiselessly through the brush and used their bows and arrows with appalling effect when they chose to use weapons, which would not reveal their presence. Sanchez hurled his men in vain into the thicket; the foe faded away but dealt death as they disappeared. The fight lasted all day and at sunset Sanchez withdrew. The next day he again vainly strove to win the battle but was forced to give up and go home.[14]

General Mariano Guadalupe Vallejo was placed in chief command of the operations against Estanislao. His force consisted of cavalry, infantry, and artillery. He proceeded from Monterey to San Jose, where he added the discomfited Sanchez to his command. The San Joaquin

Engraving of
General Mariano
Guadalupe Vallejo,
leader of the fight
against Estanislao's
Indian uprising in
1829. *Fresno County
Public Library,
California History
and Genealogy
Room Collection.*

River was crossed near the stronghold of Estanislao on
May 29, 1829, and Vallejo promptly set fire to the woods
containing the Indians. When the over-heated natives
finally fled from the forest fire to the river, they were
met by equally hot fire from the three-pound cannons
planted on the opposite bank. A few reached the water
safely, but their bobbing heads made easy targets for the
soldiers. The next morning the troops closed in on the
fire-blackened thicket, and the few Indians who had
escaped the holocaust of the previous day fought
desperately. Very few evaded the sentries posted outside
the thicket by Vallejo; the destruction of Estanislao's
band of warriors was well nigh complete. The center of
the stronghold was a wooden fort and here only three
squaws were found alive. From all this misery
Estanislao escaped with his life. He fled to Father Durán
at Mission San José, confessed his sins, received official

pardon for his crimes from Governor Echeandia, and continued to reside at the mission.[15]

The first Smith in California was a gentleman of the finest type; the second, was in many ways the antithesis of the first. The latter was a horse-thief and a ruffian, but he had some redeeming features.

Thomas L. Smith was born in Kentucky and belonged to that class locally known as "poor white trash"; according to some writers they are the descendants of the indentured servants sent to America during colonial days. The home life of this lad was unpleasant and at the age of sixteen he ran away because "I didn't keer about the old woman walloping me, but the old man and the schoolmaster had no right to treat me so blamed bad." His career from that time until he died at San Francisco surpassed the exploits of any fictitious character ever created by the author of a wild western thriller. He carved up his white enemies with a knife in Natchez-under-the-Hill, he was mangled by grizzlies, he scalped innumerable Indians with reckless abandon, and then finally died peacefully in bed of old age.[16]

The following incident will indicate that his life, replete with tales of cold ferocity, was not devoid of praiseworthy acts. In a skirmish with some Indians near the headwaters of the Platte River a man named Joe Pratt was killed and left out on the plains. Smith was not present at the time but heard about it from the survivors. He prepared to go out after the body in order to bring it back for decent burial. The other men tried to dissuade him from his dangerous and perhaps futile mission. To their arguments and entreaties Smith made reply: "That is all very true; but, then, you see if I was laying out there and he was in my place he would see that I was covered with sod." It was the spirit of noblesse oblige in wild-western garb; Pratt had been his friend.[17]

While this discussion was going on an Indian, hidden behind a distant copse, shot Smith through the ankle. Smith fired at the smoke and a dead Indian was found with Joe Pratt's rifle beside him.

> The first shot had entered Smith's leg a little above the ankle, fracturing both bones in an ugly manner. Smith desired his companions to cut the leg off, but none of the hardy fellows had courage to perform the act. Calling for a sharp knife, Smith performed the operation himself, and fortunately for him, the jagged manner in which he performed his amateur surgical duties prevented the arteries from bleeding a great deal, and in twenty-four hours the flow of blood had entirely ceased. The following day his companions placed him on a rude litter and carried him one hundred and fifty miles to the Utah village, where Smith was nursed by the squaws. Three or four weeks afterwards, Smith discovered a spicula of bone protruding from the wounds, and with a pair of bullet-mounds or forceps, he drew it out. A few days later this operation was repeated; after which the wound healed, and in the spring Smith came out of his buffalo-robe bed with a stout oak stump, which he had whittled out of a sapling, for a leg in lieu of the one he had lost. On his first appearance his friends dubbed him "Peg-leg" Smith, a name he retained until the day of his death.[18]

He was one of the Rocky Mountain hunters who followed the trail made by Jedediah Smith through Cajon Pass into southern California. In 1829 he and some comrades took pelts to Los Angeles and returned to the Rocky Mountains by way of the San Joaquin Valley. In the early months of 1830, "Peg-leg" and his cronies were in the Tulare Lake region giving the Indians post-graduate instruction in the art of horse stealing. Smith made friends with the Indians and utilized them to secure horses from the Spanish along the coast. These animals he drove east and sold to the Americans engaged in the Santa Fe trade. On their way home they camped along Kern River. One of "Peg-leg" Smith's comrades failed to appear, and a search revealed that he had met a grizzly bear with results fatal to both contestants; they were found side by side, both dead. A rude, wooden cross was erected over the grave with an appropriate inscription and this cross was frequently seen by the early cattlemen of the vicinity in later years. It was finally destroyed by miners in the Kern River gold rush of 1856.[19]

In later life Smith loafed along Montgomery and Clay Streets in San Francisco and, when drunk, he frequently astonished and greatly startled passing pedestrians by giving the terrific war-whoops of the different Indian tribes he had met during his hectic existence.[20]

The same year that "Peg-leg" Smith was engaged in horse trading, another Southerner appeared in the valley. He was a young man of good family and his name was Ewing Young. In 1829 he led a group of trappers from Taos, New Mexico, into the San Joaquin Valley, which he entered from the south by way of Tejon Pass. Ewing Young chose his trappers with the same care that a modern football coach uses in the selection of the players on the first string. Brawn, brain, speed, and combativeness were prerequisites. Therefore his selection of a cherubic-looking, twenty-year-old stripling, only five feet four inches tall, must have seemed anomalous. He was the great-grandson of Daniel Boone and answered to the name of Kit Carson. He had the face of an angel, but he could fight like one of Lucifer's drill sergeants. Although a mere youth, Carson was already famous as a trapper in the Rocky Mountains and in northern Mexico. George Creel described him as follows:

> Always, however, the unknown drew him as a magnet, and when the winds blew warm he cast his lot with some rovers, who had heard great tales of California rivers black to the very brim with beaver.

General Christopher (Kit) Carson, who visited the San Joaquin Valley with the Ewing Young fur-trapping and Fremont exploration parties. *Fresno County Public Library, California History and Genealogy Room Collection.*

It was in the days when the old Spanish missions still flourished, and at San Gabriel and San Fernando the adventurers saw hills and plains covered with horses, cattle, and sheep, vineyards and white-clad monks moving like lords through fields where a thousand Indians worked for the greater glory of the Lord. A golden land, an Eden, but a few weeks exhausted its charms for the driving Americans, and they turned to the north, following the San Joaquin Valley to the upper reaches of the Sacramento.

On every hill burned the signal fires of the Indians, and when it was seen that the savages meant war Carson urged the wisdom of a bold stroke that would instill a wholesome fear. Picking a handful of the best riflemen, he fell on an Indian village in the night, wiping it out. Then, following with the tenacity of a hound, he gave successful battle to the broken remnants of the tribe in a mountain gorge.

Trapping in peace, the Americans went from stream to stream, and when they returned to Santa Fe in the spring of

1830, the sale of the furs gave them $24,000 to divide.[21]

Ewing Young and his men trapped along the Kern River and Buena Vista Lake and proceeded up the San Joaquin Valley. There they met Peter Skene Ogden, in command of sixty Hudson's Bay trappers. The two rival groups moved amicably northward, trapping as they went. Hudson's Bay had sent a representative named John McLeod to California in 1828, and the next year Ogden had arrived. This trip in 1830 was his first venture into the San Joaquin. Ogden and Young led their combined forces to the Sacramento River, and then Young re-traced his steps through Tejon Pass to Taos.[22]

The Hudson's Bay Company thought so highly of the quantity and quality of the fur in the San Joaquin that in 1832 they established a permanent camp in the northern part of the valley near Stockton. Since most of their trappers and hunters were French-Canadian coureur-de-bois, their rendezvous became known as French Camp and this name it bears to the present time. Frequently as many as four hundred trappers gathered there at the annual rendezvous.[23]

These French trappers ranged far and wide in California. One of these wanderers was Peter Lebec, who was killed in 1837 by a grizzly bear that he had wounded. His companions buried him under the tree where he died and carved his name in the bark. The bark grew out and filled in the cuts. Years later a portion was removed from the tree, showing the name of Peter Lebec in reverse on the inside. This section of bark was then placed in the Beale Library at Bakersfield. The tree still stands (1938) near the present highway south of Bakersfield, and about four miles north of the place known as Lebec.[24]

In 1832 Ewing Young returned to the valley and secured another profitable catch of beaver and otter furs. The

The inscription commemorating the death of Peter Lebec in 1837, carved on an oak tree located near the later site of Fort Tejon and later removed from the tree. Thelma Miller, *History of Kern County, California.*

huge herds of elk supplied the trappers with meat and an extra supply of dried meat, called "jerky" from the Spanish word *jarque*, which means dried meat, was secured. On this tour Young continued north to Klamath Lake; from this point he retraced his steps through the valley and returned to the east by way of the San Bernardino Valley. [25]

By 1837 Ewing Young had become a resident of Oregon. That year he and other settlers, under the direction of Lieut. William Slacum, organized the Willamette Cattle Company. The purpose of this company was to break the stranglehold of Hudson's Bay Company on the cattle industry in the Oregon country. This British company refused to sell cattle to American settlers, even though in some cases $200 was offered for a single cow. The Willamette Cattle Company, the first of its kind organized west of the Mississippi River, proposed to bring in cattle from California for the American settlers. A fund of $5,225.36 was raised and Ewing Young ventured south in search of cattle. Seven hundred Spanish longhorn cattle were bought at an average of $8.50 a head and, in spite of beasts of prey, hostile Indians, and inclement weather, Young and his cowboys delivered more than six hundred of the original herd of seven hundred. The arrival of this herd enabled the Rev. Jason Lee to provide cattle for his missions and for the incoming American settlers. The latter were to take decisive steps in securing for the United States a part of the disputed Oregon country a few years later.[26]

Joseph Reddeford Walker, like Young a native of Tennessee, was a famous Rocky Mountain man. In 1833, he was sent on a fur-gathering expedition by Captain Benjamin L. E. Bonneville, the man who was immortalized by Washington Irving. Walker followed the tributaries of the East Walker River, near the present site of Carson City, across the range to the headwaters of the Tuolumne River. He led his frozen and famished men to the edge of the Yosemite Valley, but its grandeur proved appalling rather than inspiring; they needed soup, not scenery.

According to the journal kept by Zenas Leonard "some of these precipices seemed to us to be more than a mile high."[27] The same diary reveals the fact that they visited the Merced Grove of Big Trees. Leonard wrote that these trees were "a redwood species sixteen to eighteen fathoms around the trunk at the height of a man's head from the ground."[28] On their way down the western slope of the high Sierra, the fatigued men received an additional shock when the very firmament of heaven seemed to descend in a blaze of glory: this was the meteoric shower of November 12, 1833.

Walker went directly to Monterey and asked the governor in a manly fashion for permission to trap in the valley. The Spanish-Californians were centaurs and took no interest in any task impossible to be performed on horseback. Since it was manifestly impossible to trap or fish while mounted the obvious thing was to refrain from such menial tasks. They did. Hence the governors of California were not envious of the American trappers; they merely wanted them to refrain from violence and political agitation. The rough and tough hunters with Walker began a carousal in Monterey, which almost proved disastrous to his plans, but Walker finally led a cavalcade of fifty-two men, three hundred horses, fifty cattle, and thirty dogs into the San Joaquin. That year a terrible pestilence had broken out among the Indians in the valley and in many places Walker found it almost depopulated. His men trapped along the various streams and in the spring of 1834 he led them out through a pass which is now known as Walker's Pass, due east of Bakersfield.[29]

In 1834 the central government of Mexico sent an order to California that all the missions should be secularized. Aside from the grief this order may have caused the Franciscans, the results of secularization were twofold: first, no more missionary expeditions were ever sent into the interior; second, hundreds of neophytes were released who thereupon returned to their former homes in the valley. Their mingling with the wild Indians produced new problems and startling results. The supply of wild animal life in the San Joaquin had been greatly depleted by American trappers and hunters. The released neophytes knew of an excellent substitute. These neophytes had been trained as vaqueros; they knew cattle and their ways; and they knew just where to get them. So they led their wild comrades on raids to the coast settlements. These cattle drives were well organized and the herds were sent to Tulare Lake, which became a terminal. American adventurers established a rendezvous near the lake in 1837 and forwarded stolen cattle to the east by way of New Mexico.[30]

On September 1, 1838, while Dr. John Marsh was absent from home, some Indians ransacked and looted his ranch house on *Los Meganos*. Marsh was of New England birth but had become a naturalized Mexican citizen. He was a combative individual who had been a pioneer on six frontiers. He was of Puritan ancestry, had been graduated from Harvard, had served under Zachary Taylor and had commanded the Sioux scouts in the Black Hawk war. He was the first permanent American resident and the first medical doctor in the San Joaquin. His patients paid him for his medical services in cattle. One time he charged a Spanish-California rancher fifty cows for treating his little daughter sick with a fever; the rancher's wife washed the doctor's shirt and charged him twenty-five cows. Each thought the other had made an exorbitant charge, but the doctor finally had to content himself with a twenty-five cow fee for his visit.[31]

Marsh resented the presence of Hudson's Bay trappers in the valley because he knew the value of fur and objected to their competition. He had altercations with their leader, Michael La Framboise, which led indirectly to the withdrawal of the company. But in 1838 he was particularly indignant with the Indians and accompanied the expedition, which chased them from Brentwood to the Sierras, killed eleven natives, and recovered five hundred stolen horses.[32]

The governor of California from 1836 to 1842 was Juan Bautista Alvarado. In the last year of his administration he sent Don Santiago Estrada into the San Joaquin Valley

Engraving of General John C. Fremont, great frontiersman and early explorer of the San Joaquin Valley. *Fresno County Public Library, California History and Genealogy Room Collection.*

in command of troops with orders to subdue the Indians along the foothills to the east. Estrada held the sector from Mariposa south to the point where the San Joaquin debouches into the plains. He explored the territory thoroughly and gave to Alvarado such information concerning it that the latter, after his term of office had expired, secured a grant of land there which was named *Las Mariposas.* Later this was sold to John C. Fremont.[33]

The next year Micheltorena became governor of California. He sent General José Castro to the foothill region of the San Joaquin north of the present Fresno. Here Castro established a permanent camp. He managed to hold the Indians in check and liked the country sufficiently well to secure a land grant on the plains opposite his military camp.[34]

A new type of American reached California in 1844. He led an expedition, not in search of fur, but in quest of information of a topographical and geographical nature; it has even been asserted that political news concerning California would be welcomed at Washington. If the California plum was to fall from the Mexican tree, the United States wished to forestall England, France, and Russia.

This was General John Charles Fremont's second trip to the Far West, and his first to California. His official guide was Thomas Fitzpatrick, usually called "Broken Hand"; the hunter for the party was Alexander Godey. Kit Carson was also a member of the force. Fremont led his men directly against the high Sierra barrier and found it a difficult hurdle indeed. After a month of floundering in the snow, the men were in danger of starvation. On the night of February 13th Fremont made the following entry in his journal:

> The meat train did not arrive this evening, and I gave Godey leave to kill our little dog (Tiamath) which he prepared in Indian fashion—scorching off the hair, and washing the skin with soap and snow, and then cutting it up into pieces, which were laid on the snow. Shortly afterward, the sleigh arrived with a supply of horse meat; and we had tonight an extraordinary dinner—pea soup, mule and dog.[35]

The next day, February 14, Fremont beheld a beautiful mountain lake set like a diamond in a platinum ring; this has since become famous as Lake Tahoe. Eventually the ridge was crossed and the descent made into the Sacramento Valley without a mishap.[36]

When Fremont reached Sutter's Fort he was hospitably received, royally entertained, and finally, on March 24, 1844, bidden a fond adieu by the famous Swiss "lord of the northern marches." The evening of the same day Fremont

Engraving of Alexiz Godey, scout for John C. Fremont and early rancher of Kern County. *Fresno County Public Library, California History and Genealogy Room Collection.*

camped along the Cosumnes River. On March 28 his force reached the Mokelumne River. The Calaveras River was crossed without difficulty, but the next day the Stanislaus River proved less tractable. Fremont followed it from its mouth, toward the Sierra and then back, but no ford was located. They finally crossed it near the point where it empties into the San Joaquin. On April Fool's Day they crossed the Merced, and in his journal Fremont wrote that along this river tracks of numerous grizzlies were seen. By April 6th they had come to the San Joaquin River, where it flows in a westerly direction from the mountains. Two days later, they made their camp along Kings River at a point which Fremont gave as latitude 36°24'50" and longitude 119°41'40." This would be near Kingston or modern Laton.[37]

Fremont's ride down the San Joaquin Valley during the balmy month of April caused the famous Pathfinder to become enamoured of California; he was one of its earliest boosters. The winters may be foggy; the summers may be hot; but that the springtime in that region has a peculiar potency none can deny. Fremont's horse moved noiselessly over a thick, velvety carpet of green alfilaria dotted with decorative pink blossoms. Acres of beautiful blue lupines appeared like islands set in a golden sea of poppies. No plow had ever desecrated the soil or destroyed its native grasses and flowers. His poetic nature responded to the charm of it all. He knew that soon the hot summer winds would cause the flowers to shrivel and die, but that in dying they would sow themselves and reappear each successive spring in merry troops until the landscape would ripple with them. He may have pondered that life is like that. In dying men abide not alone, but they sow themselves by their thoughts and words and acts and thereby reincarnate themselves in the generations yet unborn. Perhaps he began to covet the land for his people and to scheme for the overthrow of the government, which then ruled it. He has thus been accused. The flag at the head of Fremont's column had white stripes representing honor, red stripes indicating sacrifice, and a cluster of stars set in a sky of blue which to him was both a picture and a promise of heaven. Four years later this flag waved over all California and Fremont himself was a cattle-king residing in the San Joaquin Valley. Thus do dreams sometimes come true.

Fremont reached the Kern River on April 12. In this region he saw numerous bands of pronghorn antelopes with a cloud of coyotes hovering on the outskirts and feasting on the young antelopes which were at that season incapable of speed and therefore helpless. The expedition left the valley by way of Tehachapi under the guidance of an Indian who led them along the route now followed by the railroad to Mojave. When Fremont saw the desert spread out before him he sadly contrasted it with the charming region he had just left. He commented on the yucca trees, which appeared grotesque both in the day and the dark. He wrote as follows in his journal:

> It was indeed dismal to look upon, and hard to conceive so
> great a change in so short a distance. One might travel the
> whole world over, without finding a valley more fresh and
> verdant—more floral and sylvan—more alive with birds and
> animals—more bounteously watered— than we had left in
> the San Joaquin; here, within a few miles ride, a vast desert
> plain spread before us, from which the boldest traveler turned
> away in despair.[38]

When they reached the San Bernardino Valley they met
Joseph Reddeford Walker, who was returning from Los
Angeles with a drove of horses for the Santa Fe trade. The
two forces made the rest of the journey together, and the
next year Walker accompanied Fremont to California. It
will be remembered that Walker had been on a trapping
expedition to the San Joaquin a decade before Fremont
got there.

In 1845 Fremont led a second exploring party to California.
He was a shrewd judge of men and insured the success of
his venture by employing Kit Carson, now a mature man,
and Joseph Walker as guides. His chief assistants were
Theodore Talbot, Alexander (or Alexis) Godey, and Richard
Owens; his topographer was Edward M. Kern.[39]

The party was divided at East Walker Lake, near modern
Carson City. Kern, accompanied by Talbot, Walker, and
Owens, led his force of men south through the valley
thereafter known as Owens Valley. They passed by way of
Inyo Lake, Bishop, and Lone Pine to Walker's Pass.
Fremont had instructed them to wait for him at the River
of the Lake. By this he meant Kings River, but Walker
took it for granted that he meant Kern River. Each river
at that time emptied itself into a lake and the
misunderstanding is thus easily explained. Incidentally
Kern River received its present name at this time for
reasons which are obvious.[40]

While Kern proceeded southward in a leisurely fashion, Fremont, Godey, and Carson led their men along the Truckee River and over the grade to Sutter's Fort. This was the route later followed by the Forty-Niners and the Pony Express. When Fremont reached Sutter's Fort, he felt that his reception was less cordial than on the previous occasion. He had difficulty in securing fresh mounts. Sutter may have been given orders for political reasons not to aid Fremont. John Bidwell, later founder of Chico, tried to mollify the Pathfinder. Fremont made a hasty trip to the presidio of San Francisco and then led his men south through the San Joaquin Valley over the same route as the preceding year. He noted in his journal the tremendous bands of beautiful, wild horses capering disdainfully beyond reach. His own fatigued and dilapidated beasts made a sorry contrast to this cavalcade which swept gracefully over the grassy plains.[41] The camp was frequently disturbed at nights by their wheeling and trumpeting as they gamboled in the moonlight:

> We waked in our brief camp and watched them,
> Wrung with a joy that was nameless.
> There is a dark time coming; sorrow and age will come soon.
> But beauty is ours to remember; how in the night on the desert
> Wild horses of the Mojave go playing under the moon.[42]

Kings River was reached on December 22, 1845, and Fremont waited two days for the appearance of Walker and his party. Thinking that their encampment might be upstream, Fremont left his camp on December 24th and followed the right bank of Kings River into the foothills and then scaled the mountains to the incredible height of 11,000 feet. Topographical maps published by the United States Geological Survey would indicate that this altitude was probably encountered along the South Fork of Kings River. At that time there existed an Indian trail along the South Fork of Kings River which led through Kings River

Canyon to Bull Frog Lake and thence to Bubb Creek
where the altitude is 11,000 feet. This trail continued
through Kearsarge Pass to the other side of the
mountains.[43] Besides being a civil engineer and a
scientist, Fremont was a poet by instinct. He gazed with
awe on Nature's handiwork and, like Othello, was
overwhelmed by:

> Antres vast, and deserts idle,
> Rough quarries, rocks, and hills
> Whose heads touch heaven.

To go farther would have been foolhardy and Fremont
gave orders to return to the valley. Swirling snow
hampered the descent. The New Year came in as they
were going out. Fremont wrote that the New Year came in
rough like the mountains in which they found themselves.
It was a happy day for them when they reached the valley
floor and safety. Fremont remained near Tulare Lake from
the 7th to the 15th of January and then went to Mission
San José. In the meantime Talbot's party waited in their
camp in the hills along Kern River, a hundred miles to the
south of Kings River. Acting on information received from
natives that Fremont was at Mission San José, Richard
Owens and Joseph Walker went scouting for their
comrades and met Kit Carson and Alexander Godey out
on the plains who had set out on a similar mission. The
reunited parties then had an unfortunate affair with
Castro at Hawk's Peak, left California, went to Klamath
Lake, were overtaken by Lieutenant Archibald Gillespie
with orders from the United States Marines to return, and
arrived in California in time to take an active part in the
war against Mexico.[44]

The same autumn that Fremont made his second trip into
the San Joaquin an Indian attack was made on the
Campo de los Franceses ranch owned by William Gulnack.

One of the ranch-hands was killed and a man named James Williams carried the news to Sutter's Fort. Sutter equipped a troop of mounted men, placed Williams in command, and succeeded in thoroughly trouncing the Indians in a running fight. This battle occurred southeast of Stockton.[45]

A cattle ranch had been established along the banks of the Stanislaus River named the *Rancho de Rio Estanislao*. One day in the fall of 1847 the ranch foreman, B. K. Thompson, arrived at the Weber ranch in a disheveled condition. The Indians had stolen his cattle and destroyed the buildings. Weber sent Thompson back with a mounted party who chastised the natives and secured the stolen cattle.[46]

In 1848 John Woodhouse Audubon organized a party of one hundred men and traveled through Mexico and up into California on an exploring tour. To the coarse hunters of the frontier his purpose must have seemed ridiculous; he was studying birds. His father, John James Audubon, had classified many of the birds of the Mississippi Valley, and the son carried on the work of the father as an ornithologist and naturalist. The portion of the journal which deals with the march of the Audubon party through the San Joaquin Valley is of value because the writer observed things which failed to interest the ordinary explorer. While camping along the banks of Kings River near the present Reedley, he made the following entry that is of interest in the light of present conditions there:

> Today I ran on to a herd of about 1,000 elk; so close was I that I could see their eyes perfectly; these elk must be greatly harassed by wolves, which are very numerous, and so bold at night that we have had several pieces of meat, and a fine goose stolen from over my tent door. Their long, lonely howl at night, the cries of the myriad of wild geese, as well as Hutchinson's goose (which is very abundant), and the discordant note of the night herons, tell the melancholy truth

all too plainly, of the long, long distance from home and friends.

There is no trail but that of the wild horses and elk, all terminating at some water hole, not a sign of civilization, not a track of a white man to be seen, and sometimes the loneliness and the solitude seem unending.[47]

The United States acquired California officially in 1848. Two years later Lieutenant George H. Derby, a literary wit and a member of the Topographical Engineers, made a long exploring tour of the valley. Although Derby was a well known army officer and the trusted friend of Jefferson Davis, Secretary of War, he is best remembered for his humorous sketches written in San Francisco during the 1850s which appeared in the San Francisco *Herald* under the name of Squibob or John Phoenix. He was the Will Rogers of the period. Like most of the regular army officers, he despised the state militia. At a banquet he offered this toast: "Here is to our citizen soldiery! Invincible in peace, invisible in war!" He was the first scientifically trained observer to enter the valley since Fremont and the first to explore it officially after California had become a part of the United States.[48]

As Father Martin had done half a century earlier, he left for the Tulare country from San Miguel. He camped near the slough at the southern end of Tulare Lake and then marched to the Visalia region by way of a village on the east shore, which he called Sintache. He reported that the chief of the village "or captain was an old Indian from the San Luis Obispo Mission."[49] Then he circled by way of Chumtache, Tache, Deer Creek, south of Bakersfield, and finally reached Buena Vista and Kern Lakes. The old Indians in the vicinity told him that this was the wettest season within their memory and yet he noted that with all this evidence of a high-water mark the two lakes did not join.[50] From the southern part of the valley he moved north and east and followed the foothills across the Kaweah, Kings, and San Joaquin Rivers. He followed the latter river west to the slough connecting it with Tulare Lake and then down the west side of the lake to Avenal Creek and over the Coast Range back to San Miguel.[51]

To Derby it was apparent that a great change had been wrought in the Indians since the coming of the white men. Men of all nations had passed that way during a half-century and the appearance of Indian posterity was a mute evidence of their conduct. Then, too, a racial change had been accompanied by a revamping of social customs. Horses and cattle had greatly modified Indian culture. After 1850 another force, disturbing to the Indians, entered the valley. Gold had been discovered and prairie schooners, entering the valley from the south, lumbered along the valley floor to the north. By 1853 regular wagon roads traversed the San Joaquin in all directions. Wild animals and wild Indians found it increasingly hard to subsist. The era of exploration was over.

Today men may long for the wide open spaces of the untrammeled West, but they find it only in their imaginations as they sit by their radios and listen to John Charles Thomas as he sings:

Oh, give me a home
Where the buffalo roam
And the deer and the antelope play,
Where seldom is heard a discouraging word
And the skies are not cloudy all day.[52]

Dr. John Marsh, one of the first Americans to settle in California and a renowned citizen of the state. George D. Lyman, *John Marsh, Pioneer.*

5 The First
Settling

Away, away from men and towns
To the silent Wilderness.

Percy Bysshe Shelley *To Jane the Invitation.*

"A cattle ranch which I am maintaining at Las Mariposas is in danger of destruction any moment from the Indians."[1] This statement was made under oath by John Charles Fremont before the United States Land Commission at San Francisco in January, 1852. This testimony by the famous Pathfinder, made two years after California had been admitted to statehood, indicates that existence on the California frontier was dangerous.

The Indian menace retarded the development of the San Joaquin Valley and explains the difficulty of the first cattlemen in maintaining themselves and their herds. The Spanish-Californians began the movement into the valley during the decade from 1836 to 1846. In 1848, the United States secured California; the gold rush began in earnest the next year; and in 1850, California was deemed populous enough to be admitted into the American union. In spite of the rapid influx of miners and covered wagon immigrants, Fremont could truthfully state in 1852 that his ranch was in imminent danger of destruction and that neither California vaqueros nor American cowboys wanted to remain in so dangerous a locality. Vile diseases, bad liquor, deceit, and military onslaughts during a half century by Spanish, Mexican, and American forces had not yet succeeded in corrupting the intestinal fortitude of the Miwok and Yokuts Indians, who still battled with pathetic futility for a cause already irrevocably lost.

The first white man to establish a home in the San Joaquin Valley was a native of Spain named José Noriéga. He built a home and stocked a ranch with cattle in the vicinity of Brentwood in the early part of 1836. The Spanish colonies had broken away from Spain in 1823 and California had therefore severed all ties with Europe. In 1835 the foreign-born Noriéga was able to secure special permission from the national government at Mexico City to acquire land. He retained his grant until late 1837, when he sold *Los Meganos* (sand dunes) to Dr. John Marsh. At that time and for several years thereafter no other land, private or mission adjoined this grant. It lay between Mt. Diablo and the present site of Brentwood and was then as far out on the Indian frontier as even a seasoned frontiersman like Marsh cared to go. The nearest line of settlements lay thirty miles toward the coast. *Los Meganos* contained 17,712 acres and was watered by the San Joaquin River. The following testimony by Dr. Marsh before the Land

Commission will illustrate social conditions then existing in the San Joaquin:

> I have resided in the State of California since the first day of January, 1835. I purchased the rancho *Los Meganos* from José Noriega in the latter part of 1837 and I removed on to it in April, 1838. When I purchased the estate the said Noriéga gave to me the original title papers which had been given to him by José Castro of the said rancho in the year 1835. Those papers with all my other valuable deeds, papers and documents were stolen from my house on said rancho about the first of September, 1838. I was absent from my house on a journey to San José, leaving my house and farm in the care of two mission Indians who were steady, trustworthy persons. On my return and before I reached my house I met my two Indians flying from my place; they were in great distress and informed me of the robbery of my house by a band of robbers and that the robbers had stolen a number of my horses and had fled. On reaching my house I found that the story of my Indians were verified by the appearance of the house and the entire destruction of all my deeds, papers, and documents and the destruction or carrying away of all my other property in the house. I found a good many fragments of the papers torn and defaced to be entirely worthless, I could not repair them so as to make them intelligible. The said original title papers from Castro to Noriega—Noriega's deed of said rancho to me—my diploma from Harvard and all my other papers and documents were destroyed at that time. I followed on the trail of the robbers until I found where they had encamped for the night about eight miles from my house by a spring of water— it was there I found the fragments of the papers and torn clothing. It was there, as I judged from the appearance, that the robbers had divided the plunder.[2]

Los Meganos was finally patented and Marsh resided there continuously until 1857. That year he was murdered by highwaymen while on his way to Martinez. His career as a doctor and rancher in the northern San Joaquin was replete with dramatic episodes, and references to them will appear in due time.

Home of John Marsh, located on the Los Meganos land grant near present-day Brentwood. *Garden of the Sun,* 1939 edition.

A grant named *Los Medanos,* not to be confused with the Noriega tract of *Los Meganos,* was made to José Antonio Mesa, his brother José Maria Mesa, and José Miguel Garcia. *Los Medonos,* meaning, "desert plains," was the second grant to be made in the San Joaquin. It was located in the neighborhood of what is now Pittsburg. The ranch contained two square leagues (8,890.26 acres) and was granted by Governor Juan Bautista Alvarado on November 26, 1839. Cattle were placed on it immediately and two houses were erected for the families of Garcia and José Antonio Mesa. The latter planted wheat, corn, and pumpkins. Perhaps this was the first wheat grown in the San Joaquin. After a time the grantees sold their ranch to three men named Murray, Faran, and Stephenson. The latter was from New York and after his arrival *Los Medanos* began to be called the New York ranch. Many of the old maps show this designation. Jonathan Stephenson finally acquired sole control of the estate.[3]

The third grant lay only partially within the San Joaquin Valley. This ranch, named *Arroyo Seco,* lay north of

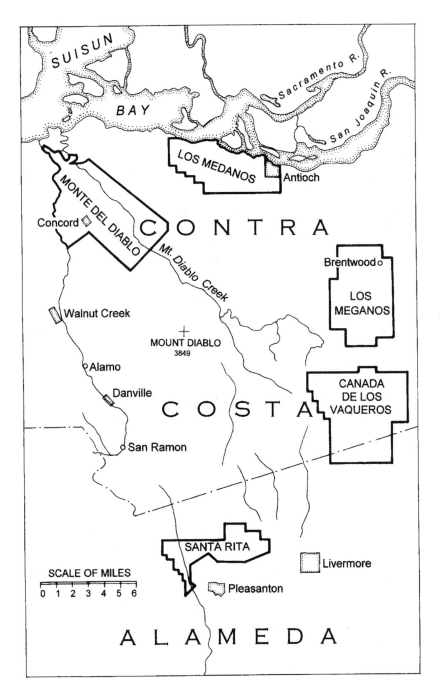

Stockton, between the Cosumnes and the Mokelumne rivers. *Arroyo Seco* consisted of eleven square leagues (48,857.52 acres) and was granted to Teodocio Yorba on May 8, 1840, by Governor Juan B. Alvarado. This region between the Sierra Nevada mountains and the road to the San Joaquin and Sacramento rivers was hostile Indian territory, and could not be permanently occupied until after 1846. Therefore Yorba did not take immediate possession. The Indians had been chastised in that region by Salvador Vallejo in 1828, but until 1847, a lonely settler faced grave danger by venturing that far inland.[4]

Francisco Soberanes received eleven square leagues (48,823.84 acres) from Governor Alvarado on September 7, 1841. This ranch was named the *Sanjon de Santa Rita* and was located in what are now the counties of Merced and Fresno. Soberanes was one of the few early cattlemen interested in improving beef stock by intelligent breeding. This was one reason for his desire to secure virgin land away from other ranches where inferior stock was common. He resided constantly on his ranch subsequent to his securing title to it. The boundaries are interesting. *Sanjon de Santa Rita* was bounded on the north by the Arroyo de los Baños del Padre; on the east by the San Joaquin; on the west by the Chamisal (thicket) del Llano; and on the south by the Dos Palos (two sticks). Apparently, the latter were placed there by some surveyor as a marker or they were already there and merely used as a starting point in the survey. The present towns of Los Baños and Dos Palos are located slightly to the west of the *Santa Rita* ranch. The grantee was driven from his ranch on several occasions and Alvarado, a former governor of California, told the Land Commission: "The country during that period was infested on all sides with hostile Indians who were fighting and committing all sorts of depredations." A member of the Land Commission interrogated Alvarado as follows: "State if in your opinion it was either safe or expedient in the year 1841 or 1842 and up to July, 1846, to occupy a grant of land lying along the San Joaquin River in consequence of the Indian difficulties and depredations aforesaid?" The answer was, "It was not safe or possible on that account to occupy land there—during the period aforesaid."[5]

Far to the south a grant was made to Antonio Dominguez by Governor Alvarado called *San Emidio*. It lay to the southeast of what is now Maricopa. The grant was made on July 14, 1842, and contained 17,709.79 acres. José Antonio Dominguez kept cattle on this ranch continuously until his death in the latter part of 1843 or the early part of 1844; he had gone on a visit to the Mission La Purisima and had contracted smallpox which proved fatal. The widow and the seven children then removed to Santa Barbara. The widow, Francesco Villa Dominguez, sold a half interest in *San Emidio* to John C. Fremont for $10,000; this deal was consummated on March 19, 1852. The other half she retained for the benefit of her growing children. The Indian menace forced the withdrawal of the livestock from *San Emidio* for a time in 1846 and they were pastured on the ranch of Octaviano Gutiérrez, which was located near Santa Barbara.[6]

The *San Luis Gonzaga* ranch (48,821.43 acres) lay to the west of Los Banos. A portion of it was located on the valley floor and the balance lay in the foothills and was drained by San Luis Creek. The original grantee was Francisco Rivera, but he made no attempt to occupy it for two years. Then José Maria Mejia denounced the land. Governor Micheltorena referred the matter to the prefect of the First Department of Monterey and on October 5th, 1843, the prefect reported the lands in question were wastelands and eligible for regranting. Mejia received the grant on November 4, 1843, and on November 7th he conveyed a

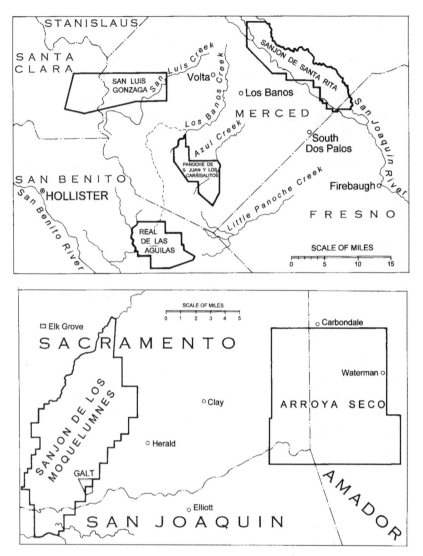

half interest in it to Juan Perez Pacheco. The latter was a
good businessman and in order to prevent future difficulty
with the original grantee he secured, for valuable
consideration, a formal release of any claims to it by
Rivera. This was done in June, 1851. José Abrego testified
before the Land Commission that Mejia and Pacheco

An example of San Joaquin Valley's earliest architecture—a tule shack lashed together with a wood frame, and with a stovepipe incongruously protruding from its roof. Photograph taken circa 1900. M. Theodore Kearney, *Fresno County, California and the Evolution of the Fruit Vale Estate.*

resided continuously on this property, built several corrals, cultivated portions of it, and constructed a house.[7]

This adobe house, built by José Maria Mejia and Juan Perez Pacheco in 1843, still remains. The Great Southern (Butterfield) Overland Mail made it one of its stage stations on their route between San Francisco and St. Louis. It is located along the present highway, which connects San Jose and Fresno. The present owners operate a gasoline service station and a quick-lunch eating place. The old ranch house consists of a single room, which is sixteen feet wide on the inside and forty-two feet long. Pieces of sandstone compose the foundation. Portholes in all the walls, five feet from the ground, offer silent testimony concerning the Indian menace, which was ever present. The Native Sons of the Golden West have placed an appropriate bronze marker on the building.[8]

The owners were annoyed by the original grantee and by

the Indians. The former, Francisco Rivera, had removed to Mexico City and on February 20, 1851, he appeared before Daniel Mendez, a national and notary public of that city, and prepared an affidavit delegating to José Abrego of Monterey the power of attorney with instructions to file a claim before the Land Commission for a share in the *San Luis Gonzaga* ranch. In the affidavit, Rivera stated that he had received the grant in December, 1841, and that a part of his rights to it had been released to Pacheco for $1200.[9]

The Indians proved annoying and dangerous. Jacinto Rodriguez, a soldier who had campaigned in the valley, told the Land Commission on September 3, 1855: "At that time the Indians attacked or came to the ranchos, even those nearest the towns, and as a soldier I pursued the Indians and knew the rancho *San Luis Gonzaga* long before it was ever granted to anyone. After the rancho was granted there was a white man killed there by the Indians." Benito Diaz, who was both a soldier and a miner, averred that the Indians from the tulares passed across this ranch on their way to the settlements.[10]

The next grant made in the southern part of the valley was called *Castaic* (from the Yokuts word meaning "my eye"). Micheltorena made the grant to José Maria Covarrubias on November 22, 1843; the latter was the alcalde at Santa Barbara. This ranch of five square leagues was located south of present Bakersfield at the point where the Grapevine road enters the foothills and included the present site of Hotel Lebec. After Covarrubias had secured it, a foreman and several Indian vaqueros were sent there with cattle. Years later, Covarrubias secured several witnesses who testified before the Land Commission that he had actually occupied *Castaic*. Among them were J. J. Warner of Los Angeles who was well acquainted with the land, had pastured stock there ten years before Covarrubias secured it, and had visited the latter there after the grant had been made. One of the famous Carrillo brothers, Pedro by name, was there in 1844 and saw cultivated fields, horses, and Indian laborers at work, but no white men. The same year Tomás Vallo arrived there with three hundred head of cattle and remembered seeing twenty men at work on the ranch. Rather irrelevantly he remarked that the mayordomo (or as he called him, "Big Boss") was named José and another man, also of some importance was called the "Corporal." He agreed with Carrillo that there were cultivated fields on the place, domestic horses, and branded cattle, all showing that earnest and immediate efforts were being made to effectively occupy the ranch.[11]

The foregoing Covarrubias, owner of *Castaic*, was one of the three San Joaquin Valley ranchers active in the framing of the first state constitution in 1850. His grandson won international renown as an astronomer and wrote a textbook still used as a standard reference work at the University of California. Another grandson, Miguel Covarrubias, was destined to win fame as an artist and caricaturist. In 1938 his famous book of sketches was published entitled *The Island of Bali*.[12]

The third grant made in the southern part of the San Joaquin was called *El Tejon* and was granted by Governor Micheltorena to José Antonio Aguirre and Ignacio del Valle on November 24, 1843. This ranch, held jointly by the two owners, consisted of twenty-two square leagues (approximately 100,000 acres) and extended from the present town of Caliente to the Grapevine highway south of Bakersfield. Aguirre was a native of Spain and had become a naturalized Mexican citizen. He had married a daughter of José Antonio Estudillo, Maria del Rosario, in 1842. The Estudillos were one of the aristocratic families of the province. Aguirre's wife died a year after their

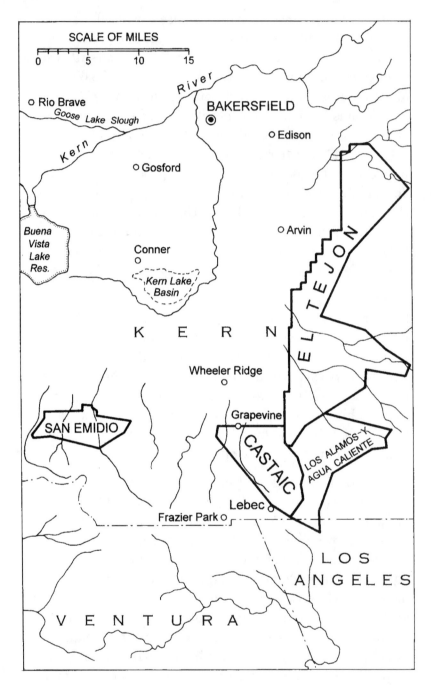

marriage and just prior to his securing *El Tejon*. His partner, del Valle, was a native of Mexico, and both were residents of Los Angeles at the time that the grant was received. They found the Indians on the *Tejon* grant hostile and occupation consequently difficult. Their ranch foreman, Manuel Jacinto Fago, and several vaqueros arrived on the ranch on July 9, 1845, with a small band of horses and remained on it until September 5, 1846. A house was erected and a corral was built; the latter was a hundred varas long and ninety varas wide, A *vara* is approximately 33 inches. Some land was placed under cultivation and two crops were harvested. The first year only corn was grown; the second, corn, beans, and vegetables. The owners sent a thousand cattle to the ranch, but fear of Fremont's approaching battalion from the north caused their return to Los Angeles. Fago went with the herd to the south but left five of his Indian vaqueros at the ranch.[13]

The same year that Aguirre and del Valle received their grant they requested Don Joaquin Carrillo, alcalde and judge of the First Instance at Los Angeles, to go to the ranch and, according to the custom of the time, give them juridical possession. He refused, due to fear of the Indians, and because the governor had ordered him to go out and purchase horses for the government. In a temporary division of the province during a small civil war, Alvarado ruled that the line between the two divisions was at San Fernando. This placed *El Tejon* within the jurisdiction of the alcalde at Santa Barbara.[14]

The alcalde at the latter place was José Maria Covarrubias, the owner of *Castaic* and the neighboring landowner of Aguirre and del Valle. He also refused to survey the ranch because of the Indian menace. This was in 1844. In August, two years later, del Valle asked Carrillo, no longer the alcalde at Los Angeles, to assume the duties of foreman at *El Tejon*. He refused. In 1850 Carrillo took six hundred cows to the Tulare Lake region for summer grazing and tarried at *El Tejon* en route. He traded twenty-two of his travel weary cows for *El Tejon* cattle. The foreman then at the ranch told Carrillo that Aguirre had five hundred head of cattle on *El Tejon* at that time. The same year a miner, Juan Gallardo, went in search of a silver mine near Tejon Pass, which the Indians helped him locate. While engaged in this venture he visited *El Tejon* and met Fago, the foreman. He saw fields of melons and corn. Another ranch visitor was Abel Stearns from Los Angeles.[15]

The grantees experienced difficulty in securing a patent to their land from the United States. In 1853 Edward Fitzgerald Beale, then the Superintendent of Indian Affairs, established five military reservations on the public domain in Oregon, Utah, and California. The Sebastian Indian Reservation was located within the *El Tejon* grant on the assumption that it was government land. Valuable improvements were made. Indians gathered there from other parts of the state, and thousands of dollars were spent by the War Department. This Sebastian Reservation existed until 1888. A fort was erected, but when the Indian reservation was reduced in size, the former was left fifteen miles outside of the reservation. The grantees finally secured the total amount of land originally granted to them.[16]

The following information was received from the Adjutant General's Office of the War Department concerning Fort Tejon:

> The official records show that Fort Tejon, about 15 miles southwest of the Tejon Indian Reservation, at the Canada de las Uvas, near Tejon Pass, in the southwest part of Kern County, California, was established as a military post August 10, 1854. It was in the process of construction September 14,

1854, and about that time was under the command of Lieutenant-Colonel Benjamin L. Beall, 1st U. S. Dragoons. The nearest post office then was Santa Barbara. An earthquake destroyed a part of the property in 1857. On June 30, 1858, it was under the command of Major George A. H. Blake, 1st U. S. Dragoons. It was evacuated June 15, 1861; reoccupied August 17, 1863, and finally abandoned as military post September 11, 1864. It was never formally declared a military reservation. No additional record has been found.

Edward F. Beale eventually became a San Joaquin Valley cattleman and secured control of both the *Tejon* and *Agua Caliente* grants. Together with his other purchases of contiguous land, his cattle ranch assumed the huge proportions of 200,000 acres. Beale was a personal friend of both Jefferson Davis and Abraham Lincoln. The former aided him in his attempt to introduce camels into the United States and Beale was appointed chief of the first and only Camel Corps in the United States Army. These animals carried freight across the so-called Great American Desert, and their first arrival at Los Angeles created a furor. Some of them finally arrived at the *Tejon* ranch. During the Civil War, Abraham Lincoln appointed Beale Surveyor-General of the State of California and the Territory of Nevada. After the war Beale joined forces with Colonel Thomas Baker, which gave them joint control of the cattle industry from Bakersfield south into the hills.[17]

A grant named *El Pescadero*, lying along the San Joaquin River due west of Modesto, was given to Valentin Higuera and Rafael Feliz by Governor Micheltorena on November 28, 1843. It comprised eight square leagues (35,446.06 acres). The prospective grantees stated in their petition for land to the governor that they possessed thirteen hundred head of black cattle, three hundred and fifty sheep, and three hundred horses which they were prepared to place on this ranch. As soon as the grant was

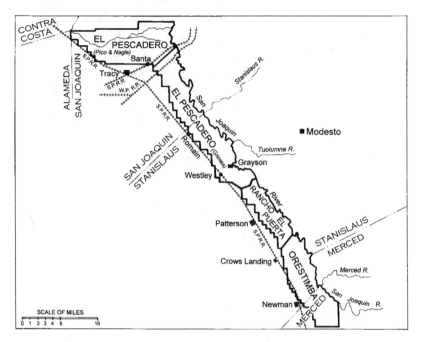

received Higuera, accompanied by José Romero, went to the ranch and built a corral. A bunkhouse, large enough to accommodate fifteen vaqueros, was also erected. A band of two hundred horses was already there. Feliz and his two sons arrived soon after with cattle and more horses. This was in September 1843. Five years later Feliz sold his share in the ranch to Don Franklin Cecara for $180, and Cecara later disposed of his part of the property thus acquired to Elizabeth Grimes. By 1850 a small town known as San Joaquin City grew up on this ranch along the river. The most important citizen at that time was William McKee; owner and captain of a steamer called the *Unit* plying between San Joaquin City and San Francisco. This little riverboat represented an investment of $15,000 and made regular runs. People found it safer to travel by water than to cross the plains among marauding Indians.[18]

The same day that the foregoing grant was made another

grant of the same name was made to Antonio Pico. The latter grant lay north and west of the present Tracy. The highway from Oakland to Tracy runs over a part of this early grant, which consisted of eight square leagues (35,546.39 acres). Pico, like other grantees in the valley, encountered the hostility of the red men. After they had killed William Gulnac's mayordomo across the river near what is now Stockton, Pico found difficulty in retaining men at his ranch. However, Pico made heroic efforts to develop his ranch although the Indians remained dangerous and, as late as 1849, terrorized the Santa Clara Valley and even approached the outskirts of San Jose. The pugnacious miners who surged into the foothills of the Sierras looking for gold were, according to Antonio Sunol, the ones who finally destroyed the last strongholds of the Yokuts and Miwok tribesmen. On April 25, 1849, Pico conveyed to Henry M. Naglee a half interest in his ranch for $2,500.[19]

José Y. Limantour received the *Laguna de Tache* grant of eleven square leagues from Governor Micheltorena on December 4, 1843. This ranch is not to be confused with the ranch of the same name later given to Manuel Castro. The latter's grant lay north of the old bed of Kings River and extended from the *Sanjon de San Jose* watercourse westward, to the intersection of Cole Slough and Kings River, for twenty-five miles. Limantour's grant lay along the south bank of Kings River and extended from the present site of the Kings River golf course, due south of Kingsburg, down the river to Tulare Lake. Claims for this *Laguna de Tache* were filed with the Land Commission and Limantour's attorneys explained that his failure to develop his ranch was due to the revolutionary disturbances in Mexico, which prevented his return from a visit to Mexico City.[20]

Limantour, a Frenchman by birth and a Mexican by

choice, received land grants in California from Micheltorena, which totaled 594,793.38 acres. The governor and this Frenchman were very friendly, and Micheltorena was under obligations to the latter; just what these were we are not certain. Limantour, like his illustrious son, was evidently a financier, and had made certain loans to Micheltorena. On May 24, 1843, he received from the government a draft on the Custom House at Mazatlan for $10,221. On May 16, 1845, he received another draft for $56,184.12 as remuneration for the confiscated cargo of the *Joven Fanita*. Both of these drafts were ordered paid by the Supreme Government of Mexico; this money, together with grants of more than half a million acres, made his California venture a great success. Incidentally, it may be of interest to note that Limantour was the first man to predict that at some future date a bridge would be built to span the bay between Oakland and San Francisco.[21]

Many of the ranchers of the San Joaquin Valley during Mexican days were men of uncommon ability. A son of José Y. Limantour became the Secretary of the Treasury under President Porfirio Diaz, and shares with Alexander Hamilton the honor of being one of the two greatest financial wizards of North America. The younger Limantour was the first Mexican elected to the French Academy.[22]

Francisco Rico and José Antonio Castro received a grant named the *Rancho de Rio Estanislao* from Governor Micheltorena on December 29, 1843. This grant contained eleven square leagues (48,886.64 acres) and was bounded on the north by the tulares, on the south by the Stanislaus River, on the east by the Sierra, and on the west by a line drawn north and south through the mouth of the Stanislaus River. Rico and Castro employed José Noriega to build them a house. The latter was the same

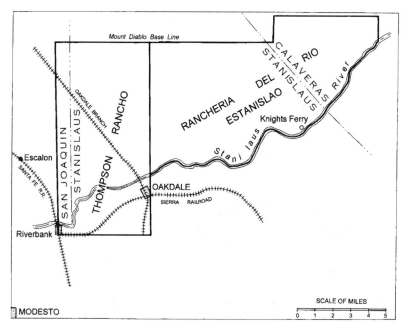

man who had first settled in the valley and was a skilled cattleman with much experience in the San Joaquin Valley frontier. The agent who handled the business affairs for the firm was Antonio Maria Pico. He sent Noriega to the ranch with a hundred head of cattle and some horses. Shortly thereafter the two owners arrived at the ranch and were actually residing there when José Y. Limantour arrived at the ranch on a visit. The latter had been on a visit to his holdings along the south bank of the Kings River due south of modern Kingsburg. Indian threats caused Rica and Castro to remove their cattle after a while.[23]

Rico had been a captain in the army under General José Castro and was well and favorably known at Los Angeles. Most of his service in the army had been in southern parts of the department. His partner, José Castro, was not General José Castro, although a relative. The general went to Mexico City from Los Angeles and had in his

133

Charles M. Weber, early settler in the San Joaquin Valley and father of the city of Stockton. George Tinkham, *History of Stockton.*

possession at that time the documents relating to the *Rancho de Rio Estanislao* land grant. Due to the unsettled state of affairs in the department, Rico had felt that his papers were safer with the general than in his own possession or filed away at Monterey. Through some inadvertence, these and other papers were lost in a camp along the banks of the Colorado River where Castro had spent the night en-route to Mexico City. In October, 1846, General Castro was stationed at Altar in the province of Sonora, Mexico, and at that time and to that place Rico wrote him a letter referring to his documents. He wrote another letter in 1847 addressed to Tepic, Mexico; in both missives he asked Castro to safeguard carefully his original copy of the grant, not knowing that it had already been lost.[24]

In the meantime Rico had employed B. K. Thompson as

foreman of his cattle ranch. The latter went to the valley in 1846 and occupied the ranch house, which was located twenty miles from the mouth of the Stanislaus River. In October, 1847, Rica sent additional cattle to Thompson, and an ounce of Mexican gold, in payment for services rendered at the ranch. Later that same fall Thompson and his vaqueros arrived at the Weber ranch, near the present Stockton, in a disheveled condition. Indian forays had scattered their cattle and rendered them destitute. Thompson's escape had been made possible by the warning of friendly Indians. Weber sent Thompson out with a force of cowboys to gather the scattered stock; some two hundred of the cattle were rounded up. A few horses were also recovered. Thompson subsequently resigned his job as foreman and joined Weber's settlement. Weber had known Thompson personally at San Jose before the latter had become foreman for Rico and Castro.[25]

During the winter months of 1847-1848 several Indian raids took place. Forays were made as far west as the San Ramon Valley, where the peaceful communities of Walnut Creek, Danville, and Dublin are now located. The perpetrators of these disturbances were Stanislaus River Indians; apparently they had not forgotten the stirring days of Estanislao and Cipriano who had, twenty years before, performed daring deeds. Captain Weber finally led a troop of mounted men after the raiders. His roughriders were employees of Weber and were paid by him. Thompson was a member of the group, which chastised the red men; another striking figure was named Rock, a professional grizzly bear hunter, a partner of Thompson in many ventures, and incidentally a shoemaker by trade.[26]

Vicente Prefecto Gómez, who had been the original grantee of *Panoche Grande*, was an important witness for the claimants when their case was filed with the Land Commission. He caused much merriment when one of the

Land Commissioners insinuated that he was receiving pay for giving testimony favorable to the claimants; he waxed both facetious and contemptuous:

> My present business is to eat, drink, and make visits, or to travel about as also in the two preceding years. I came to San Francisco because I chose to do so. I am here because I choose to be, and I will leave when it may please me. I have been here, not for the sole purpose of giving testimony as intimated, but for as long as it has been agreeable to me. I have been here for two or three months on this my last visit and as for what I have received for giving testimony, the Land Agent is welcome to it.[27]

The first grant named the *Laguna de Tache* (Lake of the Tache Indians) was given to José Y. Limantour; this lay on the south side of Kings River. A second grant of the same name was made to Manuel Castro on December 12, 1843, although a deed to secure the ownership was not issued until January 1, 1846. Castro was a resident of Monterey and knew Limantour and the location of the latter's ranch along Kings River. Limantour advised him concerning the land and Castro applied for a grant on the opposite side of the river. The latter had received land from his father, Don Simeon Castro, but his cattle had increased rapidly and he proposed to send the surplus to the frontier. Castro had been an army captain and had led several punitive forces against the Indians during Micheltorena's administration. The latter, as a reward for faithful service, issued the grant, which was later confirmed by Pio Pico. Castro had also served as prefect of the Northern District of California, residing at Monterey, for one year. In February, 1845, Castro sent Ysidor Villa to the *Laguna de Tache* as foreman. Villa was accompanied by three vaqueros. After building a small house and a corral, they returned to Monterey as the Indians began to threaten them. They soon returned to the ranch and the same year José Ramon Mesa, a resident of Santa Clara Valley, made

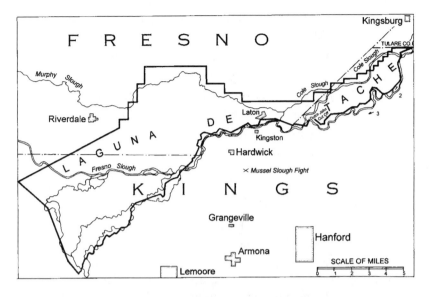

a visit to the region. Ysidor Villa and several vaqueros were herding cattle and occupied a small wooden bunkhouse that had been built about two miles west of present Laton. Melons and vegetables had been planted along the river. This *Laguna de Tache* consisted of 48,800.62 acres.[28]

A great deal of nonsense has been written about so-called "floating grants." After the American occupation, it became customary to refer sneeringly to the grants of men like Manuel Castro and Fremont as examples of "floating grants," meaning that they had originally been granted in one part of California (in this case Monterey county), and then floated to another part of the state to take advantage of better opportunities.

Therefore the following explanation may be pertinent. During Mexican days the Department of California was divided into the districts of San Diego, Los Angeles, Santa Barbara, Monterey, and San Francisco. These corresponded somewhat to our county form of government as to duties. No accurate surveys indicated the location of the boundaries of these districts. When a land grant was made in the Monterey district, it meant that the officials believed that Monterey was the nearest of the five district headquarters, or county seats. Therefore, land granted to Manuel Castro along Kings River was said to be located in the Monterey district. This caused Americans to argue later that his grant had been "floated" from what had become Monterey County to Kings River.

On December 7, 1843, Manuel Castro presented the following petition to Governor Micheltorena:

> Excellent Sir Governor: I, Manuel Castro, a Mexican by birth and a resident of this port (Monterey), with due respect, say before your justice, that being sure that in the location which was granted to Don José Limantour called Laguna de Tache there results a considerable surplus and needing this for placing cattle belonging to me which are now remaining on the testamentary land of my deceased father, Don Simeon Castro, I request of your Excellency that in consideration of the services I have rendered to the Department, you will do me the favor to grant me the same surplus in extent eleven square leagues.[29]

When Pico became governor Manuel Castro sent him a letter to safeguard his property rights and specifically stated that his land was bounded on the south by Kings River and the *Laguna de Tache* of José Limantour; on the west by the Sanjon de San José (still known as San Jose Slough); on the north by a village of the Notonoto Indians (Ysidio Villa stated that this village was four and a half leagues north of the point where San Jose Slough enters Tulare Lake); and on the east by the plains extending toward the Sierra Nevada. This gave three fixed and unchanging boundaries, but a certain flexibility was permissible in determining the eastern boundary, which was finally located about twenty-five miles to the east.[30]

On December 12, 1843, the following conveyance was made by Pio Pico:

The land granted him is eleven leagues conformable to the
sketch, bordering to the south on the Laguna de Tache and
Limantour; to the north on the rancheria de Los Notonotos;
to the west on the Sanjon de San José; and to the east by
the plains.[31]

A grant named the *Real de los Aguilas*, consisting of seven
square leagues, was made to Francisco Arias and
Saturnino Carriaga on January 7, 1844. A portion of it
was drained by Panoche Creek, which flows into the San
Joaquin Valley. It lay in the foothill region directly west of
Mendota and received its name from two brothers who
had camped on this tract while lassoing cattle there in
1827. A man named Manuel Larias, who was in the
vicinity at the same time and for the same purpose, gave
this explanation concerning the origin of the name. The
two grantees hired Ramon Anzar to herd their cattle. The
partners were merchants at San Juan Bautista and,
partly through fear of the valley Indians, they continued
to reside at San Juan. After a fire had destroyed the ranch
buildings, the merchants sold their holdings to Juan
Miguel Anzar and his brother, Maria Antonia Castro de
Anzar. Carriaga received $1,100 for his share and Arias
disposed of his interest for $1,060. The Anzar brothers
placed seven hundred cattle on the ranch. The latter was
described as being marshy and composed largely of
overflow land. Juan Miguel Anzar died and his children
remained on the ranch and continued its development.[32]

Mariano Hernandez received the *Rancho del Puerto from*
Governor Micheltorena on January 20, 1844. This grant
consisted of three square leagues (13,340.39 acres) and
was located in what is now Stanislaus County, due west of
modern Turlock and immediately east of Patterson. The
grantee and his wife, Maria del Rosaria Bernal, appeared
before Alcalde Burton of San Jose and his clerk, Charles
White, and before these two officials their claim was

approved and duly filed. These two names suggest that Americans were becoming prominent before the American conquest.[33]

Pedro Hernandez went out to his brother's ranch in the spring of 1844 and built a house and a small corral; later in the summer he erected a large enclosure. In September he brought to the ranch four milk cows and forty horses. Melons and cabbages had been planted in the spring and that autumn Mariano Hernandez and his family moved to their new home. Indian forays depleted the herds and a year later Hernandez returned to San Jose. On August 16, 1847, he sold his holdings to Hiram Grimes. Hiram Grimes was the husband of Elizabeth Grimes; the latter bought a portion of *El Pescadero* from Don Francisco Cecara. A son, Francis W. Grimes, was also an early valley rancher. The latter, a business-like Yankee, sent a surveyor, James D. Hutton, to the tract in June or July, 1847, prior to completing the purchase, and had it accurately surveyed. John M. Murphy, who accompanied Hutton as an assistant, stated that "the Indians were very bad at that time all along the valleys of the San Joaquin River. No one family would go out there to live at that time. They could not keep stock there." When questioned concerning Hernandez, Murphy told the Land Commission: "The last time I saw him he was in the custody of the sheriff of Santa Clara county under a charge of murder and he made his escape—this was in 1850 or 1851."[34]

Anastasia Chaboya received the *Sanjon de los Moquelumnes* grant of 35,509.97 acres from Governor Micheltorena on January 24, 1844. From its location in the angle of the Mokelumne and the Calaveras rivers, it was often known as the Calaveras grant. Only the southern portion of this ranch lay within the San Joaquin Valley. It had a two-league frontage on the Mokelumne

River. The acquisition of this ranch made Chaboya a neighbor of Sutter, whom he disliked most heartily. On a visit to the latter, Chaboya had been greeted cordially by the owner of the New Helvetia land grant. Sutter answered Chaboya's questions concerning vacant lands with apparent candor. As a result of the visit, Sutter, who was a government official, sent Chaboya to Monterey with dispatches which the latter had been led to believe were recommendations for his own proposed grant. Instead, it was a request favoring grants to William Gulnac, Peter Lassen, and other foreigners residing in California. Chaboya felt insulted and humiliated to think that he had been deceived. In his petition to the governor, Chaboya stated that Sutter; himself a foreigner, unduly favored aliens and discriminated against native-born Californians. Sutter, when interrogated concerning the matter, stated that Chaboya was greedy and asked for too much land and that he, Sutter, merely let the others in on the surplus. Chaboya, according to Sutter, had many cattle and abundant wealth and therefore he and his seven children would never be in want. This explanation was offered by Sutter on New Year's Day, and later in the month, Chaboya received his grant. Cattle and horses were immediately placed on the land. A large house for the overseer and bunkhouse for the vaqueros were erected, corrals were built, and some land was placed under cultivation. The houses and the corrals were located along the banks of the Cosumnes River. The cattle were sent there from the other holdings of Chaboya, which were located near San Jose. In 1846 Antonio Maria Pico visited Chaboya for two days and found a herd of three hundred sleek cattle, fifty horses, and evident prosperity. By 1859 Chaboya had made improvements on the *Sanjon de los Moquelumnes* valued at $25,000.[35]

La Panocha de San Juan y los Carrisalitos was received from Governor Micheltorena as a grant by Julian Ursua and Pedro Romo on February 17, 1844. This tract was five square leagues in area. Ursua continued to reside at San Juan, but Romo spent his time on the ranch. Juridical possession was granted by José Antonio Rodriguez, the alcalde at Monterey, but his death by drowning the next year was to cause confusion when the owners attempted to secure a patent to their land from the United States Land Commission. Finally, Ursua built a house at the ranch and settled there with his family. He employed sixteen Indian laborers, placed horses and five hundred head of cattle on the grant, and resided continuously on it until long after the American occupation. When the gold miners began thronging into the Sierra Nevada foothills in search of the golden metal, Ursua was one of the first cattlemen to take advantage of the new market thus created. He made "cattle drives" across the valley to the mines and disposed of his beef at a handsome profit.[36]

Orestimba (Bear Creek) was given to Sebastian Nuflez by Governor Micheltorena on February 21, 1844. This ranch consisted of six square leagues (26,641.17 acres) and was located along the west bank of the San Joaquin, due west of Merced. Nunez became a resident immediately and was a prominent cattleman for the next two decades.

Francisco Alviso, Antonio Higuera, and Manuel Miranda received a tract named the *Canada Vaqueros* from Governor Micheltorena on February 29, 1844. Alviso secured the interests of his two partners eventually. The former had been in the habit of grazing cattle on this portion of the national domain since 1841; he had even erected a corral on the land. After securing a formal grant to it, Alviso built another corral and erected several huts, which were occupied by his Indian laborers. The Micheltorena revolution created a lawless period during which Alviso made arrangements to range his cattle with the Livermore and Noriega herds; Alviso himself went to live with José Amador on the *San Ramon* ranch near Walnut Creek. Higuera became sick and died but Miranda, the other partner, accompanied Alviso on his trips to the *Canada Vaquero*. Shortly after Alviso had acquired the interests of his partners, he disposed of the ranch to Robert Livermore. Francisco secured Higuera's share on September 17, 1846, Miranda's interest on October 12, 1846, and sold the ranch to Livermore on April 24, 1847. The latter already owned the land lying to the south and west known as *Los Pasitos*; its general location is indicated by the present city of Livermore. The nearest neighbor to the north was John Marsh. One of the reasons why Alviso and his partners withdrew from the ranch during the Micheltorena difficulties was explained by Antonio Maria Pico: "In December, 1844, a revolution broke out in California and I, as alcalde, ordered the ranchers to repair to San Jose and arm themselves for the defense of the country and they generally came, though some complained of having to leave their families." In his testimony Pico constantly referred to his people as Californians; the Spanish-speaking people did not refer to themselves as Mexicans even during the Mexican regime.[38]

In 1843 Juan Bautista Alvarado, then governor of California, directed Don Santiago Estrada, the officer commanding the departmental troops employed in the valley of the San Joaquin, to indicate to him the most suitable place for the establishment of a new ranch home. That officer recommended the land between the Merced River and Mariposa Creek. This region was the customary camping ground of the Mexican troops employed against the Indians. Estrada pointed out that this section of the country contained many small and beautiful valleys, permanent streams that afforded sufficient water, the whole face of the country was covered with nutritious grasses and was well wooded with varieties of timber.

As soon as Alvarado's term of office had expired he petitioned his successor in office, Governor Micheltorena, for a grant of land (he could not legally grant land to himself as governor) and on February 29, 1844, he received ten square leagues (44,386.83 acres) named *Las Mariposas*. This tract was destined to become one of the most famous and valuable grants in the state. Before Alvarado could occupy his new ranch it was deemed necessary to send a military force against the red men. Governor Micheltorena's departmental troops were Mexican infantrymen used for garrison duty along the coast towns and missions; they were useless in campaigns against the mounted Indians of the plains. However, the governor agreed to recruit a troop of cavalry from among the local Californians. This force was sent to the Mariposas under the command of General José Castro and a camp was established along the banks of the San Joaquin River. Here the Indians stole the horses of the white men and lacking mounts and other resources the expeditionary force was rendered *hors de combat*.[39]

This was in 1844 and the next year Alvarado was appointed commander of the troops stationed at Monterey. Here he collected a squadron of cavalry and trained his native Californians at his ranch near Monterey. Before he had an opportunity to lead them to the Mariposa country, General José Castro, the commander-in-chief of the army in the Department of California, ordered the squadron to report for duty in the war, which resulted in the expulsion of Micheltorena. Years later when Alvarado was interrogated concerning *Las Mariposas* he answered simply: "I was never there."[40]

In April of the same year Alvarado received his grant and John C. Fremont made his first ride down the San Joaquin. Three years later *Las Mariposas* was acquired by Thomas O. Larkin, the American consul at Monterey, on

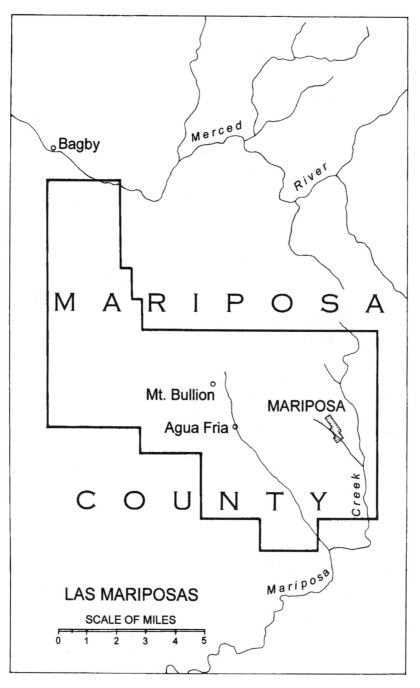

Fremont's behalf for $3,000. He was instructed to purchase a cattle ranch near the coast, and was disgusted to find that Larkin had purchased *Las Mariposas*. It remained his home for the next quarter of a century. Fremont threatened to bring suit against Larkin, but when gold was discovered he was happy to retain it. Fremont took a prominent part in the development of his mines. The Mount Ophir was among the Mariposa mines, which became nationally known.

Fremont, one of the chief American officers in California during the war with Mexico, was constantly occupied with military affairs. Difficulties with General Stephen Kearney, his superior officer, caused his arrest and a court-martial held at Washington. Subsequently he returned to California and reached *Las Mariposas* in May, 1849. Shortly after his arrival, six of his cowboys were killed by Indians. Fremont was undaunted and began active work as a cattleman and miner. In 1851 the famous Mariposa Indian War occurred near his home. The same year he told the Land Commission that the lives of his family and employees were in constant jeopardy, and that the cattle ranch and mining equipment at *Las Mariposas* were in danger of destruction any moment from the warlike red men. Concerning his grant, Fremont testified as follows before the Land Commission: "At the time this grant was made [1844] the country in which it lies was the remote frontier, occupied exclusively by hostile Indians, and considered too dangerous for occupation until nearly the present day."[41]

The Mission San José pastured its surplus flocks of sheep on a tract of land known as *Monte del Diablo* from 1828 to 1830. Thereafter Indian depredations prevented its use until Governor José Figueroa granted it to Salvio Pacheco on March 30, 1844. This place consisted of 17,921.54 acres and received its name from "The Mountain of the Devil" which lay a few miles to the south, and which had in turn been named by the soldiers who first saw its gloomy form on a dark and foggy day. Pacheco and his sons moved to the ranch immediately, built a bunkhouse, and planted corn, wheat, beans, peas, and fruit. The field, four hundred varas along each side, was enclosed by a fence to protect it from the cattle. Pacheco also brought 90 brood mares, 850 head of stock, and a flock of sheep to his estate. Aside from obstreperous Indians, Pacheco was annoyed by Julian Willis, an Englishman, who proposed to pasture his 500 cattle on Pacheco's land. The latter, then serving as the alcalde at the pueblo of Martinez, ordered Willis to refrain from trespassing. The retort of Willis sounds very much like modern slang: "The result is that I am with my stock up in the air."[42]

In the spring of 1843 William Gulnac, a native of New York, and Peter Lassen, a native of Denmark, set out from San Jose with a herd of cattle. Gulnac's name appears in some documents as Gulnack; Lassen's name was Larsen originally. No doubt they were the first two Scandinavians to appear in the San Joaquin. Each man had his own herd, but for the sake of company and greater safety they went together. Their destination was the general region of the Cosumnes River and their purpose was to secure free pasturage on government land during the summer. They passed by a site known as French Camp; here the daring and hardy French-Canadian *coureur-de-bois* employed by the Hudson's Bay Fur Company stayed during the trapping season. The grazing in this vicinity was excellent, but the Indians had developed into great cattle thieves. Therefore Gulnac and Lassen feared to remain and moved north, where the protecting guns of Sutter's Fort secured them immunity from the red raiders. During that summer their herds ranged along the banks of the Cosumnes River, and in the fall the men returned to San

The embryonic city of Stockton, founded on the Rancho Campo de los Franceses grant in 1849. Frank Soule et al., *The Annals of San Francisco.*

Jose. Gulnac realized the suitability of the French Camp region for a cattle ranch and applied to Governor Micheltorena for a grant. This was favorably acted upon June 13, 1844, and eleven square leagues (48,747.03 acres) were secured and named the *Campo de los Franceses* (Camp of the Frenchmen). This included within its boundaries the site of the present city of Stockton. At the time the grant was made Gulnac had 200 head of cattle and 40 horses and mules. He was a naturalized Mexican citizen and had married a Spanish-California girl, Isabel Ceseña, by whom he had seven children.[43]

In the fall of 1844, the same year he received the grant, Gulnac took four families to his ranch. The heads of these four households were David Kelsey, John Kelly, James Williams, and James Lindsay. A small cannon was procured by Kelsey and Lindsay; this they loaded and fired each evening as a protection against the Indians. The tremendous detonation shattered both the twilight stillness and the nervous systems of the prowling Indians, who arrived at the conclusion that the white men controlled the thunderclaps.[44]

Gulnac's hired men erected four houses, built corrals, and cared for the horses, mules, and 100 cows brought to the ranch by the owner. Every effort was made to create a permanent establishment. Peter Lassen made arrangements to pasture some of his cattle with the Gulnack herd. Two of Gulnac's men, Lindsay and Williams, planted one gallon of peach pits in the fall of 1844. They were planted in what is now the southern portion of the present city of Stockton, and this planting resulted in what was probably the first peach orchard in the San Joaquin Valley.[45]

Gulnac did not reside permanently on the *Campo de los Franceses*, but went there from time to time with cattle as they accumulated at San Jose. On these trips, he was usually accompanied by members of his family. Aside from these periodic visits Gulnac conducted a blacksmith shop at San Jose, where he shod the horses of the California dons and mended such tools as they possessed in a land where technocracy was so retarded that the "horse and buggy" age was still 'round the corner.[46]

The development of the *Campo de los Franceses* was temporarily abandoned when the Micheltorena War came to disturb the otherwise "splendid, idle forties." Gulnac left his cattle at Sutter's Fort, arranged his other affairs at French Camp, and went to war in support of the governor who had been his benefactor. So did Williams, Kelsey, and Lindsay. The other Gulnac employee, John Kelly, had died of smallpox shortly after his arrival at the ranch. The supporters of Micheltorena gathered at Mission La Soledad. Peter Lassen, John Suuer, Charles M. Weber, and John Marsh were among those present. Daniel Murphy told the Land Commission that 350

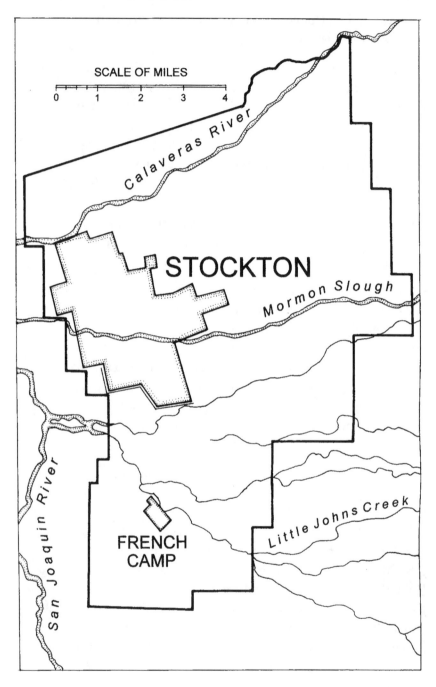

Americans from northern California participated in this civil war. Sectional feeling ran high and everyone went to war. Micheltorena's force advanced on Los Angeles whose city limits did not then extend as far north as they were to do in later years.[47]

At the conclusion of hostilities Peter Lassen returned to the north by way of French Camp with Lindsay, his "comrade in arms" during the war. This was the term Lassen used in relating to the Land Commission the circumstances, which resulted in Lindsay's death. The latter went back to his home within present-day Stockton and was soon joined by Williams. The latter went to Sutter's Fort for supplies, and during his absence Lindsay was slain by the Indians. Gulnac's cattle were either slaughtered or driven away and the ranch house demolished. When Williams learned of the tragic state of affairs, he hurriedly returned to Sutter's Fort and Sutter placed him in command of a troop of roughriders. In a running fight with the Indians they recovered thirteen head of cattle, lost one man killed and five wounded, and killed six red men.[48]

Gulnac had by this time become discouraged in his attempts to develop his cattle ranch. His work as a blacksmith paid him handsomely, but his reward came in the form of cattle rather than money. Cash was scarce and cows were valued at $2.50 each; hence he soon found his backyard overflowing with an unwieldy medium of exchange. It was to provide a place other than his city home for his growing herds that he had applied to the governor for a land grant. But the year in which he was required by law to make a permanent settlement would expire in June. If he failed within that time he might lose his claim to it. Indian depredations made vaqueros reluctant to go out to French Camp. Therefore William Gulnac sold the *Campo de los Franceses* to Captain

Charles M. Weber for a $60 grocery bill which Gulnac owed in the Weber grocery store at San Jose. This sale was consummated on April 3, 1845. Since Weber bought the *Campo de los Franceses*, it is hardly correct to refer to it as Weber's grant.[49]

Captain Weber went to work with a great display of vim, vigor, and vitality to develop the ranch which he had so cheaply acquired from Gulnac. By 1847 he had a thousand cattle on it. That year Weber began his building operations and the houses were erected close together due to the Indian danger. The residents went to their respective fields by day but returned to the village for greater safety at night. William B. Hood offered testimony before the Land Commission, which tended to minimize the Indian danger in the San Joaquin:

> I have traveled through the country of hostile Indians—
> Apaches, Comanches, and so forth, on the frontier of Texas,
> Mexico, and Missouri and have traveled among the
> mountains of California and seen a good many Indians in the
> San Joaquin Valley since I came to this country in 1850 and
> since that time. I have always considered the Indians in the
> San Joaquin Valley as harmless.[50]

Walter Herron was the county surveyor of San Joaquin County in 1850. Concerning Weber's estate he made the following deposition, which is contrary in respect to the attitude of the Yokuts and Miwok:

> I do know the rancho aforesaid. It is situated in the county of
> San Joaquin. It was first occupied by Captain Weber in 1847,
> who brought on it a band of a thousand cattle, or more. This
> is the first I knew of its occupation. He has since continued to
> occupy it; he has made improvements on it, the value of the
> improvements made by Captain Weber and those holding
> under him I should think about one million and a half. I
> passed through the ranch one year prior to Weber's taking
> possession. There were none there then. In the latter part of
> 1844 Gulnack [sic] had three or four houses on it and some

stock. The next year Weber tried to get some help but the Indians were bad, they killed Lindsay that spring; it was necessary for a person going through that country at that time to go armed and with company.[51]

In 1848 a hundred families had located on the Weber tract. Favorable inducements were offered and early settlers received many premiums in land and choice lots. By 1849 it was considered safe for the settlers to build houses on their respective holdings. Captain Weber was a naturalized citizen of Mexico and served as a captain under Governor Micheltorena. At the outbreak of the war between the United States and Mexico, Weber was suspected of American sympathies and taken prisoner. He was later released and served as a captain in the American army. Thus he was, within a period of three years, a captain in both the Mexican and United States armies.[52]

Vicente Gomez, the witness who indulged in "wise cracks" at the expense of the Land Commission during the hearing on the *Rancho de Rio Estanislao*, had been made the beneficiary of a grant made by Governor Micheltorena in 1844, shortly after the grant made to Gulnac. It was named *Panoche Grande* and consisted of four square leagues. This ranch was located near the *San Luis Gonzaga* estate belonging to Francisco Perez Pacheco. The nearest neighbor to the south was Julian Ursua of *Panoche de San Juan y Los Carrisalitos*. Gomez occupied it for a time, placed cattle on it, and in the fall of 1845 he entered into negotiations with Oscar de Grandkargue with the purpose of selling it. The latter was the master of a whaling vessel, which had put into the port of Monterey for the winter. The deal was never consummated, and Gomez remained in possession.[53]

The original documents involved in this land grant were destroyed in the following manner. When the war broke out between the United States and Mexico some of the

American officers, among them William Tecumseh Sherman, were quartered in the Custom House at Monterey. The archives containing all the papers relating to all the land grants made in California were stored in that building. Not only were officers domiciled there during the war but also James L. Ord, assistant surgeon of Company F, United States Artillery, stated that a part of the Custom House was set aside as an emergency hospital in 1847. Paper is always in demand in a hospital. In searching for this valuable commodity a great quantity, neatly rolled and ready for use, was discovered. While it had Spanish writing on it no one took the pains to have its contents translated for some time. Finally, it was discovered that the paper possessed value as documentary evidence in relation to land grants. Thus another source of future difficulty was added to those which were later to ply and belabor the harried Land Commission. The original documents relating to the grant made to Vicente Gomez were among those destroyed.

The Americans secured the Custom House in July, 1846; the emergency hospital was established there in 1847; the value of the rolls of paper was not discovered until some time later, and by that time much irreparable damage had been done. Gomez filed his claim with the Land Commission on February 9, 1853, but due to his inability to produce the necessary papers, his claim was denied on March 6, 1855. Thus Gomez found himself without a home after having spent eleven years in developing a ranch in the valley.[54]

The *Rancho of the River San Joaquin* was granted to Jose Castro on April 4, 1846, by Governor Pio Pico. This tract of land was located on "both sides of the River San Joaquin and runs with the meandering of the river from the edge of the table downward to the westward." It extended from a point a few miles above Friant to the neighborhood of

Herndon. M. B. Lewis, deputy county surveyor of Mariposa County, presented a map to the Land Commission on February 22, 1854, which represented Castro's grant. This grant consisted of 47,740 acres. General Castro built a house near the foot of the hill, some distance below the site of Fort Miller, at a later date. This ranch house was used by Castro as military headquarters while he commanded troops stationed along the river, where it debouches from the foothills. He brought to his new ranch a band of horses and 400 head of cattle.[55]

John Rowland received a grant that had no official name but due to its location it was usually called the *San Joaquin and Stanislaus* grant. Rowland was a naturalized Mexican citizen and a resident of Los Angeles. Rowland and a man named William Workman had been prospectors near Taos, New Mexico. In November, 1841, they were placed in charge of a herd of cattle and a band of sheep, which they delivered safely at Los Angeles. Some time later, after having been naturalized, they received the *La Puente* ranch of 48,000 acres near Los Angeles.[56]

The grant in the San Joaquin Valley was given to Rowland by Governor Pio Pico on May 2, 1846. The next autumn Rowland sent John Reid from Los Angeles to the Modesto region with 150 head of cattle, 50 brood mares, and 30 gentle riding horses. He drove them over the Tehachapi Mountains, across the San Joaquin Valley, and reached the Stanislaus River without mishap. To successfully complete such a drive unaided at that time was considered a remarkable feat. Reid was unable to procure men to care for the stock, and after six days at the ranch he disposed of the animals and returned to Los Angeles. This was the only attempt made by Rowland to occupy his land until after the war with Mexico had been concluded. His ranch consisted of 48,886.64 acres.[57]

The first grantee of *Los Alamos y Agua Caliente* was Pedro C. Carrillo. He failed to occupy it within the one-year time limit and thus forfeited his right to it. On May 27, 1846, Governor Pio Pico re-granted it to Francisco Lopez, Vecinte Botiller, and Luis Jordan. Lopez went to the ranch immediately with stock and tools. The coming of Fremont and his battalion caused him to abandon the place temporarily. *Los Alamos y Agua Caliente* was located east of Lebec and Grapevine and extended out toward the valley floor. It was drained by Tunis and Pastoria creeks.[58]

Los Moquelamos, consisting of eleven square leagues, was given to Andreas Pico by Pio Pico on June 6, 1846. This ranch is not to be confused with the *Sanjon de los Moquelemnes* ranch granted to Chaboya at an earlier date. The former grant was made after the outbreak of the war with the United States and no opportunity was offered to occupy it until after the end of that conflict.[59]

After the war had broken out between the United States and Mexico, Governor Pio Pico of California made land grants to his friends and relatives with reckless abandon. Many of these hastily-made grants were never patented because the Land Commission ruled that the power of the governor of California to make these grants under the Mexican law ceased with the raising of the American flag over the Custom House at Monterey on July 7, 1846. However, some grants made after the declaration of war but before the raising of the American flag were considered legal if the proper documentary evidence was forthcoming. One made during this time was given to Francisco Pico by his relative, Governor Pico, on June 11, 1846. This tract lay south of the Calaveras River near the holdings of Charles Weber. However, the final signatures to the grant were not secured until July 20th, thirteen days after the raising of the American flag. Therefore, in spite of the intercession of men as prominent and influential as John Sutter, owner of the *New Helvetia* grant; Francisco Guerrero, the namesake of Guerrero Street in San Francisco; and Manuel Castro, Prefect of the First District of Monterey and the owner of the *Laguna de Tache* ranch between Kingsburg and Laton, the Land Commission overruled Pico's claim. No patent was ever granted for the place known in the records as *Las Calaveras.*[60]

The last grant made in the San Joaquin Valley by a Mexican governor was made to Alfias Basil Thompson by Governor Pio Pico on June 13, 1846. Exactly a month earlier, on May 13, the United States had declared war against Mexico. Thompson was a naturalized Mexican citizen and prior to his making a request for a grant of land, he was a resident of *New Helvetia.* No particular name was assigned to this tract, but the transcript of the Land Commission dealing with this land referred to it as the "Land on the River Stanislaus." The attempt to take formal possession of this land was indicated by Daniel Murphy in a deposition filed with the Land Commission on November 21, 1853:

> In 1847 Alfias B. Thompson brought some 350 head of cattle from Santa Barbara to place on his ranch on the Stanislaus. He got with them as far as the Pueblo of San Jose when hearing that there was great danger from the Indians in the neighborhood of said rancho, he turned back and pastured the cattle on the Barley Ranch near San Francisco. He afterwards moved the cattle to the Carlos Castro Ranch where he kept them until 1849, when he sold them. I know at that time the Indians were very bad in that section. I do not think said ranch would have been safely occupied or settled prior to 1848.[61]

John Sutter of Sacramento, J. J. Warner of San Diego, John Bidwell of Chico, and Henry Halleck of San Francisco aided Thompson so that he was able to retain

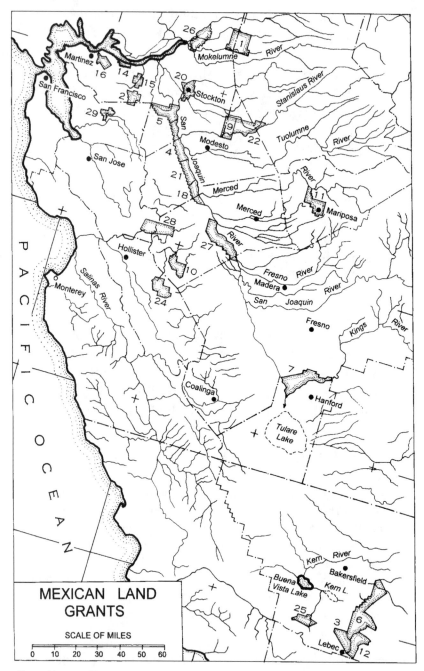

MEXICAN LAND
GRANTS

SCALE OF MILES

0   10   20   30   40   50   60

See Appendix 2, page 750

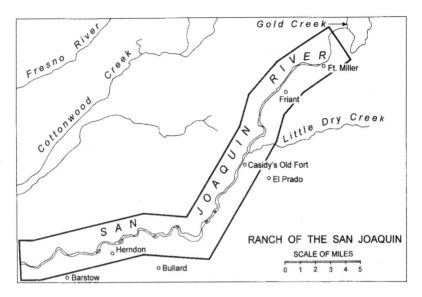

his land grant. The first three were notable men in the California of that day and thought a great deal of Thompson; Halleck was a lawyer in San Francisco and handled Thompson's claims before the Land Commission and in the United States District Court. When the Civil War broke out Halleck went to St. Louis and finally became Lincoln's chief of staff. Thompson's ranch was located west of the Rowland grant made the previous month, and was approximately north of Modesto. The City of Oakdale is situated on the line between the two.[62]

The foregoing land grants represent the holdings of the first white men to settle in the San Joaquin Valley. The maps on these pages indicate the ranches, which were finally patented by the United States government; the others were lost to the original grantees and reverted to the national domain. When the United States acquired California all the land in the San Joaquin Valley, except the thirty private land grants, was a part of the public domain of Mexico. This automatically became a part of the public lands of the United States with the transfer of sovereignty. Of the thirty grants made in Mexican days, all except six were finally patented by the United States, either through its land commission or on appeal to the federal courts.

The ranch homes established by these few cattlemen represented much expenditure of labor, disbursement of money, and sacrifice of life. The first rancher moved into the valley in 1836; exactly a decade later the advance into the San Joaquin of the Spanish-speaking people was brought to an abrupt halt by another race speaking another language. A new era was dawning. Accepting the inevitable in the gracious manner and charming fashion characteristic of their race, the Spanish-speaking California cattlemen rounded up their longhorn cattle for the last time and gradually disappeared over the horizon, musing somewhat sadly as they went:

> The present is our own; but while we speak,
> We cease from its possession, and resign
> The stage we tread on, to another race,
> As vain, and gay, and mortal as ourselves.[63]

6 Braided Riata

versus

Surveyor's Chain

Open thou mine eyes, that I may behold
Wondrous things out of thy law.

Psalms, 119: 18

"A large oak was taken as a boundary, in which was
placed the head of a beef and some of its limbs chopped."[1]
This quotation illustrates the haphazard fashion in which
land grants were made in California during the Mexican
regime. Land was plentiful and accurate surveys were
deemed unnecessary in that golden age.

One of the most interesting phases of San Joaquin Valley

history are the huge land grants made by the Mexican governors who ruled California from 1823 to 1846. No grants were made in the valley during the time Spain held the province. Yet the largest grants in California were made neither by Spanish nor Mexican governors; this honor, such as it is, belongs to the United States Congress. In Los Angeles County alone the United States gave to the Southern Pacific Railway a grant of 162,331 acres. These generous donations from the public domain were later to be the cause of much confusion and trouble.[2]

After the United States acquired California, it was found that in many cases the land grants had been made without closely defining the exact boundaries. José Y. Limantour's vast *Laguna de Tache* grant contained many times the amount of land he was supposed to receive ultimately. It was expected according to the custom of the time that Limantour would, as soon as convenient, bring out an official to measure the land. The majority of the grantees neglected or were unable to do this due to the distance and the danger of the Indians.

Even in cases where the boundaries were more specific than those of the foregoing ranch, it was found that too many perishable markers had been used. When Manuel Castro received a grant, also known as the *Laguna de Tache*, the northeastern boundary was cited as being a certain oak tree. This tree is still standing just below the Southern Pacific Railway bridge where it crosses Kings River between Kingsburg and Traver. But, in many cases, such markers were destroyed before accurate surveys could be made. The grant whose southern limits was indicated "by the place where Don Simeon Castro sits on his white horse each evening" is an exaggerated example of elusive and shifting boundary lines. Therefore, an appalling task faced the land commission established by the United States to determine private boundaries in California.[3]

Engraving of Juan Bautista Alvarado, governor of California (1836-1842), a principal figure in many of the land grants made during the Mexican era, and one-time owner of the Las Mariposas grant. *Fresno County Public Library, California History and Genealogy Room Collection*

Aside from indefinite survey lines, the Land Commission was expected to determine whether or not the grantees had fulfilled the requirements of the Mexican colonization laws. In some cases it was felt that the testimony introduced was either inadequate, or designed to unduly aid some friend. The reason for appointing a land commission goes back to the agreement made between the United States and Mexico in 1848.

The United States entered into a war with Mexico in 1846; the treaty of Guadalupe Hidalgo ending that war was signed on February 2, 1848. That treaty contained two clauses of importance to the Mexican citizens, who had been granted land in the San Joaquin Valley:

> *Article VIII.* Mexicans now established in the territories previously belonging to Mexico, and which remain for the future within the limits of the United States, as defined by the present treaty, shall be free to continue where they now reside, or to remove at any time to the Mexican Republic, retaining the property which they possess in said territory, or disposing thereof, and removing the proceeds wherever they please, without their being subjected on this account, to any contribution, tax, or charge whatsoever.

In the said territories, property of every kind, now belonging to Mexicans now established there, shall be inviolably respected. The present owners, the heirs of these, and all Mexicans who may hereafter acquire said property by contract, shall enjoy, with respect to it, guarantees, equally as if the same belonged to citizens of the United States.

Article IX. Mexicans, who, in the territory aforesaid, shall not preserve the character of citizens of the Mexican Republic conformably with what is stipulated in the preceding article, shall be incorporated in the union of the United States, and be admitted at the proper time (to be judged of by the Congress of the United States) to the enjoyment of all the rights of citizens of the United States, according to the principles of the Constitution, and in the meantime shall be maintained and protected in the free enjoyment of their liberty and property, and secured in the free exercise of their religion without restriction.

In order to fulfill the terms of the two foregoing articles, the United States Land Commission for California was organized by Act of Congress on March 3, 1851, and held its first meeting at San Francisco by order of President Millard Fillmore on December 8, 1851. The men appointed to this Commission were Hiland Hall of Vermont, Henry O. Thornton of Alabama, and James Wilson of New Hampshire. J.B. Carr was appointed secretary and George W. Cooley of Massachusetts became the Land Agent. At the first meeting of the board only Commissioners Hall and Wilson were present and they adjourned *sine die.* A second meeting was held December 31, 1851, at which the Land Agent was also present. By January 21, 1852, all the members of the Commission had arrived in California and were ready to begin hearings. Hiland Hall was chosen chairman of the Commission. This Land Commission for California continued to conduct hearings on land claims until March 1, 1856, when it was permanently adjourned.[4]

A land grant to an individual was limited to eleven square leagues under the Mexican law. These leagues were theoretically to be divided as follows: one should consist of irrigable soil, four should be dependent upon rainfall, and the remaining six should be suitable for grazing. A land grant was exempt from taxation for five years.[5]

The following testimony taken at San Francisco on October 24, 1852, in connection with the first land grant issued in the San Joaquin Valley, is typical of the cross-examinations conducted by the Land Commission in its attempt to determine ownership of land in the newly acquired territory. By this time California had already become a state in the American Union.

Question: Give your name, age, and place of residence.

Answer: My name is José Noriega. I am 53 years old, and I reside at San Jose.

Question: Did you obtain as a grant the rancho called *Los Meganos*? If yes, what time did you take possession of the same, when did you build a house thereon, and how long did you continue personal occupation thereof?

Answer: I did receive a grant from the governor of California to said land in 1835 or 1836. I took possession of said premises immediately, I believe the same month in which the grant was made. I built a house on the land the same year and also corrals and planted a garden and stocked the ranch with cattle and horses. I lived in the house myself and took care of the cattle on the place until I sold it to Dr. Marsh. While I owned the place I had on it constantly nine or ten men, and never less than seven; I kept that number because it was an Indian country and the Indians were hostile.

Question:Did you at any time request a magistrate to give you judicial possession of said rancho?

Answer: I did apply to Dolores Pacheco, the magistrate at San Jose. There was no other magistrate in that vicinity. This application was made in 1835. I applied for the purpose of getting juridical possession of it and turning it over to the present claimant, Dr. Marsh. He did not give me the possession. His reply was that he could not give me juridical

Engraving of Manuel Castro, first owner of the vast Laguna de Tache land grant situated on the Kings River. *Fresno County Public Library, California History and Genealogy Room Collection.*

possession because the danger from the Indians at the place was great and he could not go there—that it would require a large force and he could not go. Dolores Pacheco was over fifty years of age and a very large man and liked ease and comfort.[6]

The successive steps in securing land grants in California during Mexican days were simple in the extreme. The governors of the territories were authorized to make individual grants not to exceed eleven square leagues (48,712.4 acres). Larger grants for colonization purposes could be made to *empresarios*. If a man wanted land he sent a petition to the governor in which he stated name, age, country, vocation, and quantity of land desired. If possible, a description of the land under consideration was also wanted. Originally a map, usually a mere rude plat, had to accompany the petition. In time the necessity of including a map (diseño) was dropped.[7]

The second step was taken by the governor who, after scanning the petition, wrote a note on the margin assigning to the nearest prefect, or other local officer, the task of investigating the land asked for to see if it was vacant, and could be granted to the petitioner without injury to other parties or to the public.[8]

The third step was taken by the prefect whose reply, called the *informe*, was attached to the petition and both returned to the governor. If the *informe* proved satisfactory to the governor, he immediately issued the formal grant. In some cases the governor knew enough about the petitioner and the land himself, and did not need to refer the matter to the prefect, but issued the grant as soon as he received the petition.[9]

The fourth step was taken by the secretary of the government who filed the original petition with the attached *informe* (if there was one), plus a copy of the grant in the archives at Monterey. The original grant was given to the petitioner. The papers on file were placed in a roll to form one document constituting evidence of title to the grant, and was called an *expediente*.[10]

The fifth and last step was taken by the Territorial Deputation (in departments this action was taken by the Departmental Assembly), which received the governor's communication and either approved or rejected the grant. The usual procedure was to refer the matter to a special committee and approval was seldom refused. If the governor wanted to make an issue of a rejection, he could refer the matter to the national government at Mexico City. In California, the governor often considered the granting of land a trifling matter and did not report it to the legislative body, which thus took no action in the matter.[11]

When the California landowners appeared before the land commission at San Francisco to request patents to their lands, they were expected to show their original grants. In many cases these had been lost and the only other evidence was the documents (*expedientes*) in the Monterey archives, plus such testimony as the Commission would accept from neighbors and friends.[12]

The real difficulty facing the Land Commission came after

a grant had been found to be valid. This was due to the fact that neither the Spanish nor Mexican governments had ever determined by official surveys the exact location, extent, or boundaries of any grant. Prior to the American occupation, no professional surveyor had ever been in California. According to the old Spanish custom then prevalent, when a grant was made the nearest judicial officer sent out two men with a lariat or rope fifty *varas* in length (approximately 137 1/2 feet) which was attached to stakes long enough so that they could be placed in position while the men sat on their horses. These men were given rather indefinite instructions as to the general location of the new grant, and the landmarks were usually a certain hill, a river, a mountain peak, or a tree. These were to be the corners of the grant. One man placed his stake in the ground, and the other set out at a gallop to the end of the rope. Then the first man pulled up his stake and rode past his partner to the end of the rope. They continued riding and stopping in this manner until they had enclosed enough land to approximate the number of square leagues contained in the grant. In case the grass was wet, the rawhide lariat would stretch considerably and the grantee would receive rather generous boundaries. The courts later sustained this additional land under the qualifying phrase "more or less" found in all grants.[13]

After the validity of the grant had been proved, the United States deputy surveyor went out with chain and compass to run the boundaries. But he was confused by the uncertainty of the general directions of courses and distances as well as the extraordinary measurements. So the Land Department soon gave up the attempt to run boundary lines until more specific instructions could be obtained from the courts after judicial hearings upon such testimony as could be secured.[14]

Engraving of Manuel Micheltorena, governor of California (1842-1845), who presided over a number of San Joaquin Valley land grants made just before the American takeover. *Fresno County Public Library, California History and Genealogy Room Collection.*

The Mexican governors made frequent mention in their *expedientes* to the Mexican land laws and to the regulations concerning colonization. For the sake of greater clarity, these are worth reading by the student of San Joaquin Valley history. On August 18, 1824 the Mexican Congress had passed a decree on colonization. This was modified by government regulations for the colonization of the territories adopted on November 21, 1828. These laws and regulations served as a basis for the Land Commission in determining whether or not the grantees had fulfilled their obligations to the Mexican Land laws.[15]

During 1932 and 1933, the Citizens Land Association of California was engaged in challenging the validity of the Mexican grants, especially those lying within ten leagues of the sea. The contention was made that these grants had not been legally made to private owners and were therefore open to homestead entry. The directors of the Citizens Land Association encouraged homesteaders to file on land within the boundaries of former Mexican grants, and gave as their reason for so doing the official document signed by Eduardo Delhumeau, Attorney General of Mexico, on November 21, 1924:

Engraving of Don Pio Pico, governor of California just before the American conquest (1845-1846), who sanctioned the last Mexican land grants made in the San Joaquin Valley.

Eduardo Delhumeau, Attorney General of the Republic, certifies:

That the law of August 18, 1824, was in force from the date of its passage, on August 24, 1824, until the territory comprising the present state of California and other possessions ceded by Mexico to the United States, passed to the American dominion; also certifies that no Governor of the State of California, during the time said state was under the jurisdiction of the Mexican Government, had sufficient power to grant any land to anyone whomsoever within a zone of ten leagues of the sea, without first securing the corresponding approval of the Supreme Government, and, therefore, it was not sufficient the approval of the local legislature; furthermore certifies that, according to the law referred to above, no citizen or colonist could, under any circumstances, acquire an amount of land in excess of eleven square leagues; and last, certifies that no valid grant has been made in the State of California by any authorized Mexican authority since May 13, 1846.[16]

The Land Commission for California ruled that the authority of Mexican governors to make grants ceased on

July 7, 1846, with the raising of the American flag over the Custom House at Monterey. A number of grants made between May 13th and July 7th were patented by the United States. Presumably the decision made by the Supreme Court many years ago was final.[17]

During the four years of its existence the United States Land Commission for California passed judgment on 813 claims, confirmed 521, and discontinued nineteen. The federal courts later passed on many cases which were appealed. Some patents were revoked and others were confirmed; the final result was that 613 claims to land grants were patented out of the 813 presented. The 813 claims made during Spanish and Mexican days totaled 12,000,000 acres. The 604 grants finally approved by the United States through its Land Commission and Federal Courts amounted approximately to less than 9,000,000 acres. In this huge task it was impossible to give satisfaction to every claimant but, after many failures, the United States had made an honest effort to live up to the obligations incurred in its treaty with Mexico.[18]

Rise in land values accompanied the increase in population. This necessitated more careful surveys and led to increased taxation. The latter caused the original grantees to either lose or sell their holdings. Individual unhappiness was not so much the result of a change in government as it was the pain, which is a necessary concomitant to growth and development.

> The old order changeth,
> Yielding place to new;
> And God fulfills Himself in many ways,
> Lest one good custom should corrupt the Earth.[19]

Engraving of a miner with pan and rocking cradle setup, characteristic of the earliest Gold Rush days. *Fresno County Public Library, California History and Genealogy Room Collection.*

7 Helldorado

I came from Salem City
With my wash bowl on my knee,
I'm going to California
The gold dust for to see.
It rained all night the day I left,
The weather it was dry,
The sun so hot I froze to death,
Oh! brothers, don't you cry.

Oh! California,
That's the land for me,
I'm going to Sacramento
With my wash bowl on my knee.

Song of the Forty Niners
(Parody of Stephen Foster's *Oh! Susanna*)

A horseman was seen approaching at a furious gallop. The denizens of Tuleberg were puzzled, apprehensive. Were the hoof beats of the steed, rapid like a drum roll, sending forth a message of weal or woe? The rider brought his broncho to a stop in a single bound and exclaimed

173

laconically: "Gold!" A buckskin bag of gold-dust was offered as a proof and he was off in a cloud of dust. In this manner was the discovery of gold first announced in the San Joaquin Valley; the time was April, 1848.[1]

Gold was discovered from time to time in small amounts during Spanish and Mexican days in both southern and northern California. Francisco Lopez, grandfather of onetime Los Angeles County Sheriff Eugene Biscailuz, located gold about eight miles from Newhall while digging for wild onions. The date of this discovery was in 1841 or 1842. The Indians knew where gold was to be found in the San Fernando Valley. The padres cautioned Lopez and his friends against ever divulging the secret. This warning was not based on cupidity, but on their love for the natives. The friars knew from past experience what happened to the Indians when a sudden influx of miners occurred. Such things had happened in Mexico time and again. Demoralization followed in the wake of a gold rush and the work of the missions was quickly undone.[2]

In July, 1845, a group of forty-three men arrived at Sutter's Fort; they had accompanied an emigrant train of one hundred wagons from the eastern states to Oregon, and had then continued to California. One of these men was a native of New Jersey and a wagon builder by trade. He became a valuable adjunct to the Sutter estate. After a time James Wilson Marshall bought land, fought in the war against the Mokelumne Indians, served with the Bear Flag party, and later with Fremont's Battalion, seeing service chiefly in southern California. He lost his stock while thus serving his country, was re-employed by Sutter, and began the construction of a sawmill on the South Fork of the American River, where Jedediah Smith had camped two decades earlier. Marshall agreed to operate the mill and would probably have become very wealthy as a lumberman since this commodity was then

Sutter's Mill in Coloma, site of James Marshall's 1848 discovery that sparked the California Gold Rush. *Fresno County Public Library, California History and Genealogy Room Collection.*

both expensive and in great demand, but instead, he found gold—and poverty!

The mill site was located at an elevation of 1,500 feet and was about forty-five miles from Sacramento by wagon road. Many of the laborers at the mill were Mormons from the demobilized Mormon Battalion, deployed during California's conquest in 1846. One day the following entry was made in a diary kept by a young Mormon laborer, Henry W. Bigler: "Monday 24th, this day some kind of mettle was found in the tail race that looks like goald, first discovered by James Martial, the Boss of the Mill." When Sutter was informed of this discovery, he kept the news quiet, afraid that a sudden influx of gold-seekers would disrupt work at the mill.[3]

The startling news could not be hushed. Sam Brannan had returned crestfallen to California from his visit to Brigham

Young's camp along the Green River. Failing to bring Young and the Mormons to the colony along the Stanislaus River, Brannan returned to California and set up a merchandise store at Sutter's Fort. This was in the fall of 1847. He also established the first newspaper in San Francisco, which was also the second to be set up in the entire state. The Monterey *Californian*, set up by Dr. Robert Semple, had preceded it by a few months. News of the gold discovery trickled down to San Francisco by devious ways, and Semple's paper, by that time moved from Monterey to San Francisco, printed the following startling news item:

> GOLD MINE FOUND—In the newly made race-way of the saw-mill recently erected by Captain Sutter, on the American fork, gold has been found in considerable quantities. One person brought thirty dollars worth to New Helvetia, gathered there in a short time. California, no doubt, is rich in mineral wealth; great chances here for scientific capitalists. Gold has been found in almost every part of the country.[4]

The editor of Sam Brannan's paper, the California *Star*, ridiculed the rumor as a fabrication. His embarrassment may be imagined when the owner himself arrived at San Francisco, waving a bottle containing gold dust in one hand, with the other swinging his big hat over his shaggy head, and shouting the news of the gold discovery. Brannan's reputation was sufficient to cause an exodus to the diggings. Semple's paper was forced to suspend publication; advertisers, subscribers, and office force left simultaneously. Brannan's paper soon followed suit and the printer's devil arrived in the gold country almost as soon as his employer. Eventually the two newspapers were combined to form the San Francisco *Daily Alta California*, one of the state's great daily newspapers.[5]

By June 1, 1848, thousands of men were in the diggings, and by 1852 the gold procured from the California mines reached an all-time high of $81 million. The next year

Engraving of miners making their way to the California "diggin's." *Fresno County Public Library, California History and Genealogy Room Collection.*

Congress found it necessary to establish a branch mint at San Francisco.[6]

Mining during 1848 was a pleasant picnic; old time friends and neighbors changed their occupations and became miners. Gold replaced cows as a medium of exchange, and an ounce became the standard of value. There was little crime and confusion. No mining claims existed; each one dug for gold wherever he chose. However, Colonel Richard B. Mason's official report to Washington made known the gold discovery and the complexion of things soon changed. The first outsiders to arrive came from Oregon, closely followed by miners from Chile and Sonora. Then came a horde of miners from all the nations of the earth. When Brannan visited San Francisco in 1849, a cross-section of humanity passed in review:

177

He saw beneath him a variegated bazaar of all nations, crowded into a single small square; turbaned Turks and Hindus; tattooed New Zealanders; jet-black Abyssinians; fiery-eyed Malays with their short, sickle-shaped swords; swarthy but handsome Kanakas [Hawaiians]; pig-tailed Chinese in blue smocks and huge basket-hats; a few even of the hermit Japanese; fur-muffled Russians, cheek-by-jowl with shivering, half-naked Indians; Irish, their shillalahs ever ready; Frenchmen smoking little black pipes; and "Dutch Charlies" puffing enormous meerschaums; Englishmen, with and without their aitches; dark-visaged Italians; Spanish of all kinds, from grandee to vaquero, outnumbered only by Americans, each of them a walking arsenal. Native Spaniards furnished the high lights of this ever-shifting *kaleidoscope*— gorgeous in velvet and long, gaudy *serapes* trailing to their silver-spurred heels.[7]

These and many other nationalities went to the gold mines and were, in many cases, to remain as settlers in the state. The dominant element were the Forty-niners from the older states to the East. They were called the Argonauts, after Jason's ancient Greeks, who sailed in search of the Golden Fleece in a ship built by a man named Argus, and hence called the *Argos*. The Forty-niners sailed away in prairie schooners, in clipper ships, which voyaged round Cape Horn, or in vessels that carried them to Panama and made connections with Pacific Ocean vessels. When the ships arrived even the sailors deserted them and began to dig for gold. In October, 1851, there were 451 idle ships clogging San Francisco's harbor.[8]

Gold was never found in great quantities on the San Joaquin Valley floor, but mining in the adjacent foothills greatly modified valley development. No huge fortunes were made by individual miners; the gold in California was too scattered. But the total gathered by all the miners collectively was immense. The southern mines extended from the Mokelumne River to the Kern. This was the term applied to that region by the miners themselves. Tuleberg, re-christened Stockton, became the outfitting place for the miners going south; the embarcadero below Sutter's Fort, re-christened Sacramento, served a similar purpose for the northern mines.

Upon receipt of the golden news, Charles Weber of Stockton led a party to the eastern foothills and found gold along Weber's Creek; here a camp named Weberville was established. The Stockton Mining Company was organized and Weber's friend, José Jerez, who hated the Spanish but was friendly to other white men at that time, came to Weber's assistance. José Jerez was an educated Indian like Estanislao and, like the latter, had served as alcalde at Mission San José, and had then run away to the wilderness. This chief sent Weber twenty-five stalwart Indian laborers who delved for gold under the tutelage of skilled miners. Weber prospered greatly both from his mining and trading ventures. Indian miners in the early days gladly gave him a handful of gold dust for a gaudy handkerchief. Joaquin Miller saw an Indian give $25,000 in gold dust for a string of glass beads costing about fifty cents. After awhile, the Indians learned that gold dust was worth more than they were receiving for it in trade. However, unscrupulous traders managed to deceive them by manipulating the scales. The steelyards in use among the miners usually consisted of a piece of pine board for a beam, sardine cans for scales, and silver dollars for weights. Gold dust sold for five dollars per ounce at the mines and eight dollars an ounce in the coast towns. During the first months of the gold mining period, Weber sent mules laden with gold to Stockton every day.[9]

At first men looked for gold along the valley floor, but soon sagely determined to follow the streams into the hills to the original source. Both Sutter and Weber sent out Indian gold scouts. The result was that in time the miners

Engraving of miners at a typical nighttime entertainment. *Fresno County Public Library, California History and Genealogy Room Collection.*

moved up-stream into the dry diggings where each man usually averaged five ounces of gold a day.[10]

The miners moved rapidly southward from El Dorado County. The discharged soldiers of Stevenson's regiment, largely recruited from the Bowery district in New York, went to Mokelumne Hill; here a 25-pound nugget was found which, at the current value of $19 for each of the 364 troy ounces, was worth $6,916.[11] Gold was so abundant there that claims were limited to sixteen feet square. The French miners congregated there, and the attempt of the Bowery boys to expel them led to the so-called French War. The high-spirited lads from the sidewalks of New York craved excitement and promoted fights between longhorn bulls and grizzly bears. They also made Mokelumne Hill the capital of Calaveras County, a distinction that it retained from 1852 to 1866.[12]

Carson Hill, located along Carson's Creek, was named after James H. Carson. The miners who accompanied

Carson to his camp averaged 180 troy ounces a day. A 195-pound nugget, worth $43,534, ranks as the largest mass of gold found in one piece in the United States and the second largest nugget to be found in the entire history of mining. It sold for over $50,000. The Morgan Mine in this area yielded by itself $2 million within two years.[13]

George Angel gave his name to Angel's Camp and Angel's Creek, now called Angels Camp, where the famous jumping frog achieved fame. Gold dust worth $30 million was mined here. Near this mining camp was located Jackass Hill, where Samuel Clemens (Mark Twain) and his partner, Jim Gillis, dug for gold. On this hill each hundred square feet yielded $10,000 worth of gold and the quartz was 3/4 gold by weight. Associated with Mark Twain and Jim Gillis were the latter's brothers Steve, Bill, and Dick, and a man named Dick Stoker who is the Dick Baker in *Roughing It*. Clemens made a poor miner. He preferred to sit in the saloon and listen to the bartender tell yarns, of which he had a remarkable store. Among them was a tall story about an athletic frog. One drizzly and gloomy day Clemens wanted to quit work and go back to warm and dry quarters. Gillis asked him to bring just one more pail of water. Clemens replied, "Oh, hell, Jim, I won't do it. I am freezing." They returned to their cabin on Jackass Hill and left a thirty-day notice on their claim. Some Swedish miners came by and saw the gold dust which had been revealed by the down-pour of rain, camped beside the lease until the time limit expired, and reaped a fortune. But Clemens did not care; he made his fortune in another and, to him, more pleasant fashion.[14]

The camp which became known as Murphy's Diggings was founded in conjunction with Charles M. Weber's mining venture in June 1848, and was named for a partner, John M. Murphy. This camp yielded $20 million in gold dust. One of the most famous mining camps, mentioned in the writings of Bret Harte, was the place known as Poker Flat. Pioneer residents assert that this was the original name of Byrne's Ferry, the old crossing on the Stanislaus River between Copperopolis and Mountain Pass.[15]

The base towns of the gold mining region were all located below the fall line. This made it possible for river boats to carry supplies up the San Joaquin River and its affluents to distribution centers. The miners followed the streams into the hills, but they returned to these base towns for supplies and social relaxation.[16]

One evening in the latter part of 1848 the Weber trading establishment secretly disappeared. It was correctly assumed that Weber's gold scouts had located new fields. A new stampede resulted to the southern mines. A prospector named Benjamin Wood entered the Tuolumne River region and located on Woods Creek. There, in the same year, a 150-pound nugget was found by William Gulnac. Also in that same year, the Sonora Camp was founded by a group of Mexicans from Sonora, Mexico. Miners from Los Angeles and San Diego were prone to stop in the southern mines, as these were nearer to their point of departure. Sonora became the queen of the southern mines, and its Bonanza Mine alone yielded a total of $1.5 million. Other interesting mines were located at Angels Camp, Campo Seco, and Vallecito. These camps were all located in the hills east of Modesto, and yielded more than $30 million.[17]

The miners reached the San Joaquin River where it debouches into the plain in due time. The land adjacent to this stream from Millerton down into the valley bears witness to the Herculean labor performed in that district. Gold has always cost the miner more in labor than he has received for it on the market. One economist estimated that the miners, on the average, made less than one dollar per day. This was small pay, especially when the high cost of living prevalent in the mining region is considered, for their tremendous labors. A pioneer who lived at Fort Miller before Millerton had been founded, made the following statement concerning the amount of gold found along the San Joaquin: "The amount of gold recovered from the San Joaquin is traditional. No exact figure can be given; though probably a million dollars—more or less."[18]

The Dry Creek region near Fresno was first located by various American miners and a group of Spanish-Californians from the southern part of the state. These men were prone to sink deep shafts into the ground and this method incurred the ridicule of the American miners. However, they found gold and that was an effective answer to their tormentors.[19]

No gold was found along either the Kings or Kaweah rivers, at least not in paying quantities. A false report concerning gold along Kings River led to a tragedy. Mission Indians from San Miguel carried the news to Monterey. William R. Gardiner, who had been a resident of California for fifteen years at that time, organized an expedition to look for it. He secured four prairie schooners and loaded them with supplies, hired several Indians drivers, and took four Spaniards with him as partners. They left San Migúel and followed the right bank of Kings River into the hills. The Indians in the hills enticed them onward by showing them gold dust, and finally, Kaweahs and Chowchilla Indians, slew the members of the party. A diary kept by Gardiner was found and revealed the happenings up to the time of the last assault.[20]

In later years reports have persisted that gold is to be found along Kings River. One of these rumors centers about a German trapper named Shipe. One day this trapper and a small boy, related to Shipe's Indian wife, found a three-foot ledge containing gold. A specimen was taken to Visalia and shown to Sheriff Owen of Tulare County. He had been a gold miner and immediately formed a partnership with Shipe; this was in 1853. Shipe got drunk that night and in a brawl he was shot and killed by City Marshal Williams. The little Indian boy who alone knew the site of the ledge refused to talk and it was never located. The specimen which Shipe had left with Owen sold for $3,000.

In the late seventies and early eighties the Spanish-Californians around Hanford had a great deal of gold dust. It was noticed that two of them occasionally went on trips to the mountains. On one occasion they were trailed by curious ex-miners from Hanford and when they spied their trackers they refused to go on. Eventually one of them died in Mexico City and the other at Hanford. The latter, just before his death, told a personal friend named Richards that the gold came from a depression in a ridge along Kings River and was easy to get out. He left a map in an envelope for Richards, who spent five years looking for the site but never found it. Some old-timers think that this may have been the old Shipe mine.[21]

The first gold in the Kern River basin was found by members of Fremont's 1851 party who tarried at Greenhorn Gulch near the Kern River. The hills where this gold was found were known thereafter as the Greenhorn Mountains. Interest in that region fluctuated from the discovery until 1854, when Richard M. Keyes found some quartz ledges, and that year six hundred miners passed through Visalia on their way to the Kern River gold fields. Keyesville became an important gold mining center for a time. In 1864 Havilah, another mining camp, was established in the foothills east of modern Bakersfield. It derived its name from this verse in the Bible [Genesis 2:10-12]:

Engraving of a typical miner's bunkhouse of the Gold Rush era. *Fresno County Public Library, California History and Genealogy Room Collection.*

And a river went out of Eden to water the garden; and from thence it was parted, and became into four heads. The name of the first is Pison: that is it which compasseth the whole land of Havilah, where there is gold; and the gold on that land is good; there is bdellium and onyx stone."

Two years after its founding the population, was numerous enough to warrant the organization of a new county, and Havilah became the county seat. Eight years later, this mining town was supplanted by Bakersfield as the capital of Kern County.[22]

One of the chief obstacles to the development of the Southern Mines was the presence of warlike Indians. The miners either destroyed or frightened away the wild game and the Indians were confronted with an economic depression, which warranted immediate relief measures. A newspaper of the time stated the following:

Notwithstanding the existence of a murderous warfare between the Whites and Indians, throughout the entire

185

southern mining section, still, every report but confirms us in the opinion that in every placer south of the Mokelumne, the industrious miner is reaping a sure and ample recompense for his toil. From Pine Gold Gulch on the San Joaquin, to the bars of the canyon of the Merced, and the diggings of the Stanislaus, the news is in every way encouraging.[23]

Another obstacle encountered in the movement of miners to the Southern Mines was the objection of northern newspapers and leaders in the Northern Mines who resented the emigration of sturdy members from their own communities:

The tide of the population is still setting into the southern mining region. There are seven steamboats running between San Francisco and Stockton, and each trip they make to this place, they are laden to the guards with passengers and freight. In the meantime from the lower country, the Mexicans are pouring in by the thousands. From the northern mining region, large numbers are also making their way towards our placers, notwithstanding the attempt of the Sacramento *Times* to dam the stream.[24]

As long as big nuggets could be found on the surface, men took no time to study the geological formation of the mining region. But when mining became a science rather than a gamble, a study of the terrain revealed the fact that a definite formation existed which ran parallel with the Sierra Nevada for a distance of a hundred miles. This is generally referred to as the Mother Lode.

The English-speaking people were confronted with two problems in California, which they had never met with before. One was irrigation; the other, gold-mining. The former will be discussed in a subsequent chapter. Gold was discovered in January, 1848, and the treaty with Mexico by which the United States acquired California was not signed until the following month. The Mexican government came to an end and no substitute, excepting a temporary military regime, had been provided. In the meantime thousands of men went surging into the mining areas without permission and without any form of government to control them. The gold mines were on government land. What right did the miners have there? Men freed from all restraint were busy digging wealth out of the ground. Constables, sheriffs, judges, courts, and jails did not exist. The military forces were all located on the coast. Who was to provide a legalized form of control and prevent a reign of terror? The miners themselves.

Since the earliest recorded times, miners have abhorred lawyers. The latter have unjustly been accused of being the cause, rather than the result, of unhappy social conditions. Long ago an American miner wrote: "One thing I supplicate Your Majesty: that you will give orders, under a great penalty, that no bachelors of law should be allowed to come here; for not only are they bad themselves, but they also make and contrive a thousand iniquities." This writer's name was Balboa. Nevertheless, many of the California miners digging for gold along the bar opposite a bend in a river were law school graduates and were to achieve both wealth and fame before a bar of a different type in later years. They played an important part, during their career as miners, in contriving a form of government, which made the mining region more law-abiding than the cities along the coast.

The local government of the California miners was based on first principles; the old folk-moots of the Scandinavian and German forests appeared under new conditions. Each camp became a separate governmental and administrative entity and remained such even after California had held its Constitutional Convention and secured admission to statehood. Shifting mining camps were too difficult to follow in those days by duly constituted authorities. Among the miners were men of uncommon ability who took an active part in formulating local laws and regulations.

Each camp usually had a duly elected alcalde, a sheriff, and a recorder who registered mining claims. The alcalde received approximately $16 for presiding at a trial; the sheriff, who served writs, received mileage pay; and the recorder collected a fee of fifty cents to one dollar for recording a new claim. The fee was intended to cover expenses, and a specified percent was given to the recorder as his stipend. The latter amount varied in the various camps. Jurors received approximately $6 a case, and witnesses their expenses. The latter included all the whiskey used during the trial by court, jury, and witnesses. Cases were decided immediately and compliance with the decision of the court was enforced. When two Spanish-California miners disputed the ownership of a mule and were unable to prove their individual contentions, the judge ordered them to draw straws. The mining laws of the camp at La Grange were typical of those in vogue: "In event of any of the disputing parties not acknowledging the decision, then the miners of this district will assemble and compel said party to recognize the umpire's decision."[25]

When a criminal came before the jurisdiction of a mining court the news was cried from claim to claim and in thirty minutes the men had gathered. Capital punishment was meted out to any man found guilty of horse stealing, ordinary petty theft, or murder. If the miners' court found the defendant guilty, he was hanged forthwith, and the men went back to work. Such prompt action had a salutary effect and the mining camps were never as lawless as the cities along the coast. Hanging was a public spectacle and such sights together with the known fact that punishment was always swift and certain had a wholesome effect on public morals. The following public notice may be of interest:

PUBLIC NOTICE:

All citizens of Hornitos are respectfully invited to attend the *Hanging of Cherokee Bill*, Horse Thief. Meeting at Rattlesnake Ike's saloon, Miner's Court. May 12, 1851.

7 O'CLOCK—NIGHT

Hornitos *Times*, Printer
Thomas Early, Sheriff [26]

The number of mining districts naturally varied during the days of gold digging. In the *United States Report on Mineral Resources for 1866*, it was stated that five hundred organized districts were then in existence in California. These districts had been organized without authority and were solely the work of the miners themselves. They very effectively solved the problem of law and order and never tolerated anything approaching modern racketeering. The mining districts took action against foreigners on whom they usually imposed taxes, determined the size of claims, prescribed the proper size and form of notices, and in general compelled law and order. These conditions existed only during the days of placer mining. Absentee ownership of claims was not tolerated.

Some of the notices posted on claims in those days are interesting. The following are examples:

Notice: The undersigned claims this ground for mining purposes, known as the Robert McCall Claim, being a deep or shaft claim, and bounded on the northwest by the Gilchrist and Cornwell Claim, and on the southeast by the Plug-Ugly Claim, and he intends to work it according to the laws of the San Andreas Mining District.

William Irvine
John Skowalter, Recorder, August 18, 1862.

Another miner posted a notice which showed a lack of erudition but left no one in doubt as to his exact meaning:

> *Notis*:   To all and everybody. This is my claim, fifty feet on the gulch, cordin' to Clear Lake Creek District Law, backed up by shotgun amendments.
>
> Thomas Hall.

Another notice was brief and to the point:

> *Clame Notis*: Jim Brown of Missoury takes this ground; jumpers will be shot.[27]

Most districts considered a verbal conveyance of a claim legal and sufficient. This was the type of government which proved effective during the heyday of mining. The first executives in California during the American period were Stephen Watts Kearny, Richard B. Mason, and Bennett Riley. They had no correspondence with the alcaldes east of the San Joaquin River, but both Mason and Riley made tours of inspection to that region in 1848 and 1849. They reported that everything was well organized and orderly. No removals, appointments, or changes in that region were ever made by the governors during that period of the state's development.

The miners proved their ability to care for themselves but the national government was uncertain in the early months of the gold rush by what rights these miners could enter government land and extract gold. The problem was expressed by Henry George, the single tax exponent, in Progress and Poverty:

> For the first time in the history of the Anglo-Saxon race, these men were brought into contact with land from which gold could be obtained by the simple operation of washing it out—The novelty of the case broke through habitual ideas, and threw men back upon first principles; and it was by common consent declared that this gold-bearing land should remain common property, of which no one might take more

than he could reasonably use, or hold for a longer time than he continued to use it. This perception of natural justice was acquiesced in by the general government, and the courts; and while placer mining remained of importance, no attempt was made to overrule this reversion to primitive ideas. . . . Thus no one was allowed to forestall or to lock up natural resources. Labor was acknowledged as the creator of wealth, was given a free field, and secured its reward. The device would not have assured complete equality of rights under the conditions that in most countries prevail; but under the conditions that there and then existed—a sparse population, an unexplored country, and an occupation in its nature a lottery—it secured substantial justice.[28]

Similar conditions usually beget similar reactions and the English-speaking people, encountering gold in the ground for the first time, went back to the principles of the old Nordic tribes from whom they were descended. R. W. Raymond stated in "Relations of Governments to Mining" in connection with the *United States Mining Report for 1869:*

In the form of a local custom obtaining with remarkable uniformity in all the original centers of German mining, the principle of mining-freedom established itself. permitting all persons to search for useful minerals and granting to the discoverer of such a deposit the rights of property within certain limits. This principle of free mining immigrated with the German miners to all places whither their enterprise extended itself, and the original local custom became the general law. In this existence of an estate in minerals, entirely independent of the estate in soil, lies the distinctive character of German mining law. It is eminently a special law, not subordinate to civil law but coordinate with it.

Before the United States could take any definite action millions of dollars had been taken from the public domain and thousands of men were governing themselves. Local organization was functioning, and men like William H. Seward and Thomas Hart Benton hesitated to inaugurate a change. The safest course was to acknowledge the rights which had already been appropriated. Thus the possessory rights of the miners were recognized and legalized. This California system spread to the other Territories and finally to other nations. Thus did the development of the San Joaquin Valley aid in the molding of the world.

In December, 1865, the Chief Justice of the Supreme Court, Salmon P. Chase, read the majority opinion in the case of *Sparrow vs. Strong*:

> A special kind of law, a sort of common law of the miners, the offspring of a nation's irrepressible march—lawless in some senses—yet clothed with dignity by a conception of the immense social results mingled with the fortune of these bold investigators—has sprung up on the Pacific Coast, and presents in the value of a "mining right" a novel and peculiar question of jurisdiction for this Court.

After the surface diggings came to an end, tunneling became necessary, and this proved costly. Miners organized themselves into co-operative units, and some went to work at their former occupations and supported the men who worked at the mine. The miners were inclined to cooperate, although they were naturally very individualistic; the conditions of the time made such action imperative. Cooperative ventures at the mines taught these men, many of whom later became farmers, the value of that form of organization in relation to agriculture. One group of men going to the mines drew up the following agreement:

> (1) That we shall bear an equal share in all expenses.
>
> (2) No man shall be allowed to leave the company without general consent till we reach the mines.
>
> (3) Any one leaving with our consent shall have back his original investment.
>
> (4) That we work together in the mines, and use our tools in

common.

(5) That each man shall retain all the gold he finds, but must contribute an equal portion of our daily expenses.

(6) That we stand by each other.

(7) That each man shall in turn cook, and do his share of the drudgery.

(8) That anyone guilty of stealing, shall be expelled from tent and claim, with such other punishment as a majority of our company decide upon.

(9) That no sick comrade be abandoned.[29]

The men who mined for gold in California were young men; usually desert prospectors are old men, but conditions in California required youth and strength. A man over fifty was a curiosity. In many cases they were forced to work waist-deep in cold water, and the inordinate quantities of whiskey which they drank to counteract the effects of the cold water often caused delirium tremens which they, being loyal Easterners, blamed on the California climate. These young men, freed from all restraints, flung away their gold and their lives with a zest both admirable and pathetic. During the winter months they congregated in the saloons and gambling halls of the cities and by spring, they were usually financially and physically decrepit. They rested on Sundays at the mines, not because of piety but in the interest of cleanliness, which is said to be next to godliness. Shirts were boiled and clothes were mended. The hard work also made a day of rest a necessity. Father William Taylor, later a bishop of the Methodist Episcopal Church, preached to the miners who had congregated at San Francisco. Some were resting from their labors of that year; others were newly arrived. It was December, 1849. An admirer of the clergyman recounted the scene in a letter:

> It was on a Sunday morning in December when, landing from the Panama steamer, I wended my way with the throng to

Portsmouth Square. Three sides of the square were occupied by buildings, which served the double purpose of hotels and gambling houses, the latter being regarded as a very reputable profession. On the fourth and upper side of the square was an adobe building, from the steps of which you were discoursing from the text, "The way of the transgressor is hard." It was a scene I shall never forget. On all sides were gambling houses, each with its band of music in full blast. Crowds were going in and out; fortunes were being lost and won, terrible imprecations and blasphemies rose amid the horrid wail, and it seemed to me that Pandemonium was let loose.[30]

Later Rev. Taylor went to the mines and reported that he always had an attentive audience at the morning service, but that no one ever came in the evening. Another eyewitness wrote that the miners were affectionately drunk in the morning, fighting drunk in the afternoon, and dead drunk in the evening. Still another observer, according to Owen C. Coy's *Gold Days*, said:

We found that sickness prevailed to an alarming extent, particularly land scurvy, owing to the constant use of salt and greasy provisions without vegetables. In many instances it assumed a fearfully loathsome shape, swelling the limbs to an enormous size, changing the skin to a deep purple hue, contracting the muscles and main tendons of the legs and arms, so that those members were rigid and useless; enlarging the gums immensely and imparting to them a gangrenous appearance, not only disgusting to look at, but highly offensive in smell. There were also rheumatism, simple and acute, sciatica, fever, and ague, and several cases of pulmonary ailments, which generally ended fatally; all owing, I suppose, to the severity of the season, and especially to sleeping in damp clothes on the cold wet ground.[31]

The miners wrecked their lives in many cases in a joyous quest for gold and then threw their gold away in an equally glorious manner in search for a phantom pleasure. But they lived supremely and, like Edna St. Vincent

Millay in her "First Fig," they could say:

> I burn my candle at both ends,
> It will not last the night,
> But ah, my foes, and oh, my friends,
> It yields a lovely light.

Not all the miners, however, were of this type. Many a man came out of the mines with a fortune and later became famous in other fields of endeavor. Famous lawyers and great cattlemen secured their beginnings in California by "rocking a cradle" or swinging a pick. The father of William Randolph Hearst laid the foundation of the family fortune in the gold mines; so did many other men.

In the early days of gold mining, dust and provisions were transported to and from the mines by pack trains; there were no wagons. Riverboats usually carried supplies to Stockton, and from there they were moved to the south by means of mules. Goods were transported by boats for seventy-five cents a pound, and carried by mules from Stockton to the Southern Mines for $1.25 a pound. Horses became expensive after the invasion of the miners. Prior to their arrival, wild horses usually sold for seventy-five cents each. The miners were forced to pay between two and three hundred dollars for a pack animal. When the mines were reached these animals were turned loose on the assumption that "it was easier to dig out the price of another, than to hunt up the one astray."[32]

Humor was a feature in mining life. Miners delighted in weird and descriptive place names such as Gospel Swamp, Skunk Gulch, Git-up-and-Git, Lazy Man's Canyon, Wildcat Bar, Whiskey Bar, Shin-bones Peak, Humpback Slide, Bogus Thunder, Hell's Delight, and Jackass Hill.[33] At a funeral service one Sunday morning the clergyman prayed too long to please one miner and, while on his knees, he began to pick in the gravel. Walter Noble Burns

Engraving of miners attacking a Chilean settlement during the Gold Rush era. *Fresno County Public Library, California History and Genealogy Room Collection.*

has told the story in this fashion:

> On Carson Creek, a miner died and a crowd of his friends assembled about the open grave for the obsequies. While the preacher was praying, a miner with head bowed solemnly, saw a nugget sticking out of the dirt thrown from the grave and, reaching out a furtive hand, dropped it into his pocket, "Oh, Lord," intoned the parson, "forgive the sins of the departed brother—What was that you picked up, Bill?—and receive his soul into Thy Kingdom—a nugget?—Amen. This funeral's adjourned. I'm staking my claim right at this grave." It turned out to be a rich claim. The deceased was buried elsewhere.[34]

Such tales, true or false, were circulated in the camps during the days when Bret Harte and Mark Twain were digging for gold or visiting those who were.

By 1859 the old California miners began to leave for other fields. That year many went to British Columbia; in 1860 they went to Idaho and Tuscarora, Nevada; in 1862, some went to Boise, Idaho, and to the John Day region in Oregon; in 1865, the placers in the Big Bend region of the Columbia lured them. It is said that when the smallest coin in California dropped from a quarter to a dime, the miners left; forty thousand stalwart miners moved out within a period of three or four years. E. H. Hargreaves, an Australian, returned from his mining venture in California and found gold in the Antipodes. Local mining legislation and organization which grew up there were, through the instrumentality of Hargreaves and other Australians who had mined in California, modeled on that which had been developed in the foothills adjacent to the San Joaquin Valley. In 1884 California miners were still active enough to go to the Transvaal and to Siberia. When news arrived that gold had been discovered along Anvil Creek near Nome, Frank Dusy, one of the original Forty-Niners, organized a party of gold miners in the Selma district and led them to Cook Inlet opposite Kodiak Island. The men who had followed the rivers along the San Joaquin Valley floor in to the mountains searching for gold, were to continue that search in every gold mining region in the world. Their influence in method of work and in form of government was destined to be distinctly constructive in every gold field, which was subsequently discovered.[35]

The depression of 1929-1933 sent men surging into the foothill region in search of gold. On September 10, 1932, the newspapers reported a gold rush to Poso Creek, twenty miles northeast of Bakersfield. Many of these recent miners have equipped themselves with divining rods (doodle-bugs) of the type used in the search for oil. While this rush to the old gold mining region is a recent manifestation, yet mining has been going on continuously since 1848. Naturally, most of this has been done by corporations using gold dredges and other expensive machinery. The Carson Hill mines yielded $500,000 between 1919 and 1924. The Morgan Mine, between 1919 and 1924, produced $5 million worth of gold. Robert Newmeyer, a miner on Jackass Hill, made famous by Mark Twain, found a single nugget in 1929 worth $16,000.[36]

The old time California miners left their physical mark in every mining camp in the whole world. The evidence of their labor in California is still apparent. The mounds along the San Joaquin River between Fresno and old Fort Miller are an example. The traveler who tours the country along the foothill area from Sacramento to Bakersfield will see the marks of their toil in the scarred hills and up-turned gravel; he will note deserted cities and mining camps; and he will be oppressed by a region, once resounding to the bustle of intense activity, now given over to the reign of supreme silence. The red-shirted miners, with their big hats and cowhide boots, have long since passed away:

> We have worked our claims
> We have spent our gold,
> Our barks are astrand on the bars;
> We are battered and old,
> Yet at night we behold
> Outcroppings of gold in the stars.
> Though battered and old
> Our hearts are bold,
> Yet oft do we repine
> For the days of old,
> For the days of gold,
> For the days of '49.[37]

8 Bullets, Ballots, and

Tongue Lashings

God give us men; a time like this demands
Strong minds, great hearts, true faith, and ready hands.
Men whom the lust of office cannot kill;
Men whom the spoils of office cannot buy,
Men who possess opinions and a will;
Men who have honor, men who will not lie;
Men who can stand before a demagogue,
And damn his treacherous flatteries without winking;
Tall men, sun-crowned, who live above the fog
In public duty and in private thinking,
For while the rabble with its thumb-worn creeds,
Its large professions, and its little deeds,
Mingle in selfish strife—lo! Freedom weeps,
Wrong rules the land, and waiting Justice sleeps.

Josiah Gilbert Holland in *Wanted*

"This is our country; why do the Americans come here?
They are good and brave, but they come upon the lands of
my people. What do they intend to do? I want to know,

and I must know RIGHT NOW! . . . . . Heretofore my people did not permit any stranger to pass over our country or stop in it, except Mr. Savage—he made us many presents. If you will make us presents, too, you may remain in our country awhile."[1]

The speaker was José Rey (King Joseph), a Chowchilla chieftain, and his audience was composed of a few white men including Adam Johnston, the newly appointed Indian Agent for the San Joaquin Valley. This speech was similar to those made on other occasions during previous decades by King Philip, Little Turtle, Logan the Mingo, Red Jacket, Tecumseh, Black Hawk, and Chief Joseph of the Nez Percé. In each case a defeated and broken race was to meet the same tragic fate.

The United States had acquired California by treaty in 1848. John C. Fremont arrived in the San Joaquin in the month of May, 1849, to become a permanent resident of his *Las Mariposas* ranch. He brought with him forty men, of whom the Indians killed six within a few weeks. Three years before this, Fremont had been recalled from Klamath Lake by an order from the United States Marine Corps, and had taken an important part in the war against the Mexican government.

During that war, Fremont had enlisted in his battalion men of all nations. Company H, commanded by Captain Jacobs, consisted of twenty-nine Tulare Indians and eleven Walla-Walla tribesmen. This company of forty men foraged for the other soldiers. They stole food, horses, cattle, and equipment from the Spanish California ranchers. Their skill in this type of activity caused them to be nicknamed the "Forty Thieves." One of the Tulare Indians was an important chief named José Juarez, who had succeeded Estanislao as an Indian leader. After having been mustered out of Fremont's Battalion, José Juarez aided Captain Weber in his gold mining ventures.

José Juarez is also known as José Jesus and José Jerez. He is not to be confused with José Rey, the great war chief of the Chowchilla Indians. José Juarez finally surrendered to the white men, but José Rey preferred death in action. After the latter's demise, Tom-Kit and Federico became the war leaders. Another important valley chief was Vowchester, the American soldier's way of saying Bautista. One of the white men who served in Fremont's Battalion during the war was James Savage; during the campaign he made contacts with José Juarez and other influential Indians in Company H, which were to be of historic importance during the years that lay before him.[2]

The cause of Indian restlessness in the San Joaquin during the fifties and sixties was due to two things: First, the substitution of one government by another left an interregnum during which no one had the authority to take decisive action or enact corrective measures. Second, the influx of 80,000 immigrants during 1849 caused an advance along the hills to the south, which began to crowd the Indians and make them angry. The Indian menace on the frontier required federal action and on May 4, 1849, Major A. S. Miller, under orders from the military governor of California, established a camp at Taylor's Ferry on the Stanislaus River at the point where it leaves the foothills. Governor Alvarado, a decade earlier, had found it advisable to maintain a permanent garrison in this same region under the command of Don Santiago Estrada.[3]

Adam Johnston arrived in California on November 3, 1849, with instructions from the United States Government to study and direct Indian affairs in the interior valleys of California. While he was attempting to familiarize himself with conditions, James Savage had become a trader in the San Joaquin Valley. On October 29, 1850, a great celebration was held at San Francisco in honor of California's admission to statehood. Savage took José Juarez to these festivities in the hope of duly impressing the chief with the white man's power and numbers. Heavily armed soldiers, sailors, and marines passed in review. A gorgeous pageant moved past. But the chief remained impassive. The booming of cannon produced not a quiver. During much of the time Jose Juarez was in a drunken stupor and the attempts of Savage to control him and his appetite aroused his resentment.[4]

Savage returned to the San Joaquin and learned that the Indians were restless. Urgent measures were necessary if the hostile natives were to be pacified. Johnston also arrived in the valley and went in search of Savage, since this Indian trader had the most influence among the Yokuts and Miwok Indians. He located him at his trading post along the Fresno River. James D. Savage held no license from the government but operated as a trader under verbal permission from the Superintendent of Indian Affairs.

An Indian council was held at Savage's trading post along the Fresno River. José Juarez, José Rey, and Vowchester were among the chiefs present. War seemed imminent and Savage finally called upon José Juarez to tell the Indians concerning the great things he had seen and heard on his recent visit to San Francisco. To his amazement José Juarez spoke as follows:

> Our brother has told his Indian relatives [Major Savage by this time had five Indian wives] much that is truth. We have seen many people. The white men we saw on our visit are of many tribes. They are not like the tribes that dig gold in the mountains. They will not help these gold diggers if the Indians make war against them. If the gold diggers go to the white tribes in the big village they give their gold for strong water and games; when they have no more gold the white tribes drive the gold diggers back to the mountains with

clubs. They can not bring their big ships and guns to us; we have no cause to fear them. They will not injure us.[5]

Savage sprang to his feet and replied to this treacherous harangue as follows:

I have listened very attentively to what the chief, who went with me as my friend, has been saying to you. I have heard all he has said. He has told you some truth...but they [white men] are all brothers, all of one tribe. All can wear the clothing of the gold-diggers...the white men will come and fight against the Indians.[6]

José Juarez became furious but José Rey, an able and dignified chieftain, called him to order and then spoke eloquently in favor of war. A part of his speech was quoted at the beginning of this chapter.

Johnston and Savage returned to the Mariposa River, where Savage had his main trading post. On December 7th the numerous Indians employed by Savage disappeared. His wives had been abducted by their Indian relatives in order to keep them out of harm's way. Savage, after the manner of Solomon, had married the daughters of chieftains and had thereby solidified his social and political position. In personal appearance he resembled George A. Custer. He was tall and slender, and his golden hair hung in curls down over his shoulders. The Indian maidens of the Yokuts tribe undoubtedly considered him their "Fair God." Savage, a native of New York, had served with Fremont's Battalion and his magnetic personality had attracted the Indian members of that military force. After the war he had been a member of a group, including James Wood and Charles Bassett, who mined gold at Wood's Crossing. Then he led a wild and riotous existence among the Indians until the Federal Government assumed control. He promptly capitalized on his friendship with the Indians by becoming a trader among them.[7] Savage instilled in his Indian neighbors and relatives awe amounting to fear, which the following quotation may explain:

> Savage by some means had possessed himself of a small electrical machine, and having made himself acquainted with its practical workings, he used it to the greatest advantage in strengthening his power over the body and mind of the credulous and susceptible Indians, causing them to take hold of particular objects, or assist him in removing them, with the machine secreted so that it could not be seen, he would set the electric current in motion; it flashed them with lightning speed, paralyzing their physical motion, filling them with terror and dismay.[8]

By matrimonial alliances, fair treatment, and superior intellect, Savage controlled the trade of a territory greater than many a European nation. When danger threatened this region it was only natural that the Federal officials should turn to this white man for advice. Savage sympathized with the Indians and believed that vicious white men were the instigators of most of the evil. Yet he was always loyal to his own race and never became a renegade, like Simon Girty and Moses Blackstaffe. And this, too, in spite of the fact that the defeat of the Indians would mean great financial loss to him as a trader!

The desertion of his Indians on December 7th indicated a serious state of affairs. Savage and Johnston trailed them into the mountains, thirty miles west of the trading post, and finally located the natives on a hilltop. The white men were forbidden to approach, but a long-range conversation was carried on from an adjacent hill. Savage was informed that all white men, himself excepted, were hated and the Indians intended to drive all the pale-faces out of the country. He was also informed that his trading post along the Fresno River had been destroyed immediately after Johnston and he had left it. This was true. Three of the four white men employed there had been murdered, the supplies stolen, and a loss of $25,150 entailed according to the itemized account furnished the government by Savage. But profits were large in those days and Savage, at his death two years later, was worth $100,000, most of which had been accumulated since the tragedy on Fresno River.[9]

J. M. Cassity, another trader in the valley, had a post along the San Joaquin River, known as Cassity's Fort. This was situated a few miles downstream from the later site of Millerton. A stockade was built as a protection against the Indians and named Fort Washington. In more recent years the Fort Washington School and Fort Washington Golf Course have indicated the general locality of Cassity's trading post and stockade. Cassity was found with his legs cut off and his tongue pinned to his heart with an arrow.[10]

Johnston, after his unsuccessful parley with the Indians, returned to San Jose, then the state capital of California, and notified Governor Peter Burnett concerning the state of affairs on the frontier. In the meantime, Sheriff James Burney of Mariposa County organized a battalion and proceeded to chastise the Indians. At that time Mariposa County consisted of the entire San Joaquin Valley south of the Tuolumne River, all of the Sierra Nevada region facing this portion of the valley, and the deserts and valley beyond to the Nevada line. Therefore Burney's authority reached into the hills and beyond to Nevada from Tejon Pass almost to Stockton.[11]

Burney's deputies, seventy-four in number, followed the natives into the mountains. Along the headwaters of the Fresno River, the white men approached a village given over to revelry and dancing. The seventy-four volunteers engaged four hundred Indians in a battle, which lasted three hours and a half; the Indians lost fifty killed and the white men three. Burney's force finally withdrew, built a stockade, and the exhausted men slept fitfully while the Indians yelled hideously and shot arrows ineffectually into the barricade of logs. Burney and Savage rode through the lines and went to Agua Fria for supplies.[12]

One of the heroes in this little Mariposa War was a young Virginian named William James Howard, a cattleman along Burns Creek. In his later life he furnished the following humorous account of this battle:

> A hot fight ensued which resulted in the defeat of the Indians, their loss being forty or fifty killed, while the remainder, some 400 strong, took to their heels in flight. Strange to say, although I was a participant in this encounter, and was, for a part time at least, in the front rank, my recollection of the affair differs somewhat from the account given in the report and is as follows:
>
> When we received the order to charge the enemy, we did so with a rush, scattering the Indians in all directions, but they soon rallied and as many of them were armed with old Spanish rifles they commenced to make warm work for us. Suddenly it occurred to me that I could charge to better advantage from behind a tree, and, acting on this impulse, I sought shelter of a large pine tree. Evidently the same thought had occurred to others as I found that Major Burney and John Sylvester were already in possession. However, the tree was a large one and we made a point to stay close together.
>
> The first of our men to fall was Lieutenant E. Skeane [Skein , S. Skeens], then Bill Little who was shot in three different places. A little later after this Charlie Houston got a bullet through the neck and Dick Tilason had his nose shot away.
>
> Then to make matters worse (for me) I fell, with what I felt sure was a mortal wound. I exposed myself a little to much and an Indian took a pot shot at me, which tore away the whole side of my face (at least I thought so) and toppled me back behind our friendly shelter where, with my hands pressed tightly over my mutilated face, I told them of the serious nature of the wound and called attention to the blood that was trickling through my fingers. They pulled my hands down and then burst into a hearty laugh.

"Why, Howard," said the major, "you are not shot at all, you are only crying." To my intense relief I found that to be true. The heavy ball from the Indian's gun had scaled off a large piece of bark from our tree with such force that it stunned me and brought tears to my eyes. Realizing that I had come as near to being wounded as was possible without actual discomfort, I suggested to the major that we would be much safer after we rejoined the men who had remained with the horses, and a few minutes later he gave the order to fall back. Then it was that the Indians did their best running, but with commendable determination we managed to keep well in the lead, and succeeded in bringing off our wounded men safely.

Lieutenant Skeane and Bill Little both died from the wounds they had received in the fight, and as I had seen only four or five dead Indians I always felt we had come off second best until I read the official report some years later.[13]

While Indian warfare was rampant in the Mariposa country, California had been admitted to statehood, and the most prominent rancher in the Mariposa region, John C. Fremont, had been sent to Washington as United States senator. He drew the short term and remained in the Senate only a few months. During that time he introduced eighteen bills which were useful in the development of his state. The pro-slavery element in California defeated him for re-election, and he returned to *Las Mariposas* and devoted himself exclusively to ranching and mining operations. In the meantime the Indian war proceeded merrily onward.[14]

Governor McDougal, who had succeeded Burnett, issued an order on January 24, 1851, for the re-organization of the Mariposa Battalion. It was increased to 204 men. James D. Savage defeated James Burney in the election for major. This battalion was ordered to refrain from military operations until the governor's aide, Colonel J. Neely Johnson, gave them further orders. Johnson met Savage and informed him that three commissioners had been appointed by the United States Government; they had been given authority to make treaties with the Indians and were to attempt to adjust all difficulties. These three men had arrived in the state in December, 1850, while Adam Johnston and Savage were conferring with the Indians on the hill-top. They had perfected their arrangements and were now ready to go to the San Joaquin. The commissioners were Redick McKee, disbursing agent and nominal head; George W. Barbour; and Dr. Oliver M. Wozencraft.[15]

Johnson returned to the coast. While in San Francisco he was interviewed by reporters:

> Col. Neely Johnson arrived in town on Sunday. He states that in his opinion there are at least 10,000 warriors between Mariposa and the southern limits of the County, and 70,000 Indian inhabitants. The arrangements which are in progress will, he thinks, suffice for the present although the only way of effectually preventing further hostilities, is by resort to arms. The army is now acting on defense only.[16]

On February 11, 1851, McKee, accompanied by an escort of federal soldiers, left for the Mariposa country; the other two Commissioners accompanied the Indian agent, Adam Johnston, to Knight's Ferry. Here they met Cypriano, the old friend of Estanislao, who agreed to gather the chieftains of the Merced, Tuolumne, and Mariposa regions for a pow-wow to be held at the Cornelius ranchería, located up the Tuolumne about forty-five miles from its mouth. The rendezvous was set for February 24th. The commissioners gathered at the appointed place and were joined by Savage. Waiting proved irksome and the white men began to fear that Cypriano would appear with a hostile army. Even Savage became dubious about the outcome and counselled immediate action by the battalion. This apprehension was heightened by startling reports from various mining camps. Apparently a war of extermination was being carried out against the gold miners who were then surging into the foothills. Rumors concerning a massacre of white men in the Visalia region increased the tension.[17]

The oak forest surrounding Visalia was an attractive place in the otherwise dry and arid region. The first white man to become a permanent resident of the Four Creeks country was probably Loomis St. John, who built a cabin along the banks of a stream subsequently known as the St. John River. In 1849 two young Texas bear hunters, Nathaniel Vise and Gilbert Dean, arrived in that section of the valley. While Vise went to San Francisco, he left Dean at the St. John cabin. On December 1, 1850, a native of Jackson County, Missouri, and a resident of Agua Fria named John Woods, left the Mariposa country for the Four Creeks region. Woods was accompanied by fourteen men. Woods built a cabin on the south bank of the Kaweah River, eight miles east of modern Visalia. The Kawia Indians, led by a mission-trained chief named Francisco, attacked this group of white men and killed all but two. Woods barricaded himself in his cabin but was finally captured and flayed alive. Shortly thereafter a newspaper published a letter from Dr. Thomas Payne regarding the hectic state of affairs in the Four Creeks country:

> On the 4th of February I visited the Four Creeks, and found my bridges partially destroyed, as had been represented by rumor. Thirteen men were found who had been killed by the Indians at that place. Two others were wounded, but had escaped on a horse; one of them has since had his arm amputated, it having become gangrenous. The Indians doubtless skinned a Mr. Johnson who fought from my house. There were nineteen of us. We saw seven Indians driving off to the mountains about one hundred and fifty head of cattle. The Indians have all gone to the mountains to live, and will fight, if attacked, at the places they have selected as battlegrounds. We saw where they had driven off six or eight hundred head of cattle, judging by the signs.[18]

The same day, but in another newspaper, Payne's letter stated: "Mr. John G. Wood, who was at work for me at the Four Creeks, appeared to have been skinned alive, except his head, hands, and feet. There were no other signs of violence on his person."[19]

Dr. Thomas Payne was the first medical practitioner in the central part of the valley. Dr. Lewis Leach was located at Agua Fria, and a Dr. Adams, the founder of Adamsville, was the family doctor along the Tuolumne River. Another early doctor in the same region was T. E. Tynan. Dr. John Marsh was the medical expert in the northern part of the valley. These five men were the first to follow the profession of healing in the San Joaquin. Dr. Payne had built bridges across the creeks near Visalia and the prairie schooners paid toll to cross them on their way to the mines in the north.[20]

The white men attributed inhuman conduct on the part of the Indians to pure deviltry. Naturally, the Indians gave a different version of the affair. They asserted that one of the white men in the Four Creeks country was a fiend incarnate with a diabolical sense of humor, which he expressed by lassoing male Indians and performing operations upon them. The astounded natives resented this mutilation and retaliated by torturing and killing their oppressors.

Whatever the truth of this assertion may be, the fact remains that when General Patton arrived on the scene in the spring of 1851, he investigated the affair and then refused to take any action against Francisco. The chief and his Kawia warriors were permitted to live unmolested in their old haunts. Patton built a fort half a mile from the Woods cabin at the point where the Kaweah enters the valley. The same year, 1851, Nathaniel Vise and Abner, his brother, returned and settled in the vicinity of the town, which was named Visalia in their honor.[21]

While all this turmoil was going on, the Commissioners were impatiently awaiting the return of Cypriano. His appearance with two insignificant chiefs dispelled all hallucinations of impending disaster, but such meager results were nevertheless disappointing. The other chiefs had refused to come.

The Mariposa Battalion then began to round up the recalcitrant Indians. In March, 1851, Savage led his men "through blinding snow, over trails hitherto untrod by white men" in pursuit of Chief Teneiya and finally reached the Indian citadel of Yosemite, first seen by Joseph Reddeford Walker and his weary men who skirted its rim in 1833, and now actually entered for the first time by white men on March 27, 1851. Concerning this event and the conflicting claims which later arose as to the actual discovery of Yosemite, Dr. Bunnell wrote as follows: "All I have ever claimed for myself is, that I was one of the party of white men who first entered the Yosemite Valley, as far as known to the Indians."[22]

The leader of the group was James Savage. His company commanders were John Bowling, William Dill, and John Kuykendall. The first two accompanied Savage to Yosemite; Kuykendall was sent by Savage to gather the Indians along the Kaweah and the Kings rivers. Most of the men in Kuykendall's company had been recruited from sailors along the coast and were spoiling for a fight. These burly tars expressed themselves as anxious to help "shanghai the coolies and lascars," but looked askance at the strabismic quadrupeds offered them as a means of navigation. Their first attempts to remain on board the hurricane decks of pitching bronchos made them seasick and the frontiersmen hilarious.

The force led by Savage returned first and rendered a glowing report concerning the scenery at Yosemite. Kuykendall's men were led along Kings River into Kings

River Canyon. When they returned and reported what they had seen, little credence was placed in their accounts. It was assumed that they were merely trying to surpass in hyperbole the men who had told the first "tall stories." But later explorers soon verified the enthusiastic descriptions of scenic wonder-lands as reported by the rival groups.

The result of the expeditions led in various directions by the captains of the battalion was the gathering of the Indians at Knight's Ferry and at Camp Barbour. The latter was a rude log building erected as a protective barracks for the United States soldiers sent from Benecia at the time of the Indian wars. A tier of logs pierced with rifle loop-holes made it suitable to withstand a siege. It was named in honor of Colonel Barbour. The latter held a pow-wow with 1,500 Indians, representing sixteen tribes scattered from the Chowchilla River to Tejon Pass. At Knight's Ferry, commissioners McKee and Wozencraft were holding a similar confab with other natives. By a judicious mixture of force, bacon, beef, whiskey, and cajolery, fifty chiefs and sub-chiefs signed away the rights of the Indians forever. The government promised in this treaty to set aside as a reservation for the Indians a tract of land sixty miles long and fifteen miles wide, running from the Chowchilla to the Kaweah, but the United States Senate did not see fit to ratify it. This left conditions more chaotic than ever. The extermination of the Indians helped to clarify matters. During these Indian troubles the natives of the Kern area remained peaceful due largely to the influence of Don Vicente, a mission-trained Indian residing near Tejon Pass. [23]

On April 20, 1852, Tulare County was organized. The new county comprised more than half of the southern portion of Mariposa County and extended from Nevada to the Coast Range. The commissioners appointed to carry out the law and conduct the first election of Tulare County officials were James D. Savage, M. B. Lewis, John Bowling, and W. W. McMillan. Two polling places were provided in the county; one at the Woods log cabin on the south side of the Kaweah; the other, at Poole's Ferry, five miles upstream from modern Reedley, along Kings River. The election was held on July 10, 1852. The former polling place was located near one of the toll bridges owned by Dr. Payne. This place became the first county seat under the name of Woodsville. After the political adventurers had created the new county they returned to Agua Fria and civilization. Tulare County began its career in a typically boisterous, wild-western fashion. Many of the first county officials met violent deaths. Major James Savage was shot by Judge Harvey; Alonzo Edwards was killed by Bob Collins; and Dr. Everett, the assessor, was murdered by a man named Bell. In fact, all but two of the first set of Tulare County officers were killed in altercations.

A pioneer resident of Visalia furnished this account of the first election:

> The statute for providing for the organization of the County was approved in April, 1852, and the election at which the first set of County officials were elected, was held on July 10, 1852, in two precincts, one of which was at a certain oak tree, still preserved, at the foot of the foothill known as Venice Hill, and which now belongs to the County and is a part of a small park at that point. The people who held the election were adventurers who came here from Mariposa County for that purpose, and immediately after electing the officers from their parties, they all returned to Mariposa County and did not come back here to take up duties until about September, 1852.[24]

Several incidents occurred in 1853 worth recording. Lieutenant John Nugen, stationed at Fort Miller, was sent to Woodsville to put down a threatened Indian uprising. Some cattlemen insisted on corralling cattle under a certain oak tree, which the Indians considered sacred. If

The "Election Tree," under which the county of Tulare was organized in 1852. Kathleen Small, *History of Tulare and Kings Counties, California.*

an alien race had insisted on placing their livestock in a cathedral belonging to the white men, they would naturally have resented it. But the superior race considered the Indian puerile, and regarded their protestations with contempt. The Indians were willing to fight for their holy places, and went to war for as good reasons as those which sent the Crusaders to the Holy Land to rescue the Lost Sepulchre.[25]

The troops from Fort Miller restored order. The services rendered by the United States Army in the San Joaquin Valley are worthy of commendation. The troops at all times served as peacemakers. The officers made honest attempts to treat both red men and white with impartiality. The Indians never made any assault on American troops; their difficulty was always with the oncoming tide of white settlers.

A premature attempt was made to establish an Indian

reservation along the banks of the San Joaquin River. The
initial survey included the territory as far south as Kings
River. Then came the organization of the Sebastian
Reservation, in the hills south of what later became
Bakersfield. This was named in honor of William King
Sebastian, U. S. Senator from Arkansas, 1853-1861, and
chairman of the Senate Committee on Indian Affairs. The
reservation was located on the Tejon grant made to
Ignacio del Valle and Jose Antonio Aguirre in 1843. The
grantees had not yet secured a patent to the land and
Beale, the Indian superintendent, built a fort and made
provisions for establishing a reservation after due
consultation with his advisers in California. The
assumption was that if the grantees secured a patent to
their land, Congress could purchase the amount needed
from them. The law at that time specifically stated that
reservations could only be placed on public lands. An
attempt was made to bring all the Indians south of the
San Joaquin to this reservation. Beale went to work with
a will, and travelers who visited the Sebastian
Reservation were enthusiastic concerning its progress:

> He lays out a field and tells them to plant it; and he explains
> to them that the fruits of their labor inure to themselves
> alone . . . . By his presence, his encouraging words, his
> prompt decisions, and his kind assurances he has gathered
> about him a host of dependents from far and near.[26]

The bringing of Indians to this reservation proved to be an
expensive undertaking. Most of them did not want to
come. Beale encountered much of the difficulty which had
faced the Franciscan friars years before when they sought
neophytes for the missions. After spending thousands of
dollars, Beale was dismissed, the reservation reduced
from 100,000 acres to 10,000, and Fort Tejon, built by
Beale, was left fifteen miles outside the boundaries.[27]

Fremont and his wife, the former Jessie Benton, had gone

to Europe in March 1852. Fremont had built a huge dam across the Merced River and was using running water to operate the Benton Mills, a new and expensive ore-crushing apparatus. His Mariposa mines were returning a handsome profit in those days, and the Fremont's were able to entertain lavishly while in London and Paris. While in Europe the Fremont's met the famous Duke of Wellington, the victor at Waterloo, and were entertained by the nobility of many nations. The exploits of the picturesque miner and rancher from the San Joaquin had made him famous in Europe and he found himself a social lion.

Then came the report that Jefferson Davis proposed to survey possible railway routes to the Pacific. Fremont returned and offered his services. Davis declined them. Only officers in the regular army were to be employed. But Fremont enjoyed making surveys and financed a private expedition. He attempted to do for the railroads what he had done years earlier for the prairie schooners. This, his fifth and last pathfinding venture, was his least important. He reported that the central route was the most feasible for a railroad (this was the one later selected), and then returned to *Las Mariposas*.[28]

In 1854, Stanislaus County was detached from the original Tuolumne County. Adamsville, located along the Tuolumne River four miles downstream from the present Modesto, became the first county seat. The election determining this was held on June 10, 1854. On October 21 of the same year, another election shifted the county seat to Empire City, located ten miles upstream from Adamsville. On December 20, 1855, a third election sent the county capital to La Grange. In these meanderings of the county seat, it was customary to place a strongbox containing the money and the records on a big wagon and haul it to the new capital, as dictated by the volatile population of the period. In 1860, a legislative act caused a part of San Joaquin County to be transferred to Stanislaus County. Included in this cession was Knight's Ferry, which became the county seat, and the big wagon was again called into service. A decade later, the railroad reached the Tuolumne River and the new town of Modesto secured the county seat on September 6, 1871. This time three large wagons were necessary to transfer the courthouse records to their new home. But the wanderings of the strong box were over. Modesto has remained the county seat since that time.[29]

Merced County was organized in 1855. It consisted of all that part of Mariposa County lying on the valley floor. Its early history is fascinating:

> The first governmental proceedings were conducted at a place about seven miles east of the city of Merced, on what was known as the Turner and Osborne Ranch and the records show that the Grand Jury held their meetings on the creek bank in the open plains where they found indictments against several men for cattle stealing. The court was held under an oak tree on the opposite creek bank, using nail kegs, boxes, etc., for chairs and a rough board table for the judge's bench. It is further recorded that no one was convicted.
>
> In the year 1855 an election was held to locate the county seat of the new county, and at the election held in May, Snelling Ranch, on the Merced River, was voted the first county seat, where a court house was erected in 1857 and here the seat of government remained until December, 1872, when by another election it was moved to Merced, a new town, established by the railroad then being constructed through the valley.[30]

Then came the year 1856. Fresno County, the third and the last of the counties to be carved out of old Mariposa County, was organized and the capital established at Millerton. Merced and Tulare also donated a part of their territory to the new county. The same year the Indians

The Murray flour mill, one of Merced County's pioneering business concerns. John Outcault, *History of Merced County, California.*

stole cattle from the Four Creeks country and drove them to Frazier Valley. The result was that Sheriff W. J. Poindexter of Visalia sent Captain David DeMasters, with sixty mounted riflemen, in pursuit of the cattle thieves. The Indians had entrenched themselves at a place called Battle Mountain, about twenty-five miles above present Porterville, along the banks of the Tule River. Here DeMasters tried vainly to dislodge them for two days. About sixty Indians left the Tejon Reservation to help their kinsmen. J. W. Williams followed these absconding natives with nine men. He succeeded in dispersing the Indians before they were able to join forces with the natives on Battle Mountain. Then Williams went to the aid of De Masters. The latter sent Williams to Keysville on the Kern River for aid and sixty miners led by William Linn of Linn's Valley came to the aid of the attacking party. In the meantime the sheriff of Tulare County, Captain Poindexter, arrived with an additional force of a hundred and forty men. With these combined forces a terrific assault was made on the Indian fortifications on the hill-top and the white men received the same treatment that the British did at Bunker Hill. Captain Livingston arrived from Fort Miller with fifty regulars and Alonzo Ridley, the Indian Agent at Fort Tejon, brought a squadron of cavalry. The total force of the whites now numbered four hundred men. Captain Livingston, in chief command, solved the problem easily by occupying a neighboring hill and dropping shells from his howitzers into the Indian camp, which destroyed a hundred Indians and sent the rest of them running for their lives. Beale was appointed a brigadier-general in the state militia by Governor J. Neely Johnson and arrived at Visalia in June, 1858, with instructions to adjust matters. He did. Beale understood the Indians and they trusted him.[31]

Two diametrically opposed systems of society clashed when Indians and white men met. A correct theory concerning their relative rights was the first theory of relativity and as difficult to understand as the one later advanced by Einstein. White men on the frontier, regardless of their European derivation, usually had neither the wit, wisdom, nor will to follow the example of the mythical hero of the American lumberjacks, Paul Bunyan, who announced: "The hero inspires, but the thinker leads. I shall now think." The American cattleman generally indulged in no philosophical cogitations concerning the Indian. He preferred a type of direct action which inspired hero-worship among the youth of his time and furnished the credo: "The only good Indian is a dead Indian." This solved the problem for him; perhaps it solved it for the Indian too.

The story of the Indian has generally come from the lips of his white conqueror. Most races and individuals would object to be judged by posterity solely on the verdict of their enemies. The life of the Indian in the San Joaquin

Courthouse at Snelling, seat of Merced County's government from 1857 to 1872. John Outcault, *History of Merced County, California.*

changed with vertiginous rapidity as soon as the Americans acquired California. The coming of these white men, less sympathetic toward the Indians than their Spanish predecessors, destroyed the wild game and the grass seeds, the Indians' only source of food supply. When the Indian women and children became famished, the desperate Indian procured for them the only food available, the white man's cattle. Cattle rustling, whether engaged in by Indians or white men, has always been a crime punishable by death in the cow country. But the Indian was merely hungry; the white cattle rustler usually mercenary. That may be a distinction without a difference. Years after the difficulties in the Visalia region, an educated Indian woman expressed herself with rare understanding concerning an Indian cattle thief who had been killed by so-called Christian white men:

> You say your cattle are not ours,
> Your meat is not our meat;
> When *you* pay for the land you live in,
> *We'll* pay for the meat we eat.

Give back our land and our country,
Give back our herds of game;
Give back the furs and the forests
That were ours before you came;
Give back the peace and the plenty.
Then come with your new belief,
And blame, if you dare, the hunger
That *drove* him to be a thief.[32]

Conditions in California during the Civil War were rather unhappy for a time. Three things caused disloyalty; first, the native Spanish-Californians felt that they had been unjustly treated in the matter of land grants; second, a wild and foreign element had entered the state during the gold rush; third, most of the Americans in the state were of Southern derivation. However, the West had changed their preconceived notions concerning slavery. This benignant influence of the frontier prevented secession. Mexico had abolished slavery in 1829 and the constitutional convention of 1849 had made California a free-soil state. These things exerted an influence hard to estimate.

On April 25, 1861, Abraham Lincoln, at the instigation of James McClatchy, editor of the Sacramento *Bee*, relieved Albert Sidney Johnston from command of the Federal troops in California. McClatchy was a staunch Union man and furnished Lincoln with valuable information concerning conditions in the state.

> Primarily, James McClatchy saved California to the Union. That is a matter of record in the War Department. It was at the bedside of Edmund Randolph, before the first gun was fired on Fort Sumter, that the editors of the *Bee* learned that General Albert Sidney Johnston, in charge of the Department of the Pacific, would turn the stores and munitions of war over to the rebels when the time grew ripe. It was "pony express night." James McClatchy immediately wrote a letter to Senator E. D. Baker, informing him of the plot, and begging that he see that Johnston be summarily removed.

Out into the arms of the night sped the little pony, across the Sierra and Rocky ranges dashed the relays, and soon the momentous news was in the hands of that gallant "gray eagle" whose last rallying cry for Liberty was soon to be his funeral knell at Ball's Bluff. Baker immediately placed the letter in the hands of President Lincoln, a Cabinet Council was called, and General Sumner was then and there ordered to California to dispossess Johnston.

As fast as steam could carry him over the waters, Sumner came. Arrived at Johnston's headquarters, he demanded an immediate surrender of the office. Johnston begged for one day of grace, for one hour. Sumner was adamant. His orders were imperative: they were to take charge at once. Chagrined and baffled, Johnston gave up the office, and General Sumner assumed command. Soon thereafter Fort Sumter was fired upon, and Johnston, already in the South, joined the rebel army. California was saved, and the honor thereof belongs to James McClatchy.[33]

Johnston, who owned a ranch on the present site of Pasadena, was suspected of disloyalty to the Union. Other officers of Southern sympathies turned over forts and munitions of war to the Confederacy when war began. Johnston might have done likewise. The distance from Washington would have made such an act of treason fatal to the Union element in the state. However, Johnston's friends have asserted that he was a true gentleman and took no part in the plottings of the men who schemed to form a Republic of the Pacific; neither did he join the secret organization known as the Knights of the Golden Circle which at one time numbered 50,000 men. Later Johnston made this terse statement in his own defense: "If I had proved faithless here, how could my own people ever trust me?" When General Sumner was appointed to succeed him, Johnston resigned his commission and reported to Jefferson Davis, who appointed him a lieutenant-general in the Confederate Army. He became the hero and the martyr of Shiloh, the bloodiest battle of the Civil War.[34]

The majority of the newspapers of the valley were edited by Southern sympathizers. Three modes of attack were used to weaken Union sentiment. Through their columns they justified the South, ridiculed the Union successes and defeats, and lambasted the northern leaders, especially President Lincoln, with invective and vituperation. The reader can easily determine into which category the following quotations belong. The first overt act against federal authority occurred at Stockton. The San Francisco *Alta California* for January 19, 1861, stated:

> Mr. Duncan Beaumont, a resident of Stockton, on Wednesday, hoisted a flag at that place, intended to represent a Pacific Republic. One effect of his demonstration was a general hoisting of the Stars and Stripes. The Stockton *Republican* says Mr. Beaumont was the sole person engaged in hoisting the flag. The Stockton *Argus* says:

> It is rumored that the getters-up of the Bear Flag yesterday, intended to raise it on land in the city but the excitement created by it showed that such a procedure would not be allowed; and it was concluded to hoist it on private property, on a vessel in the slough. As it was, the halyards were soon cut, and a boy was sent up the mast to take it down. The Union feeling exhibited itself in various ways at sight of the flag. At first it was derided and laughed at; but, when the idea broke upon the minds of our citizens that it might be considered abroad as the work of the people of Stockton, a feeling of indignation was excited, that showed there was danger in thus trifling with the public feeling, that could not be subdued.

> Doubtless this will be heralded abroad to the effect that Stocktonians have hoisted the Bear Flag for a Pacific Republic, when there can be nothing further from their thoughts.

On April 24, 1862, the *Merced Banner* charged that "the United States officers will go to any length to sustain their master, Abe Lincoln, whose cringing slaves they are." Peter Dinwiddie Wigginton, later the legal adviser for the 76 Land and Water Company at Traver, stumped Merced County in every campaign for the secession candidates. In later years, besides being a presidential and gubernatorial candidate, Wigginton was a successful candidate for Congress (1875-1877).

The Southern, or pro-slavery wing, of the Democratic Party was very strong in Tulare County. On August 30, 1862, the *Visalia Equal Rights Expositor* stated:

> So far as the present unhappy Civil War is concerned, we neither fear nor hesitate to express the belief that the South stands justified before God and before the world, for the position she has assumed.

General Wright, who had succeeded General Sumner as commander of the federal troops in California, issued a military order on September 16, 1862, to the postmasters of all distributing offices, enjoining them to exclude from the mails the *Stockton Argus*, the *Stockton Democrat*, the *Stockton Republican*, the *Merced Banner*, the *Merced Democrat*, the *Merced Express*, the *Visalia Post*, and the *Visalia Equal Rights Expositor*.

The *Equal Rights Expositor* expressed its resentment of the order on September 20, 1862:

> This act of despotism has by no means astonished us. . . A free press has never yet been tolerated by any power that conspired against the liberties of the people. Will any one now dare say that they live under a free government, that thus outrages the liberties of the press and of free speech? . . . Men who will continue their support of such a government, steeped in infamy as it is, are fit only for slaves.

The same paper delivered its first blast against Lincoln on October 18, 1862:

> Lincoln is the President of a few eastern manufacturing corporations, and is execrated by one-half of the Union, and only commands the respect of a portion of the other by his

bastiles and confiscation bills. As a narrow-minded bigot; as an unprincipled demagogue; as a driveling, idiotic, imbecile creature, Abraham Lincoln is regarded with pity approaching contempt.

On October 25, 1862, President Lincoln was called "the cadaverous, long-shanked, mule-countenanced rail-splitter from Illinois." On November 1st of the same year, the editors returned to a justification of the seceding states:

> The sympathies of the civilized world are with them, and they must succeed. When they do so, they will be covered with immortal glory and honors, and the North will stand a monument of disgrace to the world, because she repudiated the grand principle for which their fathers fought—that of self-government.

The Thanksgiving issue of the *Equal Rights Expositor* appeared on November 29, 1862. It contained the following mock prayer:

> O Lord, we thank thee for letting the rebels wallop us at the battle of Pittsburg Landing—for letting them smite us hip and thigh, even unto the destruction of 96,000 of our good loyal soldiers, and 463 of our officers; and for giving speed to their legs through the awful swamps of Chickahominy; and, O Lord, most especially do we thank thee for the licking they gave us at Bull Run the second, and assisting our flight from that fatal field; and, O Lord, never while we live will we forget Antietam, where we had 200,000 and they only 70,000—if they, O Lord, had a happened to have had as many men as we, we'd have been a done gone in— and that friendly creek between us, the mountain that kept our men from running—and, O God of Isaac and Jacob, your special providence in sending night to our aid saved us. For the battle of Perryville, O God, when we lost 20,000 and the rebels only 2,500, we thank thee also.

This article incensed some soldiers on a leave of absence from Camp Babbitt near Visalia and rioting occurred. An army officer sent the following report to the War Department:

There are more secessionists in this and adjoining counties than there are, in proportion to the population, in any part of the United States this side of the so-called Confederate government.

Not only are they in great numbers, but they are organized and armed, ready at a moment's warning to take up their arms against the Government of the United States.

It is an everyday occurrence for them to ride through the streets of Visalia, and hurrah for Jeff Davis and Stonewall Jackson, and often give groans for the Stars and Stripes.

These things being persisted in on the part of the secessionists of this county and vicinity, in my opinion will inevitably bring about Civil War in this state.

Already there have been several fist fights and knockdowns between the citizens and the soldiers, and on Saturday, November 29, there was quite a serious difficulty occurred in which firearms were used and one soldier shot (who died from the effects of his wounds to-day) and two citizens wounded, the citizens, as the proceedings of the coroner's jury show, commencing the shooting.[35]

On December 13, 1862, the *Equal Rights Expositor* printed an article which caused the government to finally take action against its editors:

You are right, Abe. History will remember you, in spite of yourself. The record will be a fearful one. It will be written thus: Abraham Lincoln, sixteenth president of the United States of America, by accident elected to the highest office in the gift of the people, on a platform hostile to the Constitution and the rights of ten million of his countrymen, did, without cause, wage a civil and unrelenting war against an unoffending people, who only asked to be allowed to enjoy the God-given right of governing themselves as they thought would best promote their happiness. History will record, too, your repeated violations of the Constitution, your disregard of the liberties of white men, and your unbounded subserviency to the interests of the black man. Yes, Abe, the world will remember you, and your cabinet, and your congress, as the most tyrannical and corrupt crew that ever polluted the earth with their presence.

These disloyal utterances caused Captain M. A. McLaughlin of the Second Cavalry, California Volunteers, to arrest the editors of the paper, L. P. Hall and L. J. Garrison. This was done on January 6, 1863. L. J. Garrison refused to take the oath of allegiance and was kept in close confinement.[36] The other editor, L. P. Hall, took the oath with alacrity, secured his release, returned home and penned the following editorial which appeared on January 9, 1863:

> As to the oath we have taken, it conflicts with no sentiment we before entertained, and the character of the paper will undergo no change. We believe the war to be wrong, and dishonoring to the government, and shall oppose it with all the zeal we can command.

Escaping further molestation, the same editor was emboldened to write on January 23, 1863:

> Your president, who is supposed to be the representative of the honor and the dignity of a nation, has laid aside all self-respect and made himself a COMMON LIAR. Here, Black Republicans, is your president; take him; conceal him from observation. His natural ugliness is bad enough, God knows; but, when his moral deformities are added, it is dangerous to look upon.

After this outburst, the editor felt much refreshed. He made no further comments for several weeks.

The Visalia Delta, a loyal Union paper, stated on February 19, 1863, that "treason against the Constitution is preached from the pulpits, printed in the newspapers, and openly advocated in the streets and public places."

On March 7, 1863, some soldiers on leave from Camp Babbitt destroyed the printing establishment of the offending *Equal Rights Expositor*. The type was scattered in the street, the windows of the building broken, and the heavy equipment smashed. Major John M. O'Neill sent troops to Visalia to quell the disturbance and they, too, were mobbed by the citizens. Finally order was restored and the town patrolled to prevent further trouble. Some minor rioting occurred during the night and one man was arrested for cheering for Jefferson Davis. The demolition of the newspaper plant resulted in an increased local popularity for the editor, as well as an increased subscription list.

On March 21, 1863, the *Mariposa Free Press* expressed the following opinion: "What cares Abraham Lincoln for the good of his country? A traitor to God and humanity, his hands dripping with the blood of his countrymen."

During the summer of 1863 many young men with Southern sympathies and fighting proclivities enlisted in the Confederate Army. On December 21, 1863, the *Stockton Daily Independent* commented:

> The *Visalia Delta* says, on authority of a letter received in that county, that Thomas Stonehouse, David McKenzie, and Bill Skinner, late of Tulare county, are in the Confederate Army in Texas, along with Alonzo Ridley. Bill Bowers, the best of the lot, was killed in Arkansas.

The presence of local boys in the Confederate Army intensified the feeling of hostility toward the Union. Confederate sympathizers became so aggressive during the summer of 1863 that Union troops were deemed necessary in the San Joaquin north of Visalia. Fort Miller was selected as a suitable place. This post had been abandoned in 1856, the same year that Millerton had become the county seat of Fresno County. Its re-occupation was deemed a necessity on the assumption that the Confederates controlled Fresno as well as Tulare County. Threats made prior to Colonel James Olney's arrival at Fort Miller warranted such a belief. In order to be ready to meet the foe, the soldiers were halted on their march when they reached the northern borders of Fresno County, ordered to affix their bayonets, and then proceeded into Confederate territory in a battle line of skirmishers, on the lookout for rebels. No enemy force was encountered. In November 1865 the troops were permanently withdrawn from Fort Miller and some of its buildings dismantled. The previous year, a squadron of cavalry had been sent into Merced County to arrest the bellicose editor of the *Merced Democrat*, William Hall. On July 24, 1864, he was placed in the federal prison at Alcatraz Island.[37]

The loyal element, slow to act in the beginning of the conflict, became more assertive as the war progressed. A Unitarian clergyman, Thomas Starr King, then located at San Francisco, rendered such effective service to the Sanitary Commission that the loyal element in California donated $1,234,257.31 in gold; the entire amount furnished by all the states of the North during the War between the States was $4.8 million. Thomas Starr King, a Protestant clergyman, and Junipera Serra, a Franciscan friar, are the two men selected to represent California in the Hall of Fame at Washington.[38]

One of the interesting episodes of the Civil War centered around a resident of the San Joaquin Valley. He raised money for the Union cause in a rather unique fashion:

> Among the early members of this church—Modesto—was Ruel Colt Gridley. He won a national reputation in war time by the amount of money that he raised for the United States Sanitary Commission. He was a resident of a mining town in Nevada, and a war Democrat. At the time of an election he made the following wager: If his favorite candidate was defeated he would carry a sack of flour to the next mining town and sell it for the benefit of the Sanitary Commission. If his candidate was elected the other fellow was to do the same thing. He lost the wager. He carried the sack. He sold it to the

Visalia as it appeared at the time of the Civil War, 1863. Eugene Menefee and Fred Dodge, *History of Tulare and Kings Counties, California.*

highest bidder. The one that bought it gave it back and he sold it again. This process was continued as long as buyers were found, then it went to other cities and villages, and the same thing was repeated. In Virginia City and San Francisco tens of thousands of dollars were realized from its sale. Then he took it to the East, and across the States from New York to St. Louis. It is claimed that he made over $275,000 from his sack of flour for the purpose intended, though he would never take a dollar of it for himself. After the war he settled in Stockton, where, in the great revival of 1867-8 he was converted. He soon after went with his family to Modesto, where he died some years later. He was buried in Stockton, where a beautiful monument has been erected over his remains to commemorate the famous sack of flour.[39]

The Confederate general, H. H. Sibley, had conquered Arizona and New Mexico, and was threatening California. Colonel James H. Carleton organized the California Column in the southern San Joaquin, drilled them at Fort Tejon, and led 1,800 of them in a brilliant campaign which restored the two Territories to Union control.[40]

A guerilla band led by two men named Henry and Mason became obstreperous during the Civil War. The leaders were Southern sympathizers who bought or stole horses for the Confederate army. Ranchers found their bands constantly depleted. Hostlers were killed at several stage stations along the old Butterfield line and travel disrupted. The outlaw band had one retreat at Grizzly Gulch and another along the shores of Tulare Lake. Whatever their motives may have been in the beginning of their career, their patriotism soon degenerated and the Mason-Henry band became cutthroats and desperadoes. Their activities caused an army officer stationed at Camp Babbitt, near Visalia, to report to the War Department:

> There is no doubt of an organized movement among the disloyal people of this part of the State, for what purpose I am unable to find out.
>
> I have information of thirty-seven of them being together near Kern Lake, with quite a number of government horses with them . . . I last heard of these men at or near Fort Tejon, and from a letter intercepted here they seem to be moving south toward Fort Yuma.[41]

In the summer of 1865 Mason and Henry swooped down on the Hawthorne stage station, near what is now the town of San Joaquin. They murdered Hawthorne and two of his men and stole the livestock. Soon thereafter Henry appeared in San Bernardino County. Henry sent one of his men named Rogers to town to get supplies. The latter became intoxicated and was placed under arrest by the sheriff, Ben Matthews. Then the sheriff went in search of Henry. They met. Both were on horseback. Suddenly Henry swung over on the far side of his horse, intending to shoot while thus protected. But he went farther than he had intended. The sheriff put his own smoking gun back into its holster and rode away, leaving Henry where he had fallen.

Mason paid a surreptitious visit to the El Tejon ranch. Here he made threats to shoot a cowboy, Ben Mayfield, on sight. This cowboy had refused to join the band of outlaws. When he heard about the threats he went in search of Mason and found him in a cabin in Tejon Pass. Mason denied the remark, but each man sat in the cabin and watched the other. Finally Mason lay down on the bed fully dressed, but his plan to shoot Mayfield from under his blankets was frustrated when the latter shot Mason dead.[42]

Another member of the band, a man named Hawkins, was captured in Tulare County and hanged at Visalia on general principles. Such stringent measures discouraged the lesser members of the guerilla band and further depredations ceased.[43]

Secretary of War Edwin M. Stanton ruled that the draft law should not be applied to Nevada and California. To hold the frontier was almost as important as the advance against the South. The distance was too great, and the sparsely settled West needed its own men for self-protection. In order to safeguard its own people, California organized two full regiments of cavalry, eight regiments of infantry, one battalion of native Californians armed with lances and lassos, one battalion of infantry named the Mountaineers which served in Northern California, and eight companies known as the First Regiment of Washington Territory.

But many men wished to see active service in the front lines rather than on their own familiar frontier. The result was the organization of units for this purpose. The California Hundred, with Captain Reed of Grayson as commander, was recruited principally from San Joaquin Valley ranchers. They were sent to Massachusetts and became Company A, Second Massachusetts Cavalry. Massachusetts needed men to fill her draft quotas and provided the equipment, paid the fares, and furnished the bounties to the men of the West who desired to fight for the Union. The California Battalion was also organized and became companies E, F, L, and M, in the Second Massachusetts Cavalry. The few survivors of these California men attracted unusual attention during the victory parade held at Washington before the Grand Army was mustered out in 1865.[44]

In 1866 the southern part of the San Joaquin was organized into a county named Kern. This county also included the land east of the Sierra to the Nevada line. The county seat was a mining town named Havilah; the capital was moved at a later date to Bakersfield.[45]

In 1893 Madera County was organized from the northern part of Fresno County, and Kings County was detached from the western part of Tulare County. Madera became the capital of the former, Hanford of the latter. In 1907 the legislature provided for the transfer of a portion of Fresno County to Kings. The voters refused to ratify this proposed change, but modifications in the law caused a favorable vote in 1909 and this portion, located along the Coast Range south of Coalinga, became a part of Kings.[46]

In 1923 the attention of many young men was focused on a resident of the San Joaquin Valley. The American Legion was holding its annual national convention at San Francisco. Gathered there were delegates from all the states and territories of the Union. That year the three vital problems of hospitalization, rehabilitation, and adjusted compensation were confronting the members of that organization. To the amazement of many people, a San Francisco lawyer, Milton Sapiro, nominated a San Joaquin Valley cowboy as the one man in the United States qualified to solve the tasks then confronting a discouraged group of veterans:

We have had lawyers, bankers, merchants, manufacturers, we have had men of all types and men from all sections of the country except the West and the West has a man. We have got John Quinn. He is not a banker, he is not a merchant. He is a cattleman from the upper San Joaquin, a cowboy with a university education. He may not be able to preside with the charming grace, or be able to talk with the fervent eloquence of our present commander, but he can talk so every man in the world will know where he stands on any proposition that affects the Legion. He can stand with dignity before kings and he can talk with understanding to the man in the ditch.[47]

The subsequent success of Quinn justified the words of Sapiro who nominated him, and of the delegates who voted for him.

War and politics in the San Joaquin Valley from 1846 to 1924 produced many striking personalities. Most of them were builders rather than devastators. Cruelty, chicanery, and corruption were often present but never dominant. Men labored, gently or harshly, to build a great inland empire. They succeeded. The peace and the prosperity of the San Joaquin in the days that followed them exists as their monument.

Better the rudest work that tells a story or records a fact, than the richest without meaning. . . . Therefore when we build, let us think that we build forever. Let it not be for present delight, nor for present use alone. Let it be such work as our descendants will thank us for, and let us think, as we lay stone on stone, that a time is to come when those stones will be held sacred because our hands have touched them, and that men will say as they look upon the labor and wrought substance of them, "See! this our fathers did for us."[48]

9 Knights

of the Whip

Said the little Eohippus,
"I'm going to be a horse,
And on my middle fingernails
To run my earthly course!
I'm going to have a flowing tail!
I'm going to have a mane!
I'm going to stand fourteen hands high
On the Psychozoic plain!"

Charlotte P. S. Gilman, *Similar Cases*.

The Yokuts Indians, before the coming of the white men, relied on "shank's mare" as a means of transportation. Their only domestic animal, the dog, played no part in their peregrinations from hither to yon. The Indians, in their movements on the water, contributed the tule raft, which the early Spanish explorers in the valley observed on Tulare Lake and referred to as "balsas." The Yokuts and the Miwok Indians never developed anything comparable to the dugout canoe of the Santa Barbara Channel (Chumash) Indians, or the exquisite birch bark canoe of the Chippewas.

When the white men arrived they introduced boats, mules, horses, oxen, and wheeled vehicles. The first boats to be used on the rivers of the San Joaquin Valley were the launches sent out annually by the Franciscans in search of prospective neophytes. Military expeditions also made use of boats in their expeditions into the interior.

After the American occupation, boats began to ply the San Joaquin River between San Francisco and Stockton; they still do. In 1849 Alexander Todd bought a rowboat, hired oarsmen, and carried goods from Sacramento to Stockton. He charged four dollars to carry a letter, and his rates for transporting goods such as gold dust, merchandise, or passengers were correspondingly high. His profits were great, and led indirectly to the first organized stagecoach route in California.[1]

In 1850 William McKee owned and operated a $15,000 steamboat named the Unit. This boat made regular trips between San Francisco and San Joaquin City, located on the west side of the San Joaquin River, a little above the mouth of the Stanislaus River. In those days it was safer to go by boat than to travel overland. The Indian menace made a voyage preferable to a journey, as the red men had no adequate means of attacking a big steamboat. The latter, coming round the bend and belching forth volumes of black smoke, moved faster than any tule raft could possibly navigate. Its very size over-awed them.[2] Compared with the discomforts of a long ride in a stagecoach, the river steamer was indeed a floating palace. Washington Irving traveled extensively by stage-coach and wrote this about the experience: "There is a certain relief in change, even though

236

it be from bad to worse; as I have found in travelling in a stage-coach that it is often a comfort to shift one's position and be bruised in a new place."[3]

Many of the early San Joaquin Valley river-boats were modeled on the bigger craft of the Mississippi River, and their good qualities were advertised by their owners as follows:

> For she is such a smart little craft,
> Such a neat little, sweet little craft—
> Such a bright little,
> Tight little,
> Slight little,
> Light little,
> Trim little, slim little craft.[4]

Lilbourne Alsip Winchell, who arrived in the San Joaquin Valley in the fifties, stated that "a desultory steamboat service was conducted on the San Joaquin River from 1852 to 1875. The boats went regularly from San Francisco to Sycamore Point, about ten miles west of Herndon." He further stated that "the little steamer *Alta* tried to reach Tulare Lake in the winter of 1867-68, but stuck in the tules near Elkhorn; was abandoned and was finally burned by a tule fire."[5]

A part of this boat was salvaged and another pioneer, George Otis, wrote that "in later years the engine that drove the boat was chopped out of the wreck and brought to Selma and was the motive power of the planing mill that stood in the point corner of Chinatown across the street from the lumber yard to the east." The pilot wheel of the boat was taken to Kingsburg and used in the hoisting of meat in the butcher-shop on Draper Street near the schoolhouse.[6]

Until the Central Pacific line had been built through the valley, steamers landed freight regularly at the head of

Fresno Slough. A large two-story house was erected at this point called Casa Blanca (White House); this was located approximately two miles north and slightly west of the present town of Tranquillity. When Butterfield established a stage station there it was given the name Fresno City. However, there was another and earlier Fresno twelve miles to the north-northwest. At the confluence of the San Joaquin River and Fresno Slough a meeting place existed for men of more or less unsavory reputations. Since it was a junction where trails converged it was known to the Spanish-speaking part of the population as Las Juntas. However, the region in general was known as Fresno due to the ash trees, which grew along the banks of the slough. Fresno is the Spanish word for ash. Years later a bridge was constructed north of Casa Blanca and named White's Bridge after the man who built it.[7]

The steamers *Visalia* and *Harriet*, during the decade from 1860 to 1870, carried as much as a hundred and fifty tons each on a single trip. Sycamore Point was usually the terminal; from this point large wagons distributed the goods.[8] In primeval days the timber in the mountains protected the snow and it melted gradually; this caused a fairly even flow of water and made river navigation in the valley possible in those days. The reckless cutting of timber and the introduction of irrigation have reduced the volume of water in the river channels to such an extent that such a mode of transportation is now not generally feasible.

The first wheeled vehicle in the San Joaquin was the *carreta*. This was a crude ox-cart with wheels made from the sections sawed from round logs. These wheels were never exactly of the same shape or circumference, hence the carreta was not a comfortable means of conveyance. It was primarily a means of transporting goods, but along the coast it was used on Sundays to carry the Indian

Bert Belknap hauling railroad iron. *Garden of the Sun*, 1939 edition.

neophytes to church. As these carts moved ponderously over the plain, the squealing of the wheels could be heard for miles. A can of soft soap was usually carried along, and generous doses applied to the over-heated axles from time to time in an attempt to hush the unearthly din.[9]

When the blue-eyed men came to California they brought the covered wagon. Riverboats carried goods as far up the river as possible. From these indefinite and shifting points, goods were hauled in big wagons. One of the most important of the early freighters was A. O. Thoms of Visalia; his wagons transported goods from the Bay region to Visalia by way of Kingston. During the sixties Visalia, at the rate of $50 a ton, paid annually $150,000 for the delivery of goods in this fashion.[10] In the northern part of the valley, the tinkling bells which announced the approach of Ace Macholemen's twenty-four-mule freight wagon was always an event at Knight's Ferry.[11] Another famous freighter on this route between Stockton and Sonora was Henry Hoffman. These wagons were called prairie schooners.

> These big wagons were so-called because of their immense size, as they would each hold from six to ten tons of freight. One wagon was built at a cost of $1,000 and held twelve tons. The body of this big wagon was twenty-eight feet in length, eight feet wide and five feet high. Sixteen big mules drew the load. Usually smaller wagons were used, a large wagon and one or two trailers fastened to the larger wagon. In this way a teamster hauled to Mariposa 22,000 pounds of freight. He made the round trip, 110 miles, in seven days (from Stockton).[12]

The needs of the miners greatly stimulated the freighting industry. A picturesque teamster named Leif Johnson operated in the territory between Visalia and Bakersfield. He resented the arrival of the railway because it would destroy his means of livelihood.[13] Stories have been told that he matched his eight prize oxen in a pulling contest with the first locomotive to reach Tipton and that his animals, greatly to their owner's astonishment, were set on their haunches.[14] One of the stockmen in the region at that time was Harry Quinn. A letter of inquiry to his son, John R. Quinn, then chairman of the board of supervisors of Los Angeles County, elicited the following reply:

> My father knew Abe Johnson, the oxen teamster who was reputed to have hitched his oxen to a locomotive in a pulling contest, very well, as he hauled the lumber into Big Gulch that was used in the construction of my father's well and his first modest buildings there. He was a great friend of "Keech-eye" Helmench, who was also a teamster. Johnson did offer to pull his oxen against the locomotive, probably being encouraged in this by a little stimulant and the urgings of his neighbors. The engineers, however, would not permit the contest and that part of it is a myth, though my father was

there and knows that the argument got far enough along until they were ready to hitch up the oxen.[15]

The financial success of Alexander Todd in the operation of his rowboat served indirectly as the cause for the organization of the first stagecoach route in California. One of the Forty-niners was a young man in his early twenties named James E. Birch. He was a Yankee and had been a stage-driver in New England. Men who engaged in this profession developed a passion for it even as a sailor loves the sea. Birch observed the profits accruing to Todd and discerned with great clarity that an opportunity existed for introducing a more rapid means of transportation. Therefore he bought a farm wagon and four bronchos and announced one morning at Stockton: "All aboard for Mormon Island." This was the humble beginning of a very great industry. Quickly, other local stage lines were organized and during 1853 they carried $57,000,000 worth of gold dust from the various mines along the Sierra foothills. On January 1, 1854, James E. Birch and his New England friend, Frank Stevens, organized the California Stage Company. This firm became the great transportation agency of California and was soon to attract national attention. It expanded rapidly and soon the assessed valuation of its stock was over $1 million.[16]

In 1853 the interest of the nation was focused on the West. The United States government was planning ways and means of connecting California with the other states. The trans-Mississippi West was a wild and seething Indian country. While a few white settlements had been made and some cattle ranches established on the fringes, yet the only men who entered the greater part of it were Rocky Mountain fur trappers. No roads existed, excepting the trails made by the wild animals and the prairie schooners. The purpose of the contemplated road was political and military rather than commercial. To defend

Undated broadside advertising the routes of the California Stage Company. William Banning, *Six Horses.*

the Pacific coast in case of war might be difficult without a good system of transportation connecting it with the East. Before the coming of the stagecoach line and the Pony Express, the government possessed no facilities for delivering dispatches or orders to officials on the Pacific coast except by special messenger. This state of affairs explains the generosity of the government to the early railroad companies.

Jefferson Davis, Secretary of War, and subsequently United States Senator from Mississippi, took the lead in having surveys made of possible routes to the Pacific. No more energetic or capable man ever held this office. The facetious remark has often been made that he was President of the United States under Franklin Pierce. His interests were worldwide. To the Near East he sent young army officers to study the science of war as practiced by the nations of Europe and Asia in the Crimean conflict. One of these was George B. McClellan, soon to become the president of the Illinois Central Railroad and later, at the age of thirty-four, the commander-in-chief of the Army of the Potomac. Incidentally, "it is interesting to note that Abraham Lincoln was a captain of volunteers in the Black Hawk War in 1835 and that Lieutenant Jefferson Davis of the regular army administered to him his first oath of allegiance."[17] To the Far West Davis sent officers to survey five possible routes to California. The immediate purpose was to connect California with the east by stagecoach; the ultimate goal was to extend the railways, whose western terminal at that time was St. Louis, to the cities along the Pacific coast.

The army engineers sent out by Jefferson Davis located and surveyed five routes; of these, the central, followed by the prairie schooners and the Argonauts, was the most direct. The advocates of this route argued that this was the only one to which the geometric axiom "the shortest distance between two points is a straight line" could be applied. But the longest route had the strongest supporters and won. The reasons are many, and these are they.

Jefferson Davis was a slave owner of the type then dominant in American politics; Postmaster-General Aaron Vail Brown, representing the same regnant social class, was born in Virginia and had later become a citizen of Tennessee. They naturally preferred to connect California to the rest of the Union by a stage route running through Southern territory. They argued plausibly and honestly that the cold winters and heavy snows of the northern routes would be a menace to safe travel in winter; they maintained that a road near Mexico was of value both from the standpoint of peaceful trade and defensive war; and President James Buchanan, elected in 1856, was a personal friend of men interested in the southern route. Therefore it was selected.[18]

Congress, in providing $150,000 for this initial survey, required an official report to be made on or before the first Monday in February 1854. Travelers of every sort prior to this time had furnished information concerning the West; these government engineers were instructed to secure the needed detailed data. The surveying corps, aside from its specifically assigned work, gathered material on botany, ethnology, geology, and general history pertaining to the trans-Mississippi West. The final report was made in thirteen large, handsome, and profusely illustrated volumes.[19]

The general course of the southern route is interesting. From St. Louis it led south into Texas, then entered Mexico for a short distance, proceeded across the deserts to Fort Yuma, entered Mexico again after reaching California, crossed the Imperial Valley, and entered Los Angeles. It thence went across the Tehachapi range by way of Tejon Pass, through the San Joaquin Valley and to

San Francisco by way of Pacheco Pass. The total distance was 2,485 miles.[20]

After Davis and Brown had succeeded in securing the adoption of the southern route, the fact that the surveyors had swung too far to the south and had entered Mexican territory at one point was discovered. President Pierce sent Colonel James Gadsden to Mexico in 1854 to correct the problem, and Congress later ratified his purchase of 45,000 square miles for $10 million. The Southern Pacific Railroad from Yuma to El Paso later traversed the Gadsden Purchase.

Jefferson Davis set aside $30,000 from his general fund for the survey of the San Joaquin Valley. Lieutenant R. S. Williamson of the Topographical Engineers was placed in chief command. His assistants were Lieutenant G. B. Anderson of the Second Dragoons (sickness after reaching California prevented him from actually serving in the valley); Dr. A. L. Heermann, physician and naturalist; Mr. Isaac Williams Smith, civil engineer; Mr. Charles Koppel, assistant civil engineer and artist; Mr. Charles Preuss, draughtsman; Mr. W. P. Blake, minerologist and geologist; and Lieutenant George Stoneman of the First Dragoons, commander of the escort.[21]

The instruments necessary for the survey were loaded in a large spring wagon. The food, supplies, and other baggage were placed in four large wagons each drawn by six mules. Five teamsters and eight other men, to serve as cooks and field men, were employed. The military escort consisted of twenty-five private soldiers and three non-commissioned officers. The best horses and packers available were hired.[22]

Williamson's instructions called for a railway survey through the San Joaquin Valley, with special emphasis on locating the best exit to the south. The expedition left

Benicia on July 10, 1853, and entered the valley by the
way of Livermore Pass. They crossed the valley toward
the east and followed the hills southward. At Fort Miller,
Williamson reported that the thermometer registered 115
degrees in the shade. They crossed John Poole's Ferry
north of Reedley and finally reached Woodsville in Tulare
County. Here they met Alexis Godey, who had been
Fremont's chief guide to California in 1844. After resting
in the cool shade of Mooney Grove, Williamson proceeded
to the south, with Godey added to the party. Walker's Pass
was surveyed and rejected as a point of exit from the
valley. The pass itself was excellent, but the inhospitable
nature of the country to the east made it undesirable.[23]

Tejon Pass was explored and also rejected. Late in the
summer the surveyors completed their work and reported
that Tehachapi Pass was the best for the proposed
railroad. The accuracy of their surveys and the
correctness of their judgment is attested to by the fact
that this route is used by the two modern railroads in
entering and leaving the southern San Joaquin. Evidently
Jefferson Davis selected good engineers.[24]

Thomas Benton, father-in-law of Fremont and Senator
from the State of Missouri, had opposed the expenditure
of money for this survey. He may have resented the fact
that Davis ignored Fremont's volunteered aid. He argued
that the collection of additional scientific data was
unnecessary.

> There is a class of topographical engineers older than the
> schools and more unerring than the mathematicians. They
> are the wild animals—buffalo, elk, deer, antelopes, bears—
> which traverse the forests, not by compass, but by instinct
> that leads them always the right way to the lowest passes in
> the mountains, the shallowest fords in the river...and the
> shortest practical lines between remote points.[25]

However, Benton was vitally interested in the development of the West. He merely opposed what he considered a needless waste of the taxpayer's money. Another prominent leader in the East who took a part in giving the West favorable publicity was Horace Greeley. In 1859, he made a visit to the Pacific Coast, largely to stimulate interest in that region and to aid in its development. After he returned home, he wrote in his New York *Tribune*: "Go west, young man, and grow up with the country."

Since a railway to the West could not be immediately provided, it was decided by the national government to offer a six-year mail contract to the stage company, which would agree to deliver mail twice a week. In case of several bidders, the lowest bidder was to receive the contract. One of the bidders for this mail contract was the Birch and Stevens California Stage Company. But a group of men led by John Butterfield, a personal friend of President Buchanan, secured the award. His associates were William B. Dinsmore, Johnston Livingston, William G. Fargo, James V. P. Gardner, D.N. Barney, E.P. Williams, Marcus L. Kinyon, Alexander Holland, Hugh Crocker, Giles Hawley, David Moulton, and Hamilton Spencer. These men named their stage line the Great Southern Overland Mail and guaranteed to make semiweekly trips across the continent in both directions. For rendering this service the government paid them $600,000 annually. They received their contract on September 16, 1857, and were obliged to begin their activities on September 15, 1858. This contract was to run for six years. The stagecoaches left St. Louis on the 16th and San Francisco on the 15th. On October 8 John Butterfield telegraphed to President Buchanan: "The Overland Mail arrived today at St. Louis from San Francisco in 23 days and 4 hours. The stage brought through six passengers."[26]

John Butterfield proved to be a genius in the organization and administration of his huge enterprise. His task was as great as that which ever faced any railroad president of a later period. Within a year after securing his contract, he had to purchase horses by the thousands; Concord stagecoaches by the hundreds; establish more than a hundred stage stations; hire agents, stockmen, drivers; and lay in a supply of feed for his livestock. And most of the route traversed a region infested with warlike Indians. He proved equal to the task. The Great Southern Overland Mail, usually referred to as the Butterfield line, performed its task over the specified route until the spring of 1861, when the outbreak of the Civil War caused the transfer of the mail to the central route. The United States government relied on this form of carrying its mail and dispatches until the completion of the first transcontinental railway on May 10, 1869.

The horses used to pull the Western stagecoaches were usually bronchos. The thoroughbred racehorse has never been a successful harness horse, and the standard-bred horse was at that time in the process of formation and not available. Therefore, the Spanish horse had to furnish the motive power. He frequently also furnished amusement and excitement, which the following quotation indicates:

> Now and then the wild, unbroken steeds would cut up some extremely ludicrous antics. I never saw so much sport in so short a time as I once did in the spring of 1864 at Latham Station on the South Platte. A team of six wild bronchos was for the first time hitched up, late one afternoon, to the east-bound California stage destined for Atchison. When the passengers were seated and the driver said, "Let go!" the off leader immediately jumped over the near one, while the near wheeler jumped over the off one, and soon every animal was down. All were plunging and kicking and I never saw such a mixed-up and tangled lot of stage animals. Every mustang was down and not one of them could get up.[27]

A Concord stagecoach and team hurtling through a mountain pass. William Banning, *Six Horses*.

The stagecoaches were built by Abbot, Downing & Company of Concord, New Hampshire. These Concord coaches were perhaps the best wagons ever built. Even the English colonies such as Australia and Canada preferred them to the English-built coaches. The weight of a Concord was 2,500 pounds, and it could accommodate twelve passengers. An indefinite amount of baggage could be placed on the top, or on the dropboard behind the stage. The stagecoach era in America was a period of bad roads; the macadamized highways of England were unknown, especially on the frontier. Therefore a special and superior type of vehicle was developed in the United States. Nothing has ever yet been invented to equal it in solving transportation over atrocious roads. In those days antedating steel springs, leather braces were used; according to Captain William Banning, they had a value all of their own and would be used today under similar circumstances:

> The most important function of the Concord thorough braces has already been explained. It has been shown how, by

249

allowing the heavy body to rock fore and aft, they enable the force of inertia to supply the timely boost to relieve the team of strain due to obstacles of the road. The horse was the vital consideration. The less taxed, the more he could pull and the faster he could go. The coach that could run the easiest with the greatest load was the best for the horse. And the Concord was that coach.[28]

The stations situated between St. Louis and San Francisco were divided into nine divisions, with a superintendent in charge of each. The First Division comprised the stations between San Francisco and Los Angeles. According to the *Daily Alta California* for November 19, 1858, the following stations were included in this division: the number of miles between each station is also indicated.

STATION		STATION	
San Francisco	0	Packwood	12
Clark's	12	Tule River	14
San Mateo	9	Fountain Springs	14
Redwood City	9	Mountain House	12
Mountain View	12	Posey Creek	15
San Jose	11	Gordon's Ferry	10
Seventeen Mile House	17	Kern River Slough	12
Gilroy's	13	Sink of the Tejon	14
Pacheco Pass	16	Fort Tejon	15
San Luis Ranch	17	Reid's	8
Lone Willow	18	French John's	14
Temple's Ranch	13	Widow Smith's	24
Firebaugh's Ferry	15	King's	10
Fresno City	19	Hart's	12
Elk Horn Springs	22	San Fernando Mission	8
Whitmore's Ferry	17	Cahuenga	12
Cross Creek	12	Los Angeles	12
Visalia	12		

The San Francisco *Evening Bulletin* for November 5, 1858, published a letter written by a special correspondent who was making a study of travelling by stagecoach. This communication was dated Fort Yuma, October 29, and was entitled "Notes on Travel by the Overland Mail"; since it sheds light on travel through the San Joaquin Valley during that period, a portion of it has been included in this chapter.

On the morning of the 23rd, we found ourselves traversing the almost pathless Valley of the San Joaquin, our general course being southeast. The road at this point was abominably soft and wet, the late rains having made the dust very sticky and putty-like. We jogged along at a snail's pace until we reached the South Fork, or rather the Slough of the San Joaquin River, the "head of navigation," *alias* Fresno City. There we were well received by Mr. Cumming [William B. Cummings], and furnished with an ample amount of hot coffee and nicely fried venison steaks.

Leaving his hospitable mansion with regrets, we were soon driving over the plains toward Elk Horn Spring Ranch, which we reached about 12 o'clock, when we found the house burned down but a week before. The former tenants were living under a tent. They had, however, plenty of elk and deer meat ready cooked to greet our appetites. Water is of the most insipid quality along this portion of the route, and yet a little of the *ardent* renders it quite palatable.

After leaving Elk Horn Ranch, we urged our way to Kings River [Whitmore's Ferry], which we reached on the evening of the 23rd, in fine style, about dusk. We were transferred to the other side on a ferryboat, in good condition, without accident or delay. Taking in two passengers for Visalia, we reached that town at 10 o'clock where we got a weak cup of tea and a slice of beef or so—hardly enough to satisfy the inner man.

Here we were transferred to another coach, with wild Vic for our driver, who carried us along to the next stopping place— making sixteen miles in one hour and sixteen minutes. This was night driving with a vengeance, and such a growling among the passengers was never heard, as their heads were unceremoniously knocked against the staves that composed the framework of cover. The road was rough, and the night

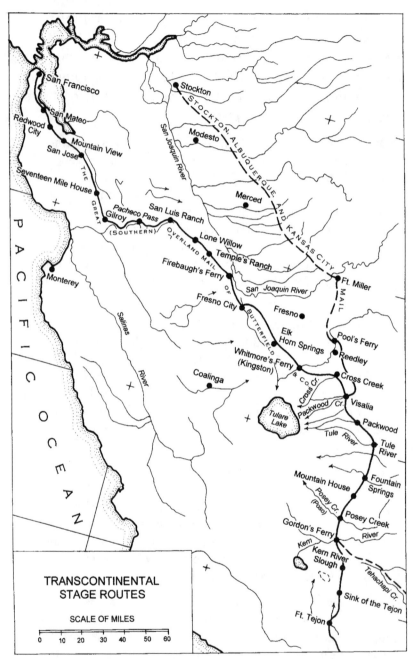

TRANSCONTINENTAL
STAGE ROUTES

SCALE OF MILES

0   10   20   30   40   50   60

dark, the mustangs wild, and all were out of humor owing to the bad supper; and you can well imagine that we had an exciting time of it, and a swift journey.

Our next stopping place was the Kern River, where we were taken across the stream, leaving the stage, and taking one of the smaller size on the opposite bank. There is a steep sandy hill to be surmounted immediately after starting, which renders it necessary for passengers to walk up it. This is soon accomplished by all, and very easily done by those who hang on to the boot-straps behind the stage. When the hill had been mounted there is no further difficulty to be encountered to delay our progress; and so away we went over the alkali plain until we met the mail coach. Then we changed horses, and after a hurried drive of some fifteen miles found ourselves along the banks of the South Fork of the Kern, where we took a late dinner, characterized by the appearance on the table of plenty of sweet milk and fresh butter.

Leaving this comfortable abode of plenty, we were hastily driven over alkali soil until we reached some alkali hills, when down we went, kiting along fast as the mustangs could gallop. Through the Devil's Gulch [Cañada de las Uvas, or Grapevine Canyon] we slowly moved along, the road being so serpentine in its course as to represent the channel of a most tortuous stream. High alkali hills enclose it on all sides, and scarcely one hundred yards of the road is visible along any part of the way. It is a stony, bold and curious formation, and worthy the attention of geologists.

A few moments, and fresh horses were added to the coach, and off again we went at a running flight of speed. After another change, we found ourselves at Fort Tejon, at the summit of the mountain pass. The weather was very cold here, and it was the most disagreeable part of the journey— owing to the agent at Tejon having crowded us with way-passengers, and the team being too light to carry us up the hill. As a consequence of the overload, and the weakness of the team, we were compelled to walk nearly through the whole of Tejon Pass, the sky being cloudy, the wind cold and piercing, and the night dark.

The correspondent who wrote the foregoing referred in another part of his letter to the fact that all the horses used by the stage company were branded with the letters "O. M." This was the official brand of the Butterfield firm and meant "Overland Mail."[29]

The other transcontinental stage-line to traverse the San Joaquin Valley was controlled by Jacob Hall. This line was named the Stockton, Albuquerque & Kansas City Mail. Hall's contract called for a monthly delivery of mail. His stages ran from Stockton to Kansas City. One clause in the contract required that the run should be made within sixty days. On the trial trip Hall's stage and six mules left Stockton on October 1, 1858; fifty-four days later, the journey was completed. The government paid Hall $79,999 for making this monthly trip across the continent. His route from Stockton led south, parallel to the foothills of the Sierra; crossed the San Joaquin at Fort Miller; crossed Kings River at Poole's Ferry, five miles up the river from modern Reedley. It joined Butterfield's Overland Mail route at Visalia, but soon diverged from this trail, passed through Tehachapi Pass to Fort Mojave, and thence went to Albuquerque and Kansas City. Indian wars eventually caused this contract to be abrogated.[30]

Besides these continental lines, several stage companies operated within the valley locally. In 1857 Thomas Heston began to operate the Rabbit-skin Express between Hornitos and Visalia by way of Millerton. Another stage company was formed by a man named Silman that served the towns of Stockton, Tuolumne City, Paradise City, Empire City, Snelling, Plainsburg, and Millerton. A man named Carter became Silman's partner and they extended the route to Visalia. These and many other lines, continued to carry passengers to various points within the valley long after the transcontinental lines in the valley had been abandoned or superseded by the railways.[31]

Butterfield Stage stable at Kingston (now Laton), Fresno County.
Photograph by Will Hollenberg. *Garden of the Sun*, 1939 edition.

There were three main traveled roads in the valley during
pre-railroad days. The first in point of time was the Old
Los Angeles Trail (El Camino Viejo), which connected San
Pedro with San Antonio, now East Oakland. The
northbound traveler entered the valley by way of San
Emigdio Canyon, skirted the eastern slope of the Coast
Range, passed through a hamlet known as Poso de Chané,
six miles east of present Coalinga (nothing now marks
this place), and left the valley by way of Patterson Pass,
located southwest of Tracy. This road was in use by the
Spanish as early as 1800 and continued to be traveled
until the completion of the railroad.[32]

The next route to come into general use was the Los
Angeles-Stockton Road, known locally along various

portions of the way as the Millerton Road and the Stockton-Visalia Road. This followed the foothills closely because most of the white people in that part of California were miners, and hence lived in the foothill area. Also, the rivers at the point where they emerge from the hills were relatively narrow and had gravel bottoms, which made crossings easier and safer than out on the valley floor, where they had a tendency to spread out and where the soil was often boggy. This road was used by the Butterfield line from Los Angeles to Visalia; at the latter place it branched off toward the west.[33]

The first important stop in California of the westbound transcontinental stagecoach from St. Louis was Los Angeles. From that point the road led through the San Fernando Valley and up the mountain pass to Fort Tejon. This was located along the banks of Grapevine Creek (Arroyo de las Uvas) and soldiers stationed there escorted the stages through the pass in early days to protect them from Indians and bandits. Cavalry units were stationed there from 1854 to 1864.

The next stop was at the Sink of the Tejon at the place where Tejon Creek sinks into the sand, but where a perpetual waterhole existed. The Spanish called it Agua de los Alamos [Los Alamitos]. Then came Kern River Slough, a substation, where horses were changed. Gordon's Ferry was located along Kern River, about five miles northeast of present Bakersfield, near the foot of China Grade. Then came the crossing at Posey Creek, where horses were changed, followed by Mountain House and Fountain Springs. The White River was crossed in what is now Range 27 East, Township 24 South.[34]

The Tule River station was located within the present limits of Porterville. From this point the road led across the present city limits of Lindsay. A station between Tule

The Grapevine area of Kern County in the 1850s, with the San Joaquin Valley floor looming in the background. *Pacific Railroad Surveys,* volume V.

River and Visalia was originally called Packwood, but was later known variously as Lone Cottonwood and the Pike Lawless Ranch. It was located about one mile south of the present Outside Creek Bridge. The hostler at Packwood was Royal Porter Putnam, a young man who had left his Pennsylvania home to seek adventure in the west. He wrangled horses for several months at a stipend of $30 a month. In time he established a hotel and trading post at Tule River, which returned the compliment by re-naming itself Porterville.[35]

North of present Farmersville the stage road swung east toward the mountains for about three or four miles to Woodsville, located along the south bank of the Kaweah River. This, as well as the St. John's River half a mile to the north, were crossed on toll bridges built by Dr. Thomas Payne. On the north side of the St. John's River the road ran between Venice Hills and the Tulare County Charter Oak toward Poole's Ferry.[36]

The regular main line from Los Angeles to Stockton did not pass directly through Visalia that lay about six miles to the west. The Butterfield stages, however, left the Stockton-Los Angeles road just north of present Farmersville and turned to the west and north and unloaded their passengers and mail at their station, located on what is now the northeast corner of Court and Main streets in Visalia.[37]

Less than a mile northwest of the Charter Oak, the Stockton-Los Angeles trail forked to form the Upper and Lower Detours. The Upper Detour ran east of the Twin Buttes, passed between what are now Yettem and Seville, continued northwest between Cutler and Orosi, and east of Smith Mountain to the ferry at Scottsburg, built in 1854. The latter was located across the river from what is now Centerville, but a flood washed it away and its exact site is now squarely in the main channel of Kings River. Senator Tom Fowler's ranch headquarters were subsequently in the immediate neighborhood.[38]

From Scottsburg Ferry the road led across the plains a mile east of modern Centerville to the San Joaquin River, which was crossed on the Converse Ferry, established in 1852. Later this was known as the Jones Ferry and was located on the site of modern Friant. About two miles north of the San Joaquin it was reunited with the Lower Detour, and continued on to Stockton.[39]

Now to go back to the Charter Oak and the parting of the ways. The Lower Detour swung to the west and paralleled the Upper Detour at a distance of from one to six miles. It ran a mile west of the present Dinuba, passed the site of the Reedley hospital, and crossed the river at Pool's Ferry, built in 1850. Smith's Ferry did not come into existence

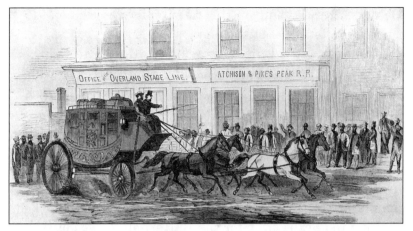

Stagecoach leaving a city for points unknown. Owen C. Coy, *Pictorial History of California*

until five years later. The road then passed over the city limits of present Sanger, and reached the San Joaquin River near the mouth of Little Dry Creek. Here the road turned upstream to the Brackman Ferry, located two miles downstream from the crossing on the Upper Detour.[40]

The combined roads now continued northward to Newton's Crossing on the Chowchilla River (on the line which separates sections 6 and 7), crossed the Merced at Phillips Ferry, about two miles below Merced Falls; used Dickinson's Ferry to cross the Tuolumne, which was located seven miles east of Waterford; and passed the Stanislaus at Knight's Ferry. This place was founded by William Knight, was later purchased by a brother-in-law of U. S. Grant, and still remains one of the most picturesque spots in California.[41]

In 1855 James Smith established a ferry about five miles downstream from Pool's Ferry. Smith's Ferry was favorably located, because the high banks on either side made it approachable even during times of high water. Therefore, it quickly superseded Pool's Ferry and became the regular crossing place for stages using the Lower

259

Detour. After crossing on this ferry, stages continued to the northwest for about five miles, where they encountered the old road. Occasionally the Butterfield stages found it necessary to use the Smith Ferry. During the wet season the road from Visalia to Cross Creek was often impassable and the ferry at Kings River (Whitmore's Ferry, later Kingston) was unapproachable. Then the Butterfield drivers sent their horses over the road from Visalia to Smith's Ferry, changed horses there, and then drove over the plains to Fresno City (Casa Blanca), approximately fifty miles away. James Smith had marked out this road especially for the Butterfield stages by digging down willow posts at regular intervals, so the drivers would have a guide to follow.[42]

Jacob Hall, who operated the Stockton, Albuquerque & Kansas City Mail, used the Stockton-Los Angeles Road going south as far as Gordon's Ferry on the Kern River. At that place, his stages diverged from the old road and turned to the southeast and left the valley by way of Tehachapi Pass.[43]

The first stop in the San Joaquin Valley was made at San Luis Gonzaga ranch. A two-story adobe house built on it in 1843, later destroyed by an earthquake in 1868, served as a stage station for the Butterfield line. This ranch was watered by San Luis Creek and a water hole near the house made it ideal as a stopping place.[44]

The next stop was made at Lone Willow, located about eighteen miles southeast of San Luis Gonzaga. This was followed by Temple's Ranch, and then came Firebaugh's Ferry, on the west side of the river, and located about where the railway station is now.[45]

The first man to operate the station and restaurant at Fresno City was William B. Cummings, and all travelers reported that his place served excellent food. Elk Horn

Springs was in charge of John Barker, later a Bakersfield newspaperman. The first Butterfield stage to reach his place found that his buildings had all burned and they were accommodated in tents. Whitmore's Ferry, sometimes called Kings River and later Kingston, was located along a river whose name is obvious.[46]

The name and location of Cross Creek is apt to be confusing. There existed by that name two small hamlets and one creek. The creek is still there. The first tiny settlement known as Cross Creek was a station established by Butterfield. It lay along the eastern banks of the creek by that name, about two and a half miles downstream from the later Southern Pacific railway. Eventually, a town by the same name was founded along the railway line; this was located a few miles south of Traver.[47]

The next stop after Cross Creek was Visalia. A few miles south of it and just north of Farmersville, the Butterfield stages made a connection with the regular Stockton-Visalia Road and continued on it to Los Angeles.[48]

The Old Los Angeles Trail, the Stockton-Los Angeles Road, and the Butterfield route were supplemented by several lateral roads running east and west. The Butterfield line itself furnished a road for many who wanted to cross the valley since it ran cater-cornered from Visalia to San Luis; it crossed the Camino Viejo near San Luis. Another road led from San Luis Gonzaga due east and crossed the San Joaquin River just south of the mouth of the Fresno River. The ferry at this point was operated for a time by Alexis Godey, Fremont's old scout. Farther north, a crossing could be made at the mouth of the Merced at Hill's Ferry. In the northern part of the valley, a trail carrying much traffic connected Sutter's Fort with San Jose and Monterey. The San Joaquin River was forded near Mossdale. In 1848 John Doak and Jacob Bonsell began to carry passengers over the river in a small yawl; this was the first ferry anywhere on the San Joaquin River. The discovery of gold caused business to boom, and Doak built a large ferryboat that he operated at a profit until its sale in 1851.[49]

A new form of transportation was introduced into California by Edward Fitzgerald Beale who was the owner of the *Tejon* Ranch of 200,000 acres in the southern part of the San Joaquin Valley. Beale believed that camels would facilitate travel across the deserts and plains of the semi-arid Southwest. He secured the active support of Jefferson Davis, Secretary of War, and the latter, in turn, solicited the aid of the Navy Department with such success that in May, 1855, David Dixon Porter was sent to Tunis, Africa, in the ship named *Supply* with orders to purchase camels. Porter was a relative of Beale and was destined to win fame in the Civil War by aiding General Grant in the capture of Confederate forts along the Mississippi River. But in 1855 he was a mere stock-buyer looking for camels in North Africa and he did not know so much about that.[50]

Every moth-eaten camel in North Africa, according to his own story, was offered for sale as a wonderful specimen. But Porter was a shrewd Yankee though entirely ignorant of dromedaries. He proceeded to Constantinople and was, for a time, an interested spectator of the Crimean War. Here English officers furnished honest and intelligent advice concerning camels, and thirty-three of the ungainly beasts were purchased and safely landed at Indianola, Texas, in April, 1856. The same year Porter was sent back in the ship *Suwanee* for another shipment and returned with forty-four camels. He also brought back native Greek and Syrian camel drivers. The two best known of these were Hadji Ali and Greek George Caralambo. The former was quickly dubbed Hi Jolly by the American "muleskinners"; later he used the name Philip Tedro, and Greek George became a citizen under the name of George Allen.[51]

The Beale Camel Corps encamped. Owen C. Coy, *Pictorial History of California.*

The camels thrived in their new environment. They liked the bitter alkali water, which was refused by horses and mules, and they waxed fat on sagebrush, greasewood, and cactus. But the American muleskinners hated the camels and took no pains to learn to understand the new animals. Horses and mules were frightened by them, and confusion reigned generally. The strange beasts shocked even human beings. Camels were introduced into the silver mines of Nevada. Dan de Quille, a newspaper reporter associated with Mark Twain, wrote that two drunk German miners were on their way home one evening when they encountered their first camels. Said one to the other: "Oh, Sheorge, yoost see dem awful big gooses."[52]

The ships of the desert were never given a fair trial because the men assigned to care for them resented their new duties; then, too, the Civil War came and engrossed the attention of the men who had sponsored their introduction. Perhaps the camels would never, even with a fair trial, have proved successful. The deserts of Asia and

263

Africa are sandy wastes and hot. The American deserts lie in most cases at a high altitude and frigid nights, even in summer, are the rule. The sharp, flinty stones, also common, would probably have ruined the soft pads of the camels. Many of them were permitted to wander off into the deserts; others were placed on sale at public auction. Some of the latter were bought by Beale and taken by way of Los Angeles to his *El Tejon Ranch* in the San Joaquin Valley. On July 25, 1860, thirty-two Mongolian Bactrian camels, distinguished from the dromedary by their double humps, arrived at San Francisco from the Amur River region in Manchuria. They were taken to Arizona and Nevada and used in the silver mines and salt works.[53]

On April 7, 1864, a camel race was held at Sacramento for the benefit of the unemployed. It turned out to be a fiasco. Camels are serious minded creatures and have a definite purpose in life. When they move they expect to get somewhere, and when it dawned on them that they were expected to run round a circular track and go nowhere, they lay down and refused to move.[54]

From time to time camels kept wandering off into the desert and hills; they kept increasing in numbers in spite of destruction by Indians and wild animals. Many a cowboy, ignorant of the fact that the United States Army once had a Camel Corps, has come in from the desert with a wild look in his eye to regale his associates with weird yarns about strange animals; on such occasions, the man's comrades generally attribute the hysteria to the heat and attempt to sooth him as they would a little child. In recent years, prospectors have complained that camels in the Mojave Desert have caused burros to run away from their camps at night.[55]

However, neither oxen nor camels played so important a part in early transportation in California as did the horse. Besides pulling the overland stages, he was used for riding. This was his most important function. Men, women, and children rode. Laws were enacted in Spanish days prohibiting the Indians from using the horse unless employed as vaqueros. This law proved futile in time. The Californian disliked any work that could not be performed while in his saddle. The rancher repaired his corral fence while mounted; if he ever cast a fish line into a stream, he did it while on a horse; and a vaquero was once observed attempting to plane a board while astride his steed. No Californian ever engaged in trapping, because his horse would then have had to remain in the background.

Naturally, constant life in the saddle bred a race of horsemen never surpassed. The gentle climate made riding possible twelve months of the year. The physical stamina of some of these Spanish-California men is indicated by the remark made by Juan Bautista Alvarado concerning General José Castro, who at one time owned a cattle ranch along the San Joaquin River between Herndon and Fort Miller: "It is my belief that Castro possessed a constitution of iron, for on occasion he was in the saddle for thirty-six hours, yet when he alighted he appeared as fresh as though he had just arisen from his bed."[56]

The Spanish-Californians who first settled the San Joaquin Valley are not to be confused with Mexicans. The latter term generally connotes peons of Indian blood. The Spanish-Californians belonging to the social class known as the *gente de razon* (the right people) were white men, usually of large stature, and frequently red-headed. William Heath Davis wrote of them: "I distinctly remember the Californians and how they impressed me when I first saw them, as a boy in 1831 and 1833—a race of men large of stature and of fine, handsome appearance."[57] Bayard Taylor visited the province in 1846; he wrote this about them:

The Californians, as a race, are greatly superior to the

Mexicans. They have larger frames, stronger muscles, and a fresh ruddy complexion, entirely, different from the sallow skins of the *tierra caliente*, or the swarthy features of those Bedouins of the west, the Sonorians. The families of pure Castilian blood resemble in features and build the descendants of the Valencians in Chile and Mexico, whose original physical superiority over the natives of other provinces of Spain has not been obliterated by two hundred years of transplanting.[58]

According to James Capen Adams, who was a professional big-game hunter in the San Joaquin Valley in the fifties, the California grizzly bear was one of the most vicious and powerful animals in the world. He followed the rivers down into the valley, where he all too often gorged himself on the beef of the rancher's cattle. Adams described this bear, now extinct, in this fashion:

> The California grizzly sometimes weighs as much as 2,000 pounds. He is of a dark brown color, sprinkled with grayish hairs. When aroused, he is, as has been said before, the most terrible of all animals in the world to encounter; but ordinarily will not attack man, excepting under peculiar circumstances.[59]

This bear was lassoed by the Spanish-California boys for amusement. When bears were wanted for bull fighting, the horsemen would go to Mt. Diablo, rope a bear, drag him to his destination, and consider it great sport. What other group of men could have done that?[60]

Perhaps the greatest single feat of horsemanship in the world can be attributed to a resident of the San Joaquin Valley. Paul Revere rode his horse, Dobbin, fourteen miles through his home community and Henry Wadsworth Longfellow made him famous; Philip Sheridan, according to Joseph Hergesheimer, actually loitered along the road from Winchester to the battlefield on his placid steed, but Thomas Buchanan Reed immortalized that ride; Buffalo Bill, then a Pony Express rider, traveled 322 miles in

Vaqueros roping California grizzly bears, one of the most dangerous early-day sports in the San Joaquin Valley. Drawing by Herbert Dunton. *Garden of the Sun,* 1939 edition.

twenty-four hours and forty minutes, but he used twenty-one horses and had the support of a score of station men along the route to aid him; Felix Xavier Aubry, a French-Canadian fur-trapper residing at Santa Fe, offered to bet a group of men, including Kit Carson, $1,000 that he could ride the eight hundred miles from Santa Fe to Independence within six days; he won the bet with a day to spare, but relay horses were provided along the way.

The California horseman, Juan Flaco (Slim John), had to contend with a different problem on his memorable ride. In 1846 Captain Archibald Gillespie found himself beleaguered at Los Angeles with fifty men. Juan Flaco volunteered to notify Commodore Stockton at Monterey. Gillespie wrote on several cigarette papers the words "Believe the bearer" and affixed his seal, which was known to Stockton. Flaco, a famous rider even in that land of great horsemen, got away in the dark about eight o'clock in the evening of September 24th. He could not be overtaken and his pursuers, as a last resort, shot his steed just as he reached the Santa Monica Mountains. But Juan Flaco escaped in the darkness, made his way on foot to the ranch of an American rancher, secured a horse, and reached the outskirts of Santa Barbara at eleven o'clock of the evening of September 25th. The next night he rode to Monterey. Stockton had already left that city but Juan Flaco, nothing daunted, borrowed horses provided for him by Thomas Larkin, and galloped into San Francisco on the evening of the 28th or 29th. Army officers at the time estimated that the route taken in this ride exceeded six hundred miles in length. The ride was made in four days and through a country generally hostile. Juan Flaco procured his own mounts and was forced to avoid the main roads in order to escape detection.[61]

Juan Flaco's real name was John Brown. He was a native of Sweden and, like his Viking ancestors, he craved excitement. According to his own account, he served four years in the British Navy and then enlisted in Simon Bolivar's cavalry. The tall, blonde daredevil became the hero of the other young hellions who surrounded the South American revolutionary leader. Finally he was captured and sentenced to be shot. But he escaped to California as a stowaway on a ship, served with the Graham and Sutter militias, and then espoused the cause of the Americans in 1846. He enlisted in Fremont's Battalion, and then, like many men of action, spent his declining years in peace and tranquillity. His neighbors considered him a man of strict integrity, with generous impulses, and a sociable disposition. He passed away at his home in Stockton on December 10, 1859.[62]

The Californians are frequently praised for their horsemanship; what about their horses? The rider has been praised for his skill in roping a grizzly bear but this dangerous pastime was made possible by a peculiar type of saddle horse. The coordination between rider and mount had to be well nigh perfect.

The Spanish claimed all of the New World and conquered most of it. That conquest was made possible by the Spanish horse. No one seems to remember the name of Paul Revere's horse; the steed of the Spaniard deserves a better fate.

The ancestry of the first horses in the San Joaquin Valley is worthy of notice. They were descendants of the horses originally imported to the New World from Spain and these consisted of two distinct breeds. The Barb was the horse of southern Spain. He had been introduced from Africa a thousand years before the Saracen Conquest although the coming of the Moors brought a fresh infusion of the same blood.[63]

In the northern sierras of Spain, another type of horse was encountered which was dun in color. He was the horse of the North, developed from shaggy Mongolian horses of the cold steppes and in Spain, he met for the first time and mixed with the Barb from the hot deserts. They matched skill and speed at Tours in France, when the Nordic chivalry under Charles Martel halted the onward march of the hitherto unbeaten Moors.

> 'Twas in seven hundred and thirty two
> That the Northern horses pounded down,
> And the feet of the Southern horses beat
> On the roads to Tours, the holy town.[64]

The northern dun was often used in the chariot races in Rome. Both Pliny and Strabo referred in their writings to the fleet Spanish horses. In his *Natural History*, Pliny the Elder wrote: "It is well known that in Lusitania, in the vicinity of the town of Lisipo and the river Tagus, the mares, by turning their faces towards the west wind as it blows, become impregnated by its breezes, and that the foals which are conceived in this way are remarkable for their extreme fleetness; but they never live beyond three years."[65]

In northern Spain, in Hungary, and in Scandinavia, the dun-colored horse was common, and horsemen in those countries are agreed that they are of the aboriginal stock and closely allied to the tarpan of Mongolia. The latter is our only primitive horse, invariably dun in color, with black stripes on the legs, a black line down the back, and a black bar over the shoulders.

The well-known eel-backed dun horse of Norway is colored like the tarpan, and Scandinavian horsemen consider this an evidence of the antiquity of the breed and its affinity with the tarpan. The dun horse of Norway was close kin to the dun horse of northern Spain, and in both the Scandinavian and Iberian peninsulas the eel-backed dun was preferred to the self-colored dun, which was considered vicious and dangerous. This was also the attitude of horsemen in Biblical times and the Apostle John, describing the four horsemen of the Apocalypse, said [Revelation 6:8]: "And I looked, and behold a pale horse; and his name that sat on him was Death, and Hell followed with him." The other horses were white, sorrel, and black, and in the original Greek the fourth horse was referred to as "hippos chloros," which means a horse of greenish yellow color (perhaps a palomino?). At any rate, it was this pale horse, the color of withered yellow grass or dun, which was imported into the New World and with him came the Barb from North Spain.

> And the Spanish horses flourished,
> to a mighty band they grew,
> They ranged and galloped all over the hills,
> for the land was wide and new.
> Strong of shoulder and fleet of foot,
> and never a man they knew.

Of the hundred and fifteen horses,
    the finest in Old Spain,
Of the hundred and fifteen horses,
    not one came back again,
But they spread over all the grand New World,
    the gallant horses of Spain.[66]

One authority on horses has stated that "roans, spotted or piebald, and yellows are not found among the Arabian horses, though roans and yellows are common among the Barbs." His investigations should quell the popular and erroneous notion that spotted cow ponies are of Arab descent. The Barb and the primitive dun were distinct breeds, but naturally they became thoroughly mixed after they reached the New World. Eventually inbreeding produced pinto horses. In time the latter became popular with the Sioux and Comanche Indians; the latter kept only pinto stallions. The Barb was the ancestor of the famous "strawberry roan" which the cowboys have immortalized in their ballads.[67]

The Spanish horses in the New World, aside from ordinary solid colors, were dun (buckskin); black and white (piebald); bay, brown, or sorrel and white (skewbald); cream colored with ivory mane and tail (palomino); or yellowish white (palomillo)[68] George Washington, while President, used eight cream-colored horses with white manes and tails to draw his coach on formal occasions; so did the King of England during Hanoverian days. In California they were the favorite riding horses of the Spanish dons and today palomino horses often appear in moving pictures made in Hollywood. They are merely a variation of the self-colored dun or pale horse. The Nez Perce Indians in Idaho developed a war-horse, also used in the buffalo hunt, which was freakishly colored. It had large black splotches on the rump, a rat-tail, and a sparse mane. Authorities differ as to its present name, but it is called variously an appaloosa or appeluchi, from the French word "pelouse" (plouse), meaning "a lawn".[69]

In time this Spanish horse, whatever his color, became known in the United States by the name of broncho, from the Spanish word *broncho*, meaning rough or wild; mustang, from the Spanish word *mesteño*, meaning wild, strayed, or belonging to the graziers; or *cayuse*, from the name of an Indian tribe and thus signifying Indian pony.

The fleet and beautiful horses which capered over the level plains of the San Joaquin during Spanish and Mexican days called forth the admiration of all travelers who beheld them. Many persons, familiar with the paintings of Arab horses, assumed that these wild horses were of that stock. Actually, they were chiefly descended from the Barb horse, and not from the Arab horse made famous in song and story. Anatomical differences prove this conclusively. The Arab horse often depicted in famous paintings is rarely encountered outside his ancestral home in the Arabian desert. Many horses have come from Arabia, but these were no more pure Arabs tracing back to the Anezeh tribe of the Bedouins than horses exported from the United States to France during the World War were necessarily Kentucky thoroughbreds.[70]

Carl Raswan wrote in 1929 that after nearly a decade of intensive investigation he was certain that there were fewer than eight hundred horses of the Anezeh breed in all Arabia, and very few elsewhere. Out of 4,351 mares examined, he found only fourteen whose pedigree indicated a pure lineage. If there are now approximately only a thousand of these animals in the whole world, it is obvious that at an earlier date Spain would not have equipped her expeditionary and colonizing forces with such animals. Even today exportation is prohibited, and the few *asil* horses outside of Arabia have been secured with the utmost difficulty.[71]

The Arab horse differs from any other horse to such an extent that a different and separate ancestry has been suggested. He has a sinuous facial profile due to a relatively large brain; the broncho is usually Roman-nosed and hammer-headed. The Arab has a high crest, even when underfed; the broncho is often ewe-necked even when well fed. The Arab lacks the sixth lumbar vertebra, which endows him with a comparatively short and strong back; this vertebra is present in the broncho and in all other breeds. The Arab has sixteen vertebrae in his tail, which he carries high like a plume; the broncho has the regulation eighteen and carries his tail low like the Barb. The Arab has a fairly level croup; the broncho's droops. The Arab is the finished product of intelligent breeding; the broncho represents the survival of the fittest. The Arab is gentle; the broncho is often cantankerous. The Arab moves like a West Pointer on parade; the broncho, like an Indian on the hunting trail. Different in anatomy and disposition, the Arab and the broncho are yet alike in their matchless courage. The broncho is not an Arab; it is enough that he is himself. To quote Admiral Sampson in another connection: "There is glory enough for both."[72]

Poets like Vachel Lindsay and Badger Clark have paid tribute to the broncho in verse; Will James, Franklin Welles Calkins, and Ernest Thompson-Seton have written stories about him; Frederic Remington and Charles M. Russell have perpetuated his likeness in their drawings and paintings; army officers have praised him; and the Plains Indians have ridden him to fame and glory in the buffalo hunt and on the war trail. With South American gauchos, Mexican vaqueros, and American cowboys he has done the hard, cruel work of a thousand circling cow camps. In the Northwest, bred to heavy draft stock, the broncho is re-appearing in another form, known as the Northwestern broncho, and is helping the homesteader in his battle with the cold and bleak prairie where only "Giants in the Earth" could win. At our annual rodeos conducted in a spirit of fun, frivolity, and frolic, the broncho is the chief entertainer and enjoys, in his own inimitable way, the hippodrome as much as does his rider.

The Indians in the San Joaquin Valley secured their horses from the Spanish. Johnnie Walker, an old-time cattleman of the San Joaquin, wrote an account for the *Western Horseman* in 1936 about the wild horses as he knew them in his youth:

> I am nearly eighty years old, and have lived in central California all my life. I used to run a thousand to fifteen hundred head of cattle and raise a lot of horses. My people followed the frontiers and were always horse and cattlemen. Sam Walker, my grandfather, took his brand from Chief Tecumseh in 1802. The old Chief told him he did not like to have the white men taking his land so if he would make writing he would sign his mark and give him land. His mark was a bow and arrow, so Sam Walker took that for his brand, and I am still using it to this day.
>
> My grandfather's brother was the Walker who served as a guide under Captain Fremont and Walker Pass and Walker Lake in Nevada are named after him. Before that the Walker boys took part in the War of 1812 and came West with the mountain men.
>
> When Jim Walker, my father, came across the plains with a party of nine mountain men in 1844, he stopped at Sutter's Fort, then went on to John Marsh's *Los Meganos* grant on the east side of Mt. Diablo. He learned there that other Walker men had preceded him, for Marsh told him that Joel P. Walker was established on the Santa Rosa grant where the town of that name stands today.
>
> When I was a young fellow we used to pick up good money catching wild mustangs out on the San Joaquin plains. My

father used to rag us because we spoiled a lot of good horses catching the wild ones. Several of the boys would start out and come into the valley at Banta's Station, a little beyond where Tracy is now, and that was where we would run into the first wild hunches. There were millions of them and that is no exaggeration. They were all the colors of the rainbow. If we could have some of them around here today the solid colored ones would be passed off as pure-bred Arabians for they looked just like them—head high, sleek coats and short backs. The Spaniards brought good horses to this country. They were small but had fire and good looks. They made the best brood mares I have ever seen. Most of the wild ones only weighed six or seven hundred pounds, but when well fed were bigger. Crossed with our American stallions they gave us nine hundred to a thousand pound horses.

The wild mares were the strongest breeders I have ever seen. The colts always came the same color as their mothers, regardless of the stallion used. I built up a fine bunch of Palomino horses from the wild brood mares. The American ranchers were glad to see us hunt them down and get rid of them, as the wild stallions ran off a good many domesticated mares each year. Often whole manadas of tame mares were taken away by wild stallions for they could lick any horse I have ever seen. I have never seen even the smallest wild stallion beaten by a tame stallion regardless of the tame one's size. They were tough little fellows and pretty as a picture...

The mustangs were not inbred. Many people will not believe this but they do not know the ways of wild horses. A wild stallion always ran all the weaned colts out of his bunch the following spring to make room for the new crop. The yearlings ran around by themselves until some old stallion picked them up. He would bunch the fillies and take care of them until some young stallion killed him, or crippled him. The vaqueros killed many a grizzled old veteran out of pure mercy, when he could no longer find a herd that would accept him, or was too crippled to get around. The yearling colts were kept away from the fillies by these old stallions.[73]

From where did all these wild horses come? The commonly accepted notion is that they ran away from the

coastal missions and ranches. If this were true, it would
be a reflection on the skill and vigilance of the California
vaqueros. Livestock clever enough to elude them probably
never existed. This is what actually happened. During the
drought of 1831-32 the government, in order to save
forage needed for the cattle, ordered all surplus horses
killed. Many ranchers, objecting to this order,
surreptitiously ran their spare stock over the hills into the
San Joaquin, planning to return at some future date to
secure them. But they never did. And so these animals,
finding good feed, plenty of water and an excellent
climate, bred like Norwegian lemmings. And soon the San
Joaquin Valley Indians had their horses.[74]

The French in Canada also secured their horses from the
Spanish. Prior to 1663 there were no horses in Canada;
that year one arrived. A brisk trade in horses soon
developed between Mexico and Canada, with the Pawnees
serving as special agents.

When the colonial gentry in Virginia, in the days before
the Revolutionary War, wanted blooded horses they sent
to Mexico for them. Patrick Henry was especially fond of
well-bred horses from Mexico. On December 12, 1778, he
wrote a letter to George Rogers Clark and sent it by
special express to Vincennes:

> I would have the horses and mares—Of the best & most pure
> Spanish Breed, Blood Bays, about five or Six years Old, &
> that have Cover'd none, or, but a few Mares. As large as
> possible, fine Delicate Heads, Long Necks, Ears small &
> pricked, & near at Ends, Deep Shoulders & chest, large Arms,
> well legg'd, Upright pasterns, & as clear of Long Hair as may
> be, in moving to go near before, Bodys good, Loins round &
> very wide, between different Turnings of the Hair, Out
> Hocked & Haunches to be as straight as possible & go wide
> behind.[75]

The Spanish grandees considered the amble the most

comfortable gait in their riding horses and the latter type of saddle stock, imported to the English colonies by way of the West Indies, produced the Narragansett pacer.[76] Concerning this type of palfrey, Pliny the Elder wrote as follows: "Galicia and Asturia are also countries of Spain; they produce a species of horse known to us as *thieldones*, and when smaller, *asturcones*; they have a peculiar and not common gait of their own, which is very easy." [77]

The English colonists did not ride the English thoroughbred because this great breed of racing horses was then in the process of formation. By 1724 two Barbs and one Arab stallion had reached England; mated to English mares they laid the foundation of the English racehorse. Progeny of this union eventually reached the English colonies but the Virginians were already accustomed to good horses before the thoroughbred arrived.

In time, the American running horses became famous for speed and performance but they are not always eligible to registration in the British Stud Book "due to some early blot, real or fancied, in the list of their ancestors. Therefore—Man-o'-War and his descendants are technically half -breeds in England as are a great many of our best horses."[78] Perhaps the bar sinister in the family escutcheon was the blood of the Spanish horse. But was this blood necessarily a taint?

In 1908, the United States Army conducted a test to determine the value of different breeds of horses for cavalry purposes. An endurance race was run from Evanston, Wyoming, to Denver, Colorado, a distance of 552 miles. The horses entered were of many different breeds. The route crossed deserts and the Continental Divide. The contestants left the starting line at six in the morning of May 30 and six days later, six big bronchos crossed the finish line at Denver. The other breeds were defeated, and the conclusion was that "the finish of this extraordinary race seems to justify the contention that for a combination of toughness, speed, and stamina, the native western pony can hold its own against any horse in the world."[79] Such was the horse of the San Joaquin Valley during its glamorous period.

The Spaniards were the most successful of all Europeans as colonizers, and two-thirds of the New World is today Iberian in language and culture. But the Spanish horse outdid even his matchless rider. His blood is still a potent factor in every province in the New World. With this tribute to him, we shall leave him to work out his own destiny. In the valley of the San Joaquin, the sound of his galloping hoofs on the distant prairie has been replaced by the roar of gasoline tractors as they labor in vineyards, orchards, and fields of golden grain. The Spaniard and his horse have departed and are now traveling the Glory Trail on the other side of Jordan River.

> "Empires, vanities, ambition, power, love—all silently pass away. There is still the memory of the golden footprints left by the faithful charger, as though to remind us, 'Here is the path which a hero trod'."[80]

10 Home

on the Range

The cattle are grazing,
Their heads never raising;
There are forty feeding like one!

William Wordsworth *The Cock is Crowing.*

Christopher Columbus brought the first cattle to the New World. Therefore, he may be considered America's first cattleman. The year 1493, the date of the second voyage of Columbus to the New World, marks the beginning of the first cattle ranches in the Western Hemisphere. In 1519, twenty-six years later, Hernando Cortez took descendants of these cattle from Cuba to Mexico. This shipment to Tabasco also included horses, which were to be used as mounts in the impending campaign. The cattle were closely guarded and the females used for breeding purposes only; they were to be the progenitors of the vast herds to roam

Mexico and the United States in later years. It was their destiny to be irrevocably linked with the indefatigable Spaniard on his march to conquest and glory.[1]

In 1769 the Spanish made the first permanent white settlement in Alta California. A little before noon on July 1st of that year Gaspar de Portolá completed his journey to what is now San Diego. In order to equip the expedition properly the various mission establishments in Baja California had made contributions; from Mission San Francisco de Borja had come "sixteen broken mules, eight horses, one stallion, ten sets of leather harness, two hundred head of cattle, most of them cows with their calves (all of which went except four head that were killed and carried jerked), a hammer and some branding forceps." This herd, augmented by the survivors of the three hundred and fifty which Juan Bautista de Anza brought overland from Mexico in 1776, was the nucleus of the only great industry of which colonial California could boast.[2]

The missions along the coast during the heyday of their youth were as large and self-sufficient as German principalities or English counties. Later, the private ranches became their equals in almost all respects. Economically, the civilization of Spanish-California rested upon cattle as surely as that of the southern states of antebellum days rested upon cotton, sugar, or tobacco. The missions were generous with their livestock, and the private rancher was permitted to borrow cattle, stock his estate, and pay his debt in full merely by returning the original number of cattle at the end of five years. Many a modern rancher would appreciate such an opportunity. This spirit of cooperation between friars and laity promoted good will and led to rapid expansion.

The first settlement was made in 1769, and the next year provision was made for the registration of cattle brands. Meat was a daily diet, and since each mission and ranch had a large population, the slaughter of cattle was a weekly affair. Sanitary rules, hygienic theories, and "clean-up" weeks were either unknown or disregarded. Hence the slaughter corral or *calaveras* (place of the skulls) smelled and looked like a cross-section of a Kansas City stockyard. Attracted to it were turkey-buzzards, condors, dogs, coyotes, and grizzly bears. On moonlight nights, roistering blades would ride out to the *calaveras*, lasso a bear, drag him snarling through the streets of Monterey, and thus rudely interrupt the young men with guitars crooning love songs under the latticed and barred windows.

The alcalde announced the time and place for the annual rodeos. A regularly appointed field judge was selected (judge of the plains) who was the master of ceremonies. Beef was used for local consumption; only hides and tallow had commercial value. Twenty-five pound bags of tallow brought $1.50 and $2.00 was paid for each cowhide. The hides were removed out on the open plains, where a squad of men trained for the purpose slaughtered the cattle. These men were called "neckers," and stabbed the cattle at the back of the horns as they rode beside them. The "neckers", at a given signal, rode into the herd and when they had finished their ride the plain looked like the Battle of Bull Run. The hides were hauled away in *carretas* and the carcasses were left. Dogs were kept as scavengers. Finally, the dogs became such a nuisance that the marines at Monterey were called out and ordered to destroy all stray canines.[3]

English and American ships called for hides annually and furnished the Californians with cargoes of clothing, finery, spices, books, and furniture. Some ships carried as many as 30,000 hides at one time. Dana's *Two Years Before the Mast* was the result of a visit to California in a ship engaged in the hide and tallow trade. The size of the herds is indicated by the fact that Mission San José owned 9,000 cattle in 1825; the neophytes at this mission consumed a hundred head each week.[4]

The missions of Alta California were located along the coast. The farthest inland penetration was at Soledad. Private land grants were made and at first they were located along the west side of the Coast Range which served as a huge Chinese wall against the depredations of the Indians from the interior. Without this natural barrier during the initial stages of the Spanish advance, the Indians of the *tulares* would have inflicted irreparable damage. But by 1833 scarcity of further available good land along the coast and the increasing size of the herds, made men willing to accept land grants on the wild frontier of the San Joaquin Valley. The men who received these grants during Mexican days have been discussed in a previous chapter. In most cases they continued to remain during the early stages of the American period. Their holdings constituted the only private property in the valley; the balance was government or public land.

New men arrived in the San Joaquin, but the old cattle remained. In the days when hides rather than beef had commercial value the old Spanish longhorn was the ideal type. But when beef found a market a new type of stock became essential; the new men were to play a part in this development. But the longhorn cow did not disappear immediately; she was to become the mother of the new type. She was a necessity in the evolutionary process, which finally evolved a graded type of beef stock. The new cattlemen were Americans, Germans, and "younger sons" from the English gentry. The "remittance man" in both Canada and the United States has often played an important part in the cattle industry. These new cattlemen imported Herford, Shorthorn, and Aberdeen-Angus bulls which were used as sires, but the longhorn

cow was the ideal mother in the days of the open range.
When a slinking coyote, with an innocent look in his eye
but a sinister thought in his heart, began circling round a
Hereford or Shorthorn cow, she nervously kept turning
around to face him, became dizzy, fell, and before she
could stagger to her feet; the coyote, laughing sardonically,
had killed her calf. A Holstein dairy cow will do the same
thing. The wise old long-horn, under similar conditions,
remained stationary, merely turning her head from side to
side until the coyote got sore feet from trotting round the
circle and, like Aesop's fox, muttered something about
sour grapes and departed forthwith.

The economic importance of Spanish cattle in the
development of the San Joaquin Valley warrants a brief
sketch of their ancestry and history. Three distinctive
breeds of cattle existed in Spain. These varieties were the
ancestors of the Texas longhorn and the cattle of colonial
California. In the north of Spain, the Gallejo and the
Navarra were the common strains. Originally they were a
uniform fawn or chestnut, but had been somewhat
modified in color due to the importation during Roman
times of stock from the Romazz Campagna. These Roman
cattle were large, long-horned, silver-gray cattle with a
white dorsal stripe and a pale ring round the eyes. They
were also distinguished by a straight profile. White
specimens of the breed were considered sacred in ancient
Rome and were used for sacrificial purposes.[5]

The cattle of central Spain were known as Castilian. The
bulls of this stock were similar to the Jersey in shape and
spirit, and from them came the famous fighting bulls used
in Spanish bullrings. Regarding their ancestry, Lydekker
wrote: "In the presence of a strongly marked fawn colored
dorsal streak the otherwise black fighting bulls of Spain
carry decisive evidence of their more or less direct descent
from the aurochs."[6] Cabrera, a Spanish authority on

283

natural history, was convinced that the Jersey and the Castilian were both descended from the aurochs.

In the south of Spain was found the third type, the Andalusian cattle. This stock furnished most of the animals that Columbus took with him on his second voyage to the New World. These were placed on ranches in the West Indies and by 1519 their progeny numbered 4,000. That year Cortez left for the conquest of Mexico and took a few head with him which were landed near Vera Cruz on March 4th. In 1587 the cattle in Cuba alone numbered 35,000. Spain's port of exit during her heyday in the Americas was Seville, and thus we may conjecture that most of the subsequent exportations were likewise Andalusian cattle. The Spanish cattle, aside from Egyptian and Roman modifications, were an autochthonous stock of aurochs derivation. The Andalusian cattle, smaller in size and often piebald in coloring, were of Egyptian ancestry and were, with slight admixture of the other two Spanish strains, the progenitors of our American range cattle.[7]

These Andalusian cattle had come from Egypt about the same time that the Barb horses arrived in the Iberian peninsula. They were of zebu (Brahma) origin. From India, they percolated into the Tigris-Euphrates valley. We generally think of the rancher in the valley of the Nile as a wheat grower, but he was also a cattleman. At a very early date, he possessed large herds of zebu cattle. About 1600 B. C. the Egyptian Pharaoh had a dream in which "there came up out of the river seven kine, fat-fleshed and well favoured; and they fed in a meadow". He also dreamed about growing grain. Joseph's interpretation is well known; these two dreams also suggest the two chief industries of the time.

By selective breeding the hump was eliminated in the Egyptian zebu cattle, while the same stock in

Mesopotamia still retained it. On the long, long trail from India to Egypt, much mixing of various strains occurred. The first cattle of the Assyrians had come from the north and were of Aurochs derivation, but when Sennacherib ruled Assyria longhorns of zebu ancestry were also common. When Tiglath-Pileser conquered Arabia and Palestine, he sent his cowboys' home with one herd of 50,000 captured cattle. Later, he secured 1,500 from Syria. Thus war and conquest played its part in the development of breeds of cattle.

The cattle of Egypt spread south into Africa, north into Spain, and thence across the Atlantic to the New World. Lydekker mentioned one ox in Africa whose horns had an expanse of eight feet, five inches; one horn measured four feet and eight inches along the curve. The Watusi giants, who live in the Belgian Congo, have developed a breed of sacred cattle, shown in Leila Roosevelt's film, *Dark Rapture*, which have horns measuring up to twelve feet from tip to tip. In the state of Sao Paulo the so-called Franqueiro cattle, descended from stock taken to Brazil from Andalusia in 1550 by Jean de Salazar, are said to exceed even the African cattle in the enormous spread of their horns. A German investigator stated that the long-horned cattle of ancient Egypt were identical with the cattle of southern Spain which had been carried thither by Phoenicians, Carthaginians, and Moors. Therefore the Texas and California longhorns can trace their ancestry back to the zebu cattle of India by way of Egypt. Today American cowboys attempt, usually with great futility, to ride longhorn and Brahma bulls at the many rodeos held at various places throughout the country. Perhaps neither they nor their highly amused audiences know that these cattle began their journey a long time ago from the same district, and have arrived at the same place after a long and circuitous route.[8]

The cattle of Egypt were light-brick red, light yellow, piebald, or dark reddish-brown in color; this was the color scheme of their descendants on the South American pampas and in the California valleys 4,000 years later. In the conformation of their bodies and in the length of their horns they were identical. Therefore King Tutankhamen would have noticed nothing incongruous had he stepped forth from his tomb in the Valley of the Kings and been transported straightway to the Valley of the Kings River in the days when a quarter of a million long-horn cattle roamed the San Joaquin Valley floor.

The rapid influx of immigrants into California during the gold rush stimulated the cattle industry. Miners need meat. One of the first to cater to this demand was a Spanish-California cattleman, Julian Ursua of *La Panoche de San Joaquin y Los Carrisalitos*, whose vaqueros drove herds across the plains from the San Joaquin river to the mines and sold beef at a handsome profit. Luis Peralta, owner of the grant now occupied by the cities of Oakland, Berkeley, and Richmond, called his sons together and dissuaded them from going to the mines. Said he: "Stay here and grow cattle and sell beef to the miners. You will find your gold mine right here at home." And the old patriarch was right.[9]

Cattle that had been worth $2.00 for their hides now became worth $35.00 for their beef. For the first time California cattle were sold by weight. A period of inflation followed, which proved fatal to the original Spanish-California grantees that had not been schooled in adversity and were therefore somewhat improvident. Many a rancher would give a boy a gold coin for merely holding his horse for a few minutes. Money was as cheap for a time as it was later to become about 1920, during the post-war inflation period. But while the demand lasted cattle were a source of wealth and other ranchers followed

Vaqueros dragging in a steer during the matanza, or slaughter day.
Edward Vischer, *Vischer's Pictorial of California.*

the example set by Ursua and Peralta. The growth of
coastal cities created another and still greater demand
which sent cattlemen surging into the valley.

The quality of the beef then available in California was
poor according to a newspaper article of the time:

> The beef and veal in San Francisco markets are rather
> inferior in quality to that found in the markets of the older
> cities in the Atlantic States, although they continue to
> improve in quality, great pains being taken to improve the
> stock imported from the Atlantic States, and there is no doubt
> but in a few years they will rival in quality any raised in
> older cities of the Union. Pork and mutton are abundant, but
> the quality might be greatly improved.[10]

The cattle selected to pull the prairie schooners across the
plains to California were of great size and strength; in
time they modified the range cattle of the West. In
addition to these draft animals, herds intended for
breeding purposes were also brought from their old home
in the East by the immigrants. These heavy, ponderous
cattle formed a decided contrast to the swift-running,
light-footed longhorns that they were eventually to

replace. The impression created by the arrival of a herd of these beef cattle has been well-expressed in Kipling's *Alnaschar and the Oxen:*

> Level-backed and level-bellied, watch 'em move—
> See those shoulders, guess that heart-girth, praise those
>   loins, admire those hips,
> And the tail set low for flesh to make above!
> Count the broad, unblemished muzzles, test the kindly,
>   mellow skin,
> And, where yon heifer lifts her head at call
> Mark the bosom's just abundance 'neath the gay and clean-
>   cut chin,
> And the eyes of Juno, overlooking all!

In 1849 Walter Crow of Missouri paid a visit to California. He decided to locate in the San Joaquin Valley. He returned to his native state and came back to California with his four sons and five hundred head of large Durham cattle. The term "beef cattle" is used in this discussion in preference to the more literary designation of "neat cattle". The word "neat" refers to bovine cattle collectively and is not to be confused with the word "meat". Crow's sons established a cattle ranch along Orestimba Creek, and Crow's Landing perpetuates the name of these pioneer cattlemen. Crow brought with him from Missouri perhaps the first large Winchester rifle seen in California and he used it skillfully and efficaciously in hunting grizzly bears. Tradition says it was this same gun which his grandson and namesake, Walter J. Crow, used with such deadly accuracy in the Mussel Slough fight.[11]

In 1852, E. Lodtman and F. Meinecke went to the East and returned to the northern San Joaquin with heavy beef stock for breeding purposes; these sold for $150.00 each. The same year William J. Kittrell also brought large American cattle, as they were called, into the Stanislaus region. Doctor John Marsh was a prominent rancher under both Mexican and American administrations and helped in improving stock. He had bought *Los Meganos*, near the present Brentwood and due east of Mt. Diablo, from José Noriega for $500; having no cattle, he resumed the practice of medicine, collected his fees in cows, and thus rapidly acquired a herd, which roamed, over his 50,000-acre estate. He was the first and only doctor in the valley at that time; perhaps no family physician during the horse and buggy age ever covered a wider territory or worked harder than he.[12]

In 1852 the *San Diego Herald* reported that "Mr. Caruthers informs us that there is a drove of about 1,200 head of Texas beef cattle on the road between here and the Colorado, which will be in next week. Part of them are already at Warner's Ranch." The same year, the correspondent of the *El Dorado Republican* wrote: "Immigrants continue to arrive daily. They are universally in good health, but look wearied, from the effects of their long and tiresome journey. A large amount of stock is also coming in, looking as a general thing in fine condition. Stock commands a fair price in this market." Evidently both northern and southern California were receiving importations of livestock from the older states.

One of the most important ranches in the northern part of the San Joaquin was the grant made to Alfias Basil Thompson in 1846. William Tecumseh Sherman, Fred Billings, A. C. Peachey, and Henry W. Halleck acquired this land on the Stanislaus after the Mexican War. Sherman was a banker at that time, and the other three men were all lawyers. All were residents of San Francisco but took an active part in the development of their San Joaquin Valley ranch; a few years later, Sherman and Halleck were to take leading roles in the Civil War.[13]

The region lying between the Tuolumne and the Merced Rivers was known as Paradise Valley; at an early date

100,000 acres of government land in this district came into the possession of John W. Mitchell. Turlock was founded on Mitchell's ranch. The latter was primarily a sheepman and used this type of livestock to clear the land of brush after which he sowed it to wheat. The coming of the railroad was to increase the value of land, and eventually this large estate was subdivided. After Mitchell's demise, the Fin De Siecle Investment Company was organized for the express purpose of handling the estate, a proportionate share of stock being given to each legatee.[14]

One of Mitchell's neighbors to the south was H. B. Stoneroad. He was one of the gold miners who saved his money and found it possible by 1853 to secure a large cattle ranch. He used the entire southern half of the present county of Merced as his grazing grounds. Prior to his becoming a cattleman, he had been a resident of Agua Fria. Other cattlemen in the general area to the south were Marshall D. Atwater, who settled near the present town of Atwater in 1869; J.M. Montgomery who settled first on the Merced in 1849, with Colonel Samuel Scott, and later near Bear Creek, in 1857; Charles V. Snelling, whose name is perpetuated by the modern Snelling; Harvey Ostrander of Planada; and Eleazer T. Givens, whose ranch along Mariposa Creek became the site of Merced's first county seat.[15]

The original owner of the Madera region was Isaac Friedlander, a San Francisco capitalist. Eastern promoters who subdivided their holdings and founded the John Brown Colony later secured part of his estate. William Chapman also acquired a large tract of land south of Madera. The Alabama Colony was later located on land originally held by Friedlander and Chapman. The big sheepman in the surrounding country was Ambrose Caldwell.[16]

Jefferson M. Shannon and S. B. Coffee engaged in the

raising of another type of livestock in 1854. They procured a ranch along the San Joaquin River between Fresno and the foothills. Shannon and Coffee catered to the desire of the Chinese, who dug for gold in the adjacent foothills, for pork. The two men waxed opulent due to their fair treatment of the Chinese; the latter were both astonished and gratified that there were white men who would be both fair and friendly. Later Shannon, a personal friend of the "Big Four," was given a position of responsibility with the Southern Pacific.[17]

The Chinese were not the only miners who asked for a change of diet. The American miners tired of constant meals of "bull mahogany," as they termed beef. The result was a rapid development of the hog-raising industry. The *Stockton Journal* for June 22, 1852 printed the following news item:

> The rearing of hogs is daily attracting increased attention in this section of the State, and has already become an important branch of business. The stock is rapidly increasing, and still the price of sows continues high. The importance of possessing animals of a superior breed is fully appreciated, and hogs of this description are eagerly sought after.
>
> A few days since we were invited by Mr. A. D. Wallace, the bookseller, on El Dorado street, to see two sows and a boar, of the celebrated Leicestershire breed, for which he paid $1,000 in San Francisco. They are by far the best-formed and heaviest hogs we have seen in this country. The weight of the three can not be far from 1,800 lbs. They were lately received direct from England, and are said to be the first of their kind imported. Mr. Wallace purchased at the same time a splendid Berkshire sow for $100. Those who succeed in getting this stock, to cross with hogs from China and the Pacific Islands, will be fortunate. There is no branch of business that pays more generously than the raising of animals from stock possessing most superior qualities.

The San Francisco *Daily Alta California* printed a

communication from Stockton on June 24, 1852:

> Stockton is becoming a town of some note as a stockbreeding
> place. Large herds of swine are driven there constantly. The
> city, says the *Journal*, is swarming with hogs, many of them
> owned by persons living in the country, who consider Stockton
> a good place for pork raising.

One of the men who took large droves of hogs to Stockton
and Sacramento was Bud Akers, a rancher at Centerville
along the banks of Kings River. He owned about 1,200
hogs, which were fed on grass and mast in winter and in
summer were taken to Tulare or Summit Lake, where
they were fattened on tule roots. On these drives to
summer feeding grounds, the hogs were driven only at
night; the hot summer days were always disastrous to
hogs on the march and for a peculiar reason. The hoofs of
the animals would become excessively hot, and if the
animals reached water during the day it was impossible to
keep them from plunging into it. When they emerged, the
suction generated by yanking their legs out of the mud
often caused the shells of the hoofs to come off due to the
peculiar formation of their pedal extremities.

Hog drives were made to the mines and as far north as
Sacramento. No other form of transportation existed, and
the hogs were forced to carry themselves. Men on
horseback, never dogs, were used on the drives and from
three to four hundred constituted the usual drove; more
hogs could not very well be fed along the way. The average
distance traveled was six miles daily; this enabled the
hogs to feed without loss of weight. When urban centers
were reached, the animals often lost their footing on the
slippery streets and the startled porcine brutes often
stampeded. At one time, 300 head stampeded for Akers in
Sacramento, and during the melee many were stolen;
some actually ran through the back doors of restaurants
in their terror and were soon served to the customers out

A large flock of sheep grazing in the Fresno County foothills, circa 1895. *The Interior (Fresno).*

in front without payment to the owner. In those days most of the hogs were razorbacks, called in the San Joaquin "tule splitters," but later Berkshire and Poland China boars were imported. Hog drives came to an end with the passage of the No Fence Law in 1874. Thereafter no feed was available along the trail.[18]

One of the chief sheepmen in the Fresno region was William Helm. He settled along Dry Creek in 1865 and grazed his sheep over the surrounding plains. At one time his bands numbered 22,000 sheep. In the San Joaquin a flock of sheep is always referred to as a band, and a shepherd is always called a sheepherder; a drove of horses is also called a band.[19]

Frank Dusy used the plains between Fresno and Kings River as a pasture ground for his band of 15,000 head. Dusy had come to California to dig for gold. He became one of the outstanding leaders of Fresno County and was at different times gold miner, rancher, photographer, oil promoter, sportsman, and soldier. During the Civil War he enlisted in Company H, 3rd California Volunteers, and saw service in Fresno and Merced counties. One time Dusy went hunting in the mountains and Dinkey, his pet dog, met a grizzly bear and immortality; the stream beside which he fell appears on the map as Dinkey Creek.[20]

William (Yank) Hazelton was one of the big cattlemen of the Upper Kings River region. Hazelton arrived in the Mariposa section in 1849 and became a gold miner and later a monte dealer. He soon invested in river bottomland, about four miles northeast of Centerville. This was in 1853. He subsequently went to southern California and Mexico to obtain herds of Spanish longhorn cattle. Thus he was one of the earliest cattle barons on upper Kings River; only Manuel Castro of the lower Kings River was ahead of him. Hazelton remained the undisputed ruler along the upper reaches of this river until Moses J. Church arrived in 1868 with a band of 2,000 sheep. Cattlemen and sheepmen have always fought over the open range. Cattle will not graze where sheep have been; hence the warfare. While Church was absent from his camp a group of cowmen, including Hazelton, tore down his cabin and corral, and let a herd of hogs destroy his provisions. At another time, according to Church, some of Hazelton's cowboys tried to kill him at the Centerville store. The cowboys said that one of their fellow buckaroos had a fistfight with Church and they did not really consider that fighting in those days. Finally Hazelton told Church to get out. He did. The sheep were moved farther down Kings River. Hazelton and the other cattlemen disliked sheep, sheepmen, settlers, and "sand lappers" in general on the assumption that they would destroy the open range and the cattle industry.[21]

Downstream from Hazelton's ranch were the joint holdings of Louis Haas and James S. Williams. Their ranch house, erected in the early sixties and still standing (1939), is typical of the California homes of that period. It is a low, one-story, whitewashed structure, with a veranda on all sides. Haas and Williams occupied it in the days before the Civil War; later it became the headquarters for the various ranches owned by Crawford W. Clarke in that section of the San Joaquin; it later became the residence of Peter Mueller, in whose backyard the Kingsburg Promotion Company erected its test oil well in the fall of 1931. Louis Haas was of Pennsylvania-Dutch extraction and his daughter, Pennsylvania Haas, became the wife of Walter J. Crow, who was to play a major role in the Mussel Slough fight.

In time Haas moved to the Mussel Slough country and Williams was left in sole charge of the sheep ranch. He borrowed money from Crawford W. Clarke and found himself unable to meet the payments when due. This led to a transfer of a part of the ranch to Clarke, "not by foreclosure on the mortgage, but by deed direct."[22]

For many years thereafter the territory located upstream from the railroad bridge south of Kingsburg and on the east side of the stream was known as the Clarke Ranch. The land lying west of the river in the vicinity of Clarke's Bridge was also added to this estate. Clarke also acquired thousands of acres in the Cross Creek section north of Goshen. When Miller & Lux were engaging Haggin & Carr in their gigantic legal duel over the Kern River lands, Clarke was an interested spectator in the San Francisco court room. Treadwell, who wrote a dramatized biography of Henry Miller, made this comment: "Crawford Clarke, a picturesque character who was driven by a desire to own land quite as strong as the motive that drove Henry Miller."[23] Clarke was interested in many things besides cattle but, in spite of his diversified interests, he must rank with Henry Miller as one of the greatest cattlemen of the San Joaquin.

East of the Clarke Ranch were located the joint holdings of Amaziah Clark and Robert Kennedy. The latter's daughter married an apprentice druggist at Traver named E.A. Cutter, who eventually founded the nationally known Cutter Laboratories at Berkeley. Kennedy had a brother-in-law named Ross who had been his partner in the carpenter business in San Francisco. In those days the state of California was disposing of its school lands and utilizing the proceeds in the development of educational facilities. This school land consisted of sections 16 and 36 in each township of 36 sections. Ross located on a school section east of Selma; Kennedy, on a similar section southwest of Dinuba. In more recent times the Ross and Kennedy schools marked the general locality of these early ranch headquarters. Both Ross and Kennedy expanded their holdings, and in time they agreed to consider Kings River the boundary line between their respective grazing grounds. Kennedy later formed a partnership with Amaziah Clark. The Clark-Kennedy Ranch comprised what later became known as the German-Mennonite Colony west of Dinuba.[24]

The nearest neighbor of Clark and Kennedy was Olli Skeene Wilson who first settled on Kings River in 1874, and relocated to the territory just south of the present site of Dinuba in 1877. Wilson had served during the Mexican War under General Zachary Taylor. In those days Kennedy, Clark, and Wilson could ride over the plains surrounding their ranches for hours and meet no one save an occasional Mexican vaquero.[25]

The Haas & Williams land between the Southern Pacific line and Burns Park was aquired by Francis Rea in 1874.

Vaqueros lassoing a steer. Edward Vischer, *Vischer's Pictorial of California.*

He was a progressive type of pioneer who kept abreast of his time and furnished constructive leadership. He saw the rise and the fall of the town named Cross Creek Switch (Grand View), its eclipse by the phenomenal growth of the city of Traver, and the less rapid but more permanent development of Kingsburg. These three places were located within a few miles of one another. Rea took an active part in the development of each. Unlike many of the early cattlemen, he cooperated with the new settlers and adjusted himself to new conditions. He aided in the building of the old "76 Canal", now the main artery of the Alta Irrigation District, and served for many years as a director of the latter. On April 12, 1875, he had the honor of opening the first headgate of the People's Ditch, which he had helped organize and construct. Francis Rea was successfully and successively a cattleman, wheat grower, dairyman, and fruit grower. In his later years this veteran of the Grand Army of the Republic became a great favorite with his young comrades of the American Legion.[26]

David Burris held the land lying down the river below Francis Rea. Burns Park indicates the general locality of his estate. Burris was one of the Forty-niners who in time turned cattleman. He returned to the East in 1852, drove a herd of cattle across the plains to California in 1856, and the next year located in Tulare county along Kings River. Eventually he sold his cattle for $75,000 and threw in the land for nothing. He removed to northern California, where he became a banker. After having organized several banks, including the ones at Santa Rosa and Ukiah, he returned to his original site along Kings River in 1884. The Burris ranch consisted of 4,160 acres.

Burris was an imposing man both physically and mentally. He proved to be a shrewd rancher, and riches crowned his efforts. During the summer months he employed forty men and kept ten mowers constantly at work in his hayfields. From a village of 500 Indians located on the ranch were secured cowboys who made annual cattle drives to San Jose. His thoroughbred racehorses were campaigned on every racetrack in California. Later he specialized in pacers and trotters.

The 76 Land & Water Company's canal needed a ditch to take away the surplus water. Burris built such a ditch with the understanding that all wastewater be turned down it to irrigate the Burris meadows. When the hayfields needed water the most, the owner found that his coveted water was being diverted into other fields. Perhaps the farmers near Traver had reasons why they did not want to donate water to him. They watched their dam night and day, and finally Burris led his men, including his giant Negro foreman, toward this dam with intent to blow it up. The farmers had built a triangular fort overlooking the dam, but the base of that triangle was open and unprotected. Two of the Burris sons tried to ride their horses across the ditch back of the fort. Their horses

A typical cattle-branding scene from the pre-American period of California history. Owen C. Coy, *Pictorial History of California.*

bogged down in the mud, but they continued on foot and threatened to shoot the farmers in the back. Among them was Francis Rea. Burris then ordered his Negro foreman to pull all the boards out of the head-gate. The farmers cheerfully promised the colored man instantaneous death and he fearfully ran away. For a brief space of time it seemed as if another Mussel Slough fight was about to begin but finally Burris, to his everlasting credit, ordered his men away. The water dispute was later settled amicably.[27]

Perry Phillips held much of the land between the Burris holdings and Kingston. He was a bitter foe of the "sand-lappers" and the Settlers' Land League. The latter organization he accused of burning one of his ranch houses which, at the time of the fire, was occupied by a renter named Hodges.[28]

Daniel Rhoads was one of the neighbors of Phillips. His land lay south of Kings River in the neighborhood of

Grangeville. Rhoads and his wife came to California from Illinois in 1846. He was one of the seven men who finally succeeded in rescuing the survivors of the ill-fated Donner party. Like most of the early Americans in the state, Rhoads had been a gold miner. When he had accumulated gold dust amounting to $8,000 he purchased a herd of cattle, drove them over the hills from Gilroy to lower Kings River, and became a cattleman.[29]

Below Kingston, John (Jack) Sutherland owned 14,000 acres on the south side of the river and several thousand acres on the north side. The latter part of his ranch he acquired from the original *Laguna de Tache* ranch belonging to Manuel Castro. Sutherland was an Englishman and a great cattleman who settled in the San Joaquin in 1857. When the state legislature enacted the famous "No Fence Law" in 1874, he made arrangements to fence his holdings on the south side of Kings River. William Sutherland, a nephew, was the majordomo of the ranch; he was sent to Stockton to purchase the necessary materials. As a result of this order, Simpson & Gray, lumber dealers at Stockton, shipped eighty carloads of fencing material to Kingsburg, from whence it was hauled by teams to the ranch. Although the railroad cars in use in 1874-5 were relatively very much smaller than those in use in 1939, this shipment of eighty carloads is undoubtedly the largest single shipment ever received at Kingsburg. The order consisted of 15,510 Coast redwood posts of an extra large size and 413,600 feet of Oregon pine boards. The latter were 1 1/2 inches thick, 8 inches wide, and 24 feet long, and entirely free from knots or other imperfections. The fence was built four boards high; no wire was used (barbed wire did not then exist) and was twenty-three miles and a half in length. Sutherland did not fence the land on the north side of the river, but relied on his riders to keep the cattle within bounds. When it is considered that in those days it cost $2,240 to fence 160 acres, it is easily understood why the cattlemen resisted so fiercely the passage of the "No Fence Law."

In 1874 Sutherland had 12,000 head of cattle on his land; he also had approximately 5,000 horses, and one dry summer he sent a band of 12,000 sheep to Texas; they were merely a part of his flock. Sutherland was the biggest taxpayer in Fresno County at that time. All of his livestock was shipped from Kingsburg.[30]

North of Kings River and directly opposite the ranches owned by Sutherland and by his neighbor John Heinlen was located the *Laguna de Tache*, granted to Manuel Castro in 1846, and patented to him on March 6, 1866, by the United States. The rise of land values and increased taxation made the subdivision of these huge land grants inevitable. The rapid shifting of ownership on the *Laguna de Tache* illustrates what happened to the other land grants and their Spanish-speaking California owners. On November 22, 1852, Castro sold two square leagues of his ranch to Jeremiah Clark, Edward W. Taylor, and Gustavus W. Beckh for $10,000; these men were the attorneys who had argued his case before the United States District Court. On January 29, 1857, Castro sold an additional two leagues to the same parties for $1,000; they, in turn, leased these four square leagues to John Sutherland on November 1, 1866. This lease expired in two years and on September 23, 1868, the lease was acquired by Edwin St. John, Theodore H. Hatch, and Richard M. Brangon. These men operated a cattle ranch under the name of St. John & Company.

A subsequent series of sales caused a rapid shifting of nonresident owners. James B. Haggin secured one square league on June 6, 1871, which he sold to Jeremiah Clark on September 8, 1872. On October 4, 1872, Hatch and

Brangon, partners to Edwin St. John, conveyed their shares to John and Alonzo Abbott. These two brothers, in turn, sold out to Edwin St. John on November 26, 1872.

Manuel Castro found himself in financial difficulties from time to time. At 2 P. M. on April 18, 1868, Sheriff James H. Walker sold the *Laguna de Tache* at public auction in front of the Courthouse in the town of Millerton to Jeremiah Clark for $20,000; Edward Kane was the plaintiff. No redemption was made within the specified six months and Castro's claim to the *Laguna de Tache* ended forever.

John Sutherland purchased several hundred acres of the *Laguna de Tache* ranch for which he paid $30,000; this deal was consummated on April 1, 1874. This land lay north of Kings River and was the portion of his huge ranch which Sutherland did not fence after the passage of the "No Fence Law"; he kept cowboys on its outskirts whose duty it was thenceforth to prevent cattle from straying.[31]

A large portion of the *Laguna de Tache* was leased by August and Adolph Heilbron, wholesale butchers of San Francisco, and a man whose great ambition it was to become a cattle baron, Sinon (not Simon) C. Lillis. He was a veteran of the Union Army and after the Civil War had bought and shipped mare mules to the sugar plantations of Louisiana. Mare mules, having less bare skin than geldings, possessed greater immunity against the gnats and flies of the tidewater country of the bayou state.

Lillis, in spite of being a newcomer into the West, soon became the dominant member of the firm. He bought range cattle in Mexico, shipped them to the ranch for fattening, and made big dividends for the firm. He began to irrigate the land, planted the first alfalfa in that region, and was also a banker. He and his foreman established a bank at Kingsburg in 1891, the first institution of its kind in that part of the valley. The dislike of the settlers for the

Vaqueros herding cattle on the California plains, in preparation for a rodeo. Edward Vischer, *Vischer's Pictorial of California.*

big cattlemen perhaps prevented them from patronizing the new bank.

> The Bank of Kingsburg had a rather interesting history. It was chartered on November 7, 1891, with S. C. Lillis, president, and W. S. Hopkins, cashier. It had $50,000 capital stock fully paid up. Seemingly Kingsburg did not offer the opportunities desired by its stockholders as a consequence of which the bank was moved to San Francisco in October, 1895, but it did not operate as a bank until 1903, at which time it opened as the Market Street Bank. It was closed by order of the bank commissioners on February 21, 1908."[32]

A daughter of Sinon C. Lillis, Helen C. Lillis, subsequently acquired interests in banks at Hanford, Lemoore, and Oroville. She became the first woman bank president in California. Her custom of signing all communications "H. C. Lillis" did not reveal her gender, and some histories of banking refer to H. C. Lillis as an able and enterprising man.[33]

Jeremiah Clark, who had acquired a large part of the *Laguna de Tache* ranch, finally passed away. His heirs, for a promissory note of $252,000, turned the land over to

Charles A. Laton and Llewellyn A. Nares. This deal was consummated on February 12, 1896. The origin of the names of the towns of Laton and Lanare is obvious. L. A. Nares was, like John Sutherland, an Englishman, and Laton was a San Francisco capitalist. They developed the land and brought in colonists.[34]

The land lying between Minkler and Visalia was leased or grazed over by Thomas Fowler, who was sent to the California State Senate as the representative of the cattle interests of the "cow counties" of the southern San Joaquin. Senator Fowler led the fight against the "No Fence Law" with great adroitness, but was defeated for re-election on this issue by Tipton Lindsey in 1874. Stephen Barton, editor of the *Visalia Delta*, used his paper effectively during the campaign in the support of the settlers and their candidates. The settlers and the sandlappers had located out on the plains away from the river and were experimenting with dry farming in the days before irrigation. The only hope of the cattle industry lay with Senator Fowler, who was an inveterate foe of the Southern Pacific Railway and battled valiantly against the land grants made to that corporation in the valley. Accused by his foes of being an ignorant "shanty Irishman," he nevertheless proved a man of much native intelligence.[35]

The cattlemen usually held the river bottoms and the river frontage. The settlers pre-empted a quarter section for which they paid $1.25 an acre, or they homesteaded eighty acres. They sowed grain and relied on the winter rains to provide moisture. This grain furnished a luscious feed that the cattle devoured with zest. Should the rancher enclose his cattle, or should the settler enclose his field? That was the issue in 1874. The cattlemen were the more powerful; the settlers, the more numerous. Ballots won. The "No Fence" bill was enacted into law. This naturally meant that no fence was required of the settler. Barbed wire had not then come into general use.

In 1861 a form of barbed wire had been introduced. But the tedious process of fastening barbs to plain strands of wire by hand made this fencing material too expensive for a large acreage. Joseph Glidden of De Kalb, Illinois, invented a barbed wire machine the same year that the "No Fence Law" was passed, but this machine-made product came just too late to influence the results of the "No Fence Law" in California. Lacking the relatively cheap barbed wire fence, which was destined to come into general use as soon as the Glidden invention had time to be manufactured in sufficient quantities, the San Joaquin Valley ranchers could use only board fences. Stephen Barton, the editor of the *Visalia Delta*, who had opposed the cattle barons, stated that the cost of fencing material at that time for 160 acres was $2,240. A few opulent cattlemen, like John Sutherland, were able to fence their holdings. But most of them were either forced to sell their big ranches, or engage in other forms of agricultural endeavor that required no fences.[36]

When the Central Pacific Railway had been built to a point just south of Fresno, Senator Fowler, who owned an immense acreage, drove his cattle to that point, built a corral, and loaded his stock on the cattle cars. This became known as Fowler's Switch; later it was shortened to Fowler. The Fowler cattle brand was a "76"; this name was applied to an irrigation district in Tulare County which had received a donation of land from the Senator. This company later became the Alta Irrigation District, but the main canal is still known as the "76".[37]

Senator Fowler's only son, Leonard B. Fowler, won international attention on April 16, 1920 when he filed a 7,000 word complaint against the decree of divorce granted by Judge Frank P. Langan of Minden, Nevada, on

March 2nd of that year, to Mrs. Owen Moore (Mary Pickford). Fowler was at that time Attorney General of Nevada and asked the court to set aside the decree.[38]

In 1857 Elijah T. Colvin, a native of Alabama, established a cattle ranch in the region due east of Visalia. The same year William Weldon and J. V. Roberts placed their stock in Walker's Basin and along the South Fork of Kern River. Their neighboring cattleman in the South Fork area was William W. Landers, George Clancy and J.L. Mack.[39]

A picturesque figure in early days near Visalia was Pat Murray. Aside from his skill as a cattleman, he enjoyed the distinction of having eliminated rival suitors in an original manner. A young lady of great charm and popularity resided with her parents on a ranch beside the affluent of the Kaweah River. A large log was used as the approach to the house over the stream. Murray thoroughly soaped this log, and then sat undisturbed on the front porch and heard his rivals periodically splash into the water during the long summer evenings.[40]

Harry Quinn, a native of North Ireland and a miner from Australia, was a pioneer stockman in the northern part of Kern County, east of Delano. He brought 8,000 sheep into the valley and acquired 20,000 acres of land. His son, John R. Quinn, who was the national commander of the American Legion in 1924, conveyed the following information after an interview with the elder Quinn:

> Dan Murphy brought the first well-bred cattle into the upper San Joaquin Valley, and a man by the name of Brannan also brought in some cattle. He was the man who built the first road into Mineral King. Jewett and Troy brought the first well-bred sheep into the valley, although Holby, after whom Holby's Meadows in the Sierras are named, imported some sheep from Vermont.
>
> My father came into the valley in '66, having brought a band

Cattle herd grazing in Kern County, circa 1910. Wallace Morgan, *History of Kern County, California.*

of sheep over from Gilroy over the Pacheco Pass, and settled around Alila and over where our old ranch is now.[41]

N. P. Peterson, a miner at Havilah, in 1864 became a cattleman along the South Fork of the Kern River. He was an enterprising citizen and secured a contract for carrying the United States mail over the route traveled by his line of stagecoaches.[42]

Staniford and Dunlap had their ranch headquarters in Linn's Valley. Their cattle ranged the foothills from Porterville to Tehachapi. Their neighbor to the south was General Edward F. Beale of Fort Tejon. His ranch extended from Tehachapi Pass to Tejon Pass. Beale was the officer who had introduced camels into the Southwest and who established the Sebastian Indian Reservation. The two old Mexican land grants of *El Tejon* (the ranch of the badger) and *Los Alamos y Agua Caliente* (the ranch of the cottonwoods and warm water) were included in Beale's ranch of 200,000 acres. When Abraham Lincoln refused to re-appoint Beale Surveyor-General of California and

Nevada he is said to have made the droll remark: "Beale becomes monarch of all he surveys."[43]

Colonel Thomas Baker arrived in the valley on September 20, 1863. The descriptive cognomen of Bakersfield suggests the location of Baker's field of 89,120 acres. Another Baker, Colonel R. H. Baker of Los Angeles, acquired the *Rancho de Castaic* in 1864 from Samuel A. Bishop, who had bought it from José Maria Covarrubias some years before. The ranch house was located at Fort Tejon. In time Baker and Beale found it profitable to join forces. A few years later (1874) they owned 10,000 cattle and 125,000 sheep.[44]

Considerable shifting of ownership occurred in this region until the concerted action of James B. Haggin and Lloyd Tevis consolidated land holdings and water rights. Then they entered into a battle royal for supremacy with the Miller & Lux enterprise. Each of the two rival forces claimed a prior right to the waters of Kern River which were essential "and the land was not able to bear them, that they might dwell together; for their substance was great, so that they could not dwell together; and there was a strife between the herdsmen of Abram's cattle, and the herdsmen of Lot's cattle." Finally, the owners realized that cowboys and six-shooters could not settle their difficulties, and the matter was settled in a San Francisco courtroom with the greatest legal talent in California arrayed for the fray.

James B. Haggin was a romantic figure. He was a Kentuckian of Arabian descent. The Bedouin Arab of the desert loves a horse; so does the bluegrass Kentuckian. Haggin was both and he did. He was one of the greatest horsemen and cattlemen of California. At one time he operated a thoroughbred-breeding establishment consisting of forty stallions and six hundred mares, all pedigreed. This exceeded in size and value any other similar establishment in Kentucky or elsewhere. His partner, Lloyd Tevis, was a capitalist of San Francisco.[45]

John McCray occupied the region south of Bakersfield. He and some partners drove 1,000 head of purebred Durham cattle across the plains from Missouri in the early fifties. Most of these cattle were placed on ranches in the northern part of the valley. McCray lived for a time along the Tuolumne River. Later he moved to Centerville along Kings River, and finally, in 1859, he built a ranch house three miles south of the present city limits of Bakersfield. Two hundred Durhams were taken to this locality.

In the vicinity of Bakersfield a tenderfoot was sold 110 bull calves and solemnly assured that they would form an excellent nucleus for a herd of cattle. A year later, the victim came to town with 1,200 head of fat cattle that he asserted with equal solemnity to be the increase from his 110 bull calves. Evidently he had not remained a tenderfoot long. Thenceforth he rejoiced in the cognomen of "Bull" Williams.[46]

The old *San Emidio* land grant, at one time in the possession of John C. Fremont, was later owned for a time by Fremont's old scout, Alexis Godey. The house, which he built and first occupied in 1885, is still standing (1939). Don David Alexander acquired another portion of this grant in 1861. Soon his 20,000 Spanish cattle grazed over the foothills from Tejon Pass west to the Temblor Range and down the valley floor to Buena Vista and Kern Lakes; they also ranged along the lower reaches of Kern River. McCray's herd of Durhams was rapidly increasing, and Alexander purchased all of the bull calves that were eventually mated to his Spanish cows.[47]

In the southwestern corner of the San Joaquin Valley, around Temblor, J. C. Crocker had entered into a loose partnership with Henry Miller. When Crocker felt old age coming on, he asked for a reckoning and wanted to dissolve the partnership. Miller objected. Finally he sent Crocker to the main office, where the latter was informed to his amazement that he owed the firm $100,000. However, this story may be apocryphal because Crocker finally secured one of the finest Miller & Lux ranches in the Kern River delta and another near Panama (just south of Bakersfield). The first was known as the Crocker Ranch thenceforth; the second as the Balfour-Guthrie.[48]

North of Tulare Lake and Kings River a man named Cuthbert Burrel established the Elkhorn Ranch. Burrel was the grandson of an English squire, had served with Fremont, had been a gold miner, and in 1860 had moved from Solano to the region mentioned with 1,311 cattle. The Elkhorn Ranch consisted of 20,000 acres and the present sites of Burrel and Elkhorn suggest the general location. Cuff Burrell, a relative of the pioneer Burrel, later maintained the spirit of the Old West in a modern fashion on his ranch near Hanford. He provided outlaw horses and Brahma steers for the rodeos held throughout the nation. He furnished this type of stock for the rodeo and wild west show held at the World's Fair at Chicago in 1933, where he was named All-Around Champion Cowboy.[49]

Jefferson Gilbert James was of Virginian ancestry. He was one of the Argonauts and, by 1857, had found enough gold to buy 960 cows. These he took to the "25" Ranch near Kingston and pastured them along Kings River and the San Joaquin. In 1858 he rounded up his stock and moved them to a plot of ground consisting of 60,000 acres along Fresno and Fish sloughs. He sold beef to the miners until 1867. Then he entered the wholesale meat business in San Francisco. However, he still retained the so-called James Ranch. This was subdivided after the World War.[50]

The land lying to the east of Burrel's Ranch was devoted

to sheep. William T. Cole, who had come from Missouri in 1849, brought the first band of sheep into Fresno County; this was in 1862. Besides his own sheep he handled those owned by Edwin St. John. His camp was maintained in the Laton area. From that point the wool was hauled to Stockton by wagon. In 1868 he cut a trench south of Kingsburg in order to divert a stream of water from Kings River for his livestock. The flood of that year, angrily tossing its yellow mane, came down one night in a fury and tore through the trench forming a new channel, known since that time as Cole Slough. The latter has carried the main current since that time and rejoins the old bed of Kings River just below the bridge that spans the river, about six miles due north of Hanford. Some time later Cole moved up the river and built a brick residence on the north bank of Kings River midway between Reedley and Sanger. The Millerton courthouse was under construction at the same time, and the windows not used in the courthouse went into the Cole residence.[51]

In 1876 the Kreyenhagen family acquired a large tract of land in the vicinity of Kettleman Hills. Their cattle ranch, known as the Posa Chené, was incorporated and four brothers, Emil, Charles, Hugo, and Adolph, were engaged in its management. Their general store located on the ranch was the trading center for the entire Pleasant Valley prior to the founding of Coalinga. On this ranch was located much potential oil land and the family name has been indelibly impressed on the oil industry of the state by being applied to the Kreyenhagen Hills and the Kreyenhagen shale.[52]

The "down-east" Yankees have always been considered hardheaded but in the early years of the nineteenth century they developed an incomprehensible mania for the possession of Spanish merino sheep. C. A. Stephens, in his "Stories of the Old Farm" in Maine, which were published originally in the *Youth's Companion*, related the fabulous prices paid by his grandfather and other New Englanders for these animals. The merinos were developed by the Spanish from fine-wooled sheep introduced from Africa by the Moors. Yankee skippers first brought them to New England. In 1802 Colonel David Humphrey, then in Spain, sent merino sheep to his farm in Connecticut. His writings and political influence popularized the breed. Between April 1, 1810, and August 31, 1811, the New England farmers imported 19,651 merino sheep from Spain.

Samuel Brannan, the founder of the Mormon colony along the Stanislaus River in 1847, returned to his native New England in 1857 and brought back with him from Vermont a flock of these sheep. Some of them were acquired by Alfred Stonesifer, who operated a large sheep ranch along the Stanislaus and the San Joaquin rivers. In the neighborhood of Hill's Ferry Richard M. Wilson owned 16,000 acres known as the Quinto Ranch; this was stocked with 7,500 sheep. In 1857 another big sheepman in the Stanislaus River country was John Carpenter.[53]

Besides the importation of merinos from the East, other importations arrived from other places. The *Placerville Herald* stated in July 1853, that Robert Cary had sent fourteen men with 1,800 Spanish merinos from Taos, New Mexico, to California; 50 were lost on the way. The *San Diego Herald* during the same year reported: "There have been entered at the Custom House here, during the past week, over 35,000 sheep which have been driven in from Sonora." Even Kit Carson, after the depression hit the trapping business as a result of the invention of the silk hat, became a sheepherder and devoted himself for a time to driving sheep to California.

The greatest cattleman in the San Joaquin Valley measured in terms of acreage and astuteness was Heinrich Alfred Kreiser. When he was a little peasant lad in Germany, he herded pigs and calves. One day he lay in the grass watching his charges and, like Little Boy Blue, he fell fast asleep. His mind went on a journey and he saw countless herds of cattle with a double H (H. H.) mark on their left hips. Such marks and such long horned cattle had never been seen in all Germany. Suddenly a huge, long-horned bull prodded him and he awakened to find a little calf playfully disturbing his slumber. The telling of his dream aroused the jeers of those who heard it, excepting only his mother. But the vision persisted. Might not one "H" represent Heinrich; what about the other? He was puzzled. No Joseph appeared to interpret his vision.

This boy eventually went to New York, worked in a meat market, met an American-born German shoe salesman named Henry Miller, and when the latter was unable to utilize his ticket to California, Heinrich Kreiser bought it at a reduced price and went by boat via Panama to San Francisco. The ticket carried the name Henry Miller and was non-transferable. So Kreiser became Miller and Miller became the guiding genius of Miller & Lux, and Miller & Lux became the cattle kings of the San Joaquin Valley. The accidental change in name seemingly brought also a change in good fortune.

The new Henry Miller arrived in San Francisco with $6.00, secured a job in a butcher shop, made and peddled sausages; and finally decided in order to improve the quality of beef that he must become a producer as well as a retailer and wholesaler. One day he saw a hide and on its left hip was the Double H! Was he a little boy back in Germany fast asleep?

Later on, Miller must have reached the *Sanjon de Santa Rita* ranch somewhat agitated. But he did not show it. He calmly discussed with Henry Hildreth, a fourth owner of the ranch, the local conditions of the cattle industry. Hildreth was dissatisfied; he wanted to go back to the gold

Henry Miller, the undisputed "Cattle King" of both California and the San Joaquin Valley. Hubert Howe Bancroft, *Chronicles of the Builders*, III.

mines. He offered to sell his 8,835 acres for $1.15 an acre and his 7,500 cattle for $5.00 each. With his cattle would go the Double H (Henry Hildreth) brand. Miller accepted—after awhile. He could not be hurried, even to make dreams come true.

This visit to the valley was made in 1857; the big cattlemen then in the valley were men of importance. Across the valley from Miller's new ranch lay *Las Mariposas*, then occupied by John C. Fremont. Along the Stanislaus River William Tecumseh Sherman was a joint owner of a big ranch. Far to the south, in territory soon to be invaded by Miller, Edward Fitzgerald Beale owned 200,000 acres. On his return to San Francisco Miller visited a cattleman, a tall Alsatian named Charles Lux, whose ranch lay along Baden Creek. At that time they were competitors in the markets of San Francisco. Soon they were to pool their interests, increase their holdings, and make the firm of Miller & Lux famous. They agreed on a policy of buying and never selling land. Each man possessed what the other lacked, and the combination proved irresistible. The first land purchased by Miller in the San Joaquin was Hildreth's interest in the *Sanjon de Santa Rita*, which had originally been granted to Francisco Soberanes about sixteen years before Miller made his purchase.[54]

Congress passed the Swamp Land Act on September 28, 1850, and under its provisions the State of California acquired 2,000,000 acres of so-called overflow land. This land sold for $1.25 an acre with the provision that if the purchaser would prove before the Board of Supervisors that he had spent $1.25 an acre on reclamation the purchase price would be refunded. Miller took advantage of this opportunity and built innumerable ditches and canals for the draining of land contiguous to the rivers on the west side of the valley. Claus Spreckels, a fellow German, offended Miller at one time and the latter sought revenge. Spreckels, a San Francisco banker, had demanded security on a loan needed by Miller. A few years later Spreckels proposed to build a railroad down the west side of the valley in order to compete with the "Octopus," as many people then called the Southern Pacific. Miller gladly granted Spreckels a right-of-way through his overflow land, and Spreckels built a high road bed a hundred miles in length. Then Miller granted another right-of-way along a higher, dryer and better route to the powerful Southern Pacific. Spreckels was forced to withdraw, but the hundred miles of grade remained and Miller had a huge levee to hold the overflow water in check. It had been donated by his enemy.[55]

According to certain legends, many a rancher in those days placed a boat on a wagon, sat in the boat, and then proceeded to drive merrily over many square miles of territory. Then he could truthfully swear before any court that he had ridden over the land in a boat. In due time proper officials would inspect the land and, finding it dry,

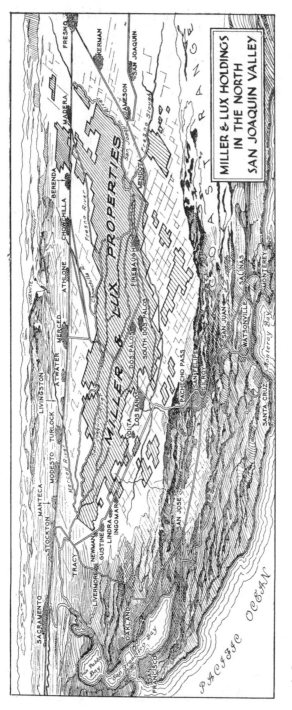

Garden of the Sun,
1939 edition.

would assume that it had been reclaimed. Land was relatively cheap then and official supervision scanty or indifferent. Therefore this form of reclamation might have been possible.

In 1871 the San Joaquin and Kings River Canal and Irrigation Company was organized. Capitalists were interested in the promotion of the project and stock was sold. The venture proved abortive. The Fresno scraper had not yet been invented, and the old style slip scraper made the work difficult. Finally, the company quit in disgust, and Miller acquired control for one-third of the money already spent on the canal by the promoters. Miller completed the canal, which was an important step not only in the progress of his own ranching operations, but in the development of irrigation in the valley.

Miller not only dealt with big projects; he was also a master of details. When he visited one of his ranches and saw mice he procured cats, sent them to the place, and when the mice had been destroyed, he ordered the manager to box the cats and ship them to another ranch. Gradually his holdings extended into the southern San Joaquin, where he fought over the water rights to Kern River with Haggin & Carr. Leaders of the California bar wrangled over riparian rights while the greatest cattlemen in the world listened impassively in a San Francisco courtroom. During the progress of the trial, Miller proved as skillful on the witness stand as on the cattle range. But he suffered a nervous breakdown, went to Germany on a visit in order to recuperate, and found himself famous in his native land. The Franco-Prussian war had just been fought, and a new Emperor had been crowned at Versailles. Henry Miller had a long interview with the creator of the German Empire, Prince Otto von Bismarck. Honors were showered upon him. A street was named after him in his native city. Then he returned to

California and learned that he had lost his case. For this he blamed his partner. Then Miller took charge. And won. When the trial was over, the papers and documents relating to it made a stack four feet high.

Miller remained an active figure in California until the Panama-Pacific Exposition held at San Francisco in 1915. The next year he passed away. The little boy from the Black Forest of Germany left to his heirs two large banks and their branches, many reservoirs and irrigation systems, a million cattle, and deeds to a million acres which carried with them control of many times that amount of land. The dream of his boyhood had been abundantly realized.[56]

The foregoing cattlemen and sheepmen were some of the prominent men in the livestock industry after the American occupation. In most cases, they bought government land and were therefore the first private landowners in their respective localities. In 1853, the counties in the San Joaquin Valley reported that they had 15,621 head of cattle. Seven years later, 226,248 cattle roamed the valley floor and the adjacent foothills, and the sheep in the same area numbered 78,568. In 1870, the cattle had increased to 288,483 and the sheep to 901,892. The report by counties showed that the livestock industry was rapidly moving southward and in time the southern counties were derisively called the "cow counties of the southern San Joaquin."[57]

Four things were to terminate the ascendancy of this form of development: first, overstocking of the range; second, drought; third, a fall in prices; and fourth, the passage of the "No Fence Law." When this law was enacted, it meant that a majority of the voters had determined that no fence would be required of the farmers; henceforth, the cattle barons would be held responsible for damages done by their stock. They were forced to either fence their land, or

Early-day California vaqueros roping wild horses on the plains. Edward Vischer, *Vischer's Pictorial of California.*

employ enough cowboys to herd their stock night and day. The latter was physically impossible; in most cases the cost of the former alternative was prohibitive. The open range in California came to a definite close. On the great plains it continued for another generation, and then the invention of the relatively cheap barbed-wire fence made it possible for the homesteader and the nester to fence his fields; thus the open range came to an end in that region in an entirely different fashion. Immediately after 1874, men in the San Joaquin Valley began to turn their energies to other things and the era of the open range came to a close.[58]

The cattle industry, although the open range passed away, continued to be much alive. As the years went on people became increasingly more conscious of the romance to be found in this occupation. Visalia inaugurated an annual Frontier Day celebration, which has compared favorably for many years in color and picturesqueness with similar affairs held at Cheyenne and Pendleton. It has attracted the presence of the state's governor and the elite from

Hollywood's moving picture colony. Clay Carr of Visalia and John Bowman of Oakdale are among the nation's greatest riders; each has been crowned one or more times the national champion broncho buster by the Rodeo Association of America.[59] Large ranches are not a thing of the past, although they are all enclosed by barbed wire fences. They are to be found even in the raisin country. In the San Francisco *Call-Bulletin* for January 15, 1932, was found the following news item: "Fresno, Jan. 15. Jack Holt, film star, today announced he had acquired a partnership with C. E. Green, wealthy San Joaquin Valley rancher, in a 20,000 acre cattle ranch near Fresno." Millerton, the first capital of Fresno County, was located on this ranch and the ranch house was formerly the headquarters building of old Fort Miller.

George Weston Pierson founded the Pierson Dude Ranch, the first establishment of its kind in California, in 1912. It consists of over 1,500 acres and is located in Wonder Valley, thirty-four miles east of Fresno, on the west slope of the Sierra Nevada mountains. Guests have registered at this ranch from every state in the union and from seven foreign countries.[60]

The saddle used by the stockman was an important part of his equipment; it was in fact his throne. All stock saddles were derived from the Spanish saddles brought over by Cortez in 1519 which, in turn, traced back to the heavy saddles used by medieval knights. An Englishman riding a flat park saddle was astonished, when he first visited the West, to see a stock saddle with its high horn. He ridiculed it by saying he would hate to have to ride to hounds in that thing and try to jump a fence. The long stirrups would catch in the fence, and the big horn would puncture the rider's belly. To which the cowboy retorted, "I'll jump as many fences in this saddle as you will rope cows with your postage stamp."

The first improvement in the stock saddle was made at Hornitos in 1868 in the harness and saddle repair shop maintained there by Juan Martarell. A Spanish saddle of the type then in common use was brought in for repairs and inspected by Ricardo Mattley, one of the workmen in the shop and a native of Sonora, Mexico. He disliked the construction of the saddle, re-built the tree, and so pleased the owner that other riders began to beg for the same improvements. In 1869 his employer, Juan Martarell, moved to Visalia, then the center of the cattle business, and opened the Visalia Saddle Works. Mattley went along and, for more than twenty years, built every tree that went into the famous Visalia saddle. His under-study and later his successor was Cipriano Martinez.

In addition to building a better tree, stronger and more comfortable for the horse, Mattley added the skirt that prevented the rider's legs from becoming chafed. The cantles were made from Visalia oak, the sidepieces from Kaweah willows, and the fork and horns from oak crotches secured from the woodchoppers about Visalia. In the days before the shop was removed to San Francisco, men from Idaho and Montana often rode to Visalia after the fall round up to secure the famous Visalia saddles. Today they are used by American cowboys, Canadian riders, Mexican vaqueros, and South American gauchos.

Another young workman who accompanied Martarell from Hornitos to Visalia was Alsalio Herrera, who had learned to make bits and spurs, both plain and silver mounted, in his father's blacksmith shop in Hornitos. Both he and Mattley moved to San Francisco with the shop, and the former worked for the Visalia Saddle Works until 1928 when failing eyesight caused him to retire.

The moving of the business from Visalia to San Francisco took place gradually after 1887 and into the early 1890s. An official of the company gave the following explanation:

321

Our reason for moving from Visalia to San Francisco was to get closer to the shipping center, as our saddles were getting so much in demand that we were shipping to practically every section of the Western country, besides foreign countries. Today the D. E. Walker Visalia saddles are to be found among the equipment of the lowliest ranch house, as well as in the elaborate tack rooms of royalty.[61]

In order to be equipped for work a cowboy needed a Western stock-horse, a Visalia saddle, a Colt's revolver, a Stetson hat, and a pair of Levi overalls. These jeans were named after Levi Strauss, a dry-goods wholesaler, who landed in San Francisco in 1850 with a shipment of denim overalls. These were sold to miners, who found that they kept ripping in the hand-stitched seams. One of them, Alkali Ike of Virginia City, Nevada, made five visits to his tailor, a man named Davis, and the latter, infuriated by Alkali Ike's sarcastic remarks about the stitches, took the pants to the blacksmith and had them riveted. To his amazement, the other miners liked the idea and demanded that he put copper rivets in the corners of their pockets also, regardless of cost. Davis made a trip to San Francisco and convinced Strauss that he should rivet the overalls at the factory. This was done, and Strauss also made an additional improvement by discarding the baggy pantaloons and cutting his overalls thenceforth from regular dress trouser patterns. These Levis, tailored and streamlined and copper-riveted, caught the eyes of the cowboys and became standard equipment on the range.[62]

Perhaps no group of men in the United States ever developed a greater pride in their occupation than did the old-time cattlemen. Neither has any other group appealed quite so much to the imagination of American youth. The moving picture industry has found that a type of picture, known to their trade as "a Western," is a certain moneymaker. Their very assurance in this respect has prevented them from employing the most skilled directors in such productions; the subject has been enough to insure capacity houses. The open range, the stampedes, the longhorned cattle, the rambunctious horses, and the gaily caparisoned cowboys who are usually depicted performing strange gymnastics on the screen, have furnished an atavistic symbolism which city-bred youth could enjoy vicariously. The contempt of the cattlemen for the homesteaders, the nesters, and the sheepmen was measured by the pride they had in the dignity of their own vocation. The cow was supreme.

> If civilized people were ever to lapse into the worship of animals, the Cow would certainly be their chief goddess. What a fountain of blessings is the Cow! She is the mother of beef, the source of butter, the original cause of cheese, to say nothing of shoehorns, hair combs, and upper leather. A gentle, amiable, ever-yielding creature, which has no joy in her family affairs which she does not share with man. We rob her of her children that we may rob her of her milk, and we only care for her when the robbing may be perpetrated.[63]

Cattlemen have been the forerunners of civilization since the days when Abraham, Laban, Jacob, and Lot herded cattle along the Jordan River in the Holy Land. Clustered about the industry and the men who engaged in it are startling tales of daring, courage, romance, and war. Badger Clark, the favorite poet of the cowboys, wrote *From Town*, which contains the following lilting lines:

> Since the days when Lot and Abram
> Split the Jordan range in halves
> Just to fix it so their punchers wouldn't fight,
> Since old Jacob skinned his dad-in-law
> Of six years crop of calves
> Then hit the trail for Canaan in the night,
> There has been a taste for battle
> 'Mongst the men who follow cattle,
> And a love of doing things what's wild and strange.

323

And the warmth of Laban's words
When he missed his speckled herds
Still is useful in the language of the Range.

In that kaleidoscopic procession of figures woven into the
tapestry depicting the development of the San Joaquin
Valley, the old-time cattleman was the most picturesque.
He can be seen following the Indian, the Franciscan friar,
the Spanish soldier, the Hudson's Bay and Rocky
Mountain fur trapper, and the topographical engineer
through the San Joaquin Valley, tarrying for a brief period
of time, and then moving over the western hills until his
silhouetted figure is lost to view beyond the waving
skyline. He has fought a good fight, and he has finished
the course. Through it all he has been diligent in his
work, true to his calling, and faithful even in little things.

He was twenty-five years a cow-puncher,
And never did things by the halves,
And the last thing he said
On his dying bed
Was to round up the cows and the calves. [64]

11   The Iron Horse

Said the Central: "I'm Pacific;
But, when riled, I'm quite terrific.
Yet, today we shall not quarrel,
Just to show these folks this moral,
How two Engines—in their vision—
Once have met without collision."
Bret Harte *What the Engines Said.*

"I am going to be elected the next governor of California and as soon as elected I shall kick the Southern Pacific Railway out of politics." This prediction was uttered with convincing earnestness by a famous San Francisco lawyer. The time was the autumn of 1910, the place was a small town in the San Joaquin Valley, and the audience was composed of a motley gathering of fruit-growers, cattlemen, small-town businessmen, and high school students excused from their classes in the little rural high school for the occasion.

This candidate for political preferment had become nationally known during the famous trial at San

Francisco that finally resulted in the conviction of Eugene E. Schmitz, mayor of San Francisco and Abe Ruef, a political boss. Now he promised to cleanse the entire state of corruption. He spoke in such a fashion that day that many a farmer, dulled by toil, understood his meaning and gained new hope for the future. Frequently political candidates make glorious promises while haranguing the crowds on the hustings and then, after election, suffer a lapse of memory forthwith. But Hiram Johnson was different.

The development of the San Joaquin Valley was made possible largely through the instrumentality of the Southern Pacific Railway. Then why should threats of a political nature arouse so much enthusiasm among the voters of that region? Let us see.

One evening in 1861 a hardware merchant, two dry goods merchants, and a lawyer held a meeting in the back room of a hardware store on K Street, Sacramento. These men were Collis P. Huntington and Mark Hopkins, owners of the hardware store where the meeting was held; Leland Stanford and Charles Crocker, owners of a general merchandise store. The previous year Stanford had been a delegate to the National Convention of the Republican Party at Chicago and had cast his vote for Abraham Lincoln. He was destined to be the war governor of California, and during the nineties he served as a United States Senator. With the exception of Hopkins, who had studied law, they were all uneducated; without exception, they were all poor. They were to become the "Big Four" of the Central Pacific Railway and were to dominate California politics for the next half century. Each man was unique in at least one respect. Huntington was a financial genius; Stanford, an incomparable political manipulator; Crocker, a splendid manager of men; and Hopkins, the possessor of an uncommon amount of common sense. Each possessed a tremendous energy, a dominant will, and a great vision. All were natives of New York and of New England Yankee descent. Never did four men co-operate more effectively to secure their desired ends.[1]

While these four men were preparing to connect California with the eastern states by rail, another group of men determined to construct a railway within the state itself. Their proposed road was to extend from San Francisco to San Diego through the counties of Santa Clara, Monterey, San Luis Obispo, Tulare, Los Angeles, and San Diego. These men who incorporated the Southern Pacific were T. G. Phelps, C. I. Hutchison, J. B. Cox, B. W. Hathaway, William T. Coleman, J. W. Stephenson, Benjamin Flint, W. S. Rosencranz, Charles N. Fox, and B. G. Lathrop. The Southern Pacific Railroad Company, as they named their organization, was incorporated on December 2, 1865; a map was filed with the General Land Office on January 3, 1867, which designated the proposed route through the valley; this route was approved by Congress on June 28, 1870.[2]

In the meantime, a small local railroad had been organized which bore the name of the San Francisco & San Jose Railroad Company. Its name indicates its route. On April 21, 1868, this little road was acquired by the Southern Pacific, and the latter then made immediate provisions for extending the newly acquired road from San Jose to Gilroy. The following July 11, the "Big Four" of the Central Pacific in turn secured control of the Southern Pacific. The annual report of the Southern Pacific, transmitted to the Secretary of the Interior on September 25, 1866, was prepared by Collis P. Huntington, vice-president of the Central Pacific. On December 31, 1869, the Central Pacific began construction of a road into the San Joaquin Valley.[3]

Comparative map illustrating the initial routes built through the San Joaquin Valley by the Southern Pacific, San Francisco/San Joaquin Valley and Atchison, Topeka and Santa Fe railroads. *Stuart Daggett, Chapters in the History of the Southern Pacific.*

Stockton had originally been selected by the Central Pacific as its junction, but the city refused to make as liberal donations of land and money as the "Big Four" demanded. The result was that the latter surveyed and laid out a new railroad town that they named Lathrop in honor of Stanford's wife, whose maiden name had been Lathrop. The building of a railroad into the valley was begun at this point.[4]

Building operations were pushed rapidly, and by the end of 1870, the rails had been laid to the Stanislaus River.

During the month of September of that year a hundred mechanics were busily engaged in constructing a bridge across this river, while a hundred Chinese were grading south from the river. The editor of the Tuolumne *News* wrote in his paper on September 2, 1870: "The locomotive runs as far south as the Stanislaus River and looks bravely into Stanislaus County as if anxious to try his speed through the wheat fields of Paradise."[5]

No land grants were given to the Central Pacific in the San Joaquin Valley. Therefore the railroad financed itself in the building of the road from Lathrop to Goshen. When the latter point was reached new conditions developed which will be considered in due time. The directors of the Southern Pacific purchased 160 acres along the north bank of the Tuolumne River and laid out a town that they named Ralston in honor of one of the directors. The new town did not long exist under the name of Ralston because William C. Ralston refused to permit his name to be used and his modesty in the matter caused a group of assembled citizens to re-christen the town Modesto. The next year this railway town succeeded Knight's Ferry as the capital of Stanislaus County.[6]

The amazing construction work which had carried the Central Pacific across the Sierra and over the deserts to Promontory, Utah, where the former road had been connected with the Union Pacific, had been under the personal direction and supervision of Charles Crocker. This had been completed on May 10, 1869; thereafter he was free to turn his men and energies into the San Joaquin. The result was that the laying of rails proceeded rapidly southward and the railway towns of Merced, Fresno, Kings River Switch, and Grandview came into existence. Kings River Switch was the name of the station, but local denizens referred to it as Draperville; Grandview was always called Cross Creek, although the

old maps all show the name of the station to be Grand
View. The latter was the first regular stop south of
Fresno, and was located midway between Traver and
Goshen; it is not to be confused with the Butterfield stage
station of the same name, which lay about two miles to
the west.[7]

During the late summer of 1872, the Central Pacific had
extended its valley line to the survey of the route
originally proposed by the Southern Pacific. This point
was given the name of Goshen. This junction, a hundred
and forty-six miles south of Lathrop, marked the southern
point of construction done in the valley under the name of
the Central Pacific. The government had given to the
original Southern Pacific a grant of land consisting of ten
alternate sections of land on each side of their road for
each mile constructed. In order to take advantage of this
grant, the Central Pacific directors continued their
building operations south from Goshen under the name of
the Southern Pacific, the little road that they had
acquired some time before 1868.[8]

In recent times, men have marveled or complained anent
the generous donations of land made by the United States
to the railway companies. But in those days only the most
optimistic hopes and enthusiastic visionaries could prompt
any corporation to project a railroad into the San Joaquin.
The great, broad plains were unoccupied save for the few
stockmen then residing there. The lonely rancher lived
out of sight of his nearest neighbor in that sparsely
settled world. Leland Stanford, accompanied by Mark
Hopkins and their engineers, rode horseback over the
proposed route. They carried their provisions on pack-
mules and camped out. They saw no signs of habitation,
save an occasional sheepherder's cabin or a lonely ranch
house. Between Lathrop and Los Angeles were only three
towns of any importance on the valley floor. Visalia, a

station on the Butterfield Overland Mail, had become a
cowtown catering to that industry in the central part of
the valley. It had also been the outfitting place for the
miners going to the Kern River mines. Bakersfield was
the cowtown of the southern part of the valley. It was
merely a hamlet with a few stores and saloons. Kingston,
located along lower Kings River, was originally a station
along Butterfield's stage line. A few stores and saloons
catered to the wants of the cowboys of the surrounding
ranches. The prosperous modern cities of the San Joaquin
were born as railroad towns and owe their development to
that new mode of transportation.

Undoubtedly the "Big Four" had faith in the future of the
valley. They must have caught a vision of a teeming
countryside dotted with happy homes and thriving cities.
They planned to attract farmers and orchardists who
would ship their goods to market over the road which they
were providing. The government furnished no loans or
land grants in the territory north of Goshen. The Central
Pacific paid its own way. The raw country at that time
gave no indication of the vast volume of traffic that would
later bring profits to the coffers of the company. Therefore
it would be unfair and ungenerous to deny that the
directors of the company built their road with hope, faith,
and borrowed money. They deserve much credit.

One of the railroad town sites platted and surveyed in
1872 received the name of Fresno. Stanford reputedly
traveled through the valley and selected town sites. At
first he planned to make Sycamore Point along the San
Joaquin River the chief town of the central part of the
valley. He also seriously considered placing his railway
yards and roundhouse at the site of modern Kingsburg.
The subsequent selection of the barren plain with water
no nearer than the San Joaquin River, ten miles away,
was due to Stanford's appreciation of the action of another

The first locomotive to enter the new town of Reedley, Fresno County. *Garden of the Sun,* 1939 edition.

visionary. In March, 1872, he journeyed over the Fresno area and saw the plans for irrigation then under way. Moses J. Church had succeeded in bringing water from Kings River by way of the Fancher Creek channel to a 2,000-acre wheat field which appeared that summer as a green oasis in a dry and dreary waste. The sight of this grain field proved two things to Stanford. First, the soil was of good quality; and second, irrigation would transform the arid region into a fertile and productive community. He promptly chose the vicinity of this grain field as the site of one of his new railroad towns.

Jefferson M. Shannon was appointed land agent for the company in that part of the valley. However, few persons at that time shared the dreams of the promoters concerning the future of the proposed city. When choice lots were offered for sale at a public auction, there were few bidders. A town can hardly exist without residents, and therefore the Central Pacific directors permitted men to settle on the townsite without purchasing lots. The understanding was that if they chose to remain they must eventually pay for their sites.[9]

As soon as a section of the new railroad was completed, a regular schedule for trains was provided to the end of the

Railroad bridge over the Kings River, Fresno-Tulare counties, circa 1895. *The Interior (Fresno).*

line. Train service on a regular schedule began into Modesto on November 8, 1870; was extended to Merced on January 25, 1872; to Sycamore Point (Herndon) on April 1, 1872; and to Fresno on May 28, 1872. The section lying between Goshen and Tipton was begun independently of the other work under the name of the Southern Pacific. Naturally the same men were in control, as they owned both roads. Train service between these two points began on July 25, 1872. The road between Fresno and Goshen was not ready for traffic until six days later. The only stop between these two stations was at Grandview (Cross Creek). Thomas Fowler and Jefferson Gilbert James used the switch nine miles south of Fresno as a place for loading livestock. It was called Fowler's Switch. Another flag station, located twenty miles south of Fresno, was called Kings River Switch. Here, goods destined for Kingston were unloaded and freighted across the plains by Josiah Draper. John Sutherland also shipped his cattle from this point.[10]

Construction work by the railroad company, which will henceforth be referred to as the Southern Pacific, rested at Tipton until the spring of 1873. From this southern terminal a bull-whacker named Lief Johnson freighted goods to White River and other points. His contemptuous remarks concerning the small locomotives of the period, which he feared would destroy his means of livelihood, resulted in a wager which, according to popular tradition, caused his eight prize oxen to be defeated in a pulling contest.[11]

The twenty-mile section between Tipton and Delano was placed in operation on July 14, 1873. Great bands of sheep ranged that portion of the valley, and sheep men brought their animals to the new towns of Tipton and Delano for shearing. The wool was then packed and loaded on the cars. This industry naturally stimulated the growth of the embryonic towns.[12]

Delano remained the terminal of the Southern Pacific until August 1, 1874. On April 6th of that year, work was resumed from Delano. South of Famoso the road was built following a curve to the east. The chief engineer, a man named Hood, had noticed trees and other debris scattered over the plains north of Bakersfield. He feared that subsequent floods from the Kern River might prove dangerous to the railroad and therefore followed the higher ground to the east. This search for a suitable elevation prevented the road being built directly into Bakersfield. The station was located east of Bakersfield, which was then a small cowtown. This new station was named Sumner, later rechristened Kern, and is now a part of the city of Bakersfield. On August 1, train service was begun to the Kern River, and a few weeks later the completion of the Kern River bridge made possible this service into Sumner.[13]

The road running through Stockton, Farmington,

Oakdale, and Merced was completed on February 2, 1891.
A road connecting Visalia with Goshen was completed on
August 14, 1874, and extended to Exeter on November 29,
1889. Another branch line was built from Fresno through
the towns of Reedley, Dinuba, Exeter, Lindsay, and
Porterville, this was opened to traffic on July 1, 1888, and
completed to Famoso on December 24, 1890.[14]

The construction of a railway through the valley had been
comparatively easy. One observer wrote that "a few
furrows are made on each side, the dirt thrown to the
center and the grade is made. Then the ties are laid, and
the rails, a few spikes driven, and the road is complete."[15]
But the road from Bakersfield through Tehachapi Pass
required the most skillful engineering before it could be
built. However, the exit from the San Joaquin Valley of
the Southern Pacific line does not come under the
province of this discussion. The route had been selected a
quarter of a century before by the group of army engineers
detailed for that purpose by Jefferson Davis.

The biggest floods that ever occurred in the San Joaquin
Valley in historic times, exceeding even the amazing flood
of December 11th and 12th, 1937, sent their brown,
swirling waters over the wide, open spaces in 1868. That
year Lou Wagner, living a few miles southwest of
Kingsburg, built a boat and rowed to White's Bridge for
supplies; a few days later, he rowed to Visalia. Aside from a
few slight elevations, the entire plain was inundated. When
the railway engineers and surveyors arrived the next year,
they saw logs and debris scattered over the plains and
decided that they had better build a high railway dump.
The result of their conclusions may explain the exceedingly
high railroad fill between Selma and Traver.[16]

The main line of the Southern Pacific thus constructed
ran from Lathrop to Tehachapi. Subsequently other lines
were constructed in the valley, which served as "feeders"

335

of the main artery of transportation. On February 1, 1877, the line between Goshen and Huron was opened to traffic. The original Southern Pacific survey provided for land grants in this region, and here occurred the famous Mussel Slough fight. The bitterness engendered then and there smoldered for a generation, and occasionally burst into flames of lawlessness that cost the railway company and the disgruntled taxpayers men, money, and many mirthless months.[17]

In the late 1880s and early 1890s, the Southern Pacific received right-of-ways through the Miller & Lux and other land holdings, and began construction of a railway along the west side of the valley. This line extended from Tracy through Newman, Los Banos, Kerman, to Fresno. It was completed on July 1, 1892. The Spreckels brothers of San Francisco began the building of an independent road along the west side of the San Joaquin in 1895, but the entry of the more powerful Southern Pacific forced them to abandon their work. They transferred their attentions to the east side of the valley and built a road that was later acquired by the Santa Fe.[18]

The organizers of the Central Pacific were originally poor men. Boundless energy, ruthless determination, public demand for a railroad, government subsidies and land grants, gifts of money from cities, counties, and states—all these made possible the building of the Central Pacific and the later Southern Pacific. But millions of dollars were needed. Huge sums were borrowed and the land grants offered as security. These tracts were thrown open to settlers who often located on this land before the railroad had secured its patent to it. In such cases the settlers believed they were pre-empting government lands. A pioneer in the Mussel Slough area stated : "They (the settlers) did think that the land was owned by the Government at the time they filed."[19] In other cases, the settlers bought the railway land on the assumption that they would pay for it the same price they paid for government land. The circular issued by the railroad company contained the following information:

> The company invites settlers to go upon their lands before patents are issued, or the road is completed, and intends, in such cases, to sell to them in preference to any other applicants, and at a price based upon the value of the land without the improvements put upon them by the settlers.
>
> If the settlers desire to buy, the company gives them the first privilege of purchase at a fixed price, which, in every case, shall only be the value of the land, without regard to improvements.
>
> The lands are not uniform in price, but are offered at various figures, from $2.50 upward per acre; usually, land covered with tall timber is held at $5.00 per acre, and that with pine at $10.00. Most of it is for sale at $2.50 to $5.00 per acre.
>
> In ascertaining the value, any improvement that a settler or other person may have on the lands will not be taken into consideration; neither will the price be increased in consequence thereof. . . .
>
> Settlers are thus assured that, in addition to being accorded the first privilege of purchase, at the graded price, they will also he protected in their improvements.[20]

A careful perusal of the foregoing will make it apparent that the circular was indefinite in its statements. Most of the land was said to be for sale at a certain stipulated price; no one could be certain just which lands came under this provision. The portion pertaining to improvements appears clear enough in meaning and yet this was the one most flagrantly violated.

The arrival of the railroad increased land values, and the corporation felt itself entitled to a share in that increment. But the exact amount was hard to determine. To satisfy both the settler and the Southern Pacific was perhaps humanly impossible. When the land-grader appeared to appraise the value of ranch land he often found himself in a quandary. He may have recalled John Morley's dictum that "though right and wrong may be near neighbors, yet the line that separates them is of an awful sacredness."

The railway directors had to maintain a huge enterprise during a formative period. They were conducting a tremendous experiment in a new form of transportation. The corporation supported itself financially, expanded, and eventually paid the debts incurred in its original construction. Someone had to pay. The railway land grants were sold, freight was hauled, and passengers were carried. To control taxation and protect itself caused the corporation to effectively enter politics. Friends of the railroad were supported before election and controlled thereafter. Governors, legislators, and jurists were generally dominated, coerced, bribed, or defeated. Lobbies were maintained at Sacramento and Washington. A Railway Commission existed in the state, but its members were decidedly not friends of The People. Hiram Johnson, in his campaign for United States Senator in 1914, stated: "You had the railroad and the railroad was the commission. The railroad commission did one work. . . . It drew its salary every month for thirty years."[21]

The Southern Pacific brought prosperity and civilization to the valley. In so doing, its directors had spent much money. To safeguard their interests, they were forced to protect themselves by political machinations against unappreciative taxpayers. The railroad company was not always considerate; neither was the settler. The "short-haul" rate caused endless grief and misunderstanding. So too, did the custom of billing eastern freight to only the main points in California. Machinery destined for Tulare or Traver would pass through these stations and the rancher paid the additional "short-haul" rate from San Francisco to his home. He wondered why this was necessary. In time, men began to murmur and say that the Southern Pacific had its tentacles snarled around every department in the state government, and citizens began to lose faith in constituted authority. They maintained audibly that an octopus stifled justice in legislature, courts, and governor's mansion.[22]

By a judicious mixture of force, funds, and finesse, the so-called Octopus managed to dominate the two major political parties in California. The "Iron Horse" had entered the valley a hero; now, it threatened to become a villain in the eyes of the people. But it was not entirely to blame. The railway directors were constantly plied and belabored by other apparently insoluble problems:

1. The large cities in California wanted *low* westbound rates on large shipments in order to secure eastern manufactured goods at a minimum cost.

2. The large cities in California wanted *high* westbound rates on small shipments in order to secure profits on the reshipments necessary at distribution centers. Obviously, the small town merchants would not order directly from the eastern manufacturer or wholesaler if the freight on a small shipment was exorbitant.

3. The farmers and ranchers wanted *low* eastbound rates on livestock and grain.

4. The California manufacturing firms, then in the process of development, wanted *high* westbound rates in order to discourage shipments of eastern machinery, implements, and vehicles.[23]

Naturally, the Southern Pacific could not accede to all of these diverging demands. Furthermore, the corporation made no pretense of doing so; neither did it attempt to mollify any group or faction. Crocker, Huntington, Hopkins, and Stanford had originally been small-town

Babbitts who are prone to consider the "rustic cackle of their burg the merriment of the world." Suddenly they had been transformed into glorified and enlarged copies of village merchants, with the same attitudes and ethics as of yore. They were conducting an establishment, which sold a single form of goods. That commodity was transportation. They argued that the sale thereof was governed only by the law of supply and demand. Their definition was correct. No one has ever improved upon it. In fixing freight and passenger rates, the standing order of the directors was: "All the traffic will bear."

The Southern Pacific was not intended to be an altruistic organization or a philanthropic society. It sold transportation, but no one was forced to buy. If a customer disliked the service or objected to the price he was welcome to go elsewhere. But where should he go? The teamster was forced, in order to realize a profit, to charge $40 a ton for transporting goods from Oakland to Visalia; the railway did it for two dollars. The riverboats were excellent for bulky articles, but not generally available except at certain points. The pack mules were incompetent. The first farmers in the valley were wheat growers. Their wheat needed a market and the road to that market lay by way of the Southern Pacific rails. The Southern Pacific knew it; so did the farmer. Under the circumstances the amazing thing is that the corporation was as lenient and gracious as it actually was; both railroad and farmer were to suffer much before peace and amity were to prevail. Both the Southern Pacific and the settlers had to pass through the purging flames of suffering before they became cognizant of the unsuspected truth that true prosperity is based on cooperation.[24]

Oftentimes the fight waxed acrimonious and the air became acrid with vicious verbosity. Concerning those hectic days, one writer expressed himself thus: "There was nothing but law; and constitutions; and provisions; and amendments; and orders: and fresh statutes; and then came more law; all aimed and shaped to regulate, restrict, and control this monster, and the monster never gave a hoot for all of them."[25]

What to do? The tragedy at Mussel Slough focused attention on conditions in the valley. After this battle, lawless acts, directed against the railroad, were committed sporadically. Chris Evans was one of the settlers who were unable to pay the high prices set on his land by the railway land grader. Attempts to prove him a train robber made him an outlaw. The Dalton brothers, then visiting in the valley, were also accused. The general antipathy of the populace toward the Octopus made the detection and capture of the hold-up men difficult. The apathy of the people toward law and order, as far as train robberies were concerned, was indicative of the common attitude of the time. Political conditions in California were putrid. Then came the organization of the Lincoln-Roosevelt League, the first steps that were taken in the Hotel Oakland on August 1, 1908, largely through the instrumentality of Chester Rowell, then editor of the Fresno *Republican*. Another type of man began to assert himself.[26]

Another event of like significance occurred which Owen Wister explained as follows:

> In time C. P. Huntington, a giant type of peddler, was gathered to his fathers, and a civilized man of higher constructive genius took hold of the Southern Pacific—E. H. Harriman. The personality of the head of any corporation, no matter how extensive, permeates it from top to bottom. Almost in the twinkling of an eye, train service improved, employees ceased to be indifferent and brutal, and the Southern Pacific was transformed. It was firmly established by now, and ready to get out of politics.[27]

When popular feeling against the Southern Pacific was at

The first train of the San Francisco and San Joaquin Valley Railway wends through its namesake valley for the first time in 1896. *The Interior, (Fresno).*

its height Claus Spreckels, the sugar-king, proposed to build another and independent road through the valley. Henry Miller, the cattle king, granted him a right-of-way through his swamplands on the so-called West Side of the valley. When Spreckels had built a high roadbed a hundred miles in length, Miller donated a similar right-of-way to the Southern Pacific through a more favorable territory, and Spreckels was forced to withdraw from the West Side. But he persevered and constructed a road along the eastern side of the valley. The route of this new railroad is indicated by the cities of Oakland, Richmond, Stockton, Riverbank, Merced, Fresno, Hanford, Corcoran, and Bakersfield. It was given the legal name of the San Francisco & San Joaquin Railroad, but residents of the valley affectionately called it The People's Road.

When the first shipment of tools arrived at Stockton for construction work, the crates were marked Atchison, Topeka, and Santa Fe. This led to the suspicion that the Spreckels brothers were being secretly financed by the latter company. Construction work was begun in 1888, and Belmont Avenue, Fresno, was reached in August,

1895. The first locomotive to enter Fresno bore the name "Claus Spreckels" emblazoned on it in gold letters. The engineer was J. H. Adams and the fireman, his brother Sol G. Adams. At Blackstone Avenue this train was met by a joyous Fresno delegation, with wagonloads of liquid refreshments. This new road had no outlet from the valley to the south, but as it commenced to ship more and more cattle and wheat to the Bay region, it forced the older and established Southern Pacific to become polite.[28]

During the 1870s, an eastern company styling itself the St. Louis and San Francisco Railway proposed to build a road between the two places suggested by its name. The Atchison, Topeka and Santa Fe followed a similar plan. The first road encountered financial difficulties before it reached Albuquerque, and the Santa Fe acquired a half interest in it. The two railroad companies jointly built a road from that place into California under the name of the Atlantic & Pacific. It entered California at Needles and reached Mojave via Barstow, and thence to Los Angeles. A branch road was extended from Deming, New Mexico, to Guaymas, Mexico, which was coveted by the Southern Pacific. The latter secured it by granting a 99-year lease entitling the Santa Fe to the use of its tracks from Mojave to Bakersfield through the Tehachapi Pass. This then made possible the purchase of the People's Road by the Santa Fe and a southern exit from the valley for the Spreckels-built railroad.[29]

From December 1, 1911, to January 6, 1918, the Santa Fe sent two trains, the Saint and the Angel, through the San Joaquin Valley at the fastest timetable schedule of any trains in the nation. The Pennsylvania system sends its Pennsylvania Limited across the Alleghenies from Chicago to New York. The route of the New York Central between these two points is a hundred miles longer. However, the latter's roadbed is laid on relatively level ground. In order to compete with the more direct route of the Pennsylvania lines, the Twentieth Century Limited of the New York Central attained a speed of seventy-five miles an hour. When the Southern Pacific inaugurated its Daylight Limited between Los Angeles and San Francisco with a twelve-hour schedule, the Santa Fe made a bid for passenger traffic by reducing this time over a longer route. A schedule of fifty miles an hour including all stops was maintained. Since this involved crossing the Tehachapi Mountains, an actual running speed of eighty miles an hour was consistently maintained through the San Joaquin Valley. This service between Oakland via Barstow to Los Angeles was discontinued when William Gibbs McAdoo became Director-General of Railways during the World War. The subsequent use of the automobile, both as a stage and touring car, prevented further competition for passenger traffic.[30]

One definite purpose of the Lincoln-Roosevelt League was to end the Southern Pacific domination of California politics. A definite result was the raising of the moral tone of state politics. Hiram Johnson became the candidate of the reform groups for governor of California in 1910. The various city political machines were his sworn foes, but he toured the rural districts and received an amazing ovation. One of his innovations was the use of the automobile. Concerning this, he wrote to the author as follows:

> I doubt if I was the first candidate to make use of the automobile in a political campaign, but I do know that up to 1910, there had never been a more extensive use of it than I made. The machine I used was a Locomobile roadster, the motor of which possessed unusual strength, and for that day, speed.[31]

The newspapers reported Johnson's defeat the day after election. The conservative factions were gleeful. But their joy was premature. His automobile had carried him into the byways, and his speeches had proved convincing. When the returns from the rural districts began to arrive, it was apparent that a new regime stood on the threshold; the prediction uttered by Johnson in the first sentence of this chapter was soon to be realized.

Today, the common people and the corporations are working in peace and harmony to develop the San Joaquin Valley. The old difficulties have been adjusted. The farmers in Mussel Slough, whose fathers may have been among those settlers who died heroically at the behest of a corporate power, now go to the station agent at Hanford and give the following orders: "We want a car to send our goods to the market tomorrow." The answer is courteous and the service is prompt.

California field dreadnoughts in action, undated and presumably from Wallace Smith's collection. *Garden of the Sun*, 1939 edition.

12 Staff of Life

Besides that, when elsewhere the harvest of wheat is most abundant, there it comes up less by one fourth than what you have sowed. There, methinks, it were a proper place for men to sow their wild oats, where they would not spring up.

Plautus *Trinummus*, IV, 4, 128.

"The plows, thirty-five in number, each drawn by its team of ten, stretched in an interminable line, nearly a quarter of a mile in length, behind and ahead of Vanamee. They were arranged, as it were, *en echelon*, not in file—not one directly behind the other, but each succeeding plows its own width further in the field than the one in front of it. Each of these plows held five shares, so that when the entire company was in motion, one hundred and seventy-five furrows were made at the same instant. At a distance, the plows resembled a great column of field artillery. Each driver was in his place, his glance alternating between his horses and the foreman nearest at hand. Other foremen, in their buggies and buckboards, were at intervals along the line, like battery lieutenants. Annixter himself, on

347

horseback, in boots and campaign hat, a cigar in his teeth, overlooked the scene."[1]

The foregoing paragraph from *The Octopus* by Frank Norris is a description of a scene common in the San Joaquin Valley in the days of the bonanza wheat farms. Leo Rogin, in his *Farm Machinery in Relation to Labor*, has defined them as follows: "By bonanza wheat farms we have in mind capitalistic agriculture (as opposed to the family farm) pursued on units so large and with methods so much like those of large industrial enterprises as to make them relatively notorious even in the regions where they were located."[2]

The Spanish-California cattlemen who settled in the San Joaquin Valley planted various varieties of cereals in small plots for home consumption. One of William Gulnack's employees, James Williams, sowed some wheat in the vicinity of Stockton in the spring of 1845. The same year, at the other end of the valley, Manuel Jacinto Fago, foreman of the *Tejon* ranch, sowed corn and wheat. Many years later Miller & Lux planted thousands of acres of wheat, but this grain was used solely in the fattening of livestock. The growing of grain by these cattlemen was merely incidental and did not directly affect the market or influence the economic conditions in the region.[3]

On the first day of the year 1847 a Mormon colony was planted on the north bank of the Stanislaus River. Samuel Brannan, the leader of the advance guard to California, sent William Stout to this region with twenty men. They erected homes, built a small town, and seeded eighty acres to wheat. That fall Brigham Young ordered the return to Salt Lake of these Mormons and only a part of the wheat was harvested.[4]

Harvesting, as it was practiced by the Spanish-Californians during the "splendid, idle forties," was a

decided contrast to the era of mechanical contrivances
that was soon to follow. John Bidwell, in his *Echoes of the
Past*, has described an early California harvest scene:

> Harvesting with rude implements was a scene. Imagine three
> to four hundred wild Indians in a grain field armed, some
> with pieces of hoop iron, roughly fashioned into shapes like
> sickles, but many having only their hands with which to
> gather up small handfuls, the dry and brittle grain; and as
> their hands would become sore, they resorted to dry willow
> sticks, which were split to afford a sharper edge with which
> to sever the straw. But the wildest part was the threshing.
> The harvest of weeks, sometimes of a month, was piled up in
> the straw in the form of a huge mound in the middle of a
> high, strong, round corral; then three or four hundred wild
> horses were turned in to thresh it, the Indians whooping to
> make them run faster.
>
> Suddenly they would dash in before the band at full speed
> when the motion became reversed, with the effect of
> ploughing up the trampled straw to the very bottom. In an
> hour the grain would be thoroughly threshed and the dry
> straw broken into a chaff. In this manner I have seen 2,000
> bushels of wheat threshed in a single hour.
>
> Next came the winnowing which would often take another
> month. It could only be done when the wind was blowing, by
> throwing high into the air shovels full of grain, straw and
> chaff, the lighter material being wafted to one side, while the
> grain, comparatively clean, would descend and form a heap
> by itself. In this way all the grain in California was cleaned.[5]

The cost of flour reached ridiculous heights during the
gold rush. Men were so obsessed by the idea of finding
huge nuggets that they preferred to dig for gold and,
rather than sow wheat, they willingly paid a dollar a
pound for flour. But soon the glamour of a futile search for
gold became tarnished and caused miners, either more
enterprising or less successful than their fellows, to turn
their energies from yellow metal to yellow grain and
thereby reap a more abundant harvest. These miners

made poor farmers. They had no expectation of remaining in the valley; they merely intended to provide bread for other miners and thus secure wealth, which would enable them to return to their eastern homes. The result was that they made no efforts to replenish the soil, they plowed carelessly, and permitted the fields to become foul with noxious weeds.[6]

The most common weed in early days was the tumbleweed. It grew to the size of a bushel basket and was sufficiently round in form so that in the fall, when it had become dry and brittle, it would roll for miles over the wind-swept plains. In 1869 Ransome McCapes built a fence in the Manteca region, which was laid flat by the tumbleweeds which piled up against it.[7]

Weeds native to the San Joaquin Valley were easily controlled. But other noxious weeds were soon introduced which have had a pernicious influence on agriculture since that time. One of these was Bermuda grass.

> The date of the introduction of Bermuda grass has not been definitely ascertained. It is a native of India and perhaps other parts of the Old World in tropical and sub-tropical localities. Some authorities, for example Hitchcock, state that it is a native of the Mediterranean region. Spillman gives an account of its introduction at Greensboro, Georgia, in 1812. However, Mease in *Geological Account of the United States*, published in 1807, gives a well substantiated record of Bermuda Grass growing in the United States at that time.[8]

There is no connection between the West India islands known as the Bermudas and Bermuda grass, other than that both derived their name from the same person. As a naval officer, the Count de Bermudas discovered some islands that still bear his name. As one of the largest landowners in Spain, he was interested in growing horses, cattle, and forage grass. Settlers leaving his community for the New World took grass seeds from the estate of this count to their new homes in America, hence the name. It did not spread rapidly in the San Joaquin until intensive cultivation and irrigation became prevalent.[9]

In 1830 Governor Means of South Carolina sent a planter to Turkey to instruct the Turks in cotton culture. This planter brought back with him several new seeds. Among them was a forage grass that became known as Means Grass. Colonel William Johnson secured seed for his plantation near Selma, Alabama. As seed from this plantation moved west with the settlers, it acquired the name of Johnson grass. Finally a man named Sanders, the central figure in the unsolved murder mystery case which occurred near Reedley, imported Johnson grass seed into the San Joaquin Valley. Credulous settlers, who visited his farm between Kingsburg and Parlier, paid him a dollar a pound for this seed to secure forage for their livestock. Many have since learned to rue their bargain. One juryman objected to hanging Sanders on circumstantial evidence in the William Wooton murder case, but favored his execution for introducing Johnson grass. However, Sanders is not alone to blame. The California Experiment station distributed this seed to settlers as a valuable forage in 1884-1885.[10] Another noxious weed of uncertain origin, the puncture vine, was spread throughout the entire valley by the automobile, whose pneumatic tires provided a natural carrier. County supervisors now spray the roadside with an oil preparation in an attempt to eradicate this pest.[11]

Shallow plowing by the first wheat growers caused deterioration, which later farmers in subsequent years had to correct by intelligent methods. The assumption had been that the dry seasons common to the valley would prevent wheat growing. The chief contribution of these miners, turned wheat farmers, was their proving that the winter and spring rains were sufficient to produce crops of amazing quality and quantity.

The result of this demonstration was the quick development of wheat growing. Another stimulating factor was the coming of the Central Pacific railway. Wheat was at first hauled to the mines by freight wagons drawn by horses or mules. The riverboats carried small tonnages to the coastal cities. But neither of these two forms of transportation were sufficient to warrant a rapid expansion of wheat growing. Then came the railway.[12]

The first Americans to grow wheat in the valley confined their activities to the region between the present cities of Stockton, Manteca, Modesto, and Escalon. Grain could be shipped by boat from Stockton to the coast cities. The base towns of the gold mining region were all located to the east along the Green Hills, as the miners designated the foothills, where they could be reached by river boats from Stockton and San Francisco. The proximity to markets made this section, known as the Stockton sand plains, an ideal location for the first wheat growers.

The plow in use in California when the first Americans arrived was hewn out of a block of wood, usually the boll of a small tree. One branch was left to serve as a handle. One end of the block was shaped into a V and shod with a piece of iron. This rude implement functioned more like a modern lister than a plow.

The wheat growers from the United States were of an inventive turn of mind. One investigator has stated that "the nature of the soil and the superficial character of the seedbed preparation made for the utilization of the gang plows almost from the beginning of the extensive cultivation of wheat."[13] The famous Stockton gang-plow was invented near the present site of Manteca. Wheat growing in this region was largely due to the initial

Plowing and seeding on T. L. Reed's wheat ranch in 1888. This scene shows 192 mules hitched to Stockton gang plows. *Garden of the Sun,* 1939 edition.

experiment of John Wheeler Jones, who planted 160 acres to wheat in 1855 within the later town site of Manteca. He plowed his field with an old-fashioned walking plow. No harrows were available in California then and branches from trees were used to cover the seed. Harrows did not come into general use in California until after 1866, although Settle & Cottle of San Jose perfected a combination seeder and harrow in 1860. This contrivance was attached to a plow, and with it one man and six horses could plow, seed, and harrow four to five acres a day. Since the harrow immediately covered up the grain, it prevented any loss of seed due to the depredations of blackbirds and other fowls of the air. But his machine was not available to all, and for many years big boughs from trees were used in covering the seed with fresh, warm earth. The boughs had a tendency to drag the seed around in such a fashion that erratic growth resulted. The wheat field harvested by John Wheeler Jones in 1855 was important, because it furnished a precedent for other men who now began to grow wheat in the region lying between Stockton and the Stanislaus River. Jones harvested his crop that year with a crude handrake McCormick reaper. Chinese labor did the work of binding and threshing.[14]

The men who followed the example of Jones and planted wheat on the sand plains all used the single bottom plow, locally known as a "foot burner." Lack of labor, and the exhilaration which came to them when first they beheld the vast and fertile plains, caused men familiar with the stony fields of eastern states to ponder ways and means to increase their holdings and harvests. The old-fashioned walking plow was too slow. But until 1860 this was the only one available. That year, Cronkite & Beale of San Jose invented a gang plow with four shares that could be handled by one man and eight horses. The next year, the Challenge Gang Plow was placed on the market by W. B. Ready of Sacramento. This plow proved easy to handle and soon became a favorite among wheat growers. No further inventions or improvements were made by implement dealers until after the Civil War.[15]

Independently of these commercial plows, the wheat growers of the San Joaquin busied themselves with the invention of a plow that was to become famous throughout the world wherever wheat was grown. In 1860 Westley Underwood, a wheat grower near the present Manteca, secured two plows from his neighbors and bolted them to his own. Each plow had a ten-inch share. In his experimentation, Underwood was aided by his wife's brother, Henry Mills. This three-bottom plow was used for the first time in the fall of 1861. The next year John A. Perry, a New England Yankee and the grandson of a Revolutionary soldier, came to California in search of health. Although he arrived late in the season, he decided to plant some wheat. In order to make haste, he bought Underwood's three-bottom plow. He employed three yokes of oxen to pull it and finished on scheduled time. The plow did excellent work, but was hard to handle on the turns.

The three heavy timbers bolted diagonally across the beams of the three plows made it cumbersome and at that stage of its development it had no wheels. One of the phenomena of the San Joaquin that impressed Perry was the absence of stones. In his native New Hampshire, he maintained that each hundred square feet of field contained more than a thousand large stones. The unobstructed soil of the San Joaquin Valley was a marvel to eastern men, and was to project itself through them into a series of mechanical inventions pertaining to agriculture.[16]

A wheat grower on the west side of the valley, Lowell Alexander Richards, improved the Underwood plow, which had been used in 1861 and 1862, by placing the standards of the three plows on a single beam. The patent rights to this plow were then sold by these men to H. C. Shaw of Stockton, who operated a foundry, and Matteson & Williamson, implement dealers of the same city. Additional improvements were then made by adding wheels, reversible shares, and levelers to adjust the depth of plowing, and a gauge to adjust the width. Thereafter, no improvements were necessary; it was complete. It was manufactured and shipped to all parts of the world under the name of the Stockton Gang Plow and brought the first fame of this type to the Delta City. Much of a similar nature was to follow.[17]

In 1869 a Marysville resident, A. Ellison, perfected the leverage on the old Buckeye Plow by giving it a drop of twenty-one inches. He also raised it in such a fashion that it would clear the highest stubble and thus prevent clogging with brush and straw that often retarded the progress of other makes.[18]

The invention of the Stockton Gang Plow resulted in a new and unique manner of handling the several spans of horses required to pull it. An improvisation of the vocal method of driving oxen together with the system of checks and lines then in vogue among freighters was combined to develop the first jerk-line team in the world. The first method could not be adopted entirely, since horses are not as amenable to control as oxen; the second was too cumbersome and costly. The farmer who walked all day beside his plow did not want to carry the many reins necessary to handle his teams.

In 1868 Stephen V. Porter, Henry W. Lander, and Ransome McCapes, all natives of Wisconsin, rented land near the present site of Manteca, later moving south across the Tuolumne River and renting 1,280 acres from John W. Mitchell, including the present site of Turlock. Irwin S. Wright, employed by Lander as a teamster, went to the Coast Range and procured four wild mules, which he broke to the plow. Lander owned a strawberry roan broncho mare named Hannah. She and her teammate were placed at the head of these four mules. A long baling rope was attached to the left ring of Hannah's bit. This line was then inserted through the rings in the hames of the near pointer and wheeler, and fastened to the lever of the plow where Wright could reach it easily. A steady pull on the rope naturally turned Hannah to the left. The other members of the team, each fastened by a head-strap to the singletree of the preceding animal, followed the leaders. In order to turn the team to the right, a strap was fastened between the right ring in Hannah's bit and the ring in her hame. This was barely long enough for her to walk comfortably. A quick jerk would cause her to throw up her head and the short strap then pulled her to the right. A sharp command "Gee!" at the same time finally taught her to turn right without any undue pressure or pain. She was then "broken to the word." Her teammate was forced to turn at the same moment by a short jockey stick extending from Hannah's hame to the right ring of the off-leader's bit. In order to enable the near leader to take precedence on the turns, the off-leader was held back by a check strap extending from his bridle to the near leader's singletree.

The off-wheeler, unlike the other horses, was usually not fastened to the animal in front of him. This enabled him, when the plow showed a tendency to crawl out into the unplowed ground, to swing out and pull it back into place. Sometimes this wheeler swung out too far and failed to get back into the furrow. Then he was either crippled or killed by the heavy plow. This caused a strap to be snapped into the single tree of the off-pointer, which permitted only a forty-five degree turn. Since the rancher or teamster always walked in the hard, unplowed ground, it became customary to designate the horses to the left as the near horses; those to the right then became the off-horses. This jerk-line form of driving a long string of work stock won favor immediately and was adopted, not only by other wheat growers, but replaced the old form of hitch on the big freight wagons throughout the nation.[19]

The first quadrupeds hitched to the Stockton Gang Plow were inferior as draft stock. Usually they were bronchos, or mules out of broncho mares. They were as hard to handle as dynamite. Young men who crave excitement in modern times are too prone to jeopardize the lives of pedestrians by the reckless manner in which they manipulate the long, low cars that come so high. In those days, they found ample vent for surplus vitality by taming these vicious brutes who, besides leaving their footprints in the sands of time on the Stockton plains, also left their marks on the broken bodies of the men whom they maimed or killed.[20]

In time native California and San Joaquin horseflesh was supplemented by the excessively tall Cleveland Bay mares, originally imported from England as carriage horses for wealthy, urban residents. Together with Percheron mares, they produced mules that weighed from 1,400 to 1,600 pounds, and stood six feet or more at the withers. They walked twenty-five miles a day with the Stockton Gang Plow and had enough energy left at nightfall to run away, if opportunity offered. These great animals were matched by the rangy young men employed as teamsters. The latter often walked to the nearest town of an evening to get tired enough to sleep. So they said. There may have been other attractions. A few old-time freighters, who became gang plow teamsters, followed their old custom of riding the near wheeler. Occasionally a rude seat was improvised on the plow. However, as a general rule, the teamsters walked beside their plow.[21]

Grain was first sowed by hand from a box placed on top of the frame of the Stockton plow. The seed was scattered on the unplowed ground to the left of the plow. Then it was covered on the next round or, if more than one plow was in operation, by the plow which followed the first. Another system in vogue was broadcast sowing by hand from a wagon. One man drove the team and another sat beside a tub containing the seed, which he scattered in a swath ten to twenty feet wide. Both of these methods were laborious and resulted in uneven sowing. End-gate seeders were invented in the Middle West. They were rotation machines attached to the rear end of a wagon and were driven from a sprocket on one of the rear wheels. They must have made their appearance at an early date, because it was stated in 1859 that these rotation machines "can be attached to any wagon within twenty minutes."[22]

About 1867 a man, whose name is now unfortunately forgotten, planted a 3,000 acre wheatfield near Crows Landing. The first day, he and his hired man sowed by hand from a box placed on a wagon. The hired man then suggested that a tub be placed on a raised platform, a hole cut in the bottom, and a fan placed under it which could be operated from one of the rear wheels. This resulted in a more even sowing, as well as a saving of labor. At the end of the season, this contrivance was taken to the Benicia Agricultural Works to be perfected. This firm acquired the rights to it, and from this invention by two unknown farmers was developed the California Gem and also the Pacific Seed Broadcaster which are still in use in the valley and elsewhere.[23]

Another popular machine of this nature in California wheatfields was the Gorham Broadcast Seeder and Cultivator. This was made in different sizes; the standard size sowed an eight-foot swath and was designed for two horses. Its average capacity was fifteen acres a day. During the seventies, the combined seeders and cultivators were largely replaced by the hand rotary broadcast seeders. The most popular of this type was Cahoon's Broadcast Seed Sower. During the eighties this machine was able to sow a hundred acres a day. [24]

The amazing increase in agricultural efficiency which was brought about in a few years is indicated by the records kept by a wheat grower in Tulare County in 1885. That year Daniel Spangler harvested 1,500 acres of wheat. Seven men, each with an eight-horse team and a Stockton plow and one man with a two-horse team on an end-gate seeder, put in a crop in thirty days. Plowing was begun on January 24, 1885, and seeding was completed on February 24th. Rogin, basing his computation on a basis of twenty-seven working days of ten hours each, concluded that 2,160 man-labor hours were consumed in putting in the 1,500 acres, or one-hour and twenty-six minutes for each acre. The crop was harvested by an equal number of hired men in twenty-six days using two Houser combines. The same year Spangler harvested 2,000 acres outside of the 1,500 under consideration and the next year he seeded 5,000 acres. This example of efficiency is not typical; Spangler, a pioneer irrigationist in the Mussel Slough region, was ahead of his time in more ways than one. His use of Houser combines in 1885 is proof of this. They did not come into general use until the late eighties and the nineties. But his case illustrates the possibility of rapid and efficient work; the machinery was now available.[25]

The drag harrows proved to be too light to cover the seed properly except when used on freshly plowed soil. A man in the Middle West named Mallon invented the rotary disc cultivator in 1878. A few of these found their way into the San Joaquin, but they were small machines and utterly inadequate on the wide sweeping plains of the San Joaquin. But they were useful in furnishing the basis on which new inventions were modeled. Lowell Alexander Richards, then a wheat grower on the West Side of the valley, patented a disc cultivator that could turn a swath twenty feet wide. This patent was dated September 7, 1886. This new disc was used solely to cover sown seed. Its use as a cultivator came much later. H. C. Shaw, the Stockton foundryman and implement dealer, furnished the castings for the Richards invention. Additional improvements resulted in the granting of a second patent to Richards on May 15, 1888. This disc was soon found on all the bonanza wheat farms, and is identical in principle with those now used in large orchard cultivation. With it a man and ten mules could cover fifty acres a day. This, and other inventions, made it possible for Richards to handle the largest farming outfit in the world in 1890. That year, it was said the Richards force of men cut and threshed a continuous and unbroken field of standing grain from the Sierra Nevada foothills east of Ripon to the Coast Range foothills west of Westley.[26]

Land along the rivers of the San Joaquin Valley yielded a

hundred bushels for each one sowed. No need for deep plowing existed, and the Stockton Gang Plow and the seeders of various types caused more land to be planted than could be harvested. This led to further inventions in order to redress the balance. One man and ten mules was expected to sow and cultivate 160 acres in less than twenty days. But the harvesting was still done by the McCormick reaper, the grain bound by hand, pitched into the wagons by hand, and finally pitched by hand into the separator. This tedious and old-fashioned process has continued down to the present time in the Midwest, where manpower is available, but it involved too much labor in a land where labor was a scarce commodity.[27]

In 1858 Rugg's Reaper was invented at Napa; this was propelled instead of drawn. Placing horses behind the machinery prevented trampling of the wheat. The same year stationary threshing machines were developed in California. Thomas Ogg Shaw made improvements of a mechanical nature on the old Manny Reaper. The interest and activity in machinery during 1858 indicated that wheat farming was becoming of economic importance. The next year Thomas Ogg Shaw invented a clod crusher. The dry summers caused clods to form after a wetting and this resulted in a rapid evaporation of moisture. To prevent this fatal action in a dry climate, this newly invented crusher was run over the fields after the sowing and clods thereby eliminated.[28]

Circa 1860, a new machine was used in the harvest on the Stockton sand plains. A McCormick reaper had been rebuilt to be pushed instead of drawn, and a spout and draper had been attached. The inventor is unknown. Lowell Alexander Richards, one of the inventors of the Stockton Gang Plow, farmed in the valley opposite Livermore Pass and Paso de Buenas Aires. Here, the strong west wind mitigated the success of the new headers. The winds common to that region blew the grain away from the header spout, and Richards added a second draper to run above the grain and hold it against the lower draper until it was delivered into the wagon. Daniel Houser of Durham's Ferry and a man named Denton began to build and improve the first headers. This was the type of harvesting machinery that was to be supreme from that time until 1880.[29]

The invention of the header required auxiliary machinery. A header wagon was originated to run alongside the header and receive the heads of wheat. The wagon box at first glance looked lopsided. One side was six feet high or more, and the other side was eighteen inches. The wagon was driven with the lower side toward the header. Richards further improved this wagon by placing the rear wheels ten feet apart and outside of the wagon bed. The front wheels were set far to the front and connected with the low body, which bad been set two feet above the ground, by a long, curved iron brace. From the latter, the wagon became known as a "goose-neck" and was the forerunner of the "goose-neck" wagon used in the orchards in later years in Santa Clara County. The last invention in connection with the header was made by Thomas Powell, also a resident of the sand plains, who made a rolling net which was placed on the wagon to receive the cut grain. It had a tight mesh and was similar to a huge fishnet. This made possible the unloading of the cut grain into stacks by horsepower.[30]

At the beginning of the nineteenth century Thomas Maithus, an English economist, frightened England into abolishing the Corn Laws by his gloomy prediction that in time every man over forty years of age must be put to death. According to his proclamation "the ultimate check to population is the lack of food." Wheat growers in the San Joaquin answered this challenge by saying, "Don't guillotine people, but let us devise a quicker way to cut off the heads of grain and thus provide food." They did. According to Rogin: "Ideal climatic conditions, the extensive scale upon which wheat was grown, the exceptionally enterprising type of men engaged in agriculture, all combined to bring about the development of the harvester-thresher in California and its widespread introduction in that state."[31]

The first combined harvester-thresher was patented by Samuel Lane of Maine in 1828 but it never got beyond the patent stage. In 1836 Ehakim Briggs and George G. Carpenter, both of Franklin County, New York, secured a patent on another combine. Their patent was dated February 5, 1836, and sixty days later Hiram Moore and John Haskall secured a patent and built a combine at Kalamazoo, Michigan, which was the first harvester to actually operate in a grainfield. A son of Hiram Moore, Andrew Y. Moore, who later settled in Tulare County, built an improved combine in 1843 which was successfully operated in Michigan until 1853. James Fenimore Cooper, the celebrated author of the famous *Leatherstocking Tales*, wrote a novel entitled *Oak Openings* which was published in 1848. He referred to this combined harvester as follows:

> The peculiar ingenuity of the American has supplied the want of laborers, in a country where agriculture is carried on by wholesale, especially in the cereals, by an instrument of the most singular and elaborate construction. This machine is drawn by sixteen or eighteen horses, attached to it laterally, to work clear of the standing grain, and who move the whole fabric on a moderate but steady walk. A path is first cut with the cradle on one side of the field, when the machine is dragged into the open place. Here it enters the standing grain, cutting off its heads with the utmost accuracy as it moves. Forks beneath prepare the way, and a rapid vibratory motion of a great number of two-edged knives effect the object. The stalks of the grain can be cut as low or as high as

one pleases, but it is usually thought best to take only the heads. Afterward the standing straw is burned, or fed, upright.

The impelling power which causes the great fabric to advance also sets in motion the machinery within. As soon as the heads of the grain are severed from the stalks, they pass into a receptacle, where, by a very quick and simple process, the kernels are separated from the husks. Thence all goes into a fanning machine, where the chaff is blown away. The clean grain falls into a small bin, whence it is raised by a screw elevator to a height that enables it to pass out at an opening to which a bag is attached. Wagons follow the slow march of the machine, and the proper number of men are in attendance. Bag after bag is renewed, until a wagon is loaded, when it at once proceeds to the mill, where the grain is soon converted into flour. Generally, the husbandman sells to the miller, but occasionally he pays for making the flour, and sends the latter off, by railroad, to Detroit, whence it finds its way to Europe, possibly, to help feed the millions of the Old World. Such, at least, was the course of trade the past season. As respects this ingenious machine, it remains only to say that it harvests, cleans, and bags from twenty to thirty acres of heavy wheat, in the course of a single summer's day! Altogether it is a gigantic invention, well adapted to meet the necessities of a gigantic country.[32]

In 1853 George W. Leland acquired an interest in this combine and shipped it to California by way of Cape Horn in a windjammer. Andrew Moore accompanied Leland to California, and eventually Moore became a resident of Tulare County. This combine was used in the harvest of 1854 in Alameda County, and operated in the wheat-fields of Mission San José. The next year, the owners went to the gold mines and the machine stood idle. In 1856 Moore operated it; lack of lubrication caused it to catch on fire, and it was burned down in the harvest field. This machine must be considered the ancestor of the many harvesters who were soon to appear. The memory of the juggernaut persisted. In 1858 the Hon. S. B. Bell of Alameda County alluded to it in an address to the California State Agricultural Society.[33]

In 1858, Strong & Taylor built a combine that they offered for sale at $2,000, and two brothers, John M. and William Y. Horner, also built a machine of a similar type. Both were evidently modeled after the original Moore combine. During the early sixties wheat growing was engaged in extensively and on a huge scale in the valley. In 1860 Marvin & Thurston won the award at the Stockton Fair on the Marvin combine. The patent rights to it were purchased by Stockton implement dealers Matteson & Williamson in 1869. During the previous year, B. F. Cook of Napa had also built a harvester. Cook estimated that it cost $1.50 a day to operate his combine, which cut, threshed, and sacked the grain as it proceeded down the field. This proved more economical than the use of the stationary threshers. Such big equipment could only be utilized in the wide, open spaces where the fields were of great size and the ground level and free from stones. A combine requiring thirty-six horses to pull it was of little value in a field of a few acres.[34]

In 1868 the wheat growers of the San Joaquin took the initiative in the building and perfecting of the combined harvester. They are the sole inventors of all the types now in use. Richard Wilson, then residing two miles west of Hill's Ferry, decided that the grain was dry enough to be threshed without being stacked. He therefore ordered his men to pitch it directly from the header wagon into the separator. This eliminated the manual labor involved in pitching it into a stack. The temperature was 110 degrees in the shade, and his hired men thought the idea was good. Their enthusiasm inspired Wilson to have another idea equally good. He placed big wheels under his separator, attached it to his header, and threshed as he proceeded down the field. Daniel Houser, then a resident of Durham's Ferry, and Rufus R. Moore, later of Modesto, approved of Wilson's plan, and both of them built machines of a similar type.[35]

All combines built prior to 1876 were made to order and according to specifications furnished by the individual wheat growers. Parts were not interchangeable and were thus costly to replace. That year, Matteson & Williamson began to manufacture a standard combine based on the patent rights they had acquired from Marvin. Dr. E. W. Hilgard, a University of California professor, referred to "a wondrous and fearful combination of header, thresher, and sacking-wagon moving in a procession side by side through the doomed grain" and concluded facetiously: "If this stupendous combination and last refinement shall prove successful, we shall doubtless see the flouring mill itself form a part of the pageant."[36]

Rogin assumed that Hilgard referred to the Centennial combine, which had been invented in 1876, and had harvested 1,400 acres that year. The *Pacific Rural Press* stated in 1879 that "it came into prominence in the San Joaquin Valley last year."[37]

Another combine placed on the market in 1876 was built by Daniel Houser and David Young, which consisted of header and separator constructed in a single unit. But neither of these combines found favor immediately. In 1879, the California wheat crop amounted to 28,946,000 bushels, and it was practically all harvested by headers. But the combine inventors were persistent. In 1881 Houser formed a partnership with a man named Haines, and began at Stockton that year the manufacture of the famous Houser & Haines combine. This proved to be more popular than the Marvin combine built by Matteson & Williamson, also of Stockton. Some of the men who

contributed to making the combine a success were
Benton, Gaines, Haines, Houser, Ingersoll, Kincaid,
Meyers, Minges, Moore, Preble, Richards, Tesch,
Tretheway, and Young. All were wheat growers in the San
Joaquin Valley.[38]

Businessmen and manufacturers were not the originators
of the combine, but they recognized its value and most of
the ranchers soon sold their patent rights. Rufus R.
Moore disposed of his rights to L. U. Shippee, a Stockton
banker, and the Shippee Harvester Works were
established at Stockton in 1883. Houser & Haines,
established at Stockton in 1881, built and sold fifteen
machines, and then combined with Shippee in 1884 to
form the Stockton Combined Harvester & Agricultural
Works. Although both firms had made pretentious
beginnings, they could only claim that their machines
harvested 50,000 acres that fall.[39]

The expensive machinery did not win favor immediately.
The header was fairly satisfactory and remained the chief
harvesting machine in the valley from 1854 to 1884. In
1884 Traver, a pioneer region in the use of the combine,
possessed only one of them. But the sales of the various
combines gained momentum, and in 1889, the Traver
Advocate could report twenty-one huge combines at work
in the wheat fields of the 30,000 acre colony founded by
the 76 Land & Water Company.

The relatively cheap header, and the vast improvement
in the stationary threshers, retarded the sales of the
combine for a time. In 1875 a fifteen horse-power Case
steam thresher "thrashed for Dr. Glen, of Colusa
County, we believe, last season, 5,745 bushels of wheat
from sun to sun." Five years later, it was officially
reported that "a Mr. Hoag threshed 2,748 sacks, or
6,183 bushels, on July 16, 1879."[40]

The Shippee combine, based on the Rufus R. Moore invention, won the award at the California State Fair in 1884 and 1885. But the committee on awards indicated that the use of combines in the state was very limited at that time. While honors were coming to the Shippee plant, they were also annoyed by a series of lawsuits instigated by ranchers, who demanded damages for alleged poor performance of the combine. The Stockton Works therefore discarded the Shippee and built only the Houser in 1886. In 1887 the firm built the Shippee again, in addition to the Houser, the Powell, and the Minges. The latter had a twenty-six-foot cutting bar. Three of these must have proved faulty, since only the Houser was manufactured thereafter.[41]

During the 1880s the twine-binder, an invention of the Middle West, became common. But in spite of the advent of this machine, there was no perceptible increase in grain acreage throughout the nation. The only great increase occurred in California and this was based, not on the twine-binder, but on the header and harvester.

Daniel Best, who had been building fanning mills in Oregon for re-cleaning grain, came to Alameda County in the eighties. He organized the Best & Drivers Improved Combined Harvester Company and began the manufacture of his machine at San Leandro. In 1886 the Stockton Wheel Company, owned by Benjamin Holt, began the manufacture of the link and V-belt combined harvester. The same year Matteson & Williamson, who had bought the old Marvin combine, introduced the Harvest Queen. But in spite of new competitors, the Houser continued to lead the field. In 1887 there were 300 Housers at work in the wheat fields; in 1888, there were 400; and in 1889, the number had been increased to 500.

Eventually Benjamin Holt purchased the rights of

Matteson & Williamson and also bought the patents of Houser, Haines, Preble, Kincaid, Ingersoll, and Tesch. The result was the incorporation of the Holt Manufacturing Company. By 1889, the transition from headers to harvesters was taking place with great rapidity, and during the nineties the change was complete on the bonanza farms. In 1900 these huge farms were in the process of subdivision, but in spite of changing conditions two-thirds of all the wheat was harvested by combines.[42]

The huge combines of the San Joaquin Valley were never introduced into the grain fields of the Mississippi Valley, the old South, or New England. Three reasons explain this. First, the relatively small size of the fields. To attack a wheat field of a few acres with such a contraption would have been equivalent to hunting quails with a cannon. The cost of it would also have been prohibitive. Second, the presence of stones, gullies, and draws would have made its operation difficult. Third, climatic conditions in a region where rainfall occurred during the summer and autumn made it impossible to thresh the grain the same day it was cut. This was made clear by a manufacturer of eastern farming equipment.

> It should be remembered that the combine method of harvesting was developed for the dry-farming districts. If wheat contains more than fourteen per cent of moisture by weight, it cannot safely be binned. It will "sweat," and its grade, or quality, will be depreciated by the elevator man or the miller who will ultimately buy it. This moisture can be external, caused by rain or dew or the evaporation of a muddy field, or it can be internal, like the sap of a tree. Externally induced moisture seldom harms a crop and dries quickly. I have seen Canadian wheat combined in the spring after it had lain all winter under the snow. Where the sun burns, as it does from West Texas to Montana, the internal moisture is unimportant. In Kansas, hail rather than rain is the enemy to be feared. But east of the Mississippi River, the climate

Horse-drawn combine in field with Smith Mountain (Fresno county) in background. *Garden of the Sun*, 1939 edition.

until recently has been thought too humid for the harvester-thresher. There, it has been said, grain must be placed in the shock to dry before it can be threshed.[43]

Ordinarily, thirty-six horses were required to pull a combine. The extreme heat of the valley during the harvest season caused several casualties among livestock each season. Men began to experiment with other forms of motive power. The first mechanically motivated harvesting equipment in the world was invented by a man in Tulare County, George Stockton Berry, a native of Missouri, who had settled in Mussel Slough in 1874. The next year he purchased land adjoining the present site of Lindsay. At that time the entire eastern half of the valley between the Southern Pacific railway line and the foothills, and from Tulare to Deer Creek, was farmed by five men. Prior to the invention of the combine, stationary threshers and portable steam traction engines had been used in connection with the headers. Berry found on his new ranch a discarded Mitchell & Fisher portable steam engine standing beside the corral. That year heat killed several of his work stock and Berry determined to make use of his unemployed engine, which was a late model of its kind. The Benicia Agricultural Works furnished parts for it, as specified by Berry. These were shipped to Tulare and hauled by wagon to the neighborhood of Lindsay. This was a long and difficult haul, but no railway then existed between the mainline and the foothills. F. F. Latta, who investigated this invention, described its essential features as follows:

> The wheels were removed from the portable boiler and engine. Cast fittings attached large drive wheels to the front of the boiler. Movable wheels were fitted to the rear of the boiler. A tiller wheel provided means of steering the front wheels. The patented feature of the tractor connected the engine to the drive wheels. The differential was constructed of a bluff-type clutch then common on combined harvesters.[44]

This steam tractor was set between the header and the separator and was run backwards. The crew consisted of eleven men: one engineer, two firemen, two water bucks, one sack buck, one steersman, one separator tender, one header tender, one sack tender, and one sack sewer. The firemen worked by shifts forking straw into the firebox. The hot sun which often killed hard working horses and mules, coupled with the fierce heat from the firebox, added to the warmth engendered by their arduous toil, caused them to say, in the vernacular of the time: "This invention is plenty hot."[45]

But the machine was a success from the first. It was utilized for the first time in the harvest of 1886; the only difficulty experienced was with the bluff clutch differential, which wore out before the end of the season due to the constant turning. Berry then devised a heavy set of gearing that ran in a cast-box filled with oil. The men who worked with this invention called it a "jack-in-the-box." This, the most valuable of Berry's inventions, was never patented. It was identical with the differentials now in use on all tractors and automobiles; Berry's neglect in this respect lost him a mammoth fortune.[46]

The success of this venture caused Berry to employ his new tractor in the plowing which followed. In this work he ran the engine forward instead of backward. The California State Agricultural Society, in its *Transactions for 1888-89*, reported that Berry hitched his tractor to five Stockton Gang Plows, each plow having five bottoms and cutting a furrow five inches deep, and worked it day and night. A huge headlight was fitted to the engine for use at night. In those days, a shift was considered to be twelve hours long and two crews kept the locomotive busy until the fields had been plowed. The straw not used as fuel during the harvest was stacked at regular intervals in the field and used during the plowing season. By this method, Berry's men plowed 160 acres every twenty-four hours. After this work had been completed, the plows were replaced by a seeder and harrow, and four hundred and fifty acres were planted each day. The cost of plowing was estimated to have been thirty-five cents an acre.[47]

A few of Berry's machines were built to order by the Benicia Agricultural Works and sold for $7,000 each. Then Berry sold his patent rights to Daniel Best of San Leandro and entered politics. He was elected to the California Assembly in 1888 and two years later became a state senator, representing the district comprising the counties of Tulare, Kings, Kern, and Inyo.[48]

In 1889 Daniel Best's Steam Harvester, based on the Berry patent, made its appearance. Several were sold that year. An auxiliary feature was a small engine that took steam from the boiler of the tractor and operated the sickle and separator independently of the locomotion through the fields. In 1891 Best advertised steam harvesters with sickles ranging in size from fourteen to twenty feet long. About the same time, Holt also began to manufacture mammoth outfits. These steam harvesters were never common in the valley. The fire hazard was too great in the tinder-like fields of the dry regions. Only in the Tulare Lake bottom did they take precedence over the horse-drawn harvesters. But they pointed the way toward a new type of tractor that was soon to follow.[49]

The amount of grain that could be harvested by a combine was truly amazing. In 1880 C. H. Huffman, the owner of a huge farm at Merced, used a combine which was drawn by twenty large mules. It had an eighteen-foot cutting bar and cut thirty-six acres a day. The Housers in use in 1886 had cutting bars ranging from fourteen to sixteen feet; the standard length was usually fourteen feet. The 16-foot machine was expected to cut 29 acres a day. During the 1890s, both the horse and steam harvesters were increased in size. In 1900, it was officially reported: "The average standard horse machine commonly used cuts a swath from 16 to 20-feet wide."[50] Such a machine harvested and threshed 25 to 45 acres of wheat a day depending on local conditions. Such machines aroused envy in the Eastern States:

> The harvester-thresher is the most spectacular of the instruments of power farming. An early machine of this type was introduced to serve the dry wheat districts of California and the hilly benches of the Pacific Northwest. It was a monster, made after the fashion of threshing machines, principally of wood and pulled by as many as thirty-six horses. Publications in the East were accustomed to print picturesque photographs of the huge mechanism and its long train of straining horses laboring along a wheat-sheathed hillside rising up to a crown of pines. This, the urban editors thought, was expressive of the bigness of the West; and uninstructed people used to wonder how small farms could compete with the masters of such a mechanical marvel. But

the large combine, like the large tractor, was to pass into the discard before lighter, less expensive, more serviceable equipment.[51]

More serviceable equipment was destined to make its appearance in due time. But inventions making such equipment possible were to come, not from those who ridiculed the large combines, but from residents of the San Joaquin Valley who had invented the large combines and continued to use them because they fulfilled a need in a region where they were valuable.

Daniel Best's New Steam Harvester, in use during the late 1890s, had a 25-foot sickle that cut 60 to 70 acres a day. Holt's Steam Combine, with a 42-foot header, harvested 90 to 125 acres a day. In 1903, the largest wheat farm in the world, owned by Barbour and Clauson on the reclaimed bottom of Tulare Lake, was served by Best's New Steam Harvester. This machine had the regulation 25-foot sickle and according to Rogin, who studied the work done on that ranch in 1903, the average cut was 45 acres a day. This was no essential gain over horse-drawn combines. The steam harvester needed seven men to operate it; the horse combine utilized four, and harvested 30 acres daily with an 18-foot sickle. In 1904, Holt built four machines for the Kern County Land Company of Bakersfield. One of these machines in one day cut, threshed and sacked 2,460 sacks, or more than 5,000 bushels.[52]

By 1905, about 60,000 acres had been reclaimed from Tulare Lake. Steam combines were used there entirely, but not extensively elsewhere. The publicity given to the reclamation project, and the spectacular appearance of a huge fleet of land dreadnoughts, gave them a fame that was not in proportion to their general use and value. Horses remained supreme until the invention of the gas tractor. That, too, was a San Joaquin Valley invention.[53]

The delta of the San Joaquin River is composed of tule peat soil. According to scientific tests, it is the richest soil in the world. If set on fire, it will burn to a depth of several feet. In drying out after a flood or an irrigation, it will form huge cracks several feet deep. Wheat often yielded 75 bushels to the acre and potatoes 700 bushels. Such was the land which men wanted to domesticate. But neither animals nor wheel tractors could be utilized because of the powdery substance of the soil, and the huge cracks that formed after an overflow.[54]

Benjamin Holt experimented with many forms of machinery on Mormon Slough and especially on Roberts Island. He built a tractor with three wide wheels on each side. The total dimension of the six wheels was over forty feet, and this tractor buried itself in the powdered soil of Roberts Island. One evening, rather discouraged, the thought came to him of his father's old treadmill. He may have shouted "Eureka" or the American equivalent thereof. He used the traveling portion of the old treadmill as a model; this was laid on the soil and wheels traveled over it. A tractor with two large sprocket wheels on each side was devised. The two wheels on each side of the tractor carried an endless chain with wooden blocks laid across it. A single front wheel was used in steering. This new tractor was hitched to two steel wagons each loaded with eight tons of pig iron. The new invention hauled this load without difficulty across the softest parts of Mormon Slough.

At that time Daniel Best was experimenting with gas tractors. He recognized the value of the new track-lay invention and realized he would be forced out of business. Therefore he sold his patent on the gasoline tractors to Holt in 1908; the latter had been using steam tractors. The steering wheel was used until the World War. Then it was eliminated, and directions changed by shifting the

Caterpillar tractor hauling grain, circa 1910. Owen C. Coy, *Pictorial History of California.*

drive from one track to the other. The Holt Manufacturing Company had a monopoly on this type of tractor for several years.[55]

In 1910 C. L. Best, a son of Daniel Best, organized the C. L. Best Gas Tractor Company with headquarters at Elmhurst near San Leandro. He manufactured wheel tractors for a time and then invented a track-lay tractor similar to the Holt. For several years these two firms were competitors, but in 1925 they pooled their interests and formed the Caterpillar Tractor Company. A company photographer who had seen the first Holt track-lay cavort and creep around the Holt backyard at Stockton had dubbed it so, and the name caught the public fancy. This machine, with tracks geared to the ground, was a new departure in locomotion and transportation. Its use became widespread and, finally, a nationally centralized location for its factory became a necessity. Therefore it was moved from Stockton to Peoria, Illinois, in 1929. Its most salient features have been summarized as follows:

Caterpillar lays its own track wherever it goes—putting the

track down ahead and picking it up behind—endlessly and with the minimum of slip and friction. On blow sand, in slick mud, in gritty dust, on ice and snow, the Caterpillar bites a foothold. A high percentage of its generated power is delivered to the drawbar and converted into useful work.[56]

Aside from its tractor, this firm has since its establishment at Peoria, Illinois, continued to manufacture a harvester-thresher under the name of the Caterpillar Combine.

Another great manufacturing firm, the International Harvester Company, representing a consolidation of the Cyrus McCormick and John Deering interests, has gone on record as recognizing the value of the example set by the inventive San Joaquin Valley wheat growers.

As you probably know, the early California type combines were the first practical expression of a machine used to cut and thresh the grain in one operation. Their use dates back to the early 70's and even earlier. The so-called California type combines, however, were mostly large, cumbersome outfits, practical only in the big wheat-growing ranches of California and the Pacific Coast region. A few scattered machines of this type were introduced into the Great Plains section but proved to be too cumbersome and expensive to be practical in this region. What was needed was a lighter, simpler, and less expensive machine—one better adapted to the smaller power and labor units available on the prairie farms.

This led to the development of a distinct type of machine now commonly referred to as the prairie combine. The Harvester Company was one of the leading pioneers in the development of a practical prairie-type combine and its introduction into general use.

The first International Harvester combines were invented during the period of 1913 and 1914 and went into factory production in 1915. The early machines were driven from a "bull" wheel, had a 9 and 12 foot cutting width, straw walker type of separating mechanism with a cleaning shoe underneath. They were usually drawn by eight or ten horses and required but one or two men to operate. Their construction was practically all steel.

The essential difference between this type machine and the California combines were in their size and weight, the simplicity of their design, and the fact that they were constructed of steel. The basic principles of cutting the grain by means of a header platform, threshing it by means of a revolving cylinder, and separating the straw and chaff from the threshed grain were very much the same, though the manner of application was somewhat different.

Just as California may be said to have been the birthplace of the huge combine used during the early days in the Far West, so the modern prairie type of combine had its start in the Great Plains area of the Southwest. The use of the harvester-thresher in this section spread rapidly during and immediately following the Great War. As advances were made in design and construction, the use of the combine gradually spread to other parts of the country, until today there is hardly a section where grain is grown that has not witnessed the benefits of combine harvesting.

With the increased interest in harvester-threshers came the development of various models and types to meet the requirements in different localities. Thus today we find the large 16-foot machine used primarily in the West, Southwest, and Northwest; the medium-sized combines used largely in the Central States; and the small 8-foot combines popular in the East, South, and North Central States or in what is often referred to as "binder" territory.[57]

During the storm and stress of the World War, Englishmen who had during peace times used the Holt caterpillar tractor in farming operations applied it to military operations. A British army officer, Major-General Swinton, invented a method whereby these caterpillars could be armored. In order to keep their true purpose a secret, the military authorities permitted rumors to be circulated that the machines under construction were designed to carry water across the sandy deserts of Egypt and Mesopotamia to the British armies operating there. At first, they were called cisterns or reservoirs; later they were dubbed tanks and this appellation stuck. The tanks proved to be the big surprise of the World War, and offset the initial superiority of the Central Powers in machine guns and neutralized their greater mobility based on maneuvering inside the circle.

Soon Frank Simonds, a war correspondent, was able to write: "The enemy still occupies strong positions, but he has now neither the moral nor the physical power to hold these positions, and the development of the tank tactic has incalculably diminished the value of positions." More recent tanks attain a speed of more than a mile a minute, and crash through all obstructions excepting only stone walls, and these they usually climb. Pontoon attachments and propellers make them navigate bodies of water. Cavalry units throughout the world are in the process of mechanization. Spectacular charges in future wars will be based on the propelling principle of the caterpillar farm tractor invented by Benjamin Holt of Stockton.[58]

The inventions and patents of the San Joaquin Valley ranchers form the basis on which rests the fame of the Caterpillar Tractor Company. Patents on headers, combines, and steam tractors secured by a score of valley farmers passed through the hands of either Daniel Best or Benjamin Holt into the Caterpillar Tractor Company. The Caterpillar Combine owes the gas tractor to Best; the friction clutch, chain belt, and caterpillar track to Holt. This firm, basing its greatness on the inventiveness of a few San Joaquin Valley wheat growers and on the business acumen and probity of Best and Holt, are now building the small tractor-combine units which Eastern manufacturers predicted would some day replace the ponderous combines of the Pacific coast:

Obviously any small machine can be cheaper than one of several times its size. By its use the farmers of the semiarid prairie States were immediately enabled to accomplish the same savings in wheat production cost as the land barons of the Pacific Coast.[59]

The first extensive wheat growing in the San Joaquin took place on the sand plains in the region between Stockton and Manteca and on the west side of the valley between Tracy and Newman. Some of these towns did not then exist but are used for purposes of identification. An attempt to grow wheat was made by the Southern planters in the Alabama Colony at Arcola in 1868 but the hostility of the cattlemen and the distance from markets made this attempt abortive. The vitalizing influence of the Central Pacific Railway was to determine the extent of the new development in wheat growing.

In September, 1870, the construction crews of the Central Pacific worked along the north bank of the Stanislaus River. They looked to the south and beheld Paradise Valley. The entire region was a golden wheatfield. One of the chief ranchers in that primeval territory was John Mitchell. He employed sheep to clear his thousands of acres from weeds and brush. When the land had been pastured clean, and sheep are ideal for this purpose as the cattlemen were willing to testify, he planted it to wheat. On October 27, 1870, the first trainload of grain ever to leave the San Joaquin Valley by rail, left Ralston (Modesto) for the tidewater (Oakland) by M. McClanathan. As the Central Pacific pushed its rails down the valley toward Goshen more and more land was sowed to wheat until by 1874 the entire valley was one huge wheat field.[60]

In 1870 Ransome McCapes left his wheat-growing partnership, held with Henry W. Lander and Stephen V. Porter, and settled independently near Fairview, about five miles northwest of modern Sanger. Aside from his family, McCapes took with him to Fresno County two things of historic importance. One was the famous horse, Hannah, the first jerk-line leader; the other was the first Stockton Gang Plow, produced in 1868 and sold by Matteson personally to Ransome McCapes. These two men had been schoolmates in Grant County, Wisconsin. The mare Hannah died in 1873; the plow, equipped with six eight-inch shares and called a "Yankee fiddler" by the men who operated it, was used on the McCapes ranch until it was worn out.

In the fall of 1870 McCapes and his son, Eugene L. McCapes, planted the first wheat in Fresno County. They prepared twenty acres for seeding, but could secure seed for only fifteen acres. Australian white wheat was planted and after the harvest in the summer of 1871 buyers, chiefly miners from the foothills along the San Joaquin River, paid McCapes $100 a ton in gold dust weighed out on the steelyards. The next year, A. Y. Easterby harvested his first crop near Fresno. Fancher Creek, which furnished the water for that wheat field, flowed through the McCapes ranch at Fairview. The McCapes were of pioneer stock. The father of Ransome McCapes, Cyrus McCapes, had planted the first wheat grown in Grant County, Wisconsin. He brought the seed from Illinois and also introduced the first plow and reaper into Wisconsin.[61]

Two San Francisco capitalists, William S. Chapman and Isaac Friedlander, had acquired thousands of acres of government land between Madera and Fresno. It was on a portion of their holdings that the Alabama Colony was founded. Later, they were to dispose of another division to eastern capitalists who promoted the John Brown Colony. But in the meantime, with the coming of the railroad, they became wheat growers to demonstrate the land's fertility to prospective purchasers. A. Y. Easterby engaged

Charles Lohse, an experienced grain farmer from San Jose, to experiment with wheat growing on the Easterby holdings near Fresno. Lohse planted 2,000 acres to wheat; the success of this venture was insured by irrigation water brought by Moses J. Church from Kings River by way of Fancher Creek. This green oasis impressed Leland Stanford sufficiently in May, 1872, to cause him to locate the railway town near the wheat field that was destined to become modern Fresno.

The land south of Fresno proved ideal for wheat growing. Most of it was shipped from a station known as Wheatville, later renamed Kingsburg. South of Kings River, the 76 Land & Water Company developed a tract of 30,000 acres, which by 1886 was one continuous wheat field. West of Goshen, the farmers of Mussel Slough devoted themselves to wheat growing in a manner that was later to be dramatized by Frank Norris in The Octopus. Tulare became the center of another wheat district and appeared in The Octopus under the fictitious name of Bonneville. Traver was the chief shipping point during its heyday; later, its place was usurped by Terra Bella, south of Tulare. Bonanza farms were common in those days. Even in later years, when diversified farming had become the vogue, Clovis Cole had a 10,000-acre wheat farm east of Fresno. The site of Clovis indicates its location. The new railway towns served as loading points for the wheat growers. Huge warehouses were erected at Modesto, Turlock, Merced, Fresno, Kingsburg, Traver, Tulare, Hanford, and Goshen. Life as it centered on these wheat towns was often gay and boisterous.[62]

Traver holds the world's record for the amount of grain shipped from a producing point during a single season. Five reasons explain the tremendous activity that centered at that place from 1884 to 1888. First, the vast nearby acreage included in the holdings of the 76 Land &

Water Company; second, the extreme fertility of the soil, which was then uncontaminated by alkali; third, a series of seasons with an adequate rainfall, combined with warm weather, which produced bonanza crops; fourth, the attempt to avoid the obnoxious "short-haul" rate caused farmers in the Mussel Slough area and in the Four Creeks country around Visalia to haul their grain to the main line of the Southern Pacific; and fifth, the wheat farmers between the Sierra Nevadas and Traver were without railway facilities, and Traver was their nearest shipping point. The Kaweah Co-operative Commonwealth, a unique experiment in colonization, was located forty miles east of Traver and yet considered this town its nearest shipping point. The only bridge across Kings River between Traver and Kingsburg was a toll bridge. This caused the wheat growers south of the river to haul their grain to Traver, although the Kingsburg warehouses were much nearer to them measured in terms of miles.[63]

When the grain wagons from this vast territory began to converge on Traver, the resulting congestion can better be imagined than described. A resident of Traver at that time stated that one morning the line of grain wagons waiting to unload extended out into the plains for more than a mile. Two days were ordinarily required for a wagon to work its way to the place of unloading. There were three warehouses in Traver, and the three lines of loaded wagons extended in parallel columns a mile or more. Occasionally, men spent a full week waiting in line before they could unload. John C. McCubbin has left the following pen picture:

> During the grain season it was a daily sight to see the three long wagon trains, the front of each lined up at a separate warehouse, and the rear of the column extending several blocks away. On one particular occasion, one of these trains reached from the 76 Warehouse to the corner of Eleventh and

Hershey Streets. It was practically a mile long.

At such times a team would take its place at the rear of the column and be two days working its way up to the front where the wagons could be unloaded. Those who could not wait so long, would unload alongside the railroad and later haul to the warehouse or load on the cars from where it lay. Hundreds of tons were handled in this manner.

Since the advent of the motor truck, the long wagon trains with their beautiful animals have gone forever. No words can do justice to one of these trains in motion, nor can the imagination of one who never saw its counter-part produce more than a dim picture of that rare spectacle.

In memory we see the dust-begrimed "mule-skinner" at the rear of the long string of animals that draw the three loaded wagons. There with drooping shoulders, partially shaded from the scorching sun by his broad brimmed sombrero, he patiently sits in his saddle astride the off wheel horse, jerk-line in the left hand, brake strap in the right, and black snake hanging by a loop to the right wrist. Now the wagons alongside the warehouse are emptied and move on. The whole procession prepared to advance the length of the building, which is five hundred feet. The crack of black snake, the clank of "fifth" chains as they tighten, and the "chuck" of the wheels are heard, along with the beautiful chimes of the numerous hame bells that adorn the leaders. Over all is heard, sharp and clear, all up and down the long line, the volley of oaths poured forth by the teamsters. Many a good Christian name worn by these long-eared beasts of burden would be used as a nucleus around which vile epithets and profane language would be grouped, with revolting effect upon the ears of those who might be unaccustomed to hearing such disgusting abuse.[64]

A magnificent picture of wheat farming in the San Joaquin Valley was penned by Frank Norris in his novel, *The Octopus*. The climax of his story was the fight at Mussel Slough. Although not a resident of the valley his facile mind saturated itself quickly with the great subject.

The Octopus, on the other hand, gives the impression of having been written by a man raised in gigantic pastoral backgrounds. One can see him following the harvester from childhood, growing up in an atmosphere of seed-time and harvests and foreclosed mortgages. The only preparation that Frank Norris ever had for this colossal story was three weeks spent upon the famous Miller & Lux ranch in lower San Joaquin County.[65]

The bonanza wheat farms which Norris described with a master's hand can still be seen in all their pristine glory. A newspaper article printed in 1929 carried the following caption: "Grain Ranch in Corcoran Area is Small Empire." The description of this bonanza farm will substantiate the accuracy of the earlier descriptions of Frank Norris.

With the harvest season opening in the San Joaquin Valley, the large scale farming done on the A. H. Wolfsen ranch, fourteen miles west of Corcoran, containing 12,000 acres of wheat and barley, has proved of considerable interest to farmers.

His camp alone is a small town in itself, located in the center of a section of grain. His camp is equipped with all modern conveniences such as electric lights, electric refrigerators, running water, electric stoves for cooking, and radios. He feeds fifty-two men at the camp.

The water used in irrigating this enormous ranch comes from nine deep wells, ranging from 1,800 to 1,950 feet in depth. 100-horse-power motors lift the water. In this section, one irrigation is sufficient to produce unusually heavy yields. Barley on the Wolfsen ranch averages from twenty-five to thirty sacks to the acre.

Wolfsen does his work with five harvesters, which are able to cut and thresh two hundred acres of grain in a day, or 6,000 sacks of wheat.[66]

Most of the ranches in the reclaimed Tulare Lake bottom still embrace huge acreages at the present time (1938). Wolfsen farmed 12,800 acres that year, the Von Glahn wheat field consisted of 25,400 acres, and the D'Artney brothers had 29,500 acres. The kinds of wheat discussed in connection with the early days of the industry have been entirely superseded in the Tulare Basin by Baart wheat, listed by the government as hard but by the trade as semi-hard. Two other varieties, Onis and Federation, are also grown, but to a lesser extent.[67]

Barley in this area, regardless of the variety, contains a higher protein than does the same variety elsewhere. Atlas barley has proved ideal for the requirements of the English brewers who manufacture a heavy beer and the result is that "British brewers come all the way to California for their brewing barley because they know it is the best in the world." Some Marriott barley is also grown since it gets along with less water than any other variety.[68]

The fertility of the soil is such that 70 bushels to the acre is not unusual. The floods of 1937 caused many of the huge levees to break and thousands of acres of wheat were ruined. On the ranch operated by Arthur H. Wolfsen, fourteen of the twenty sections were flooded. When the water rose to a height of thirteen feet against the sixteen foot levee surrounding the other six sections, he rushed his combines into the field in an attempt to save at least a part of his crop. In spite of the haste and waste necessary at such a time, he harvested twenty-five bags to the acre (2 1/4 bushels to the bag).[69]

The Harris Combine, the largest in the world, is used in the Tulare Basin almost exclusively. These machines are manufactured at Stockton, have a 24-foot cutting bar, and will harvest forty acres a day. Caterpillars have replaced the old-fashioned steam tractors.[70]

Under modern conditions in the Tulare Lake region, it is estimated that it costs $4 an acre to get the seed into the ground. This includes the cost of the seed, the working of the soil, and the drilling. During the years when irrigation is necessary an additional $6 an acre is needed. Thus the maximum cost per acre until harvest time is $10 per acre; usually it is only $4. Wolfsen reported that his power bill usually amounted to $65,000 a year.[71]

The coming of the railroads made wheat the staple crop of the valley. Its economic importance relegated the old haphazard methods of farming to the limbo of the past. Men began to care for their soil even as they cared for their livestock and their machinery. The plowing was done in February and March. After the harvest, they began the practice of summer fallowing. This gave the soil a needed rest, fertilized it by permitting the absorption of ammonia and fertile gases from the atmosphere, destroying foul weeds, and permitted early planting in the fall before the first rains fell. Where the fields were not summer-fallowed, weeds grew profusely and the hot, dry summer hardened the soil to such an extent that it could not be plowed for sowing until the fall rains had softened it. This naturally delayed planting. Conditions governing wheat farming in the San Joaquin were entirely different from those prevailing in eastern states and men had to experiment and could only learn by the old, expensive method of "trial and error."

Great care was taken in the preparation of seed wheat. First it was cleaned from chaff and foul weed seeds. Then it was washed in water, and if evidence of smut appeared, it was soaked in water for twenty minutes and placed in a solution of bluestone, dipped in freshly slaked lime, and sacked to await the sowing time and germination. It was customary to sow fifty pounds to the acre, but the chief mistake of early San Joaquin Valley farmers was a too-bounteous sowing. The fertile soil of the valley caused a remarkable stooling and tillering. Not even the valley of

1880s harvesting scene from a typical San Joaquin Valley farm. Owen C. Coy, *Pictorial History of California*

the Nile surpasses the San Joaquin as a grain country and the first wheat growers in the latter valley, familiar with the soil of less fertile eastern states, were too generous in their broadcasting of seed. The result was a choked field. However, they learned by doing.[72]

In 1868 W. H. Parks, then president of the California State Agricultural Society, was able to state:

> I may, however, congratulate you upon the proved position our State occupies today. Although young in years, she has taken place with the first of the older States in importance as a grain growing state. At the late Paris Exposition, she stood first for her cereals, and her mechanics carried off more prizes, in proportion to the number of exhibitors, than did those of any other portion of the world. This, then, would argue that we not only have the soil, climate, and natural wealth, but that we have also the genius and enterprise so

necessary to the speedy development of our country.[73]

Ten years after California had been admitted into the Union, it was beginning to rank with the best of the grain-growing states. It still led all others in the production of gold. That year, 1860, wheat sold for an average price of $1.50 a bushel, and the quantity can be gauged by the following quotation:

> Were you to place all the bushels reaped in 1860 by the combined states of Massachusetts, Connecticut, Rhode Island, Louisiana, Florida, Texas, Mississippi, New Hampshire, Missouri, Arkansas, and Alabama, and the San Joaquin Valley crop of 1860 in one, and were you offered either heap for the same price, you would make a profit of 59,444 bushels by taking our pile.[74]

California exceeded any other state in the production of wheat in 1874 and in 1875. Wheat growing reached its zenith in 1884; the founding of colonies and the introduction of horticulture and dairying then began to change the aspect of things. During the heyday of this form of farming, the average price per bushel was $1.15; from this, there was but a slight deviation.

An official report rendered to Governor Markham by the State Board of Agriculture is illuminating:

> While wheat has been declining in price for several years, by our improved system of farming, and especially of harvesting crops, there is as much, if not more, profit in the business than for many years preceding the advent of improved machinery. For instance, we do all our summer-fallowing (more properly speaking, spring plowing) with gang plows. As large farming is done with these gangs, which consist generally of four plows attached together, or four plows in one frame, one man with a team of six or eight horses can plow six acres per day. In seeding the ground, we use the common broadcast seeders, followed by an eight-horse harrow. Under this system of seeding a great saving is made. In harvesting

our crops we use the combined harvester, which cuts from 28 to 30 acres per day. A harvester with an 18-foot sickle, will, in an average grain field, cut and thresh from 350 to 400 sacks, or 800 to 900 bushels, per day, at a cost, counting wear and tear of machinery, feed of animals, wages and board of men, not to exceed $1.00 per acre.[75]

In 1852 the San Joaquin Valley produced only 112,309 bushels of wheat. By 1874 this had been boosted to 7,521,096, and that year the state of California led all others in the production of wheat with 21,840,000 bushels. California continued in the lead for several years. In 1876 the San Joaquin had 960,721 acres sowed to wheat, which produced 12,096,041 bushels, with an average price per bushel of $1.92 1/2; in 1893, during Cleveland's administration, it dropped to $1.01 1/2. The high price of 1876 caused wheat growing to boom, and the greatest expansion of the industry in the San Joaquin came in 1884—the year Traver was founded—when 1,300,631 acres were planted, and 17,997,212 bushels were gathered. The acreage planted; to wheat began a steady decline at this time, and by 1895 production had dropped to 7,146,148 bushels.[76]

The climate of the valley is ideal for wheat raising. The average rainfall is 9.92 inches per year. Of this amount, 65 percent falls from December to the following March, and 85 percent from November to the following April. The rainfall during the months of June, July, and August is .14 of an inch. Sufficient rainfall during the winter and spring, followed by a dry summer, produces wheat of marvelous quantity and quality. The average yield per acre was about thirty bushels. When the river bottoms along the Kern River were first sowed to wheat, the harvest yielded seventy-five bushels to the acre.[77]

Several varieties of wheat were grown. All of these belonged to a group known collectively as white wheat.

Soft winter wheat was grown east of the Mississippi River. Hard spring wheat was produced in Minnesota and the northern states of the trans-Mississippi West. In this region the typical variety was durum wheat, often called macaroni wheat, since it furnished the flour for this product. The states south of the Dakotas and west of the Mississippi were devoted to the growing of hard winter wheat. California was to complete the cycle of varieties grown in the United States by specializing in the production of white wheat. This is a soft grain and almost as light in color as unhulled rice. The kernels of this grain are club-shaped or square-headed. In the production of this type the San Joaquin Valley was supreme.

The San Joaquin Valley farmers experimented with many varieties of white wheat. The White Australia was a shy bearer, but of superior quality. It was suited to a dry climate and produced wheat of a hard, dry quality. The White and the Red Chile were both of average good quality; the White Chile was noted for its heavy yield. The Chile Club was also a heavy bearer. The prime favorite in the San Joaquin was the Sonora. This was introduced by the Spanish. It ripened early and yielded heavily. A warm dry climate was its natural habitat. Other varieties deserving honorable mention were the California Club, Oregon Red Chaff, Foise, Palouse Blue Stem, Palouse Red Chaff, White Winter, and Little Club. In many cases, their names indicate their original home. Conditions in the San Joaquin produced a hard kernel of wheat with a thin skin, which could be shipped to the ends of the earth without bruising. Another unique tendency was the inclination of the kernel to wrap itself tightly into its sheaf, and the shelling common in eastern wheat was unknown. The grain could wait in the harvest field from June until October. There was no shelling, no haste, no rain, and no lodging.[78]

A bearded variety known as "red wheat" was brought to Kansas by Moravian, Dunkard, and Mennonite immigrants from Russia. This wheat, grown originally along the Volga and the Danube rivers, was planted in the river bottoms of the San Joaquin and the Kings. It was one of the few kinds, other than white wheat, to achieve prominence in the San Joaquin. It was used for blending due to its hardness and high gluten content. Two varieties of recent years have been Defiance, a hard white wheat, and Early Baart, which will produce twenty sacks to the acre during a drought where other wheat would fail to even grow.[79]

Life in the wheat growing era of the San Joaquin Valley was comparable to the life made famous by Gertrude Atherton in *The Splendid, Idle Forties*. After the plowing and seeding, which was usually done in January and February, there was not much to be done until the harvest in the summer and autumn. Many months of each year were comparatively carefree for the grain men. Summer rains and autumn frosts were unknown. The nervousness and haste rampant in eastern states during the harvest did not exist in the San Joaquin. A harvest scene on the Middle Border was often a madhouse, according to Hamlin Garland's *Main Traveled Roads*. The degrading toil often left human wreckage in its wake. But such scenes were never necessary in the San Joaquin. The grain fields were left until such time as it was convenient to harvest them. And then labor-saving machinery made the work less strenuous than similar activities east of the Rocky Mountains.

A feeling of peace and well being pervaded the land. The church and the lodge were all-important to the people of that time. When the popular Methodist clergyman of the Stanislaus countryside, Father Bishop, announced services to be held at early candle-lighting time, he was sure of a large and attentive audience. Men of the cloth, regardless of their denominational affiliations, were honored by the flocks in a fashion which men of their ilk now might well envy. People went to church then, perhaps at times, due to a lack of other attractions, but they were never indifferent. The Ladies' Aid, the lodge, the church sociable, and the neighborhood dance made life and its amenities glide along like a song. No radios, phonographs, or jazz existed, but when youth gathered at a large home of a bonanza wheat grower, a rollicking fiddler was always present to furnish the music as the young men and women danced the polka, waltz, schottische, mazourka, quadrille, or the Virginia reel. Happy hearts vibrated in complete harmony with the soothing landscape that surrounded them. Sol P. Elias, who knew those days well, has recorded his impressions of his own locality in *Stories of Stanislaus* which may well serve for the entire valley, which was then one continuous and unbroken wheat field:

> In the summer, the entire country was a wavy wheat-field from one extremity to the other. To the wayfarer as he journeyed along its dusty roads and traveled among its well-kept farms wherein the ancient hospitality still found lodgment, the vibrating fields, animated by the gentle northern breezes, resplendent in the varied tints of the growing sun, gave a rich carpentry to Mother Earth that was charming to the eye.

A beautiful place was Old Stanislaus in these by-gone wheat growing days—beautiful in the simple vocation of its citizenry, in the contentment and prosperity of its inhabitants and in the social intercourse of its people.[80]

But a mistral arrived to chill the sunny scene. Life in the country where the grain was grown was sweet and wholesome; in the towns where the grain was stored and shipped, it was often putrid and corrupt. The saloon element moved into the railroad towns and assumed political control. The tillers of the soil have often been the victims of malefactors of wealth and political power. For a time, reform was impossible. Jury trials were a farce, since shyster lawyers could secure as witness's disreputable loafers who prostituted their souls for a pittance. At that time Walpole's cynical remark was veracious: "Every man has his price." The local newspapers, willing enough to be the molders of public opinion and the leaders in moral reform, were nevertheless not endowed institutions. They had to consider advertising space, circulation lists, and paid-up subscriptions. The retailer feared the wholesaler; nothing must interfere with sales. The saloons and the red-light district paid cash. The druggist sold more medicine, drugs, and perfume to the red-light district than to all of the decent part of the citizenship. What could he do? Sol P. Elias, who resided at Modesto during that period and later served as its mayor, has left a description of those days:

> Like every frontier village that grew up with a rush and experienced unexampled prosperity from the start—thereby attracting to its confines the rougher elements of society who sought opulence without honest endeavor amidst the primitive customs and the open life of a rudely and rapidly constructed town—Modesto, in its infancy, suffered its period of open lawlessness, its era of unbridled gambling, its reign of brutal thuggery, its sway of the malign saloon influence, and its season of brazen, flaunting vice. The liveliest mining camp, situated upon civilization's extreme verge, in the height of its most wide open activities, possessed no edge upon Modesto in the years 1879 to 1884. Such was the strenuousness of its night life that it held the reputation throughout the state of being a place in which there was literally a man served for breakfast every morning.

> At this period Modesto was an extremely prosperous village. The wealth that was garnered from the bountifully productive virgin soil poured into the city as though the fabled mines of

Ophir had been tapped. From the offices of the warehouses that contained the grain that rolled in from the prairies and from the vaults of the bank that stored the gold into which the wheat had been transmuted, even unto the tables of the gambling halls, the counters of the barrooms, and the parlors of the gilded palaces, it permeated every avenue of communal activity. Money in plentitude was spent with a recklessness and prodigality that baffled understanding. Young Modesto manifested the spirit of the youth who had suddenly acquired affluence and was frittering away his substance like a nabob possessed of an inexhaustible spring of riches. Modesto was in its golden age.

Modesto then presented the spectacle of a town in the grip of those elements whose activities were antagonistic to the written law as well as to the mandates of decency. The Front was wide open both day and night. It became the rendezvous of the most daring sports, gamblers, and saloon habitues that could be found in the state. Gambling and drunkenness were rampant. Hardly a night passed during which some derelict who floated in from the country to enjoy a rest from labor or a season of joy was not fleeced in a game of cards, robbed and beaten up, or plied with liquor until he became insensible and his pockets picked by the light-fingered gentry. The Front [Front Street, Modesto's Tenderloin district] displayed a continuous round of gaming, thievery, and thuggery. Shooting scrapes were frequent. Drunken carousals made the night hideous, courts and lawyers were busy with the flood of criminal business that originated on the Front. In fact, in these days criminal practice was the most profitable portion of legal work.[81]

Modesto was not an isolated example of conditions as they existed in the towns during wheat growing days; it was typical. Traver, lying 120 miles to the south, experienced exactly the same affliction at the same time. John C. McCubbin, who served as an official of the 76 Land & Water Company, wrote a series of newspaper articles entitled "The Rise and the Fall of Traver" which pictured conditions as being similar to those in the north:

There were more than a half score saloons and gambling hells, together with other places of evil, that were running unrestricted in that wide open town. Hundreds of laborers, employed in the warehouses, at the ditch camps, and on the ranches, collected their wages every Saturday night, and the scene witnessed along Front Street on Sundays beggars description. Scores of men would stagger up and down the street trying to keep track of all the gambling games that were running, and the drunkenness would increase as the day advanced. Crowds would assemble where an exciting game was in progress, and not only fill the building but extend clear out across the sidewalk, forcing pedestrians to take to the street.

Two places "across the track," where men without self-respect and women without shame congregated. served as a legalized way station on the road to ruin. The resorts mentioned, one of which was a dance hall, housed fifteen to twenty women. At that time there were no speed regulations in California that applied to traffic on the highway to perdition except the single one strictly enforced against every owner of an empty purse.[82]

The boisterous life prevalent during wheat growing days was a direct result, like many other evils, of idleness. After the men employed on a bonanza farm had completed the seeding in the spring, they were practically unemployed until harvest time. Even then climatic conditions made haste unnecessary. Where should they go and what should they do during the summer months? Traver, Modesto, and the other wheat towns beckoned to them. The saloons and the gambling "joints" offered amusement. During the long, tiresome wait incidental to the delivery of grain the teamsters wanted solace and they found it.

In August 1879, the law-abiding element of Modesto and its environs organized a secret and masked vigilance committee known as the San Joaquin Valley Regulators.

These men wore black masks and robes, similar to those worn by the members of the old Ku Klux Klan of the South that was organized to combat the carpetbagger and the scalawag immediately after the Civil War. The Regulators, in one fell swoop, drove the lawless element from the town. The next year, 1880, a similar Vigilance Committee was formed at Hanford, largely at the instigation of Rev. N. W. Motheral, which drove the gamblers and prostitutes from that city. This shows the similarity of conditions throughout the valley towns. The lagan refused to stay down and a recurrence of evil conditions prevalent in those "bad old days of sin and gin before Volstead took our breath away," caused the Regulators to subject Modesto to a second dry-cleaning in 1884. This extra-legal and organized attempt to combat vice was final. A repetition was never necessary. In time the work of the church, the program of the school, the growth of civic pride, and the influx of additional doughty settlers, transformed the cities along the Southern Pacific railroad into models of propriety and virtue.[83]

The development of wheat growing in the San Joaquin Valley kept pace with the ever-advancing terminals of the persistent Central Pacific Railway. Mushroom towns sprang into being overnight, and attracted from the wild gold camps of the Sierra and the shrieking seaport towns a kind of men who flung their primal passions into the face of humanity and laughed. For a time, wantonness stalked unchecked. But opposed to them were the settlers, the workers who actually reaped the wheat, who possessed in their souls the germ of law and order. Bitter was the struggle and great was the price, but license finally succumbed to law. The tumult and the strife, which was rampant for a time, should not be taken as an indication of general lawlessness. Dramatic episodes and deeds of violence naturally attract more attention from the novelist, the historian, and the settler himself, than does the law-abiding conduct of kindly souls, whose purposeful lives were based on positive convictions of right and wrong.

The material excellence of the San Joaquin Valley is equaled by the fine quality of its citizenship. To succeed under the trying conditions which confronted the first wheat growers in the San Joaquin required a clear vision of the future, a sublime courage in overcoming hardships, an adroitness in avoiding disaster, an ability to solve new problems, an inventive turn of mind able to devise improvements, a charitable attitude toward their neighbors, and a simple faith in the omnipotence of Divine Providence which led them to believe that:

> Back of the loaf is the snowy flour,
> And back of the flour the mill;
> And back of the mill is the wheat and the shower,
> And the sun, and the Father's will.[84]

13 The

Mussel Slough

Fight

Here have we war for war
And blood for blood.

William Shakespeare *King John*

"I heard ten shots fired altogether; it lasted about three-quarters of a minute." This was the description by an eyewitness of the greatest battle fought between white men in the San Joaquin Valley.[1] The United States Marshal, Alonzo W. Poole, also an eyewitness, reported what he saw in this fashion: "The party, all on horseback, began circling about me. Suddenly there was a rush, and I was struck on the foot by a horse, and fell to the ground. Firing commenced and I should think twenty or thirty shots were fired. By the time I got up the firing had ceased."[2] These two testimonies by reputable men show a disagreement as to the number of shots fired. The same difficulty is encountered in determining almost every important event in the entire Mussel Slough episode.

The bloodiest battle of the Civil War was fought at Shiloh where five hundred men out of each thousand engaged were hit. At Mussel Slough, a miniature battle it is true, eight men were hit and eight men died. The court determined later that eight men carried weapons. Such an affray was sheer annihilation and worthy of the comment of Pierre Bosquet, the French general, as he watched the Charge of the Light Brigade: "C'est magnifique, mais ce n'est pas la guerre." (It is magnificent, but it is not war).

This battle took place a few miles north of Hanford in the district then known as Mussel Slough and now called Lucerne. The site, according to A. T. Ellis, who opened the gate for the United States Marshal just prior to the fight, was in Section 4, about 150 yards from the southwest corner. The owner of the land in recent years has been Henry Doggett.[3]

Eight men lost their lives, and the tragedy of it sent a wave of horror throughout the state. The number of men killed was relatively insignificant. Had eight men been slaughtered in a barroom brawl, it would have caused scarcely a ripple in California at that time. Homicides were taking place every night during those years in the wheat towns lying along the Southern Pacific main line. It was not the quantity but the quality of the slain citizenship that caused consternation. Those eight men were property holders and taxpayers, heads of households and fathers of families, men without guilt or guile, spotless in reputation and flawless in conduct, members of

Fresno Republican

SATURDAY..........MAY 15, 1880.

Communications on topics of local interest or items of local news will be welcomed from any quarter. Correspondents are requested to write briefly upon one side of the paper only, to send in their favors as early in the week as possible and give their full names and addresses, not for publication, but as a guarantee of good faith.

BREVITIES.

The Democratic primary election in this county takes place to-day.

Strawberries, green peas and new potatoes are abundant in our market.

A new trial has been denied in the case of S. C. Booth vs. W. S. Chapman.

The new town lately laid out between Fowler's Switch and Kingsburg is called Irwin.

A. H. Statham has added some new teams and elegant buggies to his livery stock.

Fresno county is now assured of

Mussel Slough Tragedy.

An Attempt to Eject the Settlers results in the death of seven men.

The terrible tragedy that was enacted near Hanford on Tuesday last, and the intense desire of all our people to learn the facts and incidents attendant, induced the REPUBLICAN to dispatch a special reporter to the scene on Thursday morning. A careful investigation reveals the following to be substantially the facts, as given by eye witnesses: On Tuesday morning, about 9 o'clock, U. S. Marshal Poole, W. H. Clark, grader of railroad lands, accompanied by W. J. Crow and M. D. Hartt, left Hanford in buggies and drove out to the residence of W. B. Braden, who was not at home. His household goods were removed by the Marshall and those with him to the public highway, and Hartt was placed in possession. The party then entered their carriages and drove to the place occupied by Dick Brewer and ——————— and a

One of the first newspaper accounts of the Mussel Slough tragedy.

churches and lodges. Suddenly, a short circuit in the main current of their lives caused lambent lights to flicker over a frenzied scene for a few moments, and eight lives were burned out, leaving darkness in the hearts of their families and friends. Not death but the cause makes the martyr. They were big men, but the force, which catapulted them into sudden internecine strife, was greater than they were. Thinking men throughout the nation were startled into ejaculating: "Something is wrong somewhere!"

Only a few embattled farmers at Concord Bridge fired the shots heard round the world; only five men were killed in the Boston Massacre of March 5, 1770, but it convulsed a whole nation; only eight men were killed in the Mussel Slough fight of May 11, 1880, but it aroused an entire state. Death in the forenoon in a certain wheat field

marked the time, and ominous red stains among the
stubble marked the place from whence resolute men were
to begin the forward march on the long political crusade
which, thirty years later, resulted in the restoration of the
lost sepulchre of popular government to The People. That
is the real significance of the Mussel Slough fight.

The cause of it all was a contest over land titles with the
Southern Pacific Railroad representing one side, the
settlers the other. The railway had a legal right to the land
according to the decision of the United States Circuit Court;
the settlers had a moral right based on fair promises. The
company fought for its property; the settler, for his home.
The railway invoked the aid of the federal courts in the
state and won; the settler maintained that the Southern
Pacific dominated both state and federal courts in
California at that time, and that justice was dead. The
president of the Southern Pacific was also the governor of
California. The legislature continued to be dominated by
the railway corporation, and several years after the Mussel
Slough fight it elected Leland Stanford, the ex-governor,
United States senator from California. Corruption was
seated in high places—so argued the settler.[4]

Frank Norris has told a part of this story in *The Octopus*,
a novel. In this book Norris did for Hanford, Visalia, and
Tulare (Bonneville in the novel) what Owen Wister had
done for Medicine Bow. To millions of readers, these
towns became definite places on the map. Each of these
authors dealt with a specific phase of frontier
development. After the courts of Wyoming had become
corrupt, the cattlemen sought to enforce justice by
extralegal methods. The wheat growers of the San
Joaquin attempted to remedy a similar condition in a
similar fashion. Wister's cowboy hero with the Southern
drawl typified one element in that development; so did
the cantankerous Buck Annixter. The villain in one novel

was Trampas, a cattle thief; in the other, S. Behrman, a land thief.

After President Theodore Roosevelt had read The Octopus he wrote to his friend, Owen Wister: "What I am inclined to think is that conditions were worse in California than elsewhere." Using this sentence as a text, Wister developed the theme:

> In that surmise, Roosevelt was entirely right—unless my own sufferings on the Southern Pacific were exceptional; and unless what my friends in San Francisco had to say of the sufferings of California in general in the huge grasp of the Southern Pacific were very much overstated; and I don't think they were. I did not hear these complaints once, I heard them season after season during those years of the early nineties when I was constantly, and for weeks together, in San Francisco. Unless you came by sea you could not get into or out of California, except by the Southern Pacific, until the much later arrival of the Santa Fe. Every passenger over land, every head of stock, every grown fruit or vegetable, every manufactured article, had to travel over the rails built and controlled by C. P. Huntington and his small group of associates, who also controlled the legislature. Consequently, the rates that shippers had to pay, with the arbitrary discriminations against which they had no redress, did constitute a very oppressive tyranny indeed.[5]

Many of the settlers in the Mussel Slough area have asserted that Frank Norris favored the railway in *The Octopus*. Owen Wister thought that he was unfair to it:

> *The Octopus* presents no proportionate recognition of the fact that the courage, the vision, and the ability of C. P. Huntington created the original railroad, the Central Pacific, pushed it across the barrier of the Sierra Nevada, and linked California with the rest of the country. This put the State on the map of reality instead of the map of romance; it touched commerce and transportation to life. The man who does this for any community is an enormous benefactor to that community, no matter how much he may afterwards abuse

403

his power, which C. P. Huntington undoubtedly did.[6]

The entire matter of the land grants made to the Southern Pacific by the United States is confusing. On July 14, 1868, the Secretary of the Interior, Orville H. Browning, wrote to the United States Land Commissioner: "The designation of the general route of the Southern Pacific Railroad not conforming to law, my order of the 19th of March, 1867, directing you to order a withdrawal of lands (from the public domain) for said road is hereby revoked." Orville H. Browning and Abraham Lincoln, both Kentuckians, became lawyers in Illinois. They were great friends and endowed with the same high ideals. When Lincoln received the nomination for President, Browning conveyed the official thanks of Illinois to the assembled Convention. Browning was "a Kentucky gentleman of the old school, a compendium of gracious manners and fine codes."[7]

The original Southern Pacific had planned to build a road connecting San Francisco with Los Angeles. Its route, approved by Congress, led from Gilroy down the west side of the valley to Goshen and thence to Los Angeles. When the Central Pacific secured control, the "Big Four" disapproved of the barren hills and plains of the west side. Therefore, construction was discontinued at Tres Pinos. However, they built a road from Goshen to Coalinga eventually, which left the gap between Coalinga and Tres Pinos minus a railroad. It still is. The question then arose whether or not the Southern Pacific could legally claim the twenty alternate sections per mile along the route actually constructed in view of the fact that they did not complete the terms of their contract.[8]

General William Starke Rosecrans, of Civil War fame, was a friend of the railway corporations. He secured a suspension of Browning's revoking order and thereby prevented the immediate return to The People of the railway grants. While this perplexing question was baffling the best minds of the country, settlers began to arrive in the Mussel Slough country. In 1869 they prepared to file homestead and preemption claims. Among the early wheat growers were John Chambers, Louis Meyers, Peter Kanawyer, Robert N. Howe, and many others whose names will appear hereafter. Mrs. Sarah Railsback, prominent in social and political circles in Hanford and Kings County for many years, was a daughter of John Chambers and niece of Archibald McGregor, one of the men killed in the Mussel Slough fight. They secured land prior to the coming of the railroads. But the land was still unsurveyed and ownership uncertain. Was it government or railway land?

The Land Commission maintained an office at Visalia but until matters were clarified the settlers could get little satisfaction from it. This they naturally resented. In those days a pre-emption claim could be made on a hundred and sixty acres and paid for at the rate of $1.25 an acre, or a homestead claim could be filed for eighty acres involving three years actual residence before full ownership was granted. The railway land office was at Sacramento and from it issued many of the circulars inviting settlers to buy its lands.

On November 20, 1869, Jacob D. Cox, then Secretary of the Interior, wrote to the Land Commissioner:

> I have carefully considered the papers filed by the company (Southern Pacific) and I can come to no other conclusion than that, in the location of their road, they entirely disregard their charter from the State of California, which in the Act of Congress, is given as their authority to build a road in said state. The withdrawal (of land) not being on the route the company was authorized to construct a railroad, the suspension of Mr. Secretary Browning's order of August 20, 1869, is hereby revoked.[9]

The Secretary of the Interior, a friend to the farmers, thus sustained the original action of the former secretary and decided against granting the disputed land to the Southern Pacific.

The railroad company then took the matter to court and won its case. The settlers appealed the case. One of the leading characters in *The Octopus* was called Magnus Derrick. To him all the other wheat growers depicted by Frank Norris looked for leadership and guidance. This character in fiction had a prototype in real life named Thomas J. McQuiddy. He had much of the strength and none of the weakness of Magnus Derrick. Another leader and organizer among the settlers was John J. Doyle. The latter's land case was finally taken to the Supreme Court of the United States. While this case was pending, the railway company began a series of dispossessions on writs issued from the federal circuit court at San Francisco. The settlers decided that before they permitted themselves to be dispossessed, the railroad must prove its superior right to the lands. One of their arguments was based on Section 8 of the Act of Congress dealing with land grants to the Southern Pacific:

> That each and every grant, right and privilege herein are so made and given to and accepted by said railroad company upon and subject to the following conditions:

> That said company shall commence the work on said road within two years from the approval of this Act by the President, and shall complete not less than fifty miles per year after the second year, and shall construct and equip, furnish and complete the main line of the whole road by the 4th of July, 1878.

The settlers pointed out that the main line was not completed until three years after 1878 and thus the lands were legally forfeited. They further argued that not a stroke of work had been done along the original route from Tres Pinos to Huron, a distance of a hundred and ten miles. The third argument was based on what they called the deliberate falsehoods of the company which issued circular pamphlets inviting settlers to go upon their lands before the patents were issued or the road completed; that the road promised to sell them the land in preference to any other applicants, and at prices based upon the value of the lands *without regard to improvements*. These settlers then spent $400,000 on irrigation and dredging systems and then the agents who graded the value of the land charged the settlers for their own improvements.[10]

These were some of the problems demanding solution in the weeks preceding harvest time in 1878. A meeting was called at the Grangeville schoolhouse, and about sixty settlers were present. William L. Morton was elected temporary chairman, and John J. Doyle secretary. Morton never attended a settlers' meeting after this one; evidently he was uninterested or disapproved of their purpose.

That night a Settlers' Land League was organized. Conflicting stories were afterwards told concerning its purpose. Prior to the formation of the League, a Vigilance Club of seven members had carried on a legal battle with the railroad. The Settlers' Land League attained a membership of four hundred settlers. The Grand League had its headquarters at Hanford, and six subordinate leagues existed in adjacent towns. John J. Doyle was one of the deputy marshals appointed by the Grand League to organize the settlers for the purpose of making a legal fight for their lands. An assessment of ten cents an acre was levied on each member to finance the contest.

The Settlers' Land League had a constitution and a pledge that they would remain together for mutual protection. The chief officer administered the obligation. The meetings were held in secret. According to L. C. Hawley, secretary of the Grand League, the objects of the organization were to make a legal fight for their lands and not to remain by force.[11]

Not all of the settlers were in favor of the organization. When one of the subsidiary branches was organized in the Selma district a man named Winfield Scott Hopkins, a native of Virginia and a sympathizer with the cause of the Confederacy, was told that he must take a solemn oath to obey the League officials without question and above all other authority. He replied: "You men do not know what you are attempting to do. I have lived in a state where the people, my people, thought they could whip Uncle Sam. I have seen the result of that attempt, and I have learned my lesson well. I will never take part in such an attempt. I cannot join you."

Most of the settlers in the Mussel Slough region were, like Hopkins, Southerners by birth or extraction. Reared in the faith of Jefferson and Patrick Henry, they valued liberty above life, and justice above law. The written law favored the railroad but that law had been unjustly drawn. The settlers had no desire to rob anyone; they simply refused to be robbed. The railway land agents and station agents were arrogant and officious. Had they kept off the toes and out of the light of the settlers the latter no doubt would have remained polite. They resented any one, even a corporation, biting a thumb in their general direction and were willing to fight without wages. The owners of the Southern Pacific were New England Yankees by descent, and sectional hostility had not died down during the decade that had elapsed since the Civil War. The settlers may have felt that the Yankee "Octopus" was doing to them what the Reconstruction program was doing to their kinsmen in the Old South. Then, too, the entire nation at that time was permeated with hostility toward the railway corporations. No doubt the railroad was coarse, crude, and to blame; it is equally true that many of the settlers were of an emotional type, willing to join the Settlers' Land League, the Ku Klux Klan, or any other mysterious organization where they could "wrap their faces in a diaper" if it only provided fun, excitement, and immunity from detection.[12]

The preliminary meeting held at the Grangeville schoolhouse was attended by three men who were violently opposed to the movement. They were Walter J. Crow, Louis Haas, and Theodore Marsh. As these men are to be mentioned occasionally hereafter, it is well to say something about each. Crow's family, natives of Missouri, founded Crow's Landing west of Modesto. Haas, at one time a member of the sheep firm of Haas and Williams, had owned the ranch east of Kingsburg later known as the Clarke Ranch. His daughter, Pennsylvania Haas, had married Walter J. Crow. She is Hilma Tree depicted in *The Octopus*. Marsh's sister was the wife of Louis Haas and the mother of Pennsylvania. According to Marsh, Doyle's explanation of the proposed League was the need for concerted action in retaining their lands pending the final decision of the Supreme Court. Apparently no force was premeditated.[13]

One of the bitter opponents of the Settlers' Land League was Dr. George de Wolf, admittedly a railway partisan. His vocation was the practice of medicine, and his avocation the gathering of local news for the Associated Press. In the latter capacity he attended open meetings of the League. In a meeting at Lemoore a member inquired if the statement "violators of the League obligation shall be left to the League" meant death. Doyle answered, according to De Wolf, that "it could mean nothing else." The latter accused Doyle of making facetious remarks concerning the burning of a ranch house belonging to Perry Phillips, a sheep man, which was occupied at the time of the fire by a renter named Hodges. According to the report circulated at that time, the incendiaries were red men, but whether they were Indians or white men dressed in red was not made clear. Dr. de Wolf assumed that the Settlers' Land League was guilty because Doyle jocularly remarked that these men might be heard from again.

Doyle denied in court that the violation of the League oath would incur the death penalty. He also explained that an Indian had been killed in a card game with some cowboys or sheepherders from the Phillips ranch. The tribesmen had then held a war dance on the Tom Thornton ranch, after which they avenged their friend's death by burning a house belonging to Perry Phillips. Since the latter was a big stockman and a foe of the settlers, he naturally placed the blame on the Settlers' Land League.[14]

The three wheat growers appointed to negotiate with the Southern Pacific concerning ownership of land were John J. Doyle, James N. Patterson, and Major Thomas J. McQuiddy. Doyle, besides being a wheat grower, was a justice of the peace and a notary public. He was also a director of the Grangeville & Antioch Railroad. He wrote a petition to Congress in behalf of the settlers in 1874; in December 1875, after his return from Washington, a preliminary meeting was held at Grangeville which resulted in the definite organization of the Settlers' Land League at Hanford on April 12, 1878.[15]

The organization of the League was followed by the formation of a military squadron under the command of Major McQuiddy. The latter was an able man, a native of Tennessee, and had served as a major of cavalry in the Confederate Army. Companies of settlers were drilled at night in the towns of Grangeville, Lemoore, and Hanford. In subsequent years, many pioneers have vehemently denied the existence during those years of any form of military organization. However, the verbatim reports of the court testimony printed in the various San Francisco newspapers during 1880 indicate that even the defendants admitted such an organization. They merely denied the purpose attributed to it by the prosecution. The defense lawyer, Edward C. Marshall, made the final plea to the jury. He ridiculed the charge that his clients had organized a force with intent to resist the United States Government; however, he did not deny that a semi-military group existed and that it had a legitimate aim in view. He asked this ironic question: "Was it possible to think that the chivalry of Mussel Slough, even with black masks and mules, were going to array themselves against that power? Was an army of forty men and forty mustangs which occasionally deployed through the streets of some poor little village going to do that?"[16]

The settlers held formal parades and contended that the squadron was a local necessity due to the forays of outlaw bands then operating from the west side of Tulare Lake. In 1873 Vasquez and his desperadoes visited Kingsburg and Kingston. Later, they raided Grangeville. Procopio, an accomplice of Vasquez and a nephew of Murieta, committed a holdup in the Huron vicinity one evening and during the melee a prominent settler, Solomon Gladden, was killed. These events aroused the Mussel Slough settlers and the result was a protective semi-military organization.

Enemies of the Settlers' Land League accused them of plotting against the United States Government and of planning physical resistance against it and the Southern Pacific. They contended that the drilling of men on horseback indicated a conspiracy against the nation. The settlers stoutly asserted that forays, theft, the burning of houses, and other lawless acts were the work of Indians and outlaws then flourishing in adjacent regions and to

blame them for the very things which they were
organizing to prevent was unjust.

A renter named Ira A. Hodges occupied a house belonging
to the sheep man, Perry Phillips. This house was located
four miles east of Hanford and eight miles from
Grangeville. One evening, about 150 men dressed in long
gowns and wearing red masks formed a circle around the
house and ordered Hodges, his wife and their little child
to get out. Their furniture and personal belongings were
then quickly removed to the road and the house set on
fire. The men explained to Hodges that Phillips was
claiming too much land, and that this piece of ground
belonged to the government. Then the masked men
returned along the road to Hanford. Such was the version
of the fire made in court by Hodges.

The settlers maintained that an Indian had been killed in
a card game on the Phillips home ranch near Kings River
in the vicinity of Kingston and that the other red men had
wrapped themselves in red blankets and burned his
renter's house in a spirit of revenge. But Hodges testified:
"I saw the mustache and the chin whiskers of one man
through the disguise. Obviously such foliage did not grow
on an Indian.[17]

In the spring of 1879 the famous Irish labor agitator from
San Francisco, Denis Kearney, had made a public address
at Hanford. Some time before this he had coined the
slogan: "The Chinese must go!" The settlers vociferously
applauded him when he concluded his address by saying,
"Don't give up your lands; we shall come to your aid with
40,000 men." He may have been of a combative
disposition, that man; but he was the soul of generosity.
Needless to say, when the crisis arrived he was too busy
agitating elsewhere to be of aid to the embattled farmers
of Mussel Slough.[18]

Dr. de Wolf brought another charge of lawlessness against the League. He stated that between one and two o'clock on a July morning in 1879 a crowd of masked men called him to the door of his house and the leader asked him, in a disguised and gruff voice if he knew Buzzard or Gizzard or Crow, De Wolf replied that he knew Crow, but did not know his whereabouts. About thirty or forty men were present and all wore black gowns. They rode away when the doctor went out to count them.[19]

Jerome Madden, the Southern Pacific land agent, made repeated visits to Hanford. On one occasion he was accompanied by Collis P. Huntington; on another visit, Leland Stanford went along. The latter visit was made on March 11, 1880. On that occasion, a sightseeing tour was organized in order to give Governor Stanford an opportunity of seeing the land under dispute. Madden and Doyle rode together in the same buggy. On that occasion Madden informed Doyle that the Southern Pacific was preparing to send the United States Marshal to evict settlers who had refused to pay for their lands. Doyle replied: "That will be very bad work; there will be trouble. There are a great many members of the League that are very desperate, determined and reckless persons, and they have an idea they are fighting for their homes and are capable of doing anything."[20] Madden was nonplussed and deprecated the use of force. He told Doyle: "It would be an act of insanity. Don't you know that the army and navy of the United States are behind the Marshal, and resistance can only make matters worse?" The sum and substance of Doyle's remarks at that time, according to Madden, were: "The Southern Pacific directors want that which is wrong, and I want that which is right."[21]

On April 10, 1880, Daniel W. Parkhurst visited Hanford. He was employed by the Southern Pacific to sell and rent railroad patent lands, and to collect crops or grain rents.

On that occasion Doyle, Patterson, and McQuiddy advised him to leave town and work elsewhere until the Supreme Court had rendered its verdict. They told him frankly: "It is impossible for us to hold back some members of the League." The committee wrote a telegram that they dispatched to Governor Stanford: "Parkhurst is here. We consider it a want of good faith." Stanford evidently did not deign it worthy of a reply. Late the next night, Parkhurst was called to the door of his hotel and confronted by several masked and armed men. The spokesman asked, "When do you intend to leave?" Parkhurst answered, "Tomorrow." The speaker then said, "You must leave, you cannot live in this country. We will hold you to your word."

Concerning this visit to Hanford, Parkhurst made the following statement in court:

> I was told to desist from selling land, inasmuch as there was a great feeling in the League against such proceedings. No personal threats against me were made. They acted very gentlemanly. I was told by Major McQuiddy that I must leave. We were alone. He said, "I think it is best for you to go." It was said in a very friendly way. He considered it best for my personal interest that I should leave. The whole conversation appeared to be for my benefit.[22]

In evicting settlers, it was natural that the railway would proceed to place other men on the land. When the settlers had refused to pay the big prices finally determined by the land grader of the company, the land was declared forfeited and sold to other men. These could not take possession without aid from the company. The original settlers had taken the matter to court and had lost in the United States District Court and also in their appeal to the Circuit Court. They were waiting for a final verdict from the Supreme Court. In the meantime, the Southern Pacific, on writs issued by the United States Circuit Court, proceeded to dispossess the settlers. A group, somewhat similar to the Settlers' Land League, known as the Committee of 19, consisted of the recent purchasers of railway land and was naturally antagonistic to the League.[23]

Two men who bought railway land that they were unable to occupy were Walter J. Crow and Mills D. Hartt. Naturally, they disliked the settlers who refused to give them possession. Crow was a peaceable and law-abiding citizen, but his land difficulties with the settlers had aroused his ire. In July 1879, a cattleman named T. M. Kennan went to the home of Louis Haas at Grangeville.

> Crow and Hartt were not in, but subsequently they came up. They remained all night and so did I. We had breakfast with Haas in the morning, and then I got my wagon ready, and they came out, got their horses, and took their arms with them. Inquiring as to the reason they were going about armed, they answered that they were in constant trouble with the settlers, and then they pointed out the upper portion of the house, saying, "We've got an armory there, and there are not less than 300 shots."[24]

On this occasion, Kennan accompanied Hartt and Crow to Cross Creek and then to Smith Mountain. During the ride they regaled him with stories concerning the settlers and what they proposed to do with them. They threatened to scatter the settlers like a flock of quails if they failed to secure possession of their land within a short time.

Kennan, who had known Crow since the latter's boyhood, described him in this fashion to the Circuit Court sitting at San Francisco:

> He was a man who was bound to drive ahead when he thought he was right. He would go to much greater extremes than the rest of the human family under similar circumstances. He often told me that he had trouble with sheep-herders and others in travelling where it was a question as to who should occupy the main road when both

415

parties were travelling in opposite directions. He said that if they had not given in he would have shot them. I think I would hold on if I was in the right, but not about sheep (Laughter).[25]

The attitude of Hartt toward the settlers was emphasized by Cornelius (J. H.) Paddock, a resident o the Mussel Slough vicinity since 1866. He related that on October 23, 1879, the year preceding the fight at Mussel Slough, he and Hartt were practicing shooting at a target. Paddock complimented Hartt on his skill as a marksman, and Hartt replied: "I am practicing because there is a probability that I will have to shoot some sand-lappers." According to a newspaper reporter present at the trial:

> This new word caused quite a commotion in the court. The audience and the jury tittered audibly and a smile even passed over the countenance of the Judges as the witness proceeded to explain what a sand-lapper was. It was a word in everybody's mouth; originally, from a stock-raiser who said he feasted the whole lot of sand-lappers with one ox. Hartt used the term with reference to settlers.[26]

The United States Marshal, Alonzo W. Poole, left San Francisco on May 10, 1880, for the Mussel Slough country. He carried with him writs of possession for Crow and Hartt which had been issued by the federal circuit court. Poole was accompanied by William H. Clark, the land grader for the Southern Pacific, who was to direct Poole to the proper ranches. Clark knew the temper of the settlers and was apprehensive of what might occur during their visit. He told Poole that Crow, Hartt, and Phillips were hostile toward the settlers and that trouble might ensue. The Mussel Slough settlers were facing a double-barreled opposition. Men who had bought land from the railway desired their eviction; stockmen, who have always hated homesteaders and nesters and dry-land farmers were their traditional foes. Anticipating an unpleasant reception at Hanford from the settlers, Poole and Clark

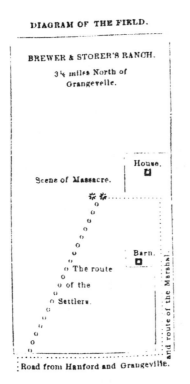

DIAGRAM OF THE FIELD.

BREWER & STORER'S RANCH.

3¼ miles North of
Grangeville.

Scene of Massacre.

House.

Barn.

The route
of the
Settlers.

and route of the Marshal.

Road from Hanford and Grangeville.

Crude sketch map of the Mussel Slough tragedy site and what happened there, taken from the May 21, 1880 issue of the *Visalia Weekly Delta*.

decided to leave the train at Kingsburg. Here they hired a livery rig from Josiah Draper and appeared in Hanford on the morning of May 11. John L. Sullivan, who was a druggist at Grangeville in 1880, furnished this information: "In answer to your letter of recent date, I wish to say that the Marshal hired a rig at Kingsburg to go to the Brewer ranch. On his return trip McQuiddy and someone else accompanied him to Kingsburg where they took the train."[27]

After locating Crow and Hartt, who had been waiting for them, they proceeded to the ranch of William B. Braden. The latter was absent from the house (Braden was a

417

bachelor and no one else was around), and the marshal ordered the furniture removed from the house. Hartt was then officially placed in possession. Then the four men drove along the road toward the ranch occupied jointly by Henry Dexter Brewer and John Storer. Shortly after leaving Braden's ranch they encountered the latter and the marshal informed Braden that he had been dispossessed. Then they proceeded on their way and soon met Storer. He had been a personal friend of the marshal in Monterey County, and Poole told Storer that he was sorry to find his old friend in trouble, but that he was merely obeying orders. Crow offered to adjust their difficulties, and Storer rode out to discuss the matter with his partner, Brewer, who was plowing, and was just at that moment in the act of turning his team at the other end of the field. While Brewer and Storer were conferring together concerning Crow's proposal, the Mussel Slough battle started. Incidentally, it may be stated here that Henry Brewer was considered one of the best shots in that part of California but this day he was unarmed and took no part in the Mussel Slough fight.[28]

Poole and Clark had left Hanford in their buggy at seven in the morning. Some time thereafter they had found Crow and Hartt northwest of that city. The latter duo were riding in a wagon. The two vehicles had then proceeded to the Braden place, and thence to the Brewer and Storer ranch.[29]

Among the settlers who planned to attend this picnic was James N. Patterson, a son of Joshua Patterson. The former was one of the most level-headed men in that region. On the way to Hanford he met his friend, Wayman L. Pryor, who announced to him the startling news that the United States marshal had arrived. Pryor feared trouble, but Patterson was of an unexcitable temperament. However, he yielded to his daughter's importunities and returned to Grangeville. On his way thither he met Major McQuiddy, who informed Patterson that the news of the marshal's presence had reached the picnic and that great excitement prevailed. Patterson saddled his horse and left home with the intention of serving as a peacemaker. He met Archibald McGregor, who was riding with some friends in a wagon. When Patterson told him the news McGregor mounted his horse, which was tied behind the wagon, and the two men rode to the ranch home of John D. Pursell. From there they went to William Braden's home and saw the furniture piled up in the road. The news of the evictions was rapidly spreading, and soon a score of men, mounted and armed, were following Patterson to the Brewer ranch. The tragedy did not begin until they got there.[30]

One of the most reliable witnesses during the trial of the Mussel Slough settlers was Rev. N. W. Motheral. This Presbyterian clergyman had arrived in Hanford in February 1880 from Nashville, Tennessee. He was a favorite among the cowboys and settlers. Like Ralph Connor's "Sky Pilot," he had interested them in the building of a church. Mingling with the people had taught him much concerning their troubles. He soon became a figure of importance and influence. Shortly after his arrival he organized a vigilance committee which expelled from Hanford some lawless men, mostly Mexicans, and some lawless women, mostly prostitutes. Some time prior to May 11 he heard about the judgments which had been obtained against the settlers, and he noticed the subsequent pessimism. In order to meet this crisis, a picnic was planned by the settlers to which every one was invited. This social affair was held in one of the big grain warehouses at Hanford, where the tables were set for the community dinner. Judge Terry of San Francisco was to have been the speaker, but he was unable to be present. He had sent his written opinion concerning the judgments, and this was to have been read to the assembled wheat growers. But the guns, which now began to boom out at Mussel Slough, prevented its ever being read.

Regarding that fateful day, Rev. Motheral stated: "There was a cloud hanging over all the community after the judgments were obtained. The people did not know what would be done. About thirty minutes before the shooting took place I heard a gentleman say, "We will send them all off like a lot of chickens."

The Court asked Rev. Motheral whether or not the burning of the house occupied by Hodges was the act of the Settlers' Land League. He replied: "I would not like to endorse every man belonging to a League of 300; I spoke of the reputation of the defendants, and not of all the members of the League."[31]

When Patterson reached the southwest corner of the Brewer ranch, he and his men broke down a section of fence. The marshal and his party had entered from the northeast corner. When Crow saw the men tearing down the fence he reached for his gun, but Poole advised him not to use it except in self-defense. Then the marshal walked rapidly toward the cavalcade. When he met them, he had walked about sixty yards from the wagon where Crow and Hartt were sitting. While he was introducing himself and explaining the purpose of his visit, someone interrupted him and said, "We don't want to hear any more; we know you have papers, but you can't execute them. We have appealed to the United States Supreme Court and have equities which have never been heard." When the marshal said he was willing to admit that they had equities, Wayman Pryor retorted: "Then what in hell are you here for?" During the conversation a settler said they were going to defend their homes. And a nervous young man added, "Yes, and make a tombstone of my heart." This remark struck the marshal as somewhat peculiar.[32]

Several settlers pointed their pistols at the marshal and James Harris demanded that his party give up their weapons. When Poole protested, several men cocked their pistols but Patterson intervened by saying calmly, "Oh, never mind, he is a United States officer, and has a pride in keeping his weapons." While this parley was going on, some of the horsemen had been circling towards the buggy occupied by Clark and the wagon in which Crow and Hartt were sitting. Hartt was lolling back in the seat, with his feet on the dashboard; perhaps his indolent position proved maddening to the tense and overwrought settlers. Suddenly a rush was made toward the two men in the wagon and the marshal, accidentally struck by a horse, fell to the ground. A bullet apparently struck the dirt in front of him, throwing sand into his eyes. The battle was on.[33]

The details of the Mussel Slough fight are both gruesome and hard to determine. What weapons were used? This is a controversial matter. Pioneer settlers, who have been interviewed personally, have disagreed. Most of them have insisted that only pistols were used. But the United States marshal, chief witness for the prosecution and presumably a friend to Crow, testified as follows: "The horsemen were breaking down the fence. Crow reached down and picked up his shot-gun. I told him not to touch his weapons unless an attack was made." In regard to the presence of rifles on the field, he added:

> I know there were arms in the wagon as I saw, when at the Braden place, a shotgun and a rifle, which were taken out before we loaded the wagon with furniture. Previous to that time the guns were concealed under the sacks in the wagon. I saw a pistol in Hartt's possession but whether at that time or afterwards, I cannot say. I did not see Crow have a pistol. I think the rifle was a Winchester, but whether the model 1873 or 1876, I cannot say.[34]

Patterson, chief witness for the defense, corroborated the marshal's testimony in this respect:

> I am under the impression that Crow and Hartt both fired while in the wagon. Crow got out of the wagon with his shotgun and fired. Pretty soon I heard him say to Hartt, "——— ———- it, bring me that rifle." Hartt got out of the wagon in a clumsy way, as though he was wounded, and the team ran away. He took the gun to Crow, who said. "——— ———- it, this is not the rifle." It was a double-barreled shotgun, and commenced loading. I went up to the bodies and found the men dead. I took the pistols from the bodies.[35]

From contemporary evidence it can be adduced that the settlers were armed only with pistols, which all men in that region carried as a matter of course, but that Crow and Hartt had in their possession two shotguns and one Winchester rifle. It is also proved that the three guns were actually used. This was the testimony during the trial, and no attempt was made in court to refute it.

Who fired the first shot? In attempting to solve that query one is reminded of the eternal question propounded by Pontius Pilate: "What is truth?" Reputable men, who tended Hartt during his last extremity, later gave conflicting testimonies concerning Hartt's dying statements. According to Daniel Spangler, Hartt said that Harris rode up and aimed at Crow. There was bad blood between these two men, based on a quarrel when both were residents of the northern part of the valley. When Harris fired, his unruly horse threw the shot out of alignment and it struck Hartt in the abdomen. William L. Morton asserted that Hartt said, "I never fired a shot." Dr. J. A. Davidson, who tended the wounded men, said that Hartt moaned in his delirium, "I shot only once." Just before he died Hartt told Hugh Robinson: "Without any enmity, Jim Harris fired the first shot, so help me God!" In the first fusillade, Hartt was shot in the groin and a heavy bullet from Crow's 1876 model Winchester crashed through the stomach of Harris. Crow then jumped out of the wagon and fired his double-barreled shotgun point blank at Harris, and twelve heavy buckshot entered his chest with sufficient force to come out through his back.[36]

Crow yelled at Hartt, "———- ———- it, bring me that rifle." Hartt, trying to control the half-crazed team, had difficulty in getting out of the wagon. He shuffled toward Crow in a clumsy fashion because of his wound. The frightened team promptly ran away. The animals on which the settlers were riding became unmanageable due to the sudden and rapid firing. Hartt managed to hand Crow the shotgun and Crow shouted angrily, "———- ———- it, this is not the rifle." Hartt, already in a semi-comatose condition, had fumbled around in the wagon-box and picked up another double-barreled shotgun by mistake.[37]

McGregor had been told to guard the marshal, and the two men were standing some distance away. Suddenly a bullet from Crow's pistol struck McGregor in the front; he spun around, threw up his hands, and his cry of pain was cut short when another round entered his back. Then Henderson, a settler, went wild with grief and rage, and charged Crow, fired, missed, fired again and received Crow's bullet in his chest. Every man who was hit that day died, although Hartt lingered for almost four days.[38]

At the beginning of the fight Crow's team ran away toward the west, returned on a wild run, and then left again toward the west. Clark's livery team from Kingsburg also ran away to the west, but wheeled quickly and nearly upset the buggy. Clark was powerless to hold them; finally, some of the settlers halted the team and disarmed Clark. The shooting was now over.

Crow came up to Clark's buggy and leaned against the wheel, breathing heavily as if exhausted. Hartt also came up and, saying that he had received a mortal wound, lay down on the grass. The marshal testified later:

> Crow came up, much excited and bareheaded, with his
> shotgun in his left hand. He turned Hartt over, and Crow
> changed his gun to his right hand. I asked him if he was
> wounded. He said, "No," but that they had tried to murder
> him. I told him to catch a horse standing near, and break for
> the woods. Another party of horsemen was coming up from
> the direction of Hanford. Crow said, "No, that won't do." He
> then started off in a stooping position.[39]

Regarding the aftermath of the fight, Patterson made the
following statement:

> Afterwards I said to Crow, "Walter, you ought not to have
> done this. The settlers did not come here for anything of this
> sort." Major McQuiddy came up and said to me, "This is bad
> work. How did it happen ?" He asked for the marshal, and I
> pointed him out. A little later I attempted to ride over to
> where McQuiddy and the marshal were talking, but Crow
> pointed his gun at me and said, "____ _____ you, one at a
> time." There was no intention on the part of the settlers to
> resist the marshal.[40]

By this time a large body of horsemen were seen
approaching from Hanford. Crow left the battlefield on
foot and in a stooping position in order to avoid detection.
He entered a wheat field and hid. No one dared approach
him in ambush. In the meantime a settler, supposedly
Caleb W. Flewelling, captured Crow's runaway team, took
out Crow's rifle (which Hartt had failed to bring him
during the fight), and waited for the owner. When Crow
left his hiding place in the wheat and approached his
home, he was shot and killed by his own rifle in the hands
of the waiting settler who, according to some accounts,
had climbed a tree in order to get a bird's-eye view of the
surrounding territory. William Morton told the court that
Crow was found two miles from the battlefield and that he
had been shot between the shoulder blades. Joseph
Fraters, one of the many deputies looking for Crow,

chanced to meet Flewelling on the road and was told to go home if he did not want to get shot; the young man went. Later, Fraters saw Crow's body and said that he had been shot from the side and that the bullet had pierced his body at right angles, going through the biceps of both arms. One of the first men to venture out into the wheat field to see if Crow was really dead was Nis Hanson.[41]

During the fighting the men had scattered over the field. McQuiddy, who had not been present during the fight, now assumed command and detailed a group of men to escort the marshal and Clark to the Kingston road as it was considered dangerous for them to go to Hanford. The marshal said that "McQuiddy conveyed to me the impression that I had better get out of the way, as there were men in the party who had been so much excited that it would be difficult to control them. I went by way of Wild Flower to Kingsburg."[42]

The evening following the fight was a tragic one in Mussel Slough community. Men were deputized to look for Crow; others were needed to care for the wounded settlers. Dr. A.J. Davidson, an elderly doctor from Hanford, rendered medical assistance. This doctor was used to scenes of bloodshed. He was a graduate of Johns Hopkins, had done post-graduate work in London, and had served with the British Army in the Crimean War where he labored with Florence Nightingale to improve sanitary conditions. He was present on that dramatic occasion when Lord Cardigan, having received a ridiculous order from a superior officer, mounted his chestnut thoroughbred stallion, made the flippant remark: "Well, here goes an earldom and sixty thousand pounds a year," and straightway led the Charge of the Light Brigade into the dark valley of death and up the higher sunlit slope to immortality. He returned to the United States, served as a surgeon with the Army of the Potomac during the Civil

Major Thomas J. McQuiddy, ex-Confederate soldier and one of the heroes in the struggle for settlers' rights in the Mussel Slough district. *Elliott's Hisory of Tulare County*, 1883.

War, and then settled down to what he hoped would be the peaceful life of a country doctor. At different times he resided in Kingsburg, Kingston, and Hanford, and served these communities as the kindly family physician in that horse and buggy era.[43]

In spite of Davidson's skillful ministrations, Kelly died quickly, and McGregor in the morning of the following day. The latter, a tall, handsome, and good-natured man, had thirty-six buckshot holes in his back, and the air came out of these holes in his back when he breathed. Joseph Fraters, a young clerk employed in the Herman Nathan grocery store at Grangeville, was assigned to stuff cotton wads into these holes to prevent the air and blood from oozing out. Crow; Harris, Henderson, and Knutson had all been killed on the battleground. The last-named was friendly with Crow, and it is thought that in the excitement Crow had mistaken Knutson for Mike White, a personal enemy and similar in appearance to Knutson. Hartt died four days after the fight. Pioneer settlers disagree concerning the cause of Haymaker's death. The usual story is that worry over a scalp wound, plus the grief over the death of his friends and neighbors caused his death. However, his son, H. A. Haymaker, made the following statement:

> My father as, shortly before his death, an innocent spectator, was shot on that day when a flying bullet went through his hat rim and cut a scalp wound. A week after the incident, he was none the worse, but the fact he died thirty days later of pneumonia has led writers to believe his death was due to the shooting, which it was not.

Chris Evans was not a Mussel Slough settler. Before this time, he had experienced some difficulty with the railroad over land in the northern part of the valley. Then he had moved to Visalia. Several pioneer settlers have stated that he attended the picnic at Hanford on May 11th, and went out with the other men to the battlefield after the shooting. They have also stated that he was one of the four or five men composing the group which took Crow's rifle from the wagon and waited for him to emerge from his hiding place in the mixed field of wheat and alfalfa, and that it was Evans who shot him at a distance of half a mile as Crow was climbing over the board fence which separated the Haas property from the place where he was hiding. The first men to approach Crow did so warily. He lay over the fence with arms outstretched, as if reaching for his shotgun, which lay on the ground before him. They feared that he might be playing possum.

Old timers who have been interrogated have all agreed that in the "public thinks" of the period Caleb Flewelling was the man who pulled the trigger in the shooting of

Crow; in the "private thinks" of that time, there might have been found another story. Since the few men who were present when Crow was shot were all tight-lipped, the reader may draw his own conclusions. After Evans had become a notorious outlaw, enemies of the settlers found it easy to hold him up as an example of the kind of people who had resisted the railway. His only comment on the Mussel Slough fight was made while he was held in the Fresno jail after the fight at Stone Corral.

> Crow opened the battle with a shotgun. He had been promised a 160-acre ranch for his dirty work. All he got was a 6x4 grave. He came near getting away though. He got through an alfalfa patch and over some hay . . . when somebody blew the top of his head off with a shotgun.

One result of this tragic affair was the indictment of seven men for resisting a United States officer in the performance of his duty. The case was not now between the settlers and the Southern Pacific: it was between the settlers and the United States government. The men indicted were John J. Doyle, James B. Flewelling, James N. Patterson, William Braden, John D. Pursell, W. L. Pryor, and Courtney Talbot. The trial was held at San Francisco and presided over by Judges Ogden Hoffman and Lorenzo Sawyer. About thirty settlers were summoned as witnesses, and they remained during the entire trial. The jury panel was completed on November 30, 1880, and the verdict was rendered on December 23, of the same year. The attorneys for the prosecution were United States District Attorney Phillip Teare and his assistant, A. P. Van Duzer; for the defense, Mr. Highton and Edward C. Marshall.[44]

The United States Circuit Court before which the Mussel Slough settlers were tried is not to be confused with the present U.S. Circuit Court of Appeals, which was not organized until 1891. In 1880 there were only two regular federal courts, the district and supreme. President Pierce had recommended the creation of a new federal intermediate appellate court, but the slavery question engrossed the attention of Congress to such an extent at that time that no notice was paid to the president's message "except that far-off California was given a circuit court and a separate circuit judge."

In his statement to the jury, Mr. Highton paid a tribute to his clients that a later generation is perhaps willing to accept:

> The defendants were not outlaws, nor members of the criminal classes, but are, and will be proved to be, God-fearing Americans, of that type which settled the country, whose actions were perpetuated throughout its history, and who have brought civilization out of the wilderness; men who have identified themselves with the progress of the country. They had taken up their residence on a desert, comprising thirty miles of land, built their homes, improved and beautified the soil, turned rivers into heretofore arid country, introduced educational facilities, expecting to found an American community of settlers.[45]

Patterson's version of the Settlers' Land League, of which he was an active member, received considerable attention in the newspapers the day following his testimony. The metropolitan press wrote about him as follows:

> In response to an inquiry by Judge Hoffman, the witness replied that his land was not in any way involved in the controversy, and his motive in taking part in the League was that he thought it was just and right on the part of the people who were members. He described elaborately the circumstances of the affray, and attributed it to the precipitate action of Crow and Hartt. As he told how his friends and long-time neighbors fell, killed and wounded, he was very much affected, and once had to leave the witness stand, take a drink of water and rest for a moment.
>
> He said he had endeavored in every possible way to act as a

peacemaker; had reasoned with Crow; had drawn a small pistol, which he had only in self-protection, and then had it out but a short time. He turned his attention to the killed and wounded, and was conscious of doing nothing except what he considered to be the duty of any good citizen under similar circumstances. His testimony evidently made a strong impression upon the jury, and every juror seemed to pay the closest attention to every word of it.[46]

An element of facetiousness was introduced into the trial during the cross-examination of Wayman L. Pryor. While relating the story of the fight, the presiding judge interposed the following question: "Why did you carry a pistol?" To which the rancher replied, "What does any man carry one for? Did you ever carry one? (Laughter). It is the custom of the country. We wished to persuade the marshal if we possibly could. We thought perhaps if we laid the case before him possibly he would not serve the process— that there being a number of us perhaps it would have more influence upon him."[47]

Naturally the United States District Attorney would cross-examine John J. Doyle, one of the chief leaders in the Settlers' Land League, concerning the aim and purpose of that much maligned organization. The following news item appeared the day after Doyle had testified:

> J. J. Doyle, one of the defendants, was then sworn, and his direct examination occupied the most of the afternoon session. He testified in a clear, straightforward manner, answering all the questions asked coolly and deliberately, and with apparent frankness. He gave a complete history of the organization of the Settlers' Land League at Hanford, and the six subordinate Leagues, and, so far as allowed by the Court, a statement of the difficulties with the railroad which led to the formation of the society.[48]

Assistant United States District Attorney A. P. Van Duzer made the concluding argument for the prosecution:

> While you are trying these defendants, yet, in a larger sense,

the good name and fame of the State of California is on trial to ascertain if this is a land of law and order or of mob rule. The offense here to be submitted to your consideration in the indictment consists of two counts: First, a conspiracy to resist the United States Marshal; second, actual resistance of that officer in the attempt to execute a legal process.

In the first place, let us segregate such points as are admitted on both sides to be true—facts in regard to which there is no controversy, before examining the disputed points. First, it is a fact about which there is no controversy, that A. W. Poole, a duly commissioned and acting United States Marshal, armed with a legal writ, issued upon a solemn judgment of this Court, went on the 11th of May last to the County of Tulare in this State, to the place known as the Brewer and Storer ranch, to place W. J. Crow in possession of the north half of Section 9. There is no dispute about that. Second, that he was resisted by force, and by force compelled to leave without making any service, is also beyond dispute. There is no controversy on this point.

The next inquiry is: Who committed this offense? What is admitted by both parties in regard to this important inquiry? Let us inquire. What are the admitted facts relative to the second count, or count for resisting a United States Marshal?

First, that all the defendants were present at the scene of the conflict in company with a large number of other persons with deadly weapons in their possession who surrounded the United States Marshal, demanded his surrender, and refused to allow him to read the writs; subsequently, under armed guard, marched him a long distance from the place where he was met by the defendants, and enjoined to leave the county at once, on peril of his life; which injunction he was not slow to obey. No dispute about this.

Second on this point, the defendants, Patterson, Pryor, Pursell, and Braden were on the ground and took part in all the acts that resulted in the obstruction of the marshal, the defendants Doyle and Talbot arriving on the ground before the marshal was conducted off the field.

Third on this point, there were at least ten of the party acting with the defendants, who were armed with weapons, to-wit: Harris, Knutson, Henderson, Pryor, Kelly, Patterson, and Breeding. In addition to these, four armed men were detailed by McQuiddy to conduct the marshal out of the county, making eleven armed men proved by the defendants themselves. How many more we cannot state.

Now, these are the facts admitted to be true and proved by the witnesses on both sides. These facts are sufficient to convict the defendants on the second count for actual resistance, and from this there is no escape.

We now come to the points on which the defendants attempted a defense. The evidence of the defendants in this case is divided into two branches. First, while not denying their presence at the scene of the conflict they attempt to say that they were not there to obstruct the marshal but to preach to him. Second, that they were peaceful and intended only to protect Brewer from Crow, and in the attempt to do this, they try to establish that Hartt fired the first shot and precipitated the unhappy conflict. Third, that so far as the charge of conspiracy was concerned, counsels for defendants claim there was none; that the League was harmless and peaceful as a Sunday School.

Let us examine the evidence on this point. In the first place, you will agree with me that the circumstances connected with and surrounding the legal controversy in regard to these lands did not require any such oath-bound, elaborate, secret organization with a Grand and subordinate organizations; with a Grand Master and Deputy Grand Master, a Grand Secretary, and a Grand Organizer, and a system of laws empowering the League to levy assessments on all the lands known as odd sections in two counties, and holding the power to enforce their decrees with the awful penalty of death. The questions in dispute were not of such intricate character as to require any such paraphernalia.

Patterson, who is the Grand Deputy Master, says there were but two questions in the issue with the conspiracy, to-wit: First, that the Railroad Company had no title at all and the League would hold the lands without paying anything at all.

Second, the price asked by the Company was more than the League was willing to pay. The settlers fixed the amount at $2.50; the Company wanted more. The first of these questions was simple and short. The Company held the lands by the highest title—a patent from the Government of the United States. Doyle had contested that question before the Land Office and the Department at Washington, and the title of the Railroad Company had been decided to be valid. In addition to this, these men came into this Court and after a fair trial the title of the Company was held valid. To raise funds to do this was the object of the League. This was simple and short. The question of the price does not seem to be of a similar character. Was the League in sympathy with the illegal acts narrated here, and which narration and publication brings a blush of shame to the cheek of every good citizen and soils the honor of our State in the eyes of the civilized world?

The first pregnant fact in this connection is that all these acts of midnight terror were in the direct line of the objects of the League. The visit of masked men to de Wolf, hunting for Crow and Clark, were just the thing to do to accomplish the object of the League. Talbot says the League had appointed a committee about that time to request Clark's removal from the Railroad Company. The visit of the armed men to Parkhurst on the night of the 14th of April last is a remarkable coincidence, for on that very day, in the afternoon, a Committee of the League, consisting of McQuiddy, Doyle, and Patterson, told this very man he most go at 8 o'clock on the next morning. And that night came a masked man and mob, which, in the identical words, made the identical demand of Parkhurst. In fact, they first ask him the very question of the supremacy of law over the mob—a question of whether the edict of this Court or the League is supreme in this State.

These defendants have violated the law. Now, let them be dealt with as the law provides.[49]

Edward C. Marshall made the final plea to the jury for the defense. The following summary of his address was printed in the newspapers:

The facts in the case are few and simple, although evidence has accumulated until we can hardly follow it. It was the old fight between the productive and the non-productive; between the slow, laborious methods of those who conscientiously upbear upon their shoulders the world's progress by labor, and those who, without labor, reap, as from the very dawn of tradition, the fruits of other men's toil.

It was strange that a Land League should exist in this country. The power of steam, which makes modern life look, in contrast with ancient life, as heaven, nevertheless in this instance seemed like the bat in the Indian swamp that fostered upon the artery of the traveler and sucked out his life blood as it fanned him with its wings. There were only two simple questions in the case, easy of solution. There were two counts in the indictment, the one for conspiracy with an overt act, the other for an overt act without any conspiracy. The jury would have to determine whether these men were conspirators or not, and whether the people of this district were engaged in a conspiracy to resist the laws of the country.

He argued that it was monstrous to think that the settlers would endeavor to overthrow the authority of the United States, when ten states had found it impossible to do so unitedly. Was it possible to think that the chivalry of Mussel Slough, even with black masks and mules, were going to array themselves against that power? Was the army of forty men and forty mustangs, which occasionally deployed through the streets of some poor little village going to do that? Twelve locomotives would not draw a second breath thinking of it. They would whistle with contempt and leave at a 2:40 pace from anybody that would try to persuade them.

He recollected once passing over the Mussel Slough country when a crow would have to pack its provisions; when the mosquitoes were impoverished on the shores of Tulare Lake, and all the ants and intelligent insects had left it years before. Now, he was told, it blooms like Naboth's vineyard, and like Naboth's vineyard it has become a temptation to the bad, self-grasping Princes of Samaria.

These men were not criminals, and there was no taint of

434

agrarianism or socialism among them. They were willing to pay for everything except their own work. They were not jumpers or squatters for they came by invitation. The Railroad Company shot out a tentacle from Goshen to Huron and gobbled up the land upon which these men had been working for years. The settlers had a right to combine together, saying to the Company, "If you have a good title, you have got to put me out some other way than by selling land from under me." The resolution adopted by them was right and proper, for they had a right to say that they intended to fight it out. "If you get it, you get it at the end of the law."

It was no conspiracy to establish their rights, but a legal defense. He argued that there was no attempt at interference with the marshal in the execution of his duty. He maintained that Crow and Hartt went upon the ground prepared for a fight, with two shotguns, a repeating rifle, and four loaded revolvers; while on the other hand, there was an assemblage of citizens that came to persuade the marshal, if by chance he could be persuaded, and had any discretion. He contended that, seeing the fight had started, the settlers asked the marshal for his arms in order to prevent his participation in the affray. Harris, seeing these men handling their guns, rushed on the wagon. Crow and Hartt thought it well to begin early, for it was a California maxim, "If you are going to fight, begin early." It was proved in Court that Hartt fired the first shot. Ellis, sitting on the gatepost, saw a shot coming from the wagon. Brewer also saw it. In conclusion, Mr. Marshal said: "Gentlemen, these men are in your hands. Deal with them as you would be dealt with here and hereafter."[50]

At one o'clock on December 23, 1880, the foreman of the jury, R. W. Osgood, handed the Court a written verdict, which found five defendants guilty of resisting the marshal as charged, but not guilty of conspiracy. The five men sentenced to serve eight months in the San Jose jail were Patterson, Doyle, Braden, Pursell, and Pryor. Charges against Flewelling had been dropped earlier, and Talbot was granted a new trial.[51]

The settlers were kindly treated by the San Jose jailer.

Apparently, even those who were forced to incarcerate them did not consider them criminals. The jail sentence served by these San Joaquin Valley farmers was certainly the oddest one in the history of American penology. San Jose, a former state capital, had one of the few large jails in the state, more like a penitentiary. There was a large tank for the riffraff, while better quarters were located on the third floor of an adjacent building. No sooner had the settlers been assigned to their rooms than telegrams of sympathy began to arrive from all parts of the Union; the first day, two cablegrams were also received from England. The jailer, William Curtis, soon tired of running up the stairs with each fresh batch of messages, so he provided the settlers with a fish-line to which he hooked the telegrams; these were then pulled up through the open window. Even this proved too much of a chore and Curtis said, "Well, if the good people here and in Europe think so much of you, I guess you are all right and won't run away, so here is the key to the jail. Get your own mail." And they did.

Thereafter the men went to the post office daily, and each Thursday evening they attended the meetings of their lodge, the Ancient Order of United Workmen. On Sundays they went to church. James N. Patterson was an elder in the Christian (Campbellite) Church, and four hundred of his fellow church members called on him during his first day in jail. Actually, Patterson spent only four months in jail. He was in poor health, and was permitted to spend the second half of his sentence in more comfortable quarters in San Jose, being requested merely to report to the jail daily.[52]

Braden and Doyle were bachelors at the time of the Mussel Slough fight, but Doyle had married just before being sent to jail. After the birth of his son on April 16, his bride and baby joined him at the jail and remained there until his release. The other men brought their wives and

Mussel Slough settlers (left to right: John D. Pursell, John J. Doyle, James N. Patterson, Wayman L., Pryor, and William Braden), photograph taken in 1880 while serving their sentences at the San Jose jail. *Garden of the Sun*, 1939 edition.

children, and three rooms were set aside on the second floor for housekeeping purposes. Visitors called every day and during the evenings games were played. They acted as paying guests at a hotel. Patterson's young son, Bart, was given a uniform and a toy pistol and solemnly assured by the sheriff that he was a full-fledged deputy. He had a grand time. Fred Black, founder of a chain of stores known as Black's, sent groceries free of charge. The St. James Hotel of San Jose provided breakfasts each morning for the group without cost.

The jailer had a daughter named Susie. William Braden courted her, and his technique and approach must have been flawless, because the day he left the jail a free man, the St. James Hotel management donated a large wedding dinner and the jailer's daughter became the settler's wife. For Braden, the eight months in jail had turned out happily and he had no regrets. That the jailer would permit his girl to marry one of his erstwhile prisoners is indicative of the attitude of public opinion toward the Mussel Slough settlers. Naturally, the lenient treatment accorded the prisoners infuriated the directors of the Southern Pacific, and they saw to it that both the sheriff and the jailer lost their jobs.[53]

When the settlers finally turned their faces toward home, the San Jose City Band escorted them to the edge of the city. Here they were the guests of honor at a huge barbecue provided by the city. Refusing to travel over the Southern Pacific railway, they drove down the old Butterfield stage road by wagon until they reached Kingston. Here they were met by a happy delegation from Hanford and, amid cheering and singing they drove down the main-traveled road toward home.[54]

In April 1881, in the spring following the Mussel Slough fight and while the settlers were still serving their sentences, the *Argonaut* published an editorial that was hostile in tone to them. A petition had been circulated to secure their pardon and within two weeks more than 40,000 people in the state had signed it. This was forwarded to President Rutherford B. Hayes. The *Argonaut* maintained that the settlers were well aware of the fact that the land on which they had settled was railway land; that they were thus repeatedly informed by the United States Land Agent at Visalia; and that they had purposely squatted on it in order to benefit by the raise in land values. They had also located on the 14,000-

acre tract owned by cattleman John Sutherland. This
land, lying south of Kings River and north of Grangeville,
was all fenced. In spite of Sutherland's unquestioned
ownership, the "squatters" refused to vacate until
Sutherland caused their eviction in a series of lawsuits.
The *Argonaut* resented the attempt to get a pardon for the
incarcerated settlers.

The attitude of the *Argonaut* was apparently not reflected
in the public opinion of the time, because the release of
the settlers, after having served the full term of their
sentence, was greeted by statewide applause. When they
reached Hanford after their exit from the San Jose jail,
three thousand people gathered to celebrate their
homecoming. This was a huge gathering for that time and
place. Their fight with the Southern Pacific was over, but
no man asked which side had won.[55]

In some individual cases, the Southern Pacific
compromised with the settlers by reducing the appraised
valuation of the land by 12 1/2 percent; this concession
was final. However, most of the farmers were either forced
to pay the original price set by the land grader, or vacate.
Some were able to pay the high prices; others left. John J.
Doyle paid $30.60 an acre for land, which he and the
other settlers maintained, had been offered for sale at
$2.50 an acre. Doyle soon left the Mussel Slough country,
with its unhappy memories, and removed to the
mountains. The scene of his later activities is indicated by
Doyle's Camp and Doyle's Springs in the mountains east
of Porterville. The constant rise in land values made it
possible for the railway company to dispose of its vast
acreage without further difficulty. The odd-numbered
sections, or railway land, are today occupied by farmers
equally prosperous with those who reside on even
numbered, or government land.[56]

Brewer and Storer, like most of the settlers involved in

the land contest, eventually lost their land. Walter J. Crow had paid 20 percent down on the purchase price, which amounted to $1,624 on the 320 acres occupied by Brewer and Storer. Members of the Settlers' Land League argued that Crow's willingness to pay $8,120 for a half-section proved that he was merely a dummy buyer for the railroad, and that this price was exorbitant and not a true valuation. After Crow's death, the railway company refunded the 20 percent which had been paid for the land and the remaining purchase price was cancelled and the land deeded to the three children of Crow (two sons and a daughter). This land, north half of section 9, remained in the family until 1910.[57]

The climax of the land contest between the Southern Pacific and the settlers was the Mussel Slough fight. The denouement of that story was long and tedious. The end did not come until Hiram Johnson, an implacable foe of the Southern Pacific and all other autocratic corporations, was elected governor of California in 1910. One of the evil effects of the Mussel Slough fight was the bitterness engendered, and from the clinkers of that tragedy was to come much future lawlessness. The members of the Settlers' Land League dispersed and were content to abide in peace. But many younger and more quarrelsome men engaged in feuds. Settlers were shot from ambush. The return of a riderless horse with a bloody saddle was a common occurrence in the days following 1880. No one felt safe. Old scores were being paid off.

Magnus Derrick, the bonanza wheat grower portrayed by Frank Norris in *The Octopus*, was depicted as a nervous wreck after the Mussel Slough fight. Broken in spirit, he became subservient to the will of the railway corporation and lived to see his renegade son nominated as governor by the corporation. But, in real life, nothing of the sort happened. Major Thomas J. McQuiddy, the prototype of

Derrick, never compromised with the railway or deserted the settlers. He became the Greenback Party candidate for governor of California in 1882. But he was ahead of his time. Much agitation was necessary before even a modicum of change could be secured.

While McQuiddy was a fugitive, an effort was made to arrest him at Cross Creek Switch. A forged letter from Frank Dusy, on the pretext of discussing a business proposition, lured McQuiddy there. He was met in the middle of the night by a detective hired by Marshal Poole, who tried to find a lamp to identify McQuiddy. When a local storekeeper named Heath angrily refused him, he was forced to give up. He followed McQuiddy's wagon toward Kingsburg but, being unfamiliar with the territory, soon became lost and McQuiddy got away.[58]

Today, when men gather at the barbershops, the crossroads stores, or in the small town garages, one can still hear the story of the Mussel Slough fight. In those years, which immediately followed the tragedy, the citizens of the community each spring made a pilgrimage to the quiet spot where their heroes lay. A valley paper reported one of these services as follows:

> The fourth anniversary of the Mussel Slough tragedy of the 11th of May 1880 was appropriately observed by a large portion of the people of Mussel Slough on Saturday. Over five hundred people assembled at the Grangeville cemetery at the appointed time with a profusion of flowers with which to decorate the graves of the murdered martyrs. Short impromptu speeches were made by Major McQuiddy and H. F. Eagle, and a prayer by Rev. J. W. McKelvey. After the floral tribute had been placed upon the graves of Iver Knutson, Archibald McGregor, and Edwin Haymaker, a procession of over a mile in length was formed, and headed by a martial band of music, proceeded to the Hanford cemetery, where the same solemn ceremony was performed upon the graves of John Henderson, and James Harris, the

immortal five who laid down their lives at the behest of corporate power.[59]

The other settler, Dan Kelly, was buried elsewhere; Crow, buried at Stockton, and Hartt, at Grangeville, were both members of the railway faction, and not included in the services.[60]

A few farmers, who had hastily assembled in a wheat field in the San Joaquin Valley, had struck a terrific blow at corporate control. Their action transcended the bounds of their own lives. Frank Norris of San Francisco made their resolute courage the central theme of a great novel. Theodore Roosevelt, while president of the United States, expressed himself vehemently concerning conditions that had made their strenuous gesture a necessity. Rudyard Kipling visited San Francisco shortly after the trial of the Mussel Slough settlers. He may have had them in mind when he returned to far-away England and wrote his poem entitled The Settler, which closed with a prayer for the healing fullness of time:

> Here, in the waves and the troughs of the plains,
> Where the healing stillness lies,
> And the vast, benignant sky restrains
> And the long, long days make wise;
> Bless to our use the rain and the sun
> And the blind seed in its bed,
> That we may repair the wrong that was done
> To the living and the dead.

14 Prodigal Sons

Three merry boys, and three merry boys,
And three merry boys are we,
As ever did sing in a hempen string
Under the gallow-tree.

Beaumont and Fletcher,
Bloody Brother, Act III, Scene 2, Song.

The exploits and career of Joaquin Murrieta cannot be determined with accuracy. The first comprehensive account of his career, written by John Rollin Ridge, was published in 1854. Since then, a vast amount of material has been written about the famous brigand chief. A perusal of this material plainly indicates two sets of stories, two sets of characters, and a divergence in dates. But in most essentials the stories are similar.

The fate of Murrieta has been a controversial matter. The common and generally accepted story is that Murrieta was decapitated and his head preserved in a glass container filled with spirits. Many investigators refuse to accept this version and insist that Murrieta escaped to

Engraving of highwaymen holding up a stagecoach. Owen C. Coy,
Pictorial History of California

Mexico. However, the purpose of this chapter is not to
solve a mystery, but merely to tell the story of Murrieta in
relation to the development of the San Joaquin Valley.
Naturally his elimination was necessary. After the fight at
Cantua Creek he disappeared.

Joaquin Murrieta was born in Sonora, Mexico. He
reputedly arrived in California during late 1848,
accompanied by his wife, Rosa Feliz; her brothers,
Claudio, Jesus and Reyes; and Murrieta's half-brother,
Jesus. The story goes that American miners attempted to
expel Joaquin from a mining claim he had staked. He
resisted, was beaten into insensibility, and the lusty
brutes raped his beautiful young wife. This caused
Murrieta to go mad with grief and rage.[1]

No man, however well balanced, can maintain his
equilibrium if misfortune wallops him long and
persistently. Joaquin Murrieta was thenceforth an enemy
of society. To his side rallied Bernardino Garcia, a native

of the Mission Santa Clara neighborhood and onetime Mexican soldier. The absence of one finger earned him the nickname of "Three Fingered" Jack. Other Murrieta lieutenants were Reyes and Claudio Feliz, Rosa's brothers, and Pedro Gonzalez, an artistic horsethief. These men were augmented by a force of ordinary outlaws who flocked to Murrieta's standard.[2]

For a time, their outlawry took the form of horse stealing. Hundreds of horses were stolen, driven across the San Joaquin Valley, and sold by Murrieta's agents in Mexico. Eventually Murrieta began operations along the Tuolumne River. Concerning this part of his career, he made the following purported statement:

Shortly after the commencement of my bandit career, I went to Tuolumne County with my confederates, then numbering only seven, and found a convenient rendezvous in a little camp called San Diego, about a half mile from Columbia. We made it our business to rob and kill miners in the daytime, whenever we found them prospecting alone among the hills, or mining in desolate places; and a portion of the cash we obtained, we gambled away at night at saloons in town. While making these visits to monte tables, I went disguised, so that those who had known me in times past, previous to my change of character, would, if we came in contact, pass me as a stranger.[3]

Murrieta, alone or accompanied by a picturesque cavalcade, was frequently seen at Stockton, Hill's Ferry, in the various mining towns, and along Tulare Lake. They took gold from the miners, money and valuables from the stages, robbed and killed solitary travelers, and sent huge bands of horses to Sonora regularly. Headquarters were maintained in the inaccessible Cantua Canyon, about sixteen miles north of present Coalinga.[4]

In mid-1852, Murrieta and some of his followers had a ridiculous experience. After a series of raids in the

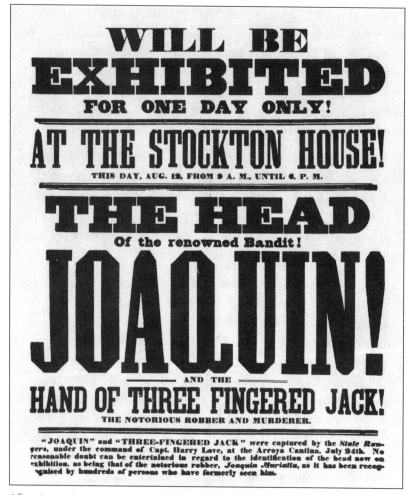

After Joaquin Murrieta was killed at the Arroyo de Cantua in 1853, his head was exhibited throughout California and advertised through posters such as this. *Collection of William B. Secrest.*

northern part of the valley, he led his men south to elude his pursuers. He made camp one evening among the Yauelmani Indians at Tejon. With him were Reyes Feliz and Gonzalez. Suddenly Chief Jose Zapatero and his Indians pounced upon the unsuspecting bandits and seized their horses. The bandits were forced to walk more than 100 miles to Los Angeles.[5]

After this episode, Murrieta was staying at the San Gabriel Mission when General Joshua Bean was murdered; he may have been the triggerman although Reyes Feliz, also present at the time, was captured by a local vigilance committee and hanged for the crime. Bean had a brother in Texas, Roy Bean, who won national fame as the sole representative of "the law west of the Pecos." Murrieta escaped afterward and returned to the mining country.[6]

Chinese proved easy victims. Three-fingered Jack had a fiendish mania for their destruction and perfected a system whereby he slaughtered them expeditiously by snatching the victim's queue with the left hand, pulling the head back, and slashing the throat with a knife held in his right. Reportedly, Murrieta protested at wholesale slaughter. Garcia protested that he was addicted to this bloodthirsty form of execution.[7]

On May 17, 1853, the governor of California signed a bill creating a company of mounted rangers, whose sole duty would be to destroy the Murrieta band. Harry Love was elected captain. Acting on information furnished by various informants, he led the rangers to a camp of mustang hunters located along Cantua Creek on July 20. He was astonished to find many heavily armed men at the rendezvous. Murrieta was absent, which probably saved the lives of the rangers. The Mexicans made no attack. Love and his men pretended to be looking for horse thieves, confiscated several stolen equines, and rode away unharmed. A few days later, on July 25, Love and seven of his men rode into the camp and found an equal number of outlaws lounging there. William Byrnes, a former friend of Murrieta, recognized the outlaw leader and the shooting started.

Murrieta quickly mounted his horse (which lacked both bridle and saddle), raced down the trail, jumped over a fifteen-foot embankment, was pursued by Ranger William T. Henderson whose thoroughbred performed the same strange gymnastics, and was finally captured when his horse was shot. Murrieta died as a result of body wounds; his head was removed for the purpose of identification, taken to Millerton in a gunnysack and preserved in spirits, and placed on exhibition in San Francisco. Three-fingered Jack was killed by shots through the head, which quickly caused decomposition, so his maimed hand was retained as a gruesome trophy. Bud Akers, one of the first settlers along Kings River, stated in a personal interview that he was present when these trophies were presented at Millerton; he saw it all and said there was no doubt but that Murrieta and Three-fingered Jack had been killed.[8]

Morbid curiosity caused people to willingly pay a dollar admission for a sight of these hideous objects. Men maintained that Jack's fingernails and Murrieta's hair continued to grow after death. It was venomously asserted that this phenomenon indicated supernatural contacts with evil spirits. Certain writers have argued that there is nothing strange in this matter as the occasional exhuming of bodies from cemeteries has revealed similar conditions. A letter from the Mayo Brothers Clinic at Rochester, Minnesota, may be of interest in this connection:

> In the legend which you relate in regard to the outlaws, there is repeated the long existent superstition amongst many people that the hair and fingernails of the dead continue to grow. Manifestly growth is a sign of life and while sometimes

Sketch of Joaquin Murrieta's head, as it was seen under glass by thousands of Californians until its apparent loss in the 1906 San Francisco earthquake and fire. *Collection of William B. Secrest.*

for variable numbers of minutes following death life is existent in some parts of the body, very rapidly after death all life ceases and it is scientifically impossible that there should be growth of any kind, beyond the infinitesimal multiplication of a few cells.[9]

Whether or not Murrieta was actually killed by the California Rangers at the battle of Cantua Canyon is of more interest than importance. Suffice to say that he never again rode the trails of the San Joaquin Valley, or engaged in any work which hampered the peaceful development of that section. But the influence of his charming and dynamic personality persisted. Many of his followers, left leaderless, roamed the state and secured honest employment. But they spoke with regret of his passing.[10]

One of the young vaqueros influenced by Murrieta's glamour was Tiburcio Vasquez, born at Monterey on August 11, 1835. In 1852, when Murrieta's career was approaching its height, this boy, then sixteen years of age, began a career in crime which was to rival that of his predecessor.

The following account, written by Mary Austin for the *Youth's Companion* in 1908, is an excellent description of the man and his methods:

> Thirty years ago there were broad-tired ore-wagons, drawn by eighteen- and twenty-mule teams, going between the mines and Mojave. There were long strings of burros with water-barrels, and rumbling, rocking stages racing between the stations that squatted by the waterholes. There were solitary prospectors going up and down, very often going blind and wide of the trails, waterless, and lost to every knowledge except the ken of the broad-winged buzzards that dip and swing in the high, keen atmosphere; and in the early sixties there was Vasquez.
>
> Vasquez was the handsomest, the most conscienceless, the politest and the cruelest bandit who ever rode the California trails...He could keep an outlook who, whenever the ore-wagons came in with bullion or the Mojave express came up with coin, would by a signal-smoke call up Vasquez and his men from the water-holes, where they made their lair. For in that clear air, on the level, treeless track, the moving dust of the mule-teams could be sighted four hours away. The bandits came down slinking and swift as coyotes, and rode back through secret passes in the Sierras to the San Joaquin, before the lumbering mule-teams could reach any possible point from which a sheriff's posse could be set in motion.
>
> But in fact sheriffs were not very hot on the trail of Vasquez until late in his career, when many killings were counted up against him, for gold came and went very easily in those days; and men were more anxious to go to find a mine than to hunt a man who had robbed one. Besides that, Vasquez was of Spanish California blood, and there were a great many of that stripe scattered about southern California in the early sixties.
>
> Vasquez had a way of making friends among his own people. No doubt many of them would have followed his way of life,

but they lacked the courage for it. He had all the characteristics of the popular bandit since the time of Dick Turpin; he was courteous to ladies and liberal to his followers; he stole only from the rich, and never forgot either a favor or a slight. There was a dash and go about his methods, which appealed to the imagination. He rode a white horse, and rode him very well. He would appear with his mounted followers, holding up a bullion-wagon in Salt Wells, and before the confounded teamster and his escort could get anywhere to tell anybody, the white horse and his rider would be robbing stages in the Coast Ranges behind Temblor.

If one is to believe all the stories that are told about him, Vasquez must have had a white horse at every station between San Diego and Tejon. But when he was finally taken and hanged, as he deserved to be, there appeared to be only one of them, whose subsequent career, as long as he lived and even after he left off living and became a ghost to haunt the old trails of Vasquez, would make a story of itself.[11]

In 1854 Tiburcio Vasquez attended a fandango at Monterey and became involved in an altercation with some Americans of the type whose favorite indoor sport was to insult "greasers." Vasquez was not to be intimidated easily, as Mr. Caspar Milquetoast. Constable William Hardmount attempted to quell the disturbance by arresting Vasquez and another horse-thief and robber, Anastacio Garcia. They protested. A man named Higuera came to the aid of his friends and, during the melee, someone killed the constable. Since Vasquez and Garcia escaped, Higuera was hanged for the crime. Later on, in 1857, Vasquez was captured while trying to sell stolen horses in Los Angeles, and sent to the state penitentiary at San Quentin. After his final release in 1870, Vasquez defied the law and all its minions.[12]

The chief aid of Vasquez was a nephew of Murrieta named Procopio. The latter had served a term in San Quentin for cattle rustling. On his release from the penitentiary he went to the region now known as Kings County and terrorized the Mussel Slough country. When Major Thomas McQuiddy organized a squadron of cavalry for the Settlers' Land League at Hanford, it was assumed that the presence of these outlaws was the reason for its existence. In 1878, after Vasquez had been hanged, Procopio robbed the store at Grangeville. He and his band tied up the men present in the approved Vasquez manner. Among them was James N. Patterson, later a leader in the Mussel Slough episode. After the robbery, Procopio and his men headed on horseback with their loot for the Poso Chane, several miles east of present Coalinga. Procopio's horse was drowned while he was trying to swim it through a slough. The so-called military squadron of the Mussel Slough settlers found the trail at the sheep camp owned by Frank Woods and Theodore Draper. When they reached the Gus Kreyenhagen store, they learned that Procopio had headed for the cabin of the Higuera brothers, two miles distant. In a room of this shack they found the bandit leader asleep. Joel A. Whiteside, one of the posse, left a man on guard while he went outside to call the others. However, Procopio was too fast on the draw, shot his way out of the cabin, and made his escape. Solomon Gladden, a Mussel Slough rancher, was killed during the fight.[13]

Another lieutenant of Vasquez was Clodovio Chavez, distinguished by his physical size and decorative goatee. Other important members of the band were Abdon Leiva, Romulo Gonzales, and a Frenchman named August de Bert. Their first raid on a settlement of any size occurred at Firebaugh's Ferry on February 26, 1873, where the stage station and store there were relieved of their money.[14]

The presence of outlaws in the community produced a nervous tension, which was both pitiful and ludicrous at times. One evening, a cattle buyer named Bill Hope was spending the night at the Josiah Draper home in Kingsburg. He had in his possession a quantity of gold money (checks were not used then) intended to be utilized in the purchase of livestock. Naturally, he was nervous. A sudden rush, a squawk, and silence sent him into a panic. He ran into the back yard and threw his $1,500 of gold pieces into a large woodpile. But Vasquez and his men did not appear; it was a false alarm. The next day, the chagrined cattle buyer had to hire two men to help him carefully sort the woodpile. It took them over six hours to recover the gold, and they worked as hard as the original miner did in extracting the precious metal.[15]

The biggest single venture of the Vasquez band took place at Tres Pinos on August 26, 1873. The leader taught his men a new technique that consisted of forcing his victims to lie down and permit themselves to be tied. This prevented injury to any one and provided leisure for a thorough search of the victims and the premises. This system worked smoothly at Tres Pinos and several men had been securely tied and were being carefully examined for money and valuables when other men unfortunately appeared on the scene. A Portuguese sheepherder, Bernal Berhuri, appeared and was greatly astonished to see several of his acquaintances flat on their backs. He failed to understand the command to halt and lie down and was promptly killed. George Redford, a teamster, was both deaf and combative, and died. Leander Davidson, a merchant, appeared in the doorway of the hotel next door, attempting to close and lock it. His wife hampered his progress by pulling at his coattails. A sudden shot through the door sent him reeling backwards into his wife's arms. His death induced Andrew Snyder, the postmaster and competing merchant, to open his safe without argument, and Vasquez left with the plunder.[16]

At that time Captain J. H. Adams was campaigning for re-election as sheriff of Santa Clara County. He was electioneering at Gilroy. Accompanied by Sheriff Wasson of Monterey County, he gathered a large posse that trailed the bandits across the Coast Range to the Cantua region. From there they went to Tulare Lake. Wasson returned home and Adams traveled south down the San Joaquin Valley. The latter continued to Bakersfield, but here the trail disappeared.[17]

After the hue and cry had subsided Vasquez callously appropriated Abdon Leiva's wife and the latter, in a spirit of revenge, had turned state's evidence. Vasquez, believing that shooting was too good for such a wretch, plotted to poison the traitor through an associate, Blas Bicuna.[18]

Failing in his evil purpose, Vasquez and his band skimmed like martial birds over the landscape between San José and Monterey. The choicest meats and finest mounts were theirs for the mere taking. They lived like the Lord's anointed. William Curtis, whose son Gene Curtis later settled at Kingsburg, had come to California with the Donner party and had served with Fremont's Battalion. Later, he was appointed the first postmaster of Monterey. One afternoon he left his home and went for a ride on his favorite mule. The hybrid steed, ambling along in her meditative way, was as rudely startled as her rider, when the Vasquez outlaws swooped suddenly out of a thicket and surrounded man and mount. The mule, resenting the jostling of the horses, emitted a disdainful bray, turned her back on her mother's relations, and churned through the atmosphere toward Monterey at a rate of speed which her rider, judging her by past performances, considered truly amazing and, under the circumstances, highly commendable. In the distance Curtis could hear the mocking laughter of the outlaws, who relished the exhibition of a runaway mule and her hapless rider, although it was an unexpected ending to their surprise party.[19]

Then word arrived that gold had arrived by stagecoach at Kingston, in payment for cattle that had been sold from the ranches along lower Kings River. Thither Vasquez led his men. The outlaws arrived at Selma the day after Christmas. The city of Selma did not then exist, but the Southern Pacific had built a switch at that point. Pat Reardon, the section foreman, occupied the only house in the vicinity. He was told to get up and prepare breakfast for his unbidden guests. It was five o'clock in the morning, cold, and Reardon refused to feed them. He was horsewhipped and left for dead. From Selma the band rode south about six miles to the Livermore ranch, located two and a half miles west of the Kingsburg cemetery's later location. The owner, Wilson Livermore, was absent at the time, and the only ones at home were his wife and little daughter. Mrs. Livermore was a tactful and hospitable woman and agreed to serve the men breakfast; the result was that no one was harmed. The following account of this incident was furnished by the lady who was the young daughter at the Livermore home, and who eventually became Mrs. Frank Draper:

> In reply to your letter, I will gladly give you any information I can in regard to the Vasquez crowd. I was only a girl of thirteen years of age at that time. My mother and I were home alone as my father was away working. It was about six o'clock in the morning when the Vasquez band came and asked for something to eat; they said they would be satisfied if they could get only a cup of coffee. They had just come from Selma where the section boss, Pat Reardon, had refused to give them anything. He had been severely beaten, but naturally we did not know anything about this until they had left. My mother used good judgment and treated them in the best possible manner. We prepared coffee and a fresh batch of biscuits and also gave them fresh cream and butter. They

The settlement of Kingston, a few years after the Vasquez raid. Note, in the lower right-hand corner, the bridge traveled by the bandits. Wallace W. Elliott, *History of Fresno County*, 1881.

seemed very much pleased. Upon leaving they asked us how much we charged and my mother said, "Nothing." They insisted upon paying, so my mother said they could give her fifty cents; thereupon Vasquez gave her a big silver dollar. They all thanked us and treated us very nicely. There were seven of them. They all got on their horses, which were very fine animals, tipped their hats to us, and left. Vasquez was a nice looking man with black hair and mustache.[20]

After leaving the Livermore ranch, the outlaws rode south and west in the direction of Kingston. In 1873 this place was a bustling little cow town and river town. The coming of the railroad to Kingsburg retarded its development; the later arrival of the railroad at Laton, across the river from Kingston, sounded the death knell of Kingston. The stable used to house the stage-coaches and horses of the old Butterfield line remained until 1937 to mark the site of Whitmore's Ferry, and a place rich in the memories of the southern overland mail.[21]

The outlaws hid among the willows along Kings River until dusk. Then they made a sudden sally across the toll bridge owned by Oliver H. Bliss and held up the town. Several men were chopping wood along the south bank and a boy hunting cottontails gave the alarm.

> I suppose that I was the boy you refer to who was present
> when Vasquez robbed the town of Kingston. In answer to your
> second question, I will say that I did not take a shot at the
> robbers, but the men that were with me did. In answer to
> your third question, the time of day that the robbers came
> was just early in the evening or just after dusk. Answering
> your fourth question, I will say that Kingston at that time
> had two stores, a hotel, and a couple of saloons. As I
> remember, the main stores were owned by Jacobs and Sweet
> [Einstein], they were both Jews. The stage-line was still in
> operation at that time. The location of the store was probably
> 500 feet southeast from where the barn still stands on the old
> Kingston town site. I now own the property.[22]

Soon after the attack, the victims had been tied and laid
on their backs. This was the approved Vasquez method.
The owner of the bridge, Mr. Bliss, flat on his back,
complained of a headache. Vasquez solicitously placed a
blanket under the throbbing cranium, after which Bliss
rested Bliss-fully. Edward Douglass of Visalia offered
resistance, and was knocked out by a blow from a pistol in
the hands of the giant Chavez. In the hotel lobby a female
guest looked up from her crocheting, and saw a villainous-
looking man gliding into the room. In her horror, she
emitted a screech that would have earned a draw with a
steam calliope. Launcelot Gilroy of Fresno, sitting a few
feet away, must have heard her because he jumped to his
feet and knocked one of the outlaws unconscious with a
blow from a chair. Another outlaw, entering the room just
then and observing this parabolic use of furniture,
reciprocated heartily by slapping Gilroy alongside the
head with a heavy dragoon pistol.

Meanwhile Edward Erlanger, employed by Jacobs &
Einstein as a clerk, had locked the safe and had run over
to warn the owner of the other store. This merchant,
Solomon Sweet, was leaning inquisitively out of his

window, and Erlanger arrived just in time to see a bandit slip out of the shadows, apply a reverse headlock to the proprietor, throw him, and tie Sweet *tout de suite*. At the other store, Einstein was pretending that the clerk had run away with the only keys to the safe. Vasquez arrived in person and put an end to this nonsense. While Vasquez and his men were going through the pockets of their prostrate victims a sympathetic little dog, merrily wagging his tail and anxious to do his part, went from man to man and cheerfully washed their noses, ears, and faces with his tongue, which ablutions the men, tied and supine, were helpless to avoid. They asserted afterwards that this part of the cleanup was the most annoying of the entire affair.

Sweet, who had been forcefully jerked from his window, was saved from pecuniary loss by the basso profundo tones of the heavy Henry rifles in the hands of John Sutherland and James E. Flood, neighboring ranchmen, who had been notified of the raid. These two doughty cattlemen were well-qualified to care for themselves and others. They made a dash for the toll bridge to intercept the retreat of the bandits, but arrived just as the latter were mounting their horses on the north side of Kings River. Sutherland, in spite of the low visibility, succeeded in shooting Gomez in the neck and Chavez in the right leg. The total amount garnered in the raid was $2,500 in gold, besides jewelry in the form of rings and watches. The only outlaw who failed to cross the bridge was a new recruit named Monterez. He followed the river up-stream about eight miles, and was captured the next day. Constables Blackburn of Kingston and Andrew Farley of Kingsburg took him to the county jail at Millerton.[23]

On the morning of December 27, 1873, which was the day after the raid at Kingston, Vasquez and his men galloped into the little cow town of Kingsburg. The only store in

"Gentleman Bandit"
Tiburcio Vasquez,
whose raids at
Firebaugh, Kingston
and Jones' store
remain among the
most notorious crimes
ever committed in the
San Joaquin Valley.
*Collection of William B.
Secrest.*

the village at that time was owned by White Davis
(Davids), an Austrian Jew from Richmond, Virginia. He
and his sons, Solomon and Samuel, were pioneer
merchants in the San Joaquin Valley. When White Davis
saw the band of horsemen ride up to his store and
dismount, he hurriedly prepared for them such food as the
place afforded. Assisted by his wife and sons, Davis
hastily opened cans of sardines, beans, oysters, fruit, and
meat; cheese and crackers were placed on the counter
until it resembled a modern cafeteria. Cigars and drinks
were also furnished the entire group. The bandits,
grateful for the hospitality, made no attempt to rob the
till. While the outlaws were eating, Vasquez divided
among them the money acquired the previous evening.

Having given to each man his just portion, Vasquez shoved his glass back across the counter to be re-filled, remarking, "It's good stuff."

"Yes, it will keep us in tortillas and frijoles until our next job," answered Procopio, combining two thoughts in one expression, which is brevity.

Directly across the track from the store was the Southern Pacific station. The agent, Ianthus E. Marshall, had in the express office a shipment of $10,000 in gold. This money represented payment on livestock recently shipped to the markets by the cattle barons along lower Kings River. Recognizing the nature of the men across the street, the agent hurriedly dug a hole in the coal bin and hid his precious metal. By the time he had removed the evidences of his burrowing, the bandits mounted their horses, and without deigning the station worthy of an investigation, they rode away to the south. Vasquez was credited with possessing an unerring instinct for the detection of gold; this time his reputed ability to scent it was at fault.

The station agent had been under a severe nervous strain during the preceding minutes, and when he saw the outlaws riding away his mingled emotions of fear and relief caused him to deliver an oral dissertation on Vasquez and all his family down to the remotest ancestors, which lacked nothing in fervor or eloquence. When the Wells Fargo express agent, who had gone for a walk, returned and learned of the narrow escape, he turned his vocabulary loose and earned a draw.[24]

On December 29th, the bandits were sighted near Visalia, riding in a westerly direction; from this region, they swung south and were next detected in the Spanish-speaking settlement of Panama. Soon after the Kingston raid, on January 24, 1874, Governor Newton Booth issued a proclamation providing $15,000 for the capture of Vasquez.[25]

Roughly two months after the Kingston episode, on February 25, Vasquez appeared at Coyote Holes Station, located on the stage route between Los Angeles and Owens River. Here the outlaws tied and robbed twenty men. The stage arrived and they promptly relieved Wells Fargo & Company of its treasure box. An element of comedy often broke the strain of an otherwise tragic set of affairs. One of the men employed at Coyote Holes Station was W. P. Shore. As Vasquez entered the stable Shore was in a rather inebriated condition. When the outlaw chief made the usual demand that he lie down, Shore felt insulted and profanely refused to prostrate himself in the stable drainage for anybody. A shot in the thigh produced the desired posture.[26]

The restaurant of Greek George (George Allen), onetime driver for Jefferson Davis' Camel Corps, served as headquarters for Vasquez; here he disported himself in what would later become the Hollywood neighborhood of Los Angeles. William Rowland, sheriff of Los Angeles County, watched this place and was in turn watched by the outlaw. The sheriff organized a posse while he remained quietly and ostentatiously at home. This posse was composed of Emil Harris, a detective; H.M. Mitchell, a special deputy; F. Hartley, Los Angeles chief of police; Sam Bryant and W. E. Rogers, constables; Albert J. Johnston, under-sheriff; D.K. Smith, a farmer; and George A. Beers, reporter for the San Francisco *Chronicle*. These men offered Greek George's wife, Cornelia Valenzuela, $250 for information concerning the whereabouts of Vasquez, (She did so, and Vasquez was captured, but the sheriff's office never reimbursed the lady for her part in the capture of the outlaw.) The posse intercepted two Mexicans riding in a farm wagon, placed themselves like sardines in the bottom of this wagon, and ordered the nonplussed peons to drive slowly and carefully to the restaurant of Greek George. Since several rifles were pointed at their backs, the Mexicans obeyed. Vasquez, eating his dinner, saw nothing threatening in the slow approach of this bucolic vehicle. He was astonished when he was called outside to meet the determined-looking posse; he made a break for liberty, was wounded, and surrendered. Vasquez was arraigned before the court at San José, convicted, and sentenced to be hanged on March 18, 1875.

Just before Vasquez was to be hanged he was asked if he had a last request to make. To the amazement of all, he inquired, "Who is that funny little Irishman down in Los Angeles who is tax-collector?" Some one mentioned the name. "Well," said Vasquez, "one day I met him as I was riding down the road; he was alone in a buggy. He stopped me and asked if I had paid my poll tax. I told him no. He got mad and said he'd send me to jail if I didn't pay. So I gave him two dollars and when I signed my name on the receipt blank he took one look at me and hit his horse a terrific lick with his whip. The last I saw of him he was tearing down the road in a cloud of dust and I never did get my receipt. Now, he was a funny little Irishman, wasn't he?" And having made this irrelevant remark, Vasquez was hanged by the neck till dead.[27]

The first outbreak of lawlessness in the San Joaquin Valley came as a result of the racial prejudices arising from the Mexican War; the second outbreak was a heritage of the evil passions aroused by the Civil War and the entrance into the valley of the Southern Pacific.

In the days before the Civil War, Kansas was the scene of border warfare: fanatical abolitionists like John Brown battled for free soil against equally cruel border ruffians. William Clarke Quantrill, a native of Ohio, moved to the Kansas prairies. For a time, he was a teacher in a little log schoolhouse. He soon became an adept in the border warfare then raging. Though born in the North, he aligned himself with the other side and opposed the Free-Soilers. Then came the Civil War, and Quantrill became a notorious guerrilla leader. His career has caused him to be described as the "bloodiest man known to the annals of America."[28] Many of the partisan leaders ignored the official surrender at Appomatox Court House; they had private reasons for continuing the horrors of guerrilla warfare. One excess led to another, and a new generation grew up in an atmosphere charged with hatred and fury. In this region lived the James family, the Youngers, and the Daltons. The boys in the two former families were tutored by Quantrill. If we are to judge a pedagogue by his success in molding students during their plastic years, undoubtedly "Quantrill was a good teacher in a little log schoolhouse out on the Kansas plains before the war."[29]

Jesse James and Cole Younger were first cousins. Adeline Younger, an aunt of the outlaw Younger brothers, married and in due time became the mother of the boys who were to achieve notoriety as the Dalton gang. The Daltons were respectable people in their community. The boys in that family were not inherently vicious; they were merely high-spirited and the product of their environment. Francis Bacon claimed that "a man's nature runs either to herbs or weeds." From the inside out, the Dalton boys were like other boys; from the outside in, there was much at that time and place to make them different. Grattan Dalton served as a United States Deputy Marshal in the Western Arkansas District when conditions there required unflinching resolution and dauntless courage. But he learned that public officials are not always honest; he also learned to his sorrow what many a man has since learned, that when a subordinate attempts to expose cupidity and peculation in a superior officer it is generally fatal—to the honest subordinate. Therefore he resigned and went west. In Oklahoma Territory, he and his brothers Bob and Emmett began careers in horse thievery that proved injurious to the reputation of the Daltons. They fled to the San Joaquin Valley.[30]

When Grattan and Bob Dalton arrived in the valley, a brother named Littleton resided on a ranch near Clovis. Another brother, William, owned a ranch in the foothills near Paso Robles. A cousin, Sam Oldham, was a wheat grower residing a mile due east of Kingsburg. Reports had come to California concerning the pugnacious proclivities of the Dalton boys. Grattan was especially combative, and willing to fight for the sheer joy of the battle. In the San Joaquin, he found men willing to accommodate him. For a time they lived with Sam Oldham. The latter at that time employed two teamsters named Charles Flewelling and Eugene Curtis. One evening these two young men and the two Dalton boys attended a dance at the Brick Hotel in Kingsburg. Both Grattan and his exceedingly handsome brother Bob went armed at all times. Their weapons proved cumbersome during a dance, and they hid their revolvers under the front porch, with the remark to their two companions: "We want to place our guns where we can find them in a hurry in case we need them." But no one present knew that the Daltons had been implicated in any difficulty with constituted authority, and so a pleasant time was had by all.[31]

Grattan and Bob remained with Sam Oldham for a time and then, accompanied by William McElhanie, they went to visit their brother William near Paso Robles. While they were amusing themselves in the vicinity of Bill's ranch, the Southern Pacific passenger train was held up near Alila, located within a mile of the present Earlimart, on February 26, 1891. Who did it?

Sheriff O'Neil and Detective Will Smith thought they knew. They had heard reports about the Dalton brothers. Therefore these two officers suddenly appeared at Bill Dalton's ranch and remained all night. The two accused men, Bob Dalton and William McElhanie, fretted and fumed in their hiding place in an adjoining room. After the officers had departed the next morning, Bob mounted his horse and followed the rim of hills to Tehachapi, crossed the Mojave desert, and finally reached Oklahoma. Grattan was arrested at Fresno by Will Smith, but proved that he had not been at the robbery scene during the exact time of the hold-up.[32]

Neither the Dalton boys nor Evans and Sontag ever confessed to train robbery in the San Joaquin. Their accusers never proved their guilt. Chris Evans and John Sontag were finally convicted on other charges. No one denies that trains were being held up during those years, and the curious must be pardoned for wondering who actually did the deeds. It has been stated that ranchers living between Kingsburg and Dinuba, in the vicinity of the famous John C. McCubbin gum tree, did it. Others have said that Cross Creek men, needing money, helped themselves at the expense of the Southern Pacific. In those days, to rob the Octopus was not considered a heinous offense.

Grattan was re-arrested at San Francisco, brought to Visalia, and convicted on circumstantial evidence. While waiting final sentence in the Visalia jail, a trusty smuggled a file into the jail, and Grattan and three fellow prisoners escaped. They secured a fleet team of gray horses hitched to a spring wagon and belonging to George McKinley, who was attending a prayer meeting in the Methodist Church. The other men boarded the train at Goshen, but Grattan went to the home of Maggie Rucker at Cross Creek. Her ranch home was located at the Cross

Creek stagecoach depot, about two miles down the creek
from the Cross Creek railroad station. A rancher named
Joe Middleton drove the team to Tulare, where they were
found the next morning. This fact caused the officers to
assume that the men had all gone to Tulare and left on
the southbound train. Thereby Grattan escaped detection
at Cross Creek.[33]

Grattan and his friend Middleton went to the hills above
Sanger, and the latter returned to the valley on a pretext
and betrayed his companion. Grattan managed to evade
the posse, accosted a farmer named Judson Elwood
plowing in a field, forced him to unhitch, and mounted one
of the astonished plough horses. He rode north and sought
sanctuary with a friend and sympathizer, Judge W.W.
Gray, near the town of Livingston in Merced County. The
latter furnished Grattan with a saddle horse and he rode
south along the Coast Range, through Tehachapi Pass and
back to Oklahoma. The rapidly shifting course of events
had made outlaws of the Daltons, and when they re-
assembled at their mother's house, the scene was one of
extreme pathos. It was a rainy and dismal evening as they
rode up; she was preparing supper and the older brothers
ate with their rifles across their knees while a twelve-
year-old brother, Sam, watched the road for possible
pursuers. The mother's emotions may be imagined:

> She was standing in the door as we mounted and wheeled
> away. I had never seen her weep before. Perhaps it was the
> rain washing against her face as she lifted her hand toward
> us while the youngsters clustered about her. Mother of
> outlaws, extending a hand of final blessing toward her
> renegade sons. Looking for the last time, through lightning-
> riven rain, upon the living face of Bob.
>
> I felt unutterably cruel and despicable as our horses splashed
> through the muddy road. I saw her next from the cot where I
> lay fighting for life in a bullet-riddled body. [34]

Emmett Dalton: "I am sending you a photograph of myself taken about a year ago, dressed and equipped just about as we were in the days of our activity." *Garden of the Sun*, 1939 edition.

After a thrilling career as bad men of the Wild West, the Dalton gang was "wiped out" at Coffeyville, Kansas, on October 5, 1893. Within ten minutes after they had attempted to hold up two big banks simultaneously six men had been killed, including Bob and Grattan Dalton, and several had been wounded. The lone survivor was Emmett Dalton. He received a bullet through his upper right arm, another in the back hip that emerged in the groin, and twelve buckshot in the back from a shotgun while stooping to help his brother. He survived, was sentenced to life imprisonment, and pardoned in 1907 after having served fourteen and a half years.[35]

Trains had been held up before the Daltons arrived in California, and they continued to be held up after they had left. Long before the Daltons had been suspected of

467

robbery, on February 22, 1889, a southbound train had
been stopped just south of Pixley. When the expressman,
J. R. Kelly, refused to open the door, a dynamite bomb was
placed under the car. The concussion caused it to heave
convulsively. James Symington, the conductor, and Ed.
Bentley, a deputy-sheriff from Modesto, who happened to
be a passenger, ran down the west side of the train to
investigate. The deputy thought he heard some one on the
other side and stooped to peek; so did the bandit, who
fired a load of buckshot in the general direction of the
deputy. Bentley ran to the rear of the train, but was out-
distanced by the conductor, who ran the entire two miles
back to Pixley. Reports that $5,000 had been looted were
received with glee by many residents of the valley, who
generally referred to the railway as an Octopus.[36]

On January 20, 1890, the southbound train was held up
two and a half miles south of Goshen. The same style was
employed, which indicated that the same bandit was at
work. Reports were circulated that $20,000 had been
stolen. Again, the guilty man escaped. A third hold-up
occurred on February 6, 1891; this was at a point half a
mile south of Alila. This was the holdup that led to the
accusation of the Daltons, and may have indirectly been
responsible for their subsequent career. The ineffectual
attempts of the officers to locate the bandits resulted in a
great deal of criticism, and they writhed under the jibes
directed their way. That explains their anxiety to pin the
guilt on some one and their apparently unjust treatment
of the Daltons. A fourth train was forcibly halted seven
miles south of Modesto. A passenger had been let off at
Ceres and before the train could gain momentum, two
armed men crawled from the tender into the cab and the
engineer was forced to halt the locomotive. Two railway
detectives, Len Harris and Lawson, were passengers, and
they entered the fray with sufficient enthusiasm to thwart

the bandits. They escaped in the darkness and were later traced to Newman, where the trail ended.[37]

Three tramps had been riding on the brake-beams and they testified that one bandit was tall and lean, the other short and fat. This description caused men of this conformation much annoyance during the next few days. The following facetious editorial was penned by the editor of the *Modesto Herald*:

> Constable Parker and his deputy, Spiers (from Ceres), arrested a dozen men in Modesto on Friday morning because they were either short or tall—one of the robbers being large and the other small. Only the middleweights of Modesto escaped these lynx-eyed officers of our neighboring town.
>
> They arrested a barber here and as the fellow clearly proved an alibi, Spiers was in favor of turning him loose, but Parker pointed out that the barber was a small man, as was one of the robbers. As the barber couldn't explain this away, Spiers concluded it was suspicious and they had the fellow crawl into their buggy and go with them to the scene of the robbery. Arriving on the ground, the barber declared that he had never been there before, and as, as Spiers pointedly remarked, he couldn't have stopped the train without having been there, and as he didn't appear to be so very short after all, Parker reluctantly turned him loose, with the admonition that he guessed he wasn't guilty, but not to go doing it again.
>
> The barber walked back the five miles through the heat to Modesto and was mad enough when he got here to waylay the first train that came along.[38]

The fifth hold-up occurred on August 3, 1892, at Collis. This station, named in honor of Collis P. Huntington, has since been renamed Kerman. The robbers secured, according to reports, between $30,000 and $50,000. The Daltons were again accused of the act, but during that time they were in Idaho and impartial citizens scoffed at the deductions of the would-be Hawkshaws.[39]

Then Christopher Evans was suspected. He was a native of Canada, a veteran of the Union Army, and a pioneer settler who enjoyed the respect and confidence of his neighbors in Visalia.

> It is said that Chris Evans is used to the smell of gunpowder. He served in the Civil War when a mere boy, and was wounded in the foot at the battle of Winchester. He also served against the Indians after the war and was under Reno at the time Custer was killed. He says he heard the firing at the time of the Custer massacre.[40]

The story has been circulated that Evans was one of the Mussel Slough settlers dispossessed of his lands in the year 1880. There is no proof of this although it makes a pretty story. J. J. Doyle, one of the organizers of the Settlers' Land League and the man who knew more of the Mussel Slough troubles than any one else, said emphatically years later that Evans had nothing to do with that episode, either as a settler or member of the Land League. Evans seems to have worked for the Southern Pacific as a laborer and teamster on construction work. He also worked as a laborer in the grain warehouses of the California Bank, which at that time exerted an influence in the valley comparable to that of the Bank of America in more recent years. This bank held mortgages on much of the wheat land in the valley, and interest and rentals were collected in the form of grain and stored in their warehouses at Pixley, Tulare, and Goshen. Evans claimed to have served as a warehouse foreman for a time. Wells Fargo frequently sent gold to these places. Perhaps Evans knew when these gold shipments were due. Eventually, he left the central part of the valley and removed to Modesto and bought a livery stable. A fire destroyed his stock and he became very despondent. Then came the holdup at Ceres and Evans returned to Visalia, his old home. Evans was

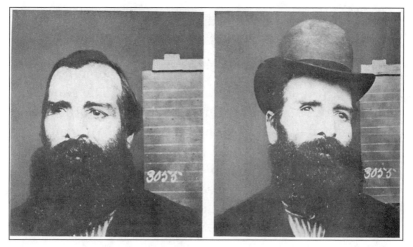

Mug shots of Chris Evans, taken after his final capture. C. B. Glasscock, *Bandits and the Southern Pacific.*

accused of being a train robber; Evans never admitted it and no one ever proved it.[41]

After his return to Visalia, Chris Evans overheard a man cursing the Southern Pacific luridly. He paused and was introduced to John Sontag. The latter was born on a farm near Mankato, Minnesota, and while serving as a brakeman at Fresno, his foot had been crushed. The political doctors employed at the railway hospital discharged him while still unfit for work. He lost his former place and failed to get other duties. He was filled with a bitter hatred. A brother, George Sontag, was also in Visalia. These three men were under surveillance by Will Smith, the railway detective who had arrested Grattan Dalton and followed Bob Dalton to Paso Robles. One day George Sontag was taken to the sheriff's office for interrogation; in the meantime, Will Smith and Deputy Sheriff Witty went to the Evans home. The Evans and Sontag story begins at this point.

Chris Evans had a daughter, sixteen years of age, named

Eva. She was a beautiful girl and, in later years, would have been a logical candidate for Miss Visalia or Miss California. She also possessed an indomitable will and strength of character. The Evans family and John Sontag were preparing for a trip to the mountains. The two men and Eva had been engaged in target practice in the back yard. Eva had just entered the house when Witty and Smith arrived at the front door. Evans had walked across the back lot to visit a neighbor. When he saw the two officers approaching his house, he turned and went back to his own back yard. Eva did not know this, and in response to Will Smith's query, she answered: "My father is not at home."

The detective had seen Evans turn back to his own yard and perhaps thought that Eva was trying to shield him. So the officer answered harshly: "You're a damned little liar." This was Eva's testimony during the trial. Smith insisted unctuously that he had said, "Little girl, I think you are mistaken." At any rate, Eva ran to her father, and what she said to him brought Evans into the house on a run. He still carried the gun used in the target practice, and the two officers fled precipitately. Had they merely walked away, or even run in a straight line, perhaps nothing would have happened, and this story need not be written. But they wiggled and zigzagged, and Evans could not resist the temptation to "wing" Witty, the deputy sheriff. Sontag, hearing the roar of a rifle outside his bedroom door stepped out and, without asking any question, blemished Smith, who had "zigged" when he should have "zagged." Evans and Sontag became outlaws that day.[42]

They appropriated the sheriff's wagon and raced for the mountains. That evening they returned to the ranch for food and clothing. Deputy Sheriff Dan Overall had posted a guard around the stable. (Incidentally, it may be stated here that Overall's son Orval, together with Frank Chance of Fresno, became the stars years later of the Chicago Cub's baseball team.) When the outlaws returned, they walked into the posse. The second battle of the first day was fought there. Men aimed at flashes in the dark. Deputy Sheriff Oscar Beaver was killed. Presently, no answering shots came from the barn where Evans and Sontag had taken shelter; only groans were heard. The morning light revealed that the groans came from a wounded horse; the outlaws had eluded the would-be captors for the second time in one day.[43]

The hunt for Evans and Sontag attracted statewide attention. United States Deputy Marshal Vernon C. Wilson arrived in Visalia from San Diego. His initials caused him to be referred to as "Vic." He had been a Texas Ranger, and sent to the San Carlos Reservation in Arizona for two Apache trackers named Jericho and Pecon. These Indians attracted much interest in Visalia.

> Pelon (Pecon?), the Apache trailer, was the first witness called in the Clarke Moore trial yesterday. Pelon is a copper-colored, sinewy, straight man, dressed in brogans, overalls, and blue coat and brass buttons. Around his neck he wears a string of beads, and his coarse, straight black hair, like a horse's mane, hangs down in three or four plaits between his shoulder blades. He is an ugly customer, with a cool, cat-like mouth, and with black eyes that burn like fiery coals.[44]

Besides Wilson and his two Apaches, the posse included Andy McGinnis of Modesto, a deputy-sheriff; Alfred Witty, a deputy sheriff from Visalia and a brother of the Witty wounded by Evans; Constable Warren Hill of Sanger; Will Smith, the railroad company's detective; and Frank Burke. Some time before the battle of Young's Cabin, the Indian tracker Jericho was replaced by another arrival from Arizona known as Cameño Dulce.[45]

The two fugitives were warned by a message from Eva

Posse surrounding the dying John Sontag after the battle of Stone Corral, June 13, 1893. Left to right: Jud Elwood, Hi Rapelje, U.S. Marshal George E. Gard, George Witty, Thomas Burns, William Stuck, Jo P. Carroll, Harry Stuart, and an unidentified. C. B. Glasscock, *Bandits and the Southern Pacific*.

and they were alert. According to Eva Evans' testimony, Wilson rather brazenly said in her hearing that his gun had twenty-seven notches, and after he had met Evans and Sontag it would hold two more. The posse trailed the hunted men into the hills and back to the plains. At Traver, Evans and Sontag fed their horses in Harrison Peacock's livery stable. The stableman was weary and sleepily accepted fifty cents for the feed. The next morning, he was astounded to read the note which his visitors had left for him: "We are sorry to have disturbed you at this time of the night, but owing to the urgency of our business and the necessity of our progress, we cannot help it. Evans and Sontag."[46]

While the two fugitives were feeding their horses in Traver, their pursuers had made camp for the night six miles from that place in the direction of Visalia. The Apaches followed the trail the next morning to Dunlap and thence to Sampson's Flat, where Evans had a gold claim. Near this place was located Jim Young's cabin. Mainwaring, a handsome Englishman, who resided in another cabin half a mile away, kept some of his supplies in the larger Young cabin. When he entered the Young cabin one morning he found the owner absent, but Evans and Sontag were sitting there. They forced him to prepare breakfast while they watched him and the trail. Some miles away the posse stopped at the Barton ranch, and Vernon Wilson profanely asked the housewife: "Have you seen *Christ* Evans?" The woman thus addressed answered with asperity: "No, but when you see him, you will see Hell."

While the two outlaws were eating, they spied thirteen men approaching the cabin. Evans ordered Mainwaring to take a pail and walk slowly to the spring two hundred yards away. He admonished the Englishman: "If you turn your head to warn the posse, or start to run to show we are here, I'll drill you between the shoulder blades." The nervous young man, trying to reconcile his instructions with his fear of impending doom, executed a fantastic cakewalk to the spring, and the approaching posse assumed the cabin to be unoccupied. As they approached the door, they were thinking only of breakfast. When Wilson was within ten feet of the door, their appetites vanished; Evans swung it open, and the roar of his shotgun and Wilson's death were simultaneous. Sontag wounded McGinnis; the others scattered. Evans walked over to McGinnis, who begged piteously for his life. Evans testified later that he had compassion on his former friend and neighbor from Modesto, and turned away, whereupon McGinnis fired hastily, inflicting a nasty flesh wound. Then Evans promptly blew out the brains of the man whose life he had just agreed to spare. McGinnis may have had another story to tell.[47]

The Apaches refused to follow the trail any longer. They collected their pay at Visalia and returned to Arizona. But other men took their places as manhunters. The officers who pursued the fugitives were honorable men doing their duty. But they were often augmented by braggarts from the saloons and pool halls, who were anxious to collect the blood money offered. Their charges into the hills were always futile and often artificially stimulated.

From Sampson's Flat the chase led to Eshom Valley, lying to the southeast; thence to Squaw Valley, ten miles southwest of Sampson's Flat. Emil Tretten, a rancher in Squaw Valley, fed the two outlaws one day, but feared to report their presence to the officers. In sparsely settled districts, it was dangerous to deny food and shelter to outlaws; it was equally dangerous to report their presence to officers. During the winter of 1892-1893 the chase lapsed. The manhunts spent their time comfortably in the saloons of Sanger, Reedley, Dinuba, and Visalia. Evans and Sontag eked out an existence in the snow-clad hills. Maggie Rucker, who had harbored Grat Dalton at Cross Creek, now rendered a similar service to Evans and Sontag. Aside from her Cross Creek ranch, she had a cattle ranch in the mountains near Badger. She was an excellent rifle shot and hunted cougars, bears, and bobcats with zest and success. She had a soft spot in her heart for those in distress, and never failed to come to their aid. During the Christmas holidays, Evans and Sontag glided into Visalia and spent several days with the Evans family. The small Evans children never revealed by word or look the fact that their father was at home. Their suppressed excitement can be imagined.[48]

In the meantime, George Sontag had been sent to the

Folsom State Penitentiary for life. Evans conceived a
grandiose plan for his rescue. A released convict named
Fredericks called at the Evans home at Visalia. At Eva's
suggestion, he stole the weapons stacked in Si Lovern's
saloon at Visalia while the toughs inside were boasting of
their conflicts, past and future, with Evans and Sontag.
These weapons, used in many a futile search for the two
outlaws, were actually smuggled into Folsom prison. Such
is the irony of fate. But Fate took another trick when it
caused a man to trip on a pebble at the psychological
moment, and the attempt to escape was frustrated.[49]

From time to time, Evans and Sontag took advantage of
the friendship of the lumberjacks at Sequoia Mills. Here
they secured food and rest. United States Deputy Marshal
J. S. Black followed them. He had come from San Diego
and was accompanied by Tom Burns, a detective. They
camped at Badger. One evening Black entered his cabin
and received a shot in the thigh. Evans and Sontag denied
that they were the assailants but before he died, Sontag
said he and Evans had tried to kill Black. Evans always
said he was elsewhere that night and placed the blame on
a lumberjack, jealous of Black's attention to his wife.[50]

The successful defiance of all constituted authority by
Evans and Sontag became such a scandal in California
that finally United States Marshal George E. Gard,
appeared in the valley. He entered the foothills with a
posse that included Hi Rapelje, a deputy-sheriff from
Fresno; Fred Jackson, an officer from Nevada; Tom Burns,
a detective; and many others. They stationed themselves
in a cabin near a landmark called Stone Corral. This place
is located in the hills due east of Yettem. The battle of
Stone Corral was the reverse of the one that occurred at
Young's Cabin. In the former the outlaws were on the
inside; in the latter, on the outside. At Stone Corral the
officers saw the two outlaws walking down the hill toward

the cabin. Had they waited, the fight would have ended there. But Jackson used poor judgment and fired too soon. His shot shattered Evans' left arm, and the two outlaws jumped back of a sheltering straw-stack. The first shot was fired just after sundown, but the summer evening was clear and the contest raged throughout the night. Jackson, whose premature shot had precipitated the battle, crawled outside in an attempt to get behind the outlaws. He was shot through the ankle and eventually lost a foot.[51]

An interesting incident occurred during a lull in the battle. William W. Ward of Kingsburg had a cattle ranch in the neighborhood of Stone Corral. A cowboy in his employ named George Boyer died and Ward was obliged to go to the ranch with a coroner and make provision for the removal of the body. Lewis Draper owned a light wagon and a fast team of standard-bred mares; Ward engaged Draper to accompany him to the ranch. The morning train of June 11, 1893 brought to Kingsburg from Fresno a coroner and a coffin; the former rode in a buggy with Ward, the latter was placed in Draper's spring wagon. They turned east on the first road south of the Southern Pacific Railroad bridge, passed through Monson and the present site of Yettem, and then ascended the hills to Stone Corral. They performed their sad duties at the ranch and then proceeded on their homeward way. Ward and the doctor preceded the wagon and reached the valley floor without mishap. Under the circumstances, it was natural that Draper should drive more slowly. As he approached the head of the grade he heard rapid firing, then silence. Suddenly both he and his team were greatly startled when two deputies, armed like walking arsenals, stepped from behind a huge rock and ordered Draper to stop. He did.

One of them said, "Evans and Sontag are lying behind

that straw-stack yonder (about a hundred yards away) and if you try to go on they will probably shoot you." Draper was ordered to turn his team and go back. He protested. To spend the night in the hills with a corpse was unpleasant. The other deputy said, "If you try to go on, Chris Evans will probably send your wagon home with two corpses instead of one." Draper then attempted to turn his team but the mares, which were angry because they had been frightened by the sudden shooting, now decided to balk. The deputies had walked up to the wagon and were standing beside the front wheel. Chris Evans, peering from his hiding place, saw his chance, stepped out with his heavy rifle, and hurriedly fired three shots. Two bullets splintered the spokes in the front wheel between the two deputies; the third scarred the thill.

The high-strung team, slightly unstrung by the previous shooting, were now promptly re-strung, and exercising the prerogatives of their feminine persuasion, changed their minds about balking and departed forthwith. Their exit was so sudden that the seat jumped off its hinges and fell to the bottom of the wagon floor, but fortunately the doubletree was made of tough old hickory, and a real horseman held the reins.

In the midst of the sudden turmoil, another deputy behind another rock shouted, "Hey, wait a moment. I've got a wounded man here (Fred Jackson); take him to Visalia." The team was gaining momentum at every bound, the bullets were whining angrily, and to stop would have been both impossible and suicidal. Draper called back through the din, "Got one corpse, can't use another." He drove unscathed through an enfilading fire, managed to turn his team at the foot of the grade, and traveled the intervening thirty-five miles to Kingsburg at a rate of speed not customary in the transportation of cadavers.

After blanketing his horses, Draper left the livery stable without comment. The next morning an irate liveryman accosted him and related with gusto his emotional reactions during the night, when he discovered the contents of Draper's wagon. Draper had known Chris Evans before the latter became an outlaw. After Evans had been taken into custody, Draper went to visit him and reminded Evans of the fracas at Stone Corral. Evans said, "Lew, I did not know it was you in that wagon, but even if I had, it would have made no difference. I was shooting to save my own life."[52]

After the exit of Lew Draper, the battle of Stone Corral continued with unabated fury. The hero of that fight was Hi Rapelje. He shot Sontag, hidden behind a straw stack, through the right arm. A little later he shot him through the right side. Evans, in trying to aid Sontag, was shot through the right arm by the ridiculously accurate Rapelje. Then this amazing sniper sent a charge of buckshot from his shotgun in the general direction of Evans, and the latter lost his right eye. This was followed by a rifle shot that perforated Sontag's right shoulder. The latter was now riddled like a sieve.

Evans crawled away through the brush. Sontag, as game a man as ever lived, maintained a wild and desultory fire throughout the night. More than a hundred shots were fired during this battle. The next morning the officers cautiously closed in on the haystack and found Sontag unconscious. Evans was gone. After walking six miles from Stone Corral to the home of a Mrs. Perkins, Evans was glad to rest. Mrs. Perkins lived in the district known as Elderwood in Wilcox Canyon, south and east of Boyd's Grade and northeast of Stone Corral. Her daughter had married Perry Byrd, a brother of Chris Evans' wife.

The presence of an outlaw in the Perkins home was

embarrassing, and word was sent to the officers. A race ensued between the Fresno and Tulare county officials to see which group should collect the reward; the latter won. One of the younger sons of Mrs. Perkins, Al by name, was offered $100 by the deputies from Visalia if he would go up into the loft in the attic and disarm Chris; they feared for their lives as Evans had promised to shoot any man who showed his head. Al Perkins did so, and found Evans unconscious. It may be of more interest than importance to say that the young man did not receive the reward that had been promised him.

The officers, led by William Hall, undersheriff of Tulare County, entered the attic where the battered Evans lay. The latter was taken to Visalia, and medical practitioners strove to save the life of the man whom duly constituted officers of the law had so recently tried to destroy. They succeeded.[53]

The Evans family was financially decrepit. But Eva Evans refused to permit their destitution to act as a deterrent to the employment of legal aid. She adored her father and was a girl of uncommon business acumen and sense. In those days there were no moving pictures. But the legitimate stage had its devotees. A dramatization of the stirring Evans and Sontag episode was a "natural." A theatrical producer wrote a play called *Evans and Sontag*. To make the play more spectacular, Eva and her mother, Molly Evans, were coached to portray themselves in the play. An excellent professional cast supported them. Just before the first night of the play, an incident occurred which was either a remarkable coincidence or a clever bit of advertising. A chubby baby boy was lost on Market Street, and a burly policeman picked up the little fellow and asked him his name. The lad answered tearfully, "I'm looking for Tris Evans." To which the cop made the only possible reply, "What, another deputy! I guess you're a little bit young to be looking for Chris Evans." But the infant insisted that "Tris" was his daddy and a good daddy, too. He was returned to his mother, then rehearsing her lines at the National Theatre. The newspapers made the most of the incident. The opening night at the National Theatre of San Francisco was an overwhelming success. The applause was deafening. The proceeds were used to procure legal aid for Chris Evans.[54]

The trial began at Fresno on November 20, 1893, with Judge M. K. Harris presiding. In the meantime, John Sontag had died in the hospital at Fresno. Evans possessed remarkable poise and never lost his buoyancy. The success of his wife and daughter as actresses and the resultant financial rewards, which provided excellent attorneys, encouraged him. Eva made a hurried visit to Fresno and met a waiter at the restaurant who usually carried the meals into the jail for Evans. This waiter, Ed. Morrell, was fascinated by Eva and her father. He was young and impressionable, and truly believed that they were the victims of oppression.[55]

A friend of Morrell purposely circulated a false rumor that a train was to be held up near Porterville. This clever ruse sent most of the officers of Fresno out of town. Then Morrell placed two loaded revolvers under the napkin and carried the supposed meal past the unsuspecting jailer into Evans' cell. Evans and Morrell then marched the dumbfounded deputy to Mariposa Street. Here they met an ex-mayor of Fresno and added him to the procession. A fast team, provided by an accomplice of Morrell, waited for them along O Street. Conversing beside this team were John D. Morgan, Fresno's chief of police, and W. M. Wyatt, who was on his way to attend a chicken dinner at his church. The approaching procession aroused their curiosity because two of their acquaintances had their arms in the air. When Morgan refused to indulge in

Ed Morrell, the Fresno waiter who helped Chris Evans plot his jailbreak and hid out with him for months in the depths of the Sierra Nevada. Morrell's autobiography, *The Twenty-Fifth Man*.

similar antics he received a shot in the side, which required first aid treatment from Dr. Maupin. The frightened team ran away, and Evans and Morrell disappeared down the alley between O and P Streets, reached Tulare Street, and on the corner of Mono and Q they relieved an astonished newsboy of his horse and Petaluma cart.[56]

When the officers returned from their futile trip to Porterville, they followed Evans and Morrell to Sanger. The Sangerites remembered what had happened to Wilson and his men, and refused to join a posse. Meanwhile, taxpayers raged over the mounting expense account of this ridiculous manhunt. Evans and Morrell followed the Hume-Sanger lumber flume along Kings River into the mountains.[57]

On January 11, 1894, the station agent at Fowler and three other men sat beside the stove in the waiting room. A masked bandit entered and relieved them of $30; two other men came in and contributed an additional $40. The bandit marched these six men to the Kutner-Goldstein store. While robbing the till, he was interrupted by the entrance of Charles Ochs, the constable, and another man. Ochs hastily fired two shots. One struck the section foreman, Pat Lahey, in the arm; the other lodged in the shoulder of H. A. Mulligan. The bandit shot Ochs in the hip, and the latter fell to the floor and rolled out of the door. The bandit followed erectly.[58]

On January 15th Evans and Morrell were seen riding in a buggy between Traver and Reedley in the vicinity of Clarke's bridge, near the Clarke Ranch. Irresponsible persons circulated ridiculous rumors. The harassed officers, anxious for a clue, went from hither to yon but most of the information they received proved figments of the imagination. Finally, Fresno deputy sheriffs L. P. Timmins and Charles Boyd went to Badger. Timmins walked up a steep hill in order to rest the horse; he took a shortcut over the hill and when Boyd, riding in the cart, reached the top of the grade, he saw a cabin with Evans standing in the doorway. When Boyd refused to stop and enter, Evans opened fire with his Winchester and neatly placed a bullet midway between Boyd and the seat on which he was sitting; this left a scar on cart seat and anatomy that proved annoying, but not fatal. Timmins opened fire on Evans long enough to permit Boyd to escape. Then the two officers left for Reedley.[59]

Special newspaper correspondents were often seen in Visalia. They were all anxious to interview the outlaws. Some of them succeeded. Perhaps the most colorful of these would-be war correspondents was Joaquin Miller, the famous Poet of the Sierras. He reported his visit to

Camp Defiance, where Evans and Sontag spent the
winter. Contemporary witnesses doubted that he ever saw
the two hunted men. However, he did make a visit by
stage to Millwood, Grant's Park, and Sequoia Lake.
Perhaps he did see them. At any rate, he was friendly in
his attitude.

> Joaquin Miller; the Poet of the Sierras, tells in the Sunday
> *Examiner* of interviewing Chris Evans, one of the Tulare
> bandits. Miller makes a much abused hero of the fugitive
> train robber, and takes much pains to show his disapproval of
> those malicious persons who wish to arrest Evans and
> Sontag, and put an end to the business of holding up trains
> and stages. The poet expresses his admiration for the
> gentleness, bravery, and generally inoffensive character of the
> bandits, and seems to be imbued with an idea that shooting
> men from ambush is the most natural and meritorious thing
> in the world.
>
> Probably the strait of Evans excites a fellow feeling in Miller.
> It may serve to recall the time he was a fugitive from justice
> himself. It excites memories of the time when he was indicted
> for horse stealing in Siskiyou County, and had the shirt shot
> off him by the late General Colton, who was then sheriff.
> After his hegira into Oregon, Miller took to poetry and let
> horses alone, but it is said he never sees a lariat without
> instinctively feeling his necktie. Since he has seen and talked
> with Evans, the public had better have a change of heart. He
> has only killed people who were trying to rob him of his hard
> earnings. He is the great and good man much
> misunderstood.[60]

The metropolitan press was far more tolerant of the
Evans and Sontag affair than were the valley papers.
Naturally the latter felt that conditions were a reflection
on life and manners in the San Joaquin. The former often
took time to be facetious. It was not their ox that was
being gored.

> The statement of the San Jose *Mercury* that Chris Evans was
> last seen on his way to Honolulu where he will marry Queen

485

Lil and hold up the provisional government, is not confirmed
by the latest news from Camp Badger. Chris is much too
smart to tackle the Queen Lil proposition with only one
arm.[61]

The cabin occupied by Evans, when Timmins and Boyd
exchanged shots with him, was located in Slick Rock
Canyon, seven miles west of Badger. William Henry,
another deputy, scouted in the region and creased Evans'
scalp, burned the cabin, but lost the fleeing outlaws,
Evans and Morrell, in a fierce mountain blizzard. The
latter reached Eshom Valley and would probably have
reached the state line and safety if deception had not been
effectively employed.[62]

A friend of the Evans family, overcome by cupidity, sent
word to Evans to come home, as his little child was
dangerously ill. Evans was an affectionate father. He
went. His paternal instinct proved fatal. Eva and Molly
were away on a theatrical tour. Officers surrounded the
house. No shots were fired. Notes were carried back and
forth by emissaries, and finally Evans agreed to
surrender. Evans stepped out on the porch and shook
hands with Sheriff Eugene Kay of Tulare County and the
other officers. He was the coolest man in the group and
showed no tenseness.

Talk of lynching developed among the rabble in the
saloons. The fastest standard-bred team in Visalia was
hitched to a light wagon, and Evans was taken for a ride.
In the parlance of modern racketeering, to take a man for
a ride is synonymous with murder. But on this occasion,
Evans was taken for a ride to save his life. George Witty,
deputy sheriff, was the driver; Sheriff Kay, who had
received Evans' surrender on his front porch, watched the
prisoners; and Sheriff Jay Scott of Fresno County peered
into the darkness alert for possible pursuers. The mob
mounted their horses and chased the fast trotters. The

latter lived up to their reputation as the fastest
Hambletonians in that part of the valley, and a good
Hambletonian is the best horse in the world for such a
task. The cow ponies of the mob were not evenly matched
in speed and bottom, and their riders were unable to
approach the wagon in a compact body. They dropped out
of the race at Goshen and stopped for liquid refreshments.
This wild ride occurred during the night of February 19,
1894.[63]

Judge M. K. Harris of Fresno sentenced Evans to Folsom
for life. When this news was received at Visalia, Evans'
hometown paper came out with the following editorial:

> The jury in the case of Chris Evans has rendered a most
> outrageous verdict. By what method of reasoning they arrived
> at the conclusion that Evans ought not to be hanged, we are
> at a loss to imagine. There never has been a more heartless
> murderer tried in the State of California; and his punishment
> should have been death.
>
> If such a thing were possible, he should have been ordered
> hanged for murder committed while robbing the train at
> Goshen; he should have been hanged for a similar crime
> when the Pixley robbery occurred; he should have been
> hanged for robbing the train at Collis; he deserved hanging
> for shooting George Witty at Visalia; he should have been
> hanged for killing Oscar Beaver; he should have been hanged
> twice for the double murder of McGinnis and Wilson; he
> should have been lynched for trying to assassinate Black at
> Camp Badger. In spite of these crimes, nearly all of which
> were brought to the attention of the jury; they found him
> guilty and fixed the punishment at imprisonment for life. It is
> such miscarriages of justice that make law-abiding people
> resort to lynch law, and the jurors who rendered the verdict
> ought to be ashamed of themselves.[64]

It was recalled that Evans had been in sympathy with
other accused train robbers as far back as the time when
Grattan Dalton was on trial at Visalia. It was his attitude

at that time which first caused Will Smith, the Southern Pacific detective, to suspect him.[65]

> Chris Evans was one of the most indefatigable attendants during the trial of Grattan Dalton for complicity in the Alila train robbery. The trial took place in the courthouse here, and day after day, Evans sat outside the railing, drinking in every word. He had little to say, however, to the general public concerning the evidence.
>
> But after Detective Smith's testimony had been given, the usual taciturnity of Evans was overcome by his manifest hatred of the detective, whose testimony proved so damaging to Dalton's cause. Evans declared to an acquaintance that Smith's story was a pack of lies. "I would not hesitate a minute to shoot down a ———- ———- ———- ———- like that detective if he'd lie on me as he's lied on Dalton," Evans growled out, an evil gleam discernible in his eye.

Evans served seventeen years in Folsom. In 1910 Hiram Johnson was elected governor of California. He, too, was an inveterate foe of the Southern Pacific and sympathized with the battered Evans. Johnson explained his attitude:

> I am not clear that I pardoned Chris Evans. I was rather under the impression that I obtained his parole from the prison directors, and that one of the special reasons for doing so was his physical condition. He had one eye shot out and one arm shot off, and he was suffering various ills, which within a year after his release terminated fatally.[66]

Ed Morrell, another member of the gang, served nine years. His hero-worship of Evans proved disastrous for a time. But his youth permitted him to begin life anew. During the first five years, he lay in a dungeon in Folsom. The next four years were spent as a trusty in San Quentin. His experiments with thought transference and spiritualism while in solitary confinement aroused the interest of his friend, Jack London, who subsequently wrote a book based on Morrell's experiences called *The*

Star Rover. After his release Morrell devoted himself to prison reform and his book, *The Twenty-Fifth Man*, was sponsored by the American Crusaders, who are striving for a new penology.[67]

Chris Evans, after his parole had been granted, came out on the streets of Sacramento and was dazzled and bewildered by the new civilization that had developed during those seventeen long years behind the gray walls of Folsom. He still hated the Southern Pacific and was pleased to find that he could ride on a new invention, the automobile, which he now saw for the first time. He went to join his family in Portland, Oregon, and passed away at that place on February 9, 1917, at peace with himself and the world. During his last days he was more charitable toward those who had harmed him than were many of those who had suffered with him. Retributive justice overtook many of those who had mistreated him.[68]

If we take Al Smith's advice and look at the record, we find that we cannot tell the whole truth about train robberies in the San Joaquin Valley; not because it is not known, but because it would not be advisable to do so. After sufficient years have elapsed the truth might be told, but by that time no one will be left alive who possesses the information. Pioneer residents, men of irreproachable character and judgment, can today offer proof that not all the train robberies were committed by Evans and Sontag. They assert that these two men held up trains; masks and worthless Peruvian silver dollars, taken by John Sontag from the train at Collis on the assumption that they were twenty dollar gold pieces, were found buried in the Evans' yard at Visalia. But they also know that other men were involved at times when Evans and Sontag were the only ones accused.

The following incident, well authenticated, may hint at

the reason why all cannot be told, and it will also point to the fact that many otherwise law-abiding citizens felt that an open season existed on the express coaches of the Southern Pacific. One evening, the northbound train out of Goshen was stopped by two masked men at Cross Creek. The express messenger heard them walking on the roof overhead, and thought they were hoboes. They climbed into the coal-car, held up the engineer and fireman in the same manner as other hold-ups had been staged, left the main part of the train on the Cross Creek bridge, and forced the engineer to drive the locomotive and express car a mile up the track toward Traver. Here a group of men and a buckboard awaited them. The expressman said he had lost the keys, but a stick of dynamite forced the safe open.

A rancher named Adam Heimrod; living south of Traver, heard the explosion and rode down to investigate. He lay prone in the grass while the men in the party passed; he recognized the men in the buckboard as well as the men on horseback. They were all residents of the community. Twitting them one day at Traver resulted in a threat and warning so stern that he did not dare to sleep in his own home for a year for fear of violent and sudden death. He bought a watchdog, tied him in the yard, and slept in his blankets on top of a huge haystack behind the barn. Incidentally, during this whole year he took his Winchester to bed with him each night.

The Southern Pacific sent guards to the scene of the hold-up from Fresno that night to watch the property that the hold-up men had thrown out of the express coach. Crates of chickens, sacks of mail, and thousands of silver dollars had been thrown on the right-of-way; only gold coins had been taken. Until the debris could be cleared away, it was necessary to watch it. The school children at Traver were much excited, and pleaded with the teacher to dismiss school so that they could go to the scene of the excitement. But no dice. The men took their spoils to Harry Burke's saloon, where in an inner room they divided $70,000 in gold coin.

John Sontag was not suspected this time; he was dead. Chris Evans was not blamed; he was in Folsom. The Dalton boys were not accused; they were all dead excepting Emmett and he was in Leavenworth. Question: had these men robbed trains before this? The technique was the same as previous holdups. These men needed money; they borrowed it from the Southern Pacific, no doubt to square the account over excessively high shipping rates on grain, and they never borrowed money in this way again. So much is certain. Some of them derived little good from the money although one man, poor at this time, invested his proceeds in good farm land, became a leader in the community, and died honored and respected at Kingsburg in 1937.[69]

Today the San Joaquin Valley is one of the most peaceful regions in the world. The majority of its residents, comparatively recent arrivals from eastern states or European countries, are not even aware that outlaws once terrorized the peaceful countryside. Murrieta, Vasquez, Procopio, the Dalton brothers, Evans, Sontag, and Morrell are mere names to them. These men were not entirely wrong. They pointed out by their very excesses the need for certain reforms. In time, conditions were ameliorated by ballots rather than by bullets. These men possessed courage above the average, a spirit that could not be broken, and ability which made them successful in other fields of endeavor. After Emmett Dalton was pardoned, he married Julia Johnson, his boyhood sweetheart, and became a highly successful building contractor at Hollywood. His verdict concerning the life of an outlaw is the mature judgment of an expert and is a fitting close to this chapter:

> It was not because we changed from train robbery to bank robbery that brought about the gang's destruction. There is a law of Nature or God that intervenes. There is no such thing as a successful outlaw. The end of all violators of the law has been the same right through history. It is impossible for the few to pit their brains against the world for any length of time. This is being demonstrated daily in the lives of the big city racketeers.[70]

> If a lot of ward heelers were thrown into jail, the backbone of racketeering would be broken, for racketeering is simply a combination of money and politics. I have made more money in a single real estate deal, than out of all the robberies of the Dalton Gang.

15 Smokestacks

and Pavements

Sweet Auburn! loveliest village of the plain,
Where health and plenty cheered the laboring swain,
Where smiling spring its earliest visit paid,
And parting summer's lingering blooms delayed.

Oliver Goldsmith *The Deserted Village*

"What's the use of bragging about being from the North,
or the South, or the manor house in the dale, or Euclid
Avenue, Cleveland, or Pike's Peak, or Fairfax County,
Virginia, or Hooligan's Flats or any place? It'll be a better
world when we quit being fools about some mildewed town
or ten acres of swampland just because we happened to be
born there."[1]

Thus spoke E. Rushmore Coglan, a true cosmopolitan, but
a few minutes later he was engaged in a furious fistfight

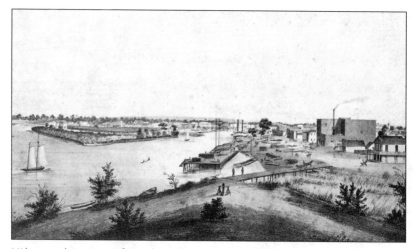

Lithographic view of Stockton by Kuchel and Dresel, 1885.

with a man who had spoken disparagingly about the sidewalks and water supply of his hometown, Mattawamkeag, Maine. The moral to this story is the keynote of the chapter, and was bluntly stated by Aristotle long ago: "Man is by nature a civic animal."[2]

Five distinct kinds of civic communities grew up in the San Joaquin Valley: fur posts, river towns, gold camps, stagecoach stations, and railway towns.

The first place in the valley where a large body of people located, even for a temporary period of time, was at French Camp, about five miles south of present-day Stockton. In 1827-1828, Jedediah Smith blazed a trail from the San Joaquin Valley to Oregon. After the massacre along the Umpqua River there, he and the men who had escaped with him found sanctuary with Dr. John McLoughlin, the factor of the Hudson's Bay Company at Fort Vancouver, north of present-day Portland. Smith gave the latter information concerning conditions in California, and McLoughlin immediately commissioned a new expedition led by Alexander R. McLeod, which back-tracked Smith's trail to California. A river, known today as

Engraving of Sam Brannan, founder of the San Joaquin Valley's first planned community, New Hope, located near the confluence of the Stanislaus and San Joaquin rivers. *Fresno County Public Library, California History and Genealogy Room Collection.*

the McCloud, was named in honor of the expedition's chief on this trip. McLeod's report led to the sending of Peter Skene Ogden to California in 1829; and the next year he and his trappers entered the San Joaquin for the first time. Aided by a brigade of thirty men, he trapped down the length of the San Joaquin River. In 1832, a permanent camp was established which took the name French Camp, due to the racial composition of the group which worked for the company. Here about four hundred trappers gathered annually at the rendezvous.[3]

The first city of any importance in the San Joaquin was Tuleberg. The tules growing profusely along the river in the vicinity suggested the name. On April 3, 1845, Captain Charles M. Weber acquired the *Campo de los Franceses* land grant from William Gulnac in exchange for 200 pesos paid in silver, and "effects." Almost immediately Weber began the erection of buildings, and a settlement developed. During the Mexican War the name was

495

changed to Stockton, in honor of the American naval commander. After the war, the United States appointed a land commission for California, which attempted to determine the validity of the grants made by the Mexican governors. Eventually Gulnac's grant was approved and Weber's title to it made secure. When the patent confirming Weber in his rights to the *Campo de los Franceses* ranch of nearly 50,000 acres was presented to President Lincoln for his approval, the latter was greatly astonished and hesitated before signing.[4]

During the gold rush Stockton became the chief point of departure for the Southern Mines. In 1850 Rev. James Woods, a Presbyterian missionary, built the first church at Stockton. Land for this edifice and for a parsonage was donated by Captain Weber. A little later in the same year, Rev. Oscar Harriman organized the first Protestant Episcopal Church in the valley. In 1857, Father Joseph A. Gallagher, on land also donated by Charles Weber, erected a Catholic church, which survives as the present St. Mary's Church of Stockton.[5]

Stockton's rail and water connections surpass those of any other inland city in California. A network of eleven railway lines serve as carriers. These roads are owned by the Southern Pacific; the Atchison, Topeka & Santa Fe; and the Western Pacific Railway. The latter, when its connections were completed with the Great Northern, made Stockton the nearest California seaport to points along the line of the Great Northern. The port of Stockton is also served by the Stockton Ship Channel, constructed by the United States government, which has a minimum width of 100 feet, a surface width of 300 feet, and a depth of 26 feet, and is 90 miles long. One half of its length consists of fresh water. The channel is lighted and navigable at night. The wharves at Stockton are 14,000 lineal feet in length, and capable of docking twenty-eight vessels simultaneously. The industrial water front acreage consists of 10,000 acres.[6]

The inland waterways surrounding Stockton exceed 1,000 miles. In allurement they surpass the Everglades of Florida or the picturesque regions of Ontario. These waterways lead through a hunter's paradise not visible from the highways. Much of the countryside resembles the lowlands of Belgium or Holland. Edible turtles, pheasants, quail, doves, ducks, and opossums abound. Striped bass come up from the sea and black bass, planted in the eighties, have thrived ever since. Beaver dams and otter slides exist as they did in the days of Hudson's Bay and Jedediah Smith. All of these waterways are adequately signed and the few shoals are marked. This section is given over largely to big ranches, and habitations are few and far between. In 1930, according to the United States Census, Stockton had a population of 47,963, but the contiguous area within a radius of fifty miles contained 720,000. Its growth since gold-mining days has been steady, and Stockton remains the metropolis of the northern San Joaquin. The College of the Pacific, a Methodist denominational college, is located there.[7]

William Knight, one of the frontiersmen who had accompanied Fremont on his exploring expeditions to the San Joaquin, built a trading post and ferry along the Stanislaus River in 1849. The stampede of gold diggers to the southern mines made the ferry a profitable venture. A little settlement grew up near the ferry and became known as Knight's Ferry. Following Knight's murder at the ferry in November 1849, the property was purchased by Dent, Vantine & Company. In 1852 Vantine apparently sold his share in the firm to his partners, the Dent brothers. That year and in 1853, a brother-in-law of the latter paid them visits. He was a captain stationed at a military post in Oregon and, since he was a graduate of

View of the Dent House in Knights Ferry, owned by the in-laws of U.S. Grant. George Tinkham, *History of Stanislaus County.*

West Point and a skilled engineer, he likely aided them in surveying and drawing plans for the bridge, which finally replaced the ferry. But no one paid any attention to the name. Few people in those days did pay any attention to the name of Ulysses Simpson Grant.[8]

The first county seat of Stanislaus was Adamsville, founded along the Tuolumne River in the winter of 1849 by Dr. Adams, one of the first medical practitioners on the plains. This little city was located six miles down the river from Modesto. In the election of October 21, 1854, the capital was moved up the river to Empire City, which lay about four miles above Modesto. Empire City had been surveyed and laid out by John S. Marvin sometime in 1850. The latter was a Harvard Law School graduate, and became the first state superintendent of California schools. For a time he also had charge of Indian affairs in the state.[9]

Burneyville was laid out by Major James Burney, the first

498

sheriff of Mariposa County. Burney commanded the first body of men sent against the Indians by an American governor of California. The old town of Burneyville lies next to the modern town of Riverbank.[10]

A trading post was located on the southwest bank of the San Joaquin River, opposite the mouth of the Merced. The founder of this place was Judge D. D. Dickenson. In 1849 he sent a boat up the San Joaquin with supplies and men. In time, a small settlement grew up around his trading post and assumed the name of Hill's Ferry from the name of the man who operated the ferry, Jesse Hill. The operator also owned saloons and other places decidedly notorious. Mexicans on their way to the southern mines crossed the river on the ferry at this point and stopped at the town for amusement. French and Basque sheepherders from the hills and cowboys from the plains made Hill's Ferry their rendezvous. The Oasis, one of the dance halls of the town, employed fifty girls. For a time Hill's Ferry was the most lawless spot in California. Watts & Boyce conducted the general store in the days when cattle and sheep engrossed the attention of the citizens. The development of wheat culture brought in Simon Newman and the Kahn brothers, who became shippers of wheat as well as merchants. The combined capacity of their grain warehouses was 10,000 tons. The more staid agricultural town of Newman, a few miles south of Hill's Ferry, made the latter and its wild type of life a mere memory.[11]

John M. Murphy conducted a ferry across the Stanislaus River. The little settlement which grew up at that point took the name of Murphy's Ferry. It was located a few miles northwest of Modesto. The Central Pacific and the building of bridges finally supplanted ferries. The settlement known as Murphy's Ferry is marked by the present site of Salida.[12]

In early 1850, Captain Andrew Jackson Grayson settled the site of Grayson, two miles above the mouth of the Tuolumne River. This city was prosperous during the days of the cattlemen, but the founding of Modesto along the railroad line caused its decline. During the Civil War, the town of Grayson furnished men for the California Hundred, as well as the first captain of the company. This captain, named Reed, and the fifteen subsequent captains were killed while serving with the Army of the Potomac. Captain Grayson was an ornithologist, and his drawings of birds were presented to the University of California, where they now repose at the Bancroft Library.[13]

Several mining towns grew up in the foothill region due east of Grayson and modern Modesto. Many of these were of a transitory nature and ceased to exist after the gold in the adjacent hills had been extracted; others changed their names in order to conform to a more conventional nomenclature. Fiddletown became Oleta; Freezeout was rechristened Ione; Bottileas, a Spanish term referred to empty beer bottles and descriptive of conditions during mining days, was converted to Jackson; American Camp retained its connotation by becoming Columbia; and Jimtown attained a new dignity by assuming the formal address of Jamestown. Northeast of Turlock was located a place known as Murphy's Diggings. Dramatic scenes were enacted there by picturesque personalities who moved in and out among the hills like characters out of a storybook.[14]

Chinese Camp, south of Sonora, was the scene of the mining activities of Ah Sin and his kin. This camp furnished Bret Harte the material for his famous poem usually referred to as *The Heathen Chinee*. Harte's cabin was located at Second Garrote and is still standing. The famous short story by Bret Harte entitled *Tennessee's Partner* was allegedly based on a wonderful friendship of two miners, J. P. Chamberlain and J. A. Chaffee, who lived together in a cabin in the hills northeast of Turlock. When the latter became sick and was taken to a hospital, Chamberlain could not endure the loneliness and took his own life. His grave in the cemetery near Jamestown can still be pointed out.[15]

A burro disappeared from camp one day. His owner went in search of him and found the beast standing beside a gulch. Stooping to pick up a rock to hurl at the donkey, the miner discovered gold in sufficient amount to cause a stampede and the establishment of a new camp known thenceforth as Jackass Hill. Samuel Clemens and his partner, Jim Gillis, were gold miners at Jackass Hill for a time. This camp was located between Sonora and Angel's Camp. Ben Coon, a bartender distinguished by skill as a raconteur, entertained Clemens and Gillis during the evenings with his quaint yarns. One of these, with a few added frills and embellishments, became famous as Mark Twain's *Jumping Frog of Calaveras County*. Dan'l Webster, the original jumping frog of Calaveras County, was a native California red-legged frog (*Rana aurora draytonii*). Recent contestants have been aliens imported from the East. Each individual weighs more than a pound. This gigantic frog is known as the Bullfrog (*Rana catesbeiana*).

Angel's Camp still exists. In 1930 it had a population of 915. Most people have forgotten that this place produced $100 million in gold dust, but the memory of the jumping frog still persists. In May of each year, highly trained jumping frogs are entered in the Angel's Camp steeplechase. Each frog is allowed three hops from taw, and the winner is the recipient of much attention. This holiday lasts for three days. When the Stockton frog won the tournament, the mayor and officials of the city held a reception for the frog at the city hall.[16]

A few miles south of Hill's Ferry, two Germans named Herman Widman and Ernest Voight built a racetrack and ran an establishment which brought an influx of gamblers and touts. The coming of the railroad and the birth of Newman ruined this place, known as Dutch Corners, just as it had killed Hill's Ferry. Progress and civilization invariably followed in the wake of the Iron Horse.[17]

Another Dutch Corners grew up in Tulare County. Four Germans secured homesteads and built a cabin where their lands joined; their names were Ben Spuhler, Chris Joos, Fred Schmidt, and Gotlet Etley (or Utley). This was known as Dutch Corners until the Santa Fe railway established a station in the immediate vicinity and shortened the name to Ducor.[18]

Irishtown was settled by North of Ireland immigrants. Some of these early settlers bore the name of Quinn, Gilligan, McCabe, McKee, Monroe, and Griffin. A later settler, Captain Slover, disliked the name and was instrumental in having it changed to Woodville, not to be confused with the Woodsville which had served as Tulare's county seat; this was located several miles to the north.[19]

Dr. Thomas Payne built a bridge across the Kaweah River about 1850 and collected tolls from the prairie schooners that entered the San Joaquin by way of Walker's Pass and proceeded north toward the gold fields. When Tulare County was organized in 1852, one of the polling places was situated at Payne's Bridge. A little settlement grew up along the stream, which became known as Woodsville and became the first site of Tulare County's county seat. The coming of the Butterfield Overland Mail made Visalia more important, and Woodsville ceased to exist.[20]

The prairie schooners on their way to the north were forced to cross Kings River. John Pool built a ferry and operated it at a point three miles upstream from present-day Reedley. When Jefferson Davis sent his army engineers to survey the valley, they crossed Kings River at

Pool's Ferry. The little hamlet which grew up there ceased to exist long ago.[21]

In 1855, James Smith established a ferry at what is now the northwest point of the Reedley cemetery grounds. This remained the most important ferry on Kings River during the next nineteen years. When freshets occurred, all travel had to be routed by way of Smith's Ferry because the high land on either side of the stream made it possible to approach the ferry when land adjacent to the river at other points was submerged. The minutes of the Board of Supervisors for Fresno County contained the following item for the year 1857:

> The petition of James Smith to run a ferry across Kings River at the place known as Smith & Crumbly was read; and proof of his having posted notices required by law, it was ordered:

> That license be granted to James Smith to run a ferry at the above named place, and to pay for the same the sum of five dollars per month, bonds to be executed in the sum of twenty-five hundred dollars ($2,500) to be approved by the county judge.

Smith built a ferry sixty feet long and sixteen feet wide, and attached it to a cable extending across the stream. The course of the boat was controlled by a block and tackle. The Smith family operated a hotel in connection with the ferry in order to care for stage passengers. By 1874 the Central Pacific had penetrated far enough into the valley to diminish stage travel, and the hotel and ferry service were discontinued. The floodwaters of 1875 tore the old boat loose from its moorings, and it floated downstream about twelve miles, where it was stranded. Soon it was demolished and the lumber used by the 76 Land & Water Company in the construction of the Wahtoke Dam.

James Smith was more than a mere ferryman. He was a popular man in the community and served his assembly district in the legislature during 1861-1862. Like all other office holders from the San Joaquin during the Civil War he was a Democrat, but he made no disloyal statements. However, the Union soldiers stationed at Camp Babbitt resented the sarcastic editorials of the Visalia *Equal Rights Expositor*, and vented their spleen on prominent Democrats. When these soldiers had occasion to cross Smith's Ferry, they never paid for the food they ate in his restaurant, nor the grain they took from his barn; they considered all Democrats fair game and punished Smith for the sins of others. The latter died in December 1862, and was buried at the brow of the hill overlooking the site of the old ferry. An ailanthus tree, planted at the foot of the grave, stands a silent sentinel on the heights overlooking the countryside, which has undergone a magical change since the days of Smith's Ferry. Only Smith Mountain, five miles east of Reedley and perpetuating the memory of the man who served as its namesake, remains the same.[22]

A few miles upstream from Pool's Ferry was located the town of Scottsburg, named after the third man to serve as sheriff of Fresno County, William Y. "Monte" Scott. This speck on the map served as a social and business center for the cattlemen of the upper Kings River region. The flood of 1862 washed away the town, and it was rebuilt on the opposite side of the river on higher ground and re-christened Centerville. The latter place was frequented by William "Yank" Hazelton's cowboys in the days when Moses J. Church was taking his initial steps in his irrigation project. It was in the Centerville store that Church was assaulted by cowboys, who hated settlers and sheepmen with good reason. For a short time this place became the mecca for the county's intelligentsia. The first Teachers' Institute to be held in Fresno County was held there on December 7-9, 1870. According to the records of the superintendent's office, the school children that year totaled 436; the teachers, 15. A 100 percent attendance of teachers at the Institute was reported.[23]

Agua Fria was the first county seat in the San Joaquin Valley. It is now defunct, but its site is discernible along Highway 140, about five miles below Mariposa. Agua Fria was the capital of Mariposa County when the entire valley floor was a part of this huge county, as well as all the mountains and deserts to the Nevada line. This wild little town served as headquarters for the Mariposa Battalion. It is now a faded memory.[24]

In April, 1851, Colonel George W. Barbour arrived with a military escort and began erection of a fort along the south bank of the San Joaquin River. The locality was named Camp Barbour in honor of the Commissioner who negotiated the treaty with the Indians there. However, when the fort was formally dedicated on May 26, 1851, Lieutenant Tredwell Moore named it Fort Miller in honor of Major Albert S. Miller, then commanding officer at Benicia. This fort, the oldest structure in Fresno County, is still standing (1939). A boisterous little mining camp grew up along the river a mile below the fort and took the name Rootville. Ira Stroud erected the first tent there and built the first saloon. In time this little gold town became known as Millerton, due to its proximity to the fort. In 1856, when Fresno County was organized, Millerton became the county seat.[25]

L. A. Whitmore was placed in charge of the stage station on the Butterfield line where it crossed Kings River. He was also the operator of the ferry. This station, located near the present Laton, was known as Whitmore's Ferry. In 1861, the Butterfield transcontinental line was discontinued. However, local stage lines operated within the state and these used the ferry and the old Butterfield roads. Still later, Whitmore's Ferry assumed the name of Kingston. This place served as a distribution point for the cattlemen and settlers of the Tulare Lake region. Teamsters freighted goods along the stage road to Kingston which contained two large merchandise stores. When the railroad reached Kingsburg, merchandise was hauled by teams from that point. The coming of the railroad to Laton, located across the river, sounded the death knell over Kingston.[26]

Hornitos was settled accidentally. One evening a vigilance committee made one of those sporadic attempts to purify the mining camps, which was one of the characteristic features of western life. The gamblers, prostitutes, and dance hall girls were expelled. They left the settlement, but finally stopped to prepare food in some little ovens which they burrowed out of a clay bank. This furnished the basis for the story which Bret Harte later wrote called *The Outcasts of Poker Flat*. Most of the miners were less puritanical than the members of the Vigilance Committee; the former wanted to gamble and play, even though they lost and suffered. Therefore they followed the outcasts to the little ovens (*hornitos*) and a new town developed along the clay bank. In 1856, Domingo Ghirardelli established a store where he sold chocolate candies, coffee, and spices. In time, this firm developed into the famous San Francisco-based Ghirardelli (say Gear-are-delli) corporation.[27]

Visalia was an important station on the overland mail route. Both the Great Southern Overland Mail and the Stockton, Albuquerque & Kansas City Mail had stations there. The stage buildings were located near the northwest city limits of the modern city. Visalia was originally settled by Southerners and retains many of the aspects of a Southern town. A Frontier Day celebration, held each spring, rivals similar events held at Cheyenne or Pendleton. Visalia is the county seat of Tulare County. During its early years it was the center of many stirring events and scenes that have been discussed elsewhere.

During the Civil War period, Visalia was the base of
supplies for an area more than two hundred miles in
extent. While Stockton was the chief trading center in the
northern part of the valley, Visalia took care of the needs
of the central and southern sections. Its population during
the Civil War was 1,500. When the boys in blue stationed
at Camp Babbitt secured passes to town, they observed
the following places and persons: two public schools, one
private school, three churches, two drug stores, eleven
mercantile stores, one wholesale liquor store (this place
sold goods annually worth $1.25 million), four blacksmith
shops, one steam flour mill, two tinshops, two shoemaker
shops, two meat markets, three lumber yards, three
barber shops, seven physicians, four lawyers, two printing
offices, eight saloons, two breweries, two hotels, one
courthouse, one jail, and two newspaper offices. One of the
latter interested the Union soldiers very much, as it often
called them vile names.[28]

One of the prominent pioneer residents of Visalia was
Judge A. J. Atwell, who gave his name to Atwells Island in
Tulare Lake. The judge was a member of the California
legislature in early days, and the author of numerous
measures in the interest of irrigation. His son, Allan Lee
Atwell, became a well-known actor on New York's
Broadway. He has also appeared on the English stage
before Great Britain's royal family. Atwell became
America's greatest impersonator of Chinese and Japanese
characters. His first appearance on Broadway occurred in
1904, when David Belasco produced *The Rose of the
Rancho*. This play ran for one year in New York, and was
on the road for one year. He appeared in the silent movies
back in 1916, when he played opposite Alice Brady in
Bought and Paid For, and won fame in his portrayal of
Sam Shew Sing, a Chinese fellow, in *The Man Who Came*

Back. Atwell modeled his part after a man whom he had known in California. His first opportunity to play an American part came in 1931, when he played opposite Lois Moran in *This is New York*. In recent years Atwell has been featured on radio programs.

Broadway has secured many of its scintillating stars from the San Joaquin Valley. The original New York company which first presented *Paid in Full* consisted of Allan Lee Atwell from Visalia, who played the Japanese part; Lillian Albertson, the leading lady, from Tulare; Oza Waldrop (Mrs. Edgar MacGregor), from Visalia; and Tully Marshall, from Stockton. In 1925 Atwell was a member of the troupe which secured the Pulitzer award at New York with the presentation of *They Knew What They Wanted*. Pauline Lord, the leading lady, was born on a ranch near Hanford. She has been for many years one of America's greatest actresses on the legitimate stage.

The moving picture industry at Hollywood has also drawn many of its best performers from the valley. Stuart Erwin, the comedian, was born in Squaw Valley but later removed to Porterville. He won fame in *Make Me a Star*, *The Big Broadcast*, and *Viva Villa*. Spec. O'Donnell, the lad with the many freckles, is a Turlock product. Lawrence Tibbett, famous baritone of the Metropolitan Opera Company of New York, was born at Bakersfield. For a time he sang in a church choir there. According to popular tradition, Tibbett failed to win a place in his high school glee club; the invention of the Vitaphone made possible his production called *The Rogue Song*. Barbara La Marr entered the movies from Fresno and Alma Rubens from Madera. Another Fresno girl, Shirley Deane, was a decided success in *Love on a Budget*. Nan Sunderland, who won recognition in musical comedies and with Kolb & Dill, is the daughter of a former mayor of Fresno and the wife of Walter Huston, who was starred in

Abraham Lincoln and in *The Wet Parade*. Frank Clarke, born at Kingsburg, and a great-nephew of Crawford W. Clarke, the famous cattleman, has been for many years a stunt flyer at Hollywood. He was one of the aviators in *Wings*, in *Hell's Angels*, and in many other pictures. Joan Marsh, the moving picture actress who was starred in *Are You Listening?*, was born and educated in Porterville.[29]

Royal Porter Putnam arrived in the valley about 1858 and became an employee of John Butterfield. He was engaged as a hostler at the Overland Mail station at Packwood. Later, he established a trading post along the Tule River and sold goods to the Indians and the few cattlemen in the vicinity.

Putnam first wrangled horses at the Pike Lawless place of Lone Cottonwood. He, within a few weeks, went to the Tule River, and ran the station there. It stood on Sunny Side Avenue at the present north Porterville city limits. The building was long, with a fireplace in each end, and was built of split oak shakes. There are several men yet living who remember the place as early as 1857 or 1858.

Putnam was a delightful person and men usually referred to his post as Porter's trading post; later, this became Porterville. This city is located at the edge of the plain and in the center of a great citrus growing territory. It is famous for the beauty of its surroundings and the quality of its fruit.[30]

Tailholt, now known as White River, is located about twenty miles southeast of Porterville. A supercilious lady, sitting in a stagecoach, tried to prevent her poodle from jumping through the window, and succeeded in grasping his tail. He hung yelping outside the window until Mrs. Cummings, the matron at the stage station, rescued him with the amiable remark, "Well, a tail holt is better than no holt at all." Tailholt was originally a mining camp, but

View of Porterville in the 1880s. Eugene Menefee and Fred Dodge, *History of Tulare and Kings County, California.*

when most of the gold had been extracted, the once-bustling town dwindled away. On February 28, 1933, its postoffice was closed and the fifteen patrons then residing at White River were notified that thenceforth their mail would be delivered from Porterville by star carrier. Tailholt's post office was, excepting Visalia's, the oldest then operating in the county.[31]

Andrew Firebaugh, a young Virginian who had served with the First Texas Mounted Riflemen during the Mexican War and with the detachment of the Mariposa Battalion which Savage led into Yosemite, established a trading post and ferry on the San Joaquin in 1854. The same year the Murphy brothers, two cattlemen who had had trouble in driving their cattle over the hills to summer grazing in the Tulare Lake region, induced Firebaugh to begin construction of a toll road over Pacheco Pass. This was completed in the spring of 1857, and the next year Butterfield sent his heavy stagecoaches over it. This road through Pacheco Pass is still visible in places from the new highway. Pacheco Pass received its name from Juan Perez Pacheco, one of the two first men to occupy the *San Luis Gonzaga* land grant.

Firebaugh operated the stage station during the years 1858-1861. When the transcontinental stage service through the San Joaquin was discontinued due to the outbreak of the Civil War, the place known thenceforth as Firebaugh became the center of activities for the Miller & Lux firm.[32]

During the Civil War, a group of Southern sympathizers set out to sea in a ship and tried to intercept gold shipments from California to Washington, D. C. They thought they might be more successful as pirates than they had been in their land attacks on stagecoaches carrying Wells, Fargo & Company's strong boxes. But they were captured and found guilty of piracy. Under the terms of Lincoln's amnesty proclamation, they were pardoned. One of these men, Asbury Harpending, moved into the hills along the Kern River. He had been a gold miner and soon found indications of this metal:

> Realizing the importance of the discovery, I sent one of my companions to collect enough men to form a mining district under the existing laws. These assembled; we perfected an organization and elected officers.

Harpending, a native of Kentucky, was apparently a Bible student and named the new gold camp Havilah. This rapidly developed into a town and when Kern County was organized, this mining camp became the first county seat. Later, Harpending became the bright and shining light in the "Great Diamond Hoax" which deceived for a time even so great a banker and financial genius as William H. Ralston, who has been described as "the man who built San Francisco."[33]

The place known as Bakersfield was formally laid out in late 1869. On December 22 of that year A. D. Jones, the publisher of the *Havilah Courier*, moved his paper from the county seat to the new place of Bakersfield. Other residents of the foothill capital followed him, due to the expected arrival of the Southern Pacific in the new town. The rapid growth of Bakersfield will be made apparent by a perusal of the following evidence of civic enterprise as of January 1, 1870: two stores, one telegraph office, one doctor, one lawyer, one carriage shop, one printing office, one harness shop, fifty school children, two boarding houses, and one saloon. The population numbered six hundred. In September 1871, the railroad surveyors were busy running the preliminary lines in the vicinity for the proposed Southern Pacific. Efforts to move the capital of the county to Bakersfield met with stubborn resistance on the part of Havilah but, after much litigation, Bakersfield was declared the winner on January 26, 1874.[34]

The original station of the Southern Pacific was built outside the Bakersfield city limits, but in time, the city grew to include the site of the station. Originally Bakersfield was a cow town, having existed for several years prior to the coming of the railroad, and it had all the earmarks of a typical frontier village of the period. Many of the cowpunchers in that country in early days were remittance men from old England. William Henry Bishop, a writer for *Harper's Monthly Magazine* who toured the valley in 1882, noticed this:

> Strangely enough—there is a rather English tone among the herders, and young prodigals of good family are found in it, who have come here after trying their fortunes in Australia and India, and they eat their husks of repentance in true Scriptural fashion.[35]

Englishmen have always been interested in livestock, and they played an important part in the cattle industry of the American West. To them belongs largely the credit for the first importations of purebred Shorthorn and Hereford

View of the first house built in Bakersfield, a traditional San Joaquin Valley dwelling made of thatched tules. Thelma Miller, *History of Kern County, California.*

bulls used in the improvement of the American range stock. Ralph Connor (Rev. C. W. Gordon), who knew the type well, has described his first meeting with young Englishmen who had migrated to the Far West:

> I was surprised at the grace of the bows made me by these roughly dressed, wild looking fellows. I might have been in a London drawing room. . . What a hardy-looking lot they were! Brown, spare, sinewy and hard as nails, they appeared like soldiers back from a hard campaign. They moved and spoke with an easy, careless air of almost lazy indifference, but their eyes had a trick of looking straight out at you, cool and fearless, and you felt they were fit and ready. . . Well born and delicately bred in that atmosphere of culture mingled with a sturdy common sense and a certain high chivalry which surrounds the stately homes of Britain, these young lads, freed from the restraints of custom and surrounding, soon shed all that was superficial in their make-up and stood forth in the naked simplicity of their native manhood. The West discovered and revealed the man in them, sometimes to their honor, often to their shame.[36]

Many of them unfortunately brought to the San Joaquin the faults and foibles of the privileged class to which they belonged in England. George Weeks, a Bakersfield editor, has chronicled in his *California Copy* the altercations he had with younger sons of this type. On one occasion a supercilious specimen, fresh from his home across the sea, presumed to take precedence over a group of men waiting in line to purchase tickets at the railway station. His social position may have made this possible in the London of that day, but in the democratic West it was axiomatic, to paraphrase the Irishman, that one man was as good as another and often a great deal better. Hence there was a disturbance. The ticket agent stuck his head out of the window and profanely demanded the reason for the fuss. The remittance man, nettled at the uncivil query, answered with pompous dignity, "Sir, do you realize that I am a son of a lord?" To the huge glee of the bystanders, the irate ticket-agent snarled back, "I don't care if you are a son of a lord or a son of a _____, you wait until your turn comes."

A more lovable type was Lord Sholto Douglas, third son of the Marquis of Queensberry. He fell in love with a Bakersfield girl, Maggie Mooney, who was an actress in the small local theatre. Friends of the girl as well as rival suitors warned Maggie that a scion of British nobility would make a poor husband and that the Marquis, his father, would never consent to his son's marriage with a mere commoner and a showgirl. The newspaper correspondents of Bakersfield furnished the metropolitan dailies of Los Angeles and San Francisco with detailed information concerning this courtship, and many pranks were planned in order to secure additional newspaper copy. Miss Mooney was high spirited and resented the imputation that "the fruit of the family tree" in America was inferior to a "younger son" of the British nobility, no matter how ancient its lineage. Lord Sholto vainly pointed out his father's entire freedom from snobbishness, that he was England's greatest sportsman, and that he had drawn up the boxing rules which govern the manly art of

Chester Avenue in Bakersfield during the 1880s. Thelma Miller, *History of Kern County, California.*

fisticuffs down to the present time. As a matter of fact, British fashion recoiled from the reckless abandon which characterized Queensberry's association with the "great unwashed." But Maggie remained obdurate. Finally, Lord Sholto clinched matters by writing to the Marquis and receiving official permission to marry Maggie Mooney. They moved to a big ranch in Canada and lived there for many years. Lady Sholto Douglas, after the exit of her husband, married and divorced Prince Burhan-ed-Din, sixth son of the last Sultan of Turkey.[37]

One of the picturesque groups in Bakersfield's early history was the Swamp Angels. They terrorized the surrounding countryside. In some respects they resembled the Clary Grove boys of Lincoln's early manhood. A typical bad man of the period, presumably associated with the Swamp Angels, was named Percy Douglass.

> He met a friend at the railroad station one day, who had just arrived on his first visit. As the couple was walking up one of the principal streets, the newcomer said:
>
> "I have heard a great deal about Bakersfield. What sort of a place is it, anyhow?"
>
> At that moment, Douglass caught sight of an acquaintance that had just emerged from the door of a saloon diagonally across the street and was walking away without having

noticed the couple on the other side. Said Percy:

"What sort of a town is this? Well, I will show you. Just watch me shoot that_____ across the street!"

Thereupon he halted, rested his heavy gun across his upraised left arm, took deliberate aim, fired, and the object of his aim fell dead in his tracks.

And the coroner's jury brought in a verdict of "justifiable homicide." It was well known and was fully established that a "notice to shoot on sight" had been out for some time between the two, which at that time and in most frontier communities was considered ample justification for Douglass' exhibition of marksmanship.

By a strange coincidence, the enemy of Douglass had stepped out of a saloon at the very moment that the Easterner had expressed his disappointment with the tranquillity of Bakersfield. Since the circumstances were not explained to him, he must have been completely flabbergasted.[38]

Another interesting episode occurred in 1893, when the railroad strike prevented the movement of trains. The publisher of the San Francisco *Chronicle* engaged a former Bakersfield editor, George F. Weeks, to deliver the *Chronicle* to the various valley towns by wagon. The newspapers were shipped to Stockton by boat, and from there transported in a six-horse wagon up the valley through Modesto, Fresno, Kingsburg, and Tulare. and finally to Delano. At this point, thirty miles north of Bakersfield, a passenger train stood on the tracks. General William (Pecos Bill) Shafter was on board with regular United States Army troops. He proposed to carry the mail through to Los Angeles. Weeks was permitted to place the balance of his newspapers on board, and rode into Bakersfield on the troop train.

At Bakersfield representatives of the strikers held an interview with General Shafter and forbade him to move the train. The general replied, in modulated tones: "Gentlemen, I wish to inform you that this train is the property of the United States Government. It is now two o'clock. It will move south at 2:15 exactly. You may so inform the men whom you represent."[39]

Five years later, General Shafter was sent to Cuba in command of the American Expeditionary Force which included John Pershing, Leonard Wood, Joe Wheeler, Theodore Roosevelt and the Rough Riders. After the war, Shafter retired to his San Joaquin Valley ranch of 10,520 acres. His holdings were subdivided about 1914 and colonized. The present town of Shafter is the center of the colony. Shafter's son-in-law, Captain W. H. McKittrick, was also a landowner in the valley and gave his name to the town of McKittrick, now the center of a famous oil field.[40]

In 1896, the discovery of oil along Kern River made Bakersfield the large oil town of the San Joaquin. Since that time, this industry has continued to expand until the present. Natural gas proved a valuable by-product and, together with hydroelectric power developed along Kern River, has been instrumental in the development of manufacturing plants at Bakersfield.[41]

While cattle ranches still exist, the rapid development of dairying and orange growing has changed the aspect of things. The latter are successfully grown in the San Emigdio hills. Alfalfa growing has stimulated not only dairying near Bakersfield, but has proved profitable in furnishing the dairy herds of Los Angeles County with fodder.[42]

The building of the Central Pacific through the valley led to the birth of a series of new towns. Many of the older places succumbed to the lure of more favorable sites, and were transported immediately and bodily to the iron rails. Other towns remained for a time and either died lingering deaths, or were resuscitated by the arrival of branch roads from the main line.

The Central Pacific bought 400 acres along the north bank of the Tuolumne River and platted a town. Residents of adjacent towns watched the coming of the railroad with mingled emotions of dismay and elation. In most cases it spelled the doom of the older river towns. A newspaper in one of these frontier villages announced the advance of the Iron Horse:

> The cars of the San Joaquin Valley Railroad crossed the Stanislaus River and came into this county for the first time last Monday. The event was one of considerable rejoicing to many of our people and was witnessed by a large number of citizens. Only a few days more and the tracks will be completed to the Tuolumne River, the site of the proposed new town.[43]

The new town mentioned by the editor was named Ralston, in honor of William C. Ralston, a banker of San Francisco and a director of the Central Pacific. But those who had christened the new town had neglected to consult the namesake in the matter. In the meantime the name was finding favor and coming into general use. The newspaper just quoted printed an item indicating this: "The first trainload of wheat shipped from the new town of Ralston was loaded by M. McClanathan on October 27th and went direct to Oakland."[44] After writing this brief comment, the editor went out into the street and heard rumors, which sent him scurrying back to his desk to write this explanation, in the same issue as the foregoing:

> Last week we learned that the railroad company had as a compliment named the proposed town Ralston. The name looked well and pleased the generality of citizens. It looked well in print and had a pleasant sound. Ralston was the name and suited every one. It was published far and near as

such. The plat now comes out marked "Modesto." It appears
that Ralston had not been consulted and through excessive
modesty declined to submit to the use of his name.[45]

When William C. Ralston remained firm in his refusal to
permit his name to be used, a convention of citizens met
to select another cognomen. After many futile suggestions,
Judge Archibald G. Stakes arose and said, "The parent of
the infant is Modesty—then the baby's name must be
Modesto." The name was enthusiastically adopted. The
next year, Modesto became the county seat and has held
this honor since that time. In 1884 the town was
incorporated. Modesto, at that time the center of a vast
wheat growing area, selected a combined harvester with a
suitable background as its city seal. Its population in 1930
was 13,842, thus making it the third-largest city in the
San Joaquin Valley. At that time it had thirty churches.
Modesto is the center of a melon, fruit, and dairy region.
Its dairymen have organized the largest cooperative in the
United States, largely made possible by the introduction
of irrigation, which has made Stanislaus County the
banner dairy region of California.[46]

One of America's greatest poultrymen, Professor James
Dryden, spent the last years of his life as a poultry fancier
in the Modesto community. About 1903 he organized the
poultry department in the College of Agriculture at the
State University of Utah. In 1907 he performed a similar
service at the Oregon State Agricultural College at
Corvallis. At the latter place "he won fame in his chosen
work and profession that has not been thus far excelled by
anyone else, either in this country or a foreign land."
Dryden was the first to demonstrate that high egg
production was an inherited characteristic and many of
his pupils, notably J. A. Hanson of Corvallis, have since
carried on the work of their mentor. Hanson's strain of
White Leghorns, advertised by the slogan: "Handsome is

View down Modesto's 10th Street, taken sometime in the 1880s.
George Tinkham, *History of Stanislaus County.*

as Hanson does," have won international recognition in
egg-laying contests. In 1927 the Imperial Government of
Japan secured this stock, originated by Dryden, for its
experiment stations. Scientific mating and rigid culling
led to the development of White Leghorn hens which lay
more than a thousand eggs in a lifetime. Dryden was the
author of *Poultry Breeding and Management* and the
producer of the first motion picture illustrating practical
and scientific poultry farming. In 1921 Professor Dryden
retired from the teaching profession and conducted his
large poultry establishment, one of the show places of
Modesto, until his death in 1935.[47]

The first settler in the Turlock area was John W. Mitchell.
He owned 100,000 acres in what was known as Paradise
Valley, the region lying between the Stanislaus and
Tuolumne rivers. Most of the settlers in that district found
employment on his huge estate. In 1866, Stephen V.
Porter and his wife Florence arrived at what is now
Turlock from Wisconsin. Other arrivals were William
Fulkerth and his wife, Abby. Upon their arrival in
Paradise Valley, they applied to Mitchell for work. In time

they became landowners themselves. In 1871, the railway at last reached the Mitchell ranch. Warehouses were erected to handle the grain crops. A post office was established, and Sierra was suggested to the Postal Department as a suitable name. But Sierra was in use elsewhere and therefore rejected. Clark P. Lander was appointed the first postmaster of this new town of Turlock (named after Turlough in County Mayo, Ireland, after Mitchell declined having the settlement named after him). From the Lander home was distributed the first Turlock mail to local residents, as well as to the neighboring Paradise City.[48]

Turlock was the shipping point for the grain growers and huge warehouses were built for storage. Later the growing and shipping of melons began to vie with wheat growing. The introduction of irrigation in 1903 made possible a rapid expansion of horticulture and made peaches and grapes commercially important. Within a short time after the Turlock Irrigation District had begun to function, the arrival of colonists began to change conditions.

> A few years ago a whistling station, with a lonesome grain warehouse and a cluster of weather-beaten houses disputing possession of the sandy wastes with the horned toad and the lizard. Today a bustling little town, growing like a weed, new buildings on every hand and the hammer ringing through the land. More than a thousand settlers, all new, are getting their mail at Turlock; the schools are crowded out of doors; a bank building will soon appear on the main street, more settlers are coming and more. Alfalfa fields, sweet potato patches, orchards and vineyards are crowding the wheat grower back into the hills. This region is going to be famous for its sweet potatoes. The soil is just right for it.[49]

The Central Pacific trains entered Merced on January 25, 1872, and in December of the same year the county seat was moved from Snelling, located on the Charles V. Snelling ranch, to the new railroad town. The only pretentious building in the latter place in 1872 was the El Capitan Hotel. Merced was named after the River of Mercy, which Moraga and his weary men had visited in 1806. The completion of the Crocker-Huffman Canal system led to the colonization of the territory surrounding Merced, and resulted in a rapid expansion. Merced is located in the center of both the state and the valley and is the gateway to Yosemite Park.[50]

Oakdale, located northeast of Modesto, was founded in 1871. Its name was derived from the oak groves, which grew on the town site. Originally, the chief shipping point for the southern mines, Oakdale has since achieved recognition as a cotton and almond growing community. In 1931, the almond shipment amounted to 1800 tons. Three railways serve this city: the Southern Pacific, the Santa Fe, and the Sierra. The latter, a mountain road that serves Sonora, Tuolumne, and Angels Camp, has its terminal at Oakdale.[51]

Madera is a Spanish word meaning lumber. This city did not appear as an original railroad town. Borden, the center of the Alabama Settlement, was located three miles to the southeast. In 1874, two years after the railroad had appeared at Borden, the owners of the California Lumber Company secured huge tracts of sugar pine and other timber lands in the Sierras. Borden was then the largest settlement between Turlock and Fresno, and the directors of the California Lumber Company desired to secure a terminus for their flumes at this town. No agreement could be reached with the owners of the Borden lands, and a townsite to the south was procured.

This place was named Madera, and construction was begun on the flume. This V-shaped flume, sixty-three miles long, was finally completed and presently sawed lumber from the mills in the mountains floated down the flume to Madera. Here it was loaded on cars and shipped to the lumberyards of the nation. This flume carried timber for the first time on October 26, 1876, and is still in operation (1935). In recent years, it has transported approximately fifty million feet of lumber per year from the adjacent mountains. The present company is known as the Madera Sugar Pine Company. The manager of the original California Lumber Company was W. H. Thurman. He laid out the town site of Madera, selected the name, and built the first residence. It is interesting to note that the grave of the famous Major James D. Savage is located sixteen miles east of Madera.[52]

Fresno, the largest city in the San Joaquin Valley, was named after a tree so small it resembles a graceful shrub or bush. People have searched in vain for it in the area immediately surrounding the metropolis. Why was the present county seat named after a small ash tree, which grows only in the foothills and lower mountains? The Spanish word for ash tree is *fresno*, and that name was to arrive at its present location, the scene of its greatest fame and glory and far from its original habitat, by a long and circuitous route. The word *fresno* was not in use during the years that Spain and Mexico ruled Alta California. After the American occupation, gold mining became important and men from all nations flocked to the diggings. Among them were expert gold miners from Sonora, Mexico. Moving north along the foothills they came to a small stream that yielded gold in paying quantities. Unaware that in the early years of Spanish rule the explorers had already named this river the Rio Santa Ana, these miners renamed it the Rio Fresno after the ash trees (*Fraxinus oregona*) which grew along its verdant banks.[53] This Fresno River, located in what is now Madera County, and crossed by Highway 99 in the northern outskirts of the city of Madera, meanders down toward the San Joaquin River. Near its mouth a small hamlet, now practically forgotten and never shown on modern maps, came into being. It was a sinful little place, hardly more than a wide spot in the road, and its denizens—saloon keepers, dance hall girls, and gamblers—called it Fresno after the adjacent little river. Among Spanish-speaking people it was more often referred to as Las Juntas, a term meaning a confluence, a junction, or a joining together, in this case of two rivers and a slough. The local gentry, Spanish, Mexican, and/or American catered to the wants of the cowhands, sheepherders, and outlaws who passed that way. The waterlogged area to the south became known as Fresno Slough.[54]

In April, 1856, the legislature provided for a new county to be called *Frezno*. Yes, this is the way it was spelled in the legislative bill and is still the proper pronunciation of the word, although later official documents and general usage would change the spelling to *Fresno*, the correct Spanish version. However, up to now no legislative act has authorized this change. In 1858 John Butterfield established one of his hundreds of stage stations along the San Joaquin River, about seventeen miles south of the original Fresno. Sensing better business opportunities, the residents of the latter moved their activities and operations thither and took the name of their little community along. Thus came into being the historic Fresno City, located about a mile and a half north of present Tranquillity.[55]

The Central Pacific line traversed the 80,000 acre estate of the German Syndicate. Its directors decided to establish a division point in the "Sinks of Dry Creek," some twenty-odd miles directly east of Fresno City, and train service was inaugurated there on May 28, 1872. It was decided to call this whistle stop in the arid, treeless desert "Fresno Station." A man named James E. Faber, heeding the knock of opportunity, decided that the rumored site of the new railroad station would be a suitable place for a general merchandise store. Contrary to the rules of the railroad magnates, but no doubt with the connivance of the conductor, he had his goods shipped toward Fresno Station on a construction train. However, to prevent detection the railroad crew began to toss his crates, bags, and boxes out along the right-of-way, about where the Hacienda Motel and Olive Avenue are now. His consumer goods were strung out to the south along present-day Roeding Park to the underpass. It is said Faber spent two days with a mule team and wagon gathering up his stock for an appraisal and inventory. He then opened the first shop and general store just east of the original depot, then being built. The present Southern Pacific station is located on the same site as the original building and Faber's store was erected, at first consisting of canvas, just about where the Fresno County Chamber of Commerce building used to be. This was the humble beginning of the great city of Fresno. The various colonization projects which were sponsored by the German Syndicate resulted in a rapid growth of the new city.[56]

Sensing the trend, again there was a movement of people, this time from Fresno City to Fresno Station. In 1874 the county seat was moved from Millerton (the latter, a foothill mining camp originally, lay about twenty-five miles to the east) to Fresno (the word "Station" had been dropped soon after its founding). A river, a hamlet, a slough, a transcontinental stage-station, a great city, a county (the richest in the entire nation measured in terms of agricultural products), a great and extensive irrigation system, and an implement (the Fresno scraper) used in the construction of the canals and ditches of that system all bear the name of the little ash tree up in the foothills which has been left far behind and largely forgotten.

Fresno, the capital of Fresno County, is the largest city in the San Joaquin Valley and the largest inland city in California with the exception of Pasadena. Its population in 1930 was 52,513. This was an increase of 16.5 percent over the previous census. Three things determined its development: luck, climate, and soil. When Mark Hopkins, Leland Stanford, and their corps of engineers rode horseback through the valley selecting sites for future cities, they were impressed by Easterby's green wheatfield in an otherwise arid region. Therefore they discarded other sites and chose a flat and uninviting place as the site for their railway yards. That was luck.

The climate and the soil surrounding Fresno makes possible the production of dried fruits and makes the city the center of the largest raisin growing area in the world. In it are located the plants of Sun-Maid and the commercial packers which handle in the aggregate approximately a quarter of a million tons of raisins annually. Fresno is also a great shipping point for fresh grapes and dried fruits of many kinds, besides raisins.

Fresno is the wholesale and retail center within a radius of seventy-five miles. The city had 1,452 retail stores in 1930 with net sales totaling $53,007,761. The same year the manufacturing plants numbered 127, paid wages amounting to $3,974,714 and produced products worth $36,173,448. Land under cultivation in the county at that time amounted to 1,493,477 acres.[57]

The Millerton *Expositor*, edited. by J. W. Ferguson, followed the county seat to Fresno and became the Fresno *Expositor*. This paper expired in 1898. The *Fresno Weekly Republican* was founded by Dr. Chester H. Rowell on September 23, 1876. Subsequently, under the management of a nephew, Chester Rowell, this paper wielded an influence in the molding of public opinion never equaled since the days when Horace Greeley's old neighbors in the North Country of old New York State read the New York *Tribune* as they did the *Bible*. The *Fresno Morning Republican* was acquired by George A.

Osborn and Chase Osborn, Jr., on October 1, 1920. They, in turn, disposed of their paper to the McClatchys of the *Sacramento Bee* in the spring of 1932. The Fresno *Bee* was established on October 17, 1922, and has, since that time, been capably edited. The publisher at the time of its founding was C. K. McClatchy, a son of that James McClatchy who enjoyed the confidence of Abraham Lincoln during the Civil War and did much to save California for the Union.[58]

Fresno State College shares, with the College of the Pacific at Stockton, the honor of being the only two institutions in the valley permitted to grant college degrees.[59]

The parks in and near Fresno enhance the beauty of the countryside. Roeding Memorial Park, composed of 157 acres, is a horticultural paradise. Kearney Park, donated to the University of California, is located a few miles west of the city. Five thousand acres are used as a crop experiment farm, and the 240 acres surrounding Kearney's famous home are maintained as a park.[60]

The railroad between Fresno and Goshen was opened to traffic on July 19, 1872. A switch was constructed nine miles south of Fresno, and at that point Senator Thomas Fowler loaded his cattle from his ranches in Fresno County. The place was known as Fowler's Switch, and in time this name was shortened to Fowler. The introduction of irrigation led to colonization of the surrounding territory, until the census of 1930 revealed that Fowler was the most cosmopolitan community west of the Mississippi River. The first settlers were originally from the Midwest, but they were subsequently supplemented by almost every race to be found in the universe.[61]

The origins of Selma's name have long been a matter of conjecture. The best-documented account was compiled by Ernest J. Nielsen of Selma, who contributed a long, well-written article on the subject to the April 3, 1949 *Fresno Bee*, containing facsimiles of letters, documents, photographs, and statements from living witnesses. Briefly, these are Nielsen's conclusions: A young Norwegian sea captain named Michael Michelsen came to California during the gold rush. He brought his wife with him, and in 1853 a daughter, Selma, was born on the famous packet ship *Cadmus*. When in its prime, this ship had taken the Marquis de Lafayette to the United States on his famous visit in 1824. By 1853 it was anchored at the foot of Taylor Street in San Francisco, and was serving as a marine hospital. In due time Selma Michelsen became the wife of Sanford Kingsbury, chief clerk and later chief assistant to Mr. A. N. Towne, the superintendent of the Central (Southern) Pacific. Mr. Towne often solicited suggestions from his office staff with respect to names for the new railroad towns. Kingsbury suggested the name of his wife, Selma, and this was one of four names sent by A. N. Towne to the four owners of the original townsite: J. E. Whitson, E. H. Tucker, Monroe Snyder, and George Otis. The name "Selma" was selected in preference to the other names submitted.

Lew Draper, having read the Ernest Nielsen article, came to see me and insisted that Selma was named after Sally Whitson. Mr. J. E. Whitson was a first cousin of Lew Draper, and one of the original owners of the Selma town-site. Draper insisted that Whitson placed his daughter's name (Sally being short for Selma) on the first plat made of the city.

A third story suggests the Frey Brothers, pioneer millers at Selma, might also have had something to do with the naming of the town. Several names had been suggested and rejected by the directors of the Central Railway for the location. Finally, a list of names was submitted which included the name of Selma. George Otis, a member of the

View of Selma during its early days, circa 1895. *The Interior (Fresno).*

committee to select a name, favored the latter. He was influenced in his selection by the Frey brothers, who said this name was very popular in their native Switzerland. It is claimed that Max Gruenberg, a friend of Leland Stanford, chanced to visit the latter while the selection of a name for this new railway town was pending. Gruenberg showed his friend a photograph of his baby girl, and when Stanford asked the name of the little lady, he was told it was Selma. This struck the fancy of the railroad king, and he included it in the list sent to the residents of the new community. The Frey brothers liked the name, told George Otis, and he chose it from the submitted list. In 1930 this prosperous community celebrated its Golden Jubilee and received a letter from Selma Gruenberg Lewis, which is quoted in part:

> If I had been among those present when the first stake was driven on the wide open plains, and the first canvas spread bearing the name of "Selma," instead of being at school studying my lessons, I would be able to give you a true picture of the event of the naming of our little city after that little school girl who was so innocently me. My little picture must certainly have made an impression on Governor Stanford when my proud father displayed it to him, that he could confer

this great honor upon so tiny a maid at that time.

Now that fifty years of peach culture have made Selma the "Home of the Peach" and that a beautiful city has grown up to be a pride and a glory to the State of California and to me, I will confess that I have been trying with all my might to live up to my honor.

When I was in Paris last fall and Marshal Petain asked me if I had noticed how France had honored America by naming one of the Paris streets after President Wilson, I said: "Monsieur le Marechal, that is nothing! In America I will show you a whole city that is named after Me!" The Marshal asked me what battle I had won. I replied that I had captured the heart of Governor Stanford of California![62]

In time, the youthful namesake of the city of Selma became the wife of Myron Lewis. Their daughter, under the pen name of Miss Georges Lewys, achieved recognition as an author and playwright. In 1932 she instituted a $1 million damage suit against Eugene O'Neill, asserting that he had plagiarized his *Strange Interlude* from her *The Temple of Pallas Athene.*

Irrigation made the region surrounding Selma a vast peach orchard and the light, sandy loam produced fruit which made appropriate the advertising slogan, "Selma, the Home of the Peach." During the Panama-Pacific Exposition at San Francisco in 1915, the Selma Municipal Band secured favorable publicity for their city by parading down Market Street and playing the stirring music written by Bandmaster Louis Everson:

> We're from old Selma Town,
> Best one for miles around.
> Down in the valley of San Joaquin,
> Where fruit is Queen,
> Best ever seen;
> If you come down our way,
> Stop off and make a stay;
> We want to know you,

Want to show you
Selma, the Home of the Peach.[63]

Kings River Switch was established as an unloading point
for goods destined for Kingston. It also enabled Jack
Sutherland and other big cattlemen from lower Kings River
to load their cattle on the cars and thereby eliminate the
long drives over the plains to urban centers. Josiah Draper
built the first house near this switch. It consisted of four
willow posts set upright in the ground and covered with a
thatch of brush. He received a contract to haul the goods
unloaded at the switch, which were billed to the stores at
Kingston. Cattlemen along the river and settlers out on the
plains referred to this switch as Drapersville. When the
post office was established, the postal authorities gave it
the name of Wheatville. Thus this little hamlet was known
by three different names simultaneously, and at last by
Kingsburg: it was consecutively christened by railway,
settler, again by the railway, and finally by postal
department. The assumption has been that the town was
named for the Kings River. However, Ernest Nielsen of
Selma discovered that the Southern Pacific's A. N. Towne
submitted the name in honor of his chief clerk, Sanford
Kingsbury, husband of Selma Michelsen Kingsbury. He
decided to limit the name for the little town to two
syllables, hence Kingsburg. This confusing state of affairs
was finally cleared up when the Fresno *Weekly Expositor*
for December 1, 1875, stated briefly: "The post-office at
Wheatville has been changed to Kingsburg."

In those clays before specialization in industry had
become the vogue, S. H. Loomis was barber, painter,
paperhanger, grave digger, undertaker, and manufacturer
of his own coffins. Competition was not tolerated. A Negro
barber appeared on the scene, and the local barber placed
a sign on his shop which he read: "What do you think! I'll

give you a shave and a haircut for nothing". This gave the
dark and emancipated gentleman the St. Louis Blues, and
he departed forthwith. After the colored gentleman had
left, denizens of the little burg pretended that they
wanted free service which they insisted his sign offered
them. He took them outside and read it this time as
follows: "What! Do you think I'll give you a shave and a
hair-cut for nothing?"[64]

The firm of White, Davis & Sons dealt in everything
except coffins and musical instruments. The editor of the
Kingsburg Herald invented a spray to combat the San
Jose scale. This pest had arrived on a shipment of prune
trees imported from France. His spray proved effective,
and the editor acquired wealth and the cognomen of "Bug-
juice" Wheeler.[65]

Andrew Farley was appointed Kingsburg's first
postmaster in the fall of 1873; he was already the
constable. At the same time Wells Fargo provided an
express office, and Simon Harris was appointed their
agent. Grain was first planted in the vicinity the next
year. On June 21, 1875, work was begun on an irrigation
canal which, eighteen months later, brought water to
Kingsburg. Water from this irrigation canal was sold for
$250 per right, with an annual tax of $25. Irrigation
changed the aspect of things, and in 1880 about 16,000
acres were planted to grain which yielded 4,000 tons. Two
years later Kingsburg, the chief grain shipping point
between Mussel Slough and the San Joaquin River, had
two warehouses with a storage capacity of 7,500 tons. The
Kingsburg Warehouse had a capacity of 3,500 tons and
the Davis Warehouse of 4,000 tons.[66]

The fruit and grape industry had its inception about 1880.
During a period of thirty years wheat and fruit vied with
each other for mastery, but gradually the soil became
exhausted by the continuous growing of grain, and now

532

only vineyards and orchards are to be seen. In 1886, a colony of Swedes was founded at Kingsburg and they have been the creators of modern Kingsburg. Most of them came from large metropolitan areas in the East. Either their previous environment, or an obsession that their new home town would become vast some day, caused them to lay out excessively wide streets; Draper Street, the main thoroughfare, is nearly the width of Market Street, San Francisco. The city they built is the neatest and cleanest place outside of New England.[67]

The rise and the fall of Traver is one of the most hectic incidents that can be chronicled about any civic organization in the San Joaquin. Traver was named in honor of Charles Traver, a director in the 76 Land & Water Company. It was one of the late arrivals among the towns located along the main line of the Southern Pacific. A group of capitalists financed a colonization project on land located in Fresno and Tulare counties. Their 30,000 acres lay along the south bank of Kings River. A townsite of 240 acres, located five miles south of Kings River, was surveyed and lots offered for sale on April 8th and 9th, 1884. The sales of these two days amounted to $60,000. Sixty days later, the newly born town of Traver contained a post-office, an express office, a railway station, a drug store, an implement store, two merchandise stores, two lumber yards, two hotels, two barber shops, two livery stables, three saloons (later increased to fourteen), and several bawdy houses. On the west side of the railroad tracks, the ubiquitous Chinese were already contributing their share to the charm of the new town by providing an Oriental quarter.[68]

This new wheat town of Traver replaced and caused the extinction of the old cow town of Cross Creek, located four miles to the south. The postmaster at Cross Creek was C. F. J. Kitchener, a director in the newly organized 76 Land &

Water Company. He and his partner, William D. Tuxbury, conducted a warehouse and hardware store at Cross Creek. The latter specialized in "shooting irons" and ammunition for the cowboys and sheepherders of that frontier region. When Traver was established they moved thither, and Kitchener took his post office along. All the residents on the surrounding plains called the town Cross Creek, due to its proximity to a stream by that name, but the county map of the time gave it the official name of Grand View.

> Cross Creek was the name of the station to which my father (Francis Rea) came in 1874. I have heard him say that there were three saloons, a post-office, a railroad station, and a few dwellings. These saloons were the type where the sheep-herders came with three months pay and woke up the next day in the cellar, broke. Mrs. Loomis said that the big trees for the Centennial at New Orleans in 1876 were loaded on the train at Cross Creek.[69]

Eventually, the only resident remaining at Cross Creek was Mrs. William Apperson. Her sister, Maggie Rucker, lived in another Cross Creek which had originally been established as a stage station on the old Butterfield line. This lay about four miles from the railroad down the stream to the west. These two women conducted dairies and delivered milk to the residents and restaurants of Traver. When the famous outlaw Grattan Dalton escaped from the Visalia jail, he found refuge at Maggie Rucker's ranch house at old Cross Creek. Maggie Rucker, a picturesque personality, played a part in the central part of the valley comparable in some aspects to that of Calamity Jane in the Black Hills of South Dakota. She passed away at Kingsburg on January 28, 1928, at the age of eighty-four. Emmett Dalton made this statement about her: "I never had any acquaintance with Maggie Rucker of Kingsburg, but I was informed by my brother Grat, that it was at her place that he stopped for two or three days after he tore down the Visalia jail."[70]

In order to handle the bonanza wheat crops grown in the vicinity of Traver, three huge warehouses were erected. These had a combined capacity of 30,000 tons and were filled and re-filled each season. The official report of the Southern Pacific station agent at Traver for the year 1886 revealed the fact that there was shipped from that point 32,214,517 pounds of wheat during that year. An additional 34,407,100 pounds were shipped during the first seven months of 1887, and there still remained in the warehouses 30,000,000 pounds which were subsequently loaded and shipped to tidewater. No producing point in human history has ever equaled this amount in shipment during a similar period. The Southern Pacific provided over three thousand boxcars of the period to move the Traver wheat crop of 1886.[71]

Together with the storing and shipping of grain at Traver came other industries. S. K. Greene secured a patent on a certain type of windmill. In those days before gasoline and electric pumping plants had been invented, the windmill was a factor in economic life. Therefore, Greene and a partner named Kimble established a machine shop and manufactured windmills. George Lobb built another factory for the same purpose. Robert Simpson secured a patent on a cultivator which he and a partner named Burke made and sold. Wilson & Wilson, millers, erected the best flour mill in the San Joaquin in the northern part of Traver, along the 76 Canal; during the irrigating season they relied on water power, and the rest of the year the owners used a steam engine. During its heyday Traver had three newspapers: the *Traver Tidings*, owned by Hayes & Starring; the *Traver Advocate* edited successively by F. V. Dewey, F. A. Zeigler, and Harry Hurst; and the *Traver Tribune*, edited by James Macdonald.[72]

In September 1886, Worth Brown, a Traver cowboy, visited Kingsburg and engaged Pete Simpson, the constable, and Jim Allison, his deputy, in a gun battle. Brown was a man quick on the draw, and shot Allison in the mouth. This annoyed the deputy, and he retaliated by shooting Brown through the lungs. Both men recovered. This was a relief to Allison, as several of Brown's friends had vowed to kill the deputy if Brown had died. Later, this same Brown shot and killed his own brother, Luther Brown, over a woman's favor. This fratricidal act took place in Harry Burke's saloon in Traver. Worth Brown died in San Quentin from tuberculosis of the lungs, presumably induced by the wounds inflicted by Allison years before.[73]

Another item of interest concerning the lively wheat town of Traver concerns the editor of the Traver *Tidings*, Carrol S. Hayes, who went to visit a young lady in Lemoore. While they were sitting on the porch looking at the family album some unknown person fired a load of buckshot through the screen porch, and Hayes slid to the floor and across the Great Divide.[74]

But the frailties of human nature were matched by the eccentricities of Nature. Irrigation made the Traver region supreme as a wheat-growing country; the introduction of water also ruined it. Alkali was forced to the surface by the water, and a decade after its founding Traver was as defunct as dead mutton. Another demoralizing factor was the building of railways to the east, which diverted the shipments of grain to other centers. In 1888 new towns such as Reedley, Dinuba, and Monson were established, and many of Traver's residents were attracted thither. Traver had ruined Cross Creek; now she, in turn, was ruined by Dinuba. Life is like that.[75]

On April 8 of each year pioneers of that section congregated at Traver for a reunion picnic. The people who gathered there were those fine, law-abiding citizens who took no part in making the old Traver a "wild and woolly town of the Old West." Nothing now remains of the old Traver but wide open spaces. Those homecomings were fraught with many emotions, and an observer need not be a psychologist to notice "laughter which prevents one from bursting into tears." Neither is it difficult to conjecture that:

> To the pioneer of Traver who chances to visit the ruins, a more pathetic scene can hardly be imagined than the one presented to his view. Whole blocks, which at one time had exhibited practically solid business fronts on all four sides, are only a barren waste, white with alkali. The awful dreariness is intensified during the stillness of the night. The long drawn-out weird "cuck-o-o" of the little billy-owl perched on an alkali knoll, the faint response of another in the distance, the myriad sounding howl from an occasional wandering coyote, and the defiant shriek of a locomotive as it rushes past the old deserted depot and disappears in the darkness, are all calculated to produce only sad and melancholy reflections. And as if to haunt or add a more ghostly atmosphere to the uninviting surroundings, the dry bladder shaped pods of the poisonous loco weeds, when disturbed by the night winds, give back only a gruesome death rattle.[76]

Goshen was the last station reached by the Central Pacific. Thenceforth the directors operated under the name of the Southern Pacific. Goshen owes its importance to the fact that it is a railway junction. A branch line was built from Goshen to Visalia in 1874, and extended to Exeter in 1889. This line taps the great citrus belt of the San Joaquin. Another branch line was built from Goshen in the opposite direction in 1877. This line was opened to traffic on February 1, 1877, as far as Huron; in July, 1888, it was extended to Alcalde. This railway taps the oil fields of Coalinga and Kettleman Hills.[77]

The first hotel at Goshen was opened by George Walter Williams. He had been a soldier during the Mexican War and a pioneer California scout. He settled in Tulare County in 1860, and appeared at Goshen when that town was established. When the first Bear Flag was hoisted at Sonoma on June 14, 1846, it was distinguished by a flaming red border or margin. This had been made from the red shirt worn by Williams:

> George Walter Williams, according to his own story, was one of the four men responsible for the flag. He purchased three yards of unbleached domestic, with the intention of making a flag for the flagstaff, and another one for the field, but the one flag only was completed. The original design outlined was a white flag bearing the words "California Republic," but a young fellow, by name William Todd, conceived the idea of painting a bear on it with paint made from red clay or chalk. The red border made from the shirt was an afterthought. Mr. Williams was a native of Virginia, born November 2, 1819.[78]

Tulare is the largest city between Fresno and Bakersfield. Its proximity to the great lake accounts for its name. Frank Norris gave it the fictitious designation of Bonneville in *The Octopus*, and made it the setting for many of his dramatic episodes. Like other cities in the valley, it was originally a grain center. Now it devotes itself to dairying and fruit growing.

The world's largest peach and apricot orchard is located in the immediate vicinity. Hulett C. Merritt, who had made a fortune in the iron mines of Minnesota, purchased this tract in 1903. This Tagus Ranch is not an ordinary farming proposition, but an industry carefully planned. Fruit and vegetables ripen at Tulare ten days earlier than at Turlock. The first marketable products come from the semi-arid Imperial Valley; the Tagus Ranch is capitalizing on its location between the harvest seasons of Turlock and El Centro. In 1935 it produced 12 1/2 percent of the national crop; most of these were canned at the California Packing Corporation plant in Kingsburg.[79]

The history of Delano dates back to the 1870s, having been named in honor of Columbus Delano, secretary of the Interior Department in Grant's cabinet. In 1873, the Southern Pacific Railroad reached Delano from the north and this was the terminal of that transportation system for a little more than a year, after which the road was extended to Bakersfield. In its early days, Delano was an important trading point for homesteaders, sheep men and, while it was the railroad terminal, for the railroad men as well. It later became an important wheat shipping point. Since 1930 Delano has been the center of the largest cotton growing area in California. Most of this product is handled by the California Cotton Cooperative Association, located on Highway 99 just north of the city of Bakersfield. After the repeal of the "noble experiment," the production of wine and brandy has contributed materially to business. Three wineries are located within a few miles of the town, and one of these is the largest in California. Irrigation is accomplished by the use of wells drilled to a depth of 150 feet or more. The population of Delano in 1939 was more than 4,000. The name of the city is pronounced with the accent on the second syllable and a long "a."[80]

Along the branch line between Goshen and Alcalde, three important cities developed. Hanford was named after James Hanford, treasurer of the Southern Pacific Railroad. At the time of the Mussel Slough fight, this entire region was a part of Tulare County. In 1893 Kings County was organized, the preliminary meeting for this purpose being held in the office of E. E. Bush, and Hanford became the county seat. Diversified farming gradually replaced the old bonanza wheat ranches, and in 1925 the crop valuation of Hanford's trade area of 1,000 square miles was $12 million. The original settlers have been supplemented by a colony of immigrants from the Azores Islands, who have engaged largely in dairying and fruit growing.[81]

Lemoore received its name from Dr. Lovern Lee Moore, an early resident of the region. Its development has not been unlike that of the surrounding cities. During its early days the Settlers' Land League frequently held its meetings there.[82]

In the northern part of the valley the city of Tracy was founded in 1878. It was named in honor of Lathrop J. Tracy, a friend of Leland Stanford. This city is a railway junction, where the trains from the southern part of the valley connect with those going to either Stockton or Oakland. Truck farming and cattle raising are the chief occupations.[83]

On July 1, 1888, the Southern Pacific opened a road from Fresno to Porterville; this was extended to Famoso on December 24, 1890. Sanger was founded in early 1888, and owed its birth to the will of the Southern Pacific and the obstinacy of certain residents of Centerville. The men who owned the land in the latter place refused to cooperate with the railway officials, and they built a town four miles away and named it after one of their officials, who was connected with the Pacific Improvement Company, then the land holding company for the Southern Pacific. Lots were sold on May 25, 1888, and in time Sanger became the terminus of the Kings River Lumber Company's fifty-four mile flume. This V-shaped structure, filled with running water, transported lumber from the mills in the mountains to this valley town, from whence freight trains hauled it to the lumberyards of the nation.

In the vicinity of Sanger were the holdings of William B. Hazelton, Harvey Akers, and W. C. Caldwell. When the railway arrived, Sigmund Frankenau moved his store from Centerville to Sanger Junction, as it was called then. Sanger is the home of the Paxton Box Nailing Machine Company, which is the largest manufacturer of this type of machinery in the world. In recent years the people of

Sanger have sponsored the Christmas celebration at the foot of the huge General Grant, the "Nation's Christmas Tree."[84]

Thomas Law Reed, who had marched with Sherman to the sea, gave his land and his name to the city of Reedley. He conveyed to the Pacific Improvement Company an undivided one-half interest in 360 acres of his holdings. This subsidiary company of the Southern Pacific Railway was authorized to select town sites along the proposed route through the valley. The irrigation project of the 76 Land & Water Company had caused canals to be built through the territory prior to the arrival of the railway. Thomas Law Reed bought land from the 76 Land & Water Company and moved to his ranch on March 4, 1884. Two years later he was farming 15,000 acres between the present site of Reedley and Smith Mountain, and had an additional 14,000 acres at Chowchilla. That same year he introduced the first Haines harvester into that territory. The wheat crop, which usually averaged 30 bushels to the acre, was at first hauled to Cross Creek and later, to Traver.

According to a popular story, Thomas Law Reed had a Chinese cook named Li (Lee). This servant was a great family favorite. He died just prior to the naming of the new railroad town and his master honored his memory by coupling Li's name to his own; hence Reed-Li (Reedley). However, members of the Reed family have always denied the truth of this story. The fact seems to be that Thomas L. Reed objected to the use of his name for the new town. The director of the Pacific Improvement Company arbitrarily added a suffix to the name Reed, and thus originated Reedley.

The arrival of water and a railway through this section of the valley led to the founding of Reedley, and a diversification of crops. Within a few years thereafter, a

541

colony of German Mennonites settled at Reedley and helped to develop the surrounding country.[85]

The first settler near Dinuba was Olli Skeene Wilson, who owned the land south of the present city. The site itself was owned by a later arrival, James Sibley, whose partner was W. D. Tuxbury. The latter had been a merchant at Cross Creek in early days, had removed to Traver when that town was platted, and then led the exodus to Dinuba. When the railway arrived the new town site was called Sibleyville, and later Sibley. Sometime later, James Sibley and other citizens held an interview with the officials of the Pacific Improvement Company at San Francisco, and the official name of Dinuba was chosen.

The origin of the name Dinuba is still a mystery. The director of the Pacific Improvement Company who stated that Dinuba was the name of a famous Greek battlefield was either misquoted, misinformed, or a profound student of ancient history. The location of such a battlefield has not been determined. No standard reference work available in the immense library at the University of California in English, German, or French contained a name even remotely resembling "Dinuba". The only possible exception is "Danube," which is the name of a river and not a battlefield. Neither is it in Greece. Rev. M. Mandillas, priest of the St. George Greek Orthodox Church of Fresno, denied knowledge of any such battlefield; so, too, did Dr. Gregory Floredas, a member of the medical staff of the Fresno County Hospital, trained in the schools of Greece and a graduate of the University of Michigan. Dr. J. J. Van Nostrand, professor of ancient history at the University of California, doubted the existence of any such battlefield. The word is not Greek in form.

Some investigators have suggested the pronuba moth, a pest prevalent at one time, as Dinuba's namesake. Others maintain that Greek laborers were employed when the railway was being built into Dinuba, and that during a brawl one evening this word was used as a slogan to inspire the combatants during the fight. Tellers of this tale have insisted that the cry "Remember the Dinuba" will enrage a Greek, as surely as the yell "Remember the Alamo" will stimulate a Texan. The only thing wrong with this story is that no Greeks were employed by the Southern Pacific at that time.

Dinhabah, a city in ancient Edom, is mentioned in Genesis 36:32. According to *Webster's Unabridged Dictionary*, the pronunciation of this word is very similar to "Dinuba". The meaning of Dinhabah was "she gives judgment," and the city was located at the edge of the desert. To a director in San Francisco, an inland valley town may have reminded him of the desert. Dinhabah was the scene of much fighting, and since the Mussel Slough fight had occurred eight years before this, the director may have judged the name suitable. Whether the spelling was purposely changed or not is a matter for conjecture. Perhaps an Edomite city and not a Creek battlefield was the origin of Dinuba's name.

Some have suggested that perhaps the director who named the city was a doodler, and accidentally wrote down some letters while meditating on a name, and arrived at a conclusion without further ado. The story that the name came from the first syllables in the names of two teamsters, Dinsmore and Uballis, I cannot accept, although that is the one given credence in most publications dealing with the origin of Dinuba's name. Mr. John C. McCubbin, who resided at Traver during its heyday, who collected grain rentals for the 76 Land and Water Company, and who knew everyone connected with that place at that time, told me he had never heard of Dinsmore and Uballis. It is doubtful that a railroad company would name a new town after two men, if they ever existed, who were so unimportant relatively that a prominent official whose work would bring him in touch with all teamsters, had never heard of them. Invariably men of prominence were selected as namesakes, and obviously not all prominent men could have cities named after them; there were not enough to go around.

A facetious interpretation concerning the origin of Dinuba's name is as follows: A Traver merchant resented the exodus to the new town, then known as Sibleyville. In order to discourage the outgoing movement of settlers, he prophesied: "That town will die new—bah!" Hence "Die-new-bah." However, the latter is not the correct pronunciation. The pioneer founders all called it Dî-nu'-bä, and present day dictionaries so list it.[86]

Harry Hurst, editor of the *Traver Advocate*, realized that his hometown, which at one time had contained over 2,000 persons within the city limits, was shrinking fast. On McKinley's inaugural day, March 4, 1897, he changed the name of his paper to the *Alta Advocate*. During the following week he moved his entire plant to Dinuba, and on March 11 his paper appeared at that place as the *Alta Advocate*. The latter is still being published there at the present time (1949) under the able direction of 'Jake" Jacobsen.[87]

The city of Dinuba was the beneficiary of most of Traver's prosperity and business when the latter succumbed to the alkali. The quality of the soil surrounding Dinuba has made possible the production of citrus fruits and a fine quality of table grapes. The headquarters for the Alta Irrigation District, the successor of the 76 Land and Water Company, is located at Dinuba.[88]

The railway reached Exeter in 1888, but the previous year Pat Balaam had built a Good Templars Hall along the road that leads to Visalia. The site was later marked by

Kirk's vineyard. The site of the city was owned by John Franklin Firebaugh, a native of Virginia and a former Confederate soldier. Exeter developed from a wheat growing community into one devoted to citrus growing, which is now its chief source of wealth.[89]

Lindsay was founded by Captain A. J. Hutchinson in 1888. The city was christened in honor of his wife's maiden name. Lindsay is located between Exeter and Porterville. It enjoys the distinction of having the largest acreage of olives in the state, and is also the largest orange shipping point in the world. The seventeen orange packinghouses in the city hold the state record for carloads shipped from one point in a single day. These seventeen citrus packinghouses are in operation two months in the fall, while packing the navel oranges and a like period in the spring during the Valencia season. The gross selling value of the 1928 crop was $10,061,505; because of their well-organized cooperatives, the growers received more than half of this gross amount. The climate in the Garden of the Sun causes fruit to mature and ripen six weeks earlier than in Southern California.

The residents of the Lindsay community, like all other citrus growing districts in the San Joaquin, are distinctly native-born Americans, and few settlers of foreign birth are to be found. In 1931 there were thirteen churches within the city limits.[90]

In 1891, when the San Francisco and San Joaquin Valley Railroad was being constructed, its route intersected the ranch of Clovis Cole, and a half-way station between Friant and Tarpey assumed the name of Clovis. Sons of the Middle Border became farmers in this region, and Italian immigrants became the first vineyardists. Since that time orange groves have become economically important, although Clovis is primarily noted as the center of the Calimyrna fig section. Its scenic background

545

has attracted the attention of Hollywood moving picture producers; several films have been produced at the Balfe Ranch in the vicinity.

This ranch was established as a country home by Harry Balfe, owner of a hundred chain stores in New York state. During the building of the Panama Canal, he was the personal representative of President Theodore Roosevelt in the Canal Zone. Later he retired to his Clovis ranch home, where he maintains the largest thoroughbred racehorse farm in the valley. Many polo players, including Will Rogers, have secured their best mounts there. Clovis, due to Balfe, is probably the best-known small town in the valley so far as moving picture celebrities are concerned. Will Rogers was a frequent guest; so were Jack Holt and Gary Cooper. The latter was married to Sandra Shaw, Harry Balfe's granddaughter.[91]

Los Banos derived its name from the adjacent creek that was used by the Franciscan friars as a bathing place on their journeys to and from the valley. The city was founded by Henry Miller in 1889, along the route of the newly built West Side line of the Southern Pacific. This city was the center of the Miller & Lux holdings and owed its development to the activities of this firm. About 60 percent of the residents of Los Banos are Portuguese or Italian.[92]

Collis was the name of a railway junction and township west of Fresno. The land in this township was acquired by W. G. Kerchhoff and Jacob Mansar, owners of the Fresno Farms Company. They surveyed and subdivided the territory and brought in colonists of Scandinavian and German extraction from Minnesota and the two Dakotas. The name of the junction was changed from Collis to Kerman, the latter name being composed of the first syllable in the surname of each of the two partners. Diversified farming is in vogue at Kerman. One of the largest tallow plants in the state is located there.[93]

546

The town of McFarland was platted by J. B. McFarland in 1907. This place is located a few miles north of Bakersfield along the line of the Southern Pacific. Cotton, grapes, and dairying are the chief interests.[94]

Hiram Hughson, a pioneer grower who owned a ranch of 2,080 acres, gave his name to the town founded on his land in 1907. Gustine, the center of a thriving dairy community in Merced county, offers attractive opportunities to settlers and home-seekers. The large farms in its area are now in the process of subdivision into twenty- and forty-acre tracts. Ideal railway connections and the proximity of markets make its dairy and poultry products profitable.[95]

Terra Bella, meaning the Earth Beautiful, was established in 1900. The two pioneers in the vicinity were E. F. Halbert and A. S. Radcliff. After Traver had ceased to exist as a great wheat shipping point, Terra Bella became the largest interior wheat shipping point in California. In recent years, citrus fruits and grape growing have engrossed the attention of the community. Aside from the American part of its population, Terra Bella has one German and one Italian colony in its neighborhood.[96]

When oil fields were developed in the Maricopa and McKittrick regions, the Southern Pacific built a line through that territory. Midway between these two points, the company built a switch known officially as Siding No. 3. Wildcat wells were being drilled in the vicinity and a man named Stewart built a pool-hall near the siding. He came from Morro Bay and named his place the Morro Pool Hall. In time men referred to the little hamlet as Morro or Morron. Confusion between the two, and a Moron post office in Colorado, resulted in Taft obtaining the name it has held ever since. The oil promoters possessed a great antipathy for William Howard Taft, because he had issued an executive order withdrawing public oil lands from drilling operations. But it was either the name of Taft or no post office, so Morron decided to take both. Within a year after the establishment of the post office, the patrons served by it exceeded 9,000. This is the most rapid growth made by any post office in the United States with the exception of Rawhide, Nevada.[97]

In 1932 the city of Taft was the richest per capita city in the United States. The population of the city itself was 3,442. The monthly payroll of the oil workers was $1.8 million. Bank deposits exceeded $2,000 for each man, woman, and child. There were one and a half automobiles for each individual. The value of the oil produced in 1932, with low prices and the depression at its height (or depth), was more than three times the value of the gold extracted in California during the heyday of mining for a similar period. And Taft is only one of nine oil districts in the San Joaquin Valley. New fields are constantly under surveillance and in the process of development. This indicates the value of the oil industry in the valley.[98]

The Patterson family owned a 19,000 acre ranch, which finally was subdivided and colonized. The town of Patterson was founded in 1910 in the midst of the colony. The racial composition of the settlers in the Patterson Colony is American, Scandinavian, and Portuguese, named in numerical order. The town is unique in many respects. It is a model townsite possessing circular streets, a plaza, radiating avenues, and shaded driveways. The irrigation system provided for the colony surrounding Patterson is original in conception and has been widely copied elsewhere.[99]

Chowchilla was founded in 1912 and received its name from a river in Merced County. The river had been named after the warlike Chauchiles who lived there long ago. Cotton, fruit, and dairying engrosses the attention of the settlers in the surrounding neighborhood.[100]

The Kern County oil town of Taft during the boom times, 1910. Thema Miller, *History of Kern County.*

Biola, also founded in 1912, is located west of Fresno. The promoter of the colony surrounding the town was William Kerchhoff. He was an ardent supporter of the Bible Institute of Los Angeles, and selected the initial letters in the name of this religious school as the designation for his new town. The chief product of the community is a seedless raisin.[101]

Orange Cove was founded in 1914. Some years prior to that time, a tract of land in that region had come into the possession of Elmer M. Sheridan. He proceeded to subdivide the acreage owned by him, and made contacts with officials of the Atchison, Topeka & Santa Fe railway, which caused this company to build a road through that district. The directors of the Santa Fe suggested to Sheridan that he locate and name the station which they proposed to erect in that general region. Seeking a suitable name, he was led by a sudden flash of inspiration to call it Orange Cove. No orange groves existed there then, only vast wheat fields for miles around. But the new town decided to live up to its name and Sheridan's prophetic insight, and its name is now actually descriptive of its chief industry. Orange Cove is located between two projecting spurs of the Sierra Nevadas and is thus a natural cove. The second part of its name is therefore also fitting.

The Orange Cove Citrus Association, an affiliate of the California Fruit Growers' Exchange, handles the pack of the orange growers in the Orange Cove district. This organization handles more oranges each year than any other cooperative north of Tehachapi. Olives, grain, and grapes are also important products. Irrigation water is secured partly from the Alta Irrigation District and partly from wells. In the hills to the east lie some of the big cattle ranches in the state. Orange Cove is their shipping point.[102]

The California Bureau of Commerce, in an official bulletin for 1930, listed eighty-four organizations of a civic nature in the San Joaquin. The presence of this number of Chambers of Commerce, or their equivalent organizations, indicated a highly developed form of urban life in the valley. The rapid growth of these cities followed the attempt of white men to subdue nature and make it subservient to economic needs. Together with this change came the commercial development of scenic wonderlands and the destruction of alluring wilderness areas. The men who love the wide-open spaces consider the spread of urban centers a blight rather than a blessing. But the city has come to stay and the white man seems to thrive therein:

> He flung out his barbwire fences wide
> And plowed up the ground where the grass was high.
> He stripped off the trees from the mountainside,
> And ground out his ore where the streams run by,
> Till last came the cities, with smoke and roar,
> And the White Man was feelin' at home once more.[103]

16 Races, Religions, and Realtors

Seest thou yon dreary plain, forlorn and wild,
The scene of desolation?

John Milton *Paradise Lost*

The first promoter of a colony in the San Joaquin was Dr. John Marsh of *Los Meganos*. His skill as a realtor was of a high order. A California realtor has been facetiously defined as follows: "real" comes from the Spanish word meaning royal; the suffix "tor" comes from the word *toreador*, meaning bull-thrower. Hence a realtor is a royal bull-thrower. Marsh, through political friends and newspaper advertisements called attention to the wonders and glories of the "Paradise of the Pacific." The first tangible result of this activity on his part was the departure from Missouri on May 19, 1841 of sixty-nine persons, with the *Los Meganos* cattle ranch in the San

Joaquin Valley as their destination. John Bartleson and John Bidwell were the leaders of this first caravan of covered wagons to cross the plains.[1]

Since these colonists were the first to cross the plains in prairie schooners, they had no beaten path to follow. They beat Fremont, who was to win fame as a pathfinder, to California by three years. They actually arrived in California without their wagons. Bidwell wrote in his journal: "We concluded to leave them, and pack as many things as we could." These wagons were left along the Walker River. The colonists also arrived in foreign territory without passports. The Mexican authorities required an explanation from John Marsh who was their host. He had to mollify the officials and feed the colonists. His purpose was to bring enough Americans to the province to insure its acquisition by the United States. But he was not prepared to care for them personally. When the Missourians killed his prize oxen for beef, which they probably did by mistake, he expressed himself in a fashion that caused Bidwell to write: "He is perhaps the meanest man in California." The year 1841 was one of little rainfall; the summer was hot, dry, and long. The colonists arrived in the fall and saw only a dreary plain, sere and parched. However, they perforce remained. Clouds of rain soon dispelled the clouds of dust; grass replaced gloom. Five years later, these Missouri immigrants in the northern part of the valley were to take an active part in the events that culminated in the Bear Flag Republic and the acquisition of California by the United States. The plans of John Marsh were thus successfully realized.[2]

The colonists led by Bartleson and Bidwell were the first to arrive in the San Joaquin. Fourteen other caravans crossed the plains and arrived in California while the latter was still a department of Mexico. It is important to note that several thousand Americans had arrived in California before the discovery of gold, and that Bartleson, Bidwell, and their company had been Californians for almost a decade when the first Forty-niners arrived. This does not detract from the achievement of the latter, but adds significance to the planning of John Marsh.

Most of these Americans came from Pike County, Missouri, which was then the frontier county of the United States. They made a bee-line for California in such numbers during the days that California was still Mexican territory that they aroused fear not only among native Californians, but among those Americans of different antecedents who were already located on the Pacific slope. John Marsh, a New England Yankee, disliked these people. Theodore Winthrop, like Marsh a Harvard graduate, who visited California, wrote this about these colonists:

> The most vigorous of them leave their native landscape of cottonwood and sandbars along the yellow ditches of the West, and immigrate with a wagonload of pork and pork-fed progeny across the plains to California. There the miasms are roasted out of them; the shakes warmed away; they will grow rich, and possibly mellow, in the third or fourth generation. They had not done so in my time. I lived among them *ad nauseam*, month after month, and I take this opportunity to pay them parting compliments.[3]

Sectional strife in older portions of the United States, as exemplified by the Kansas border warfare and the Civil War, created a reaction that was felt even in California. Theodore Winthrop, a Boston Brahmin, described a Sacramento gambler as follows: "One was a rawboned, stringy chap—as gaunt, unkempt, and cruel a Pike as ever pillaged the cabin, insulted the wife, and squirted tobacco juice over the dead body of a Free State settler in Kansas."[4] Missourians retaliated by calling the New Englanders "sniveling, blue-bellied hypocrites who sing psalm tunes through their noses." John Brown of Pottawatomie was held up as the typical fanatical Yankee. Henry W. Grady of Georgia, in his famous speech on the New South, told the New England Society of New York City in 1886 that his people had become as penurious as "any down-easter that ever swapped wooden nutmegs for flannel sausage in the valleys of Vermont." Mutual distrust and lack of understanding continued to exist at a much later period and among prominent people in California. New England Yankees (Stanford, Huntington, Hopkins, Crocker) were heartily disliked by Missourians of equal ability (George Hearst). According to a recent writer: "George Hearst left his father's Missouri farm to join the gold rush and spent the fifties as a miner in the foothills of the Sierras, a tall, bold adventurer with the strong aquiline nose of the Southern mountaineer. He was of the Southern faction by birth and temperament, and when, loaded with millions, he married a genteel girl of Virginia-Missouri stock and built a mansion in San Francisco, he had little in common with the men from Yankeeland who lorded it over the State as owners of the new railroad."[5]

Although the Pikes were disliked by their fellow Americans from New England and other northern states, the fact remains that they were a dominant influence in securing California for the United States. They were the first white men to enter the gold fields and the first Anglo-Americans to become cattle ranchers in the valley.

> Where in California is not "Pike County, Missouri" known, and what fight or funeral, wedding or gold washing has been seen in yon El Dorado, without its array of sturdy scions of our western prairies.[6]

One of the earliest colonizing enterprises in the San Joaquin was undertaken by Captain Charles M. Weber, who had come to California with the Bartleson and Bidwell party in 1841. He secured a tract of approximately fifty sections, which he proceeded to colonize. This was the original *Campo de los Franceses* granted to William Gulnac. By 1847 Weber had 1,000 head of cattle on his tract. Walter Herron, then county surveyor of San Joaquin County, testified before the California land commission on December 21, 1852:

> I do know the Rancho aforesaid. It is situated in the county of San Joaquin. It was first occupied by Captain Weber in 1847, who brought on it a band of 1,000 cattle, or more. This is the first I knew about its occupation. He has since continued to occupy it; he has made improvements on it—the value of the improvements made by Captain Weber and those holding under him I should think about $1.5 million. I passed through the ranch one year prior to Weber's taking possession. There were no people there then. In the latter part of 1844 Gulnack [sic] had three or four houses on it and some stock. The next year Weber tried to get some help but the Indians were bad. They killed Lindsay that spring. It was necessary for a person going through that country at that time to go armed and with company.[7]

Captain Weber began his building operations in 1847, and his houses were erected close together due to the Indian danger. An early observer stated rather indefinitely that "by 1848 it had got to be quite a city." The fifty sections of land colonized by settlers under the direction of Captain Weber, a German, may be considered the first successful real estate promotion project in the San Joaquin Valley. The next attempt on a large scale was also a venture involving Germans, which resulted in the settlement of a tract of 152,480 acres surrounding what is now Fresno.[8]

The first definitely planned city and colony in the San Joaquin Valley was founded by the Mormons. It failed, not because the land was defective, but because the Mormon leaders believed it was too good. This is the only colony in the San Joaquin Valley that was abandoned because of its good qualities as a colonization site. This seemingly paradoxical statement needs an explanation.

In 1830, the same year that "Peg-leg" Smith visited California, another Smith startled his neighbors at Palmyra, New York by announcing revelations from Jehovah, which culminated in the publication of the *Book of Mormon*. This man, Joseph Smith, organized his followers into a group known as the Church of Jesus Christ of Latter Day Saints. They called their neighbors Gentiles; these, in turn, referred to the Latter Day Saints as Mormons. Smith founded a colony for his people at Kirtland, Ohio; later it was transferred to Missouri. Persecutions by their neighbors finally caused them to locate in Illinois, where they built the city of Nauvoo. Here they prospered for a time, and by 1844 Nauvoo had 12,000 inhabitants as contrasted with Chicago's paltry 4,000. Even Lincoln and Douglas recognized Nauvoo's political importance and appealed to the Prophet, Joseph Smith, for votes in their campaigns. Then Smith made the fatal mistake of running for president of the United States. The Mormons were self-sufficient unto themselves and avoided contacts with their neighbors. This caused fear and hatred on the part of the Gentiles. A mob killed Joseph Smith and his brother Hyrum. The Mormons now decided to leave the United States and seek sanctuary in the far west, much of which was then owned by Mexico. There the new Prophet, Brigham Young, decided to lead his people.

Most emigrants to the Far West were drawn thither by attractive inducements, such as better and cheaper land, better climate, or a change in occupation and environment. Two things sent the Mormons to the far west: attractive and propulsive forces. Beyond the western rim of settlement lay greater opportunities and freedom from persecution. When the ordinary covered wagon emigrants left for the far west, their Gentile friends usually patted them on the back in farewell. When the Mormons left, they were also patted on the back by their Gentile neighbors, but in most cases those pats were forcefully delivered and peculiarly located.

The Mormons crossed the Mississippi River on the ice in wagons drawn by oxen and, in some cases, by women and children. They established a camp at Council Bluffs, a place where the Pottawattomie Indian chiefs used to meet. In subsequent years, this permanent camp served as a point of departure for Mormons on their way to the West. Leaving his main group, Brigham Young picked 140 men and set out early in April 1847 to look for a permanent home for his colonists.[9]

Young had in his possession a map made by Fremont. This was his only guide. But instead of following the south bank of the Platte, where lay the road used by the prairie schooners to Oregon and California, he chose the north bank. Here there was more grass for the oxen that pulled his seventy-three oxcarts loaded with equipment for the founding of his colony. Here, too, there were fewer Indians, since they hovered along the road on the south bank, and no Gentile emigrants were encountered to annoy the party. The Mormons rode fearlessly into the unknown Indian country because "at their head rode a heavy-set man of forty-five, red of hair and gray of eye, a jut of short chin whiskers accentuating the thrust of an underjaw that had the look of granite." Young's efficiency in conducting his caravan across the plains gave no inkling of the fact that heretofore this middle-aged house painter and window glazier had spent his whole life in cities.[10]

The original destination of the Mormons was California, but Young had presumably not heard from Samuel Brannan's colony on the Stanislaus River when he left Council Bluffs. As the Saints marched along they felt they were headed for the Promised Land and they sang:

> The Upper California, oh, that's the land for me,
> It lies between the mountains and the great Pacific Sea:
> The Saints can be supported there, and taste the sweets of
> liberty;
> In Upper California, oh, that's the land for me.
>
> We'll go and lift our standard, we'll go there and be free,
> We'll go to California and have our Jubilee;
> A land that blooms with beauty rare; a land of life and liberty,
> With flocks and herds abounding, oh, that's the land for me.
>
> We'll burst off all our fetters and break the Gentile yoke,
> For long it has beset us, but now it shall be broke;
> No more shall Jacob bow his neck, henceforth he shall be free;
> In Upper California, oh, that's the land for me.
>
> We'll reign, we'll rule and triumph, and God shall be our king,
> The plains, the hills and valleys, shall with Hosannas ring,
> Our towers and temples there shall rise along the great
> Pacific Sea
> In Upper California, oh, that's the land for me.[11]

At the entrance to South Pass, Brigham Young met Jim Bridger and Peg-leg Smith. Of all that wild crew known as the Rocky Mountain men, they were the wildest. But they knew the West. Young was eagerly curious about the far west and sat with them on a wagon tongue far into the night, discussing suitable sites for a colony. Peg-leg Smith had been in the San Joaquin Valley. Perhaps he knew that Samuel Brannan was already there in the city of New Hope along the Stanislaus River. At any rate both he and Jim Bridger argued that a settlement somewhere in the lovely sweep of the Pacific Coast was the most feasible. Smith and Bridger were sincere as they expatiated on the wonders of California. Young believed them. But it failed to click. Their very enthusiasm dampened the ardor of the far-visioned leader. Young gave a reverse twist to their logic. He realized that the very qualities which would make the San Joaquin attractive to the Mormons would likewise lead to large-scale colonization by Gentile groups, followed by the hate and persecution which had already driven the Mormons from their previous settlements. For the good of his people, it would be better to settle in the forbidding Utah country with its high mountain ranges and burning plains, which would not only serve to lock out unbelievers, but lock in the Saints themselves.[12]

After crossing South Pass, Young left the Oregon Trail and went south along the Big Sandy until he came to the Green River. While the Mormons were preparing to cross this, Samuel Brannan and two companions arrived in camp from California. Brannan had heard rumors that Young had been diverted from the original plan of going to the colony along the Stanislaus.

In order to make the relationship clear which existed between Brannan and Young, it is necessary to recapitulate somewhat. While the Mormons at Nauvoo and other points along the Mississippi prepared to leave for the far west under the command of Brigham Young, the church authorities made plans for other members of their sect, located along the Atlantic seaboard, to leave for California under the leadership of Samuel Brannan. Subject to these instructions, Brannan secured the 450-ton ship *Brooklyn* and, with 258 persons, set out for California by way of Cape Horn. When the *Brooklyn* reached Honolulu, Brannan learned from Commodore Stockton, the naval commander, that war was imminent with Mexico. Brannan, a down-east Yankee from Maine, who had led his people from the limits of "this wicked nation," now suddenly decided that "blood is thicker than water" and instructed Robert Smith, a Mormon, to drill the men on deck as they voyaged toward San Francisco. Brannan wanted the honor of capturing San Francisco for his Mormons. Naturally, this would have been of psychological value in modifying public opinion in favor of the Mormon sect. But it was not to be. When he entered the harbor of San Francisco the first thing he saw was the Stars and Stripes. In his disappointment Brannan roared: "Damn that flag!" He was too late. This remark was misinterpreted in later years.[13]

The war was over as far as California was concerned, and Brannan speedily made arrangements to found his colony. A tract was chosen along the north bank of the Stanislaus River, about a mile and a half upstream from its confluence with the San Joaquin. The men were sent to this place in a launch under the command of William Stout. The party arrived on January 1, 1847; Young did not leave the Council Bluffs until April of the same year. The Mormons along the Stanislaus laid plans for a city, which they called New Hope. Due to its location, some people referred to it as Stanislaus City. Log cabins were built, a sawmill erected, eighty acres seeded to wheat, and a potato field planted.[14]

While these colonists were busily engaged in laying the foundations for their future home, a dispatch arrived from the Mormon elders ordering the return of the colonists in the San Joaquin. Plans had been changed. Brannan and two other men immediately left on fast horses to meet Brigham Young.

> Brannan's purpose in meeting the pioneers was to persuade them to pass by the barren, forbidding region of the Great Salt Lake, and join him and his colony on the fertile slopes of the Pacific. He used every endeavor to convince President Young that it would be to the advantage of the Latter-day Saints to establish themselves on the western coast; but in this he was unsuccessful. The project painted by his eloquence had its pleasing features, but was not alluring to the sagacious leader, who had seen his people despoiled and driven repeatedly, through sheer inability to hold their own against overwhelming odds, hostile to and arrayed against

them. Until they became strong enough, not only in numbers, but in influence, through a proper understanding of their motives on the part of their fellow citizens, to defend themselves against further possible aggressions, it was better for them to seek isolation, and face the hardships and dangers of the desert.[15]

Brigham Young's mind had been made up. The colonists at New Hope on the Stanislaus were ordered to return. Most of them obeyed the summons. But many remained in California and were employed by Sutter at his mill when gold was discovered. Brigham Young created a permanent home for his people in the valley of Salt Lake. He pointed out that this region fulfilled both the prophecies of their former Prophet, Joseph Smith, and the dream of a New Zion:

> The deserts, valley rivers, and salt lakes realized the visions of the wilderness, of the Jordan and Dead Sea of ancient Palestine, and stamped the country as the new Land of Promise. Here the somber and apocalyptic imagination of a modern Israel finds its home.[16]

If "Peg-leg" Smith had not made his haphazard visit to California, he would have talked less fluently to Brigham Young about the possibilities of the San Joaquin. Without this deterrent, Brigham Young would have proceeded to New Hope, and the influx of Gentile settlers into the San Joaquin in subsequent years would have caused the disintegration of the Mormon sect. Big events in history often turn on small hinges. The State of Deseret arose, not along the flowing stream of the Stanislaus, but beside the still waters of Great Salt Lake. No flowing stream of jarring Gentile settlers disturbed the still, smooth surface of Mormonism at Salt Lake. This guaranteed the perpetuity of the Mormon Church. Perhaps for once in his sinful life, "Peg-leg" Smith had been an unwitting instrument in the hands of the Lord.

One of the earliest and most homogeneous racial units to

enter the San Joaquin was the Chinese. Their history goes
back to 1850, when individual members of that race
landed at San Francisco and soon appeared in Stockton.
From that point they moved to the Southern Mines. They
were energetic and dug for gold with a patience that often
aroused the envy and ire of their fellow miners. They
labored along the San Joaquin River, at Chinese Camp, at
Sonora, and wherever gold was to be had.

The building of the Central Pacific from California to its
junction with the Union Pacific at Promontory, Utah was
done by Chinese labor. The Cantonese proved efficient
workers, although the average weight per man of all the
thousands employed was only one hundred and ten
pounds. When the "Big Four" decided to begin
construction through the San Joaquin, the Chinese were
transferred to that region. Many of the Chinese miners
left the mines and became railroad laborers. Charles
Crocker, the construction work superintendent, was
adored by the Chinese. Both he and Leland Stanford were
great friends to them in this country, and the Orientals of
an older generation who still remain in the valley speak of
these two men with sincere affection.[17]

The completion of the railway caused the Chinese to
divert their attention to farming. Herding and shearing
sheep, pruning vineyards, and harvesting fruit, were the
kinds of work that engrossed their attention. The Chinese
merchants appeared in the railway towns as soon as their
Jewish confreres. A tourist in the San Joaquin in 1882,
W.H. Bishop, observed Chinatowns in every city of any
pretensions and compared them to the ghettos of medieval
towns. These merchants introduced gorgeous silk gowns,
beautiful chinaware, and exotic curios. Chinese cooks
were employed at the ranches and in the homes of the
wealthy city dwellers. Tea gardens popularized Chinese
dishes such as noodles and chow mein.[18]

The American cuisine was further enriched by a food
which it is claimed was never heard of or seen in China;
this was chop suey. Carl Crow, in his *Four Hundred
Million Customers*, has stated that chop suey restaurants
are found everywhere except in China, and that no
Chinaman ever eats it. According to his story, some early
American miners forced their way into the first Chinese
restaurant in San Francisco to learn what the pig-tailed
yellow men ate. It was past the regular meal-time and the
frightened proprietor, forced to feed his unwelcome guests,
picked up all the scraps left in the kitchen, added a dash
of Chinese sauce, and told them it was chop suey (beggar's
hash). To his astonishment the miners liked it, told
others, and the increasing demand for it built more
Chinese fortunes than were ever dug out of the gold
mines. The Chinese to this day consider it a culinary joke
at the expense of the white men.[19]

Richard Dow, a Hanford Chinese, was shown the foregoing
account and made the following comment concerning it:

> In regard to what you heard about the origin of chop suey in
> this country, it is all wrong. The one who gave an account of it
> simply used his imagination and intended to write
> humorously about the subject in order to attract attention.

He went on to say that this dish was popularized during
the visit of Li Hung Chang to the United States during
the administration of William McKinley. The former, in
response to the hospitality extended to him officially,
invited the president and members of his official family to
a Chinese dinner.

> There were bird's nest soup, shark's fins, abalones, oysters,
> mushrooms, Snow-white lichens, and Yunan hams. These were
> easily recognized. But American names for certain Chinese
> dishes are hard to find. Thus when a dish appeared which
> consisted of sliced chicken, bamboo shoots, mushrooms, lichens,
> ginger sprouts, and eggs, the interpreter did not know what

American name to give it. After scratching his head, he finally shot out: Chop Suey! An uproar rose from the diners, and they all said this was the dish they liked the best. The newspapers the next day described the famous dinner prepared by Li Hung Chang's Chinese cooks for the members of the White House and the government officials and chop suey was reported to have been the most popular dish. The Chinese in this country were serving chop suey, but they capitalized on the publicity and served Li Hung Chang chop suey from then on. Chop suey is a mandarin (not common) dish, and to prepare it properly takes several days. "Chop" means "everything." and "suey" means "chopped into small pieces."[20]

The foregoing stories do not agree and the reader may use his own judgment.

In time, Chinese herb doctors entered the valley and proved successful in the treatment of many diseases. At first they encountered the hostility of the allopaths, but finally the Rockefeller Foundation sent a corps of medical doctors to China to collect the prescriptions deemed worthwhile by the Chinese medical experts. One of the outstanding medical schools in China was the Kwongtung Medical Development Society of Canton whose graduates, notably Dr. L. T. Sue of Hanford, have won recognition in the battle against disease.

The Chinese played an important part in the development of the San Joaquin Valley. Their good qualities have been appreciated in recent years. During mining days their presence lent an Oriental color which Bret Harte was quick to perceive. In the valley cities, that quarter of the city known as Chinatown became and has remained a picturesque section. The passage of the Exclusion Act reduced their numbers. San Joaquin County, according to the census of 1930, had the most Chinese; Fresno County ranked second.[21]

In 1868 a colony was founded at Woodville which consisted of Irish immigrants. These people hailed from the North of

Ireland and were Protestants in religion. In regard to this colony, John R. Quinn made the following comment: "My father (Harry Quinn) was in that settlement, which was made up of the Griffin, Gilligan, and Monroe families largely." The original name of this community was Irishtown. The first settlers were sheep men.[22]

The same year that the northern Irish immigrants settled at Woodville, the Alabama Colony was founded near what is now Madera. The Civil War had impoverished many of the old Southern slaveholders, and they sought new homes in the far west. In the spring of 1868, some cotton planters held a meeting in Alabama and elected three of their number to journey to California in search of a suitable location. The committee consisted of Judge Samuel A. Holmes, Major C. A. Redding, and L. A. Sledge. They chose a tract of government land near the Fresno River. They returned to Alabama and made their report. The result was the removal of several Southern planters from Alabama and Mississippi to the San Joaquin.

But these heroic people seemed born to misfortune. The Civil War had destroyed their wealth and social position. When they reached the San Joaquin, they found their government land had been gobbled up by Isaac Friedlander and William Chapman, two San Francisco capitalists, for speculative purposes. In order to secure their chosen tract, the Southern planters were forced to pay twice the government price. They applied the name Arcola to their little civic center, after the Alabama home plantation of one of the settlers, T.A. Strudwick. The school district south of Madera still retains the name.

The new homes established around Arcola were named after the fashion prevalent in the Old South. The "Cradle of Innocence" was owned by two brothers, both former Confederate cavalry captains, Joseph A. Pickens and Henry A. Pickens. Another former Confederate officer, Major C. A.

565

Redding, named his "Elkhorn." The old Mississippi judge, R. L. Dixon, named his estate "The Refuge." This was ironically done, since it was no refuge at all. Even since the day when Cain slew his brother Abel, cattlemen and farmers have been unable to agree as to what constituted their respective birthrights. The open range was menaced by these Southern planters. The "No Fence" law had not yet been enacted and the longhorn cattle, as well as their owners, were glad to utilize for their own benefits the wheat fields of the Alabama colonists.

When Leland Stanford and Mark Hopkins rode down the sparsely settled valley to chart their proposed railroad route, they were entertained at the home of Dr. Joseph Borden, one of the Alabama settlers at Arcola. The urbane manners and gracious hospitality of this transplanted Southerner were a decided contrast to the rudeness often prevalent on the frontier. Stanford was delighted with his host and erected a station right there which he named Borden, and appointed Dr. Borden's son the first station agent. This remained the chief shipping point in that region until the California Lumber Company, failing to get a donation of land at Borden, built its own city of Madera two and one half miles to the south.

The settlers of the Alabama Colony, unsuited by temperament and previous experience to make good tillers of the soil, nevertheless planted the first wheat grown between Paradise Valley and Tejon Pass. This was done before the arrival of the railway. The surrounding cattlemen, opposed to all settlers and in this case capitalizing on the prejudices existing against "rebels," permitted—nay, encouraged—their cattle to destroy the plantations, as the colonists called their wheat fields. Cattlemen in those days used purple adjectives when describing settlers. No irrigation, no transportation, and no friends made these members of the Alabama Colony restive, and Borden and its citizenship soon gave up the struggle. The settlers scattered. But they had a flair for law and politics and many of the valley counties, especially Fresno, drew from this stock some of their ablest leaders. The colony exists only in the files of very old records.[23]

Portuguese whaling vessels from the Azores Islands appeared in Golden Gate harbor as early as 1840. This port served as their haven of rest after their long voyage around the Horn. Many of the Portuguese sailors, after the fashion of sailors, left their ships without permission and remained in California. They saw no future in the sand dunes of San Francisco and moved across the bay where they helped to develop the so-called East Shore Empire. Many of their first permanent homes were made at San Leandro, and from there they gradually moved into the San Joaquin.

In 1849, the Portuguese in California were augmented by large numbers who arrived from New England. The latter group had been engaged in the fisheries of the North Atlantic coast. Many of the Portuguese went to the gold mines, but the adventurous life of that region was not to their liking. They then secured employment as sheepherders on the large sheep ranches of the valley. A man named M.F. Silveira had a sheep camp on the present site of the Fresno County courthouse. He returned to his native Azores Islands but his sons, having heard tales of the land called California, emigrated and became merchants at Hanford. Another early settler in the Fresno area was Antonio Joseph.

The first Portuguese wheat grower in the valley was Frank Silva, who resided north of Grangeville at the time of the Mussel Slough fight. Another of the early Portuguese settlers in the Mussel Slough country was A. F. Nunes. In 1869, Perry Phillips employed a sheepherder named Joseph V. Rodriguez. The latter became a wheat grower, an influential citizen, and had much to do with attracting other people of his nationality to the Hanford community. The first Portuguese woman to be seen in the Tulare country was the wife of Manuel Senter, a wheat grower. When she arrived the neighbors were prompt to make their calls; they were curious to see a woman of her nationality.

These early Portuguese, invariably beginning life in the San Joaquin as sheepherders, saved their money and became farmers. They were almost all from the Azores Islands and, due to the heterogeneity of their racial antecedents, they are listed in the census as Azores Islanders and not as Portuguese; the latter term is reserved for those who have come from the mainland. These Azores Islanders have shown a strong predilection for dairying. In 1930 they controlled 75 percent of this industry in California. Settlements of Portuguese are now found in the counties of Stanislaus, San Joaquin, Merced, Madera, Kings, Tulare, and Fresno. One of their largest colonies is at Hanford, where they outnumber any other ethnic group.[24]

The Italians who settled in the San Joaquin were all from the north of Italy. The Italians from Sicily and Naples generally congregated in the large cities. The first Italians in the valley came during the gold rush. Subsequently, they became farmers in the vicinity of Jackson and Stockton. Their chief interest since that time has been in agriculture, especially viticulture and dairying. The wineries located throughout the San Joaquin are nearly all in the hands of northern Italians. The widespread activities of the Bank of America, founded by A.P. Giannini and formerly the Bank of Italy, naturally attracted men of this nationality, who have taken a leading part in the phenomenal success of that banking institution.[25]

The Swiss entered the valley about 1870 in isolated groups. Beneditto Ardizzi settled at Delano and engaged in merchandising, and a colony of German-Swiss later settled to the south, at Bakersfield. Andrew Mattei arrived in Fresno in 1887 and purchased the nucleus of his later holdings in the valley at that time, although he continued to reside in Los Angeles until 1890. Mattei, a native of Ticino, Switzerland, became interested in wine making and by 1910 had 1200 acres set to vines. He produced his first wine in 1892 and by 1902 his winery produced 300,000 gallons of wine and 1,000 gallons of brandy. His memory and success as a figure in the development of Fresno is perpetuated by the Mattei building of that city.

In 1877 Auguste Sandoz became a cattleman in Cummings Valley. In the early eighties Joseph Cerini, Silvio Zanatini, and Peter Gabbi settled at Riverdale. By 1900 there were Swiss scattered over the entire valley, but no special colony existed in any one place. These people have engaged in all industries, but are particularly devoted to dairying. They came, in most cases, directly from Switzerland to the valley. The Frey brothers, pioneer millers at Selma, represented the quality of people sent to the New World from Helvetia. They came with the intention of becoming American citizens, they have taken the obligations of their new citizenship seriously, and all have quickly amalgamated with the other settlers in the communities where they have located.[26]

Perhaps the biggest real estate promotion project undertaken in the San Joaquin Valley was the work of William S. Chapman and his associates. Chapman organized a syndicate to purchase Agricultural College Scrip that they located on unappropriated land in the San Joaquin Valley. He interested a number of German capitalists of San Francisco in the project and they advanced the money. Hence this group of real estate men were known as the German Syndicate. By 1870 Chapman had purchased scrip representing 152,480 acres within Fresno County. Each certificate was limited to 160 acres.

This land was held in trust by William S. Chapman, Edmund Janssen, and Frederick Roeding. The members of the syndicate were required to join in execution of a deed whenever land was sold, and this proved inconvenient and cumbersome. Therefore, the syndicate was dissolved in 1873 and each of the interested parties received his share of acres.

This huge tract of land, completely surrounding the modern city of Fresno, then became the center of a series of colonial settlements. In 1874 Chapman developed the Central Colony located southwest of Fresno; this consisted of six square miles of land. The average farm consisted of twenty acres. Chapman gained community support in this venture from prominent citizens such as Dr. Lewis Leach, Otto Froelich, William Faymonville, and J. W. Ferguson, then editor of the *Fresno Expositor*. The majority of the settlers in this colony were Scandinavians. The chief opponents of colonization in those early days were the cattlemen, who resented the apparent end of the open range. Bernhard Marks, a former gold miner and a school teacher at San Francisco, was largely instrumental in the initial steps being taken in this colonial venture. The Central Colony was doubly important, because it both achieved success as a colony and served as a model for later colonies.[27]

A tract of land lying between Fresno and Fowler and east of the Central Colony was placed on the market under the name of the Malaga Colony by G. G. Briggs. He proved an efficient promoter, and soon colonized his ten sections. The present town of Malaga is located on this tract.[28] Due

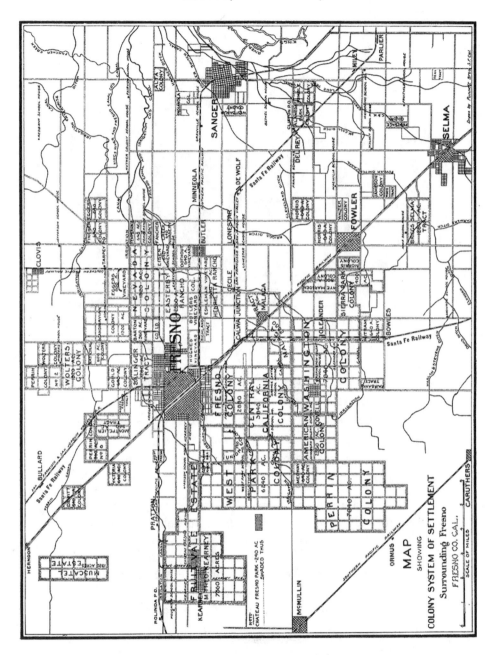

Map showing the different agricultural colonies of Fresno County, circa 1900. M. Theodore Kearney, *Fresno County, California and the Evolution of the Fruit Vale Estate*, and *Garden of the Sun*, 1939 edition.

Farm of Bernhard Marks, founder of Fresno County's Central California Colony. *Wallace W. Elliott, History of Fresno County.*

south of the Malaga Colony was located a tract of 7,000 acres known as Washington Colony. This colony, like the Central, was settled chiefly by Scandinavians. Washington Colony still retains many of its early characteristics. Rev. Oscar W. Ostrom. one of the original settlers, made this statement concerning it:

> The Colony in which I live and which comprises the Easton-Oleander district, is called Washington Colony. Scandinavian Colony is as far to the north of Fresno as Washington Colony is to the south (about five miles). Washington Colony was founded in 1878 by Wendell Easton, [J.P. Whitney] and George Covell. What is now the village of Easton is properly called Covell, Easton was the post office name only.

> Among the very first settlers was Charles Erickson, who by Swedish newspaper correspondence here in California, as well as in eastern papers, made known to the Swedes the wonders and possibilities of a colony. In 1879 Charles Erickson, Mathilda Peterson, and F. D. Rosendahl organized

the Swedish Methodist Episcopal Church. This was the first and only church ever organized in this colony.

The people (Swedish) came because men like Charles Erickson and Judge Frank D. Rosendahl led the way and sounded the call over the United States. Good land, good climate, plenty of water, good promoters, and then just plain California were the inducements that led so large a number of the Swedes to Washington Colony.[29]

Approximately five miles northeast of Fresno, the Scandinavian Home Colony was organized. This consisted of 1,920 acres and was colonized between 1879 and 1882. This attracted Swedish and Danish families. E. Swensen, Erick Johnson, and William Kanstrup were pioneers in this colony, which has long since ceased to exist as a separate entity. At first, only Scandinavians were admitted by the promoters but, eventually, the ban on other nationalities was lifted. Today practically none of the original stock remains.[30]

The American Colony was founded due west of the Washington Colony. This settlement consisted of 3,840 acres and was limited to old-line Americans. It experienced about the same fate as the Scandinavian Colony. The ban on foreign-born citizens was soon lifted, and the colony now exists only in name.[31]

Other colonies developed from the original holdings of the German Syndicate were the Morris, Pacific, Church, Wolters, and Nevada. The last-named colony was developed under the direction of S. A. Miller, then editor of the *Fresno Republican*. The lands of this colony were placed on the market in 1877. The Temperance Colony was promoted by Moses J. Church. The latter was a staunch Seventh-day Adventist and a firm believer in temperance, hence the name and aim of his colony. Due south of Fresno were the holdings of Edmund Janssen. This tract of 6,080 acres was acquired by Thomas Hughes

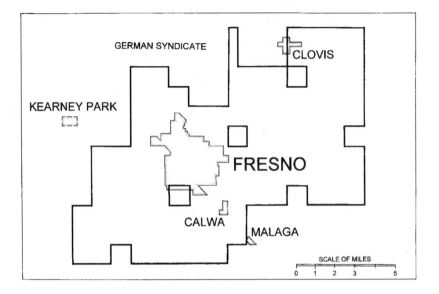

and sons, who colonized it in 1881. Their memory is perpetuated by the Hughes Hotel of Fresno.[32]

One of the chief promoters of colonization in the Fresno district was Frederick Roeding. The career of this German in California is a cross section of the early development of the state. Born in Hamburg, Germany, he arrived in San Francisco during June 1849 to join the gold rush excitement. In 1869, he became a member of the German Syndicate which acquired the land surrounding Fresno; in 1873, this tract was divided and Roeding secured 5,000 acres as his share; in 1877, he sold the lands which later became the Nevada Colony; and in 1883, he organized the Fancher Creek nursery, which subsequently furnished trees and vines and shrubs to the thousands of settlers who swarmed into the valley during the next decades.[33]

German settlers naturally followed prominent leaders of their race into the San Joaquin. By 1889, enough German Lutherans had settled at Fresno to warrant the organization of a church. Rev. J. M. Buehler of San

Francisco, who had come to California in 1860, and Rev. J. H. Theiss of Zion Lutheran Church, Oakland, took the initial steps in the movement. Formal organization of Emanuel Lutheran Church, Fresno, took place on March 9, 1890, with Rev. H. Meyer as pastor. This was the first German Lutheran church in the San Joaquin. German settlers of the same faith later organized churches at Lodi, Stockton, Tracy, Valley Home, Modesto, Newman, Livingston, Selma, Visalia, Delano, Terra Bella, Bakersfield, and Dinuba.[34]

The founding of the colony at Traver was largely due to the vision of P. Y. Baker, a civil engineer. He conceived the idea of building a canal system, which would irrigate a tract of 30,000 acres in Fresno and Tulare counties that lay along the left bank of Kings River. Baker succeeded in securing the financial support of several capitalists and on June 7, 1882, the 76 Land & Water Company was incorporated. C. F. J. Kitchener, the postmaster at Cross Creek, was elected president, and he served until 1887 when failing health caused his retirement and the election of I. H. Jacobs. D. K. Zumwalt was elected secretary and served until March 1, 1884, when S. F. Earl succeeded him; the latter remained in office until his death in the spring of 1916. H. P. Merritt had charge of the funds until July 1888, when Jacob Levi. Sr., was elected treasurer. P. Y. Baker, the original promoter, was appointed superintendent of canal and ditch construction. He severed his connection with the company in January 1884 and was replaced by Joseph Peacock, who held this position until the sale of the canal system to the Alta Irrigation District on July 1, 1890.

The capital stock of the 76 Land & Water Company was fixed at $280,000 and was divided into fourteen shares of $20,000 each. Eight men subscribed to the stock in this company. The six following subscribers owned $40,000

The town of Traver, Tulare County, before the turn of the century, when the surrounding lands turned to alkali and rendered the place into a ghost town. Kathleen Small, *History of Tulare and Kings Counties, California.*

worth of stock each: H. P. Merritt, Charles Traver, I. H. Jacobs, C. F. J. Kitchener, Francis Bullard, and Thomas Fowler. The other two men, D. K. Zumwalt and P. Y. Baker, were credited with $20,000 each.

Thomas Fowler, for many years a State Senator, was the owner of the famous "76 Ranch." His brand was well known throughout the state. A portion of his land was turned over to the new company in return for $40,000 worth of stock, and the name of his cattle ranch and brand applied to the water and colonization company. The main canal, now the property of the Alta Irrigation District, is still officially known as "Big 76."

The 76 Land & Water Company began construction in the month of October 1882, on what was to become the largest irrigation canal in the state of California. At the headgate it measured one hundred feet wide at the bottom. The new intake is not as large as the original. The undertaking proved expensive. The first assessment on the capital stock amounted to $70,000; when this had been spent, a loan of $150,000 was made from the San Francisco Saving Union and a mortgage on all the company's land given as security. This loan was carried for many years. The rate of interest was 8 percent, payable semi-annually, and was equivalent to $1,000 per month.

Water was turned into the new irrigation canal on trial on December 1, 1883, and flowed down to the Wahtoke Dam, but the canal bank broke a mile below the head gate and the water had to be turned off immediately. Irrigating was actually begun in early April 1884, when Joseph Peacock opened the headgate and sent the water flowing to the new town of Traver, named after Charles Traver, one of the stockholders. Excepting for a limited acreage surrounding Traver, only a small portion of the 30,000 acres in the colony was irrigated until 1888. An abundant rainfall made possible bonanza wheat crops during this four-year period without the aid of irrigation.

The first man to buy land from the 76 Land & Water Company was Emil Tretten. On the last day of the year, 1883, he bought forty acres located three miles northeast of where Reedley is now located. Tretten paid $15 an acre for the land and $5 an acre for the water right. The second sale was made to Samuel Theall, who paid $50 an acre for ten acres adjoining the city of Traver.

Aside from its land sales, the company secured a profit by selling water rights to settlers living on land contiguous to company land. The first sale of this nature was made on October 1, 1884, to A. E. McClanahan. The same day similar sales were made to Emerson Bloyd and his son, L. Jefferson Bloyd. Exactly a month later a water sale was made to G. W. Barnes, on whose forty acres was later to be planted the famous McCubbin Gum Tree (Eucalyptus viminalis), said to be the largest tree in the world for its age.

The 30,000 acres of the 76 Land & Water Company had never been touched by a plow, although it had been grazed for many years. Colonists were dilatory in coming. None of the stockholders possessed the intimate contacts and personal following needful in attracting large numbers of colonists, the value of which was to be illustrated two decades later in the amazingly rapid settlement of the Turlock Colony under the direction of Nils O. Hultberg. However, they finally offered five special inducements to attract settlers: First, leases to cover a term of years; second, rental to be one-fifth of the crop; third, delivery to be made on the land (the company was to haul its own share of the grain from each tenant to the warehouse which, in some cases, was twenty miles from the field); fourth, tenants were to get all the sheep feed (stubble); and fifth, the privilege of purchase of the leased land at any time during the life of the lease and at a stipulated price.

The result of these attractive inducements was a rapid colonization of the virgin lands. Soon the entire 30,000 acres were a green and beautiful wheat field. The little city of Traver entered into its glory and boomed. The fertile soil yielded bounteously, and land rose in value. It was a period of local inflation. The 76 Land & Water Company, astounded at the mounting prices of real estate, regretted its "privilege of purchase" clause. The stockholders naturally wanted to share in this increment. Therefore, they attempted to avoid fulfilling the terms of the very clause that had been the most important inducement in their agreement with their tenants.

The legal counsel for the 76 Land & Water Company was P. D. Wigginton, who had been a presidential candidate of the United States in 1884 on the American Party ticket. He devised a plan whereby the company could evade the "privilege of purchase" clause although, at the same time, he advised the company to effect a compromise with the

Hauling grain beside Thomas L. Reed's home in 1884, the first house erected in Reedley excepting only the ferry house at Smith's Ferry. Notice bells on leaders. *Garden of the Sun*, 1939 edition.

holders of leases. His suggested compromise, which many of the more timorous tenants accepted, gave them a portion of the land for the original stipulated price if they would relinquish all further claims. Others of the tenants brought suit for a "specific performance of contract" and finally won their cases. This caused the tenants who had compromised to regret their action, and they also brought suit against the company. But these latter litigants were doomed to disappointment; the company won.

During these land disputes, which in some cases lasted many years, the court ruled that the company was liable for all damages incurred by forced collection of rentals. This led to endless litigation, which, in turn, led to ill feeling on the part of both tenants and company. The original agreements with the tenants were rescinded, and new leases made more exacting. Leases were now limited

Elaborate engraved view of George Malter's St. George Vineyard, located east of Fresno, during its heyday in the 1890s. *The Interior (Fresno).*

to one year; tenants no longer received the stubble; instead of a fifth, they were required to pay a fourth and in some cases a third rental, which they were also forced to deliver to the company's warehouse at Traver; and they were ordered not only to poison the ground squirrels, but also to buy the poison and do the work connected with this onerous task.

This breaking of faith with the tenants seemed to inaugurate an era of bad luck. Litigation, several successive short crops, low prices, and a financial depression all arrived at the same time. These things delayed the progress of the 76 Land & Water Company and brought financial ruin to many of the pioneer settlers.

The water for "Big 76", as the company's main canal was called, was taken from Kings River at the mouth of Dennis Slough. Later a new intake, not as wide as the first, was made farther upstream, which was called Upper Head. This was twenty-seven miles from Traver. In those days a watchman at the Upper Head was a necessity. The company built a road from Traver to Upper Head; this was at that time the edge of civilization, as only an Indian trail existed from that point up the river. Reedley and Dinuba had not then been founded, so Traver was the only town of any pretensions within miles, and its enticing lights could be seen twinkling across the intervening plains. To find a man willing and reliable enough to remain there in the awful loneliness was difficult. Supplies were sent up once a month, and Indians occasionally passed that way. These were the only breaks in the monotony. After a few weeks the beautiful scenery palled on the average watchman, and he regretted his rashness in having assumed this position of trust. Invariably, he either deserted his post or demanded to be relieved.

Soon he hurried to Traver and civilization, either with or without leave, and sought forgetfulness by justifying Nietzsche's dictum that "the mother of debauchery is not joy, but joylessness" as he imbibed freely from "the bouzing can," as Herbert Spenser in his *Faerie Queene* designated a container of alcoholic beverage. Finally, a sturdy and somewhat mysterious character called Bob Sanford was engaged to guard the dam at Upper Head. He did not apparently mind isolation, and remained faithful to his trust until the 76 Land & Water Company sold its canal system to the Alta Irrigation District, and withdrew from the valley.

Long before the question of abrogating the "privilege of purchase" clause came up for discussion, four original stockholders had severed their connection with the

company: Thomas Fowler, P. Y. Baker, D. K. Zumwalt, and
C. F. J. Kitchener. In justice to their memory, it must be
said that they therefore had nothing to do with the so-
called "76 Turmoil" which followed. Most of it must be
blamed on new stockholders who were primarily
financiers from metropolitan areas with no interest in the
settlers or the community.

John C. McCubbin, who knew conditions in the Traver
Colony from intimate association with both the settlers
and the officials of the 76 Land & Water Company, wrote
this about those interesting days:

> I was rather intimately connected with the company's affairs
> during the peak of "the 76 Turmoil." Acting as assistant to the
> superintendent, the work of collecting the rentals devolved
> upon me, and this work kept me on the "firing line" during
> those troublous times. This experience furnished me with
> first hand information as to the conditions as they actually
> existed through that unpleasant period.
>
> There was one gentleman with whom I was associated, of
> whom it is a pleasure to make special mention, and that is
> Joseph Peacock, who served as Superintendent for the 76
> Company for many years, though never a stockholder. In the
> discharge of his duty he always showed good judgment, a
> high degree of intelligence, and an efficient leadership. His
> kind and modest manner was in marked contrast with the
> bigotry exhibited by other officials.
>
> This noble characteristic won for him the universal
> admiration of both friend and foe of the company. He went
> through the strenuous period described above, and came out
> without a known personal enemy. A warm welcome always
> awaited him, either in the humble wooden shack of the settler
> out on the plains, or in the palatial city residence of the
> millionaire. He was equally at home in both places. His
> memory is revered to this day by all of his old acquaintances.

The headquarters for the 76 Land & Water Company was
at first located at Visalia. Then the company established

its own city of Traver and moved the office to that place on April 1, 1884. Here business was transacted for nine years and then, in 1893, the office was moved to Reedley. The last transfer took the office to San Francisco in 1895. The return of several parcels of land to the company prevented its liquidation; otherwise it would long since have passed into history. McCubbin further stated:

> Had it been possible for the officers of the 76 Land & Water Company to have looked into the future in 1888, and foreseen conditions ten years ahead, it would have prevented one bad case of greed. A proposition from a tenant to exercise his option and purchase every acre that his privilege covered, would have been welcomed, and this somber chapter in the history of the Alta District would never have been written.[35]

Perhaps the most unique and the most enduring of the early colonies as a separate entity was the one founded at Kingsburg. On July 28, 1885, Judge Frank D. Rosendahl, one of the original settlers in the Washington Colony, moved to Kingsburg. He was a graduate of Rosendahl College, and had been employed as a division gardener in Central Park, New York City. Subsequently he went to California by way of Panama and was employed as a landscape gardener in Golden Gate Park, San Francisco. In 1878 he became a member of Washington Colony, where he engaged in fruit growing and conducted a nursery. In the latter capacity, he made the acquaintance of Samuel Moffett of Kingsburg. When the latter left Kingsburg to become a feature writer on William Randolph Hearst's San Francisco *Examiner*, he sold his quarter section of land to Rosendahl. The second Scandinavian to arrive at Kingsburg was a relative of Rosendahl named C. A. Johnson.[36] However, the man who actually promoted the colony at Kingsburg was Andrew Erikson, who made the following statement concerning that venture:

> We were tired of the cold winters in Ishpeming, Michigan, and when we read in the newspapers about the government

land to be had in California we organized a little emigration society which subscribed enough money to send out a man to investigate. I was elected. I started on my trip the first part of August, 1886, and traveled extensively, both in the north and the south of this glorious state of California.

May I say that the State looked a whole lot different then from what it does today. When I came from the south I decided to stop off at Kingsburg and see Mr. C. A. Johnson and through him, I met Judge Frank D. Rosendahl for the first time. He took me to the Washington Colony, south of Fresno, where the orchards and vineyards, then in bearing, as well as other types of farming, made a good impression on me.

But I was not through with my investigation of government land. I started for the northern part of the state but I found no other land that I thought suitable for colonization. Then I went home and rendered my report. After a lengthy discussion a few persons decided to move to Kingsburg and try fruit farming. On November 26, 1886, two families and two single men arrived in Kingsburg in the sunny San Joaquin Valley; other members of the emigration society were to come later on. This was the beginning of the Swedish Colony at Kingsburg. A church organization was founded at Kingsburg on September 6, 1887, and this was the first Swedish Lutheran Church in the San Joaquin Valley.[37]

Incidentally, this was the first Lutheran church founded in the San Joaquin Valley; the Danish Lutheran church at Easton did not come into existence until December 2, 1888. The first Swedish church of any denomination was the Swedish Methodist, founded in Washington Colony in 1879. Prior to that time, religious services had been held by Rev. Andrew Farrell in the homes of the various Swedish Methodists in that colony, and to him goes the distinction of being the first Swedish-speaking clergyman to officiate in the San Joaquin Valley.

Other Swedish churches subsequently organized at Kingsburg were the Swedish Methodist; the Swedish Christian Mission (Congregational); the Scandinavian

Evangelical Free Mission; and the Swedish Baptist (First Baptist Church of Kingsburg). After half a century, these churches began gradually to employ the English language in their worship and to affiliate with the American branches of their respective denominations.[38]

Kingsburg has been a unique colony in two respects. First, it has been distinguished for racial homogeneity and second, for its religious tone. It has been the nearest equivalent in modern times to the old Puritan commonwealths which were characteristic of early New England. Religious fundamentalism and moral austerity have been much in evidence. The early Spanish were homogeneous, but their settlements always contained a large proportion of Indian servants. The later Americans from the older States were always heterogeneous in racial antecedents. The first pure racial units in the valley came into being with the founding of colonies. Today these colonies are in the process of Americanization, which is entirely changing their original racial and linguistic traits.

In 1921 a special writer for the Sun-Maid organization, with headquarters at Fresno, made the following observation on Kingsburg:

> Within a radius of three miles of Kingsburg, 94 percent of the population is of Swedish descent. One hundred per cent pure Americans, every one of them, but that thread of hard working industrial heredity has had much to do with Kingsburg's unusual prosperity. We count Kingsburg one of our most loyal districts. In the campaign just completed, 98 percent of all the acreage was signed with our Association. We are indeed proud of Kingsburg.[39]

Exactly a decade later Percy Nordstrom, then postmaster at Kingsburg, made a survey of the racial composition of the people of the Kingsburg community and made the following report:

> In response to your letter dated October 15th, pertaining to

the population, or patrons, served through this office, I will state that by a careful check I find that we are serving 5,179. As to those of Swedish ancestry or birth, 61 percent is all that can be thus figured on the result of said check. Should this question have been asked two years ago, 85 percent would have been the answer. We have had an influx of people from Oklahoma and elsewhere that has reduced the percentage of Swedish folk considerably.[40]

This is an interesting commentary on the tendency of colonists to disperse. The melting pot still functions in the San Joaquin.

The second thing, which has distinguished the Kingsburg Colony, has been the large percentage of its members affiliated with churches. The census for 1930 credited the city of Kingsburg with a population of 1,322; at the same time, the combined membership of the nine churches located within the city limits was 1,736. The total church membership exceeded the total population of the incorporated city. These figures do not include the membership of the three religious organizations located outside the city limits but in territory contiguous to Kingsburg.[41]

One of the settlers in the Central Colony was H. M. H. Kaarsberg, a Dane. He settled in this colony in 1876 and then transferred his interests to Selma. Later, he was followed by John Miller from Washington Colony Other Danish settlers in the Selma district were John Peterson, Myers Rassmussen, and the Lauritzen family. These first settlers stimulated an interest in their fellow countrymen in eastern states and in Denmark, which caused Selma to become largely Danish in culture and race. The first Danish religious service held in the Selma area took place on March 6, 1895, in a schoolhouse five miles north of that city. Eventually the Pella Danish Lutheran Church was organized in the vicinity; later, a church of the same name was established within the city. More recent settlements by Danes is indicated by the presence of Danish churches at Easton, Fresno, Parlier, Del Rey, and Reedley. There is also a colony of Danes at Modesto, and individual Danes have settled throughout the length and breadth of the valley.[42]

The Kaweah Co-operative Commonwealth was organized in 1886 and thereby hangs a tale. Charles Ferdinand Keller, a native of Germany, accompanied his parents to Pennsylvania. When the Civil War broke out he enlisted, although only a mere lad. He served four years and vividly remembered "marching through Georgia" with Sherman. After the war he settled at Eureka, California, and ran a meat market there until 1881. Then he moved to San Francisco and accidentally read about the activities of the 76 Land & Water Company, which was developing a tract of 30,000 acres in Tulare County. An auction was to be held a few miles north of the Grand View post office (Cross Creek station), at a place destined to become known as Traver. Keller attended this auction, bought several lots, and also acquired twenty acres of farmland. On the way to the land auction he rode behind two men interested in the Traver lands; they were P. Y. Baker and D. K. Zumwalt. He overheard them during the trip talking about the wonderful timberlands in the mountains east of Visalia. This gave him an idea.

Keller had been depressed by the fraudulent methods used by capitalists in obtaining the wonderful stands of timber to be found in Humboldt County. He decided that such lands should belong not to entrenched greed and corporate wealth, which squandered and destroyed these specimens of age and beauty, but to the common people, who would try to preserve them. Therefore he went to Visalia, hired a guide named Nort Tharp, whose father had discovered what is now Sequoia National Park, and went on foot to see this remarkable forest of *Sequoia gigantea*.

Upon his return to Visalia Keller telegraphed to some of his friends in San Francisco, and they responded by quickly appearing in Visalia. Keller secured powers of attorney, and he and his friends filed on lands containing the famous redwood forest. Forty filings were made; subsequently, seventeen additional filings were made. These fifty-seven constituted the sum total of the land secured by the Kaweah Co-operative Commonwealth. Other land was later filed upon, but these had nothing to do with the colony.

Keller's assistants were John H. Redstone, James J. Martin and Burnett Gregor Haskell; the two last-named were labor leaders in San Francisco. The individual members of the colony filed on land located on both sides of the Kaweah River and thus secured approximately 9,000 acres. The Halstead Ranch, consisting of 960 acres, was purchased outright by Keller; on this has been situated, in recent years, the Kaweah post office. The purpose of the colonists was to engage in horticultural and agricultural pursuits, irrigate the land, and protect the redwoods. When they first saw these immense *Sequoia gigantea*, these city-bred colonists were filled with awe. Since all of them were Socialists, they approved of Keller's action when he named the biggest tree in the forest after the great apostle of their movement, Karl Marx. This name the tree retained until the government authorities re-named it the General Sherman.[43]

The colony elected a president and a superintendent; these officers were to hold office for one year. The first president was P. N. Kuss. The routine business of the colony was conducted before the Referendum, a popular assembly consisting of all the members of the colony. In many ways, this body was similar to the old time New England town meeting. Nothing was said about religion, but it was understood that full religious freedom existed.

When a man joined the colony his wife and minor children automatically became members; major children were voted on separately. The cost of admission to this colony was $500. Of this amount $100 was payable in cash and the balance could be paid in labor. A member of the Kaweah Co-operative Commonwealth was not required to work, but the drones were denied wages and a share in the profits of the enterprise.[44]

One of the articles of the covenant of the Commonwealth read as follows:

> A membership in this Association consists of an equal share in the emoluments, profits, privileges, and hereditaments of the colony. It means that every member shares equally in all that the bounteous soil will yield and all that improved machinery can produce, measured by the amount of time he has usefully employed, or the proportion of energy he has himself expended in producing the general result, whatever it may be.[45]

One of the projects attempted by the Kaweah Co-operative Commonwealth was the building of a road from Traver to what is now Sequoia Park. Traver, situated forty miles due west of the Kaweah Colony, was the nearest shipping point. Keller resided at Traver during most of the time that he was active in the colony's affairs, and Martin also spent much time there. Keller Hall, the municipal auditorium of Traver, was owned by the original promoter of the Kaweah Cooperative Commonwealth.

Kaweah, as the colony was called, consisted of a dining and meeting hall, store, print shop, blacksmith's shop, and a barn and some sheds. From the village, located at an elevation of 1,500 feet along the north fork of the Kaweah River, an eighteen-mile road was built into the granite-clad hills to an elevation of 8,000 feet. Anarchism and free love had no place in this colony. The members were native-born Americans interested in pure democracy.

Property was owned as a whole, affairs were administered by a board of five trustees elected by the membership at large, and each branch of industry had a superintendent appointed by the trustees, but removable by the workers in his department. A weekly four-page newspaper, the *Kaweah Commonwealth*, was published on what was apparently Tulare County's first steam-powered press. Regarding party affiliations, the officers stated: "The colony has not recognized any party in politics. Its members have voted for those whom they have considered to be the most fit for office." The colony officers consisted of the following: secretary, James J. Martin; treasurer, William Christie; trustees, James J. Martin, Burnette G. Haskell, William Christie, Horace T. Taylor, Richard Corbett; industrial superintendents, Irvin Barnard, W. B. Hunter, James Bellah, William Howard, William Christie, James J. Martin, Burnett Gregor Haskell, George B. Savage, and Mrs. Candace E. Christie.[46]

Tulare County officials, suspicious because so many filings were so suddenly made, brought suits of ejection. The resulting court trial on these ejection suits resulted in a victory for the colony, but the federal government was antagonistic and finally the colony disbanded and went to the Kettleman Plains, where its members founded the Esperanza Improvement Company. Here they encountered hostility at the hands of the Southern Pacific Railway; ejection suits and general lawlessness made them lose heart, and their second colony was also abandoned as a failure.[47]

Another Swedish colony was organized in 1886 known as the Kingsburg-Riverside Colony; locally, it was usually referred to as the Mission Colony due to the preponderance of settlers belonging to that church. This was located along Kings River, directly across the river from the city of Reedley. Some of the original settlers in this colony were C. A. Erickson, Andrew Olson, Hans Hanson, and Rev. John Gilberg. The latter organized the Swedish Mission church in the colony in 1890; this became the parent church of the congregation organized in Kingsburg in 1907.[48]

In 1890, the Rosedale Colony was organized near Bakersfield. The majority of the settlers were from England, and their farming methods aroused a great deal of hilarity among the Americans who were their neighbors. The latter ploughed their fields with a gang plow and six to ten horses controlled by a single jerk-line. The Englishman used one horse and hired a boy to lead him, while a man handled the plow. But these Englishmen were tenacious settlers, the peanuts and vegetables that they planted brought handsome returns, and the colony flourished.[49]

Several Canadian families settled near Wasco, but they were not numerous enough to be considered a colony. In the northern part of the valley, the Orange Blossom Colony was organized east of Modesto. Another colony in the north was the Temperance Colony, founded at Ceres. The name of the colony suggests the type of settler and the nature of the experiment. Seven miles from Ceres some English colonists settled at a place called Westport.[50]

The founding of the colony at Turlock is closely related to the discovery of gold in Alaska. In 1903 Jack London was sitting beside a table in the corner of Johnny Heinhold's *First and Last Chance* saloon at the foot of Webster Street in Oakland. London was writing a book; its title was the *Call of the Wild*. The first two sentences that he wrote were as follows:

> Buck did not read the newspapers or he would have known that trouble was brewing not alone for himself, but for every tide-water dog, strong of muscle and with warm, long hair, from Puget Sound to San Diego. Because men, groping in the

591

Arctic darkness, had found a yellow metal, and because steamship and transportation companies were booming the find, thousands of men were rushing into the Northland.[51]

The same year that London wrote these lines, one of the men who had been "groping in the Arctic darkness" was promoting in the dazzling sunlight of the San Joaquin the Swedish Colony at Turlock. His career as a pioneer in Alaska and in the San Joaquin Valley warrants a brief summary. The publicity given to his adventures in Alaska brought him the fame that, in turn, made possible the successful completion of the pretentious Turlock colonization project.

Rev. Nils O. Hultberg, under the auspices of the Swedish Mission Church, had gone to Alaska as a missionary to the Indians; he was also a government teacher. His mission station was located at Golovin Bay. A part of his duties was to teach the natives of Alaska the care of reindeer. He described his social service work, prior to the gold rush, as follows:

> The reindeer were kept in the hills some distance away from the coast back of Port Clarence, and one herd was kept back of Golovin Bay and was in my charge. I drove the first herd of fifty over the mountains from Port Clarence to Golovin Bay in the winter of 1895-1896. The first reindeer were brought over from Siberia by the Government in 1892 and were placed on the Unalaska Islands. In 1893 they brought fifty more which were left at Port Clarence. After that the Russian Government stopped the export and the now almost uncountable thousands existing in Alaska are all an increase from the fifty head imported in 1893.

> This move by the Government was made at the instigation of Dr. Sheldon Jackson, then head of the educational department of Alaska. The first reindeer were transported over in the revenue cutter *Bear*, with Captain Healy in charge, and Lieutenant Jarvis, afterwards Captain Jarvis, second in command. Both of these men have long since passed away, after having rendered great service in Alaska.

Turlock, Stanislaus County, as it was in 1904, the hub of a settlement founded by Swedish immigrants. *Fresno County Public Library, California History and Genealogy Room Collection.*

In those days in Alaska the only industry was fishing and hunting by the Eskimos and some trading in fur and ivory. This trade was taken care of by a few white traders in the employ of the Alaska Commercial Company that was at that time the dominant element in Alaska.

My study in mineralogy and information obtained from miners I had met, led me to the positive conclusions that gold existed. Gaining more and more knowledge by experimentation, I soon became a first rate prospector. I sometimes instructed the Eskimos to bring me sand and quartz from their fishing and hunting trips. In this I sometimes found colors of gold.

The first bag of sand brought to me from the Nome district was brought in by an Eskimo we called Lincoln and contained black sand and numerous colors of gold. This was in 1897 and I at once made a trip to investigate. This trip was nearly disastrous as I was caught in a severe storm lasting three weeks; part of the time I existed on frozen, raw dog meat, and nearly froze to death. No success was made of prospecting on

593

this trip. The winter was too severe and I was glad to get back home alive.

In the meantime I had sent out to friends asking them to send me two experienced miners. These two came from Michigan in the spring of 1898. But lo! they were not gold miners, but coal miners and did not know gold from sand. These men were John Brynteson and John Hagelin, both of whom I at once took to the Nome district, and we found gold everywhere. Not being fitted out to stay long at this time, we went back to Golovin Bay. It being time for me to get out that year, I left everything in their hands, arranging for Lindblom and Lindeberg to go with Brynteson back there again. The result is common history.[52]

Jaffet Lindeberg had been imported from Finland by the United States government to help train the Eskimos in the care of reindeer. He broke his contract and became a gold prospector. Erik O. Lindblom was a deserter from a whaling vessel and Tlingit Indians, finding him wandering alone in the forest, had taken him to Hultberg's mission station at Golovin Bay. He found riches in the northland and returned to Berkeley, where he bought the Claremont Hotel in the Berkeley Hills, overlooking the University of California campus. The discovery of gold along Anvil Creek at the point where it enters the tundra, about three and a half miles north of Nome, led to the gold rush of 1898 and 1899, which rivals the gold rush to California in 1848 and 1849. The stampede to the Canadian mines occurred at the same time. These were located in a region known as the Klondike, and were about a thousand miles from Nome.

Nels O. Hultberg, like James Wilson Marshall, failed to profit by his discovery to any great extent. Two of his children had died in Alaska due to lack of medical attention and in August 1898, after having placed his friends on claims along Anvil Creek, Hultberg left for "the outside" in the interests of his surviving child's health.

Returning from his furlough, Hultberg learned that other miners had jumped his claims, and he found himself destitute, while other gold-diggers were taking out $10,000 a day from ground he had discovered and staked. Such hard luck might have discouraged a man of smaller caliber. Unlike Marshall he did not become an object of charity, but turned his attention to other fields of endeavor. Whatever proceeds accrued to him from his other claims on the Seward Peninsula were invested in the promotion of a colony at Turlock. Concerning this project, he made the following explanation:

> The Turlock colonization scheme was wholly my own plan. No, it was not my purpose to make it a colony purely for people affiliated with the Swedish Mission Church as, of course, the different denominations established there would show. My dream was to establish the largest Swedish Colony in the State and possibly in the United States.
>
> The fact that the majority of the oncoming settlers at that time were Mission Friends was due to the reason that I was well known among them, having been in the service of that church as a missionary in Alaska for a number of years. Also, because of the publicity given this venture in all the Swedish papers and on account of the further fact that I was the actual discoverer of gold in the Nome district.[53]

John Mitchell had secured about 100,000 acres of government land some time in 1848. The present city and colony of Turlock is located on that quondam ranch. Mitchell's heirs organized the Fin-de-Siecle Investment Company, with Horace Crane as secretary-treasurer. Part of their holdings were acquired by Hultberg. In order to realize his pretentious plans, it was necessary to find a stenographer and secretary well versed in both the Swedish and English languages. Miss Esther Hall, a graduate of a commercial college at Minneapolis and at that time on a visit to San Francisco, was employed on December 26, 1902, and proceeded immediately to Turlock.

Literature advertising the possibilities of this new locality were sent to eastern papers and advertisements were inserted in the *Sunset Magazine*, in *Missions Vännen*, and in *Västkusten*. Rev. Andrew Haliner, pastor of the Kingsburg-Riverside Mission Church, was engaged as manager of the project. Hailner was superseded by David F. Lane in 1905.

Hultberg conducted a boarding house, where the prospective purchasers of land were fed free of charge until they had completed their business deals. In many cases, people came to look at the land but failed to buy. The price of land at that time was $25 an acre. In the spring of 1903, Rev. J. O. Boden brought his entire congregation intact from Youngstown, Ohio, to Turlock. These settlers were mostly steelworkers from the iron mills. They were entirely ignorant of agricultural pursuits, and their first attempts at horsemanship were somewhat ludicrous. This colony, located due south of Turlock, is still known as Youngstown.

But no large project ever functions smoothly at all times. Photographs of the older settlements at Kingsburg and Washington Colony accompanied the advertisements that appeared in the magazines and newspapers, and usually carried this caption: "Turlock will soon look like this." But when the settlers arrived and saw the sandy wastes and felt the hot, stinging winds of their new homes, they believed themselves thoroughly duped. A pioneer wheat grower in that region asserted that the sand drifted against the stables in such huge piles that pathways had to be shoveled before stock could be taken out. The board fences used in early days often broke from the weight of the sand piled against them by the winds surging through the passes in the Coast Range mountains.

Then came the grasshoppers. They were hatched in April, they appeared in full bib-and-tucker in May, they defoliated the vineyards and orchards in June, and only the bare peach pits, glistening like gnawed bones, were left on the trees in July. No vestige of plant life remained. Naturally, Hultberg was blamed even for the grasshoppers. But the plague was upon them, and the poor settlers can not be condemned harshly for sitting down in their misery and murmuring (Exodus 16:3): "Would to God we had died by the hand of the Lord in the Land of Egypt, when we sat by the flesh pots, and when we did eat bread to the full; for ye have brought us forth into the wilderness, to kill the whole assembly of hunger."

In 1904 an indignation meeting was held at Hilmar (likely named after Hultberg's son) to protest against the alleged misrepresentations of the advertisements and circulars which had been sent out to prospective colonists. The assertion had been made that the sandy plains in the hot interior valley needed only water and the right kind of people to make them a horticultural paradise. A wag rose to remark: "Plenty of water and the right kind of people will also transform Hell." But eventually the grasshoppers were destroyed by grass fires, night fires, and hopperdozers; water demonstrated the wonderful fertility of the apparently sandy soil; and homes were erected. The thousands of happy and prosperous settlers now residing in the Turlock area bear out the assertion that the Turlock colonization project of Hultberg was fundamentally sound in its original conception.[54]

One of the unique racial groups in the San Joaquin Valley are the Armenians. The first member of this race to reach the valley was probably a man named Mardiros Yanikian (Frank Normart, after the Armenian for "new man"), who settled in Fresno in 1874. Perhaps the first permanent settlers were the Seropian brothers, who left Turkish Armenia and bought land near Fresno in 1881. They became fruit growers and wrote enthusiastic letters to their kinsmen and friends in Marsovan (Marzifoun), as well as to Armenians who had settled in New England.

The settlement of Armenians in New England was due to the work of missionaries who had gone from there to Armenia shortly after the Civil War and established schools and colleges. Graduates from these missionary schools gradually began to appear at Harvard, Yale, and Princeton. Political conditions within the Turkish Empire caused an exodus to the United States during the years 1874 to 1894. The Huntchaggist (revolutionary) movement was organized in 1883; its sympathizers were forced to flee. These fugitives congregated near Boston and labored in the shoe factories; others secured employment in the New Jersey silk mills at Paterson. One of the Seropians had settled in the San Joaquin Valley in search of health; he had found it. It was to these political fugitives in New England to whom he wrote glowing letters concerning climate and soil in the years following 1880.[55]

The lot of the Armenians in Turkey and Russia continued to be unhappy, and the influx from New England into the San Joaquin was augmented by a continued immigration from the Caucasus Mountains, from the headwaters of the Tigris River, and from the plains of Mesopotamia. The majority of the Fresno colonists hailed originally from the communities of Harput, Diarbekir, Aintab, Antioch, Adana, Erzerum, and Van. Another group of Armenians claim descent from the sons of Sennacherib and refer to themselves as Assyrians. They base their claim on Isaiah 37: 37-38. "So Sennacherib, king of Assyria departed, and went and returned, and dwelt at Nineveh. And it came to pass, as he was worshipping in the house of Nisroch his god, that Adrammelech and Sharezer his sons smote him with the sword; and they escaped into the land of Armenia; and Esarhaddon his son reigned in his stead."

However, there is a race of people in the valley called

Assyrians who are different from the Armenians in race, language, and culture. The Assyrians have no language of their own now; they speak the language of the people among whom they lived in the old country. Those who came from the Mosul (Dikranagerd) region had dwelt among the Arabs, and hence speak Arabic. Those who were originally settlers in Harput, Turkish Armenia, speak the Turkish language.[56]

The national church of Armenia has been the Gregorian (Nestorian). The majority of the original colonists were members of this organization. Those trained at the mission schools were either Congregationalists or Presbyterians. A few affiliated with the Roman Catholic and Greek Orthodox.[57]

In the San Joaquin their chief interest has been in horticulture. Henry Markarian was one of the pioneer fig growers of the valley. His method of planting trees thirty feet apart has since been generally followed by fig growers. The first fig-packing plant in the valley was established by the Seropian Brothers at Fresno. These packers shipped fruit to the urban centers over the Southern Pacific. They, like the wheat growers, were soon involved in altercations with the railway authorities over the continual increase of shipping rates. The Seropian firm solved its own troubles by buying pack mules, loading them with crates of dried figs, and sending these donkey caravans to market, as had been done years before in the valley of Mesopotamia. These long mule trains to San Francisco aroused curiosity in the small cities along the way between Fresno and San Francisco. The metropolitan newspapers contributed their share of publicity. The revolt of wheat growers and fig growers against the only railway in the valley received much attention. A Spanish journal printed in Mexico City carried the tidings to the hacienda of a wealthy Mexican hidalgo. He promptly sent a courteous message to the Seropian brothers informing them that he had excellent pack mules for sale.

Horticulture owes much to the arrival of the Armenian colonists. They introduced the yellow watermelon (ice-cream melon), the Armenian cucumber, the Diarbekihr melon, the Turkish melon, and the casaba. The latter derives its name from the town of Kassaba, near Smyrna.[58]

The only Syrian colony in the valley is located near Reedley in the Navelencia district. These people are not to be confused with Assyrians. The first Syrian to reach California was no doubt Hadji Ali (Hi Jolly) who was one of Jefferson Davis' camel drivers. The first one to locate permanently in the valley was Joseph A. Lawand, who arrived in Fresno in 1899 and settled on a fruit farm three miles east of Reedley in 1909. Most of the early Syrian immigrants were peddlers in the city, and in the summers they would pass through the valley selling imported rugs and other curios. Here they met Lawand, who prevailed upon many of them to buy land in the Navelencia district, Section 10 being colonized by them in time. They found that their new valley home was almost identical in all things with their old home in Syria: Soil, irrigation, and fruits all reminded them of Lebanon, the district from which most of them came. In religion the Syrians near Reedley are either Roman Catholic or Greek Orthodox although most Syrians in the homeland are Muslims. Their language is Arabic.[59]

The founding of the Finnish colony near Reedley took place in 1904; in 1939, it numbered four hundred and twenty-five persons. Prior to that time, a senator in the legislature of Finland named Aksel Wahren had resisted the increasing autocracy of the Russian imperial government that then ruled Finland. He was forced to flee and finally arrived in the United States, residing for a time in Oklahoma, looking for a suitable agricultural colony district. He then moved on to the Pacific coast, visited the Reedley district, and began to promote it for Finnish settlement. While in San Francisco he attended a meeting of Finnish carpenters, longshoremen, and sailors who met on Sunday afternoons to discuss the possibility of founding a farm colony. They had corresponded with the Department of Agriculture, but had not found a suitable location. Senator Wahren suggested they settle near Reedley. Further investigation caused the site to be approved, and land was bought along Kings River from the 76 Land & Water Company. The first house was built by Gust L. Laine, who became the leader in the colony. The only Finnish-speaking churches in the San Joaquin are in Reedley; one, a Congregational; the others, Lutheran and Laestidian. The United Finnish Brotherhood, a local lodge, provides sick benefits. The nomenclature of Reedley has been enriched by names such as Tiura, Loukonen, Panttaja, Lehtonen, Korsinen, Multanen, Nurmi, Hongola, Kangas, Kallio, and Rintala. Amnesty was finally granted to Wahren, and he returned to his political duties in Finland.[60]

Men of German blood like Charles Weber and Frederick Roeding were followed in 1903 by German colonists of a different type, who made Reedley and the Clark-Kennedy ranch between Dinuba and Kingsburg the scene of their activities. Many of these German Mennonites came from Kansas and Minnesota, others directly from Germany or the German colonies in Russia. A Mennonite colony had been founded at Upland, California, near Los Angeles, but many of the residents at that place were dissatisfied with orange growing. The Atchison, Topeka and Santa Fe Railway Company maintained an immigration bureau at that time, which attempted to colonize the lands along its San Joaquin Valley line. This bureau was instrumental in causing Daniel T. Eymann and his son, August, to visit the city of Reedley and its environs in August 1903. They purchased land and removed to Reedley. The following year many of their friends and relatives followed them from Upland. Their favorable report concerning that part of the valley brought Jacob Bergthold and other colonists from Minnesota in 1904. Mennonite communities in Kansas sent their quota, and colonists of the same faith came directly from Germany and the German colonies in Russia.[61]

These people were uniformly Mennonites in religion. The most similar, though not identical, American church is the Church of the Brethren (Dunkards). This Mennonite church consists of three varieties: the General Conference Mennonites, the Mennonite Brethren, and the Krimner Mennonites. According to Rev. H. J. Krehbiel, a prominent clergyman of Reedley:

> The Mennonites were originally called Anabaptists and started in 1525 at Zurich, Switzerland. Persecuted there, they fled to Germany and Holland. In Holland a Catholic priest by the name of Menno Simons was converted and joined them. He became a great leader and preacher among them. He also wrote much in their defense and soon his followers began to be called after his name.

> It may interest you to know in what manner the Mennonites differ in their teaching from other Protestant denominations. Briefly the following: first, baptism upon confession of faith; second, they forbid the taking of an oath according to Matthew 5:33-37 and James 5:12; third they are opposed to war and the killing of a human being under any circumstances.[62]

This German colony surrounding Reedley is a populous and prosperous colony at the present time. Four Mennonite churches are located in the vicinity. The location of other German-Mennonite colonies in the valley is indicated by the existence of churches of their faith at Rosedale, Dos Palos, Lodi, and Shafter.[63]

The first Yugoslav to enter the present state of California was Father Ferdinand Konsciak, a Croat, who arrived in Loreto, Baja California in 1732 to begin work as a Jesuit missionary. On his tour he crossed the Colorado River into Alta California, and his maps and missions paved the way for Junipero Serra. The first Yugoslavs to settle permanently in California were gold miners, who formed a mining district around the town of Jackson in the Mother Lode region. Many of these miners came from the areas of Istria, Slovenia, Croatia, Dalmatia and Montenegro. The building of the San Joaquin & Kings River Canal by Miller & Lux brought the first Yugoslavs into the valley as laborers. After this canal and other similar irrigation works had been completed the Yugoslavs remained as fruit growers. To one of them, Stephen Mitrovich, goes the credit for importing the first Adriatic fig cuttings to the San Joaquin. The Yugoslavs are homogeneous racially, but definitely divided as to geography and religion. In the present kingdom of Yugoslavia the Serbs, Greek Orthodox in religion, are the dominant element; the minority groups, Croats and Slovenes, are Roman Catholics. The Yugoslav population in the San Joaquin is concentrated about the city of Fresno, although individual members of this race are scattered up and down the entire valley. The first actual Yugoslav settler in the valley was Jacob Kocerar, a Slovene gold miner, who began to farm in Tulare county in 1885, and finally acquired thousands of acres. It was his successful venture that attracted other members of his race to the valley.[64]

A Japanese colony was promoted near Livingston in 1906 by Kyuntaro Abiko, the manager and editor of the *Japanese-American*, a Japanese newspaper published at San Francisco. On January 14, 1907, this colony went into the official records of Merced County. The members of the colony all espoused Christianity rather than Buddhism or

Shintoism. One of the leaders in all community enterprises was Nobutada Satow, a merchant.

Fierce winds swirling over the hot sands of that unirrigated region had literally blown away an American colony founded there twelve years before. The story of the Japanese effort to succeed is an epic struggle with nature. The hot winds, unhindered by windbreaks, orchards, or vineyards, swept away the soil that had been loosened by cultivation. This was the original Dust Bowl. Trees and vines shriveled and died. Grasshoppers, having devoured plant life in the Swedish colony at Turlock, advanced in mass formation on Livingston. Drinking water had to be carried two miles. In 1909 the Japanese-American Bank at San Francisco, which held mortgages on their land, was forced to close its doors. In those days the colonists were friendless and poverty stricken, but not hopeless. They marched to their little Methodist Church and sang, "Hold the fort for I am coming," and their faith saved them:

> For Livingston is a Christian colony, and that fact has, in more than one way, profoundly influenced its development. It is that fact that prevents Livingston, the highest example of a Japanese farming community in California, from being taken as the most typical example. The fact that many of its members were Christians has had so much to do with the success of the community that it has in a measure set this colony apart from other Japanese agricultural settlements.[65]

In time the colonists managed to organize the Livingston Cooperative Society, capitalized at $25,000, and built a packinghouse at a cost of $10,000. They bought their own supplies and materials in bulk as a united community, and marketed their own crops. In 1906, they owned less than nothing; in 1917, the colonists shipped 260 carloads of fruit from Livingston. In 1921 the colony owned 1,730 acres with an average of 40 acres to each farmer.[66]

In spite of the many colonization projects which engrossed

Stephen N. Mitrovich, pioneer fig grower of Fresno County. Paul A. Vandor, *History of Fresno County, California.*

the attention of promoters between the administrations of James K. Polk and Woodrow Wilson, the San Joaquin Valley still remained largely a section of wide open spaces. The point of saturation had not been reached by 1920. In 1916 the tax commissioner reported that 310 landed proprietors owned 4 million acres in the state. In the San Joaquin Valley, four companies held a million acres. The Kern County Land Company alone owned 356,000 acres. In Merced County, Miller & Lux controlled 245,000 acres. The great size of the valley made such big ranches a possibility.

The San Joaquin Valley, 250 miles long and 40 miles wide, comprises the largest continuous block of agricultural land in the state. On the vast plains of the valley floor are 6.6 million acres of land having gentle slope and flat surface conformation favorable for agriculture. The marginal foothills to the east and south add 1.8 million acres more, making a total of 8.4 million acres of agricultural land in the San Joaquin Valley, one-third of all the agricultural lands in the state.[67]

In the early years of the twentieth century, several private colonization companies established settlements in various parts of the valley. The more important of these were at Kerman, Patterson, Laguna de Tache, Chowchilla, Wasco, Shafter, and Oakdale. General William H. Shafter's Kern County ranch was subdivided in 1914. The settlers in this Shafter Colony, north of Bakersfield, were mainly of German birth or descent. Most of them were Mennonites, Seventh Day Adventists, or Reformed Lutherans. Near Shafter is located a federal government experiment station, and between Shafter and Wasco lay the tract of land developed by Herbert C. Hoover. At Oakdale, the best success was achieved by the Rodden Brothers Colony. These promoters were attempting to fill a need once supplied by the government. In former generations "a homestead of 160 acres was a mirage of hope. It was the voice of opportunity calling to the pioneer." But suitable homestead land was gone.[68]

Changing economic conditions and the end of free land brought to the United States a new type of immigrant. Elwood Mead, a veteran in the land settlement program, explained changing conditions as follows:

> Good people were driven out by cheaper people just as bad money drives out good money. If this policy of securing farm help wherever it can be had is to continue, then we must have some organized effort to lift these people up to American standards of life and living and to endeavor to instill in them some of the ideals that have made this country what it is. From the landing of the first settlers at Plymouth Rock and in Virginia, the people who made this country were noted for their fortitude, their coolness in danger, their orderly habits of life, consideration for the weak and interest in government. They were people whose morals and standards of living made

their children men and women of strength and beauty. The good looks of the descendants of American pioneers of Massachusetts, Virginia, Kentucky, and California had their origin in both ancestry and right living.

So long as there was free land, rural America was largely made up of this fine type of people. The first immigrants from Great Britain and France were followed by other waves of immigrants from the Scandinavian countries, Germany and Ireland. They were being fused into a harmonious rural society when free land disappeared and a new type of immigrant appeared.[69]

The studies of Elwood Mead caught the attention of the Commonwealth Club of San Francisco, and it sponsored a movement to place the right kind of people on the right kind of land. In 1917, the legislature passed the Land Settlement Act and appropriated $260,000 for the venture. California thus entered into its first colonization project. Dr. Elwood Mead was appointed director of the movement. In 1919 the legislature added an additional $1 million to its first appropriation and inserted a provision giving ex-service men preference as prospective settlers.

A tract of approximately 6,000 acres, thenceforth known as the Delhi Settlement, was chosen in 1920. This site lay in Merced County, six miles south of Turlock, and within the Turlock Irrigation District. The State Land Settlement Board was guided in its choice by advice from the University of California College of Agriculture, the United States Department of Agriculture, and the State Engineer. The state paid an average of $120 an acre, made certain improvements, and sold the land to the colonists for $229 an acre.

The contract for the first building was let on March 4, 1920. The Delhi townsite was planned by Professor J. W Gregg, Professor of Landscape Gardening at the University of California. It's curved streets and beautiful location on the highlands bordering the Southern Pacific railway made it an attractive place for the settlers. While the private buildings were under construction, Edgar M. Wilson of San Francisco donated a $10,000 community hall. This place was used as a community center where the settlers met in a social way at their parties, dances, socials, plays, lectures, and religious services. The bronze plaque in the entrance hall carried an inscription that was written by Benjamin Ide Wheeler, president emeritus of the University of California:

> Wilson Hall typifies the neighborhood spirit wherein men are social beings rather than machines, dwell in homes not laboratories, and lead the old Town Meeting out into the service of the new economic democracy.

> From the beginning of human civilization, the irrigation trench, in Egypt and Babylonia, taught men to work together. Today history is written in terms of such works as the hospital, the library, the church and the schools. Joint credit, security of life, and community health have laid the basis of a cooperation, rich in sympathy and keen to serve. For what is a man profited, if he shall gain the whole world and lose his own soul?

Two years after the Delhi Settlement had been formed, 220 settlers had secured allotments; at that time, 208 remained. Of this group 82 percent were Californians; the other colonists had come from fifteen other states, and from Canada, Australia, and England. About 50 percent of the total group were ex-service men of the World War. The Veterans Welfare Board cooperated with the Division of Land Settlement in aiding the veterans with expert advice concerning livestock, horticulture, and the orientation of vineyards, orchards, and buildings. A federal training officer paid weekly visits to all the ex-servicemen in the colony. Other agencies acknowledged by the Division of Land Settlement to have been contributory factors in securing settlers and rendering assistance to the movement are indicated in the following official report:

> The Santa Fe and the Southern Pacific railroads have been of
> great assistance in securing a desirable type of settlers.
> Through their agents and in other ways they have done much
> to make the country acquainted with the opportunities
> offered by the state settlements. The same is true of the state
> press which has kept the public informed regarding the
> progress of these settlements and the opportunities they
> present. In the main, however, the chief magnet has been the
> fact that the state offers men of industry and thrift, who have
> a little capital, a better chance to succeed, and gives them a
> more attractive social life, than can be secured under any
> unplanned development.[70]

The result of the Land Settlement plan in California was
watched with keen interest by thinkers throughout the
nation. The *Review of Reviews* for October 1921 printed a
favorable comment:

> A few years ago California was wise enough to recognize the
> fact that the future well-being of the state called for the
> settlement of land upon the basis of the associated group or
> neighborhood and not merely the location of the isolated,
> independent farmer.

Collier's for July 29, 1922 contained the following:

> Already firmly established in California, the community land
> settlement idea is now sweeping the country—the
> governments of many eastern states are studying the plan
> with a view to its adoption in reclaiming abandoned New
> England farms and the great stretches of unused land in
> Maryland and the Old South.

An August 1922 article by Arthur Ruhl in *Harper's
Magazine* contained a defense of the land settlement plan.
He asserted that in it was "nothing untried or unduly
paternalistic. We have merely done what has been done in
Europe long ago—loaned to the individual for the benefit
of all some of the state's surplus capital and expert
intelligence."

A new interpretation of conditions was supplied by the September 1922 issue of the *Sunset Magazine*:

> The state (California) already has an excess of irrigated land for which settlers are required. It needs money to finance new settlers far more than it needs additional irrigation facilities. Also, through established channels funds are steadily flowing into new irrigation enterprises but for scientific colonization of these new irrigation projects the available funds are totally inadequate.

Elwood Mead served as administrative head of the Land Settlement Board until 1924, when he was succeeded by C. M. Wooster. During the next few years, the economic fabric of the nation was being rent and torn, and American industry strutted into the debacle of 1929. Old established farmers became bankrupt; that the inexperienced settlers at Durham, in the Sacramento Valley, and at Delhi could succeed was not within the realm of reason. When the Department of Agriculture took over the administration of the colonies on July 29, 1927, the "responsibility amounted to a virtual receivership, involving 14,600 acres of land, 300 settlers and their families and an investment of some $3 million on the part of the state."

A legislative committee rendered the following report:

> The Project as a whole has been, and now is, a financial failure. The settlers were led to expect too much; in several instances they were granted greater loans than the Land Settlement Act permitted.
>
> In a number of instances chattel mortgages were made by settlers to the board securing loans made by the board. Later the mortgaged chattels were sold by the mortgagors and the loans were not repaid to the board.
>
> Furthermore, in addition to the general expectation that more help would be given than is economically sound or larger loans made than were financially or legally proper, many of the settlers came to the colony with the distinct belief that

the state would act as a sort of guardian angel or Santa Claus and "see them through," as they expressed it.

> The final consideration of this problem has led your committee to recommend that the State of California should never enter into another land settlement scheme.[71]

When the economic conditions in the Dust Bowl caused an exodus from that region many of the refugees turned their faces and Fords toward California. They arrived in such numbers that they became a social and economic problem, and highway patrolmen and Los Angeles city policemen were assigned to duty at the state line with orders to turn them back. To many neutral observers, this net seemed to savor of despotism and was no doubt a violation of the Bill of Rights. While many of these "uncovered wagon" migrants to California during the depression decade of 1929 to 1939 were from Kansas and eastern Texas, the great majority were from Oklahoma. Since they had been chiefly cotton sharecroppers, they headed for the cotton fields of the San Joaquin. The growing of cotton seems to leave poverty in its wake everywhere. Picking and chopping cotton are seasonal jobs, and the rest of the year the destitute Oklahomans eked out an existence by fishing for catfish and carp along the banks of the various rivers as well as by the shores of Tulare Lake. Unable to secure new license plates for their automobiles, their cars were attached and stored, but the storage costs threatened to break the county, and in time the jalopies were returned with or without licenses. An excess of cheap labor, growing numbers on relief, and mounting tax rates caused friction. The pitiful conditions of the poor Oklahomans caused heartless persons to invent ribald and unkind jokes at their expense. The C. I. O. was said to mean "California Importing Oklahomans." The genius of John Steinbeck has given us in *The Grapes of Wrath*, a dramatic and sympathetic story of the trek of the Oklahomans from the Dust Bowl to the Garden of the Sun. It also includes a

dire prophecy concerning the ultimate outcome of the
graceless manner in which the established Californians
"took them in" when they arrived.[72]

Another group which modified life in the San Joaquin
Valley are the Mexican peons. They are usually of Indian
blood and are not to be confused with the Spanish-
Californians of an earlier day. The Mexicans are excellent
laborers and follow the fruit harvest. Under present
conditions they are a necessary adjunct to a successful
development of the San Joaquin Valley. Many of them
aspire to improve their lot in life and that groping after
something better than they now possess has been
expressed by Amado Nervo, their favorite poet, in *A Peon's
Prayer*:

> I'm only a spark,
> Make me a fire.
> I'm only a string,
> Make me a lyre.
> I'm only an anthill,
> Make me a mountain.
> I'm only a drop,
> Make me a fountain.
> I'm only a feather,
> Make me a wing.
> I'm only a peon,
> Make me a king.[73]

A family of Yokuts Indians, employed on a fruit ranch
along Kings River, were visited one evening by Mexicans
from an adjoining ranch. The Indians spoke only English;
the Mexicans, only Spanish. No conversation was possible,
and the offended Mexicans returned home and told their
employer that the Mexicans on the other place were
inhospitable and snobbish. Informed that their neighbors
were Indians, they expressed great astonishment. The
moral is this: The last group of people to arrive in the

valley are physically indistinguishable from the aborigines. Every racial type in the world is to be found in the San Joaquin. The last group to arrive cannot distinguish itself from the first. The circle has been completed.

The frontiersmen who attempted to hew homes out of the great forests of the Ohio Valley have often been apotheosized. A few years later their sons and daughters subdued the prairies. The agony and the heartache which often darkened life on the Middle Border has been delineated by a master veritist, Hamlin Garland, in his *Main Traveled Roads*. Then came the advance into the trans-Mississippi west. Another literary genius, like Garland familiar with life on the frontier from first-hand experience as a pioneer, attributed to the prairie that irresistible force with which Frank Norris was wont to endow the forces of nature that appeared in his novels. This man, O. E. Rolvaag, caused the Dakota Prairie to express herself as follows in his *Giants in the Earth*:

> That night the prairie stretched herself voluptuously; giantlike and full of cunning, she laughed softly into the reddish moon. "Now we will see what human might may avail against us! Now we'll see."

The same challenge was blared forth by the plains of the San Joaquin Valley, as many men and women who have been mustered into the service of its conquest and domestication have testified. Just what human might has been able to achieve in the battle against the semi-arid plains, this chapter has attempted to show.

A laboratory of races is found in the San Joaquin Valley. No racial group has thus far revealed a monopoly of either good or bad traits. A social worker among the submerged tenth in California has insisted after years of active service that "no railing accusation is to be brought against a whole nation nor even against a whole class in a nation." Each race has contributed much to the development of the valley and each has, at times, been handicapped by scoundrels and inferior specimens. Within each race is to be found a striking study in contrasts:

> The two images farthest removed from each other that can be comprehended under one term, are, I think, Isaiah. "Hear. O Heavens, and give ear. O earth!"; and Levi, of Holywell Street, "Old Clothes!"; both of them Jews, you'll observe. Immane quantum discrepant![74]

17 Spillways and Headgates

Water is the mother of the vine,
The nurse and fountain of fecundity,
The adorner and refresher of the world.

Charles Mackay *The Dionysia*

When the American settlers from the Eastern States reached California, they were confronted with a new problem in agriculture. The Spanish felt at home in semi-arid regions because these resembled southern Spain; irrigation was no mystery to them. The blue-eyed men who acquired California came originally from northern Europe, and their sojourn in the eastern part of North America had taught them nothing new in the form of cultivation. Both North Europe and the Atlantic States relied on the annual rainfall in the production of crops.

One of the first attempts made in the building of dams were those built across rivers to divert the flow of water and make it available for the panning of gold. The miners organized themselves into cooperative units for such purposes. At the end of that time most mining and water rights had been acquired by capitalists, who invested money in the building of dams and relieved the miners of that task. When the gold mining era drew to a close, many of these claims were available for the purpose of irrigation. One of them was located on the Tuolumne River, situated one mile above the town of La Grange. In 1854 it was bought by Milton A. Wheaton, a San Francisco lawyer, who intended to use it to provide irrigation. Unfavorable conditions in the state prevented any action being taken. Eventually, it was acquired by the Modesto and Turlock Irrigation District and became the site of the La Grange Dam.[1]

The bringing of water to a mining town in the early days was as big an event in the lives of the miners as the successful completion of an irrigation system was to the farmers of a later period. The following quotation may illustrate this elation:

> The hills on three sides of our town are now supplied with water, and a view of the panorama is most cheering. The flume embracing and changing into a source of wealth those seemingly barren hills, stretches around, from which hose and sluice extend down the hill, affording the means of extracting the golden treasures which lay there embedded. Each of these latter is attended with a number of workmen and the busy sound of labor echoes from hill to hill.[2]

The first irrigation canal reported in the valley was built by Edward Fitzgerald Beale on the Tejon ranch in 1851.[3] Two years later Lieutenant Williamson visited Beale and stated that 1,900 acres of wheat were under irrigation at that time. [4] The first irrigation canal in the middle part of the San Joaquin of any significance was built by Dr. Reuben Matthews in 1854. A dam was constructed across Upper Mill Creek and the canal extended to Visalia. The running water was utilized in turning a mill, as well as for irrigation purposes. Water rights were sold, and smaller lateral ditches carried the water to the settlers. This canal remained in use until 1870. Some of the original ditches still carry water as part of the works of a later system.[5]

In 1868 Moses J. Church arrived in the San Joaquin Valley with a band of sheep. On August 9 of that year, he began construction of the Centerville Ditch and incurred the enmity of the big cattleman in that region, William (Yank) Hazelton. He and his fellow cattlemen in the river bottoms naturally resented the intrusion of another type of settler, and the introduction of another form of industry.

On July 7, 1870, Moses Church recorded his intention of appropriating 3,000 feet of water from Kings River; this move resulted in the definite organization of the Fresno Canal & Irrigation Company, locally referred to as the Church Ditch. This system carried water to what is now the city of Fresno by way of Fancher Creek. A. Y. Easterby, who had encouraged Church to come to the valley, was waiting for that water. He had traveled extensively. From personal study and observation, he was well acquainted with the orchards and vineyards along the Mediterranean shore, the grain fields of the Nile Valley, and the rice lands of India. These all depended upon irrigation, and Easterby believed that a similar system would transform the arid wastes of the San Joaquin Valley.[6]

In 1871, the San Joaquin & Kings River Canal Company was organized by San Francisco capitalists. They invested money in its stock as a speculative venture. A dam was erected at the junction of the San Joaquin River with Fresno Slough. The intention was to irrigate the land between Firebaugh and Newman. This was the most pretentious canal construction venture since the building of the Erie Canal. The latter had been dug in the days when only picks, shovels, and wheel-barrows were available in the moving of earth. Since that time the slip, or scoop, scraper had been invented and teams could move the soil. But even this implement proved wholly inadequate in solving the problem of excavation, and leveling necessary to prepare the land for irrigation and leave a marginal profit for the investors.

The discouragement always attending ventures into new fields of endeavor proved too much for the speculative capitalists, and they sold their holdings in the company to Miller & Lux for one-third of the amount already invested in the project. This firm organized camps of Chinese, Mexicans, and Americans along the line of work from Mendota to Los Banos. About four hundred men were employed, and the canal was completed in 1878. The men almost broke their backs as they walked in a stooped position holding the short handles of the slip scraper. But their heroic toil made possible this great West Side canal, and in time, it became one of the chief sources of wealth in furnishing Miller & Lux with water for the arid plains. The firm began to grow wheat on a huge scale—not for sale, but for the fattening of their own livestock. They remained stockmen to the end of their regime.

The year 1875 was one of great activity among the irrigationists throughout the length and breadth of the great valley. The members of a farmer's grange on the West Side organized a public meeting that was held at Grayson on April 20 of that year. Its purpose was to agitate for the passing of an irrigation bill. Certain men, among them J. R. McDonald, were approved by this convention of farmers to formulate a measure and present it in due time to the lawmakers at Sacramento. As a result of their labors Governor Irwin signed a bill on April 3, 1875, which created the West Side Irrigation District.

The new law provided for a board of commissioners, who investigated the matter of irrigation in the region and reported the result of their findings to the legislature. The specifications finally presented for this cooperative system called for a headgate at Tulare Lake; a canal from there to Antioch, 190 miles away; and an outlet at Fuller's Point, a quarter-mile east of Antioch. This grand trunk canal would carry water to 503,717 acres, of which 490,917 were irrigable. It would bisect the San Joaquin & Kings River Canal owned by Miller & Lux.

After the commissioners had rendered their report, an election was held in the district. The result was an overwhelming vote in favor of building the canal. This required bonding the district for the construction cost. A permanent board of commissioners was also elected which included J. R. McDonald, usually referred to as the father of irrigation on the West Side. These commissioners were to direct the construction of the canal.

But now came the jolt. The judge of the Third Judicial District of California, S. B. McKee, promptly issued a writ against the entire proceedings. He contended that the organization of a public irrigation district was unconstitutional. Thus this premature attempt ended in failure. It was against his ruling in the matter that Samuel Moffett of Kingsburg directed his articles dealing with riparian rights and irrigation problems, which caught the attention of William Randolph Hearst and finally led to a change in the attitude of the lawmakers and the law itself. But that happy day lay in the future, ten years away.[7]

A decade elapsed. During those ten years much water had flowed under the bridge. Then came a similar attempt and success. This will be discussed in due time. Meanwhile, the various kinds of private irrigation companies continued to carry on this particular phase of developing the San Joaquin Valley.

South of Kings River, several irrigation companies were organized at an early date. Settlers moved into the Mussel Slough territory in the late sixties and the early seventies and occupied both government and railway land. The land south of the river opposite Kingsburg and down the river to Kingston was irrigated by three canal systems. Included in this territory were the present sites of Hanford, Grangeville, and the locality known as Mussel Slough. Additional canals and ditches were built, and the new system was officially dedicated on April 12, 1875, when Francis Rea opened the headgate for the first time, and in the presence of a large gathering permitted the thirsty soil to be refreshed by artificial means. Another irrigation system developed in the same region was the Last Chance Canal Company.[8]

Lyman Brown Ruggles, later a merchant at Traver, was a rancher between Traver and Hanford during the 1870s. He took a leading part in completing the Settlers' Ditch, which carried the water from Cross Creek to Mussel Slough. At the celebration held when the work was completed, a song written by Ruggles was lustily sung by the settlers:

> Oh, we've now got done our ditching,
> And now let's have some fun,
> We'll celebrate and jubilate
> O'er the labors we have done.
> The work was long and tiresome,
> But we pushed it right along,
> So we'll celebrate, then irrigate,
> And this shall be our song,

Then blow, ye winds, aye-ho,
Let fall the rain and snow.
Through old Cross Creek and the Settlers' Ditch
The water now may flow with melted snow and rain,
And we'll all get rich with the Settlers' Ditch
To grow the golden grain.

Then honor to the pioneers
Who first conceived the plan
To use the waters of Cross Creek to irrigate the land.
With Urton for the engineer, and the rest to lead the way,
They laid the grade where the ditch was made
For they saw that the thing would pay.[9]

In 1875, Haggin & Carr built a dam across the Kern River due north of Bakersfield. Their canal was called the Calloway Canal, although it was incorporated as the Kern River Land & Canal Company. The water was carried through it for thirty miles and watered an area of 13,000 acres. Miller & Lux invoked the aid of the courts and the riparian law in an attempt to prevent this irrigation project. If their attorney was veracious, according to the following summary, the holdings of the latter firm were seriously damaged by this diversion of Kern River water:

> In reference to the comparative interests at stake here, which perhaps is not a matter of any importance—but I simply call attention to the fact that the swamp land along Buena Vista Slough consists of 200,000 acres, and those 200,000 acres are worth about $40 an acre—with this affluent coming down in the early spring and making that a place for pasturing cattle, stock, and hogs. There is about $8 million dollars in that swamp land district of property, providing we have this annual flow of water coming down there, for the purpose of making that swamp what it has been for the last twenty years, a place of general value when the dry season comes, because it is the only large tract of land in that neighborhood where cattle can be pastured in a very dry season.[10]

This contest between the two greatest cattle firms in California attracted national attention. The civil code, based on the common law of England, forbade interference with the waters of a flowing stream. In the initial legal skirmish, Miller & Lux lost. Miller was in Germany on a visit when the decision was rendered. He returned in a rage, censured his partner for the defeat, and carried the fight to the Supreme Court of California. By a vote of four to three, this high tribunal decided in favor of the English common law and Miller & Lux.

When California adopted her first constitution, the common law of England served as the basis of her civil code. England, having no need of irrigation, provided for a riparian law, which meant that the waters of a flowing stream could not be diverted from its natural channel. When Haggin & Carr built a dam across Kern River, they thus violated the constitution of California. But the same constitution stated that all water "now appropriated, or that may hereafter be appropriated for sale, rental or distribution is hereby declared to be a public use subject to the regulation and control of the state in the manner to be prescribed by law." This presupposed the right of appropriation.

Furthermore, Section 1410 of the Civil Code, stated: "The right to the use of running water flowing in a river or stream, or down a canyon or ravine, may be acquired by appropriation." Here was sufficient material for endless litigation. The irrigation companies already in existence were placed in jeopardy by this court decision. Great excitement prevailed in 1886 over this case of *Lux vs. Haggin* (69 Cal. 255). An extra session of the legislature was called on July 20, 1886, but no definite action was taken. In time, the lawmakers repealed entirely that section of the Civil Code dealing with riparian rights, but protected those who already had vested interests by

Engraving of an artesian well and pipe system, as was used in the San Joaquin Valley around the turn of the century. *Fresno County Public Library, California History and Genealogy Room Collection.*

exempting them from the application of this new provision. Aside from this single act by the legislature, the irrigation law of California rests entirely upon court decisions. Miller & Lux, and all other ranchers who owned land along the rivers prior to the enactment of the repeal act, were secure in their rights to water under the old riparian law. That remains the law of California until the present time. On January 27, 1933, Superior Judge Haines entered a judgment granting Miller & Lux, Inc., an injunction against the storage or diversion of San Joaquin river waters by the Madera Irrigation District. Judge Haines ruled that Miller & Lux were entitled to the full and undisturbed customary flow of the San Joaquin River, its branches and channels, through its lands, all of which were declared to be riparian to the stream.

The State of California surveyed narrow strips along the river after all this legal squabbling and called them "lots."

623

These carried with them riparian rights. This was done to prevent huge estates along the rivers becoming dominant. Many landowners had filed applications for water rights to huge acreages facing these streams and many of these, recorded at an early date, are still in effect (such as that of Miller & Lux).

Miller, having won his fight, graciously compromised with Haggin & Carr, aided them in the building of dams and reservoirs in Kern County, and thereby secured protection against drought. The legislature, by its repeal of the civil code dealing with riparian rights, had taken a step that greatly influenced valley development. Riparian rights to the exclusion of appropriation rights were no longer to exist after this repeal, with the exception of those belonging to ranchers who had, prior to the passage of this repeal act, recorded their intentions of appropriating water. This did not affect Miller & Lux. Many other ranchers also enjoyed this special type of riparian rights. The Civil Code held that the first in time were the first in right as between riparian proprietors. The act of the legislature legalized the building of irrigation systems by private companies, providing these did not interfere with riparian rights already in existence. It was over these rights, guaranteed them by court decisions and legislative acts, which Sinon C. Lillis and John Sutherland fought with the settlers along Kings River during the early days of the irrigation era.[11]

John S. Urton, a civil engineer and a graduate of the University of Tennessee, had been one of the original settlers in Mussel Slough. He arrived there in 1874 and almost immediately was employed to make surveys for the various canals built south of Kings River. The area along the north bank of this river was next to receive his attention. In 1876 the Emigrants' Ditch was organized, and a headgate installed on land belonging to the cattle barons of the *Laguna de Tache* ranch. From this point it extended west to Wildflower and thence out over the plains.[12]

The success of this venture led to the organization of the Centerville & Kingsburg Irrigation & Ditch Company. John S. Urton was employed as surveyor and engineer. Two of the leading promoters in this work were Captain Bratton and Major Sides. The venture was begun with a great deal of enthusiasm and shares in the irrigation company were sold to the ranchers in the region who would be served by the proposed canal. The ranchers, after having bought shares in the company, were each assigned a certain distance to excavate and grade. The allotments were measured and grade stakes posted with a number designating each. These were drawn for by lots. One of the men employed on this ditch construction wrote the following:

> The company work could be done by any shareholder and his time was a sort of legal tender and passed as cash in the early days and if one could not go personally on the canal he could go to the storekeeper in Kingsburg and buy ditch time and turn it to his individual credit to the superintendent of the company. Such time had been accepted in the store for supplies and was honored as valuable as cash.[13]

The work was hard but the men sponsoring the attempt were persistent. Most of them were descendants of stock originally hailing from the British Isles; a few were Scandinavians and Germans. These closely related strains are not prone to surrender. The result of their labor was made apparent in 1879 when water ran in the ditches from Centerville to Kingsburg, a distance of thirty-five miles as the valley quail flies. Concerning this pioneer venture on a big scale, an early historian wrote as follows: "Twenty-four men, some of whom could not get credit for a plough, banded together to take water to Kingsburg and vicinity, a distance of twenty miles. The estimated cost of the work was $40,000."[14] Among the leaders in this project were John S. Urton, whose name has already been mentioned in connection with the Peoples' Ditch emanating from Cross Creek; W. J. Berry, whose son later became an Alaskan gold miner and the owner of the Los Angeles Coast League baseball team; Charles and John Traber; Lemuel Harp; John B. Fowler; George B. Otis, who later wrote *Reminiscences of Early Days*; and W.T. and T.R. Garner.[15]

At the beginning of this ditch construction, the old type of slip scraper was used. In the rocky and stony ground of eastern states it was the only implement workable. But its difficulty of operation, and the vast amount of clear soil to be moved in canal work, caused men to ponder on other ways and means. Necessity is the mother of invention. Eventually a new scraper was perfected, which was built in sizes for either one or two spans of horses. One of the men active in the Centerville & Kingsburg Irrigation & Ditch Company wrote this about the new scraper:

> It was invented in Selma, in the shop of Mr. Diedrick, situated where the Selma Brick Stables are now. The perfection of it was worked out on the canal and irrigation works here and has since been so fully recognized as the "best scraper" that it is now used all over the world and the Fresno scrapers are to be seen in every railroad and grading camp.[16]

In those days, the minds of inventive men actually and literally ran in the same ditch. The same year the Herndon Ditch, in the region north of Fresno, was under construction. Henry Hawn, Clovis Cole, and Stockton Berry secured contracts for the scraping and leveling to be done. Each of them used a hundred teams. At the beginning of ditch construction, the old-type railroad slip scraper was used. In the rocky ground of eastern states, it was the only implement workable. But its difficulty of operation, and the vast amount of clear soil to be moved in canal work, proved inefficient as it always did in this type of work. At first the ground was plowed deeply and Hawn then devised a buck scraper of wood, formed like a heavy drag, with runners at each end. Where the soil was moved downgrade, this contrivance made it possible to move a yard of earth on each trip. This was three times as rapid, and a hundred times as easy, as a similar amount of work with a scoop scraper.

At this time there entered the field of invention a man named Abijah McCall, who had come to California via Panama in 1856. He invented the cross-reaches used on the early buckboards, the same as are now used on vineyard trucks. Then he and his son, William, on their own initiative entirely, began to work on a sheet-iron scraper. After experimenting with various sizes, they decided that a five-foot width was suitable for a four-horse team. This remained the regulation size, as long as horses were used. In order to secure the $150 necessary to get a patent, a half-interest was given Frank Dusy. In perusing an old copy of that patent one reads: "Frank Dusy and Abijah McCall have invented an Improvement in a Dirt-Scraper; and we hereby declare the following to be a full, clear, and exact description of what is known as the Fresno Scraper." This dirt-scraper was listed as Patent No. 320,055, was witnessed by William Faymonville and J. W. Coffman, and dated June 16, 1885. Abijah McCall received royalties on his scraper until his death in 1886.

James Porteous, a blacksmith in the new railroad town of Fresno, saw it. Hawn released his rights to the invention to Porteous and received in payment ten new sheet iron scrapers and a discount of $10 on the next forty to be purchased. These were identical with the modern Fresno scraper. Shortly thereafter, Frank Dusy sold his half-interest to Porteous for $5,000, and the two sons of McCall subsequently disposed of their interest to Porteous for $1,000; $500 in cash, and $500 worth of farm machinery. Porteous added wheels to the scraper; however, these prevented tipping the load while in action and were soon discarded. Then Porteous built a second scraper minus wheels, and used heavy sheet metal instead of wood in its construction. Diedrich, a Selma blacksmith who had helped in making the first McCall scraper, made one of similar design, and secured a caveat on it, but it did not prove successful and was never manufactured commercially. To protect his own interests, Porteous bought out Diedrich and secured a patent.

Felix Moore, a Hanford blacksmith, and Stockton Berry, who had cooperated with Hawn in the building of the first "buck-scraper," continued to build wooden scrapers for the next decade. But it was James Porteous and his Fresno scraper, modeled on the McCall invention that was to win fame and fortune. Porteous began to manufacture Fresno scrapers on a big scale. They formed the principal element in his subsequent success and, in time, his plant developed into the Fresno Agricultural Works. These Fresno scrapers found their way into all parts of the world. The French have used them in railroad construction work in Syria, the British in South Africa and India, and the Japanese and Russians in the Far East. The Fresno scraper, often simply referred to as "a fresno," was destined to become the proud parent of the modern bulldozer of World War II fame.[17]

The coming of water brought new settlers and a different type of agriculture. But no pioneer movement is as pleasant and smooth in reality as when seen in retrospect. When the settlers mixed water with their soil and proceeded to become husbandmen, it might be taken for granted that, "The wilderness, and the solitary place shall

Branch irrigation canal located near Fresno, circa 1895. *The Interior (Fresno).*

be glad for them; and the desert shall rejoice, and blossom as the rose." (Isaiah 35:1.) But often war and strife entered into this peaceful domain.

One of the directors in a certain irrigation company was Samuel E. Moffett, a nephew of Samuel Clemens (Mark Twain) and a resident of Kingsburg; the superintendent of the same company was William H. Shafer of Selma. These two men, when their dam was placed in jeopardy by another dam, drove to Sweet's store in Visalia, purchased dynamite which they placed in their buckboard, drove along the foothills to the rival company's dam, sent the watchman scuttling into the brush, planted a charge of dynamite which sent the water of Kings River higher than the hot spray of Old Faithful geyser at Yellowstone, and then went home. In those pioneer days men were never guilty of innocuous desuetude and adhered to the Spanish adage well known in the San Joaquin Valley long before it was popularized by Theodore Roosevelt: "Walk softly but carry a big stick"—of dynamite. But after the fighting comes the armistice; after the war, the peace. These two companies, together with several other small irrigation companies, eventually consolidated to form the great Consolidated Irrigation District, with an irrigable area of 149,047 acres and a population of 24,000 in 1930. The district had 300 miles of canals in 1933 and within its territory lay the towns of Fowler, Selma, Kingsburg, Del Rey, Sanger, Parlier, Caruthers, Monmouth, Bowles, and Conejo.[18] The superintendent of the company in 1933 was the same William H. Shafer who held a similar position with one of its component irrigation systems in 1883. His statesmanlike comment concerning changing conditions and developments in the San Joaquin is worth quoting:

> The blowing out of a dam on Kings River was a necessary (under the circumstances) act of war. War is not glorious, however dramatic it may be. We have a League of Nations; or rather, a League of Interests, on Kings River composed of the same interests that fought that war. We are trying to get all parties to live up to their part of the contract. I am probably the only survivor living here of that fight of 1883. The memory had better die.[19]

In 1902 the Centerville and Kingsburg canal system, the Fowler Switch Canal, the Emigrant Ditch, and ten lesser irrigation companies were consolidated; hence the name for the Consolidated Canal Company. In 1921 the district was formally organized and subsequently farmers in the area, who now own the district's property in fee, approved a bond issue to purchase the district's canals, which were owned by a syndicate of British insurance companies.[20]

Samuel Moffett realized that blowing up dams would not permanently solve the vexatious problem of riparian rights and its resultant corollaries. Accompanied by his mother, a sister of Mark Twain, Moffett had sought to improve his health by a residence under a kindly, southern sky. Both mother and son were a welcome addition to the social life of the little frontier village of Kingsburg. In those movie-less, radio-less days, people furnished one another entertainment and instruction by debating current topics and live issues. Two men were particularly skilled in debate. One was Samuel Moffett, a Harvard graduate and a brilliant student; the other was John Forney, whose cogent reasoning and remarkable faculty of speech, made the debating team of Moffett and Forney invincible. Moffett, a director in the Centerville and Kingsburg Irrigation Company, was naturally interested in riparian rights. Forney, a recent arrival from the old plantation home in North Carolina, wished to understand the problems of his new home in the West. Other excellent debaters of the period were Lemuel Harp, later undersheriff of Fresno County; W. F. Allender, a blacksmith; and A. A. Smith, the postmaster.[21]

The result of their studies and debates transcended the bounds of their own lives. Eventually Moffett was led to write a series of newspaper and magazine articles advocating the rights of the irrigationists, on the assumption that the justice of any issue must be determined on the basis of what constitutes "the greatest good for the greatest number in the long run." Articles by Judge McKee and Justice McKinstry were answered by Moffett. His reply was so convincing in argument and unanswerable in logic that William Randolph Hearst, then beginning at San Francisco his amazing career as a newspaper publisher, telegraphed to A. A. Smith, then postmaster at Kingsburg: "Who is this man Moffett?" Smith told him. The result was that Moffett sold his ranch at Kingsburg to Frank D. Rosendahl, became a feature writer on the San Francisco *Examiner*, and when Hearst acquired the New York *Journal*, Moffett was transferred to that metropolis.[22] John Forney, who was his comrade during his residence in Kingsburg, stated: "Sam E. Moffett was a Harvard graduate and wrote for *Harper's Magazine* during the years 1882 and 1884. He is known today for his articles on the tariff, which are standard reference books in the Library of Congress to this day."[23]

The irrigation companies thus far discussed were owned by stockholders, and controlled by boards of directors. In time the arguments of Samuel Moffett and others bore fruit, and men began to agitate effectively for a modification of the California law which would permit the organization of publicly owned and controlled irrigation districts by The People.

In 1886 C. C. Wright, a Modesto lawyer, was elected to the legislature. He introduced a bill that was enacted into law on March 7, 1887; this Wright Act was perhaps the greatest single step ever taken in the development of the San Joaquin Valley. Provision was made for the bonding of organized districts. Henceforth, the taxpayers were to own their own irrigation projects; democracy was asserting itself, and irrigation corporations were to be replaced by The People. Distinctive features of the new system which was thus inaugurated were:

> The districts are public corporations managed and controlled by officers elected by the voters; and the works are constructed with money raised by the sale of bonds that are paid by the taxation of the land in proportion to the tax paid. Under this plan the irrigation of the soil becomes a public service, and there is a joint ownership of the water and the land. This plan for distribution of the water has been more or less modified as the result of experience.[24]

When Assemblyman Wright returned to Modesto after his maiden term at Sacramento, he was greeted with an ovation commensurate with the service he had rendered to the public weal.

An immediate result of the Wright Act was the organization of the Modesto & Turlock Irrigation District. The discouragements in the forming of this first public district were many, but Turlock finally got its water in 1900; Modesto was equally fortunate in 1903. The lapse of time between 1887, when the law was enacted and 1900 is accounted for by a series of lawsuits instigated against the new venture. While the case of *Tregea vs. The Modesto Irrigation District* was pending, the United States Supreme Court upheld the constitutionality of the Wright Act in *Bradley vs. The Fallbrook Irrigation District* (164 U. S. 112), in Southern California. The former case was then dismissed.

James A. Waymire, a former superior judge of Alameda County, was the chief leader in the successful completion of the Turlock Irrigation District. Worn out by his labors, he died a martyr to the cause of irrigation. Two men who were indefatigable workers for the welfare of their community in carrying on the work of the Modesto Irrigation District were James H. Maddrill, editor of the *Modesto News*, and T. C. Hocking, editor of the *Modesto Herald*.

The joint Turlock and Modesto districts drew water from the Tuolumne River. When the new La Grange Dam, 126 1/2 feet high, had been completed and water flowed in the canals on the south side of the river to Turlock, and on the north side of the river to Modesto, a great Jubilee Celebration was held. The days of April 21 and 22, 1904 were momentous to that region. Thirty railway coaches arrived with celebrities and friends of the community. A tour of the two districts was made, and at the great open air meeting in the Modesto park, a roster of distinguished men delivered prophetic and congratulatory addresses. They included George C. Pardee, governor of California; Benjamin Ide Wheeler, president of the University of

Irrigation check drop on a Fresno County canal, circa 1895. *The Interior (Fresno)*.

California; Henry Morse Stephens, chairman of the history department at the same institution; Professor Elwood Mead, representing the United States Department of Agriculture; and last, but not least in the eyes of his fellow-citizens, a young lawyer named C. C. Wright, who was largely responsible for it all.[25]

The organization of irrigation systems in California during the twentieth century has followed four distinct lines. The most important type is the irrigation district made possible by the Wright Act of 1887. Its first representative was the Turlock Irrigation District, which began to function in 1900. Under state law such an irrigation district is a public corporation, empowered to issue bonds, to levy and collect taxes, and to maintain and operate its works. The Wright Act provided for a board of directors to be elected from among the residents of the districts, in a manner similar to the election of school boards. Sparsely settled communities and lack of experience caused irrigation bonds to clog the market. In 1911 the legislature provided for a commission consisting of the attorney general, the superintendent of banks, and the state engineer, whose duty it would be to pass on the feasibility of the proposed districts. If a favorable verdict was rendered, the bonds were registered at the office of the state comptroller and were then considered legal investments for insurance companies, banks, or trust funds, and thereby given the same consideration as school, city, or county bonds.[26]

Edward Hyatt, State Engineer of California, made the following report on the result of the Wright Act:

> Since the passage of the Wright Act in 1887 there have been organized in California 166 irrigation districts, embracing within their boundaries approximately 6,104,000 acres, or an area of about 27 percent of the total agricultural lands of the State. Through proper legal procedure 49 of these districts, containing 2,104,000 acres, have been dissolved, and of the remaining 117, two are in the process of dissolution. Of the 117 districts now existing, 22 may be said to be inactive, in that they have not built irrigation works and no water is furnished to the included lands through the district organizations. Of the 49 districts dissolved, 33 voted bonds in the total amount of $13,839,000. Approximately $6 million of the bonds voted were never issued, and prior to dissolution settlements were effected which retired all outstanding bonds of the dissolved districts. Of the 117 districts now existing, 84 have voted bonds in the total amount of $156,304,558— $4,830,511 of which was refunding bonds. On January 1, 1931, the total of all irrigation districts bond issues outstanding was $96,503,091.[27]

Cooperative irrigation enterprises are operated and maintained by and for the water users themselves. These enterprises are organized as stock companies and the water users own the stock, which is always appurtenant to the land and conveyed with the land only.

Closely related to the two foregoing are the individual and partnership enterprises. An individual farmer, or a group

635

of farmers, build ditches and canals for the irrigation of their respective fields. The only essential difference between this and the cooperative enterprise is the lack of formal organization. The irrigation systems built by Miller & Lux, by Tevis, Carr & Haggin, and other individuals or groups, were typical of this form of enterprise.

Irrigation in its initial development in the San Joaquin chiefly took the form of commercial enterprises. Water was supplied for compensation by capitalists, who invested money in the building of ditches and canals. Water users held no stock in the works, but paid for water rights to their land and an additional annual charge for the water. Three distinct kinds of commercial enterprises developed: First, payment on a quantitative basis with a specific charge for second-feet or acre-feet. Second, the sale of water rights plus an annual fee for services rendered during the year in the delivery of water. Companies which at one time came under this classification were the Fresno Canal & Irrigation Company, the Consolidated, and the Crocker-Huffman Land & Water Company. The legality of the water right was tested in court, and it was held that such companies were public corporations entitled to charge annual rates only. As a result of this litigation, the legislature on April 30, 1913 passed a law that all such enterprises were public utilities under the jurisdiction of the Railroad Commission. The only exception to this new law was the mutual companies that delivered water to stockholders at cost. Third, a group of irrigation enterprises developed which had as their primary purpose the sale of their land holdings. The purchaser of land secured a share in the water system provided by the company as an inducement for the colonization of its tract. Such colonization projects are typified by the 76 Land & Water Company, with its 30,000 acres surrounding the town of Traver, and the Patterson Land Company with 19,000 acres in Stanislaus County.[28]

Cobble and brush irrigation dam, Fresno County, circa 1899. Elwood
Mead, *Report of Irrigation Investigations in California.*

The California Civil Code of 1873, stated that the first in
time was the first in right as between two riparian
owners. After the *Lux vs. Haggin* decision of the Supreme
Court in 1886, the Civil Code, Section 1410, was amended
to read: "The right to the use of running water flowing in
a river or stream, or down a canyon or ravine, may be
acquired by appropriation." This was a direct challenge to
the doctrine of the Supreme Court. Riparian rights were
judge-made; appropriation rights were legislature-made.
Irrigation law in California proceeded to march in double-
time in both directions at the same time. No wonder that
dams were built and blown up, that irrigationists and
cattlemen fought and won and lost all at the same time,
and that even the lawyers became dizzy. After the
completion of the Centerville & Kingsburg Irrigation &
Ditch Company's system, the directors were sued by John
Heinlen, a cattleman with land riparian to Kings River
west of Lemoore, and these directors were forced to pay a
fine of $100 each. Sinon C. Lillis also brought injunctions

637

against them. After repeated trips of this nature to the court at Visalia, the directors chose jail sentences in lieu of fines. Their decision in this respect ended annoyances of a legal nature. The foreman of one of the large cattle ranches rode to the headgate of the Emigrant Ditch and ordered his cowboy to burn the dam and the house of the watchman. When the latter refused through fear, the foreman ordered him to ride down the road until he was out of sight. In a few moments the house and dam were burning merrily and the irrigationists were put to the expense of their replacement.[29]

The "compromise judgment of 1897" served as the basis of settlement in most water disputes on Kings River during subsequent years. In time, constant litigation over water rights led the opposing interests to appoint a water master. Included in these various private systems and public districts were 940,000 acres. The following is the membership of the Kings River Water Association: Alta Irrigation District, Cuthbert Burrel Company, Consolidated Irrigation District, Corcoran Irrigation District, Crescent Canal Company, Fresno Irrigation District, James Irrigation District, Laguna Irrigation District, Lemoore Canal & Irrigation Company, Last Chance Water Ditch Company, Riverdale Irrigation District, Liberty Mill Race Ditch Company, Reed Ditch Company, Liberty Canal Company, Peoples Ditch Company, Stinson Canal & Irrigation Company, Tranquillity Irrigation District, John Heinlen Company, and Foothill Irrigation District. All agreed to abide by the decisions of the water master, and assessed themselves to pay his salary. These groups, organized into the Kings River Water Association, adopted the following resolution:

> That the Water Master to be employed by the Board of Directors of said Association for the purposes provided in this Agreement shall be a competent hydraulic engineer nominated

by the Chief of the Division of Water Rights of the Department of Public Works of the State of California and appointed by the Board of Directors of said Association; but no such person shall become such Water Master until his selection shall have been approved by at least two-thirds of the whole Board of Directors of said Association, such approval to be made at a regular meeting of said Board or at a special meeting thereof called for the purpose; and said Water Master shall keep at all times and during all seasons correct and accurate records of the flows of the waters of said River and of the amount or quantity of water turned to each and all of the parties hereto, and, as far as practicable, accurate records of all waters diverted from the said River by persons, districts and corporations not parties hereto, and make accurate reports of all such matters to said Board of Directors.[30]

The first man selected to fill this responsible position was Charles L. Kaupke. He assumed office on January 1, 1918, and was still serving as chief arbiter on January 1, 1939. The most technical and important duties of the water master are to regulate the diversion of water at the various headgates, and make a fair apportionment when the stream drops to less than 2,000 acre-feet per second.[31]

According to the report of the State Engineer for 1930, Kings River furnished more water for irrigation purposes than any other river in the world with two big exceptions. The Indus River in India irrigates about 2,500,000 acres; the Nile, somewhat more; and Kings River has within its irrigation districts 1,791,880 acres, of which 1,100,000 have actually been irrigated. Fourteen irrigation districts draw water wholly or in part from this stream. The following data pertaining to the irrigation districts of the San Joaquin Valley are based on statistics as of 1930.

The Alta Irrigation District, with offices at Dinuba, is the successor by right of purchase, to the old 76 Land & Water Company's water system. Its territory comprises an area of 129,300 acres lying within the counties of Fresno,

Tulare, and Kings. Its total population, including the cities of Reedley and Dinuba, was 13,500 in 1930.[32]

The Consolidated Irrigation District is a combination of several old time irrigation companies. Within its system were consolidated (hence the name) the Fowler Switch canal, the Emigrant Ditch, the Lone Tree Channel, and the Centerville & Kingsburg Irrigation & Ditch Company. It was against the latter that Sinon C. Lillis and other cattle barons of the *Laguna de Tache* brought suit in early days. The settlers had refused to co-operate with Lillis and he usually won his many court battles directed against them as the following statement by C. E. Grunsky would indicate:

> On September 12, 1885, judgment was entered against the Centerville & Kingsburg Canal Company, decreeing that its canal take no water, remove all dams and other obstructions from Kings River, and fill in the head of its canal.[33]

Two men who rendered great service to this irrigation system were William H. Shafer and William Martin. Each spent many years as an official of the company. In forming this district $1,175,875 was spent in purchasing water rights, canals, and other property. The farmers of the area, who own the district's property in fee, approved the bond issue for this amount in 1922, and the last installment was paid on January 3, 1933.[34]

Two irrigation districts have their headquarters at Corcoran. Both lie solely within Kings County. The Corcoran Irrigation District contains 51,616 acres, with 1,500 residents. Its water is secured through the Peoples' Ditch supplemented by wells. The Lakeland District, organized in 1923, consists of 23,285 acres owned by ten ranchers.[35]

At Laton are located the offices of two districts. Island No. 3 District consists of 4,620 acres, with 320 inhabitants;

and Laguna, 34,858 acres and 3,000 residents. The towns of Laton, Hardwick, and Helm indicate the general location of these districts. The land they irrigate lies in Fresno and Kings Counties.[36]

The Lemoore District serves 1,500 persons with irrigation water, and the Lucerne, with offices at Hanford, renders a similar service for 1,900.[37]

In the Riverdale District 1,000 persons occupy 11,150 acres. A man named Sanborn Young, a state senator, acquired a ranch in the Riverdale community. His wife, under the pen name of Ruth Comfort Mitchell, gave a tinge of romance to the coming of water, by writing a novel entitled *Water*, which had its setting in the Riverdale country.[38]

The Foothill District, with headquarters at Orange Cove, consists of 85,875 acres lying in Fresno and Tulare counties, occupied by 1,200 residents. This was organized in 1921 and included within its boundaries Orange Cove, East Orosi, Citrus Cove, Navelencia, Tivy Valley, and extended as far south as Stone Corral, being twenty-five miles long and six miles wide. It was planned to provide water for the lands lying between the mountains and the Alta Irrigation District and was allotted 30,000 acre-feet per annum under the proposed Pine Flat Water Storage project. When it became apparent that this enterprise was being held in abeyance, the district officials and engineers began to look for water that would be available at an earlier date. After considering several sources, negotiations were concluded with certain companies on the West Side of Kings River some fifty miles downstream from Orange Cove, known as the Murphy Slough Association, which had legally established rights to water.

In 1928 and 1929, a deal was consummated with the association whereby the Foothill District would drill certain wells on about 10,000 acres of land it held under option near where the Murphy Slough Association took its water from the river. The district would pump water into the canal of the association in exchange for water owned by it in the river, which river water would in turn be taken out of the river some 25 miles farther upstream, and adjacent to the upper end of the Foothill District.

Irrigation districts near the site of the proposed "well field" brought an injunction suit against the Foothill District. It was argued that the pumping of underground water would draw from the supply in the river, and that removal of the diversion which transferred the Murphy Slough Association's entitlement would disrupt the various schedules and water rights in the Kings River area.

The result was much litigation and, although the Foothill District emerged victorious in each trial, the market value of its bonds was impaired. This led to discouragement on the part of the farmers, and in 1933 the Orange Cove Chamber of Commerce voted to support a movement to dissolve the Foothill Irrigation District. This was done.[39]

The James Irrigation District, drawing water from both the Kings and the San Joaquin rivers and supplementing these sources by eighty-one wells, had a population of 175 in an area of 26,266 acres. Its headquarters are in the town of San Joaquin.[40]

Offices for two districts are maintained at Fresno. The Stinson has an area of 11,150 acres with 200 residents. The Fresno Irrigation District, successor to the Fresno Canal & Irrigation Company (Church Ditch), was organized on June 26, 1920, largely through the efforts of S. Parker Frisselle, John Fairweather, J. C. Forkner, and Wylie Giffen. Included within its exterior boundaries of 243,100 acres are the cities of Fresno and Clovis, and the towns of Kerman, Herndon, Rolinda, Biola, and Malaga.

Fresno Canal and Irrigation Company dam, circa 1895. *The Interior (Fresno).*

This district has over 600 miles of canals and ditches. In 1930, its population was over 50,000.[41]

Aside from these irrigation systems, the Kings River supplies water for the Tulare Lake Basin Water Storage Company. This reservoir is used as a storage place for water utilized by twenty-five large grain growers. The office of this company is at Hanford.[42]

Nine irrigation districts draw their water from the San Joaquin River. Of these, four are located in the vicinity of Tracy and have their office headquarters in that city. The Banta-Carbona consists of 15,624 acres, with 750 residents. The Naglee-Burk, with no record of its population in 1930, consists of 2,871 acres. The Tracy-Clover contains a population of 140 and an acreage of 1,084. In the West Side Irrigation District are 1,340 residents and 11,828 acres. All of these districts lie solely within San Joaquin County.[43]

Brentwood is the headquarters for the East Contra Costa Irrigation District. Its 20,000 acres contained 1,200 inhabitants in 1930. The Linden District, lying within San Joaquin County, has its offices in Stockton. Linden

consists of 13,700 acres, with 450 landowners. The West
Stanislaus District comprises 22,137 acres in Stanislaus
and Merced counties. The Tranquillity Irrigation District
lies in Fresno County, had 450 residents in 1930, and
10,750 acres. At Byron are located the offices of the
Byron-Bethany Irrigation District. Its acreage is 17,200,
its population 1,500. It furnishes water to land in the
counties of Contra Costa, San Joaquin, and Alameda.[44]

The Stanislaus River furnishes water for two districts.
The Oakdale Irrigation District has a population of 6,500
and an area of 74,240 acres. The land served by it lies in
Stanislaus and San Joaquin counties; its offices are at
Oakdale. The South San Joaquin District, lying in San
Joaquin County, comprises 71,112 acres, with a population
of 8,000. The city of Manteca contains the office of the
company, and the towns of Ripon and Escalon are also
within its borders.[45]

Both the Turlock and the Modesto Irrigation Districts
draw water from the Tuolumne River. These two districts,
the first in the state to be organized under the Wright Act,
have been discussed elsewhere. The Modesto District
consists of 81,203 acres in Stanislaus County, with a
population of 23,000; the Turlock, of 181,556 acres in
Stanislaus and Merced counties, with a population of
20,000. The Waterford Irrigation District, with offices at
Waterford, consists of 14,110 acres in Stanislaus County,
and has a population of 900.[46]

Five irrigation districts relied on wells for water,
according to the official report made in 1930. The Alpaugh
District, with offices at Tulare, consists of 8,133 acres in
Tulare County. Its population was 150. The El Nido
District, lying in San Joaquin County, had a population of
300, an acreage of 9,330, and its offices at Stockton. The
Madera Irrigation District, with 352,000 acres in the
county of the same name, was the largest in the state.

Within its boundaries lay the cities of Madera and Chowchilla; its 1,750 private pumping plants pulled wells, which furnished the water for the district. The Madera District was engaged for years in litigation with Miller & Lux and others, relative to water rights on the San Joaquin River. On January 27, 1933, Superior Judge Haines of Madera granted Miller & Lux, Inc., an injunction against the storage of water or its diversion in any form by the Madera Irrigation District. Other cases were at that time still pending.[47]

The Terra Bella Irrigation District has its offices at the city of the same name. Its water is drawn from forty-seven wells, most of them located along Deer Creek. The average depth to water in this district in 1933 was 400 feet. The water supply was adequate for 3,000 acres out of the 12,285 in the district. Its population was 650. No ditches are used to convey the water; instead, a network of eighty-one miles of pipelines is used. In Tulare County another district, known as the Tulare Irrigation District, consists of 34,000 acres with a population of 8,400.[48]

The Wachumne River supplies the water for the Lindsay-Strathmore Irrigation District of 15,246 acres lying in Tulare County. Offices are in Lindsay; the population was 4,500.[49]

The Woodbridge Irrigation District draws its water from the Mokelumne River. It comprises 14,164 acres in San Joaquin County, with a population of 200. Offices are located at Woodbridge, and the cities of Stockton, Lodi, and Thornton are adjacent to the district. The people of this district purchased the old Stockton & Mokelumne Canal Company's system. The first appropriation of water was made by Byron D. Beckwith in 1886, and the Woodbridge Canal and Irrigation Company was organized in April, 1889. The present district was organized in 1924 and reorganized in 1926.[50]

The Buena Vista Storage Company draws its water supply from the Kern River. Its acreage is 78,596 and its population 400. Offices are maintained at Buttonwillow.[51]

The Vandalia Irrigation District, with offices at Porterville, relies on the Tule River and wells for its water supply. Its area is 1,276 acres, occupied by 150 persons. The district purchased the rights of the Vandalia Ditch, which was the basis for its water rights. Prior to the beginning of any construction work, an agreement was made with the Tule River Water Users Association setting forth the rights of the Irrigation District in regard to its operation. Prior to that time, fifty protests had been filed against the organization of the company and its proposed program; after this settlement, no further trouble or interference was brought to light. Eleven wells set in the bottoms of Tule River provide water.[52]

The Merced River furnishes water for the Merced Irrigation District. The rights of the old Robla Canal and the Crocker-Huffman Land & Water Company furnished the basis for this system. Its population was 13,000 and its gross area 190,025 acres.[53]

The largest district in gross area was the Madera with 352,000 acres; the smallest, the Tracy-Clover, with 1,084. Fresno Irrigation District ranked first in population, with 50,000; Lakeland was inhabited by only ten ranchers.[54]

The total approximate area under irrigation in 1930 of the 6.6 million acres of the San Joaquin Valley floor was 1.8 million acres. Most of the irrigation districts reported at that time a lack of sufficient water and a rapidly receding water plane. In the days before irrigation, the depth to water varied in direct ratio with the proximity to rivers. At Kingsburg, it was sixty feet to water in 1930; at Selma, somewhat farther from Kings River, it was seventy feet. At points more distant than these from flowing streams, it

Headgate on the Crocker-Huffman Canal, Merced County, circa 1895. *The Interior (Fresno).*

was often 150 feet to the underground water. A pioneer rancher stated that on his ranch, located within two miles of Kings River, the depth to water was between 32 and 35 feet before the coming of irrigation. Fifty years later, or in 1933, it was 37 feet. This would lead the superficial observer to conclude that irrigation had had no effect on the level of underground water. But in such a conclusion he would be in error. Immediately after the introduction of irrigation, the water level rose to 13 feet on the place under consideration. The dry sand hollows located in various parts of Fresno County became partially filled with water, became sloughs, produced a rank growth of tules, and furnished natural duck preserves for sportsmen. In time these stagnant pools, often acres in extent, became a menace to public health and a detriment to agriculture. Public dredging districts were organized to rid them of their superfluous water.[55]

These sloughs furnished irrefutable evidence, for the

irrigation companies against landowners who attempted
to avoid the payment of water taxes, that irrigation had
raised the water level and made horticulture possible. In
subsequent years, the almost universal use of pumping
plants to lift the underground water to the surface
resulted in a rapid lowering of the water table until in
1933, it was almost identical with the figures available for
the pre-irrigation era. The rapid receding of the water
level was most pronounced on land far from rivers. Land
riparian to the streams has naturally maintained a water
table equal to the riverbed, due to seepage and percolating
water. This has been especially true of land located on the
side of the river toward the watershed.

Just who was the first man to employ a pumping plant for
the purposes of irrigation is somewhat debatable. Pumps
for lifting water were apparently built in the early
eighties. The sales manager for Worthington Pump and
Machinery Corporation reported that "John Richards and
the Krogh Bros., whose ranch and shop I believe was at
Woodland, built pumps as early as 1882 for irrigation. In
fact they patented and built the first *2 stage* single case
pump in 1882. This pump I bought for Worthington in
1898 for use in a patent suit." This same man further
stated:

> With reference to the use of centrifugal pumps prior to 1894,
> would state that in August, 1895, I went to Lindsay which, at
> that time, was a settlement only and saw and reported to Mr.
> Sehwashausser about several centrifugal pumping plants in
> that territory, used for irrigating in that territory. The water
> table in that territory had fallen on account of several dry
> years, and the ranchers who were just beginning to grow
> oranges, to save their trees, were obliged to get water "which
> previously had flowed" for their young trees. The water level
> had dropped about 30 ft. and several (about 20 plants) had
> been installed using horizontal shaft belted single stage (the
> multiple stage had not at that time been used). The pump

was placed in a pit and the engine and boiler on the surface with a long belt to the pump.[56]

Mr. W. W. McLaughlin, Chief of the Division of Irrigation, United States Department of Agriculture, stated: "Your inquiry was referred to Mr. C. E. Grunsky, who probably is better qualified to answer it than any other man known to us, and a very informative letter was received from him. However, he was not able to answer your question directly." In this letter Grunsky, at one time a city engineer of San Francisco, said:

> In 1893 I visited Captain Hutchinson, who some five or more years before had placed a steam-driven pump in a pit about 30 feet deep and was drawing water from a single well in the bottom of this pit for the irrigation of about 160 acres of orange grove. He was a pioneer at Lindsay, about 10 miles northwest of Porterville.

I have no specific reference to the first well drawn upon by a pump actuated by a gasoline-driven engine, steam, or electricity located in the San Joaquin Valley, with irrigation as its prime purpose.[57]

The Hutchinson referred to was the man who founded and named the city of Lindsay. He used the plunger type of pump, with the bailer set upon the surface and the pump in the pit. Both of the authorities just quoted agree that the first attempts at irrigation from underground water was tried in the Lindsay country.

A man named Epinger, residing near Visalia in the vicinity of Mooney Grove, experimented with a steam driven pumping plant. While he was trying to pump the well free from sand the topsoil caved in and the steam engine was buried in the huge excavation that had been formed.[58]

In the eighties William De La Grange, a veteran of the Union Army, settled on the plains west of Selma. He had been an oil driller in Pennsylvania, and utilized this experience in drilling water wells for settlers on the arid plains. Tools were made to order by Diedrich, the Selma blacksmith who had contributed his share to the invention of the Fresno scraper. De La Grange drilled a well on his ranch and struck water at 130 feet. An 8-foot bailer, 4 inches in diameter and with a leather valve at the bottom, was dropped down the casing to water, and pulled to the surface with a rope and pulley. An old horse furnished the motive power. In regions where the underground water was nearer the surface, the old-fashioned plunger pump and a perforated casing were used to provide water for domestic purposes. These perforations in the casing were made in those days with a cold chisel or a hatchet. These crudely made apertures, since the galvanizing was destroyed, rusted quickly. The casings had to be replaced and the well often re-drilled.

Eventually De La Grange bought a ranch at the corner of Bethel and Manning, four miles northeast of Selma. His land lay within the confines of the irrigation system then known as the Centerville & Kingsburg Irrigation Ditch Company. But when De La Grange tried to irrigate his land in the daytime, he found that his neighbors farther up the ditch utilized most of the water. At night they retired to a well-earned repose, and the water flowed unchecked and uncontrolled down the ditches to flood and damage the De La Grange improvements. The latter then determined to provide an irrigation system for himself. The result was the development of the first pumping plant seen in that part of the state. Undoubtedly, it was one of the very first ever used anywhere for the purpose of irrigation.

A 10-inch well was drilled to a depth of 60 feet. At this point a hard clay landing was located. An additional 20 feet of drilling perforated this stratum. A 60-foot casing was inserted into the hole and left standing on the hard foundation. Under this clay landing was found a mixture of sand and water. This was pumped out until a natural reservoir was created under the clay superstructure. Into this the clear underground water quickly collected. The cost of drilling this open-bottom well, the first of its kind on record, was $22. This well was able to furnish a continuous flow of water for irrigation purposes. A steam engine, which had been used by a son of De La Grange in the mountains for sawing box shook and tray material, was attached to the 3-inch centrifugal suction pump. A steady and continuous flow of water at the rate of 350 gallons a minute was thus provided for irrigation purposes.

Settlers for miles around came to view the invention. In time, a new method of perforating casings was to make them applicable to the use of irrigation, but for many years the open-bottom well remained supreme. It still is the most reliable, although in areas where sand strata are more numerous, the perforated casings economize on power since the lift is distributed over a wider range. No further inventions were ever made, although in subsequent years pumps were increased in size. A modern 5-inch pump throws 700 gallons a minute; a 6-inch, 900 gallons; and a 7-inch, 1,200 to 1,400 gallons a minute. The 6-inch pump is the most common. In favorable localities, pumps of this size will lift water to the surface continuously for days and nights without running dry.

The success of the De La Grange pumping experiments caused similar equipment to be installed in due time throughout the valley. Some time in 1896 Thomas G. Martin, also a resident of the Selma district, applied a gasoline engine to lift water from a 70-foot well. This 5-horsepower engine, equipped with dry cells, was unique in one respect. After it had become warmed up, the engine continued to run after the electric current had been switched *off*. Soon, the use of gasoline engines supplanted the old-fashioned steam engines. Later they, in turn, were replaced by electric motors, which now furnish the motive power for most of the pumping plants in the valley.[59]

Walfrid Larson, a Kingsburg rancher, secured a patent on May 15, 1923, on a contrivance known as the Larson Box-Booster-Pump. This was a low-lift pump designed for drainage work, and for lifting water directly out of a flowing stream for irrigation uses. Unlike most centrifugal pumps, it revolved like a windmill set horizontally. The tremendous volume of water it could throw caused it to win favor with irrigation companies as a means of lifting water from canals and ditches to higher ground. Three years after the invention of the Larson Box-Booster-Pump, the superintendent of the Alta Irrigation District stated: "We have installed in different parts of the District several Larson pumps and we find them very satisfactory in every respect." Since that time this irrigation district saw fit to install an additional 25 of these pumps.

This San Joaquin Valley invention soon came into general use in other states. Bridge builders in Eastern States found these pumps useful. At Bonners Ferry, Idaho, several drainage companies were organized. After several discouraging years, two Larson Box-Booster-Pumps were installed. Within a short time the superintendent of Drainage District No. 1 made the following report: "The two pumps we got from you are doing wonderful work. In three days they pumped dry 160 acres of lakeland that we had tried for six years to drain." Other drainage districts in the same locality immediately followed suit. So did similar districts in the Tulare Lake bottom. These pumps were made in sizes ranging from fourteen to twenty-two inches.[60]

By 1933, pumping plants for irrigation purposes had become almost as numerous as houses and barns. Their general use was due to two things. First, it made possible irrigation late in the summer, when the rivers were running dry. This new form of irrigation made possible the planting of trees and vines in localities hitherto unfavorably situated with regards to water. Second, this rapid increase in the use of pumping plants resulted in a rapid lowering of the water level. Ranchers, who at first refrained from their use, were eventually forced, due to the rapid lowering of the water table, to compete with their neighbors and install pumping plants as a means of self-protection. In an attempt to keep pace with the rapidly receding water, it became necessary to sink wells lower and lower, and eventually some of these deep-water wells produced salt water. They thus proved worthless for irrigation purposes.

A brief recapitulation of irrigation as it existed at the time the census was taken in 1930 is as follows: The San Joaquin Valley contained 6.6 million acres of relatively level land, of which 1.8 million were served by water from streams and wells. Of the 39 irrigation districts then in operation the Madera was the largest with 352,000 acres; of these 222,000 were irrigable. The Fresno District contained the largest irrigable area; 239,000 out of a total of 243,100 acres. Rivers and wells furnishing water for these districts, either wholly or in part, were as follows: Kings River, fourteen; wells, twelve; San Joaquin River, nine; Tuolumne River, three; Merced River, two; Tule River, two; Stanislaus River, two; Kern River, one; Mokelumne River, one; Fresno River, one; and Wachumne River, one. These rivers can do no more, and if the fertile land of the San Joaquin Valley shall all be irrigated adequately, the water must come from some source outside the valley itself.[61]

The California State Engineer proposed a coordinated plan that would forever solve the water problem of the San Joaquin. This plan involved the building of fourteen dams across the San Joaquin River, with a pumping station located beside each. These pumps would boost the water of the Sacramento River up the channel of the San Joaquin for two hundred miles. The proposed dams would be collapsible, and would furnish no obstruction during times of high water. Another purpose of these dams would be the conservation of water during drought. Whatever water was then available would be caught and redistributed by pumps located beside the dams. During the irrigating season, the entire volume of water from the San Joaquin would be diverted to the south and this would confine the water of the Sacramento to the lower reaches of the San Joaquin Valley. This would reduce pumping to a minimum.

Levees would be a necessity along the lower San Joaquin, but at some intermediate point upstream the natural banks would be sufficient. The coordinated plan called for the construction of dams in the mountains, which would conserve water during floods, and could readily generate electric power for use in the pumps along the dams as well as for commercial sale. Trunk canals are also contemplated. One from Kings River and one from the San Joaquin would run due south into the area where the water plane is rapidly receding. The amount of water necessary for navigation in the Sacramento would also be sufficient to serve as a saltwater barrier.

Zealous supporters of the coordinated plan have suggested the possibility of continuing the main canal to Bakersfield. This would make the channel capable of carrying ocean-going vessels which would, at some remote future date, sail majestically down the San Joaquin Valley, and unload their cargoes at the wharves of the seaport city of Bakersfield.

This proposed plan by the state engineer was later supplemented by a federal plan called the Central Valley Water Project. This called for the disbursement of national funds in the building of huge dams to catch the surplus water during floods, which would be stored and used during the irrigating season. One of the proposed dams was to be built across the San Joaquin River, a short distance downstream from the site of old Fort Miller and the former county seat of Millerton, at a place called Friant. Action on this was moving forward in 1938. This proposed dam was to be nearly 300 feet high and 3,430 feet long. The Friant-Kern Canal would skirt the foothills to the south for a distance of more than 150 miles. It would carry 3,500 second-feet of water to Kings River, 3,000 second-feet from Kings River to the Kaweah, and a lesser amount from that point to the Kern River. The Madera Canal would skirt the foothills to the north for 40 miles. It would carry 1,000 second-feet to the Fresno River and 500 second-feet from the Fresno to the Chowchilla River. The storage capacity of the Friant Reservoir will be 520,000 acre-feet, making a lake 15 miles long.

The chief objection offered by critics of the coordinated and federal plans, aside from the cost, has been the apparent folly of developing intensive cultivation in new tracts of land while older and established regions are already more than supplying the demands of the market.[62]

The story of irrigation in the San Joaquin Valley is an epitome of human life: the insolent floundering of youth, the draining away of the elixir of life during maturity, the approach of senility, and the search for a Fountain of Youth. These phases are analogous to the initial irrigation attempts, the draining away of water for all irrigation areas, and a later need for water from an outside source. It was stated facetiously, in years gone by, that the rivers of the San Joaquin Valley were a mile wide and an inch deep. When irrigation companies diverted most of the water and several successive dry seasons had reduced the customary flow to a mere trickle, it was said rather lugubriously that the river had turned on its edge and was running an inch wide and a mile deep. The variable flow in valley rivers is illustrated by the volume in Kings River has had at different times. When it drops below 2,000 cubic feet per second, the water master begins to carefully apportion it. In the late summer, the flow is reduced so that irrigation is impossible. During the flood of 1914, this same river carried 57,000 cubic feet per second during approximately 24 hours. This was exceeded in December 1937, when Kings River carried the unprecedented amount of 80,000 acre-feet per second.[63]

Men have gone, in the interests of irrigation, to the headwaters of every stream in the Sierra Nevada. They know now that no further supply of the life-giving fluid exists in the ranges lying opposite to the San Joaquin Valley. They all bring back the same story, and they have all traveled far, for "you will find the marks of their feet, where the broken rivers meet."

At the present time, the people of the San Joaquin Valley are conducting a great experiment in irrigation and intensive farming. Judging the future by the past, it may safely be assumed that they will encounter many fortunes, but never that of defeat.

18 Cabbages

and Kings

Each tree, laden with fairest fruit
That hung to the eye tempting,
Stirred in me sudden appetite
To pluck and eat.

John Milton *Paradise Lost*, Book VIII, L. 30.

"James Williams and James Lindsay planted one gallon of peach pits in the fall of 1844." This information was conveyed to the Land Commission by William Gulnac as evidence that he had made an effort to settle his *Campo de los Franceses* land grant. The location of this first peach orchard in the San Joaquin Valley was in what is now the southern part of Stockton.[1] Peach pits were carried in the pockets of the various Spanish-California ranchers from ranch to ranch, as they penetrated the vast interior valley. The resulting seedling trees grew and flourished along the rivers wherever a land grant was located. The fruit, undoubtedly poor in quality, was nevertheless greatly relished in season by the pioneer settlers.[2]

The "sand-lappers" followed the cattlemen, and these began to experiment with a better type of trees. They sent to the nurseries of the eastern states for improved varieties, and these were grafted on the old seedling trees. Newspaper accounts during the fifties and sixties referred to the delicious Crawfords and Susquehannas then appearing in the markets of the coastal cities. One of the first men to plant a superior variety of peaches in the central part of the valley was Charles Walker of Selma. His stock was secured from the Bloomington nurseries of Illinois. The Chinese brought in the White Heath peach. None of the foregoing varieties have any commercial value at the present time. The Crawfords and Susquehannas are excessively juicy, and too fragile to withstand the rigors of transportation. They lacked sufficient texture to be of value as a drying peach at any time. The White Heath is in demand for domestic use, but its white color militates against its use in the market.[3]

A striking peculiarity of the peach is the fact that each variety has its youth, maturity, and old age. The Crawford of fifty years ago was superior to the same variety of the present time. This is the opinion of professional canners. Each variety goes through a complete cycle and then loses the qualities that made it delectable, desirable, and profitable. Therefore the Canners' League of California employ experts who experiment, graft, and search for the possible development of new varieties. This Canners' League is composed of ninety-five percent of all the commercial canners of California. Their high salaried horticulturists are able to furnish growers with trees that supply the fruit demanded by a critical market. They have demonstrated that grafts secured from the original Phillips Cling peach tree, still growing (1931), will not produce the quality of fruit which made that variety the supreme canning peach for a quarter of a century. Hence the need for new varieties.[4]

Irrigation was introduced into the area lying between Fresno and Kingsburg before 1880 and into the Modesto-Turlock country about 1903. Crawfords and Susquehannas were planted in both sections, and peach growing began to assume importance in the economic scheme of things. Today, the San Joaquin Valley is supreme in the production of peaches for drying, canning, and fresh shipment. The successive varieties of peaches grown for each of the three industries will be discussed briefly.

The first dried peaches placed on the markets were the Crawfords and Susquehannas. They were quickly supplanted by the Muir; this peach, due to a high sugar content and a low drying-out ratio, has never been equaled as a drying peach. Its closest rival is the Lovell that contains less sugar and ripens later in the fall. At that season of the year many growers need their trays for curing their raisins. The Elberta, which ripens earlier than the Muir, is a popular drying peach, due to its fine flavor and great size. Dried peaches are graded according to size and the price varies accordingly. Freestones are generally used in green shipments. The Elberta is also a factor in this trade. Its large size and beautiful color make it attractive to the shoppers. In recent years, it has been superseded by the Hale peach propagated by J. H. Hale of Missouri. This Hale freestone is larger than the Elberta and stands shipments equally well. Fruit, whether it be water melons or peaches, which stand shipment the best are not always the best in quality; obviously the toughness of skin and rind which permits rough usage is not usually indicative of the best quality. The Lovell has also been placed on the fresh fruit markets but its arrival late in the season and its tart flavor has rendered it a poor seller. Many kinds of clingstones are also offered for green shipment. These same varieties are in demand by the canners.[5]

The original commercial canning peach in the San Joaquin was the Lemon Cling. This was quickly followed by the Orange Cling. The latter was the best shipping peach of all time. These peaches, ripening in August, were augmented in more recent years by the Tuscan Cling, which ripened in June. From 1900 to 1920 these three varieties were supreme in the canning trade. Their gradual deterioration has been evidenced in five ways: increased size of pit, red discoloration of the flesh surrounding the pit, coarse texture of the flesh, increasing paleness of color, and lack of firmness. The same faults eliminated the Levi Lates and the Salways. A later arrival, the Phillips Cling, is now in a similar condition of senility. The Phillips Cling, increasingly subject to gum disease which growers find difficult to combat successfully, is now definitely on the downgrade. The canning peach now in its heyday of youth is the Palora, which possesses a small pit, an excellent flavor, a yellow color, a symmetrical form, a medium size, and a firm flesh which successfully survives much bruising and resists decay.[6]

Since 1930, the canning season has been divided by the commercial canners into two divisions: the early midsummer and the late midsummer. The former begins on August 1, the latter on August 12. The varieties listed and accepted, as "early mids" are the Palora, Hauss, Johnson, Madison, and Van Emmon. The "late mids" are the Gaume, Libbee, and the Sims. The latter was propagated by a Visalia resident whose name it bears. The Gaume has been considered an exceedingly desirable canning peach since 1930. Three new varieties were added in 1939; the Stewart,

Halford, and Stabler. Few freestones are canned in the San Joaquin Valley, although the canneries south of Tehachapi still use them for this purpose.[7]

The growing of apricots for canning is of relatively slight importance in the San Joaquin. Fruit grown along the coastal regions is larger, ripens more uniformly, and is richer in color. However, the interior, due to climatic conditions, produces the bulk of dried apricots. The largest apricot grown is the Moorpark. This has a high sugar content, but is a poor producer. The Tilton, originated in the Hanford vicinity by J.E. Tilton, is next in size and a better producer, but lacks the sugar content of the Moorpark. The Royal is the heaviest producer of all, but lacks size. The best drying apricot is the Blenheim— rich in sugar content, medium in size, and a sure producer.[8]

In 1930 Fresno County had 2,800 acres in apricots valued at $417,956. The peach acreage the same year was 19,686, valued at $2,632,018.20, while the territory devoted to grape culture was listed as follows: raisin vineyards, 165,000 acres worth $10,428,760; table grapes, 32,000 acres, worth $2,671,680; and wine grapes, 15,520, worth $1,249,204.[9]

Before the coming of the white men, a variety of small, blue, wild grapes grew along the river bottoms. In favorable seasons, these produced a quantity of grapes that were eagerly devoured by the red men and their feathered neighbors. When Jefferson Davis sent surveyors to the San Joaquin in 1853 to locate the best route for a proposed railway, the commander of the expedition wrote this about the wild grapes:

> It is probable that grapes could be cultivated in this valley with success. The borders of the creek were overgrown in places by thick masses of grapevines, loaded with long and heavy clusters of fruit. This grape is deserving of attention, as

it is probable that it will be found an exceedingly valuable variety for the manufacture of wine. The berry is small and round, and much resembles the ordinary "frost grape" of New England; but it is larger, more juicy, and rich in flavor, and also has a high color, yielding a juice of a rich claret-color.[10]

These grapes, once found along the rivers in the valley, gradually disappeared due to the diverting of water for irrigation purposes. Another factor was the cutting of trees that had provided natural trellises. But in the lower foothill country they can still be found, clinging to the sycamore trees along the streams. Valley residents, having at their disposal the finest grapes brought into the valley from the ends of the earth, yet prefer to journey to the foothills to pick these wild grapes for domestic purposes. Apparently they merited the praise bestowed upon them by Lieutenant Williamson in 1853:

> Several persons from valley points visited the river section of the foothills in the past week in quest of wild grapes, which matured in abundance this season. Quantities of wild grape jelly have been put up by local housewives.
>
> The wild grape season is nearing its close and only the fruit hanging at the highest point, where the vines near the tops of the sycamore tree, to which they cling, is left.[11]

The Franciscans brought bundles of grape cuttings to California which, in due time, furnished wine for the sacraments and solace to the priesthood. The Spanish-California ranchers along the coast secured cuttings from the Mission vineyards and eventually produced wine for their own consumption, as well as an inferior kind of raisin.[12]

The first vineyard in the San Joaquin Valley was planted in 1852 by Harvey Akers. He was a native of Arkansas, had lived in Texas for a time, and in 1850, accompanied by his four brothers, had left for California in covered wagons. They traveled by way of El Monte, Elizabeth

662

Lake, and Tejon Pass to Visalia. The spring floods of 1852 detained them for a time at Visalia, but as soon as the water had subsided, they continued to Kings River and settled at Centerville where the five brothers became partners in the purchase and operation of a large cattle ranch. In the fall of the same year, Harvey Akers rode horseback to Mission San Gabriel and returned with a bundle of cuttings tied to his saddle. This resulted in the first vineyard in the valley.[13]

Ira McCray in 1859 secured 7,000 scions from the vineyard at Mission San Jose. Some of these were planted along Kings River and were destroyed in the flood of 1862. The others were planted along the San Joaquin and developed into a vineyard.[14]

In 1869 Billy Christy, a gambler and racehorse man at the county seat of Millerton, planted a vineyard and fig orchard along the bank of the San Joaquin River, just below the county court house. The figs were still bearing fruit in 1938. Incidentally, the padres were responsible for the introduction of the little pink roses that were typical sights of the early California landscape. The golden poppies were native to the country and their profusion lent a flaming appearance to the valley which caused the first padres to name it "the land of fire."[15]

The first vines planted by California ranchers, both Spanish and American, were secured from the missions and hence became popularly known as Mission grapes. The value of this Mission grape for the making of wine has been summed up by one expert in this fashion:

> The Angelica made from this grape has never been excelled by wine produced from any other variety, and as a general utility grape we have never had any to take its place. The white wine produced from it, while taking longer to mature, developed qualities equal to some of the finest German types, the saccharine in these grapes maturing at no less than 24

degrees. The Sherry produced from these grapes also had a fine quality and Brandies were always considered desirable. In a blend, as a Port Wine, it always met with favor.[16]

The Mission grape is still of value commercially. From 1917 to 1924 (except in 1922) it outsold the Zinfandels in the New York market. The chief difficulty in marketing the Mission lies in the fact that it ripens later than other varieties and frequently encounters a glutted market. In many cases the crop is not harvested. The acreage in 1931 was 10,000 acres.[17]

The quality of California wines is indicated by what happened at one time in San Francisco. A European expert in wines appeared and annoyed his American friends by his sneering remarks concerning California wines. At a public dinner they asked him to test (taste) a European variety and a similar American brand. He did not know that the wines had been exchanged and so he pronounced the wine from the bottle with the foreign label as far superior.

> After sampling this (the California wine) the expert grew enthusiastic. Here, now, was a wine that *was* a wine. He compared the two vintages, swallow by swallow, almost drop by drop, always to the disparagement of what he supposed was the California product and in praise of the French, little thinking that his pretensions were being given a disastrous test.
>
> He was listened to patiently, and evidently did not detect or understand the covert glances of amusement exchanged by those who were in the secret. He was apparently very well satisfied with the manner in which he had discouraged the ambitious California wine makers.[18]

In 1851 Colonel Agustin Haraszthy planted some muscatel grapes at San Diego which he had secured at Alexandria, Egypt. Ten years later the vineyards propagated from these vines together with those brought in by the Franciscan padres were producing wine of

Views of the La Favorita raisin vineyard, adjacent to M. Theodore Kearney's Fruit Vale Estate, taken in 1890 and 1896. The photographs graphically document how agricultural operations quickly altered the San Joaquin Valley landscape just before the turn of the century. M. Theodore Kearney, *Fresno County, California and the Evolution of the Fruit Vale Estate.*

sufficient quantity to warrant the appointment of a commission by Governor Downey. The purpose of this commission was to encourage the growing industry by the importation of better vines. Hopes were entertained that wines comparable to the best vintage of France or Spain would soon be produced in California.

665

Colonel Haraszthy was one of these commissioners. He visited Europe and imported 200,000 cuttings composed of several varieties. Among them was the Gordo Blanco (muscatel). The latter was similar to the Alexandria and most vineyards, which are known today as Muscats, contain both of these closely-related varieties. These Muscats moved north from San Diego, and in 1873 a few vines were planted near Fresno. The railroad, irrigation, wheat, and Muscats appeared simultaneously at Fresno. The Muscats were slow in gaining momentum, but they were to bring Fresno its greatest fame.[19]

A rancher in Sutter County named William Thompson recalled with poignant longing the grapes that he had eaten during his boyhood days in England. These were grown in a hothouse and pleased his palate better than any grapes he could find in California. The name this variety had escaped his memory, but he wrote to the nursery firm of Ellwanger & Barry of Rochester, New York, and the catalogue which they sent him in response to his inquiry contained a description of the delectable grapes which he desired to purchase. They bore the name of Lady de Coverly, and were natives of Constantinople. Three cuttings arrived in 1872, and these were grafted on Muscat vines. The next year, the Sacramento River overflowed its banks and washed away two of the vines. The remaining vine became the parent of the millions of Thompson Seedless vines now growing in the two inland valleys.[20]

The first vine proved disappointing because of its failure to produce grapes. Thompson pruned it as he did his Muscats; that is, he cut the canes back to three buds and provided no trellis. Eventually he became disgusted and refused to either prune or cultivate his Lady de Coverly vine. This inattention resulted in the vine climbing an adjacent tree and presenting her astonished owner with fifty-six pounds of grapes. Thompson saw the point, apologized to Lady de Coverly, and thenceforth left her with canes three or four feet in length and provided her with a trellis. Soon, cuttings from that vine were at a premium. Had this vine been destroyed, or had it lacked a tree during its testing period, one of the big industries of interior California might never have developed. In 1930, with low prices, the Thompson Seedless raisins in the valley sold for $6,293,684.76—such was the importance, measured in monetary returns, of one little vine.[21]

The Zante Currants are a third type of raisin commercially important. The misnomer of currant was caused by the fact that these raisins, originally grown near Corinth, Greece, were referred to as Zante Corinths. Poor enunciation quickly corrupted this term into its present name.[22]

Raisins came originally from eastern Persia. From there, they spread to Greece and the region around the Mediterranean. The medieval knights acquired a taste for raisins on the Crusades, but not until the mass production of the San Joaquin Valley placed thousands of tons on the market did raisins become a staple article of food for the ordinary "common garden" variety of folk. Shakespeare referred to this type of fruit when he credited Falstaff with this quip while conversing with bluff Prince Hal: "If reasons (meaning raisins) were as plentiful as blackberries, I would give no man a reason upon compulsion."[23]

Juice grapes used for wine making are usually not suitable for table purposes; even those possessing delicious taste do not stand shipment. Raisin grapes are all good to eat and can be transported long distances. Aside from these, Malagas and Emperors are the special table grape varieties in the valley. Tokays are confined to the Sacramento Valley around Lodi.[24]

The State of California requires a sugar content of eighteen percent before fresh grapes may be placed on the market. Grapes are crushed, the juice extracted, and then placed in a saccharometer (sugar meter); the latter is a cylindrical glass tube about fourteen inches long and an inch in diameter. Grapes intended for raisins are not picked until they contain twenty-four percent; a ton of grapes with a sugar content of this amount will produce 131 pounds more raisins than grapes with nineteen-percent content. The drying-out ratio of grapes with twenty percent is 4.3 to 1. Drying is facilitated by placing the trays on an incline tilted to face the south. This incline is prepared by a V-shaped drag. After the grapes have been dried in the sun on these trays, they are stacked and then placed in "sweatboxes," which serve as equalizers.[25]

The first oranges to reach the San Joaquin were imported in the form of fruit by way of stagecoaches. The Franciscans had planted orange trees at their missions, and a limited amount of fruit from these small orchards was available. Thrifty housewives carefully planted the seeds contained within these rare and expensive oranges. Usually, they were doomed to disappointment; the seeds either refused to grow or failed to survive the early frosts. In 1862, Mrs. William Hazelton succeeded in growing orange trees that eventually produced fruit. This first orange grove was located on the Hazelton cattle ranch, five miles above Centerville, along Kings River. Harvey Akers, who twelve years before this had planted the first vineyard in the valley, was a near neighbor and a brother of Mrs. Hazelton.[26]

In 1866, orange seeds sprouted in the backyard of the old headquarters building at Fort Miller and these grew successfully and formed the second small orange grove in the valley. Both of these groups of trees were bearing fruit

Orange groves located near Centerville (Fresno County), circa 1895, with eastern foothills in the background. *The Interior (Fresno)*.

in 1938. In the early eighties, an orange grove at Knight's Ferry also began to produce fruit.[27]

From time to time, frostless belts and coves were located where oranges and lemon groves could be planted, and thus this form of industry began to contribute its share to the development of the San Joaquin Valley. The citrus industry is based on the production of oranges, lemons, pomelos (grapefruit), and mandarins. The soil and climate of the valley floor adjacent to the foothills and the slopes of these foothills proved ideal for this type of fruit-growing, and has produced citrus fruit equal to the best grown in the world. Citrus growers have adopted the following self-explanatory slogan: "Above the Fog—Below the Snow." Cities whose prosperity is largely based on this industry are Orange Cove, Lemon Cove, Exeter, Lindsay, and Porterville. The two chief varieties of oranges grown in these districts are the Valencia and the Washington Navels. The latter has had an interesting history.[28]

The Portuguese, sailing round the Cape of Good Hope to India, and thus earning the distinction of being the first Europeans to reach the Orient by an all-water route, established a colony at Goa. The original home of the

669

orange is in eastern Asia. A variety, known to the
Portuguese as the Selecta, flourished in their Indian
colony. Soon, it was transplanted to the Portuguese colony
of Brazil. In the Bahia district, a Selecta tree put forth a
sport limb bearing seedless oranges with a formation at
the end opposite the stem resembling that portion of the
human anatomy known as the umbilicus. Hence this new
orange was indelicately referred to as the "navel" orange.
A Portuguese gardener propagated buds successfully from
this sport about 1820 and, in time, the results of his
menial labors circumnavigated the globe. In 1868 William
Saunders, then superintendent of the gardens maintained
by the United States Department of Agriculture at
Washington, learned about these navel oranges from a
friend at Bahia. Here, the story varies. According to one
version, his correspondent at Bahia was the American
consul; according to another, the wife of a Protestant
missionary. A shipment was made that year, and the trees
died in transit. In 1870 twelve little trees arrived safely,
but six of them soon perished in the unfriendly climate of
Washington, D. C.[29]

About that time a man named Luther Tibbets left his
home in New York and took up government land in
California near Riverside. His wife and daughter
remained with friends at Washington, D. C. until the new
home in the west should be ready for occupancy. Mrs.
Tibbets was interested in horticulture, and frequently
visited the gardens maintained by the Department of
Agriculture. The American consuls scattered throughout
the world send to the department such plants and seeds
as they think may be of value to their home country. The
attempt is then made to acclimatize them. One day Mrs.
Tibbets viewed the six small navel orange trees. The
rigorous climate of the Atlantic seaboard was unsuited to
these trees from the southern hemisphere. When the
department officials learned that Mrs. Tibbets was

Interior of a fruit packing house, circa 1900, depicting the intensive labor necessary for the enterprise in the days before automation. M. Theodore Kearney, *Fresno County, California and the Evolution of the Fruit Vale Estate.*

planning a new home in California, they were glad to send three of the small trees to the Pacific Coast. It was stipulated that the trees should be carefully tended and a report made concerning their progress. The three trees that remained in the Washington gardens succumbed to the harsh climate, and only the three on their way to California were left. Their arrival in California, which was pregnant with possibilities for the future, has been related as follows:

> More important to Riverside than any of these pioneers was Mrs. Eliza Tibbets, a neighbor of the Millers, who one day hitched her horse and buggy and drove sixty miles to Los Angeles where the postmaster presented her with a package from Washington, D. C. The package contained three live orange trees which the Department of Agriculture had imported from Brazil. They were a new variety of orange, sweet, seedless and juicy. That was in 1873.
>
> The oranges that Mrs. Tibbets' trees bore, when they had taken root in the California soil, were finer than any others grown in this country. Neighbors tasted the luscious fruit and then had their own trees grafted from her stock, and in a few years the once arid valley surrounding Riverside was covered

with thousands of thriving offspring from these two
remarkable trees.[30]

These oranges arrived at Riverside in December, 1873.
The family cow chewed one of the little trees to death, but
the remaining two thrived. In January 1879, Luther
Tibbets picked four large, well-flavored seedless oranges
from the trees. These were the first Navel oranges ever
picked outside of Brazil.[31]

From these two trees were procured the grafts which
transformed the seedling oranges of Southern California
and led to the development of Pomona, Redlands,
Ontario, and Monrovia. Grafts from these trees also
crossed the mountains to the north, and soon the San
Joaquin vied with Southern California in the production
of the luscious fruit.[32]

Another variety of orange known to the Spanish as the
"La Naranja Tarde de Valencia" was developed in the
Azores Islands. The Valencia is more oblong in shape than
the Navel, lighter in color, and without the navel
formation. It ripens in the summer, and the fruit may be
held on the trees for months after the normal summer
picking season. An unusual occurrence in fruit culture is
the presence of blossoms and ripe fruit on the Valencia
trees at the same time. Washington Navels, named so
because Mrs. Tibbets secured her trees from Washington,
D. C., and Valencias naturally supplement one another.
Navels are picked late in the fall, and Valencias early in
the summer.[33]

The Spanish brought the first lemon seedlings to
California. Subsequently a superior variety, known as the
Lisbon and developed in Europe, arrived by way of
Australia. The third, called the Eureka and now the most
commercially important, was developed in Los Angeles
from Sicilian lemon seeds. In structure, a lemon and an

orange are similar; each is composed of carpels filled with tiny juice sacks. But they differ in one respect. Lemon trees blossom, grow, and ripen their fruit without interruption year-round. Thus fresh lemons are always available.[34]

A Chinese book written 2,000 years before Christ stated that the pomelo "regulates digestion, causes the body to become light, and prolongs life." Like most of our other fruits, it was introduced by the Spanish adventurers. The Americans nicknamed it the grapefruit, due to its tendency to grow in bunches like grapes. The chief commercial variety is the Marsh.[35]

The Mandarin orange is a comparatively recent arrival in the valley. It was introduced from China and is the midget of the citrus family. Its small size aroused curiosity, which won it immediate favor; distinctive flavor enabled the Mandarin to retain its popularity. The only variety commercially important is the Dancy. The trade name for the latter is the tangerine. Uninformed people have confused terminology by applying the word tangerine to any member of the mandarin family; it belongs properly only to the Dancy.[36]

Cotton was first grown in the valley in 1866. That fall, a small shipment was made by Skelton & Turner from Snelling by wagon to the tidewater. One member of this firm, W. H. Turner, later became the mayor of Merced and remained active in civic affairs until 1912. This first cotton crop consisted of 3,500 pounds and was grown on the Albert Ingalsbe ranch near Hopetown. The cost of production for this ton and three-quarters was approximately $25. Shortly thereafter the Buckley brothers, residents of the same community, exported 23,000 pounds of native Merced County cotton. In 1871 another neighbor, Colonel J. N. Strong, produced 74,450 pounds of seed cotton from fifty-one acres which he sold for six cents a pound. In 1880 the

Woolen Mills at Merced Falls used 65,000 pounds of cotton grown in Merced County, and the planters began to agitate for textile mills.[37]

In more recent times, the cotton industry has been stimulated by the improvement of transportation facilities and by utilizing cottonseed, considered a waste in former times. Cotton cake and cottonseed oil are now important parts of the crop. Machinery has supplanted the old forms of hand labor in every respect except picking; this is still done by hand. Expert cotton pickers can gather from one to five hundred pounds, depending upon the yield.[38]

Kern County ranks first in yield per acre. This is due to the extreme fertility of the soil, plus the fact that in the southern San Joaquin Valley little rain falls between May 1 and October 1. This long period of uninterrupted fine weather, together with an abundance of irrigation water, has resulted in huge crops of fine cotton. The planting of this crop in Kern County began in 1885, shortly after the introduction of irrigation. The chief advance made in cotton culture in the valley has come from this region:

> Chief among Kern County's outstanding agricultural developments of the past few years has been the planting of the pure bred Acala strain of cotton. By reason of the fact that one and only one strain of cotton has been planted throughout the length and breadth of the San Joaquin Valley, the yield is not only exceptionally high (average yield in excess of one bale to the acre) but better prices are paid for Kern County cotton by reason of its entire uniformity. This pure bred strain of cotton seed brings from $24 to $40 per ton, while the average Kern Acala lint measures 1-3/16 inches in length.[39]

The Franciscan padres introduced the black Mission fig into California. This is still popular as a drying fig, and supreme in the making of jams. The Mission fig is a member of the Adriatic family. The other varieties of the same family were later arrivals in the valley. The White

Adriatic becomes yellow when ripe, and is the usual variety seen along the roadsides of the San Joaquin. The Kadota is the commercial canning and preserving fig of California. In recent years the Kadota has been the only fig utilized in the commercial canneries. The Calimyrna is the genuine drying fig and the giant of the family; a fig of this variety is often as big as a duck egg. It is not an Adriatic fig, but belongs to the Smyrna family and was named by a Fresno nursery after the fig wasp had been introduced into the family. These wasps (*Blastophaga grossorum*) grow in wild Capri (non-edible) figs. Capri figs are planted in Calimyrna orchards, and the wasps convey the pollen into the edible figs.[40]

How to successfully grow Calimyrna figs in California proved to be a long and tedious problem. The successful solution of this difficulty must be credited to many men working unselfishly toward a common goal. The production of figs excellent for canning, making preserves, and fresh eating was fairly easy; however, all of these figs possessed skins too tough to make good drying figs, as far as the market in the East was concerned. Smyrna figs from Italy, Turkey, and North Africa outsold California figs at twice the price. This was galling to the pride of native sons. During the 1890s, the United States imported 10 million pounds of figs a year. The Smyrna figs had been planted in California as early as 1880, but they refused to bear.[41]

One of the early sponsors of importing Smyrna fig trees was Gulian P. Rixford, a newspaper reporter, who persuaded the San Francisco *Bulletin* to finance the importation of such trees from Turkey. In 1880 a shipment of 1,500 cuttings arrived which were planted, grew, and finally bore fruit which fell off before it ripened. Furious orchardists roared: "We've been tricked. The unspeakable Turk has sent us inferior stock."[42]

Illustration showing a properly pollinated Calimyrna fig, from George C. Roeding's *Fruit Grower's Guide* of 1919.

In the late 1890s Walter T. Swingle, an American college student pursuing advanced studies at the University of Naples, spent part of his time watching Italians at work in their fig orchards. He had wondered why good drying figs could not be grown in the United States, and tried to find out from the Italians how they did it. However, the Italian gardeners did not welcome him. They were superstitious, or perhaps they used this as a pretext. At any rate, they had dark eyes and maintained that his gray eyes would put a curse on the fruit. So they hung goats' horns and other charms on the trees after he had inspected them.[43]

In time, it became known to Swingle and other American observers that the fig-growers in the older countries had a custom of going at certain times of the year to the plains and gathering fruit from the caprifig, which had a fruit resembling the edible fig. When they were asked why they did this they replied: "No hang caprifig, no have fig crop." Scientists in the old world dismissed this custom as a childish superstition. American scientists thought there might be a connection, but did not know what it was. Finally, Dr. Gustaf Eisen of the California Academy of Sciences proved that the caprifig contained wasp-like insects, about 1/32 of an inch long, which carried caprifig pollen to the Smyrna fig.[44]

After this momentous discovery, several years were spent in trying to introduce the fig insects into California. At this point Dr. Swingle took a hand. He secured hard, solid, winter-generation caprifig fruit, wrapped them in tinfoil, packed them in cotton, and sent them to the Department of Agriculture in April 1898. He did this at his own initiative and at his own expense. Unfortunately, the insects present in the fruit did not pollinate the trees. The next year, Swingle sent more figs packed in the same manner. These figs were forwarded to George C. Roeding of Fresno, who had also been active in the attempt to secure caprifigs. He had a wooden frame built over the tree, under which the caprifig fruit was placed, and suspended from this frame a cloth which covered the entire tree. The fig wasps were kept under this cloth until the trees on the outside showed signs of being ready to receive the wasps; then, they were liberated. But the reflection of the sun from the cloth had caused them to develop too early, and most of the wasps had died trying to get outside. However, the few who had managed to escape in time had pollenized enough fruit to prove the end of the mystery. Nothing then remained but to plant caprifig trees in orchards in sufficient numbers to take care of the proper production of so-called Calimyrna figs.[45]

The extensive planting of vineyards and orchards led to the invention of a new type of farm implements. The old Stockton Gang Plow was unsuited for vineyard use, since the rows were only ten feet apart. The walking plow once again became common. In time, this was replaced by "pony gang" plows. Plowing irrigated land during the hot weather led to the forming of large clods. The old clod-crusher invented by Thomas Ogg Shaw in 1859 for use in wheat fields was not designed for vineyard or orchard use. Plowing to or from vines left the soil in ridges, and the flat drag-harrow proved useless.[46]

An unknown farmer laid a buggy wheel flat on the ground and used it as a model for a new type of harrow. Being built of wood, it proved too light. Then cast-iron was employed in building an exact duplicate of this buggy wheel. Ordinary harrow teeth were inserted, at regular intervals, through the spokes and rim. A perpendicular bar of round iron formed the axle. The horses were attached to a beam, with two handles at the other end for driver guidance. A weight on one side exerted enough pressure to cause this harrow to revolve and it became

A hay-baling team in the field, probably Fresno County, circa 1900. M.
Theodore Kearney, *Fresno County, California and the Evolution of the
Fruit Vale Estate.*

known as a revolving, or circle, harrow. The cast-iron
proved too heavy for livestock, and the harrow was
discarded.[47]

Walfrid Larson, a Kingsburg blacksmith and rancher,
built a circular harrow of pipe material. Being hollow, this
material proved light enough to be pulled by one span of
horses, but heavy enough to pulverize clods and lumpy
soil. An added feature of the Larson harrow was a covered
sheath for the axle around which the harrow revolved.
This excluded sand, permitted greasing, and prevented
undue wear. This harrow soon came into general use in
vineyards and orchards throughout the state. Larson
never applied for a patent on the circular harrow but he
did secure a patent on the King Tire Bolt Wrench,
especially designed for removing nuts from old buggy and
spring-wagon tires.[48]

Larson also invented the fruit elevator used in fruit sheds
where apricots and peaches are cut, smoked, and cured.
This elevator was gradually lowered into a pit as the fruit

679

trays were placed on the truck and filled with cut fruit. When loaded, the elevator was raised to the surface and the truck run out on a track into the sulphur house. Prior to this invention, all trays placed on trucks had been removed by hand power. Olaf and Andrew Olson of Reedley patented a similar invention for use in smaller establishments in 1911. This was known as the Excelsior Fruit Cart, an appliance for conveying fruit trays, sweat boxes, and sulphur sacks, from the fruit shed to the smokehouse and about the drying yard.[49]

The cultivation of orchards and vineyards proved difficult, due to protruding spurs of the vines and low, overhanging branches of the trees. In order to get close to the stumps, an offset disc harrow was patented by Towner of Santa Ana, based on the old tandem disc invented by Lowell Alexander Richards in 1886. This offset disc was designed to run diagonally behind a tractor and could therefore work the soil near the stumps and trunks without interference. In 1931 Olaf and Andrew Olson, at that time owners of the Olson Brothers Implement Company at Kingsburg, secured a patent on a new off-set disc distinguished by its simplicity of design, lightness of construction, ease of operation, and greater versatility than previous discs. This soon came into general use among horticulturists.[50]

The members of this firm also invented a sulphur machine used in dusting vineyards with sulphur to prevent mildew. This machine, patented in 1921, was equipped with a higher speed blower than any other then on the market, the cast aluminum blast wheel making 3,000 or more revolutions a minute. Muscat vines are usually planted at intervals of ten feet. Small trucks were built to haul raisins out of vineyards and for scattering trays for the pickers. The Olson firm invented a vineyard truck equipped with spring steel cross-reaches which tracked perfectly, and made the necessary short turns with ease.[51]

In 1933 W. E. Goble, a rancher near Orosi, secured a patent on the first disc with an enclosed bearing; this prevented wear since dust, sand, and grit could not gain entrance. Goble went broke while making his first discs, and was forced to work for twenty-five cents an hour for a year in order to save the $300 necessary to further his work. In 1934 he placed 78 discs on the market; in 1935, 307; and in 1936, 587. He formed a corporation with his three sons-in-law and the Goble Disc Works was established along Highway 99, between Selma and Fowler. These discs have become famous for their ability to take hard ground, work close to rows of trees and vines, and do smooth work.[52]

Goble also invented the brush shredder (about 1924), which came into general use for a time in shredding vineyard and orchard brush after the pruning season. This patent was sold to the Valley Foundry of Fresno, but its manufacture was discontinued when it was found that the new heavy discs could be used in chopping the brush, which was returned to the soil as fertilizer.[53]

In order to prevent noxious weeds from securing a foothold in vineyards, it was necessary each spring to plow the soil away from the vines and trees. One horse and a single plow were used for this purpose. This task proved not only onerous but also deleterious to the health, happiness, and disposition of the vineyardists. During the World War some doughboys from the San Joaquin Valley, while on a furlough from the front line trenches, went to visit French farmers at work in their vineyards. The familiar scene produced nostalgia, but the Americans retained their composure sufficiently to realize that the French peasants possessed an implement superior to the ordinary American single-plow. It was a peculiar implement invented by a Frenchman named Kirpy for vineyard tillage. He had established a manufacturing firm named the Establissements Kirpy at Layrac, France. The soldiers carried the news of this plow back to California, and within a few years one of these Kirpy plows was found in almost every vineyard and orchard in the San Joaquin. One attempt to copy this plow by a firm in the Middle West was stopped by court injunction as being an infringement of the French patent.[54]

The first steps to grow rice in the San Joaquin were undertaken by John Czerny, superintendent of the Merced Sewer Farm, in 1910. His experiments demonstrated the possibility of growing this type of grain and eventually led to the planting of thousands of acres to California Japanese rice. The second step was taken by Olcese & Buchenau in 1915, who planted eighty acres and reaped a harvest of 49 bags to the acre. The El Capitan and Deane colonies then began to devote themselves to rice culture, and in 1927 the Crocker-Huffman Land & Water Company planted thousands of acres of their holdings southwest of Merced to rice. The latter enterprise was made possible by the Exchequer Dam, which provided the vast amount of water necessary for the growing of this crop. Since it is imperative that the growing rice plants be covered with fresh, flowing water to a depth of four inches during a period of a hundred and twenty days, it is evident that much water must be available. The use of this great amount of water proved damaging to other kinds of crops in adjacent fields. Numerous lawsuits resulted in the effort by certain farmers to recover damages for alleged injuries done by this form of irrigating. This led the irrigation companies to zone certain lands for rice growing, and the result was a decrease in the acreage available for this purpose. The Dos Palos, Stevenson, and Merced regions continued to grow rice after 1927.[55]

The harvesting of rice is done with reapers and binders, in the old-fashioned manner prevalent in the wheat fields of the Middle West. The combined harvesters are too ponderous to take into the muddy rice fields, which are all bisected by large levees. Rice is threshed like other grains and sacked in paddy form, which means that the hull is left on the grain. The hulling is done in the rice mills, where the grain is also polished. Most rice fields in California are planted from airplanes, and the ripening grain is protected from wild ducks and geese in the same fashion.[56]

The Spanish-California cattlemen who settled in the valley between 1836 and 1846 planted melons in the moist soil along the rivers. In 1846 Ysidio Villa, cattle foreman on the *Laguna de Tache* ranch belonging to Manuel Castro, planted a field of melons along Kings River in the vicinity of Laton. The introduction of irrigation made melons commercially important. The quality of the soil, the climate, and the proximity to large urban centers made melon growing the dominant industry in the Turlock-Modesto region for many years. Casabas, cantaloupes, and watermelons are the three types commercially important.[57]

Whatever their horticultural classification may be, melons are eaten as fruit and grown as vegetables. The climate of the San Joaquin is ideal for their propagation. Watermelons are usually planted in April. Too-favorable conditions have had a tendency to cause certain varieties of watermelons to become overly large for commercial purposes; individual melons have often attained a weight of more than a hundred pounds. The Lodi melon controlled the market during the early years of the industry. It was later supplemented by the Cuban Queen, which proved to be an excellent shipper. From 1905 to 1915 the Southern Rattlesnake, a long oblong melon with

683

decided stripes of light and deep green, dominated the market. It had an excellent pulp and was a good shipper, but possessed a rather thick rind. The Ice Cream melon is distinguished by its yellow pulp. Thomas E. Watson, a presidential candidate for the Populist Party in the nineties and a United States Senator from Georgia after the World War, was a melon grower in his native state. His fame as a publicist, and his services in securing for American farmers rural free delivery of mail, will no doubt be dimmed long before the Tom Watson melon— dark green in color, oblong in shape, and a giant of the family—will cease to be sold about the countryside of Georgia. However, in California this melon has been of little commercial value since 1920.[58]

Russian immigrants from the Volga River region settled near Rocky Ford, Colorado. They brought with them melon seeds that developed the most popular melons grown in the San Joaquin Valley since 1920. The Angeleno, a medium-sized, round melon and a native of California, was finally supplemented by these Russian melons, which assumed such names as Winter King, Winter Queen, Klondike, and Alaska. Of these closely related varieties, all medium-sized and rather oblong, the Klondike has been the most important in the San Joaquin. It possesses supreme shipping qualities. During the decade from 1923 to 1933, the Klondike was the melon demanded by the trade. These melons are often placed in salt brine and kept for months, with no appreciable deterioration in quality.[59]

The localities where melons are grown necessarily vary from year to year. Melons pollute the soil, and cannot successfully be grown more than once on the same acreage. Hence other crops must take their place. Turlock enjoyed a long period of melon supremacy. Then Dinuba attained the honor, and in the year 1936 Kingsburg

shipped more watermelons than any other producing
point in California. Attempts to grow melons on land, not
planted previously to melons for twenty years, has proved
a failure. In 1938 the experts in the University of
California department of agriculture developed the
Klondike R7, which proved resistant to fisarium wilt and
commercially superior to the older varieties of
Klondikes.[60]

In 1930 California produced more than half of all the
muskmelons produced within the nation. The San Joaquin
Valley was credited with more than one-third of the crop
grown in the state. A statistician computed that the
cantaloupes grown in California would provide one for
each resident of the nation and leave a surplus of fifteen
for every individual in California. Turlock is the center of
the cantaloupe area in the valley. The so-called Turlock
method has attracted considerable attention from melon
growers elsewhere. The fields are plowed to a depth of
twelve or fourteen inches in January. More shallow
plowing is done in March, and planting is done about the
middle of the month. The ninth row is omitted for a
driveway. This prevents mutilation of the other vines. The
quality and the quantity of the cantaloupes grown there is
an index of the efficacy of their system.[61]

Muskmelons are divided into two classes. Class I consists
of netted muskmelons, which are generally called
cantaloupes. This class is subdivided into shipping and
home garden varieties. The Rocky Ford melon, not a
separate variety but the name given to the Netted Gem
type developed at that place, is supreme in the shipping
trade. A larger variety is the improved Paul Rose, known
as Burrell's Gem. For home consumption the California
Large Nutmeg, the Large Yellow, the small Jenny Lind,
and the Hackensack are popular.[62]

Class II in muskmelons consists of winter and special

685

varieties. The first muskmelon of this type, also known as the pineapple melon, was introduced in 1869 by John Bidwell, the famous prairie schooner leader. Later, the Armenians arrived in the San Joaquin Valley and brought with them seeds of a muskmelon that they called a casaba, after the city of Kassaba in Mesopotamia. Still later, the Golden Beauty and the Winter Pineapple found ready markets because they could be stored until February. These winter muskmelons could not be grown successfully in cold, damp climates. This is true of all the varieties in Class II. Their natural habitat is a hot, semiarid region. The casaba soon took precedence over other varieties of winter muskmelons, as these melons grown late in the summer were designated, and soon the trade adopted the word "casaba" to include the entire group.[63]

In time a rival to the Armenian casaba was introduced from Europe, where it had been grown under the name of the White Antibes Winter. All winter muskmelons can be grown successfully throughout the San Joaquin, but the chief commercial product for many years came from the Dinuba district in Tulare County. The White Antibes Winter was introduced there and popularized under the name of the honeydew. The most recent arrival in the San Joaquin is the Persian or Odessa, known locally as the Santa Claus. Heavy netting on a melon indicates good shipping traits, but not good table qualities. This is borne out by the Santa Claus, which possesses rare table qualities but is poor for shipping purposes. It is sparsely netted, has a white or light yellowish green flesh, and possesses a distinct aroma without muskiness, which is pleasing to the senses. It is very difficult to grow, except in the most favored localities of the arid West.[64]

Scattered throughout the valley are groves of almond trees. These produce the famous paper-shelled almonds. The first variety, introduced about 1870, was the

Languedoc. In more recent years, the Hatch almond has largely supplanted the former. The Hatch is the variety now commercially important in the northern part of the San Joaquin Valley, especially in Contra Costa County.[65]

The English gave their name to a soft-shelled walnut that originally came from Persia, where it was known in ancient times as the King of Nuts. The walnut made its appearance in the valley about the same time as the almond. In 1930 California produced 97 percent of all the walnuts grown in the United States. The San Joaquin furnished the bulk of the fancy varieties. The walnut acreage at that time in California was 127,485.[66]

All walnuts fall into three commercial classes, namely: Soft Shells (from seedling trees); Budded (Placentia Variety); and Fancy Varieties (Concord, Eureka, Payne, Franquette, and Mayette). The Soft Shells come from the first groves in the state. Trees were developed from soft-shelled English walnuts planted in the ground as seeds. Products from these trees have been uneven in quality and quantity. A single definite variety known as the Placentia is sold under the trade name of Budded. Placentia buds were inserted under the bark of native California black walnuts. The latter are endowed with great size and strength, and have furnished the trunk and root system for the Placentia tops. The native black walnut has a plump kernel of rich flavor, but the shell is too hard to win favor on the market. The Placentia is grown chiefly in Southern California.[67]

The Fancy Varieties, the trade name for five distinct walnuts, are the finest grown in the world. Most of these are produced in Northern and Central California. The Concord, Eureka, and Payne were originated in California. The Payne is a precocious walnut and begins to bear earlier than any other. The Franquette and Mayette were developed from imported French trees. The latter is grown where the weather is excessively hot. The chief walnut districts in the San Joaquin Valley are in the counties of San Joaquin, Contra Costa, and Tulare, especially around Visalia. Walnuts are graded as to quality, size, and variety. The finest specimens are stamped with the Diamond brand; the second, not much inferior, are labeled Emerald.[68]

Bishop William Taylor is generally credited with the introduction of the eucalyptus tree from Australia to California. Locally, this tree is called a gum tree, but it is not to be confused with the gum tree of the southern states. Groves of these trees have been planted in the valley, and the wood from these has been used for fuel and timber. Individual trees, most of which grow to a great height, are found in almost any locality in the San Joaquin. The odor emanating from these trees is unpleasant to the senses of flies and mosquitoes. Therefore, these trees have been used extensively as shade trees near houses and stock corrals; eucalyptus trees have also been planted in malarial regions. The rapid growth these trees are capable of making in the San Joaquin Valley is illustrated by the records kept of the tree known as the "McCubbin Gum Tree." This is located midway between Reedley and Kingsburg and belongs to the family known as the *Eucalyptus viminalis*. This variety is often called the manna gum, because it exudes a substance thought to resemble the manna mentioned in the Bible. Its leaves have a slight sickle-shaped curve, are pendant, and identical. They have no under-surface, as do the leaves of other trees. The fame of the McCubbin tree kept pace with its phenomenal growth and Luther Burbank, at the time of his death, had trees growing in his experimental garden at Santa Rosa which were from the seeds of the great tree of the San Joaquin.

When planted, this tree was a cull that had been rejected

from a lot used to plant out a grove near by, and what was considered a defect at the time, probably resulted in giving the tree an extra good start. An injury had been inflicted under the following rather peculiar circumstances. The box containing 100 small trees, had been brought from town by a neighbor, and placed in one corner of his barn, where it remained the following day. At night I went over, groped around in the dark, and after locating the box, placed it on my shoulder and carried it home. At the end of the journey, I learned to my great surprise and disgust, that I had carried a hen's nest, with a freshly laid egg in it, all the way home. An ambitious "Biddie" having discovered what she considered a "choice building site," had appropriated the place to her own individual use, and had scratched some of the trees out by the roots in the middle of the miniature forest, and had thrashed the tops out of several others. It was one of these topless victims that have furnished the material for this sketch, and that now has grown to be the largest tree of its age in the world.[69]

Data covering the yearly measurements of this tree are on file in the office of the United States Forest Service at Washington. When planted in April 1889, it was 10 inches high and the size of a knitting needle. Ten years later it had a girth of 8 feet, 5 inches, and was 63 feet high. In 1909 its girth had increased to 14 feet, 5 inches, and its height to 120 feet. Its bough spread was 88 feet, 6 inches. In the fall of 1919 it had attained a girth of 19 feet, 1 inch, a girth at the ground of 26 feet, a height of 130 feet, and a bough spread of 114 feet. By 1929, its girth at the height of a man's head was 22 feet, 3 inches; its girth at the ground was 29 feet, 9 inches; its height was 131 feet, and its bough spread 123 feet. The influence of this gigantic tree has shown itself by the subsequent planting of groves throughout the valley. The wood of the *Eucalyptus viminalis* is suitable for fuel. But it can fill a far more important need.

In some species the grain is beautiful, surpassing the oak in hardness and elasticity; its tensile strength equals the hickory, giving it great value where fine grained, hard timber is desired. Manufacturers have long imported the wood under the name of "Australian Mahogany." Since the trees are uninjured by the borers they are ideal for sea-piles. For railroad ties the wood has proved almost indestructible. When properly cured, it is fine for house-furnishings and cabinetwork. Its leaves, when crushed, give the eucalyptus oil so extensively used; a ton of leaves yields twenty pounds of oil. From the bark of the tree a juice exudes that quickly hardens and becomes the king of commerce.[70]

Alfalfa is a native of Arabia that came to Spain with the Moors, and to America with the Spanish, but did not arrive in California until some time in the 1850s. Neither mission records nor the researches of historians have produced any evidence of the presence of alfalfa in the state during the Spanish period. In 1855, the *California Farmer* mentioned an alfalfa lawn at the Captain Walsh home in Benicia. The same issue of this paper also mentioned an experimental planting of alfalfa at Sacramento by Colonel Foreman, then postmaster at that place. Such newspaper publicity indicates that alfalfa was a new thing in the state. In 1858 the Sacramento *Union* stated that alfalfa was winning favor among the stockmen. That same year John Bigler, a former governor of California and then Minister to Chile, wrote a letter quoted by a Sacramento paper, describing its use in Chile and earnestly recommending it to the stockmen of his state.[71]

Chile alfalfa is the variety now commonly grown in the San Joaquin Valley. Peru, also known as Hairy Peruvian, is a more recent arrival. This variety produces heavier crops than the Chile, is shorter-lived, has a coarse and hollow stalk, and makes poorer feed. Arabian alfalfa has more leaves than either of the other two, and therefore makes better cow feed. It also makes a quicker start after each cutting, but is short-lived. Grimm alfalfa, due to

Alfalfa-stacking scene in the San Joaquin Valley, circa 1900. M. Theodore Kearney, *Fresno County, California and the Evolution of the Fruit Vale Estate.*

conditions of soil and climate, has been confined to the foothill slopes.[72]

In 1932 the most valuable single crop of the San Joaquin Valley was not oranges, raisins, cotton, or peaches; neither was it dairy products. This honor belonged to alfalfa. That same year, the alfalfa grown in Fresno County exceeded in value all of the other crops combined. In the hot interior valley, six crops are usually gathered during each season; in favorable localities, two tons to the acre are produced during each cutting.[73]

Alfalfa growers today owe a vote of thanks to Thomas Powell for his invention of the hayfork. He was an early wheat grower on the west side of the valley near modern Patterson, and the same man who in 1876 invented the net used in unloading grain from header wagons into the stacks by horsepower. During the depression following the

691

Civil War, he moved to Stockton and opened a cigar store in 1874. His evenings were devoted to the invention of machinery which lightened the burdens of men who stacked hay and grain on the hot plains during the summer months. His hay fork and pivoting derrick were patented in 1878, and are still in use. The Jackson hayfork, now in use in the San Joaquin, is almost identical with the grain and hayfork invented by Thomas Powell.[74]

The Mormons planted the first potato field in the San Joaquin Valley in their colony along the Stanislaus in 1847. This was irrigated by an endless chain of buckets from the river, but produced only a meager crop.[75]

The early history of successful potato growing in the San Joaquin Valley centers on one man. The delta region near Stockton was considered worthless for agricultural purposes until George Shima, a Japanese labor contractor, made it the big potato field of California. Shima had a vision, which he realized by draining this delta along the San Joaquin River. Steam engines were installed which pumped out the superfluous water. The brush and tules were replaced by potato plants. Almost every person, excepting Shima, was astonished at the bounteous crops that resulted. In some instances, 700 bushels were produced on one acre. Shima acquired 6,000 acres and cultivated additional fields under lease from American owners. During a period of twenty years, he paid these owners $8 million in rent for land which had prior to his arrival been considered worthless. The potato crops he gathered from his fields, usually 20,000 acres—more or less—earned for him the sobriquet of the "Potato King." He practically controlled the market and set his own price. The Early Rose was grown for early shipment; the Burbank for mid-season and fall demands. His probity and business acumen made him trusted and successful beyond the dreams of avarice. His holdings in Oregon were devoted exclusively to the growing of seed potatoes.[76]

Soon other men followed his example and became potato growers in the valley. According to the Census of the United States for 1930, the county where Shima conducted his initial experiment was one of the fifty leading potato producing counties in the United States. It ranked first in the average yield per acre. Yakima County, Washington, averaged 258.6 bushels per acre; Aroostook County, Maine, with the heaviest total production in the nation, averaged 314.8 bushels per acre; and San Joaquin County led all the others with 326.2 bushels per acre. Since then Kern County, especially in the region about Shafter, has come to the front as a potato center, and in 1937 shipped more potatoes than any other producing point in the nation. In 1937 the ranch of J. N. Anderson, near Shafter, produced 500 sacks to the acre of U. S. No. 1 Grade A potatoes; the average yield for the Shafter district is 350 bushels. The railway furnished 7,755 cars for moving the Shafter potato crop in 1937.[77]

Sweet potatoes found a natural habitat in the valley. A Chinese variety known as the Californian has won favor. The Southern Queen and Jersey Red are grown in Fresno County. The dairymen of Stanislaus grow sweet potatoes for stock feed, run them through a root shredder, and dry them on fruit trays.[78]

Due largely to the experiments conducted by Henry Ford, it was found that soybeans were of value in automobile manufacturing. This led to the planting of this crop in the central part of the valley. Soybeans can be raised with less water, and hence with less cost, than many other crops. The first soybean factory was erected at Tulare in 1938. That same year, a sugar beet receiving station was erected at Kingsburg, and 1000 acres were planted to beets under the direction of the American Crystal Sugar Company.

Thinning, cultivating, topping, harvesting, and hauling to the receiving station were all contracted by the company.[79]

Obviously it is impossible to explain in detail the many forms of horticulture engrossing the attention of the San Joaquin Valley ranchers. Fields of asparagus, celery, and flax are much in evidence. Olive groves and mulberry trees, destined to form the basis for a future silk industry, are common sights in the valley. The California State Department of Agriculture, and the experts connected with the University of California, have brought to the state from the ends of the earth every form of plant life which may prove of economic value to its residents. If Pedro Fages were privileged to make a tour of the valley in 1940 he would find not the wild frontier of 1772, but a smiling countryside very similar in its appearance to his beloved Spain. His people were the first to introduce domestic trees and plants, and present-day Californians are continuing that form of development.

> Read my little fable:
> He that runs may read,
> Most can raise the flowers now
> For all have got the seed.[80]

19 Black Gold

Oil is as necessary as blood
in the battles of tomorrow.

Georges Clemenceau, Premier of France

"American Indians in western Pennsylvania . . . led
Father Joseph de la Roche D'Allion, a French Franciscan
missionary, to a pool of black water. Since then this
miracle-working fluid has been used increasingly, first as
a medicant, and later as an illuminant." This visit was
made in 1699. The Seneca Indians, one of the six tribes
composing the Iroquois Confederacy of New York, held as
their traditional right the Seneca Oil Spring, located near
the present city of Cuba, New York. They valued the oil
for healing purposes, and by the Treaty of Big Tree in
1797, it was permanently reserved to them.[1]

The first man to recognize the commercial value of
petroleum products was George Washington. In 1763,
after the close of the French and Indian War, he made a
vacation and business trip to the western part of
Pennsylvania. He learned of the existence of petroleum in

that region and recognized that this mineral possessed industrial importance. Thereafter, he acquired oil lands and listed them among his most valuable assets. Concerning these holdings, he wrote in his will: "This tract was taken up by General Lewis and myself on account of the bituminous spring which it contains, of so inflammable a nature as to burn freely as spirits and is as nearly difficult to extinguish."

The foregoing quotation suggests that George Washington was the first man to recognize the commercial value of the oil in the region destined to become the first great oil-producing section in the United States. The second great discovery was to take place in the far west.

The discovery of a yellow metal in California sent millions of gold dollars out of the state; the later discovery of oil brought millions of those dollars back to California. The Golden State leads any other state today in the production of both yellow and black gold. The discoveries of these two minerals were dissimilar in one respect. The moment gold was found the rush began; however, oil was known to exist in California a hundred years before the boom began. In the case of oil, it was not the discovery of the mineral, but of the market, which led to rapid exploitation of the oil fields.

Swamps of crude oil, and the bubbling of gas in stagnant pools, revealed the presence of petroleum to the early valley residents. The Indians used asphaltum, and the Franciscan padres employed the same substance in roofing their missions. One observer, who published a book in 1868, described the region that was later to become a vast oil field:

> From Fort Tejon, on the southern extremity of the county, to the Kern River, a distance of about forty miles along the western border, the county, for about ten miles from the Coast

Range, is covered with salt marshes, brine, and petroleum springs, which, in a locality more favored with roads, would be valuable.

The same author stated that the surface of the pools was "constantly agitated by the escape of gas from below."[2]

In 1864 Frank Dusy, then a resident of the Mariposa country and subsequently of Selma, and John Clark of Bear Valley went on a hunting trip to the Coast Range mountains, west of modern-day Coalinga. Dusy was one of the original Forty-niners, and was destined later to pioneer from the Selma district the exodus of the first group of miners to Cook Inlet in Alaska. Dusy and Clark noticed oil seepage beside certain springs and ledges in the Vallecito Canyon. These two men, along with W. A. Porter, organized the San Joaquin Petroleum Company and filed a claim on 160 acres in the region on December 16, 1864. A few gallons of petroleum were extracted and peddled in the streets of the county seat at Millerton. Soon, the rush was on.[3]

Claims were filed on lands, public and private. The Elkhorn Ranch, owned by Cuthbert Burrel, became the site for wildcat drilling. The modern site of Burrel indicates its general locality. Cuthbert Burrel and other men organized the Elkhorn Oil District under mining laws, and became directors in the company. The interest in oil became a mania for a time. Lacking geological knowledge, the most ridiculous places were selected for drilling operations. However, the subsiding of interest and the collapse of the organized companies was not due to lack of oil, so much as to a lack of markets for the evil-smelling petroleum. The development in later years of oil-burning machinery was to alter these conditions.[4]

During this exciting premature oil boom period, Talleyrand Choisser of Mariposa County sold an oil claim

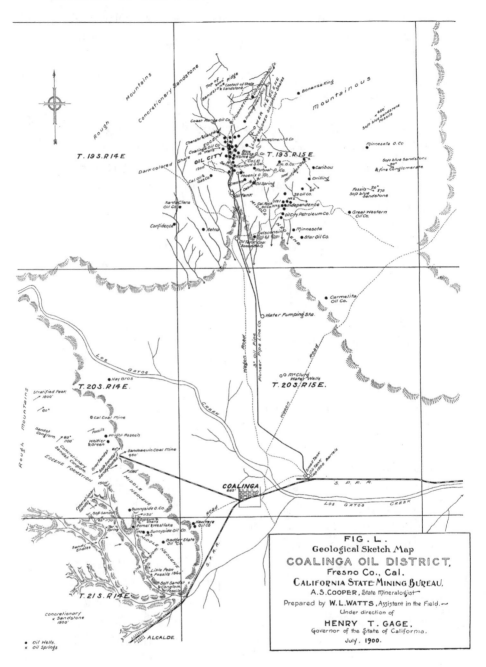

W. L. Watts, *Oil and Gas Yielding Formations of California.*

to a New York firm for $20,000 in greenbacks. This was the largest exchange of money made up to that time for an unproved oil field in California. Choisser's oil prospecting partner, in what is now Kern County, was a man named Ketton.[5]

The oil excitement reached its apex in 1865. The lands lying along the San Joaquin River were then under surveillance. An observer stated that the oil prospectors that year crossed "Firebaugh's Ferry like unto a battalion of soldiers—some in wagons, some on horses or on mule-back, and many on foot, all bound for the land of petroleum."[6]

In 1864, the same year that Dusy and Clark located oil in the vicinity of Coalinga, oil was secured and distilled about eighteen miles southeast of Buena Vista Lake. A visitor to the works located there wrote: "The company made several thousand gallons of good oil, but it cost more to send it to market than oil could be procured for from the Eastern States."[7]

This Buena Vista Petroleum Company was organized by business and professional men from Mariposa and Bear Valley, and Judge J. O. Lovejoy of Mariposa was president of the company. This company dug wells and continued to sell oil in moderate quantities, although no great demand for the product then existed.[8]

In 1882 M. L. Curtiss made a homestead entry on a tract of land in Pleasant Valley, which included within its boundaries the present site of Coalinga. At that time, most of the land in that region was controlled by the Kreyenhagen family, which had its ranch headquarters at Poso Chine. Aside from cattle and sheep, the only industry in Pleasant Valley at that time was represented by two Englishmen, Robinson & Rollins, who operated a small coalmine in the hills near Alcalde. The Southern Pacific built a branch road into that territory in 1888 in order to take advantage of its land grants. Hanford furnished a market for coal, and Robinson & Rollins loaded their product from a platform built beside the new railway at a point nearest their mine. This was appropriately named Coaling Station A, or Coalinga.[9]

The water in that region, since it was impregnated with oil, was vile. Therefore it, as well as other liquid refreshments, was shipped into Coalinga and its environs from Hanford. The railroad, closely followed by the saloon, gave to this little coal-shipping station a semblance of that type of civilization then typical of the frontier. The saloon-keeper, Frederick Tibbits, catered to the wants of the Basque sheep herders from the sagebrush plains, to the cowboys and cattlemen from the foothills, and to the Welsh miners from the nearby coal pit. The speech and dialect of the latter caused the native-born cowboys to regard them curiously. Tibbits was proficient in a game played with little pasteboards, and is reported to have bankrupted the firm of Robinson & Rollins in a rancorous tilt in which the hands dealt from the deck were not to their liking.[10]

Geologists maintain that once upon a time the coastline of California lay along the western edge of the Sierra Nevada, and that the San Joaquin was then a great inland sea. The Coast Range was then a barrier, or possibly a series of islands, between it and the Pacific Ocean. Their assertions have been borne out by the experiences of borers who have drilled wells for irrigation purposes. In 1920 Omie De LaGrange, the owner of a well-drilling firm at Selma, was engaged to bore a well for a rancher residing two miles west of Caruthers. At a depth of 150 feet, his bit bored through an oak log in an excellent state of preservation. Other well borers have reported drilling through redwood logs at various places in the San Joaquin. These experiences indicate that erosion had gradually filled the inland sea with soil of an inexhaustible fertility.[11]

In those days before the inland water had rushed out at the Golden Gate, huge rocks were placed or formed in the Coalinga region under which were deposited pools of low, specific gravity oil. But men did not know this in 1890; those who followed their premonitions in the matter were ridiculed or pitied. In that year, an attempt was made to prove that Coalinga was a prospective oil field. The few men in that community (Coalinga had not then been founded) with money, as well as business and professional men in adjacent cities, "hee-hawed" the attempt and set an example since generally followed by Babbitts in other communities during similar attempts. Not one cent could be raised among the Bakersfield merchants for the original venture sponsored by oil promoters along Kern River. Neither did they reap any of the profits; it all went to outside investors.[12]

In justice to the "hee-hawers," it is only fair to point out that the search for oil is as big a gamble as the search for gold, and infinitely more expensive. Gullible investors have frequently been deceived by dishonest promoters. A knowledge of geology is necessary, but it is not always an infallible guide. Oil has been found where geologists denied its existence. Also, the improvement of rotary drills has made possible a deeper penetration, and thus made available unknown or previously unattainable sources. Those who have ridiculed attempts to prove new oil fields have often been right in fact, if not in spirit.

The official California oil and gas report for the first quarter of 1931 revealed the fact that 169 attempts during 1930 resulted in financial loss and failure. The cost of each attempt, depending upon the depth of each well, ranged from $25,000 to $50,000; the average depth of the discarded wildcat wells was 5,920 feet. However, the State of California leads the union, and the United States leads the world, in the production of oil. The men who pioneer in this search for oil receive merely that portion of criticism that always has been the lot of the men who possess clarity of vision and strength of purpose.

The development of a new oil field has often encountered opposition in the form of propaganda sponsored by major oil companies in established fields who feared the competition of new fields, with oil in paying quantities at a possibly shallower depth. One form of veiled attack has been to send speakers to service club luncheons or Chamber of Commerce banquets in the area under surveillance. Their scheduled addresses to the credulous have been camouflaged under innocent appearing subject matter, but their boasted knowledge of oil indications has enabled them to provide the deterrent to the venture under consideration. One speaker from an oil field located along the foothills managed to squelch support from a proposed attempt in another locality by stating that it was doomed to failure since no foothills existed there. He neglected to inform his gaping auditors, and they forgot to think, that the great oil fields of Santa Fe Springs, Texas, Oklahoma, and Kansas, managed to produce oil without the aid of foothills.

The first oil well in the Coalinga region was 163 feet deep, and produced green oil which was pumped to the surface with two windmills at the rate of ten barrels a day. This was the result of the first attempt in 1890. Almost two years later Rowland and Lacy of Los Angeles drilled a 400-foot well, which averaged nine barrels a day. About that time, men residing in towns adjacent to Coalinga evinced an interest in the fields. J. A. McClurg of Selma formed a partnership with William De La Grange, who had been an oil driller in the Pennsylvania fields. The

Oil field on the outskirts of Coalinga, circa 1900. M. Theodore Kearney, *Fresno County, California and the Evolution of the Fruit Vale Estate.*

latter's name is associated with the first venture in the use of underground waters for the purposes of irrigation. Immediately after the completion of the first pumping plant, De La Grange moved his drilling rig to the Coalinga region. On October 5, 1895, he brought in the first oil well for the new Selma oil company, organized by McClurg under the name of the Producers' and Consumers' Oil Company. This well was 695 feet deep, and produced fifteen barrels a day; a second well was sunk 700 feet, and produced twenty barrels.[13]

In 1896 Chanslor and Canfield succeeded in developing a well producing 300 barrels a day. The next year, G. W. Terrill of Selma organized the Home Oil Company and the well developed by this concern, named the Blue Goose, proved that truth is sometimes stranger than fiction. This well proved a greater source of wealth than the goose that laid the golden egg. Its eventual output was 9,000 to 10,000 barrels a day. In the same vicinity, the Silver Tip gave its owners 45,000 barrels in seventy-two hours. The amazing success of these two wells caused the drilling of thirty other wells by other concerns in adjacent territory in an attempt to tap the same pool. Each of these thirty wells was drilled at a cost of $25,000 and in each case the result was a dry hole. Digging for oil is sometimes like that.[14]

The Hanford Oil Company began operations in the Coalinga district in 1898. The Caribou Oil Company, organized by C. C. Spinks, E. E. Bush, and W. A. Spinks, also began to drill in the same territory. The proving of the Coalinga fields led to the investing of both European and Eastern capital. This stimulated expansion of the oil fields region. In 1901 the California Oil Fields, Limited, an English concern incorporated for $2 million, entered the territory and invested $4.5 million; the success of their business enterprise is indicated by the fact that they paid annual dividends of from thirty to forty percent to their stockholders.[15]

This English company employed Frank Jennings as their drilling superintendent. He had been a factor in the oil fields of Pennsylvania and had brought in the Mathews Well of Allegheny County, which produced 25,000 barrels a day. Jennings developed the Twenty-Three Well at Coalinga, which produced 4,000 barrels a day. This well was equaled by a gusher named the Silver Tip, owned by Z. L. Phelps, which broke loose in September 1909 and produced, when under full control, 4,000 barrels a day. In 1908 the California Oil Fields, Ltd. sold out their holdings to the Shell Oil Company and withdrew from the fields. Jennings remained with the latter company for three years and then retired. Another pioneer driller in the Coalinga fields was Milton McWhorter who had been the first driller in the Kern area.[16]

Several large companies entered the fields about 1902. That year, an upward trend began in oil prices, and the demand stimulated great activity in the oil fields. Besides the Shell Oil Company, other big firms such as Standard Oil, Union Oil, and the Associated began to drill. Local capitalists from Fresno and other urban centers began to develop wells. W. F. Chandler and Herman H. Brix of Fresno organized companies that were very successful. Their business ventures dealt not only with oil, but also with transportation and real estate connected with development in the Coalinga region.[17]

The Berry brothers, Clarence and Henry, residing on a ranch four miles north of Kingsburg, were at different times Alaska gold miners and San Joaquin Valley oil promoters. They reaped fortunes in both ventures; Henry Berry later turned his attention to baseball, and acquired the Los Angeles franchise in the Coast League.[18]

Some Fresno men bought land in order to profit by the evident increase of land values which, they expected, would follow the demand for oil. They paid $12.50 an acre, sold 600 acres soon thereafter for $50 an acre, and a few months later disposed of an adjoining 200 acres for the tidy sum of $3,000 an acre.[19]

The nature of Coalinga's growth from 1902 to 1909 was comparable to Traver's phenomenal growth a fifth of a century earlier. The romance and lure of a typical western mining town was then found there. Faro games, with tables stacked high in $20 gold pieces, were the order of the night. The boom was at its height in 1908, when oil reached the high price of 62 1/2 cents a barrel. The Sauer Dough Well by the end of 1910 had paid $517,303.50 in dividends. The Lucile Well was equally good; others were not far behind. Joseph H. Canfield, president of the Associated Oil Company, made his fortune in Coalinga; others, too. Steady employment followed the steady demand for oil, and these conditions finally brought to the fields a steady type of labor. The boisterous old days, with all their tinsel and glamour, gradually came to an end, and were replaced by the solid worth now characteristic of Pleasant Valley.[20]

Oil seepage was frequently noticed along the banks of the Kern River. Wells used for domestic purposes often furnished water tainted with oil. These indications led two brothers, James and Jonathan Elwood, to dig an ordinary well with a hand auger, reaching oil sand at the thirteen-foot level. Business and professional men in Bakersfield leaned back in smug self-complacency and laughed. But the Standard Oil Company did not laugh. It appeared on the scene promptly. The Elwood attempt took place on a farm belonging to Thomas A. Means. It lay along the banks of Kern River, seven miles northeast of Bakersfield. In due time, the surrounding territory developed into the famous Kern River oil fields. The first driller to bring in a paying well was Milton McWhorter.[21]

The Elwood brothers discovered oil in May 1899. About that time Lyman Stewart, member of an eastern oil firm, invested $13,000 in oil properties in Los Angeles County. This was the modest beginning of the Union Oil Company. This company appreciated the significance of the Elwood discovery and moved into the Kern River area with up-to-date machinery and equipment. In a short time thereafter its wealth equaled its wisdom and judgment, and it was capitalized at $75 million.[22]

The Standard Oil Company completed a pipeline from Kern River to Point Richmond in 1902. In order to compete with the major oil companies, the many small companies associated themselves together and took the name of the Associated Oil Company. The latter then formed an alliance with the Southern Pacific Railroad and built a pipeline along the railway's right-of-way. A series of pumping stations were erected at proper intervals, to boost the oil along the way to Martinez and Port Costa. In

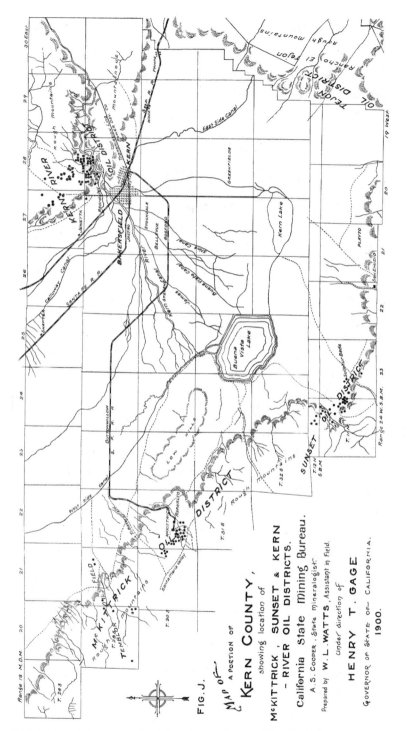

W. L. Watts, *Oil and Gas Yielding Formations of California.*

June 1909 the Union Oil Company, the Independent Oil Producers' Agency, and a similar agency at Coalinga united to form the Producers' Transportation Agency, which built a pipeline from various fields in the San Joaquin to Port Hardford. This line was completed on February 1, 1910. Port San Luis, a port of entry, contains three wharves. No. 1 Wharf is at a town called Avila; No. 2 Wharf is the Union Oil pier; No. 3 Wharf is what was known as Port Hardford. The entire port is called Port San Luis. The same group also formed a consolidated agency, which controlled and regulated sales with excellent results.[23]

After the Kern River and Coalinga fields had been developed, thinking oilmen assumed that the region lying between these points might also produce oil. They explored the territory from the southern end of the valley to Coalinga. The result was the proving of the fields at Maricopa, McKittrick, Taft, and Lost Hills. Within a few years oil derricks could be seen in that region, intermediate between the two older fields, in an unbroken line for fifty miles. This erstwhile halcyon retreat of the lonely sheepherder and cowboy was often disturbed by the roar of new gushers. Individual wells were discovered, which surpassed the wildest dream in the *Arabian Nights* by their extravagant performances.

One of the most astonishing of these was the Lakeview in the Maricopa district. When the well had been drilled to a depth of 2,500 feet the board of directors ordered the superintendent to close down but contrary to orders, he persisted a few days longer. On the night of March 14, 1910 the bailer, weighing half a ton shot out of the well and landed on the top of the derrick. It was followed by oil, sand, skeletons of prehistoric animals, and gas. The roar could be heard for miles around. Finally, it settled down to a steady discharge of oil that rose into a column three hundred feet high. The gusher could not be stopped, and the oil was finally drained away into a sump and pumped from it to Port Hardford on the coast. For two years, this well averaged about 42,000 barrels a day, and some days the output was 68,000 barrels. After having delivered between nine and ten million barrels, it finally stopped flowing in March 1912.[24]

In the official report of the California State Mining Bureau issued in 1921, the San Joaquin was credited with nine proven oil fields. (1) The West Side Fields, including the region from Sunset to Lost Hills. (2) The Midway-Sunset Fields, located in the extreme southern end of the valley. Included in this area, about twenty miles in length, are Maricopa, Taft, Fellows, and Buena Vista Hills. (3) The McKittrick Fields, which consist of the territory surrounding the city of the same name. (4) The Belridge Fields, located in a flat area four miles north of McKittrick and due south of Antelope Hills. (5) The Lost Hills Fields, which lie twelve miles north of Belridge Fields. (6) The Devil's Den Fields, located northwest of the Lost Hills Fields. (7) The Elk Hills Field, which lie northeast of the Midway-Sunset Fields. (8) The Coalinga Fields, most northerly fields thus far (1939) of those developed in the valley. (9) The Kern River Fields, which lie north of Bakersfield.

In view of later events, this report for 1921 contained an interesting prophecy concerning the Kettleman region: "Wells drilled to date indicate that there is no commercial production above approximately 4,000 feet. There are, however, sufficient favorable conditions present to make this region worthy of being tested by at least several deep wells located on the axis of the fold."

The first quarterly report for 1931 made by the California State Oil and Gas Supervisor contained a summary of the new development in oil prospecting during 1930. Two

General view of the Kern River oil field, circa 1899, with wells dotting the plains north of the watercourse. W. L. Watts, *Oil and Gas Yielding Formations of California.*

companies, the American Oil Company and the Camarillo Oil Syndicate, were each financing a test well in the Conejo district. Nothing important had been discovered at the time of the report. The same conditions existed in the Buttonwillow territory, then under surveillance. The Terra Bella Oil Company began operations on June 22, 1930, and cemented its well at a depth of 890 feet. When pumping commenced in this test well, No. "Gardner" 1, it was found that the oil was mixed with water. Twenty-four other wells were drilled by other concerns, and the same conditions developed in all of them. The wells proved of no commercial importance and they were closed on September 30, 1930. Since that time, the Discovery well of the Terra Bella Oil Company and the Bradford well of the Western Oil and Exploration Company have produced oil in paying quantities.

Two fields were proved successful in 1930 beyond the dreams of an Irish Sweepstakes ticket holder. Mountain View (Weed Patch) had been toyed with as early as 1924. Leonard Jones began to drill there in that year, and in September of the same year he sold out to the Shell Oil Company. This company penetrated to a depth of 4,393 feet, found no showing of oil, and abandoned it until April 1930. During this interval, much improvement had been made in drilling machinery, and the Shell Company again attacked Weed Patch. When their core drill reached a depth of 5,910 feet, oil was found in abundance. This

Maricopa's celebrated Lake View gusher open at full throttle, 1910.Wallace Morgan, *History of Kern County, California.*

discovery was made at 9:30 A.M. on November 15, 1930.[25]

The other famous well developed in 1930 was the amazing No. "Huffman" 1, owned by the Superior Oil Company. This was proved on September 4, 1930, at a depth of 8,323 feet. The No. "Huffman" 1 is located in the Kettleman

Hills region. The first successful well in this area was drilled by the Milham Exploration Company and its well, the No. "Elliott" 1, began to produce oil on November 7, 1928. Since then, the prophecy contained in the official report for 1921 has been verified. In 1932 oil was at an ebb tide as far as prices were concerned and yet three wells in the Kettleman Hills, less government royalties, produced oil worth $2,352,683. These wells were owned by the Kettleman Dome Association.[26]

The following report was made officially by the State Oil and Gas Supervisor in 1931:

> The No. "Huffman" 1 has demonstrated that a very large production of black oil with a comparatively low gas-oil ratio may be obtained by penetrating deep into the oil zone and excluding the upper 300 feet from production. This well was completed on September 4 and has a penetration of 1,258 feet, the depth being 8,323 feet. The average daily production for December was 11,090 barrels of oil, 37.3 degrees A. P. I. gravity, and 27,346,000 cubic feet of gas, the gas-oil ratio being 2,466 cubic feet of gas per barrel of oil. The average gas-oil ratio for other wells in the field during December was 35,675 cubic feet per barrel, and the gravity of the oil was 60 to 62 degrees A. P. I., with one exception. Associated Oil Company Well. No. "Whepley" 1 produces dark colored oil of about 43 degrees gravity A. P. I., but the upper sands are open to production and the gas-oil ratio is about ten times as large as that of the well of Superior Oil Company. In view of the fact that approximately half the gas produced in the field is being blown to the air, the importance of a low gas-oil ratio such as that of Superior Oil Company Well cannot be overestimated.

The new towns of Avenal, west of Kettleman Hills, and Kettleman City, east of the hills, are a direct result of this oil discovery that stimulated activity in Kings County generally. The Standard Oil Company entered the field and built a tank farm and pump station near Kettleman City, from which oil is pumped to their ship loading docks at Morro Bay. Here the oil tankers are loaded and carry their cargoes to the ends of the earth.[27]

The natural gas produced in the Kettleman Hills area was ready for distribution for domestic use at San Francisco in August 1929. On October 14th of the same year the company reported that the Milham Well was producing more natural gas than the cities of the bay region could utilize, and that it proposed extending the pipeline to Sacramento. Since then, additional pipelines have been built which extend into Oregon. This natural gas was in general use for heating and cooking purposes in northern California in 1930.[28]

In 1932, with oil prices at their lowest point, the oil produced in the Taft area alone exceeded the value of the gold extracted from Alaska during its most glamorous period for a similar period of time. Water equal to the oil brought to the surface in the San Joaquin annually would float three hundred battleships.[29]

In 1931 the Kingsburg Exploration Company secured a lease of 4,000 acres due east of Kingsburg. The test well was erected on the Peter Mueller ranch, and drilling commenced in September of that year. Lack of funds caused this attempt to lapse, although an official Halliburton test showed indications of oil. Professional geologists have maintained that the area under surveillance contained oil in paying quantities at a shallow depth, but two subsequent attempts at drilling failed because of financial difficulties.[30]

A number of factors have caused an ever-increasing demand for petroleum products. In 1900, the Southern Pacific Railroad discarded coal as fuel, and began to use crude oil. In the same year, county boards of supervisors began to surface public roads with it, and oiled roads became a distinct characteristic of valley landscape.

Factories throughout the nation began to install oil-burning machinery and the invention of the automobile, which came into general use after 1900, made the demand for oil constant and imperative. The tractor and the truck arrived as offshoots of the automobile's development. Finally, the Navy Department began equipping the fleet with oil-burning engines. The demand for oil suddenly became worldwide. This had its bad points as wars have, and will be, fought for possession of the precious fuel.

The United States is fortunate in its possession of the great untapped oil fields of the San Joaquin. The valley, by its richness in this respect, is not only helping in the maintenance of peace, but is insuring the greatness and prosperity of the entire nation. According to a French writer:

> He who owns the oil will own the world, for he will rule the sea by means of the heavy oils, the air by means of the ultra refined oils, and the land by means of petrol and the illuminating oils. And in addition to these he will rule his fellow men in an economic sense, by reason of the fantastic wealth he will derive from oil—the wonderful substance which is more sought after and more precious today than gold itself.[31]

20 United

We Stand

It is not the guns or armament
Or the money they can pay,
It's the close cooperation
That makes them win the day.
It is not the individual
Or the army as a whole,
But the everlastin' teamwork
Of every bloomin' soul.

J. Mason Knox *Cooperation*

"Warning—here lies the body of M. Theodore Kearney, a visionary who thought he could teach the average farmer, and particularly raisin growers, some of the rudiments of sound business management. For eight years he worked strenuously at the task, and at the end of that time he

715

was no further ahead than at the beginning. The effort killed him."

The foregoing epitaph was found among the papers of Theodore Kearney after his death. This man was a mysterious and picturesque figure. A few miles west of Fresno he developed a place known as Kearney Farm, which he proposed to transform into a baronial estate. A winding avenue flanked by palms and eucalyptus trees shaded the approach to a castle surrounded by a moat. Kearney's last will and testament passed this estate to the University of California. Since its acquisition by the state it has been conducted as an agricultural experiment station.

Kearney's effort to organize the raisin growers into a cooperative unit was not the first attempt to be made in the valley. The first growers placed their own products on the market, and the eager demand caused a rapid expansion of the industry. This resulted in the appearance of the merchant packers, who relieved the grower of the task of finding a market for his product, and in some cases also relieved the grower of most of his profits. During the 1880s the demand exceeded the supply, and profits were correspondingly high. Vineyards showed a net profit of $450 an acre, and land sold for $1,000 an acre. The result was a rapid expansion and exploitation of the raisin belt. A condition similar to the post-war period of 1919 to 1920 resulted.[1]

In 1889, the packers refused any longer to assume the risk of purchase. They advanced the growers a small sum on delivery and paid the balance after the product had been sold in the East. This commission system failed to function and an agitation was begun to improve marketing conditions by cooperation. A few small cooperative organizations were formed in 1889, but these handled only a small percentage of the crop. In 1891, a

Armenian crew picking wine grapes in Fresno County, circa 1900.M. Theodore Kearney, *Fresno County, California and the Evolution of the Fruit Vale Estate.*

movement was sponsored by O. B. Olufs to organize a raisin exchange. That year raisins sold for one cent a pound. On June 25, 1892, a mass meeting was held in the DeWitt Hall at Fresno, which drew up the following agreement:

> We, the undersigned raisin growers of California, having become fully satisfied that the present demoralized condition of the raisin market is almost, if not entirely, due to the absence of any understanding concerning uniform selling prices among the parties who have the products of raisin vineyards in their hands for sale, and from the fact that numerous established agencies in the East are in the habit of competing and thereby underselling each other without regard to prices, we believe the time is at hand when this system of disposing of our vineyard products will bring the raisin growers of this State to poverty and financial ruin.
>
> Now, therefore, in view of the facts above stated, we, the undersigned raisin growers, do most earnestly request, as a matter of protection to ourselves and families, even demand,

717

that the packers who are producers of raisins, and packers who are not producers of raisins, and, in fact, all who have raisins in proper condition for the markets of the world, join together immediately and agree among themselves not to sell any raisins during this present crop year for less than the minimum price agreed upon. And in consideration of such agreement as above, we, the undersigned raisin growers, hereby agree and mutually bind ourselves upon our honor, not to give; sell or consign any raisins subject to our control, during the term above mentioned, to any party or parties who do not enter into our agreement establishing such minimum price.[2]

Packers promised to pay 4 1/2 cents a pound for raisins in the sweat box if the California State Raisin Growers' Association thus organized could secure control of 95 percent of the crop; otherwise, the few outside packers would undersell them with enough raisins to make this price ruinous. An agreement to this effect was reached, but many growers withdrew because they wanted five cents a pound. Enough raisins were consigned to New York by outside packers and growers, which made impossible the 4 1/2 cent figure, and the result of the debacle which followed can be expressed succinctly in the terms of 1 1/4 cent a pound. The president of the California State Raisin Growers' Association at that time was Professor D. T. Fowler of the University of California.[3]

A second attempt was made on June 20, 1894, when the California Raisin Growers' and Packers' Company was incorporated. The owner of the San Ricardo Vineyard four miles east of Fresno, W. H. Hodgkin, was elected president. He issued the following circular of warning to the growers:

We must have 100 percent of the growers and packers united in order to succeed. Eighty percent is not enough. Therefore, let every man who finds that his neighbor has not joined the company impress upon him the vital importance and immediate necessity of his so doing, so that every raisin grower and packer in California will stand shoulder to shoulder to protect this great industry. In becoming shareholders, we believe you are taking the only course to save your homes and the vineyards from ultimate ruin and loss at the hands of the eastern broker and his allies.[4]

Eighty percent of the entire tonnage was signed up with the association, and a price of 3 3/4 cents per pound set for the crop. Outside packers consigned raisins from the 20 percent remaining outside the company at a lower price, and the organization and its price was thus doomed. The raisin crop of 1894 was sold for hog feed in most cases, and 10,000 acres of vines were torn out and replaced by diversified forms of agriculture. Therefore, the second big attempt at cooperation and price setting ended in failure due to treachery from within.[5]

In 1895 Robert Smith presided at a mass meeting held at Easton, at which Professor D. T. Fowler was the speaker, and a plan of future cooperation by affiliation with the California Fruit Exchange was outlined. This meeting led to a series of subsequent attempts at organization, but nothing tangible was achieved. However, the need of cooperation was becoming increasingly apparent. The result of discussing the question was educational if not definitely conclusive. Meanwhile, the grapes were ripening and the crop of 1895 was coming on to glut the market and to confuse matters.[6]

In those days, often referred to as the gay old nineties, no definite opposition to cooperation existed. The chief obstacle was the particular method to be employed. All sought the same end, but one group of men invariably blocked the method proposed by another. They all had the same destination, but chose to travel by different roads. The raisin growers then were of British, German, and Scandinavian descent, and intelligent enough by heredity

719

and training to appreciate the value of concerted action.
Since that time, the matter of cooperation has been
grievously hampered by the arrival of illiterate immigrants
whose oppression at the hands of tyrannical governments
has made them suspicious, intensely individualistic, and
opposed to the delegation of authority.[7]

On May 14, 1898, hundreds of growers assembled in
Armory Hall, Fresno, to plan another cooperative venture.
T. C. White was appointed permanent chairman. Theodore
Kearney's address that day electrified his audience:

> How did the present condition come about? We had a hard
> time to create a market for our raisins. We prospered for a
> while—as long as we sold a good quality of raisins, but in an
> evil hour we became too greedy. We were not satisfied with 6
> cents a pound and we filled our orders with goods inferior to
> the brand on the package. The result was disaster during the
> panic of 1893, and then the consignment period, with its
> stupid and reckless shipping of damaged raisins fit only for
> the wineries.
>
> The only practical remedy is to pool our crops, control the
> quality and quantity when offered for sale, and then the price
> at which the output shall be sold. I suggest the incorporation
> of the California Raisin Growers' Association with a capital
> stock of $500,000 in 100,000 shares of $5 each, shares to be
> opened for raisin growers only, and no one to have more
> shares than the proportion that his crop bears to the whole
> yield of the State.[8]

The plans formulated by Kearney were accepted, and by
September 90 percent of the growers had signed up with
the pool. A permanent organization was effected with
Kearney as president. Prices were set at 4 1/2 cents a
pound, and a large holdover from the previous year was
sold. Buyers were sent into the field to compete with the
outside packers; this venture alone netted the growers'
concern $15,000.[9]

Kearney was re-elected president in 1899 and the contract with the packers made more stringent. During the previous year, only three growers out of the 2,100 members had broken their contracts. Again, the growers enjoyed a highly prosperous season. Raisins were sold for 6 cents, and this price was increased by a fourth of a cent in October 1899. Two things began to cause Kearney difficulty at that time; first, the resentment of the growers against the high salaries of the officers; and second, the attempt of Kearney to secure warehouses in order to control packing facilities, which was thwarted by the membership. Kearney made a bitter criticism of conditions in a speech before the California Fruit Growers' Convention in the fall of 1899:

> I regret to say that the farmers as a class are somewhat inclined to an excess of suspicion at the wrong time, and to an absence of it at the right time. It is also unfortunate that in large business affairs they appear to be lacking in masterful business ability and broad views which are so conspicuous in the many large undertakings in commercial life. It requires great patience, and greater perseverance, to win the confidence of farmers, but when they secure men of ability and unswerving integrity as leaders, they can be depended upon to fall into line and stay there, however fierce the battle may rage.[10]

The directors of the Association mailed to the growers, in December 1899, a form known as the "Yellow Slip," which requested them to convey to the directors the right to deduct from next year's crop a fourth of a cent a pound. The fund thus established was to be spent in the erection of packing plants. These yellow slips became the source of difficulty, because many of the growers objected to the building of these plants. In May, 1900, Kearney asked for an increase in salary from $500 a month to $1,000; the growers refused to sanction this, and Kearney resigned and went to Europe on a visit.[11]

The packers organized the California Raisin Packing Company and came to an agreement with the Association, then composed of 90 percent of the growers, to handle the 1900 crop. The price was set at 6 1/2 cents a pound, but many growers broke their contracts and the market slumped. The result was 1,400 carloads as a carry-over, most of which eventually went to the wineries at 1 1/2 cents a pound.[12]

Kearney returned from his European vacation and informed the growers, what they already knew to their sorrow, that their failure to heed him had cost them $1million. This time they heeded and needed him, and Kearney again became president. He quickly reorganized the company but, due to ill health, returned to Europe. Vice President Biddle was left in charge. The yellow slip feature of the new contract militated against its being signed, and only 60 percent of the growers supported it. In spite of this small membership the growers managed to dispose of their crops, although the average price was only 2 3/4 cents a pound. The disgruntled growers elected a new board of directors in January 1902, and Kearney retired. The former secretary, Robert Boot, became the new president.[13]

The raisin crop for 1903 brought the growers 3 4/5 cents a pound, but 500 carloads remained unsold. In June 1904 a one-year contract was offered the growers, and 90 percent signed it. The packers offered 4 1/2 cents a pound for the raisins in the sweatbox, and the Association found itself unable to compete with these outside packers. The result was the election of a new board in March 1904, which included Kearney. The fifth member of the new board, R. K. Madsen, was on a visit to Denmark at the time of his election. Kearney refused to serve unless elected president; Madsen secured the coveted place, and Kearney resigned and went to Germany to take the baths. In

Mass meeting of the California Raisin Growers' Association, circa 1900. Organization President M. Theodore Kearney is seated at center stage. M. Theodore Kearney, *Fresno County, California and the Evolution of the Fruit Vale Estate.*

September of the same year, the Association gave all its raisins to the Central California Raisin Company, a packing corporation which, in turn, assumed the liabilities of the now bankrupt cooperative organization.[14]

The irrepressible Kearney returned from his tour of Europe and agitated for another cooperative organization. The contracts offered the growers included the yellow slips, and the result was the California Raisin Growers' Company. This was incorporated under the laws of Nevada and provided for a board of thirty-three directors. The raisin belt was divided into twenty-six represented districts, and the other seven directors were elected at large. Kearney was elected president and again went to Europe in search of health. This company controlled only 50 percent of the acreage, but the directors succeeded in

Drying raisins on trays in a Fresno field, circa 1900. M. Theodore Kearney, *Fresno County, California and the Evolution of the Fruit Vale Estate.*

disposing of their raisins through the instrumentality of the Mercantile Company for 3 1/4 cents a pound. The company paid all of its debts and had $4,500 with which to pay the fees of the directors and vice president. Then came the San Francisco earthquake, and this amount was generously donated to aid the stricken people fleeing from that holocaust. Kearney returned from Europe, requested an increase in salary, was refused, and severed his connections with all cooperative attempts thenceforth.[15]

The Farmers' Educational and Cooperative Union of America played an important part in the raisin industry from 1908 to 1912. Up to that time, it had concerned itself chiefly with the cotton and corn belts. At the instigation of Paris Henderson of Kingsburg, the Farmers' Union made its appearance in the valley. Henderson had been an

724

active member in Kansas, and upon his arrival in
Kingsburg he noted the gloom which enshrouded the
entire community as a result of the chaotic conditions in
the raisin industry. He thought that, perhaps, the
Farmers' Union could solve the problem. Therefore he
wrote to Charles Barrett, the national president of the
Farmers' Educational and Cooperative Union of America.
The latter sent W. W. Welsh, national organizer, to the
San Joaquin Valley, where 4,000 growers promptly
enrolled in the Farmers' Union. In 1908, delegates from
the entire valley between Stockton and Bakersfield met at
Kingsburg and formulated plans for the handling of
raisins. At this meeting, an organization was effected
which took the name of the California Farmers' Union,
Incorporated. A board of five directors was elected, with A.
Sorenson of Fresno as president. Local units were
organized with the proper officials. This Union handled
the raisins for its members until 1912. It helped to tide
over a serious crisis, but lack of funds prevented it from
competing successfully with the merchant packers. The
Farmers' Union could not make full payment upon
delivery. It rented or purchased several packinghouses,
which were retained until the farmers finally formed a
permanent organization.[16]

In 1908 James Horsburgh, general passenger agent of the
Southern Pacific, suggested that Fresno celebrate a Raisin
Day and stimulate an interest in the industry. The date
for this event was set for April 30 which commemorated,
appropriately enough, the planting of the first vine in
California. This celebration has remained an annual event
since that time. A local girl is selected as queen of the
Raisin Day festival. Surrounded by her attendants and
accompanied by a moving picture actor or other celebrity,
she rides in state on the beautiful float provided for the
occasion.[17]

As a result of the enthusiasm engendered by this first Raisin Day parade, a plan was promulgated to form a Million Dollar Company with shares at $10 each, and one share to each acre. This plan was adopted to the exclusion of many others offered. Wylie Giffen, campaign manager, opened an office in Fresno, but the attempt proved abortive and was abandoned in June 1910. The growers had proved apathetic and listless.[18]

In June 1911, W. R. Nutting was instrumental in the organization of the Raisin Exchange. The chief contribution of this body was the compilation of data and valuable information by its Bureau of Statistics, which later formed the working basis of the successful attempt soon to follow.[19]

In the fall of 1912, another Million Dollar Company was proposed by Ingvart Teilman. This company was to consist of ten thousand shares at $100 dollars each. This concern was incorporated under the name of the California Associated Raisin Company and is still (1939) in existence, although its name was changed in February, 1922, to the Sun-Maid Raisin Growers. Wylie M. Giffen was elected president and James Madison, vice-president and manager.[20]

In 1913, the California Associated Raisin Company handled 90 percent of the crop of the entire state; the next two years it secured only 80 percent. On August 1, 1915, the *Sun-Maid Herald* made its appearance, with the following comment from Wylie M. Giffen:

> In mailing you this, the initial issue of the *Sun-Maid Herald*, we do so with the desire and belief that it will go far toward cementing the tie that binds us together in this great organization. It is our intention to make this a monthly magazine that will be mailed to every grower in the district on the first of every month.

Its columns will be open for a free discussion of our needs by any grower who has the welfare of the raisin industry at heart. Criticism of the management will be welcome, provided it is made in sincerity and with the desire to build up and strengthen instead of to tear down.

This trade journal appeared regularly. In time its name was changed to the *Associated Grower*; finally, it became *Sun-Maid Business*. The periodical employed journalists who gave favorable publicity to the organization and created an esprit de corps among the growers. Interspersed with serious statements concerning market conditions appeared articles in a comic vein, which nevertheless contained a great deal of information. The following, written in imitation of H. C. Witwer's "You know me, Al" series, is typical:

This Valley is some place when it comes to size and possibilities for the future. Why, man alive, it is about 225 miles long and averages 50 miles wide! That means it has a total area of about 11,500 miles, and that doesn't include the land that we commonly call the foothills, but is just the floor of the Valley. I got curious one day to compare the size of the Valley with some of the States back east, and what do you think? The San Joaquin Valley is as large as Rhode Island, Connecticut, Delaware, and half of New Jersey all put together! Wouldn't it be great if we could have three brand new Governors and half of another one to make a good bargain? If Sue would let me get into politics, I believe I would be fool enough to run for the office of half a Governor.

Maybe you don't think this Valley is level, but just listen to this. The elevation above sea level at Stockton is 23 feet, and way down at the southern end of the Valley at Bakersfield it is 394 feet. That means you can drive your Lizzie flivver (if you had one) all day without shifting into low. Best of all we have dandy paved roads almost everywhere here now, so you can scatter out in style. Some different than when we used to drive the old mule team and walk back every night to find out how far we had traveled during the day.

Well, anyway, this is the Valley where most of the raisins of the United States are grown—something like 94 percent to be exact. Most of them are grown within 60 miles of the city of Fresno. Now, just because we seem to be the big toads in the puddle right now, don't think that we are going to lean on the shovel handle and let the rest of the world go by. We thought one time several years ago when we were producing something like 40,000 tons of raisins that every mother's son and his mother were eating all the raisins they could, but we growers got together and formed this cooperative organization and found out there were a lot of people who never heard of a raisin. Now we are raising pretty close to two hundred thousand tons, and a lot more vines being planted every year. You can see from this that a lot of people have learned to use raisin bread, raisin pie, and a lot of other good things they put raisins into.

Even with all this increase in production of raisins, to say nothing of a lot of other fruits like peaches, apricots, figs, prunes, plums, oranges, lemons, olives, and a few others, there is room for a good bit of development yet. One fellow made an estimate a month ago that we had only about 25 percent of the tillable area of the Valley under cultivation at the present time, so you see, Al, selling all of the raisins we can produce here around Fresno is a pretty big job.

I told you something about using the water of the melting snows up in the mountains for irrigation. You may think it strange, but we can stand on our side porch, any day in the year, even in summer when it is hot, and look right up the mountains and see all kinds of snow. You can imagine that these mountains must be pretty high to have snow on them all the year around. Well, the height at the summit varies from 12,000 to 14,000 feet above sea level. During the summer this snow melts slowly and comes down to the Valley, so the Sierras are the source of eight large streams and a number of smaller ones. The water of all these streams is used for irrigation purposes. There are plans for some large storage reservoirs at suitable places in the mountains, so the supply will be uniform all the year around, because there is more water in the early summer than we can use, and later

Stemming raisins in a Fresno plant, circa 1900. M. Theodore Kearney, *Fresno County, California and the Evolution of the Fruit Vale Estate.*

when we need the most it sometimes gets a little short. This condition will be getting worse when we develop more of the land.

It must have been a pretty big job to plan for and make all of the big main irrigation canals. They carry a few drops of water every year. If you want to look at big figures, just study this out. The annual run-off from eight or more streams is estimated at 11.5 million acre feet and there is approximately 325,850 gallons of water to each acre foot. That is enough water to make your head swim, even to look at the figures.[21]

In 1920, the raisin crop brought the growers their largest returns and amounted to $38,416,825.90; the same year, the Attorney General of the United States brought suit against the California Associated Raisin Company. It was specifically charged that the company was violating the Sherman Anti-Trust Law by monopolizing the raisin industry. The attempt was made to prove that the activities of the Company were in restraint of trade. On April 16, 1921 it was reported that 10,700 growers, or 93 percent, were members of the association. This suit, instigated by foes of all cooperatives, was dismissed in January 1922, when a decree was filed in the federal district court at Los Angeles prohibiting the California Associated Raisin Company from doing what it had never done and had never intended to do. The general effect of this trial was to strengthen the position of the association, although it caused a great deal of temporary anxiety.

The packers, instigators of this famous lawsuit, did not have a clear case, as was noted by a local Sun-Maid unit member. First, the association never at any time controlled all of the vineyards in bearing. It merely tried to market, at its own price, the raisins produced by its own membership. Second, the land lying between Dinuba and Caruthers, and between Fresno and Kingsburg, is the true raisin belt. Most of the region was not then, and never has been at a later date, devoted to raisin culture. No law or agreement prevented the planting of other vineyards to compete with those already in existence. Suitable land and irrigation water was available for that purpose. The opponents of the cooperative had the opportunity to furnish competition, which they maintained was the life of trade. The association could not, and did not, control the supply, which is the basic necessity in a true monopoly.[22]

Raisins would have brought 15 cents a pound that year if enemies had not molested the association. Some sales were actually made to independent packers for 19 and 20 cents per pound. The Association finally was able to pay 11 cents.

The damage done to the association by federal action, and the ill-will of hostile interests by this lawsuit, has been summed up by a student of this period as follows:

The fact must be borne in mind that the long legal battle that diverted so much money, time and energy of the community and of the growers' company from the problems of marketing was instigated within the Fresno District by a group of packers intent upon their immediate gain and personal survival. They must bear a heavy responsibility for the community and industry turmoil that followed.[23]

Herbert C. Hoover and Ralph P. Merritt acquired a large tract of land jointly near Wasco in 1920. A part of this ranch was planted to vines and the following January the two owners became members of the California Associated Raisin Company. In February, 1922, the name of the organization was changed to the Sun-Maid Raisin Growers. This was done to capitalize on the trade name that was well known by that time. Salesmen in the East reported that buyers did not know that Sun-Maid products were produced by the California Associated Raisin Company. Hence the change avoided explanations and confusion. The chief figure in the company at that time was a raisin grower, Wylie M. Giffen, who directed the affairs of the huge cooperative without any salary, or indirect remuneration. In January, 1923, he was succeeded by Ralph P. Merritt, who became managing director of Sun-Maid, and in September of the same year, president of the company. This position he retained through the period of depression which inevitably followed the post-war inflation period. On July 26, 1928, he retired in favor of Harry M. Creech.[24]

One of the most intensive campaigns to sell raisins took place in 1922. The budget for advertising was placed at $2,520,000 and the result justified the assertion that advertising will sell raisins. As long as the company controlled 85 percent of the crop it was possible to control the price, but the short term contracts and the necessary sign-up campaigns militated against this control and the prices of raisins steadily declined.[25]

731

Large-scale raisin drying with stacked trays, from George C. Roeding's "Fruit Grower's Guide" of 1919.

The creation of a Federal Farm Board by the Hoover administration aided the farmers in four ways: By minimizing speculation; by preventing inefficient and wasteful methods of distribution; by encouraging the organization of producers into effective associations or corporations—that is, into cooperatives; and by aiding in preventing and controlling surpluses in any agricultural community.

The Federal Farm Board did not organize cooperative associations; it merely proposed such organizations, and volunteered to assist them by furnishing cheap money. In an attempt to stabilize the raisin industry, the outstanding $4 million worth of Sun-Maid bonds were taken over at 6 percent, with payment to be made over a 20-year period by varying amounts deducted from each pound of raisins sold. This is not to be confused with the $5.25 stabilization fee subtracted from the sale of each ton of raisins sold. The stabilization fee on fresh grapes is $1.50 a ton.

The Farm Board required that 85 percent of the raisin growers join the raisin pool before aid would be forthcoming. The ensuing campaign was both educational and edifying. The requisite number of signers was secured. A Grape Control Board of twenty members was elected, which was to serve as an intermediary and intercessory group between the grower and the Federal Farm Board. In 1930, the funds furnished the growers in financing their crop was provided in the following fashion: The Government made an advance of $2.5 million to the growers. Of this amount, the Federal Farm Board furnished 50 percent at 1 5/8% interest; the Federal Intermediate Credit Bank of Berkeley, which is a branch of the Federal Land Bank, provided the other half of the amount at an interest of 4 percent. In 1931, the interest charged by the Farm Board was 1/4 of 1 percent; by the Credit Bank, 4 1/2%. The Raisin Pool cashier was required to make a monthly financial statement. The Federal Intermediate Credit Bank handled the funds used in connection with the grape industry during 1930; these amounted to $11,291,829.58, with 7,000 tons not accounted for when the report was made. The 1930 crop brought advance payments of $5,345,021.71 and a progressive payment of $948,663.05, or a total of $6,293,684.76. The varieties recognized in the raisin trade are Muscats, Thompsons, Sultanas, Feherzagos, Malagas, Currants, and Dried Grapes (including everything else). Every variety, except the currants, proved profitable during 1930.[26]

The following chart was prepared under the direction of O. A. Landstrom, who was elected to the Raisin Pool Directorate from the Kingsburg district. It illustrates the set-up of the cooperative organization as sponsored by the Federal Farm Board:

733

CONTROL BOARD

(20 members)

10 Fresh Grape representatives selected as follows:

California Vineyardists Association 3

California Fruit Exchange 3

California Fruit Industries, Incorporated 2

San Joaquin Growers & Shippers Association 2

10 Raisin Pool representatives selected as follows:

Raisin Pool directors (29) elect 3 of own number annually for three-year term. The first year 10 men were elected; these drew lots for the short term 10

CONTROL BOARD EXECUTIVE COMMITTEE

8 members

4 members elected from 10 Raisin Pool representatives on Control Board.

4 elected by other commercial interests.

RAISIN POOL DIRECTORATE

Composed of 29 directors; Wylie M. Giffen, president. Entire raisin territory divided into 29 districts; 28 in San Joaquin Valley and 1 in the Sacramento. One director elected from each district by growers signed up with Control Board.

RAISIN POOL
EXECUTIVE COMMITTEE

7 members

Raisin Pool directors (29) elect 7 of their own number.

POOL-PACKER COMMITTEE

10 members

5 members selected from growers affiliated with Raisin Pool; may be from 29 directors; only 2 may be from Sun-Maid.

5 members selected from following commercial packing concerns on following basis:

2 from Sun-Maid

1 from Rosenberg

1 from California Packing Corporation.

1 from all other commercial packers combined.[27]

The Sun-Maid Advisory Council is composed of one representative from each of the twenty-eight San Joaquin Valley districts, and one from the Sacramento Valley. The members of the council are elected from twenty-nine districts that are identical in area with those electing members of the Raisin Pool Directorate. Many growers are signed up with the Raisin Pool, which is not affiliated with Sun-Maid; therefore the voting population for the two candidates is not the same. These districts are Sacramento Valley, Stanislaus, Merced, Chowchilla, Madera, Clovis, Kerman, Biola, Fresno, Burness, Sanger, Lone Star, Fowler, Easton-Oleander, Del Rey, Parlier, Reedley, Orosi-Cutler, Dinuba, Kingsburg, Selma, Monmouth, Caruthers, Lemoore, Hanford, Tulare, Delano, Lindsay-Exeter-Porterville, and Kern County. These twenty-nine men control the destinies of the Sun-Maid Raisin Company, today in a better position than at any time since those hectic days of 1913, when the directors looked at the sun on the package of raisins and wondered whether it was a rising or a setting sun.

While raisins are the chief product of the valley, another form of income exceeds it annually and yet receives little attention. This comes from the tourist trade, which brings to the valley each year more than $50 million.[28]

The attempts of the raisin growers to form a successful cooperative concern has stimulated interest in other growers and farmers. Some of the more important attempts along these lines will be discussed briefly.

The peach growers of the valley have experienced many vicissitudes during the past generation. Their attempts to form a cooperative were modeled on that of the raisin growers. Often growers, due to a diversification of crops, were members of both organizations. Eventually a cooperative took form, and the name of the California

Peach and Fig Growers Association. This organization sold its products under the Blue Ribbon brand.[29]

The apricot and prune growers in the valley affiliated with a coast organization named the California Prune and Apricot Growers Association. This cooperative had its headquarters at San Jose. Their products were sold under the Sunsweet brand. In the late summer of 1932, the latter organization accepted the membership of the California Peach and Fig Growers Association as a local, and assumed control of the Blue Ribbon plants at Fresno, Reedley, Dinuba, and Kingsburg. Its trade journal is the *Sunsweet Standard*.[30]

The citrus industry has expanded rapidly in recent years and groves of oranges, lemons, and pomelos are located along the eastern edge of the valley floor and in the adjacent foothills from Bakersfield to Mariposa. The citrus industry has generally attracted men of a high degree of intelligence, and their cooperatives have usually functioned smoothly. They are affiliated with the California Fruit Growers Exchange, with headquarters at Los Angeles, and market their products under the famous Sun-Kist brand.

This exchange for the marketing of citrus fruits was formed at Los Angeles in 1893. On March 27, 1905, it was reorganized and assumed the name of the California Fruit Growers Exchange. A monthly trade journal called the *Blue Anchor* is issued to its members. This exchange was organized into three classes, consisting of a central exchange; district exchanges, located at strategic points; and local associations, which affiliated with the nearest district exchange. In 1933, there were 26 district exchanges with 210 affiliated local associations. At that time, there were three district exchanges in the San Joaquin Valley; two at Lindsay and one at Porterville.

Fifty packinghouses in the valley were affiliated with these three exchanges. The central figure in this great citrus organization was Francis Q. Story, who remained president of it from its beginning until his retirement in 1920, at the age of 75 years. His successor was C. C. Teague, who was serving as president in 1933.[31]

In 1912 the walnut growers organized the California Walnut Growers Exchange. C. C. Teague and Carlyle Thorpe were elected president and general manager, respectively, and were still holding those positions in 1933. Federated with the central association, located at Los Angeles, were 40 local walnut packing associations located in the walnut-producing districts. The walnuts in the central part of the valley are marketed through the Sequoia Walnut Growers Association, with headquarters at Visalia. Affiliated with this cooperative, in 1933, were 245 growers.[32]

In the northern part of the valley, the almond growers organized an association in 1899. This functioned until July 1906, when its members disbanded. In 1910 a man named Dargitz called a mass meeting at Sacramento to formulate plans for a statewide organization. Two other sponsors of this movement were John Trembath and B. L. Norcross. The result was the birth of the California Almond Growers Exchange. At the present time, the Eastern Contra Costa Almond Growers Exchange is the dominant element in the marketing of the almonds grown in the San Joaquin Valley.[33]

Dairying was relatively unimportant during Spanish and Mexican rule in California. The longhorn cow was a poor milker and not inclined by birth, breed, or previous training, to be docile.

It required the services of four men to milk one of these half-wild animals. One man would "snub" the cow's nose to a post,

737

holding the rope tightly in his hand. Two others would seize the hind legs, throw the animal to the ground, and keep the legs pinioned, while the fourth man performed the actual milking operation, carefully drawing a few ounces of milk into an earthen vessel.

In those days, churns and cheese presses were unknown, but large quantities of butter and cheese were made. Butter was made by a process of stirring milk and cream together. The method of working the mass to remove the buttermilk was not understood and in consequence, the butter soon became rancid. The only cheese made at the Missions was a sort of cottage cheese formed into cakes with the hands.[34]

The entire state of California produced only 750 pounds of butter and 150 pounds of cheese in 1850. The first cheese factory in the United States was erected in Oneida County, New York, in 1851; five years later, the first creamery was built in Orange County of the same state. This was the nucleus about which was built an industry greatly to modify the development of the San Joaquin Valley.

The first dairy farm in California was established at Colma in 1853 by I. C. Knowles. This San Mateo County farmer was the first man to serve San Francisco with milk in a commercial way. This venture, initiated by Knowles, stimulated activity along similar lines and a decade after the inconsequential output of 1850, the production of California had jumped to 3.1 million pounds of butter and 1.34 million pounds of cheese. In 1862, the Steel brothers established a string of five dairy farms in San Mateo County and specialized in the making of cheese. Until 1888 California dairying was confined to the moist pastures of the coastal region, and particularly to points within easy transportation distance of urban centers such as Los Angeles, San Francisco, San Jose, and Monterey. These cities furnished the chief markets for milk, butter, and cheese.[35]

A Swedish engineer, Alfred de Laval, invented a centrifugal cream separator introduced to the United States in 1885. Prior to that time cream was skimmed by hand from milk set to cool in shipping cans. This invention was to make dairying in the San Joaquin possible. The hot weather in that region was not conducive to the natural forming of cream on top of the milk.[36]

In 1888, D. C. Hayward, a rancher residing five miles southwest of Traver, induced J. G. Cohoe, an experienced butter and cheese maker from New York State, to install a creamery on the Hayward ranch. This was the first creamery in the San Joaquin Valley. At that time irrigation had not been introduced into the Stanislaus region which is now the banner dairy district of California. The work of Cohoe was important, because he demonstrated for the first time that good butter and cheese could be made in the hot interior valley.[37]

The Southern Pacific trainmen handled Cohoe's cheeses recklessly at the Traver station, and the latter realized that his venture was in jeopardy. Cohoe had no inferiority complex where the railroads were concerned. He came from New York, where a railway was considered a servant of The People and not an Octopus to be feared and hated. He went to San Francisco and interviewed the directors. His self-confident manner must have won the approval of the higher authorities, because the Cohoe products were thenceforth handled with the utmost gentleness.[38]

Two years after Hayward had begun his dairying operations, another improvement in the industry occurred which was of vital significance.

> The growth of the factory system of butter-making developed the need of an accurate method of measuring the percentage of butterfat in milk and cream, since the basis of payment to the farmer is the amount of butterfat in the milk or cream. Doctor S. H. Babcock, an American chemist, at the University

of Wisconsin, invented in 1890 an apparatus to test the fat content of milk, thereby placing the butter industry upon a more substantial and permanent basis. The Babcock test also enabled the producer to test the milk of his own cows, and weed out those which were unprofitable as producers of milkfat, and helped the food authorities to protect the consumer against adulterated milk.[39]

In 1900, Harrison Peacock established a creamery at Traver. In the meantime, Cohoe had transferred his business to Hanford. Peacock, a former liveryman at Traver, enlarged his creamery interests rapidly, and soon owned plants at Hanford and Bakersfield and Stockton. Eventually he became president of the Peacock Dairies Incorporated, which has supplied for many years valley retailers with milk and manufactured products, such as ice cream.[40]

Until 1888 there were no dairy cattle in the San Joaquin. The successful experiment of Cohoe at the Hayward ranch; the invention of the centrifugal cream separator; the perfecting of the Babcock tests; the elimination of harmful bacteria by pasteurization through the research work of Louis Pasteur, a French scientist; the introduction of alfalfa and irrigation; the perfecting of the tuberculin test; and the development of markets due to the growth of California cities, all led to the importation of the finest dairy cattle in the world. Today pure bred herds of Holsteins, Jerseys, Guernseys, and Ayrshires are a common sight and excite no comment.

The dairy industry in the San Joaquin has several cooperative organizations. The Swedish and Danish settlers, based on previous experience in their native lands, were to be leaders in this form of development in the San Joaquin. Their contributions were given due recognition in an account published by the National Dairy Council in 1926: "For it is a fact that for twenty years not only in state and in national, but also in international contests, people of Scandinavian blood have taken most of the prizes as butter makers." In the Fresno area in 1930, the Danish Creamery Association linked up its activities with more than 2,000 dairymen. A small leaflet, the *Danish Creamery Magazine*, was issued each month, with a statement of conditions pertaining to the industry. In a report furnished in 1933 by J. R. Murphy, manager of the Danish Creamery Association, is contained an index of this association's volume of business.

> The cooperative manufactured 7,446,669 pounds of butter in 1932, which brought $1,727,806.77; sold 280,603 pounds of butterfat for ice cream purposes for $98,987.42; manufactured 1,967,858 pounds of casein, 3,144,124 pounds of powdered skim milk and 1,142,557 pounds of dried buttermilk.[41]

One of the largest dairy cooperatives in the world has its headquarters at Modesto. This organization, named the Milk Producers' Association of Central California, is usually referred to as the M. P. A. An annual conclave of its members is held at Modesto. This creamery cooperative was organized in 1918, and was the first creamery in the state to produce more than 5 million pounds of butter in one year. This occurred in 1924; the exact output was 5,380,874 pounds. Since that time, the M. P. A. has remained the largest cooperative factory in the United States, excepting only the year of 1930. That year, much of its milk was diverted into condensed products, and honors still remained in the San Joaquin Valley as the Danish Creamery Association of Fresno outranked any other cooperative creamery in the United States. During 1931, the M. P. A. received 155,663,582 pounds of milk at its plants in Modesto and Stockton.

The president of the M. P. A. during recent years has been J. C. Jensen. *Butterfat*, the monthly trade journal, is issued at Modesto by S. J. Strauss. The correlation between a slight gain in prices and the monetary return of dairymen is shown by the effect of the Olympic Games at Los Angeles. A sudden demand for butter caused an increase of one cent a pound for butterfat. This slight increase brought an additional $4,000 a day to the M. P. A. at Modesto.[42]

During that same period, the M. P. A. and the other Challenge Creameries formed an alliance with the Interstate Creameries in Oregon and with the United Dairymen's Association in Washington. The two latter groups were already allied with the Land O' Lakes Creameries of the Mississippi Valley. As a result of this arrangement, carloads of butter and cheese are moved out of congested areas and stored by another of the allied groups. The result has been a decided increase in prices and a strengthened market. That little sod-shanty creamery out on the plains near Traver was the parent of a group of cooperative San Joaquin Valley creameries that have developed an interlocking arrangement with all the creameries of the nation.

> The Kingdom of the Cow is a constantly widening empire. Where she makes the land her own, green carpets of pasture possess the fields, alfalfa throws its perfume to the breeze and corn waves and rustles in the sunshine. There great new barns rise in place of the old, and white-walled farmsteads speak of peace and plenty. There contented farm folk found dynasties by striking the roots of their lives deep into the soil.[43]

Although dairy cattle have largely replaced beef cattle, the latter still have their devotees. The foothill country and much of the valley floor is used for grazing purposes. These cattlemen, the heirs of a long tradition, also have gone modern and have organized a cooperative known as the Western Cattle Marketing Association. Their annual meeting is held usually at Madera. A kindred organization, the Central California Live Stock Breeders' Association, sponsors a stock show at the Fresno County Fairgrounds each fall, together with contests and exhibitions reminiscent of the old west.[44]

The California Cotton Cooperative Association, with headquarters at Bakersfield, is affiliated with the American Cotton Cooperative Association. The California branch had 695 members in 1930. They produced a cotton crop of 45,850 bales that year. Another cooperative unit in the cotton industry is the Farm Bureau Planting Seed Distributors. This organization assists in the distribution of seeds for planting which are secured from the highly improved Acala variety, bred at the Shafter United States Experiment Farm.[45]

The Poultry Producers of Central California is a nonprofit cooperative egg-and-poultry marketing association; it is also a feed-and-supply purchasing organization. This cooperative, the largest in the world, is an actual selling-and-buying business concern and not merely a bargaining association. Its main office is at San Francisco and its activities, represented by forty plants, extend from Petaluma to the southern part of Merced County. In 1929, the 4,537 members owned 4,354,338 hens. The sales value of the eggs handled by the cooperative that year was $15,189,437; feed, $5,131,738; and of poultry, $840,597. The eleven elected directors are all actual poultrymen.[46]

The Porterville Poultry Association is organized like the foregoing cooperative. Its chief plant is at Porterville; an imposing branch plant was later erected at Fresno. This cooperative handles eggs, poultry, and supplies for its members in the counties of Fresno, Tulare, Kings, and Kern. Members are required to deliver all eggs, except those used for home consumption and for hatching purposes.[47]

743

In the summer of 1932, the two-year contract of the raisin growers with the California Raisin Pool was terminated. A new signup campaign directed by Wylie M. Giffen and his associates failed to secure support of the necessary 85 percent of the growers, and the government withdrew its support. Low prices, a result of the depression of 1930-1932, caused dissatisfaction with the pool and its efforts. Therefore, independent packers and Sun-Maid are now the marketing agencies of the raisin industry. The latter cooperative has been relegated to the role of an independent packing concern. When it became apparent that the Raisin Pool signup had failed, Sun-Maid was deluged with applications for membership. But this cooperative felt itself unable to handle raisins for any but its own members, and declined to accept outsiders.[48]

The "Big Five" in raisin marketing have been Theodore Kearney, James Madison, Ralph Merritt, Wylie Giffen, and James M. Leslie. The last-mentioned has been serving as president of Sun-Maid during the past decade. Wylie M. Giffen was active in the industry in the days of Kearney, and directed the campaign of 1932. He served the cooperative as president and manager during its most prosperous period and drew no salary. About him one might truthfully quote Robinson's statement concerning Father Juan Viader: "A good old man, whose heart and soul were in proportion to his immense figure." Kearney's epitaph, quoted at the beginning of this chapter, must have come to his mind after the failure of the campaign. Evidently each new generation of farmers must learn by bitter experience the value of cooperation. The Raisin Pool paid 3 cents a pound for raisins in 1930; 2 1/2 cents in 1931; and the 1932 raisin crop, without the aid of the Pool, brought the grower 1 cent a pound. In the early part of 1933, packers were offering $5 a ton for the holdover 1932 raisin crop. This was the lowest price on record during the history of the industry. It is thus apparent. . .

> ...that even among educated people slovenliness of thought
> may lead to calamitous consequences; as witness in the last
> fifty years the philosophical havoc wrought among educated
> people by so foolish a phrase as *the struggle for existence*, few
> men perceiving that a creature in existence cannot possibly
> struggle for what it already possesses, and that the real
> struggle in nature—a key to the spiritual mystery—is a
> struggle for *improvement*, and that the greatest force in that
> struggle is not egotism, selfishness, and brutal aggression,
> but a most significant cooperation.[49]

Ever since the inception of the raisin industry, many sincere men have opposed any form of marketing cooperative as being un-American and contrary to those principles of rugged individualism which had made this nation great in days past. But the frontier days are over, and society is becoming highly organized and inextricably woven together. The old system was given a last thorough trial, and its collapse in 1929 is now past history. Whether that crash was inevitable, and therefore an indictment of the capitalistic system, or one which could have been averted by adroit management, the historians of the distant future alone can determine.

Enthusiastic supporters of the National Recovery Act have asserted that this program which was typified by the Blue Eagle was a complete, definite, and emphatic repudiation of the old theory of rugged individualism and the laissez-faire doctrine of political economy. One of the great leaders in cooperative marketing in the San Joaquin Valley wrote this about the NRA and its contemplated plan:

> This is an ambitious program. It can not be put over in a day,
> especially in a democracy. But it is well worth the effort
> necessary to secure its acceptance.
>
> We tried it in the San Joaquin Valley some years ago without

745

leading industries. But at that time the federal government was against us, the outside grower was against us, and public opinion beyond the valley was antagonistic. Now the great government of the United States has taken up the Fresno plan and, though we are not claiming that they copied it from us, they have applied it to all industries in the country, instead of to a few, brought millions to see the justice and righteousness of the scheme, enlisted the services of the great economic specialists in the world in its behalf and given us a leadership in the person of President Roosevelt that all should be proud to follow.[50]

No rural section in the United States of a similar area has as many schools, churches, or miles of paved highways as the San Joaquin Valley. In many sections a beautiful home is found on every twenty or forty acres. This creates in the traveler an impression of a suburban tract. The material excellence of the San Joaquin Valley is unequalled. The direction of its future development will depend entirely upon the attitude of its citizenship:

Ships sail East and ships sail west,
While the self-same breezes blow;
It's the set of the sails
And not the gales,
That determine the way they go.

Like the winds of the Sea
Are the ways of Fate
As we journey along through life:
It's the set of the Soul
That determines the goal,
And not the calm nor the strife.[51]

Appendix 1

Indian Tribes of the San Joaquin Valley
Listed by Geographical Area (see map, page xx)

(Based on A. L. Kroeber's *Handbook of the Indians in California* and the *Journal* of Father Francisco Garcés.)

I.   Foothill Division of Yokuts Indians

A. Buena Vista—Kern Lake Group listed by tribes:
1. Tulamni—west shore of Buena Vista Lake.
2. Hometwoli—shores of Kern Lake.
3. Tohohai—Kern River near Tulare Lake.

B. Poso Creek group:
4. Peleuyami—south of Poso Creek and in Linn's Valley.
5. Komechesi—White River region, Earlimart, California Hot Springs.

C. Tule—Kaweah group:
6. Yaudanchi—Springville, Lindsay, Porterville.
7. Bokenwadi—east of Pixley and Terra Bella.
8. Wikchamni—east of Visalia.
9. Yokod—Exeter.
10. Kawia—Woodlake, Yettem, and along Kaweah River.

D. Kings River group:
11. Choinimni—Mill Creek.
12. Michahai—south of Mill Creek.
13. Chukaimina—Squaw Valley.
14. Indimbich—Dunlap region.
15. Toihicha—between Dinkey and Big Creeks.
16. Aigicha—between Mill Creek and Centerville.
17. Gashowu—Little Dry Creek and Big Dry Creek, north of Fresno.

747

E. Northern group of Foothill Division:
    18. Toltichi—in the Sierras along the San Joaquin River.
    19. Kechayi—Millerton.
    20 Dumna—north bank of San Joaquin in front of Fort Miller.
    21. Dalinchi—Coarse Gold Creek.
    22. Chukchansi—Coarse Gold Creek, downstream from the Dalinchi.

II.   Valley Division of Yokuts Indians:

A. Southern group of Yokuts divided into following tribes:
    23. Yauelmani—Tejon Ranch region near the Pass; also Bakersfield.
    24. Koyeti—Tipton and Strathmore.
    25. Choinok—south of Tulare.
    26. Wolasi—south of Farmersville.
    27. Telamni—Visalia, Goshen, Traver.
    28. Wechihit—west of Tulare.
    29. Nutunutu (Notonto)—between Cross Creek and Kings River.
    30. Wimilchi—Laton, Riverdale, Kingsburg, Selma.
    31. Wowol—along Tulare Lake, west of Delano.
    32. Chunut—Kaweah river delta along Tulare Lake.
    33. Tachi—west of Tulare Lake; Coalinga, Huron.
    34. Apiachi—Caruthers, Conejo.
    35. Wech-i-ket—Reedley, Centerville, Sanger.
B. Northern group:
    36. Pitkachi—Herndon, Sycamore Point.
    37. Wakichi—Pinedale, Friant, El Prado.
    38. Hoyima—south of Fresno River, near Madera.
    39. Heutsi—north of Fresno.
    40. Chauchila—Chowchilla.
    41. Noptinte—Mariposa.
    42. Tawalimni—Tuolumne River.
    43. Lakisamni—Knight's Ferry.
    44. Coconoon—Merced River.
    45. Chulartini—Stockton.

III.   Interior Division of Miwok Indians
(Coast and Lake Divisions do not come under the scope of this dissertation).

A. Plains group: north of Stockton.
B. Northern group: west along Stockton toward the mouth of the San Joaquin.
C. Central group: in Sierra foothills east of Stockton.
D. Southern group: in foothills area south to Fresno River.

Appendix 2

Mexican Land Grants

(see map, page 158)

Map	Grant	Owner	Acreage
1. No. 444	Arroyo Seco	Teodocio Yorba	48,857.52
2. No. 79	Cañada de los Vaqueros	Francisco Alviso, Antonio Higuera, Manuel Miranda	48,856.92
3. No. 536	Castaic	José Maria Covarrubias	21,700.09
4. No. 293	El Pescadero	Velentin Higuera, Rafael Féliz	35,446.06
5. No. 267	El Pescadero	Antonio Maria Pico	35,546.39
6. No. 240	El Tejon	Jose Antonio Aguirre, Ignacio del Valle	95,480.10
7. No. 600	Laguna de Tache	Manuel Castro	48,800.82
8. No. 781	Laguna de Tache	Jose Yves Limantour	48,888.09
9. No. 801	Land on the Stanislaus River	Alfias Basil Thompson	35,532.80
10. No. 545	La Panoche de San Juan y los Carrisalitos	Julian Ursua, Pedro Romo	22,450.04

11. No. 1	Las Mariposas	Juan Bautista Alvarado	44,386.83
12. No. 498	Los Alamos y Agua Caliente		
		Pedro C. Carrillo	26,040.14
13. No. 602	Las Calaveras	Francisco Pico	30,720.34
14. No. 616	Los Medanos	José Antonio Mesa, José Maria Mesa, José Miguel Garcia	8,890.26
15. No. 213	Los Meganos	José Noriega	30,380.12
16. No. 76	Monte del Diablo	Salvio Pacheco	17,921.54
17. No. 357	Moquelamos	Andreas Pico	48,889.45
18. No. 35	Orestimba	Sebastian Nunez	26,641.17
19. No. 569	Panoche Grande	Vicente Gómez	16,360.03
20. No. 255	Rancho de los Franceses		
		William Gulnack	48,747.03
21. No. 509	Rancho del Puerto	Mariano Hernandez	13,340.39
22. No. 232	Rancho de Rio Estanislao		
		John Rowland	48,889.46
23. No. 693	Rancho de Rio San Joaquin		
		José Castro	48,887.92
24. No. 628	Real de los Aguilas	Francisco Arias, Saturino Cariaga	30,380.00
25. No. 556	San Emidio	José Antonio Dominguez	17,709.79
26. No. 393	Sanjón de los Moquelemnes		
		Anastasia Choboya	35,509.97
27. No. 673	Sanjón de Santa Rita	Francisco Soberanes	48,823.84
28. No. 37	San Luis Gonzaga	José Maria Mejia	48,821.43
29. No.	San Ramon	José M. Amador	17,120.00
30. No. 767	Rancho de Rio Estanislao		
		Francisco Rica, José Antonio Castro	48,886.64

Of the foregoing land grants all but Nos. 8, 13, 17, 19, 23, and 30 were patented. Out of the 30 grants made wholly or partially within the San Joaquin Valley, 24 were considered to have valid titles.

Appendix 3

Folk Poems of the San Joaquin

1. An anonymous poem:

Don't go, I say, if you've got any brains,
You'll stay far away from the San Joaquin plains.
At four in the morning they're hustling up tools,
Feed, curry, and harness ten long-eared old mules.
Plow twenty-four miles through sunshine and rain,
Or your blankets you'll roll on the San Joaquin plain

They'll work you eight hours and eight hours more,
You'll sleep in a bunk house without any door;
They'll feed you on mutton, sow-belly, and sheep,
And dock you for half of the time that you sleep,
Twenty-four hours through sunshine and rain
Or your blankets you'll roll on the San Joaquin plain.

2. A young cowboy goes out to see the world.

Recited by Frank Clarke of Goshen, a nephew of
Crawford W. Clarke, the famous cattleman.

Once I was traveling, and I didn't know what to do,
So I staked my horse on Fresno Slough;
When I got there it was just before night,
So hired out to work for a man whose name was White.
The next morning I got up feeling quite merry,

751

The first job he gave me was to cross the ferry.
I pulled the boat back; I felt quite frisky,
And he asked me in the house to have a drink of whiskey
I drink at the bar until I drink my fill
And then I struck out for old Centerville.

When I got there I thought I'd had enough
But I was out a dollar and a half (right under the bluff),
I walked up and down, I felt like a whaler,
And then I struck out for old Visalyer.
When I got there I thought I'd die
For a girl went through me they called "Shoo-fly."
I walked up and down the town till I thought it was a pity,
And then I struck out for Fresno City;
I walked up and down
And fetched up in Chinatown.

Next morning at daybreak
I struck out for Tulare Lake,
When I got there the weather was fine,
I thought I'd catch some fish for I had a hook and line.
I fished all day, and I threw my line away,
Then I struck out for Pasa Jona,
When I got there around the hills I did rally,
Then I struck out for little Penoche Valley.
When I got there I was all in a quiver,
Then I struck back for old Kings River.
Now boys, I'll tell you I've had my fill,
The best place I've struck is old Centerville.

3. Written by Mrs. L. L. Wright of Reedley:

He made a dash for Miller's hash
On the banks of the San Joaquin;
The hash was hot, the hobo cold,
Though his clothes were ragged, his ways were bold
For he swore a lot, so I've been told,
On the banks of the San Joaquin.

The wild geese honked in the azure sky,
The antelopes grazed on the plains nearby,
And millions of mosquitoes were on the fly,
On the banks of the San Joaquin.
The cowboys followed their far-flung herds,
While they sang their songs with their telling words,
The air was full of migrant birds
On the banks of the San Joaquin.

And hunters came and shot the geese,
No fear then, of the State Police;
They shot the antelope, doe and fawn,
And let them lie on God's green lawn.

Mules and horses, cattle and sheep,
Lay down to rise where the grass was deep;
While the mists from the tules would over them creep
On the banks of the San Joaquin.

Another decade has passed away;
The bright-eyed antelopes have had their day,
So have the mules who ate the hay
For modern equipment has come to stay
On the banks of the San Joaquin.

Fields of rice and cotton galore,
Grow where the range herds fed before;
And tractors hum where the gray mules brayed,
Don't stop to think, or you will be dismayed
On the banks of the San Joaquin.
Miller has gone to his well-earned rest,
They say he died from a pain in his chest;
Lux, he died from a broken back,
And even Roosevelt can't bring them back
To the banks of the San Joaquin.

4. Anonymous poem

The following anonymous poem, popular among the men who operated the Miller & Lux ranches, was given to me by Mr. Arthur Safstrom of the Fresno State College faculty. He is a son of the Red Safstrom mentioned in the poem. The latter was a Miller & Lux superintendent, as were also D. W. Wallace and Daniel Leonard. William Morrison, employed as a fence rider, was known as Buffalo Bill. Rock was in charge of irrigation, and Nick was one of the ranch hands, unfortunately a hunchback; hence the reference in the poem. Tramps and hoboes were always fed at the Miller & Lux ranches to insure their good will. Otherwise they might have done great harm by leaving gates open and setting fire to haystacks. However, Miller ruled that the cook's helper need not wash dishes for the hoboes; they ate after the ranch hands had left the table and on the same dishes. This explains the reference to the dirty plate. The route connecting the various Miller & Lux ranches was known as "the dirty plate route."

A hobo once was lying in the shade of Miller's stacks,
His curly head on his bed, a roll of Miller's sacks;
He turned to his partner, this is what he said:
Can they ever run these ranches when the old time boss is dead?
When they go up to Heaven, what ever will they do?
They can't lie and take it easy, the same as me and you.
Will they keep the same old things as they do down here?
They'll surely play Hell in Heaven, the whole she-bang will be queer;
Will Buffalo Bill quit boozing when he reaches the Golden Shore?
Or ride a bucking bronco over Peter at the door?
Will Dan Leonard ride in an auto, will Wallace drive a team,
Will Rock be irrigating out of Heaven's silvery stream?
I wonder will Red Safstrom still get up at four o'clock;
Will he bawl the hobo angels when they hide behind the shock,
Will they leave the hump on Nick when he enters at-the gate,
Will they taboo the gunny sacks or use the dirty plate?

Appendix 4

So-Called German Syndicate (Fresno County)

This account was written by Mr. Jarvis Streeter, Secretary and Manager of the San Joaquin Abstract Company of Fresno.

One, William S. Chapman, conceived the idea of organizing a syndicate to purchase Agricultural College Scrip and locate it on unappropriated lands in the San Joaquin Valley. He interested a number of German capitalists of San Francisco who advanced the funds for purchasing the Scrip, and, in 1868, Chapman, having purchased scrip representing 80,000 acres, each certificate being limited to 160 acres, located these certificates on 79,921 acres in Fresno County, and U. S. Patents for each quarter section were issued to William S. Chapman in 1869, the legal description being as follows:

In Twp. 13 S., R. 20 E., Mt. Diablo Base and Meridian: W 1/2 of Sec. 1; W 1/2 of Sec. 12; All of Secs. 13, 17, 18, 19, 20, 21, and 24 to 35 inclusive.

In Twp. 13 S., R. 21 E., Mt. Diablo Base and Meridian: All except Secs, 5, 6, 7, 8, 16 and 36.

In Twp. 14 S., R. 19 F., Mt. Diablo Base and Meridian: Secs. 1, 2, 11, 12, 13, 14, 15, 23, 24, 25, 26, 27, 34, and 35.

In Twp 14 S., R. 20 F., Mt. Diablo Base and Meridian: All except Secs. 16 and 36.

In Twp. 14 S., R. 21 E., Mt. Diablo Base and Meridian: Secs. 1 to 15 inclusive and 17 and 18.

On August 4, 1868, after said Scrip had been located on said lands William S. Chapman conveyed the whole tract to Clinton Gurnee and on the same date Clinton Gurnee conveyed said lands to William S. Chapman, Edmund Janssen and Frederick Roeding in trust for themselves and the other members of the syndicate and specified the beneficial interests in the 79,921 acres as follows:

William S. Chapman	21421/79921
Edmund Janssen	5000/79921
Frederick Roeding	5000/79921
Charles Adler	1000/79921
Francis Locan	2500/79921
Christian H. Voigt	2500/79921
Emile Pascal	2000/79921
Edward Michelssen	2000/79921
William Scholle	2500/79921
George H. Eggers	2500/79921
Thomas Basse	2000/79921
Henry Schmiedel	2000/79921
Isaac Friedlander	5000/79921
Frederick Putzman	2000/79921
Henry Balzer	1000/79921
William Kroning	2000/79921
Charles Baum	2500/79921
Rudolph Hochkoffer	2000/79921
Frederic Duhring	1000/79921
Gottlieb Muecke	2000/79921
Albert L. Wangenheim	2000/79921

Subsequently some of the holders of the beneficial interests sold either all or a portion of their beneficial interests to purchasers, greatly increasing the number of those holding beneficial interests.

Owing to the inconvenience and cumbersome method of making transfers by the syndicate when any of the lands were sold, (it being necessary for all who held a beneficial interest under the trust deed to join in execution of a deed, either personally or by Attorney in fact) it was decided to dissolve the syndicate and partition the remaining lands among the beneficiaries in proportion to their beneficial interests.

For the purpose of effecting the partition in 1873, all those then holding beneficial interests conveyed to one George Harris, who was a clerk in William S. Chapman's office, and he conveyed to each beneficiary the number of acres to which he was entitled by mutual agreement of all beneficiaries, describing the land by legal subdivision, section, township and range according to the Plat of U. S. Government Survey.

Appendix 5

Written for *Garden of the Sun*
by Mr. Ernest Nielsen of Selma

On the morning of August 3, 1883, the late William H. Shafer, with the assistance of three friends, dynamited the diversion dam at Centerville on the Kings River. This act permitted much needed water to run down the Centerville and Kingsburg canal system and saved the crops of the ranchers of the Selma-Kingsburg area.

Mr. Shafer often referred to the act of dynamiting the dam as an act of war, which it was. But, in any war, there are three phases: first, unsuccessful arbitration of differences; second, hostilities or war; and third, the peace treaty. The dynamiting of the dam by Shafer was the second event of the three phases.

In order to understand the motive behind the act, an understanding of the conditions at that time is important. All of the interests which were taking water from the Kings River, by means of canal systems were doing so in what was considered good faith. Filings for water had been made and the canals had been constructed by the ranchers themselves. The future seemed bright, but they had failed to consider the basic law which governed the use of water from any stream in California. This was the Riparian Act, which briefly states that the flow of any stream shall not be diminished in quantity or quality, past a given point.

The 48,000 acre Laguna de Tache Ranch, bordered by the Kings River and at this time controlled by an English syndicate, was to become an important factor in the use of water from the Kings River. Solely to protect their own interests, the owners of the grant filed

757

suit in the superior court of Tulare County, requesting that all irrigation interests taking water from the river be restrained and, further, that headgates be closed to prevent further use of water from the river. The injunction was granted on the basis of the riparian law.

At various times, the directors of the irrigation interests were called before the court to answer charges of water use. In all cases, they denied the use and stated that, if any water was being taken from the river, it was done by the ranchers, without the directors' knowledge.

The year 1883 was an extremely dry year. The wheat crop had been a failure. A small amount of water was running in the river, but in the middle of July the Centerville and Kingsburg canals abruptly went dry.

William H. Shafer, at that time the Superintendent of the C and K System, was ordered to go to the headgates and determine the cause. He returned and reported to the directors that the Fresno system (of which Moses Church was the guiding figure) had built up a diversion dam at Centerville, and was diverting all of the water from the system into the Fresno system.

A committee from the C and K System, one of which was Shafer, called upon Church and called his attention to the fact that all of the water was being diverted into his system. They also called his attention to the fact that he was restrained by court action from diverting any water from the river, just as they were. They also stated that they had no desire to call his violation to the attention of the courts, and asked for a share of the water.

Mr. Church told the C and K committee that he was powerless to act, since the people had taken the operation of the canals from his hands.

The C and K committee returned to Kingsburg and decided to determine if the statements of Church were true. They accordingly instructed Shafer to go to the headgates and turn all of the water out of the Fresno system and back into the river, and then remain at the point and see who came to turn the water back into the Fresno system.

It was not long before Shafer was to have this question answered. It was J. M. Loveland, Church's own superintendent, who came to turn the water back into the Fresno system. Loveland remarked, "Who had the nerve to turn the water out of our canals?" To which Shafer replied, "I did and I think you have your nerve to take all the water from the river." Loveland replied, "Well, I'm turning it back into our system." Shafer replied, "I don't intend to stop you, but I'm going to watch you do it."

Shafer then returned and reported his findings to the directors. They again went to Moses Church, informed him of their findings, and asked him, as friends and neighbors, to permit some of the water to go down the C & K system. To this Church agreed, but with the stipulation that the water be taken from his waste gate. The directors immediately saw his point, since if this was done, they would have acknowledged his right to dam the river and take all the water. The C & K directors refused these terms, and Church declined to let them have any water in any other manner.

The C & K directors returned to Kingsburg for a meeting with their attorney and their superintendent, Shafer. The attorney informed them the legal advice was difficult to give. Any legal action might take years to decide. But he stated, "If it is the advice of your attorney that you seek, I cannot give you any. However, not as a lawyer, but as a man, if my family depended on the water in the ditches which you have built yourselves, if my crops were dependent on water from the river, I would blow up that dam that is keeping water from reaching my ranch, which I thought I was rightfully entitled to."

After meeting with the attorney, the directors met outside his office and Shafer remarked to Mr. T. C. Bratton, "Here is our solution." I. N. Parlier, the president of the C & K system, remarked, "How can we blow the dam with powder, since powder will not function in water?"

Shafer replied, "We can blow the dam with dynamite."

Parlier added, "But, who will get the dynamite and who will blow the dam?"

Shafer answered, "I will get the dynamite and I'll blow the dam."

While the group was still discussing the intentions to blow up the dam, the telegraph operator at Kingsburg came to the group. He was asked what he wanted. To this he replied, "A telegram is just as personal as the U.S. Mail, but in this case I feel I must tell you that a telegram has just been sent to the Fresno Irrigation Company, informing them of your intentions to dynamite the dam."

With this information, it was decided to wait at least a week, since it was certain that the directors of the Fresno Company would station guards to prevent any action at the dam.

At the expiration of the week, Shafer asked A. A. Smith, then postmaster at Kingsburg, and Samuel Moffett to go to the Sol Sweet store at Visalia and purchase the dynamite. The only other place where it might be purchased was at the Kutner Goldstein Company in Fresno. Purchase in Fresno was to be avoided, since it was certain

759

that, if this course was taken, the Fresno group would soon receive word.

Moffett and Smith made the purchase and were instructed to meet Shafer and Capt. T. C. Bratton (of Selma and a Civil War veteran) at Ray's Ford. Ray's Ford is at a point where Lincoln Avenue now ends at the Kings River, and is also a point where the Kings River makes a 45-degree turn. This crossing was at a point where the river had a hard cobble bottom. The group met on August 2, 1883. Moffett, when met, displayed his 25-pound box of dynamite, which had been wrapped in cotton and which he described as "eggs." Someone in the group laughed at the cotton wrapping around the box, and Moffett replied, "I was cautioned against subjecting it to any hard jar, so I bought the cotton. The women at home can always make use of cotton, so it will not be wasted."

On the morning of August 3, 1883, the group prepared to dynamite the dam, after having gone from Ray's Ford to the diversion dam on the east side of the river, so that they would not be detected. When they arrived at the dam site, Shafer carried Captain Bratton across the river on his shoulders. Bratton had been wounded in the Civil War, and the hip injury that he had suffered in the war caused him to be careful not to aggravate the condition by getting into cold water.

Moffett insisted on being permitted to assist Shafer in placing the dynamite. To this and other requests by his companions, he refused. Shafer contended that any injury that might be suffered by Moffett would become widely known as well as the incidents relating to such injury.

While Shafer was engaged in placing the dynamite, the superintendent of the Fresno system appeared. Again it was J. M. Loveland. When he shouted across the river, "What are you doing?," Shafer replied, "We are going to dynamite your dam."

Still shouting, Loveland replied, "Don't you men know that you will get into a pack of trouble for what you are doing?"

With this, Shafer replied, "Of course we know that, but this is war, and war is not pleasant. We are determined to get the water that we are entitled to, trouble or no trouble."

Shafer lit the fuse and ran. The dam was blown, and boulders were blown fifty feet in the air. Water rushed into the C & K canal system and remained there for a period of two weeks. Shafer had his men remain at the site, and they were told to engage in "target practice" during this time, to discourage any attempt to repair the dam. Two attempts were made during this time, when Church sent a crew of Chinese to the scene. They were frightened away.

After these two attempts J. M. McCardle, the constable of Fresno, was sent with a warrant for the arrest of Shafer. Shafer and McCardle were friends, and Shafer readily submitted to arrest.

On the way to Fresno, McCardle questioned Shafer and he was told the entire story. McCardle had no great affection for the actions of Church, and told Shafer so in a few well-chosen words.

McCardle told Shafer that he could not be brought into court until the following day and that he had no desire to place him in jail. He said that his own family was in the mountains, or he would take him to his home. He then asked Shafer, "Have you any money?" Shafer replied that he did.

McCardle then replied, "I don't think you will run away. I'll put you up at the Grand Central Hotel for the night."

On the following morning, Shafer appeared in the court of Justice of the Peace S. H. Hill. The lawyer for the Fresno system was George E. Church, later to become district attorney. Shafer was charged with "malicious mischief." Years later, Shafer often remarked "malicious, yes; mischief, no."

Church proved his case against Shafer without question; but, all during the hearing, Shafer's attorney made no objections, and offered no evidence to the contrary. Shafer became alarmed and whispered to his counsel, "When do you start defending me?" The reply was, "Relax, don't worry."

At the conclusion of the presentation of the case by Church, Shafer's attorney rose and addressed the court with these remarks: "Your honor, the case has been proved without question, but certainly you must be aware of the fact that the scene of the alleged crime was very close to the county line. The prosecuting attorney has failed, in presenting his case, to prove the jurisdiction of this court. He has failed to show whether the crime was committed in Fresno or Tulare County. In the absence of such information, I move that this case be dismissed."

Justice of the Peace Hill was smart enough to see that he had a hot potato in his lap. Had he decided against the defendant in this case, as the evidence indicated, he would have acknowledged also the violation of the Fresno Canal Company against the injunction to take water from the river. Their own violation of the injunction would have been a matter of court record by the mere act of finding the defendant guilty. He welcomed the opportunity to dismiss the case. He did so, much to the relief of all parties concerned, once they realized the importance of the case.

This single act by Shafer ended all further attempts on the part of any company to take all the water from the river, and was the actual beginning of peaceful ways and means to partition the water to all interested parties, in accordance with their legal rights.

A few years later, the courts made serious efforts to enforce the injunction. The headgates were ordered closed. Shafer was ordered to the headgates to close them, in accordance with the court order. When he arrived there, he found the woods full of men with rifles and shotguns. They had no intention of permitting him to carry out his orders. The men wore bandana handkerchiefs with their coats turned inside out. Shafer recognized none of them. One man approached him with a 30-30 rifle. He informed Shafer that they were well aware of his orders, but they would prevent him from carrying out those orders. The man also informed Shafer, "This 30-30 that I have is something that I will use if you make an attempt to close the headgate."

Shafer returned and reported his reception to the directors of the C and K. They told him that he had not used enough force. To which Shafer replied, "I would suggest that you all go with me and help me." They all went.

The same man who had met Shafer before came out of the woods, masked and unrecognized. He informed the group of the same conditions that he had told Shafer. The group returned. However on this second visit, Shafer noted a physical peculiarity about the man with the 30-30 rifle. He walked pigeon-toed.

Several weeks later, Shafer, busy with his thoughts and looking down was walking down east Front Street in Selma. As he walked, he noticed these same feet approaching him. In recalling this meeting Shafer said, "As I looked at the approaching feet, I had no idea who the man would be. When they neared me I raised my head, looked at the man, and said, 'Rev. DeMumdrum, haven't I met you somewhere before?'"

The man Shafer met, and the man who threatened to use the 30-30, was Rev. J. M. DeMumdrum, pastor of the United Brethren Church at Selma. His reply was, "It could be, Mr. Shafer, it could be."

Notes

Chapter 1

1. [Kroeber, *Handbook of the Indians of California*, 495.]
2. The spelling of tribal names and the location of the various tribes is based on Kroeber's *Handbook*. This monumental report to the Smithsonian Institute is the most authoritative work available on the subject. [Kroeber, *op. cit.*, 443, 476, 488.]
3. [Sources reliable but uncertain.]
4. [Kroeber, *op. cit.*, 488-491.]
5. [Sources reliable but uncertain.]
6. [*Ibid.*]
7. [Kroeber, *op. cit.*, 477; and reliable but uncertain sources.]
8. Latta, F. F., *Uncle Jeff's Story*, 17-18. Used by permission of F. F. Latta.
9. [Kroeber, *op. cit.*, 478.]
10. [*Ibid.*, 479.]
11. [*Ibid.*, 479, 482.]
12. [*Ibid.*, 479.]
13. [*Ibid.*, 479-480.]
14. [*Ibid.*, 480.]
15. [*Ibid.*, 480, 485.]
16. [*Ibid.*, 480.]
17. [*Ibid.*, 481.]
18. [*Ibid.*, 481-482.]
19. [*Ibid.*, 482.]
20. [*Ibid.*, 483.]

21. [Probably based on Smith's personal knowledge.]
22. [Kroeber, *op. cit.*, 483.]
23. [*Ibid.*, 484.]
24. [*Ibid.*]
25. [*Ibid.*, 485.]
26. [Sources reliable but uncertain.]
27. [Kroeber, *op. cit.*, 485.]
28. [*Ibid.*, 442-461 *passim.*]
29. [*Ibid.*, 443, 446, 447-448, 451, 452, 457-458.]
30. [*Ibid.*, 496-497.]
31. [*Ibid.*, 498-499.]
32. [*Ibid.*, 499-501.]
33. [*Ibid.*, 492-493.]
34. [*Ibid.*, 498.]
35. [*Ibid.*, 538-540.]
36. [Latta, F. F., *Uncle Jeff's Story*, 17.]
37. [Pope, "Yahi Archery," and Morse, "Bulletin of Sussex Institute."]
38. [Kroeber, *op. cit.*, 521-523.]
39. [*Ibid.*, 528-530.]
40. [*Ibid.*, 523-526, 527.]
41. [*Ibid.*, 531-538 *passim.*]
42. [*Ibid.*, 495, 498; and Latta, *Uncle Jeff's Story*, 38.]
43. [Kroeber, *op. cit.*, 502-504.]
44. [*Ibid.*, 504-506.]
45. Menefee, C.A., *Historical and Descriptive Sketch Book of Napa, Sonoma, Lake, and Mendocino*, 26.
46. [Kroeber, *op. cit.*, 519.]
47. Bryant, William Cullen, *An Indian at the Burial Place of His Father*. [Edition uncertain.]

Chapter 2

1. [Herbert E. Bolton, *Outpost of Empire*.]
2. Bancroft, Hubert Howe, *History of California*, II, 43.
3. Bushnell, Horace. *California: Characteristics and Prospects...Published Originally in the "New Englander."*
4. Bancroft, *History of California*, I, 486-487.
5. [Dates of Fages' relief of command and promotion corrected on the basis of later authorities.]
6. Fages, Pedro. *Diary*, translated by Herbert E. Bolton. In "In the South San Joaquin Ahead of Garces." in *Quarterly of California Historical Society*, September, 1931. [The account given subsequently here is taken from that work.]
7. Palou, Father Francisco, *Historical Memoirs of New California*, III, 234-235 (Herbert E. Bolton, translator and editor).
8. [Bolton, *op. cit.*]
9. [Palou, *op. cit.*]
10. [Source reliable but uncertain.]

11. Coues, Elliott, *On the Trail of a Spanish Pioneer*. [The account given subsequently here is taken from that work.]
12. [*Ibid.*, 288.]
13. [*Ibid.*, 302-303.]
14. [*Ibid.*]
15. [*Ibid.*]
16. [Bancroft, *History of California*, I, 290-291, 295.]
17. [*Ibid.*]

Chapter 3

1. Martin, Father Juan, *Visita a los Gentiles Tulareños*, 1804. Santa Barbara Archives, Papeles Miscelaneos, VI, 85-89.
2. [Bancroft, *History of California*, II, 297.]
3. [Sources reliable but uncertain.]
4. Martin, *op. cit.*
5. [Sources reliable but uncertain.]
6. [Bancroft, *History of California*, II, 35.]
7. Muñoz, Father Pedro, *Diario de la Ezpedicion hecha por Don Gabriel Moraga O los Nuevas Descrubrimientos del Tular*, Sept. 21-Nov. 2, 1806. B. C., Arch. Sta. Barb. IV, 27.
8. [*Ibid.*]
9. Zalvidea, Father Jose Maria. *Diario de una Expedicion, Tierra Adentro, 1806*. Santa Barbara Archives, Papeles Miscelaneos, VI, 50-58.
10. [*Ibid.*]
11. [Muñoz, *Ibid.*]
12. [*Ibid.*]
13. [*Ibid.*]
14. [*Ibid.*]
15. [Bancroft, *History of California*, II, 55.]
16. [Sources reliable but uncertain. Mention of another 1808 expedition to the Buena Vista Lake area, led by Jose Palomares, is omitted by Smith.]
17. Zalvidea, Father Jose Maria. "*Diario de una Expedicion, Tierra Adentro, 1806.*" Papeles Miscelaneos, Santa Barbara Archives, VI, 50-58.
18. Bancroft, Hubert Howe, *History of California*, VIII, 726.
19. Robinson, Alfred, *Life in California*, 59.
20. [Sources reliable but uncertain.]
21. [Bancroft, Hubert Howe, *History of California*, II, 338.]
22. Bancroft, Hubert Howe, *History of California*, II, 324.
23. [*Ibid.*]
24. Runeberg, Johan Ludwig, "Sven Duva." Translation by Isabel Donner in *A Selection from the Series of Poems Entitled Ensign Ståls Songs*, 37-38.
25. Alvarado, Juan Bautista, Manuscript History of California, I, 103-104.

26. Cabot, Father Juan, "Expedicion al Valle de los Tulares, 1814" in the form of a letter to the Father Prefect, dated April 7, 1815, Papeles Miscelaneos, Santa Barbara Archives, VI, 67-72.
27. [*Ibid.*]
28. [*Ibid.*]
29. [*Ibid.*]
30. [Bancroft, Hubert Howe, *History of California*, II, 470, n. 24.]
31. [Ortega diary.]
32. [*Ibid.*]
33. [*Ibid.*]
34. [Bancroft, *History of California*, II, 326.]
35. [Bancroft, *History of California*, II, 489-490.]
36. [Martínez, Father Luis. "Entrada a las Ranchería del Tular, 1816." *Archivo del Arzobispado de San Francisco*, III (1), 42-45.]
37. [Bancroft, *History of California*, II, 618, n. 12.]
38. Father Sarría to Governor Solá, June 10, 1816. *Archivo del Archbispado de San Francisco,* No. 507.
39. [Bolton, Herbert E. The Mission as a Frontier Institution in the Spanish American Colonies.]
40. [Sources reliable but uncertain.]
41. [*Ibid.*]
42. [*Ibid.*]
43. Leonard, Zenas, *Narrative: Adventures of Zenas Leonard, Fur Trader and Trapper, 1831-1836*, 230.
44. [Bolton, *op. cit.*]
45. [Sources reliable but uncertain.]
46. Sanchez, Sergeant José, *Diario*, September 10, 1819. Copy in the Bancroft Library, Berkeley, California.
47. [*Ibid.*]
48. [*Ibid.*]
49. [Sources reliable but uncertain.]
50. [Information on following campaigns from Bancroft, *History of California*, II, 339; and reliable but uncertain sources.]
51. [*Ibid.*]
52. Kendrick, T. D., *A History of the Vikings*, 64-65.
53. Neihardt, John Gneisenau, "Ashley's Hundred" in *The Song of Three Friends*.

Chapter 4

1. [Bancroft, *History of California*, II, 533-534.]
2. [Bancroft, *History of California*, II, 534, and Portilla diary.]
3. [Sanchez 1826 diary.]
4. [Sources reliable but uncertain.]
5. Fisher, Helen Dwight, "The First Smith of California," *American Mercury*, September, 1928.
6. *Ibid.*
7. Dale, Harrison Clifford, *The Smith-Ashley Exploration and*

Discovery of a Central Route to the Pacific, 1822-1829, with the Original Journal, 198-228.

8. Jedediah Smith to Father Durán, May 19, 1827, *Departmental State Papers*, Mss., II, 17-19.
9. [Sources reliable but uncertain.]
10. [*Ibid.*]
11. [Sources uncertain and not entirely reliable; corrections made based on consulting later authorities.]
12. Fisher, "The First Smith of Cailfornia."
13. [Sanchez 1829 diary.]
14. [Sanchez 1829 diary.]
15. [Vallejo 1829 diary.]
16. *Hutchings' California Magazine*, V, 421.
17. San Francisco *Evening Bulletin*, October 26, 1866.
18. *Ibid.*
19. Menefee, Eugene L., and Dodge, Fred A., *History of Tulare and Kern Counties, California*, 5-6.
20. [Sources reliable but uncertain.]
21. Creel, George, "Incredible Kit Carson." *Collier's: the National Weekly*, August 21, 1926.
22. [Sources reliable but uncertain.]
23. [*Ibid.*]
24. [*Ibid.*]
25. [*Ibid.*]
26. [Sources uncertain. Smith has "California Cattle Company" for "Willamette Cattle Company."]
27. Leonard, Zenas, *Narrative*, 174.
28. *Ibid.*, 180.
29. [Partially relies on Leonard's narrative; other sources reliable but uncertain.]
30. [Sources reliable but uncertain.]
31. [Lyman, George D., *John Marsh, Pioneer.*]
32. [*Ibid.*]
33. United States Land Commission for California, *Land Case No. 693.*
34. [*Ibid.*]
35. Fremont, John Charles, *Memoirs of My Life*, I, 336.
36. Fremont, John Charles, *Report of the Exploring Expedition to the Rocky Mountains in the Year 1842, and to Oregon and California in the Years 1843-1844.*
37. [*Ibid.*]
38. [*Ibid.*]
39. [Fremont, John Charles, *Memoirs of My Life*, I.]
40. [*Ibid.*]
41. [*Ibid.*]
42. Arnold, Adelaide Wilson, *Wild Horses of the Mojave.*
43. [Fremont, John Charles, *Memoirs of My Life*, I.]
44. [*Ibid.*]

45. [Sources reliable but uncertain.]

46. [*Ibid.*]

47. Audubon, John Woodhouse, *The Western Journal*, 182-188.

48. [Sources reliable but uncertain.]

49. Derby, George Horatio. *Report of the Secretary of War, Communicating a Report of the Tulare Valley, Made by Lieutenant Derby.*

50. [*Ibid.*]

51. [*Ibid.*]

52. Guion, David W, *Home on the Range* [Victor sound recording].

Chapter 5

1. United States Land Commission for California. *Transcript of Proceedings in Case No. 1, John C. Fremont, Claimant, vs. the United States, Defendant, for the Place Names "Las Mariposas."*

2. [———. *Transcript of Proceedings in Case No. 213, John Marsh, Claimant, vs. the United States, Defendant, for the Place Named "Los Meganos."*]

3. [———. *Transcript of Proceedings in Case No. 616, Jonathan D. Stevenson, et al., Claimants, vs. the United States, Defendant, for the Place Named "Los Medanos"; and reliable but uncertain sources.*]

4. [———. *Transcript of Proceedings in Case No. 444, Andreas Pico, Claimant, vs the United States, Defendant, for the Place Named "Arroyo Seco."*]

5. [———. *Transcript of Proceedings in Case No. 673, Francisco Soberanes, Claimant, vs. the United States, Defendant, for the Place Named "Sanjon de Santa Rita."*]

6. [———. *Transcript of Proceedings in Case No. 556, Francisco Dominguez, et al., Claimants, vs. the United States, Defendant, for the Place Named "San Emidio."*]

7. [———. *Transcript of Proceedings in Case No. 37, Juan Perez Pacheco, Claimant, vs. the United States, Defendant, for the Place Named "San Luis Gonzaga."* San Francisco, 1853.

8. [Sources reliable but uncertain. The ranch house was moved in 1962 to escape inundation by the San Luis Reservoir, and suffered great structural damage in the process.]

9. [Case No. 37, *op. cit.*]

10. [*Ibid.*]

11. [United States Land Commission for California. *Transcript of Proceedings in Case No. 536, José Maria Covarrubias, Claimant, vs. the United States, Defendant, for the Place Named "Castac."*]

12. [Sources reliable but uncertain.]

13. [United States Land Commission for California. *Transcript of Proceedings in Case No. 240, Jose Antonio Aguirre and Ignacio del Valle, Claimants, vs. the United States, Defendant, for the Place Named "El Tejon."*]

14. [*Ibid.*]
15. [*Ibid.*]
16. [Sources reliable but uncertain.]
17. [Bonsal, Stephen. *Edward Fitzgerald Beale: A Pioneer in the Path of Empire, 1822-1903.*]
18. [United States Land Commission for California. *Transcript of Proceedings in Case No. 293, Hiram Grimes, et al., Claimants, vs. the United States, Defendant, for the Place Named "El Pescadero."*]
19. [——. *Transcript of Proceedings in Case No. 267, Antonio Maria Pico and Henry M. Naglee, Claimants, vs. the United States, Defendant, for the Place El Pescadero."*]
20. [——. *Transcript of Proceedings in Case No. 781, José Yves Limantour, Claimant, vs. the United States, Defendant, for the Place Named "Laguna de Tache."*]
21. [*Ibid.*]
22. [Sources reliable but uncertain.]
23. [United States Land Commission for California. *Transcript of Proceedings in Case No. 767, Francisco Rico, et al., Claimants, vs. the United States, Defendant, for the Place Named "Ranchería Rio de Estanislao."*]
24. [*Ibid.*]
25. [*Ibid.*]
26. [Sources reliable but uncertain.]
27. [——. *Transcript of Proceedings in Case No. 569, Vicente Gomez, Claimant, vs. the United States, Defendant, for the Place Named "Panoche Grande.*]
28. [United States Land Commission for California. Documents relating to the "Laguna de Tache" land grant.]
29. [*Ibid.*]
30. [*Ibid.*]
31. [*Ibid.*]
32. [——. *Transcript of Proceedings in Case No. 628, Maria de Antonio Castro de Anzar, et al., Claimants, vs. the United States, Defendant, for the Place Named "Real de los Aguiles."*]
33. [——. *Transcript of Proceedings in Case No. 509, Samuel G. Reed, Claimant, vs. the United States, Defendant, for the Place Named "Rancho del Puerto."*]
34. [*Ibid.*]
35. [——. *Transcript of Proceedings in Case No. 393, Angel and Maria Chabolla (Heirs of Anastasia Chabolla), Claimants, vs. the United States, Defendant, for the Place Named "Sanjon de los Moquelemnes."*]
36. [——. *Transcript of Proceedings in Case No. 545, Julian Ursua, Claimant, vs. the United States, Defendant, for the Place Named "La Panoche de San Juan y Carrisalitos."*]
37. [——. *Transcript of Proceedings in Case No. 35, Sebastian Nunez, Claimant, vs. the United States, Defendant, for the Place*

Named "Orestimba."]

38. [——. *Transcript of Proceedings in Case No. 79, Robert Livermore, Claimant, vs. the United States, Defendant, for the Place Named "Canada de los Vaqueros."*]

39. [——. *Transcript of Proceedings in Case No. 1, op. cit.*]

40. [*Ibid.*]

41. [*Ibid.*, and reliable but uncertain sources.]

42. [——. *Transcript of Proceedings in Case No. 76, Salvio Pacheco, Claimant, vs. the United States, Defendant, for the Place Named "Monte del Diablo."*]

43. [——. *Transcript of Proceedings in Case No. 255, Charles M. Weber, Claimant, vs. the United States, Defendant, for the Place Named the "Campo de los Franceses."*]

44. [*Ibid.*]

45. [*Ibid.*]

46. [*Ibid.*]

47. [*Ibid.*]

48. [*Ibid.*]

49. [*Ibid.*]

50. [*Ibid.*]

51. [*Ibid.*]

52. [*Ibid.*]

53. [——. *Transcript of Proceedings in Case No. 569, op. cit.*]

54. [*Ibid.*]

55. [——. *Transcript of Proceedings in Case No. 693, José Castro, et al., Claimants, vs. the United States, Defendant, for the Place Named "Rancho of the River San Joaquin."*]

56. [——. *Transcript of Proceedings in Case No. 767, Francisco Rico, et al., Claimants, vs. the United States, Defendant, for the Place Named "Ranchería Rio de Estanislao."*]

57. [*Ibid.*]

58. [——. *Transcript of Proceedings in Case No. 498, Pedro C. Carrillo, Claimant, vs. the United States, Defendant, for the Place Named "Los Alamos y Agua Caliente."*]

59. [——. *Transcript of Proceedings in Case No. 357, Andreas Pico, Claimant, vs. the United States, Defendant, for the Place Named "Moquelamos."*]

60. [——. *Transcript of Proceedings in Case No. 602, Francisco Pico, Claimant, vs. the United States, Defendant, for the Place Named "Las Calaveras."*]

61. [——. *Transcript of Proceedings in Case No. 158, Alfias Thompson, Claimant, vs. the United States, Defendant, for the Place Named "Land of the River Stanislaus."*]

62. [Sources reliable but uncertain.]

63. Love, Thomas, *Peacock Time*, L, 9. [Precise source uncertain.]

Chapter 6

1. Baker, Charles C., "Mexican Land Grants in California" in *Annual Publications of Historical Society of Southern California,* 1914, 241.
2. [Sources reliable but uncertain.]
3. [*Ibid.*]
4. [Sources uncertain and not entirely reliable; corrections made based on consulting later authorities.]
5. [Jones, William Carey. *Report on the Subject of Land Titles in California.*]
6. [United States Land Commission for California. *Transcript of Proceedings in Case No. 213, John Marsh, Claimant, vs. the United States, Defendant, for the Place Named "Los Meganos."*]
7. [Jones, *op. cit.*]
8. [*Ibid.*]
9. [*Ibid.*]
10. [*Ibid.*]
11. [*Ibid.*]
12. Morrow, William W. *Spanish and Mexican Private Land Grants.* Los Angeles, 1923.
13. [*Ibid.*]
14. [*Ibid.*]
15. Jones, William Carey, *Report on the Subject of Land Titles in California,* 44-48.
16. Citizens Land Association, *California Lands,* 16.
17. [Morrow, *op. cit.*]
18. [Sources uncertain and not entirely reliable; corrections made based on consulting later authorities.]
19. Tennyson, Alfred, *Morte d'Arthur.* [Edition uncertain.]

Chapter 7

1. Lyman, *John Marsh, Pioneer,* 276.
2. Coy, *Gold Days,* 8-9.
3. [Sources uncertain and not entirely reliable; corrections made based on consulting later authorities.]
4. San Francisco *Californian,* March 15, 1848.
5. [Sources reliable but uncertain.]
6. [Sources uncertain and not entirely reliable; corrections made based on consulting later authorities.]
7. Scherer, James A. B., *The First Forty-niner and the Story of the Golden Tea Caddy,* 94-95.
8. [Soule, Frank, et al. *The Annals of San Francisco,* 355.]
9. [Bancroft, *History of California,* VI, 76; and reliable but uncertain sources.]
10. [Sources reliable but uncertain.]
11. [Calaveras Chamber of Commerce. *Folder for 1930.*]

12. [Sources reliable but uncertain.]
13. [Sources uncertain and not entirely reliable; corrections made based on consulting later authorities.]
14. Paine, Albert Bigelow, *A Short Life of Mark Twain*, 105.
15. [Sources reliable but uncertain.]
16. Wiltsee, Ernest Abram, *The Pioneer Miner and the Pack Mule Express*, 2.
17. [Sources uncertain and grossly unreliable; corrections made based on consulting later authorities.]
18. Winchell, Lilbourne Alsip. Manuscript Letter, Fresno, Oct. 1, 1931.
19. [*Ibid.*]
20. [Sources reliable but uncertain.]
21. [Sources reliable but uncertain.]
22. [Sources uncertain and unreliable; corrections made based on consulting later authorities.]
23. Stockton *Journal*, March 17, 1851.
24. Stockton *Times*, April 18, 1851.
25. [Shinn, Charles Howard. *Mining Camps*, chapter 14.]
26. [Sources reliable but uncertain.]
27. Shinn, *Mining Camps*,chapter 21, 249-250.
28. [Quoted in Shinn, *Mining Camps*.]
29. [Shinn, *Mining Camps*, chapter 9.]
30. Scherer, James A. B., *op. cit.,* 92-93.
31. Coy, Owen Cochrane, *Gold Days*, 156.
32. Carson, James H., *Early Recollections of the Mines,* 14.
33. [Hittell, John S. *The Resources of California, passim.*]
34. Bums, Walter Noble, *The Robin Hood of El Dorado*, 24.
35. [Sources reliable but uncertain.]
36. [Calaveras Chamber of Commerce. *Folder for 1930.*]
37. Miller, Joaquin, *The Days of '49*. [Edition uncertain.]

Chapter 8

1. Johnston, Adam, Report of March 7, 1851. *U.S. Senate Executive Documents*, No.4, 33rd Congress, Special Session, 63-67 (688).
2. Bunnell, Lafayette Houghton, *Discovery of the Yosemite and the Indian War of 1851 Which Led to that Event*, 42.
3. [Sources reliable but uncertain.]
4. [Bunnell, *op. cit.,* 4-5.]
5. [*Ibid.,* 7.]
6. [*Ibid.,* 8.]
7. Most accounts state that Savage was a native of Illinois. L. A. Winchell of Fresno possessed documentary evidence that he was a native of New York. [Sources uncertain and not entirely reliable; corrections made based on consulting later authorities.]
8. *Fresno Weekly Expositor*, May 4, 1870.
9. [Sources uncertain and not entirely reliable; corrections made

based on consulting later authorities.]

10. [*Ibid.* Smith has "Cassady" for "Cassity."]

11. [Sources reliable but uncertain.]

12. [*Ibid.*]

13. Corcoran, May Stanislaus, "William J. Howard, Last of the Famous Mariposa Battalion" in the Stockton *Record*, Dec. 3, 1927.

14. [Sources reliable but uncertain.]

15. [*Ibid.*]

16. San Francisco *Evening Picayune*, Feb. 27, 1851.

17. [Sources unknown but mostly reliable; Smith has "Cipriano" for "Cypriano."]

18. *Daily Pacific News*, March 7, 1851.

19. Stockton Journal, March 7, 1851.

20. [Sources reliable but uncertain.]

21. [*Ibid.*]

22. Bunnell, *op. cit.,* 40.

23. [Sources reliable but uncertain.]

24. Perkins, D. E., Manuscript Letter, Visalia, Sept. 23. 1931.

25. [Sources reliable but uncertain.]

26. Hayes Collection, Indians, II, 145. Quotation from Los Angeles *Star*, June 17, 1854. [Citation unclear; presumably from one of Judge Benjamin I. Hayes' compilations.]

27. [Sources reliable but uncertain.]

28. [*Ibid.*]

29. Tinkham, *History of Stanislaus County*, 92.

30. Fowler, T. W., Letter-Bulletin, Merced, Oct. 12, 1931.

31. [Sources reliable but uncertain.]

32. Johnson, E. Pauline (Tekahiowake), "The Cattle Thief," in *Flint and Feather*, 15-16.

33. McClatchy, Charles K., Manuscript Letter, Sacramento, Oct. 9, 1933.

34. Orton, Brigadier-General Richard H., *Records of California Men in the War of the Rebellion, 1861-1867*, 7.

35. *Records of the War of the Rebellion*, Series I, Vol. 50, Part H. 236. Report made by George S. Evans, Lieutenant-Colonel, Second Cavalry, California Volunteers, Commanding.

36. *Ibid.*, Series I, Vol. 50, Part II, 277. Official report made by Captain M. A. McLaughlin to Col. R. C. Drum, Adjutant-General, Presidio, San Francisco, January 1, 1863.

37. [Sources unknown and somewhat unreliable; corrected according to later authorities.]

38. [Sources reliable but uncertain.]

39. Anthony, Rev. C. V., *Fifty Years of Methodism*, 325-326.

40. [Sources reliable but uncertain.]

41. *Records of the War of the Rebellion*, Series I, Vol. 50, Part II, 386.

42. [Sources reliable but uncertain.]

43. [*Ibid.*]
44. [*Ibid.*]
45. [*Ibid.*]
46. [*Ibid.*]
47. *Fresno Morning Republican*, Oct. 19, 1923.
48. Ruskin, John, *Seven Lamps of Architecture. The Lamp of Memory.*[Edition uncertain.]

Chapter 9

1. Banning, William, and Banning, George Hugh, *Six Horses*, 12.
2. [United States Land Commission for California. *Transcript of Proceedings in Case No. 293, Hiram Grimes, et al., Claimants, vs. the United States, Defendant, for the Place Named "El Pescadero."*]
3. Irving, Washington, *Tales of a Traveller*, preface. [Edition uncertain.]
4. Gilbert, W. S., *Ruddigore*. [Edition uncertain.]
5. Winchell, L. A., Manuscript Letter, Fresno, Sept. 21, 1930.
6. Otis, George B., *Reminiscences of Early Days*, 14 [and perhaps Smith's personal knowledge.]
7. [Appears to derive from the writings/recollections of L.A. Winchell.]
8. Thompson, Thomas H., *Official Historical Atlas Map of Tulare County*, 12.
9. [Sanchez, Nellie van de Grift. *Spanish Arcadia*, 299.]
10. [Thompson, Thomas H., *op.cit.*]
11. [Elias, Sol P. *Stories of Stanislaus*, 240.]
12. Tinkham, George H., *California Men and Events*, 115.
13. [Heath, Erle, "From Trail to Rail" in *Southern Pacific Bulletin*, June, 1928.]
14. [Latta, *Uncle Jeff's Story*, 67.]
15. Quinn, John R., Manuscript Letter, Los Angeles, Dec. 19, 1931.
16. Banning and Banning, *Six Horses*, 8-14, 45.
17. Ganoe, William Addleman, *History of the United States Army*, 273, footnote.
18. [Sources reliable but uncertain.]
19. [Bancroft, *History of California*, VII, 519-524.]
20. [Banning and Banning, *Six Horses*, 110.]
21. *Senate Executive Documents, No. 78. Reports of Explorations and Surveys, to ascertain the most practicable and economical route for a railroad from the Mississippi River to the Pacific Ocean*, V, 7-8.
22. [*Ibid.*]
23. [*Ibid.*, 13, 14-16.]
24. [*Ibid.*, 18-20, 22-25.]
25. [Heath, *op. cit.*]
26. Root, Frank A., and Connelley, William E., *The Overland Stage to*

California, 13. [Additions and corrections made based on consulting later authorities.]

27. [*Ibid.*, 276.]
28. Banning, and Banning, *Six Horses*, 23-27.
29. [Hafen, Leroy R., *The Overland Mail, 1849-1869*, 96.]
30. [*Ibid.*, 115, 116.]
31. [Sources reliable but uncertain.]
32. [Appears to derive from the writings of Frank F. Latta.]
33. [Appears to derive from John C. McCubbin's then-unpublished writings on the Stockton-Los Angeles Stage Road.]
34. [Sources used by Smith uncertain and unreliable; corrections made based on consulting later authorities.]
35. [*Ibid.*]
36. [McCubbin, *op. cit.*]
37. [*Ibid.*]
38. [*Ibid.*]
39. [*Ibid.*]
40. [*Ibid.*]
41. [Sources reliable but uncertain.]
42. [McCubbin, *op. cit.*]
43. [Sources reliable but uncertain.]
44. [*Ibid.*]
45. [*Ibid.*]
46. [*Ibid.*]
47. [*Ibid.*]
48. [McCubbin, *op. cit.*]
49. [Sources used by Smith uncertain and slightly unreliable; corrections made based on consulting later authorities.]
50. [Considine, John L., "Jeff Davis and the Camels," *Columbia Magazine*, December 1929; and Bonsal, *Edward Fitzgerald Beale*, 198-210.]
51. [*Ibid.*]
52. Considine, *op. cit.*
53. [Considine and Bonsal, *op. cit.*]
54. [Sources reliable but uncertain.]
55. Oakland *Post-Enquirer*, Dec. 3, 1932.
56. [Alvarado, Juan Bautista, Manuscript, *History of California*.]
57. [Davis, William Heath. *Seventy-Five Years in California, 189*.]
58. [Taylor, Bayard. *Eldorado*, chapter 14.]
59. Hittell, Theodore H., *The Adventures of James Capen Adams, Mountaineer and Grizzly Bear Hunter of California*, 25.
60. [Source reliable but uncertain.]
61. [Bancroft, *History of California*, V, 304 n.]
62. [*Ibid.*, II, 732.]
63. [Lydekker, Richard. *The Horse and its Relatives*, 170.]
64. Parsons, K. K., "The Barb Horse in America," *Western Horseman*, Sept.-Oct., 1937.
65. [Pliny the Elder, *Natural History*, VIII, 166.]

66. [Parsons, *op. cit.*]
67. Davenport, Homer, *My Quest of the Arab Horse*, 258.
68. Dodge, Theodore Ayrault, *Riders of Many Lands*, 55.
69. [Sources uncertain.]
70. Raswan, Carl, "Drinker of the Air," *Asia Magazine*, April, 1929.
71. [*Ibid.*]
72. [Sources uncertain.]
73. Walker, Johnnie, "The Wild Horses of Early California: Where They Came From and What Happened to Them," *Western Horseman*, October, 1936.
74. [Sources uncertain.]
75. Haines, Francis. "George Rogers Clark and His Spanish Horse," *Western Horseman*, July-August, 1937.
76. *New Americanized Encyclopaedia Britannica*, Chicago, 1896, 12 volumes, article entitled "Horse", Vol. VI., 3205. [Perhaps the Ninth Edition; work cited does not appear to exist.]
77. Pliny the Elder, *op. cit.*
78. Daingerfield, Elizabeth, Superintendent at Haylands (at that time the home of Man-of-War), Manuscript Letter, Lexington, Kentucky, Nov. 26, 1930.
79. Muir, Mauchline. "The Rocky Mountain Endurance Race," *The World To-day*, August, 1908.
80. Segrelles. José, Comment by this well-known Spanish painter on his picture representing Napoleon's riderless war-horse. This famous painting interprets Beethoven's Third Symphony, *Eroica*, whose original title, *Napoleon Bonaparte*, the democratic composer destroyed when the First Consul became Emperor of France.

Chapter 10

1. [Sources reliable but uncertain.]
2. Palou, Father Francisco, *Historical Memoirs of New California*, Berkeley, 1926, I, 52 (Herbert E. Bolton, translator and editor).
3. [Sources reliable but uncertain.]
4. [*Ibid.*]
5. [*Ibid.*]
6. [Lydekker, *The Horse and His Relatives*, 170.]
7. [Sources reliable but uncertain.]
8. [Lydekker, *op. cit.*; other sources reliable but uncertain.]
9. [United States Land Commission. *Transcript of Proceedings in Case No. 545, Julian Ursua, Claimant, vs. the United States, Defendant, for the Place Named "La Panoche de San Juan y Carrisalitos."*]
10. *Daily Alta California*, August 24, 1854.
11. [Fink, George W., (Chamber of Commerce secretary), Manuscript Letter, Crow's Landing, Oct. 8, 1931.]
12. [Lyman, *John Marsh, Pioneer*, 226-227.]

13. [Tinkham, *History of Stanislaus County*, 48.]
14. [Crane, Horace S. Manuscript Letter, Turlock, Oct. 6, 1931.]
15. [Elliott & Moore, *History of Merced County*, 120-121, 147.]
16. [Lewis Publishing Co., *Memorial and Biographical History of Fresno, Tulare and Kern Counties*, 120.]
17. [*Ibid.*, 50.]
18. [Probably from a personal interview or newspaper article regarding Akers.]
19. [Lewis Publishing Co., *op. cit.*, 606.]
20. [*Ibid.*, 634-635; Elliott, *History of Fresno County*, 213.]
21. [Possibly from Hubert Howe Bancroft, *Chronicles of the Builders*, III, 227-232.]
22. McCubbin, John C., Manuscript Letter, Los Angeles, Nov. 11, 1931.
23. Treadwell, Edward F., *The Cattle King*, 85.
24. [Bondesen, Annie L., Manuscript Letter, Madera, Sept. 25, 1931.]
25. [Lewis Publishing Co., *op. cit.*, 629-630.]
26. [*Ibid.*, 538-539.]
27. [Draper, Lewis, Personal Interview, Burris ranch near Kingsburg, Dec. 31, 1931.]
28. [Elliott & Moore, *op. cit.*, 197; Menefee & Dodge, *History of Kings and Tulare Counties*, 777-778.]
29. [Railsback, Sarah, Manuscript Letter, Berkeley, Oct. 29, 1931; Elliott & Moore, *op. cit.*, 180-181.]
30. [McCubbin, John C., Manuscript Letter, Fresno, Feb. 24, 1924.]
31. [*Abstract to the Title to the Rancho Laguna de Tache*, 6, 16-17, 18.]
32. Cross, Ira B., *Financing an Empire: History of Banking in California*, II, 604.
33. [Vandor, *History of Fresno County*, I, 260.]
34. [*Abstract, op. cit.*, 69.]
35. [Sources reliable but uncertain.]
36. [*Ibid.*]
37. [*Ibid.*]
38. [*Ibid.*]
39. [Lewis Publishing Co., *op. cit.*, 330-331; Morgan, *History of Kern County*, 44.]
40. [Source unknown.]
41. Quinn, John R., Manuscript Letter, Los Angeles, Dec. 19, 1931.
42. [Lewis Publishing Co., *op. cit.*, 355-356.]
43. [Morgan, *op. cit.*, 48; Bonsal, *Edward Fitzgerald Beale*, 272-290.]
44. [Morgan, *op. cit.*, 61.]
45. [*Ibid.*, 85; Treadwell, *The Cattle King*, 80-81.]
46. [Morgan, *op. cit.*, 46.]
47. [*Ibid.*, 47-48.]
48. [*Ibid.*, 48.]
49. [Lewis Publishing Co., *op. cit.*, 407-408; some data seem to be based on Smith's personal knowledge.]

50. [*Ibid.*, 585-586.]
51. [Possibly from J.M. Guinn, *History of California* and *Biographical Record of the San Joaquin Valley*, 1483-1485.]
52. [Sources reliable but uncertain.]
53. [Sources reliable but uncertain.]
54. [Treadwell, *op. cit.*, 5-10, 26-27, 39-54, 55, 56.]
55. [*Ibid.*, 190-194.]
56. [*Ibid.*, 67-69, 78-94, 224.]
57. [California Surveyor-General's Office, Report for 1853.]
58. [Sources reliable but uncertain.]
59. [Sources reliable but uncertain.]
60. [Probably based on promotional material and Smith's personal knowledge.]
61. Latta, Frank F., "Pioneers of the San Joaquin" in the Fresno *Bee*, Feb. 6, 1935.
62. Bergen, L. B., Manuscript Letter, San Francisco, Jan. 10, 1938.
63. [Sources reliable but uncertain.]
64. British Dairy Farmers' Association, quoting *Household Words*.[Context uncertain.]

Chapter 11

1. Heath, Erle, "From Trail to Rail" in *Southern Pacific Bulletin*, June, 1928.
2. [*Ibid.*]
3. [*Ibid.*]
4. [*Ibid.*]
5. [Elias, *Stories of Stanislaus*, 42.]
6. [Tinkham, *History of Stanislaus County*, 92.]
7. [Sources reliable but uncertain.]
8. [Heath, *op. cit.*]
9. [Sources reliable but uncertain.]
10. [Heath, *op. cit.*]
11. [*Ibid.*]
12. [*Ibid.*]
13. [*Ibid.*]
14. [*Ibid.*]
15. Thompson, Thomas H., *Official. Historical Atlas Map of Tulare County*, 13.
16. Forney, John, Personal Interview, Kingsburg, Dec. 31, 1931.
17. [Heath, *op. cit.*]
18. [Sources unknown and not entirely reliable; corrected in part.]
19. Sullivan, John L., Manuscript Letter, Hanford, Oct. 30, 1931.
20. A committee appointed by the settlers issued a pamphlet which contained their version of the land troubles with the Southern Pacific; this pamphlet, a copy of which is on file in the Bancroft Library, was entitled *The Struggle of the Mussel Slough Settlers for Their Homes! An Appeal to the People. History of the Land*

Troubles in Tulare and Fresno Counties. The Grasping Greed of the Railroad Monopoly. By the Settlers' Committee. Visalia: Visalia Delta Book and Job Print, 1880.

21. [Precise source uncertain.]
22. [Sources reliable but uncertain.]
23. [Bancroft, *History of California*, VII, 625-627.]
24. [Sources reliable but uncertain.]
25. Russell, Charles E., *Stories of the Great Railroad*, 220. [Work, as cited, does not appear to exist.]
26. [Sources reliable but uncertain.]
27. Wister, Owen, *Roosevelt: The Story of a Friendship*, 84-85. Used by permission of the Macmillan Company.
28. Rowe, William, Veteran section foreman at Fresno, Personal Interview, Fresno, Nov. 11, 1933.
29. [Sources reliable but uncertain.]
30. Adams, Sol G., Personal Interview, Calwa, Nov. 26, 1933. Adams was locomotive engineer on the division between Riverbank and Fresno, and is authority for the statement that he maintained a rate of eighty miles an hour on the Angel.
31. Johnson, Hiram, Manuscript Letter, Washington. D. C., Oct 9, 1931.

Chapter 12

1. Norris, Frank, *The Octopus*, 127-128. Used by permission of Doubleday, Doran, and Company.
2. Rogin, Leo, *Farm Machinery in Relation to Labor*, 43.
3. [United States Land Commission, *Transcript of Proceedings in Case No. 255, Charles M. Weber, Claimant, vs. the United States, Defendant, for the Place Named the "Campo de los Franceses.";* and *Transcript of Proceedings in Case No. 240, Jose Antonio Aguirre and Ignacio del Valle, Claimants, vs. the United States, Defendant, for the Place Named "El Tejon.]*
4. Bancroft, *History of California*, V, 552-553.]
5. [Bidwell, John, *Echoes of the Past*, 82-83. Used by permission of the Donnelley Publishing Co.]
6. [California State Agricultural Society, *Transactions for 1890*, 189.]
7. [McCapes, Eugene L. Personal Interview, Reedley, Oct. 15, 1933.]
8. Bellue, Margaret K., Weed and Seed Botanist, California Department of Agriculture, Manuscript Letter, Sacramento, Oct. 18, 1933.
9. [*Ibid.?*]
10. [Sources reliable but uncertain.]
11. [Menefee & Dodge, *History of Kings and Tulare Counties*, 479-480.]
12. [Sources reliable but uncertain.]
13. [Tinkham, *History of Stanislaus County*, 54-57; Elias, *Stories of*

Stanislaus, 268-269; Latta, *Farm Equipment in the San Joaquin, passim.*]

14. [Rogin, *Farm Machinery in Relation to Labor*, 42; and Latta, Frank F. "Stockton Gang Plow Invented Near Manteca." California Country Life Section, *Fresno Bee*, July 2, 1933.]
15. [Latta, *Ibid.*]
16. [*Ibid.*]
17. [*Ibid.*]
18. [Source reliable but uncertain.]
19. McCapes, Eugene L., Personal Interview, Reedley, Oct. 15, 1933.
20. [Sources reliable but uncertain.]
21. [Sources reliable but uncertain.]
22. California State Agricultural Society, *Transactions for 1859*, 236 [and Latta, *op. cit.*, July 2, 1933.]
23. [Latta, *Ibid.*]
24. [Sources reliable but uncertain.]
25. [Rogin, *passim.*]
26. [Latta, *op. cit.*]
27. [*Ibid.*]
28. [Rogin, *op. cit.*]
29. [Latta, *op. cit.*]
30. [*Ibid.*]
31. [Rogin, *op. cit.*]
32. Cooper, James Fenimore, *Oak Openings*, 501-502. [Edition uncertain.]
33. [Latta, *op. cit.*]
34. [*Ibid.*]
35. [*Ibid.*]
36. Hilgard, Dr. E. W., "The Agriculture and Soils of California" in U. S. Department of Agriculture, *Report for 1878*, 498.
37. *Pacific Rural Press*, 18 (1879): 197.
38. [Latta, *op. cit.*]
39. [Sources reliable but uncertain.]
40. *Ibid*, 9 (1875): 209; *United States Census for 1880*, 3: 457. [Edition uncertain.]
41. [Sources reliable but uncertain.]
42. [Sources reliable but uncertain.]
43. McCormick, Cyrus, *The Century of the Reaper*, 216.
44. Latta, Frank F., "Auto-Motive Combined Harvester Used in Lindsay District" in California Country Life section of the Fresno Bee for August 6, 1933.
45. [*Ibid.*]
46. [*Ibid.*]
47. [*Ibid.*]
48. [*Ibid.*]
49. [Sources reliable but uncertain.]
50. U. S. Department of Agriculture, Division of Statistics, *Bulletin 20*, 27. [Uncertain citation.]

51. McCormick, Cyrus, *The Century of the Reaper*, 10.
52. [Rogin, *op. cit.*]
53. [Perhaps based on author's personal knowledge.]
54. [Perhaps based on author's personal knowledge.]
55. [Latta, *op. cit.*]
56. Caterpillar Tractor Company, *The Caterpillar Souvenir Book*, 21. [Work cited does not appear to exist.]
57. Schaedel, T. B., International Harvester Company of America, Manuscript Letter, Chicago, Illinois, October 20, 1933.
58. [Source uncertain; possibly from Simonds' *New York Tribune History of the War*.]
59. McCormick, Cyrus, *The Century of the Reaper*, 212.
60. [Elias, Stories of Stanislaus, 43.]
61. [Probably McCapes, Eugene L., Personal Interview, Reedley, Oct. 15, 1933.]
62. [Vandor, *History of Fresno County*, I, 181-182.]
63. McCubbin, John C., "The Rise and Fall of Traver," *Fresno Morning Republican*, March 5, 1923.
64. *Ibid.*
65. Caldwell, Charles, "Frank Norris, or, Up From Culture" in the *American Mercury* for April, 1928.
66. *Fresno Morning Republican*, July 27, 1929.
67. [*Ibid.*]
68. Shultz, James, Los Angeles Lumberman and San Joaquin Valley wheat grower; statement quoted by *Fresno Bee*, July 7, 1935.
69. [Source reliable but uncertain.]
70. [*Ibid.*]
71. [*Ibid.*]
72. Marten, Effie Elfreda, *Development of Wheat Culture in the San Joaquin*, 38-43. This master's thesis, on file at the University of California, is based on an intensive study of official reports and documents, and is the best available account of the wheat industry in the San Joaquin Valley.
73. California State Agricultural Society, Transactions for 1872, 234.
74. *Ibid., Transactions for 1861*, 43.
75. *Ibid., Transactions for 1893*, 15.
76. [Sources reliable but uncertain.]
77. [*Ibid.*]
78. [Marten, *op. cit.*]
79. [*Ibid.*]
80. Elias, *op. cit.*, 19.
81. *Ibid.*, 293-297.
82. McCubbin, *op. cit.*
83. [Elias, *op. cit.*, 298-299, 303-317.]
84. Babcock, Maltbie Davenport, *Give Us This Day Our Daily Bread*.[Edition uncertain.]

Chapter 13

1. William Braden's testimony in the United Circuit Court as reported by the San Francisco *Chronicle*, December 21, 1880.
2. *San Francisco Morning Call*, Dec. 9, 1880.
3. *San Francisco Chronicle*, Dec. 18, 1880.
4. [Sources reliable but uncertain.]
5. Wister, Owen, *Roosevelt: The Story of a Friendship*, 84-85. Used by permission of the Macmillan Company.
6. *Ibid.*
7. Sandburg, Carl, *Abraham Lincoln: The Prairie Years*, II, 273, 346.
8. [Sources reliable but uncertain.]
9. *San Francisco Morning Call*, Nov. 16, 1880.
10. [Sources reliable but uncertain.]
11. [*Ibid.*]
12. [Source unknown.]
13. [*Ibid.*]
14. *San Francisco Morning Call*, Dec. 3, 1880.
15. [Menefee & Dodge, *History of Kings and Tulare Counties*, 111.]
16. *San Francisco Evening Bulletin*, Dec. 22, 1880.
17. *Ibid.*, Dec. 7, 1880.
18. *Argonaut*, April, 1881.
19. [Sources reliable but uncertain.]
20. *San Francisco Chronicle*, Dec. 10, 1880.
21. *Ibid.*
22. *San Francisco Morning Call*, Dec. 4, 1880.
23. [Sources reliable but uncertain.]
24. *San Francisco Morning Call*, Dec. 15, 1880.
25. *Ibid.*
26. *San Francisco Chronicle*, Dec. 15, 1880.
27. Sullivan, John L., Manuscript Letter, Hanford, January 28, 1932.
28. [Sources reliable but uncertain.]
29. [Sources reliable but uncertain.]
30. [Sources reliable but uncertain.]
31. *San Francisco Evening Bulletin*, Dec. 6, 1880.
32. *San Francisco Morning Call*, Dec. 9, 1880.
33. [*Ibid.?*]
34. *Ibid.*
35. *Ibid.*, Dec. 19, 1880.
36. *San Francisco Examiner*, December 22, 1880.
37. [Sources uncertain and not entirely reliable; corrections made based on consulting later authorities.]
38. [Sources uncertain and not entirely reliable; corrections made based on consulting later authorities.]
39. *San Francisco Morning Call*, Dec. 9, 1880.
40. *Ibid.*, Dec. 19, 1880.
41. [*Ibid.?*]

42. *Ibid.*
43. [Probably based on Smith's personal knowledge.]
44. [Generally reliable; some information expanded according to other authoties.]
45. Cummings, Homer, and McFarland, Carl, *Federal Justice: Chapters in the History of Justice and the Federal Executive,* New York, 1937, 525.
46. *San Francisco Chronicle,* Dec. 19, 1880.
47. *Ibid.,* Dec. 18, 1880.
48. *Ibid.,* Dec. 16, 1880; a verbatim report of Doyle's entire testimony can be found in the *San Francisco Morning Call,* Dec. 16, 1880.
49. *San Francisco Bulletin,* Dec. 22, 1880.
50. *Ibid.*
51. [Sources uncertain and not entirely reliable; corrections made based on consulting later authorities.]
52. [Sources reliable but uncertain.]
53. [Sources uncertain and not entirely reliable; corrections made based on consulting later authorities.]
54. [Sources reliable but uncertain.]
55. *Argonaut,* April, 1881.
56. [Sources reliable but uncertain.]
57. Crow, Clarence, Personal Interview, Hanford, Nov. 16, 1934.
58. [Sources uncertain and grossly unreliable; corrections made based on consulting later authorities.]
59. *Visalia Times,* May 15, 1884.
60. [Sources reliable but uncertain.]

Chapter 14

1. [Original account is vastly unreliable; much has been eliminated and corrected according to later authorities.]
2. [*Ibid.*]
3. *California Police Gazette,* Sept. 17, 1859.
4. [Sources reliable but uncertain.]
5. [Original account is vastly unreliable; much has been eliminated and corrected according to later authorities.]
6. [*Ibid.*]
7. [Source reliable but uncertain.]
8. [Original account is vastly unreliable; much has been eliminated and corrected according to later authorities.]
9. Robertson, Dr. H. E., Head of the Section of Pathologic Anatomy, Mayo Clinic, and Professor of Pathology, University of Minnesota, Manuscript letter, Rochester, Minnesota, Feb. 15, 1932.
10. [Source reliable but uncertain.]
11. Austin, Mary, "Vasquez Rock" in the *Youth's Companion,* Nov. 5, 1908. [Smith's prefatory notes on Vasquez are inaccurate and have been corrected according to later authorities.]
12. [Beers, *Vasquez, or the Hunted Bandits of the San Joaquin,* 16-

34. Original account is vastly unreliable; much has been eliminated and corrected according to later authorities.]

13. [Sources reliable but uncertain.]
14. [Sources mostly reliable but uncertain; Chavez's name is incor-
rectly given in original text.]
15. [Likely based on Draper, Mrs. Frank (Florence Livermore
Draper), Manuscript Letter, Kingsburg, Sept. 24, 1931.]
16. [Sources reliable but uncertain.]
17. [Original account is vastly unreliable; much has been eliminated
and corrected according to later authorities.]
18. [*Ibid.*]
19. [Sources reliable but uncertain.]
20. Draper, Mrs. Frank (Florence Livermore Draper), *op. cit.*
21. [Sources reliable but uncertain.]
22. Bush, E. E., Manuscript Letter, Hanford, Oct. 29, 1931.
23. [Generally accurate, and perhaps adapted from the account in
Winchell's *History of Fresno County*.]
24. [Likely based on Smith's personal knowledge and/or an unrecord-
ed interview with a pioneer.]
25. [Sources unknown; corrected in part according to later authorities.]
26. [Sources generally reliable but uncertain.]
27. [Beers, *op. cit.,* 86. Original account is unreliable; corrected
according to later authorities.]
28. Connelley, William Elsey, *Quantrill and the Border Wars*, preface.
29. Love, Robertus, *The Rise and the Fall of Jesse James*, 19.
30. [Sources unknown and somewhat unreliable; corrected according
to later authorities.]
31. [Likely based on Smith's personal knowledge.]
32. [Sources unknown and somewhat unreliable; corrected according
to later authorities.]
33. [Sources reliable but uncertain.]
34. Dalton, Emmett, *When the Daltons Rode*, 127.
35. [Sources unknown and somewhat unreliable; corrected according
to later authorities.]
36. [Sources generally reliable but uncertain. Some clues for the
sources of Smith's information may be found in his later work,
Prodigal Sons (Boston: Christopher, 1951) which focuses on the
events which conclude this chapter. As many California and
national newspapers followed the activities of John Sontag and
Christopher Evans, it is difficult to ascribe the precise sources
Smith used, save for those he identified expressly.]
37. [*Ibid.*]
38. *Modesto Herald*, Sept. 5, 1891.
39. [Sources reliable but uncertain.]
40. *Visalia Daily Times*, Aug. 13, 1892 [and Glasscock, *Bandits and
the Southern Pacific*, 130-264.]
41. [Sources reliable but uncertain.]

42. [*Ibid.*]
43. [*Ibid.*]
44. *Visalia Daily Times*, March 13, 1892.
45. [Sources reliable but uncertain.]
46. [*Ibid.*]
47. [*Ibid.*]
48. [*Ibid.*]
49. [*Ibid.*]
50. [*Ibid.*]
51. [*Ibid.*]
52. [*Ibid.*]
53. [*Ibid.*]
54. [*Ibid.*]
55. [*Ibid.*]
56. [*Ibid.*]
57. [*Ibid.*]
58. [*Ibid.*]
59. [*Ibid.*]
60. *Visalia Daily Times*, June 6, 1893.
61. *Ibid.*, Dec. 29, 1893.
62. [Sources reliable but uncertain.]
63. [*Ibid.*]
64. *Visalia Daily Times*, Dec. 14, 1893.
65. *Ibid.*, Aug. 13, 1892.
66. Johnson, Hiram, United States Senator from California, Manuscript Letter. Washington, D.C., Oct. 9, 1931.
67. [Sources reliable but uncertain.]
68. [*Ibid.*]
69. [*Ibid.*]
70. Fresno *Bee*, March 31, 1931.

Chapter 15

1. Porter, William Sydney (O. Henry), "A Cosmopolite in a Cafe" in *The Four Million*. Used by permission of Doubleday, Doran, and Co. [Edition uncertain.]
2. Aristotle, *Politics*, 1, 2. [Edition uncertain.]
3. [Sources unknown and somewhat unreliable; corrected according to later authorities.]
4. [*Ibid.*; see George Tinkham's *History of Stockton* for corrective material.]
5. [*Ibid.*]
6. [Sources reliable but uncertain.]
7. [*Ibid.*]
8. [Tinkham, *History of Stanislaus County*, 73-74; and corrections according to later authorities.]
9. [*Ibid.*, 66-67; and corrections according to later authorities.]

10. [*Ibid.*, 187-188.]
11. [Elias, *Stories of Stanislaus*, 287-292.]
12. [Sources unknown and somewhat unreliable; corrected according to later authorities.]
13. [Tinkham, *op. cit.,* 59-61; Elias, *op. cit.,* 262-265.]
14. [Sources reliable but uncertain.]
15. [Sources generally reliable but uncertain.]
16. [*Ibid.*]
17. [Elias, *op. cit.,* 292.]
18. [Sources reliable but uncertain.]
19. [*Ibid.*]
20. [*Ibid.*]
21. [Sources unknown and somewhat unreliable; corrected according to later authorities.]
22. [Sources unknown; likely based on personal knowledge of Smith and John C. McCubbin.]
23. [*Annual Report of the Condition of Common Schools in the County of Fresno, 1870-1871.*]
24. [Sources reliable but uncertain.]
25. [*Ibid.*]
26. [Sources unknown and somewhat unreliable; corrected according to later authorities.]
27. [Sources reliable but uncertain.]
28. [Elliott & Moore, *History of Tulare County*, 35-36; Menefee & Dodge, *History of Kings and Tulare Counties*, 167-168.]
29. [Menefee & Dodge, *op. cit.,* 855-856; and reliable but uncertain sources.]
30. Latta, F. F., Manuscript Letter, Tulare, Feb. 22, 1932.
31. [Sources reliable but uncertain.]
32. [Sources generally reliable but uncertain.]
33. Harpending, Asbury, "The Great Diamond Hoax" in the *San Francisco Bulletin*, Sept. 27, 1913.
34. [Morgan, *History of Kern County*, 74-75.]
35. Bishop, William Henry, "Southern California" in *Harper's New Monthly Magazine*, Vol. LXV, Oct.-Nov., 1882.
36. Connor, Ralph, *The Sky Pilot*, 14. Used by permission of Fleming H. Revell Company.
37. Morgan, Wallace, *History of Kern County*, 114; and *San Francisco Chronicle*, Oct. 6, 1933.
38. Weeks, George F., *California Copy*, 177.
39. *Ibid.*, 249-250.
40. [Morgan, *op. cit.,* 181, 185.]
41. [*Ibid.*, 129.]
42. [*Ibid.*, 20-29.]
43. *Tuolumne City News, Oct. 14, 1870.*
44. *Ibid., Oct. 28, 1870.*
45. *Ibid.*
46. [Elias, *op. cit.,* 44, 324-327.]

47. [Sources reliable but uncertain.]

48. Porter, Florence, Manuscript Letter, Turlock, Oct. 13, 1931 [and Tinkham, *op. cit.,* 172-173.]

49. Elias, *op. cit.,* 133; quotation from the California Promotion Committee.

50. [Source possibly John Outcault, *History of Merced County,* 100-101, 255-260, 268-269.]

51. [Sources reliable but uncertain.]

52. [*Ibid.*]

53. [*Ibid.*]

54. [*Ibid.*]

55. [*Ibid.*]

56. [*Ibid.*]

57. [Winchell, *History of Fresno County,* 122; and generally reliable sources, corrected by other authorities.]

58. [Sources reliable but uncertain.]

59. [*Ibid.*]

60. [*Ibid.*]

61. [*Ibid.*]

62. *Selma Irrigator* (Golden Jubilee Edition), Oct. 23, 1930.

63. [Sources reliable but uncertain.]

64. [Sources unknown; likely based on Smith's personal knowledge.]

65. [*Ibid.*]

66. [*Ibid.*]

67. [*Ibid.*]

68. [Likely based on personal knowledge and/or writings of John C. McCubbin.]

69. Coughran, Neva Rea, Manuscript Letter, Kingsburg, Oct. 16, 1931.

70. Dalton, Emmett, Manuscript Letter, Hollywood, Oct. 2, 1931.

71. [Likely based on personal knowledge and/or writings of John C. McCubbin.]

72. [*Ibid.*]

73. [*Ibid.*]

74. [*Ibid.*]

75. [*Ibid.*]

76. McCubbin, John C., "The Rise and Fall of Traver" in the *Fresno Morning Republican,* March 6, 1923.

77. [Possibly based in part on Heath, "From Trail to Rail" in *Southern Pacific Bulletin,* June, 1928.]

78. Hurst, Harry, "Alta Pioneers" in the Dinuba *Alta Advocate,* n. d.

79. [Sources reliable but uncertain.]

80. [*Ibid.*]

81. [*Ibid.*]

82. [*Ibid.*]

83. [*Ibid.*]

84. [Sources unknown and not entirely reliable, corrected according to later authorities; possibly based in part on Heath, *op. cit.*]

85. [Likely based on personal knowledge and/or writings of John C. McCubbin.]
86. [Possibly based in part on Hurst, *op. cit.*]
87. [*Ibid.*]
88. [Sources reliable but uncertain.]
89. [Menefee & Dodge, *op. cit.*, 49.]
90. [Sources reliable but uncertain.]
91. [Sources unknown and somewhat unreliable; corrected according to later authorities.]
92. [Sources reliable but uncertain.]
93. [*Ibid.*]
94. [*Ibid.*]
95. [*Ibid.*]
96. [Menefee & Dodge, *op. cit.*, 49.]
97. Sheridan, Elmer M., Personal Interview, Reedley, Sept. 20, 1933 [and Morgan, *op. cit.*, 178-180.]
98. [Sources reliable but uncertain.]
99. [*Ibid.*]
100. [*Ibid.*]
101. [*Ibid.*]
102. Sheridan, *op. cit.*
103. Clark, Badger. *God's Reserves.*[Appearance citation uncertain.]

Chapter 16

1. [Sources reliable but uncertain.]
2. Bidwell, John, *A Journey to California*, 19, 47.
3. Winthrop, Theodore, *John Brent*, 10-11. [Citation unclear; no similar item located.]
4. *Ibid.*, 136. [Citation unclear; no similar item located.]
5. West, George P., "Hearst: a Psychological Note" in the *American Mercury*, November, 1930.
6. *San Francisco Evening Bulletin*, November 19, 1858.
7. United States Land Commission for California, Land Case No. 255.
8. [Sources reliable but uncertain.]
9. [*Ibid.*]
10. Creel, George, "The Lion of the Lord" in *Collier's*. Sept. 24, 1926.
11. Peery, Joseph S., President, Temple Square Mission and Bureau of Information of the Church of Jesus Christ of Latter-Day Saints, Salt Lake City, Utah, Manuscript Letter, December 5, 1933.
12. [Eldredge, Zoeth Skinner (editor), *History of California*, V, 175, 176.]
13. [Bancroft, *History of California*, V, 545-546, 550.]
14. [Sources reliable but uncertain.]
15. Eldredge, *op. cit.*, V, 176.
16. King, Murray E., "Utah: Apocalypse of the Desert" in *These*

United States: a Symposium, First Series, 74. Ernest Gruening, editor.

17. [Sources reliable but uncertain.]
18. Bishop, William Henry, "Southern California" in *Harper's New Monthly Magazine*, October and November, 1882, Vol. LXV.
19. Crow, Carl, *Four Hundred Million Customers*. Quoted by the *Current Digest*, January 1938.
20. Dow, Richard, Manuscript Letter, Hanford, January 10, 1938.
21. [Sources reliable but uncertain.]
22. [Likely based on manuscript letter(s) received by Smith from John R. Quinn; see "Essay on Authorities.]
23. [Winchell, *History of Fresno County*, 89, 91; Elliott, *History of Fresno County*, 119.]
24. [Sources reliable but uncertain.]
25. [*Ibid.*]
26. [*Ibid.*]
27. [See Appendix IV, containing Smith's likely source for this material; corrected in part according to later authorities.]
28. [Lewis Publishing Co., *Memorial and Biographical History of Fresno, Tulare and Kern Counties*, 129.]
29. Ostrom, Rev. Oscar W., Manuscript Letter, Fresno, Oct. 26, 1931.
30. [Vandor, *History of Fresno County*, I, 263.]
31. [Vandor, *op. cit.,* I, 264; Elliott, *op. cit.,* 118.]
32. [Vandor, *op. cit.*]
33. [Sources unknown and somewhat unreliable; corrected according to other authorities.]
34. [Sources reliable but uncertain.]
35. McCubbin, John C., Manuscript History of the 76 Land & Water Co., furnished by Mr. McCubbin, August 10, 1926.
36. [Possibly from J.M. Guinn, *History of California and Biographical Record of the San Joaquin Valley, 1460-1461.*]
37. Erikson, Andrew, Manuscript Letter, Kingsburg, Sept. 30, 1931.
38. [Likely based on Smith's personal knowledge.]
39. Gearhart, E. J., "A Thumb-nail History of our Plants and the Men that Make Them Go," in *The Associated Grower* for May, 1921.
40. Nordstrom, Percy H., Manuscript Letter, Kingsburg, October 16, 1931.
41. [Likely based on Smith's personal knowledge.]
42. [Sources reliable but uncertain.]
43. [Sources unknown and somewhat unreliable; corrected according to later authorities.]
44. [*Ibid.*]
45. Shinn, Charles Howard, "Co-operation on the Pacific Coast" in the *History of Co-operation in the United States*, VI, 464-470.
46. [Sources reliable but uncertain.]
47. [*Ibid.*]
48. [Likely based on Smith's personal knowledge.]

49. [Morgan, *History of Kern County*, 113, 175.]
50. [Sources reliable but uncertain.]
51. London, Jack, *The Call of the Wild*, 1. [Edition uncertain.]
52. Hultberg, Rev. Nels O., Manuscript Letter, Los Gatos, Nov. 9, 1931.
53. [*Ibid.?*]
54. [*Ibid.?*]
55. [Sources reliable but uncertain.]
56. [*Ibid.*, with some additions from other authorities.]
57. [Sources reliable but uncertain.]
58. [Likely taken from studies made by Wilson Wallis and published in the *Fresno Morning Republican*.]
59. [Sources reliable but uncertain.]
60. [Sources unknown and somewhat unreliable; corrected according to later authorities.]
61. [Sources reliable but uncertain; possibly from members of the Eymann family.]
62. Krehbiel, Rev. H. J., Manuscript Letter, Reedley, Oct. 8, 1931.
63. [Sources reliable but uncertain.]
64. [*Ibid.*]
65. Boddy, E. Manchester, *The Japanese in America*, 99-102.
66. [Sources reliable but uncertain.]
67. State of California, Department of Public Works, Division of Engineering and Irrigation, Bulletin No. 12. *Summary on the Water Resources of California and a Coordinated Plan for their Development*, 33.
68. Howe, Frederic, *Privilege and Democracy in America*, 15.
69. Mead, Elwood, *How California Is Helping People Own Farms and Rural Homes*, 8.
70. California Department of Public Works, Division of Land Settlement. *Introduction to First Biennial Report of the Division of Land Settlement*, 13.
71. California Legislature. *Report of Legislative Committee Investigating the State Land Settlement at Delhi*, 3.
72. [Sources reliable but uncertain.]
73. [Edition unknown.]
74. Coleridge, Samuel Taylor. [Reference uncertain.]

Chapter 17

1. [Sources unknown and somewhat unreliable; corrected according to later authorities.]
2. *Calaveras Chronicle*, Sept. 19, 1853.
3. *Senate Executive Document*; No. 78. Third Congress, Second Session. *Reports on Explorations and Surveys*, V., 39.
4. [*Ibid.*]
5. [Menefee & Dodge, *History of Kings and Tulare Counties*, 132-133.]

6. [Vandor, *History of Fresno County*, I, 171, 181-182; and sources reliable but uncertain.]
7. [Elias, *Stories of Stanislaus*, 32-33, 36-37, 38-39.]
8. [Sources reliable but uncertain.]
9. Hurst, Harry, "The Alta Pioneers" in the Alta (Dinuba) *Advocate*, n. d.
10. McAllister, Hall, *Oral Argument on Petition for Rehearing in the Supreme Court of the State of California, Nos. 8587-8588, Charles Lux et al vs. J. B. Haggin et al.* [Reference uncertain; no known documents coincide with this description.]
11. [Morgan, *History of Kern County*, 108-110.]
12. [Sources reliable but uncertain.]
13. Otis, George B., *Reminiscences of Early Days*, 26.
14. *History of Fresno County*, 119.[Elliott]
15. [Sources unknown and generally reliable; amended according to later authorities.]
16. Otis, *op. cit.*, 25.
17. Porteous, James, Personal Interview, Fresno, Sept. 26, 1933.
18. [Sources reliable but uncertain.]
19. Shafer, William H., Manuscript Letter, Selma, August 31, 1930.
20. [Sources unknown and somewhat unreliable; corrected according to later authorities.]
21. [Likely based on Smith's personal knowledge.]
22. Smith, A. A., Personal Interview, Oakland; July 30, 1931.
23. Forney, John, Manuscript Letter, Kingsburg, Sept. 30, 1931.
24. Elias, *op. cit.*, 62-63.
25. [*Ibid.*, 81, 107-113.]
26. [Sources reliable but uncertain.]
27. Hyatt, Edward, State Engineer of California, *Report on Irrigation Districts in California for the Year 1930*, Bulletin No. 21-B, 17. [Reference uncertain; no known documents coincide with this description.]
28. [Sources reliable but uncertain.]
29. [*Ibid.*]
30. Kings River Water Association, *Administrative Agreement*, 4-6.
31. [The report cited cannot be ascertained with precision, but is likely the source for Smith's subsequent data on irrigation district facts and figures.]
32. [*Ibid.*]
33. Mead, et al., *Report of Irrigation Investigations in California*, 277.
34. [Sources unknown and somewhat unreliable; corrected according to later authorities.]
35. [See Note 31.]
36. [*Ibid.*]
37. [*Ibid.*]
38. [*Ibid.*]
39. [*Ibid.*]

40. [*Ibid.*]
41. [*Ibid.*]
42. [*Ibid.*]
43. [*Ibid.*]
44. [*Ibid.*]
45. [*Ibid.*]
46. [*Ibid.*]
47. [*Ibid.*]
48. [*Ibid.*]
49. [*Ibid.*]
50. [*Ibid.*]
51. [*Ibid.*]
52. [*Ibid.*]
53. [*Ibid.*]
54. [*Ibid.*]
55. [*Ibid.*]
56. Eichbaum, W. P., Manuscript Letter, Glen Ellen, Sonoma County, California, February 15, 1938.
57. McLaughlin, W. W., Manuscript Letter, Berkeley, Dec. 29, 1933.
58. [Sources reliable but uncertain.]
59. [Sources unknown and generally reliable; corrected in part according to later authorities.]
60. [Likely based on Smith's personal knowledge.]
61. [See Note 31.]
62. [Sources reliable but uncertain.]
63. [*Ibid.*]

Chapter 18

1. United States Land Commission. *Transcript of Proceedings in Case No. 255, Charles M. Weber, Claimant, vs. the United States, Defendant, for the Place Named the "Campo de los Franceses."*
2. [*Ibid.*]
3. [Likely based on Smith's personal knowledge.]
4. [*Ibid.*]
5. [*Ibid.*]
6. [*Ibid.*]
7. Swenson, Aaron W., Superintendent of Plant No. 25, California Packing Corporation. Personal Interview, Oakland, February 28, 1932.
8. [Likely based on Smith's personal knowledge.]
9. [Sources reliable but uncertain.]
10. *Senate Executive Documents*, No. 78, 33rd. Congress, Second Session, *Explorations and Surveys, to Ascertain the Most Practicable and Economical Route for a Railroad from the Mississippi to the Pacific Ocean.* Made under the direction of the Secretary of War, in 1853-54, according to Acts of Congress of March 3, 1853, May 31, 1854, and August 5, 1854, 13 volumes,

Vol. V., 39. Report by Lieutenant R. S. Williamson.

11. Fresno *Bee*, October 22, 1933.
12. [Sources reliable but uncertain.]
13. [*Ibid.*]
14. [*Ibid.*]
15. [*Ibid.*]
16. [*Ibid.*]
17. [*Ibid.*]
18. [*Ibid.*]
19. [*Ibid.*]
20. Lachman, Henry, "Value of the Mission Grape" in *California Grower,* March 1932.
21. Weeks, George, *California Copy*, 247.
22. [Sources reliable but uncertain.]
23. [*Ibid.*]
24. [*Ibid.*]
25. [*Ibid.*]
26. [*Ibid.*]
27. [*Ibid.*]
28. [*Ibid.*]
29. [*Ibid.*]
30. Taylor, Frank J., "Promised Land" in *Sunset Magazine*, Feb. 1932.
31. [*Ibid.?*]
32. [*Ibid.?*]
33. [Sources reliable but uncertain.]
34. [*Ibid.*]
35. [*Ibid.*]
36. [*Ibid.*]
37. [Elliott & Moore, *History of Merced County*, 96.]
38. [Sources reliable but uncertain.]
39. Kern County Chamber of Commerce, Letter-Bulletin, Oct. 10, 1931.
40. [Sources reliable but uncertain.]
41. [*Ibid.*]
42. [Sources unknown and somewhat unreliable; corrected according to other authorities.]
43. [Sources unknown and generally reliable; corrected in part according to other authorities.]
44. [Sources reliable but uncertain.]
45. [Sources unknown and unreliable; corrected according to other authorities.]
46. [Sources reliable but uncertain.]
47. [*Ibid.*]
48. [Likely based on Smith's personal knowledge.]
49. [*Ibid.*]
50. [*Ibid.*]
51. [*Ibid.*]

52. [*Ibid.*]
53. [*Ibid.*]
54. [Sources reliable but uncertain.]
55. [*Ibid.*]
56. [*Ibid.*]
57. [*Ibid.*]
58. Wade, John Donald, "Jefferson: New Style" in *American Mercury* for Nov. 1929.
59. [Sources reliable but uncertain.]
60. [*Ibid.*]
61. [*Ibid.*]
62. [*Ibid.*]
63. [*Ibid.*]
64. [*Ibid.*]
65. [*Ibid.*]
66. [*Ibid.*]
67. [*Ibid.*]
68. [*Ibid.*]
69. McCubbin, John C., Manuscript Letter, Los Angeles, Nov. 15, 1931.
70. Hardy, Mary Earle, "Eucalyptus Trees" in *Nature Magazine,* July, 1932.
71. [Sources reliable but uncertain.]
72. [*Ibid.*]
73. [*Ibid.*]
74. [*Ibid.*]
75. [*Ibid.*]
76. [*Ibid.*]
77. [*Ibid.*]
78. [*Ibid.*]
79. [Likely based on Smith's personal knowledge.]
80. Tennyson, Alfred, *The Flower*. [Edition uncertain.]

Chapter 19

1. L'Espagnol de la Tramerye, Pierre, *The World Struggle for Oil*, 21.
2. Cronise, Titus Fay, *Natural Wealth of California*, 117.
3. [Vandor, History of Fresno County, I, 265.]
4. [*Ibid.*]
5. [*Ibid.*, I, 286.]
6. [*Ibid.*]
7. Cronise, Titus Fey, *Natural Wealth of California*, 118.
8. [Sources reliable but uncertain.]
9. [Vandor, *op. cit.*, I, 282-284.]
10. [Vandor, *op. cit.*, I, 284.]
11. [Likely based on Smith's personal knowledge.]
12. [Vandor, *op. cit.*, I, 284.]

13. [Vandor, *op. cit.,* I, 290; and likely also based on Smith's personal knowledge.]
14. [*Ibid.*]
15. [Vandor, *op. cit.,* I, 289.]
16. [Vandor, *op. cit.,* I, 291, 293-294.]
17. [Vandor, *op. cit.,* I, 291, 295, 713-714.]
18. [Vandor, *op. cit.,* I, 289.]
19. [Vandor, *op. cit.,* I, 288.]
20. [Vandor, *op. cit.,* I, 284, 289.]
21. [Morgan, *History of Kern County,* 129-130.]
22. [Sources reliable but uncertain.]
23. [Morgan, *op. cit.,* 135-136.]
24. [Morgan, *op. cit.,* 141-143.]
25. [Sources reliable but uncertain.]
26. [*Ibid.*]
27. [*Ibid.*]
28. [*Ibid.*]
29. [*Ibid.*]
30. [Likely based on Smith's personal knowledge.]
31. L'Espagnol de la Trameryе, *op. cit.,* 16.

Chapter 20

1. [Sources reliable but uncertain.]
2. [Raisin cooperative data likely adapted from a series of historical articles which ran in the Sun-Maid Herald during 1917-1918.]
3. [See Note 2.]
4. [*Ibid.*]
5. [*Ibid.*]
6. [*Ibid.*]
7. [*Ibid.*]
8. [*Ibid.*]
9. [*Ibid.*]
10. [*Ibid.*]
11. [*Ibid.*]
12. [*Ibid.*]
13. [*Ibid.*]
14. [*Ibid.*]
15. [*Ibid.*]
16. [Sources reliable but uncertain.]
17. [*Ibid.*]
18. [*Ibid.*]
19. [*Ibid.*]
20. [*Ibid.*]
21. Howard, Fred K., *Dear Al Letters,* 8-9. Mr. S. M. (Sun-Maid) Raisin grower wrote letters to his Eastern friend, A. Salesman.
22. [Sources reliable but uncertain.]
23. Bragg, James Monroe, *History of Cooperatives in Raisins to 1923,*

133.

24. [Sources reliable but uncertain.]
25. *The Associated Grower* for August, 1922, itemized the money spent that year for advertising as follows:

National magazines	$704,000.00
Newspapers	$700,000.00
Posters	$490,000.00
Materials	$56,000.00
Window displays	$100,000.00
Dealers' Services	$25,000.00
Domestic service	$10,000.00
Recipe books	$25,000.00
Trade press	$15,000.00
Moving pictures	$10,000.00
Foreign advertising	$300,000.00
Demonstrations and general expenses	$85,000.00

26. [Sources reliable but uncertain.]
27. Landstrom, O. A., Personal Interview, Kingsburg, Dec. 31, 1931.
28. [Sources reliable but uncertain.]
29. [*Ibid.*]
30. [*Ibid.*]
31. [*Ibid.*]
32. [*Ibid.*]
33. [*Ibid.*]
34. Hannay, E. Evelyn, *Dairying and Civilization*, 26.
35. [Sources reliable but uncertain.]
36. [*Ibid.*]
37. McCubbin, John C., Manuscript Letter, Los Angeles, Nov. 12, 1931.
38. [Sources reliable but uncertain.]
39. Franklin, Zilpha Carruthers, *The Path of the Gopatis*, 42-43.
40. [Sources reliable but uncertain.]
41. [Type of report uncertain.]
42. [Sources reliable but uncertain.]
43. Van Wagenen, Jr., Jared. [Citation unclear.]
44. [Sources reliable but uncertain.]
45. [*Ibid.*]
46. [*Ibid.*]
47. [*Ibid.*]
48. [*Ibid.*]
49. Begbie, Harold. *The Glass of Fashion*, 148.
50. Glass, William, "Public Thinks," in *Fresno Bee*, Aug. 21, 1933.
51. Wilcox, Ella Wheeler, "The Set of a Soul." [Edition uncertain.]

Essay on

Authorities

I. Printed Material

A. Bibliographies:

Bancroft, Hubert Howe. *History of California*, 7 vols. San Francisco: The History Company, 1884-1890. Every student of any phase of California history turns first of all to Bancroft; the latter is the starting point, not only for beginners, but for professional historians. The foregoing volumes furnish innumerable clues to primary sources and documents.

Chapman, Charles Edward. "The Literature of California History," *Southwest Historical Quarterly*, April 1919. In the part devoted to printed works Professor Chapman has listed and annotated bibliographies, source materials, periodicals, and books. The part devoted to manuscripts deals with guides to manuscript materials, the Bancroft Library, public archives, and archives outside of California.

Cowan, Robert Ernest. *A Bibliography of the History of California and the Pacific West, 1510-1906*. San Francisco: Book Club of

California, 1914. A critical bibliography of a thousand printed works arranged alphabetically, according to the name of the author. There is a chronological index according to date of publication and a title and subject index.

United States Department of Agriculture, *Bibliography of the History of Agriculture in the United States, Miscellaneous Publication No. 84*. Washington, D. C.: The Department, 1930. This pamphlet lists more than five thousand general works; of these about two hundred deal with special phases of California history. Most of the works listed are critically annotated.

B. Government Documents:

Annual Report of the Condition of Common Schools in the County of Fresno, 1870-1871. Sacramento: State Printing Office, n.d.

California Department of Public Works, Division of Land Settlement. *Introduction to First Biennial Report of the Division of Land Settlement, Department of Public Works, State of California*. Sacramento: California State Printing Office, 1922.

California Division of Engineering and Irrigation. *Summary report on the Water Resources of California and a Coordinated Plan for their Development*. "A Report to the Legislature of 1927." Typescript, 1926.

California Legislature. *Report of Legislative Committee Investigating the State Land Settlement at Delhi: As Appearing in the Journal of March 17th of the Senate*. Sacramento: California State Printing Office, 1925.

California Surveyor-General's Office. *Report*, 23 vols. Sacramento: The Office, 1855-1881. The Surveyor-General's Office has listed the annual amount of grain produced, the number of cattle in each county, the rainfall, the flow of rivers, and the production of various types of fruits.

California State Agricultural Society. *Transactions*, 1855-1890. Sacramento: The Society, 1856-1891. All forms of agriculture and stock-raising are discussed in these publications of the society. Inventions pertaining to agriculture, statistics, and problems are adequately discussed.

Derby, George Horatio. *Report of the Secretary of War, Communicating a Report of the Tulare Valley, Made by Lieutenant Derby*. Washington: G.P.O., 1852. Lieutenant Derby made a tour of the San Joaquin Valley in 1850. He made an official report concerning the quality of the soil, the condition of the natives, and the supply of water available.

Fremont, John Charles. *Report of the Exploring Expedition to the*

Rocky Mountains in the Year 1842, and to Oregon and California in the Years 1843-1844. Washington: G.P.O., 1845. The only explorer to make an official report to Washington while California was still a part of Mexico was Fremont.

Johnston, Adam, Report of March 7, 1851. *U.S. Senate Executive Documents*, No.4, 33rd Congress, Special Session, 63-67 (688).

Orton, Brigadier-General Richard H. *Records of California Men in the War of the Rebellion, 1861-1867*. Sacramento: State Printing Office, 1890.

United States Department of Agriculture. *Bulletin No. 239*. Washington: The Department, 1888. This bulletin discusses the question of riparian rights and contains a report on the rainfall of the various districts of the San Joaquin. Since the valley is elongated, the rainfall is not identical in all parts thereof.

United States Land Commission for California. Documents relating to the "Laguna de Tache" land grant. The transcripts of the hearings before the Land Commission contain the original *expedientes*, or copies of them; the testimony offered for the claimants to land grants; the subsequent decisions of the Land Commission; and the later rulings of federal courts.

——. *Transcript of Proceedings in Case No. 1, John C. Fremont, Claimant, vs. the United States, Defendant, for the Place Names "Las Mariposas."* San Francisco, 1852.

——. *Transcript of Proceedings in Case No. 35, Sebastian Nunez, Claimant, vs. the United States, Defendant, for the Place Named "Orestimba."* San Francisco, 1853.

——. *Transcript of Proceedings in Case No. 37, Juan Perez Pacheco, Claimant, vs. the United States, Defendant, for the Place Named "San Luis Gonzaga."* San Francisco, 1853.

——. *Transcript of Proceedings in Case No. 76, Salvio Pacheco, Claimant, vs. the United States, Defendant, for the Place Named "Monte del Diablo."* San Francisco, 1853.

——. *Transcript of Proceedings in Case No. 79, Robert Livermore, Claimant, vs. the United States, Defendant, for the Place Named "Canada de los Vaqueros."* San Francisco, 1855.

——. *Transcript of Proceedings in Case No. 158, Alfias Thompson, Claimant, vs. the United States, Defendant, for the Place Named "Land of the River Stanislaus."*

——. *Transcript of Proceedings in Case No. 213, John Marsh, Claimant, vs. the United States, Defendant, for the Place Named "Los Meganos."* San Francisco, 1854.

———. *Transcript of Proceedings in Case No. 232, John Rowland, Claimant, vs. the United States, Defendant, for the Place Named "Land on the River Stanislaus."* San Francisco, 1854.

———. *Transcript of Proceedings in Case No. 240, Jose Antonio Aguirre and Ignacio del Valle, Claimants, vs. the United States, Defendant, for the Place Named "El Tejon."* San Francisco, 1855.

———. *Transcript of Proceedings in Case No. 255, Charles M. Weber, Claimant, vs. the United States, Defendant, for the Place Named the "Campo de los Franceses."* San Francisco, 1855.

———. *Transcript of Proceedings in Case No. 267, Antonio Maria Pico and Henry M. Naglee, Claimants, vs. the United States, Defendant, for the Place El Pescadero."* San Francisco, 1854.

———. *Transcript of Proceedings in Case No. 293, Hiram Grimes, et al., Claimants, vs. the United States, Defendant, for the Place Named "El Pescadero."* San Francisco, 1854.

———. *Transcript of Proceedings in Case No. 357, Andreas Pico, Claimant, vs. the United States, Defendant, for the Place Named "Moquelamos."* San Francisco, 1854.

———. *Transcript of Proceedings in Case No. 393, Angel and Maria Chabolla (Heirs of Anastasia Chabolla), Claimants, vs. the United States, Defendant, for the Place Named "Sanjon de los Moquelemnes."* San Francisco, 1854.

———. *Transcript of Proceedings in Case No. 428, Augustin Olvera, Claimant, vs. the United States, Defendant, for the Place Named "Los Alamos y Agua Caliente."* San Francisco, 1854.

———. *Transcript of Proceedings in Case No. 444, Andreas Pico, Claimant, vs. the United States, Defendant, for the Place Named "Arroyo Seco."* San Francisco, 1855.

———. *Transcript of Proceedings in Case No. 498, Pedro C. Carrillo, Claimant, vs. the United States, Defendant, for the Place Named "Los Alamos y Agua Caliente."* San Francisco, 1854.

———. *Transcript of Proceedings in Case No. 509, Samuel G. Reed, Claimant, vs. the United States, Defendant, for the Place Named "Rancho del Puerto."* San Francisco, 1855.

———. *Transcript of Proceedings in Case No. 536, José Maria Covarrubias, Claimant, vs. the United States, Defendant, for the Place Named "Castaic."* San Francisco, 1855.

———. *Transcript of Proceedings in Case No. 545, Julian Ursua, Claimant, vs. the United States, Defendant, for the Place Named "La Panocha de San Juan y Carrisalitos."* San Francisco, 1854.

———. *Transcript of Proceedings in Case No. 556, Francisco Dominguez, et al., Claimants, vs. the United States, Defendant, for the Place Named "San Emidio."* San Francisco, 1853.

———. *Transcript of Proceedings in Case No. 569, Vicente Gomez, Claimant, vs. the United States, Defendant, for the Place Named "Panoche Grande."*

———. *Transcript of Proceedings in Case No. 600, Manuel Castro, Claimant, vs. the United States, Defendant, for the Place Named "Laguna de Tache."* San Francisco, 1854.

———. *Transcript of Proceedings in Case No. 602, Francisco Pico, Claimant, vs. the United States, Defendant, for the Place Named "Las Calaveras."* San Francisco, 1855.

———. Transcript of Proceedings in Case No. 616, Jonathan D. Stevenson, et al., Claimants, vs. the United States, Defendant, for the Place Named "Los Medanos." San Francisco, 1855.

———. *Transcript of Proceedings in Case No. 628, Maria de Antonio Castro de Anzar, et al., Claimants, vs. the United States, Defendant, for the Place Named "Real de los Aguiles."* San Francisco, 185?

———. *Transcript of Proceedings in Case No. 673, Francisco Soberanes, Claimant, vs. the United States, Defendant, for the Place Named "Sanjon de Santa Rita."* San Francisco, 1854.

———. *Transcript of Proceedings in Case No. 693, José Castro, et al., Claimants, vs. the United States, Defendant, for the Place Named "Rancho of the River San Joaquin."* San Francisco, 1855.

———. *Transcript of Proceedings in Case No. 767, Francisco Rico, et al., Claimants, vs. the United States, Defendant, for the Place Named "Ranchería Rio de Estanislao."* San Francisco, 1855.

———. *Transcript of Proceedings in Case No. 781, José Yves Limantour, Claimant, vs. the United States, Defendant, for the Place Named "Laguna de Tache."* San Francisco, 1855.

United States War Department. *Reports of Explorations and Surveys to Ascertain the Most Practicable and Economical Route for a Railroad from the Mississippi River to the Pacific Ocean...Made Under the Direction of the Secretary of War, in 1853-4, According to Acts of Congress of March 3, 1853, May 31, 1854, and August 5, 1854.* 12 volumes in 13. Washington [D.C.]: various printers, [1855-186-?]

———, et al. *The War of the Rebellion: A Compilation of the Official Records of the Union and Confederate Armies.* Series I, Volume 50 (Part I). Washington, D.C.: Government Printing Office, 1897.

C. Periodicals:

1. Newspapers: The Bancroft Library, that portion of the
University of California Library devoted to the history of the
West, contains rich material in its voluminous newspaper files
for purposes of research, which is not available in book form. The
cattle industry, the stagecoach period, and the Mussel Slough
tragedy are adequately treated in these accounts. In addition, I
used the private files of many San Joaquin Valley newspapers.
The following issues were consulted:

Alta Advocate [Dinuba]: [Contains "Alta Pioneers" series by the
editor, Harry Hurst, published in 1924.]

Argonaut (San Francisco), April 1881. This issue contains an
editorial which is decidedly hostile in tone to the Mussel Slough
settlers.

Calaveras Chronicle, Sept. 19, 1853 [comments on water being
brought into mining town.]

Californian (Monterey), March 15, 1848 (gold discovery at Sutter's
Mill).

Daily Alta California (San Francisco). June 24, 1852 (hogs); July 18,
1852 (miners); August 4, 1852 (cattle); August 21, 1852 (cattle);
August 24, 1852 (cattle); November 30, 1852 (sheep); January 27,
1853 (sheep); July 7, 1853 (sheep); November 1, 1853 (sheep);
August 24, 1854 (beef quality in California); November 19, 1858
(stagecoach routes).

Daily Pacific News (San Francisco), March 7, 1851 (letter on San
Joaquin Valley Indian troubles by Dr. Thomas Payne).

Fresno Bee, March 31, 1931 (contains a statement of Emmett Dalton
concerning his attitude toward lawlessness rampant in the United
States; based on an interview with the sole survivor of the Dalton
gang); August 21, 1933 (comments on National Recovery Act and
San Joaquin Valley); October 22, 1933 (news item from Springville);
July 7, 1935 (article quoting James Shultz, San Joaquin Valley
lumberman and wheat grower).

Fresno Morning Republican, October 19, 1923 [Milton Sapiro
comments on John Quinn], and July 27, 1929 [report on wheat
growing in the Tulare Lake country].

Fresno Weekly Expositor, May 4, 1870. [Account of James W.
Savage.]

Los Angeles Star, June 17, 1854 [conditions at Sebastian Indian Reservation].

Modesto Herald, September 5, 1891. The train robbery near Ceres and some amusing incidents which occurred thereafter are reported in this issue.

Oakland Post-Enquirer, December 3, 1932 (camels in the desert).

San Francisco Bulletin, September 27, 1913 [contains "The Great Diamond Hoax" by Asbury Harpending].

San Francisco Chronicle, December 2, 10, 15, 16, 18, 19, 21, 1880 (the trial of the Mussel Slough settlers, then pending in the United States Circuit Court at San Francisco, was reported in the issues of the paper here listed); October 6, 1933 [article on Lord and Lady Sholto Douglas].

San Francisco Daily Evening Post, March 31, 1881. Trial of the Mussel Slough settlers.

San Francisco Evening Bulletin, November 5, 1858 (stage routes); November 19, 1858 [comment on Pike County citizens in California gold rush]; October 26, 1866 (Peg-leg Smith); December 1, 6, 7, 14, 19, 22, 23, for 1880 (trial of the Mussel Slough settlers).

San Francisco Evening Picayune, February 27, 1851 [report on Indian troubles in San Joaquin Valley].

San Francisco Morning Call. November 16; December 3, 4, 9, 15, 16, 19, 21, for 1880. Trial of the Mussel Slough settlers.

Selma Irrigator (Golden Jubilee Edition), Oct. 23, 1930 [contains letter from Selma Gruenberg Lewis, for whom city of Selma was allegedly named].

Stockton Journal, March 7 (letter on San Joaquin Valley Indian troubles by Dr. Thomas Payne), and March 17, 1851(mining conditions).

Stockton Record, December 3, 1927 [contains "William J. Howard, Last of the Famous Mariposa Battalion" by May S. Corcoran.]

Stockton Times, April 18,1851 [migrations to the mines].

Tuolumne City News, October 14 and 28, 1870 [entry of Central Pacific Railroad into Stanislaus County and naming of Modesto].

Visalia Daily Times, March 13, August 13, 1892; June 6, December 14, 29, 1893. [Accounts of Chris Evans and John Sontag, alleged train robbers.]

Visalia Times, May 15, 1884. This issue contains a report of the ceremony held at the graves of the martyrs of the Mussel Slough battle.

2. Noteworthy Magazine Articles: These articles, most of them signed and written by experts in their particular fields, were perused in search for material bearing on the development of the San Joaquin Valley.

Arnold, Adelaide Wilson. "Wild Horses of the Mojave." [Possibly appeared in *Western Horseman*.]

Austin, Mary. "Vasquez Rock." *Youth's Companion*, November 5, 1908.

Baker, Charles C. "Mexican Land Grants in California." *Annual Publications of the Historical Society of Southern California, 1912-1914*, Los Angeles, 1914.

Bishop, William Henry. "Southern California." *Harper's New Monthly Magazine*, October-November 1892.

Bolton, Herbert E. "In the South San Joaquin Ahead of Garces." *Quarterly of the California Historical Society*, September, 1931.

——. "The Mission as an Institution in the Spanish American Colonies."

Bushnell, Rev. Horace. "Characteristics and Prospects of California." *The New Englander*, 1858.

California Police Gazette, September 17, 1859. [Portion of a serialized life of Joaquin Murrieta, based on the earlier biography by John Rollin Ridge.]

Caldwell, Charles. "Frank Norris, or, Up from Culture." *American Mercury*, April 1928.

Considine, John L., "Jeff Davis and the Camels," *Columbia Magazine*, December 1929.

Corcoran, May Stanislaus. "Robber Joaquin." *Grizzly Bear*, June, 1921. Contains a list of California statutes and legislative acts related to Joaquin Murrieta.

Creel, George. "Incredible Kit Carson." *Collier's: The National Weekly*, August 21, 1926.

——. "The Lion of the Lord." *Collier's: The National Weekly*, September 24, 1926.

Dalton, Emmett. "West of 96." *Adventure*, October 1930.

Fisher, Helen Dwight. "The First Smith in California." *American Mercury*, September 1928.

Gearhart, E. J., "A Thumb-nail History of Our Plants and the Men that Make Them Go." *Associated Grower,* May, 1921.

Hardy, Mary Earle. "Eucalyptus Trees." *Nature Magazine*, July 1932.

Haines, Francis. "George Rogers Clark and His Spanish Horse," *Western Horseman*, July-August, 1937.

Heath, Erle. "From Trail to Rail." *Southern Pacific Bulletin*, June and July, 1928. This official publication of the Southern Pacific contains an account of the construction of the railway through the San Joaquin Valley.

Hilgard, Eugene W. "The Agriculture and Soils of California." U.S. Department of Agriculture, *Report for 1878.*

Hutchings' California Magazine, III, IV and V, 1859-1860. A detailed biography of "Peg-leg" Smith appears in this magazine.

Lachman, Henry. "Value of the Mission Grape." *California Grower*, March 1932.

Latta, Frank F[orrest]. "Auto-Motive Combined Harvester Used in Lindsay District." California Country Life Section, *Fresno Bee*, August 6, 1933.

———. "Pioneers of the San Joaquin," *Fresno Bee*, February 6, 1935.

———. "Stockton Gang Plow Invented Near Manteca." California Country Life Section, *Fresno Bee*, July 2, 1933.

McCubbin, John C. "The Rise and Fall of Traver." *Fresno Morning Republican*, March 4, 5 and 6, 1923.

Muir, Mauchline. "The Rocky Mountain Endurance Race." *The World To-day*, August, 1908.

Pacific Rural Press, 9 (1875) and 18 (1879).

Parsons, K. K., "The Barb Horse in America," *Western Horseman*, Sept.-Oct., 1937.

Raswan, Carl. "Drinker of the Air," *Asia Magazine*, April, 1929.

Taylor, Frank J. "Promised Land." *Sunset Magazine*, February 1932.

Wade, John Donald, "Jefferson: New Style." *American Mercury*, November 1929.

Walker, Johnnie, "The Wild Horses of Early California: Where They Came From and What Happened to Them," *Western Horseman*,

October, 1936.

West, George P., "Hearst: a Psychological Note." *American Mercury*, November, 1930.

3. University of California Publications: These represent scholarly and elaborate reports by specialists which carry the approval and bear the imprint of the University of California.

Gifford, E.W., and W. Egbert Schenck. "Archaeology of the Southern San Joaquin." *University of California Publications in American Archaeology and Ethnology*, XXIII, Berkeley, 1926.

Kroeber, A.L. "Elements of Culture in Native California." *University of California Publications in American Archaeology and Ethnology*, XIII, Berkeley, November 21, 1922.

——. "Yokuts Language of South Central California." *University of California Publications in American Archaeology and Ethnology*, II, Berkeley, January 5, 1907.

Morse, E.S. *Bulletin of Sussex Institute*, XVII.

Pope, Saxton T. "Yahi Archery." *University of California Publications in American Archaeology and Ethnology*, III.

Schenck, W. Egbert. "Historic Aboriginal Groups of the California Delta Region." *University of California Publications in American Archaeology and Ethnology*, XXIII, Berkeley, November 13, 1926.

4. Master's theses:
Bragg, James Monroe. *The History of Cooperative Marketing in Raisins to 1923*. Berkeley: University of California, 1930.

Chaffee, Everett Barker. *Jedediah Smith in California*. Berkeley: University of California, 1929.

Martin, Effie Elfreda. *The Development of Wheat Culture in the San Joaquin Valley*. Berkeley: University of California, 1924. Miss Marten's master's thesis is based on material garnered from a thorough search of state and government reports. It is an interesting account, as well, of inventions and experiments which resulted in a rapid development of a certain form of agriculture.

D. Books and Pamphlets:

The books which have been written about California cannot all be listed here. Only those which have conveyed information concerning the development of the San Joaquin Valley are included. Most California histories ignore the valley and so the gleaning was scant. The books were all excellent, but sometimes I read twenty volumes to get one paragraph. It made me think of the man who sifted a mountain and came out with a spoonful.

Abstract of the Title to the Rancho Laguna de Tache for Laguna Lands, Ltd. Fresno: Fresno County Abstract Company, 1908. A record of land sales of this famous land grant from the time of the original grant to Manuel Castro until its acquisition by the Kings County Land Company.

Anthony, C[harles] V[olney]. *Fifty Years of Methodism: A History of the Methodist Episcopal Church Within the Bounds of the California Annual Conference from 1847 to 1897.* San Francisco: Methodist Book Concern, 1901.

Audubon, John Woodhouse. *Audubon's Western Journal.* Cleveland: The Arthur H. Clark Co., 1906. In this book, Audubon relates his experiences during a tour through Mexico and California during 1848-1849. He was an ornithologist and hence his observations differed from those of most travelers.

Bolton, Herbert E. *Outpost of Empire, the Story of the Founding of San Francisco.* New York: Alfred A. Knopf, 1930. This is perhaps the most authentic account of the Anza expeditions to California. The author covered the route traversed by Anza and located every camp site along the way. On his return from the Bay region, Anza led his party into the northern San Joaquin Valley.

Banning, William and George Hugh Banning. *Six Horses.* New York: Century, 1930. William Banning was a stage driver (whip) in his youth. Naturally he is an authority on the subject. He and his son have also written an excellent account of coaching, overland journeys, the Concord coaches, and the transcontinental routes which preceded the railways.

Beers, George A. *Vasquez, or the Hunted Bandits of the San Joaquin.* New York: R.M. De Witt, 1875. This is a detailed account of Tiburcio Vasquez and his outlaw comrades. These desperadoes terrorized the San Joaquin Valley for a decade. The author has collected material concerning their escapades, capture, and execution.

Begbie, Harold. *The Glass of Fashion; Some Social Reflections by a Gentleman with a Duster.* New York: Putnam, 1921.

Bidwell, John. *Echoes of the Past About California...* Edited by Milo Milton Quaife. Chicago: R.R. Donnelley and Sons Co., 1928.

——. *A Journey to California: With Observations About the Country, Climate and the Route to this Country...With an Introduction by Herbert Ingram Priestley.* San Francisco: John Henry Nash, 1937.

Boddy, E. Manchester. *Japanese in America*. Los Angeles: The Author, 1921.

Bonsal, Stephen. *Edward Fitzgerald Beale: A Pioneer in the Path of Empire, 1822-1903*. New York: Putnam, 1912. Beale was not only an important figure in the San Joaquin Valley, but also in the history of the United States. Abraham Lincoln appointed him surveyor general of California and Nevada; he was the only man in California capable of coping with the Indian situation. This cattle rancher of the San Joaquin was later appointed minister to Austria.

[Branch, Leonidas C.] *History of Stanislaus County, California: with Illustrations Descriptive of its Scenery, Farms, Residences, Public Buildings, Factories, Hotels, Business Houses, Schools, Churches, and Mines, from Original Drawings by Artists of the Highest Ability: with Biographical Sketches of Prominent Citizens*. San Francisco: Elliott & Moore, 1881.

Bunnell, Lafayette Houghton. *Discovery of the Yosemite and the Indian War of 1851 Which Led to that Event*. Los Angeles : G.W. Gerlicher, 1911.

Burns, Walter Noble. *The Robin Hood of El Dorado*. New York: Coward-McCann, 1930.

Calaveras County Chamber of Commerce. *Folder for 1930*.

Carson, James H. *Early Recollections of the Mines and a Description of the Great Tulare Valley*. Stockton: Published to Accompany the Steamer Edition of the *San Joaquin Republican*, 1852.

Chapman, Charles Edward. *The Founding of Spanish California*. New York: Macmillan, 1916. The author spent a considerable time in the archives of Spain and his book reveals both accuracy and careful research. His account of the northwestward expansion of New Spain from 1687 to 1783 has never been surpassed.

———. *A History of California: The Spanish Period*. New York: Macmillan, 1921. A comprehensive and scholarly treatment of a definite period in California history.

Citizens Land Association. *California lands: acquired by fraud, protected by politics, disposed of by deception, sustained by intimidation: homesteaded by citizens of the United States*. Los Angeles: The Association, 1933.

Cleland, Robert Glass. *Pathfinders*. Los Angeles: Powell Publishing Co., 1929. This book deals with the discovery, the exploration, and the development of Alta California from the coming of the first white men to the coming of Fremont.

Connelley, William Elsey. *Quantrill and the Border Wars*. Cedar

Rapids, Iowa: The Torch Press, 1910. Jesse James, Cole Younger, and Emmett Dalton were relatives and residents of the same community. They were members of good families. Connelley explains the conditions which made possible the development of these outlaw bands. His book is not a eulogy; it is an examination of a condition.

Connor, Ralph. *The Sky Pilot: A Tale of the Foothills...* Chicago, New York [etc.]: F.H. Revell Company, 1902 [c1899].

Coues, Elliott. *On the Trail of a Spanish Pioneer: The Diary and Itinerary of Francisco Garces in His Travels Through Sonora, Arizona and California, 1775-1776.* New York: Francis P. Harper, 1900. 2 volumes. Coues translated an official contemporaneous copy of the original Spanish manuscript and also furnished copious critical notes.

Coy, Owen Cochrane. *Gold Days.* Los Angeles: Powell Publishing Co., 1929. This book, one volume in the series *California*, is a collection of data dealing with the mining region of California. It is both accurate and entertaining.

Cronise, Titus Fay. *The Natural Wealth of California: Comprising Early History; Geography, Topography, And Scenery; Climate; Agriculture and Commercial Products; Geology, Zoology, and Botany; Mineralogy, Mines, and Mining Processes; Manufactures; Steamship Lines, Railroads, and Commerce; Immigration, Population and Society; Educational Institutions and Literature; Together with a Detailed Description of Each County; its Topography, Scenery, Cities and Towns, Agricultural Advantages, Mineral Resources, and Varied Productions.* San Francisco : H.H. Bancroft & Company, 1868.

Cross, Ira B[rown]. *Financing an Empire: History of Banking in California.* 4 volumes. Chicago: S. J. Clarke Publishing Company, 1927.

Crow, Carl. *Four Hundred Million Customers; the Experiences— Some Happy, Some Sad, of an American in China, and What they Taught Him.* New York and London: Harper & Brothers, 1937.

Cummings, Homer, and Carl McFarland. *Federal Justice; Chapters in the History of Justice and the Federal Executive.* New York: Macmillan, 1937.

Dale, Harrison Clifford. *The Ashley-Smith Explorations and Discovery of a Central Route to the Pacific, 1822-1829, with the Original Journals.* Cleveland: The Arthur H. Clark Co., 1918. When Jedediah Smith made his memorable journey to California, his second in command was Harrison G. Rogers; the latter kept a journal until his untimely death near Klamath Lake. The rescue party sent out by Dr. John McLaughlin, the Hudson's Bay factor along the Columbia, recovered this journal, which has since furnished much of the information concerning Smith's trip into the San Joaquin. Dale has carefully annotated his journal, as well as contributed much information concerning other ventures by Ashley and Smith.

Dalton, Emmett. *When the Daltons Rode*. New York: Doubleday, 1931. An autobiography by the lone survivor of the Dalton gang. The Dalton boys operated for a time in the San Joaquin Valley. Their activities in that region are revealed in this book. Many erroneous impressions are corrected. Dalton is not an apologist; he does not condone lawlessness.

Davenport, Homer. *My Quest for the Arab Horse*. New York: B.W. Dodge, 1909.

Davis, William Heath. *Seventy-Five Years in California*. San Francisco: John Howell Books, 1929. Davis was one of the Americans who settled in California while it belonged to Mexico; he married into one of the Spanish-California families and had the opportunity to observe society during that golden era. His book is a compilation of what he actually saw and heard; therefore it is extremely interesting and valuable.

Dodge, Theodore Aryault. *Riders of Many Lands*. New York: Harper and Brothers, 1894. Colonel Dodge was an Army officer in the old west during and after the Civil War. His duties as a cavalry officer made him familiar with horses, and his verdict concerning the quality of the Spanish horse is the opinion of an expert.

Eldredge, Zoeth Skinner (editor). *History of California*, 5 vols. New York: Century History Co., 1915. This is a pretentious work which contains much information not available elsewhere. An attempt was made in these volumes to correct errors which had been detected in the earlier works of Bancroft.

Elias, Sol P. *Stories of Stanislaus*. Los Angeles, 1924. Elias, a former mayor of Modesto, was intensely interested in his county and its environs. He collected information from pioneers and early newspapers and wove this information into a fascinating history of Stanislaus County and the cities, past and present, in that territory.

Engelhardt, Fray Zephyrin. *The Missions and Missionaries of California*. 4 vols. San Francisco: James H. Barry, 1908-1915. This is an excellent study of the Indians, the Franciscans, and the work of the Catholic church in the early days of Alta California.

Fages, Pedro. *Expedition to San Francisco Bay in 1770: Diary of Pedro Fages*. Edited by Herbert Eugene Bolton. (Publications of the Academy of Pacific Coast History, Vol. 2, No. 3.) Berkeley: University of California, [1911].

Franklin, Zilpha Carruthers. *The Path of the Gopatis*. Chicago: National Dairy Council, [c1926].

Fremont, John Charles. *Memoirs of My Life*, Vol. 1. Chicago, New York: Belford, Clarke & Company, 1887. The author planned to write another volume, but only the first was completed. This volume includes a narrative of his five journeys of western explorations and is a fascinating retrospect of fifty years.

Ganoe, William Addleman. *The History of the United States Army*. New York, London: D. Appleton and Company, 1924.

Glasscock, C.B. *Bandits and the Southern Pacific*. New York: Stokes, 1929. The author was a former newspaperman at Fresno. He collected information from newspaper files, living witnesses, and other sources, until he had material for his book. Portions are exceedingly valuable; the part describing the location and cause of the Mussel Slough fight is woefully inaccurate.

Gruening, Ernest V. *These United States: A Symposium*. New York: Boni and Liveright [c1923-24]. [Contains article "Utah: Apocalypse of the Desert," by Murray E. King.]

Hafen, Leroy R. *The Overland Mail, 1849-1869*. Cleveland: The Arthur H. Clark Co., 1926. This book was originally offered as a doctoral thesis at the University of California. An excellent and thoroughly scholarly account of the organization, problems, and importance of the transcontinental stage lines, which were a promoter of settlement and a precursor of railways.

Hannay, E. Evelyn. *Dairying and Civilization*. [San Francisco]: California Dairy Council, 1928.

History of Co-operation in the United States. (Johns Hopkins University Studies in Historical and Political Science, volume 6.) Baltimore: Johns Hopkins University, 1888. [Contains "Co-operation on the Pacific Coast" by Charles Howard Shinn.]

History of Fresno County, California, with Illustrations, Descriptions of its Scenery, Farms, Residences, Public Buildings, Factories, Hotels, Business Houses, Schools, Churches, and Mines, from Original Drawings, with Biographical Sketches. San Francisco: Wallace W. Elliott & Co., 1882.

History of Merced County, California: with Illustrations Descriptive of its Scenery, Farms, Residences, Public Buildings, Factories, Hotels, Business Houses, Schools, Churches, and Mines, from Original Drawings by Artists of the Highest Ability: with Biographical Sketches of Prominent Citizens. San Francisco: Elliott & Moore, 1881.

History of Tulare County, California: with Illustrations Descriptive of its Scenery, Farms, Residences, Public Buildings, Factories, Hotels, Business Houses, Schools, Churches, and Mines, from Original Drawings by Artists of the Highest Ability: with Biographical Sketches of Prominent Citizens. San Francisco: Wallace W. Elliott & Co., 1883.

Hittell, John S. *The Resources of California.* San Francisco: A. Roman, 1870.

Hittell, Theodore H. *The Adventures of James Capen Adams, Mountaineer and Grizzly Bear Hunter of California.* San Francisco: Towne and Bacon, 1860.

Howard, Fred K. *"Dear Al" Letters.* [Fresno, Calif.: Sun-Maid Raisin Growers, n.d.]

Howe, Frederic Clemson. *Privilege and Democracy in America.* New York: Scribner's, 1910.

Hunt, Rockwell Dennis. *Oxcart to Airplane.* Los Angeles: Powell Publishing Co., 1929. Dr. Hunt, in his contribution of one volume to the series California, has traced the various forms of transportation in vogue at different times in California's history. Transportation, communication, and traffic were the important problems facing California and the author has made a thrilling story of it all.

Johnson, E. Pauline (Tekahionwake). *Flint and Feather.* London , New York: Hodder and Stoughton, 1913.

Jones, William Carey. *Report on the Subject of Land Titles in California.* Washington: Gideon Printers, 1850. This book might possibly be considered a government document, but it was privately published and hence is listed here. Jones translated from Spanish the laws relating to land grants and other papers relating thereto. His report was made pursuant to instructions received from the secretary of state and from the secretary of the interior; it is the standard work on the subject.

Kendrick, T[homas].D[owning]. *A History of the Vikings.* New York: Scribner, 1930.

Kern County Chamber of Commerce. Letter-Bulletin, October 10, 1931.

King, Murray E. *See* Gruening, Ernest V.

Kroeber, A.L. *Handbook of the Indians of California.* Washington: Government Printing Office, 1925. California's leading anthropologist is responsible for this report to the Smithsonian Institution. It is the most authentic and the most comprehensive work yet published on the Indians of California.

La Pérouse, Jean-François de Galaup, comte de. *A Voyage Round the World : Performed in the Years 1785, 1786, 1787, 1788...* Boston: Printed for Joseph Bumstead, 1801.

Latta, F.F. *Uncle Jeff's Story: The Tale of a San Joaquin Valley Pioneer and His Life With the Yokuts Indians.* Tulare: Tulare Daily Times, 1929. The author, a former high school teacher at Tulare, is an archaeologist of note in the San Joaquin Valley. Jefferson Mayfield had been placed in the care of Yokuts Indians by his father, a soldier and widower. Latta collected the data from this man and had it published.

Leonard, Zenas. *Narrative: Adventures of Zenas Leonard, Fur Trader and Trapper, 1831-1836.* Cleveland: The Arthur H. Clark Co., 1904. Leonard accompanied Joseph Reddeford Walker into the San Joaquin Valley in 1832. His journal is the only source of information for that expedition. The book here listed is a reprint from the rare original of 1839.

L'Espagnol de la Tramerye, Pierre Paul Ernest. *The World Struggle for Oil, translated...by C. Leonard Leese.* New York: Alfred A. Knopf, 1924.

Love, Robertus. *The Rise and Fall of Jesse James.* New York and London, G.P. Putnam's Sons, 1926. Brigands and robbers appeal to the imagination. The author attempts to explain the reasons for the lawlessness rampant in the border states and the effect on the younger generation. Since the Daltons were molded by their environment and later functioned in the San Joaquin Valley, the book is of some value in this connection.

Lydekker, Richard. *The Horse and Its Relatives.* London: G. Allen & Co., 1912. The Spanish horse played an important part in every province in the New World. This English author traces the various breeds of horses and their dispersion in the Americas.

Lyman, George D. *John Marsh, Pioneer: The Life Story of a Trailblazer on Six Frontiers.* New York: Scribner's, 1931. The first medical doctor in the San Joaquin Valley had a most amazing career. The foregoing biography depicts in a charming fashion his life, prior to and after arriving, in California.

McCormick, Cyrus. *The Century of the Reaper; An Account of Cyrus Hall McCormick, the Inventor of the Reaper: of the McCormick Harvesting Machine Company, the Business he Created: and of the International Harvester Company, his Heir and Chief Memorial.* Boston and New York: Houghton Mifflin Company, 1931.

Mead, Elwood. *How California is Helping People Own Farms and Rural Homes.* (University of California, College of Agriculture,

Agricultural Experiment Station. Circular No. 221.) [Berkeley, Calif.: University of California, College of Agriculture, Agricultural Experiment Station, 1920.]

———, et al. *Report of Irrigation Investigations in California...* (U. S. Department of Agriculture, Office of the Experiment Station, Bulletin No. 100.) Washington, D.C.: Government Printing Office, 1901. [Contains article "Water Appropriation from Kings River," by Carl E. Grunsky.]

Memorial and Biographical History of the Counties of Fresno, Tulare and Kern, California. Chicago: Lewis Publishing Co., 1890. This book contains a summary of the history of the three counties indicated, and biographical sketches of the leading men and women who settled there in the early days of the American occupation.

Menefee, C[ampbell] A[ugustus]. *Historical and Descriptive Sketch Book of Napa, Sonoma, Lake, and Mendocino: Comprising Sketches of Their Topography, Productions, History, Scenery, and Peculiar Attractions*. Napa City : Reporter Publishing House, 1873.

Menefee, Eugene L., and Fred A. Dodge. *History of Tulare and Kings Counties, California*. Los Angeles: Historic Record Co., 1913. The authors have collected from the pioneers themselves the information contained in their history. It also contains biographical sketches of the men and women who took the first steps in the development of the San Joaquin Valley after the "blue eyed men" arrived on the scene.

Morrow, William W. *Spanish and Mexican Private Land Grants*. San Francisco and Los Angeles: Bancroft-Whitney, 1923. A subtitle to this book states that it is issued with the compliments of the California jurisprudence. Undoubtedly it is the best work in English for explaining the method of securing land grants in California during Spanish and Mexican days.

Morgan, Wallace. *History of Kern County, California*. Los Angeles: Historic Record Co., 1914. The southern part of the San Joaquin has had a picturesque history which has been carefully preserved in this county history. The records of the men and women who were identified with the early growth and development of this region are carefully recorded.

Neihardt, John G. *The Song of Three Friends*. New York: Macmillan, 1919.

Nevins, Allan. *Fremont, The West's Greatest Adventurer*. 2 vols. New York and London: Harper and Brothers, 1928. Hitherto unpublished sources were furnished the author of these two volumes and the result is pleasing. Access to papers, documents, and records in the private collection of the Fremont family made possible an outstanding contribution to the information extant concerning the life and career of the famous Pathfinder.

Norris, Frank. *The Octopus*. New York: Doubleday, 1901. This novel, an epic of wheat, makes Wheat the hero, the Mussel Slough settlers the innocent victims, and the Southern Pacific Railroad the villain.

Otis, George B. *Reminiscences of Early Days*. Selma: The Author, 1911. This little book portrays the pioneer days of Selma and surrounding territory in a delightful fashion. The author was an active participant in the scenes which he recounts.

Paine, Albert Bigelow. *A Short Life of Mark Twain*. New York: Harper and Brothers, 1920.

Palou, Francisco. *Historical Memoirs of New California, by Fray Francisco Palóu, O.F.M., Translated into English from the Manuscript in the Archives of Mexico, Edited by Herbert Eugene Bolton*. Berkeley: University of California Press, 1926. 4 volumes.

Pliny the Elder. *Natural History*. 6 vols. London: Bell, 1855-1858. This Roman historian wrote an account of the Spanish horse which has been quoted here.

Paz, Ireneo, translated by Frances P. Belle. *Life and Adventures of the Celebrated Bandit, Joaquin Murieta*. Chicago: Regan Publishing Corp., 1925. This book, originally written in Spanish, gives a point of view slightly different from that of the authors who represented another racial strain.

Raine, William MacLeod. *Famous Sheriffs and Western Outlaws*. Garden City, N.Y.: Doubleday Doran, 1929. A serious study of the old Wild West and its chief actors, with an interpretation of the conditions which made possible such a form of society.

Richman, Irving Berdine. *California Under Spain and Mexico, 1835-1847*. Boston and New York: Houghton Mifflin, 1911. Based on original sources in the Bancroft Library collected by Herbert E. Bolton. A readable account of the period.

Robinson, Alfred. *Life in California: during a residence of several years in that territory, comprising a description of the country and the missionary establishments, with incidents, observations, etc., etc....* New York: Wiley and Putnam, 1846.

Rogers, Julia Ellen. *Trees Worth Knowing*. New York: Doubleday Doran, 1928. The Franciscans and the Spanish soldiers went into the San Joaquin Valley looking for mission sites and reported that no suitable timber was available. The author explains what was wrong with the large trees which grew in abundance in that region.

Rogin, Leo. *The Introduction of Farm Machinery in Its Relation to the Productivity of Labor in the Agriculture of the United States During the Nineteenth Century*. (University of California Publications in Economics, Volume 9.) Berkeley: University of California Press, 1931.

Root, Frank A., and William Elsey Connelley. *The Overland Stage to California*. Topeka, Kansas: Published by the Authors, 1901. This is an authentic history based largely on personal reminiscences of the overland stage routes from the Missouri River to the Pacific coast.

Runeberg, Johan Ludwig. *A Selection from the Series of Poems Entitled Ensign Ståls Songs; Rendered into English by Isabel Donner*. Helsingfors : G.W. Edlunds, 1907.

Russell, Charles Edward. *Stories of the Great Railroads*. Chicago: C.H. Kerr, 1912. Reprinted from a series of articles which originally appeared in *Hampton's Magazine*.

Sabin, Edwin L. *Kit Carson Days, 1809-1868*. Chicago: A.C. McClurg, 1914. A biography of Kit Carson and his career in the Far West.

Sanchez, Nellie van de Grift. *Spanish Arcadia*. Los Angeles: Powell Publishing Co., 1929. Mrs. Sanchez, a sister of Mrs. Robert Louis Stevenson, married into an old Spanish-California family. Her book has added charm and luster to the romantic days of early California.

Sandburg, Carl. *Abraham Lincoln: The Prairie Years*. 2 volumes. New York: Harcourt, 1926.

Sawyer, Eugene T. *Life and Career of Tiburcio Vasquez*. San Francisco: Bacon and Company, Printers, 1875. This biography is very comprehensive. A detailed account is furnished for each of the exploits credited to the famous outlaw. Included in the book is the address delivered by Judge Collins in a futile attempt to save Vasquez from the gallows.

Scherer, James A. B., *The First Forty-niner and the Story of the Golden Tea Caddy*. New York: Minton, Balch and Company, 1925.

Settlers' Committee of the Mussel Slough Country. *The Struggle of the Mussel Slough Settlers for Their Homes! An Appeal to the People. History of the Land Troubles in Tulare and Fresno Counties. The Grasping Greed of the Railroad Monopoly. By the Settlers' Committee*. Visalia: Visalia Delta Book and Job Print, 1880.

Shinn, Charles Howard. *Mining Camps, A Study in American Frontier Government*. New York: Scribner, 1885. This is the most authoritative work available on the organization and government of the mining camps in California.

——. See also *History of Co-operation in the United States.*

Soule, Frank, et al. *The Annals of San Francisco.* New York: D. Appleton and Co., 1855.

Taylor, Bayard. *Eldorado.* New York and London: G.P. Putnam, Richard Bentley, 1850.

Thompson, Thomas H. *Official Historical Atlas Map of Tulare County.* Tulare: Author, 1892. The maps in this book were made by the author after a personal survey and a personal examination. It also contains biographical sketches of early residents. This county history is now very rare and valuable.

Tinkham, George H. *California Men and Events; Time 1769-1890.* Stockton: Printed by the Record Publishing Co., 1915.

——. *History of Stanislaus County.* Los Angeles: Historic Record Company, 1921. The official history of the county; contains biographical and historical sketches of the leading pioneers.

Treadwell, Edward F. *The Cattle King.* New York: Macmillan, 1931. A dramatized biography of Henry Miller, the dominant member of the Miller & Lux cattle firm.

Tuolumne County Chamber of Commerce. *Folder for 1930.*

Vandor, Paul E. *History of Fresno County.* 2 vols. Los Angeles: Historic Record Co., 1919. The author, very much in love with his subject, has collected a vast amount of data which is valuable for those who search after facts.

Weeks, Geo. F. *California Copy.* Washington, D.C.: Washington College Press, 1928.

Wiltsee, Ernest Abram. *The Pioneer Miner and the Pack-Mule Express.* San Francisco: California Historical Society, 1931.

Wister, Owen. Roosevelt: *The Story of a Friendship, 1880-1919.* New York: Macmillan, 1930. This study of political conditions in the United States contains the reactions of Roosevelt to the conditions prevailing in the San Joaquin Valley about 1880.

II. Other Evidence

A. Manuscripts:

1. Spanish-Era Diaries and Letters: Practically all the material in Chapter III is drawn from the writings of the men who personally went into the San Joaquin in search of neophytes. The Franciscan friars who accompanied the expeditions kept diaries, which are invaluable in studying that period.

Alvarado, Juan Bautista. *Historia de California.* 5 volumes. Copy in the Bancroft Library, Berkeley, California.

Cabot, Father Juan. "Expedicion al Valle do los Tulares, 1814." *Papeles Miscelaneos,* Santa Barbara Archives, VI, 67-72.

Martín, Father Juan. "Visita de los Gentiles Tulareños, 1804." *Papeles Miscelaneos,* Santa Barbara Archives, VI, 85-89.

Martínez, Father Luis. "Entrada a las Ranchería del Tular, 1816." *Archivo del Arzobispado de San Francisco,* III (1), 42-45.

Muñoz, Father Pedro, *Diario de la Ezpedicion hecha por Don Gabriel Moraga O los Nuevas Descrubrimientos del Tular, Sept. 21-Nov. 2, 1806.* B. C., Santa Barbara Archives, IV, 27.

Sanchez, Sergeant José, *Diario,* September 10, 1819. Copy in the Bancroft Library, Berkeley, California.

Sarria, Fr. —-, to Governor SoIá, June 10, 1816. *Archivo del Archbispado de San Francisco,* No. 507.

Smith, Jedediah to Father Narciso Durán, May 19, 1827, *Departmental State Papers,* Mss., II, 17-19.

Viader, Father Juan. "Diario de una Entrada al Río de San Joaquin, Octobre 19, 1810." *Documentos para la Historia de California,* IV, 207-212.

Zalvidea, Father Jose Maria. "Diario de una Expedicion, Tierra Adentro, 1806." *Papeles Miscelaneos,* Santa Barbara Archives, VI, 50-58.

2. Modern-Era Manuscripts:

Kings River Water Association, *Administrative Agreement.*

McCubbin, John C. *The 76 Land & Water Company.*

3. Personal Letters to the Author: My file shows about three thousand letters, which are answers to direct questions concerning phases of valley history. Those cited in the text are listed below.

Bellue, Margaret K. Manuscript Letter, Sacramento, October 18, 1933. [Weed and Seed Botanist, California Department of Agriculture, on the introduction of Bermuda grass to the San Joaquin Valley.]

Bergen, L.B. Manuscript Letter, San Francisco, January 10, 1938. [Official of the Visalia Stock Saddle enterprise, giving historical background on the company.]

Bondesen, Annie L. Manuscript Letter, Madera, September 25, 1931. Mrs. Bondesen was personally acquainted with some of the early cattlemen in the San Joaquin, including Henry Miller, and conveyed some of that information.

Bush, E.E. Manuscript Letter, Hanford, October 29, 1931. The writer was one of the organizers of Kings County and was present at Kingston when Vasquez held up that river town in 1873.

Brown, May. Manuscript Letter, Earlimart, March 10, 1932. The postmistress at Earlimart furnished information concerning the site of the quondam city of Alila.

Clarke, Frank. Manuscript Letter, Goshen, January 23, 1932. A nephew of Crawford W. Clarke, whose position as a cattleman in the San Joaquin was only surpassed by James Haggin and Henry Miller.

Coughran, Neva Rea. Manuscript Letters, Kingsburg, September 4 and October 16, 1931. A daughter of Francis Rea, one of the pioneer stockmen along Kings River.

Crane, Horace. Manuscript Letter, Turlock, October 6, 1931. Mr. Crane was secretary-treasurer of the Fin-de-Siecle Investment Company, which handled the sale of the John Mitchell estate.

Crow, C.C. Manuscript Letter, Hanford, September 3, 1931. A son of Walter J. Crow, one of the chief actors in the battle of Mussel Slough.

Daingerfield, Elizabeth, Manuscript Letter, Lexington, Kentucky, Nov. 26, 1930. Superintendent at Haylands (at that time the home of Man-o'-War).

Dalton, Emmett. Manuscript Letter, Hollywood, October 2, 1931. The only survivor of the famous outlaw band has answered questions which clear up certain obscure points.

Dow, Richard, Manuscript Letter, Hanford, January 10, 1938. [Origins of chop suey in the United States.]

Draper, Mrs. Frank (Florence Livermore Draper). Manuscript Letter, Kingsburg, September 24, 1931. [Account of Tiburcio Vasquez's visit to the author's home.]

Eichbaum, W. P., Manuscript Letter, Glen Ellen, Sonoma County, California, February 15, 1938. [Early history of irrigation water pumping in San Joaquin Valley.]

Erikson, Andrew, Manuscript Letter, Kingsburg, September 30, 1931. [Reminiscences of the early settlement of Kingsburg.]

Fink, Kenneth. Manuscript Letter, Crow's Landing, November 12, 1931. The secretary of the Chamber of Commerce furnished material concerning the early cattlemen in the Orestimba region of Stanislaus County.

Forney, John, Manuscript Letter, Kingsburg, Sept. 30, 1931. [Comments on Kingsburg resident Samuel E. Moffett.]

Fowler, T.W. Letter-Bulletin, Merced, October 12, 1931 [Concerns early history of Merced County].

Hultberg, Rev. Nels O., Manuscript Letter, Los Gatos, Nov. 9, 1931. [Early history of Turlock area.]

Johnson, Hiram. Manuscript Letters, Washington, D.C., October 9 and November 12, 1931. Senator Johnson gave his views concerning the memorable campaign of 1910 and his reasons for paroling Chris Evans.

Kern County Chamber of Commerce, Letter-Bulletin, October 10, 1931. [Cotton culture in Kern County.]

Krehbiel, Rev. H. J., Manuscript Letter, Reedley, October 8, 1931. [Religious background of Mennonite settlers in Reedley area.]

Latta, Frank F[orrest], Manuscript Letter, Tulare, Feb. 22, 1932. [Concerns history of Royal Porter Putnam and Porterville].

McClatchy, Charles K. Manuscript Letter, Sacramento, October 9, 1933. [Account of James McClatchy and his Civil War-era career].

McCubbin, John C. Manuscript Letters, Fresno, February 24, 1924, and Los Angeles, November 11, 12, 15 and December 10, 1931. This writer has the most nearly complete data on the history of the region between Fresno and Tulare counties.

McLaughlin, W. W., Manuscript Letter, Berkeley, Dec. 29, 1933. [Chief of the Division of Irrigation, United States Department of Agriculture.]

Nordstrom, Percy H., Manuscript Letter, Kingsburg, October 16, 1931. [Kingsburg postmaster, commenting on ethnic composition of area.]

Ostrom, Rev. Oscar W., Manuscript Letter, Fresno, Oct. 26, 1931. [Early settlement of Fresno County's Washington Colony.]

Patton, Lyle. Manuscript Letter, Stockton, September 6, 1931. The city engineer of Stockton defined what he considered the northern limits of the San Joaquin Valley.

Peery, Joseph S., Manuscript Letter, December 5, 1933. President, Temple Square Mission and Bureau of Information of the Church of Jesus Christ of Latter-Day Saints, Salt Lake City, Utah [Mormon emigrant trail song].

Perkins, D.E. Manuscript Letters, Visalia, September 18 and 23, 1931. Mr. Perkins arrived by stagecoach in Visalia in the 1860s. He described the original limits of the primeval oak forest and the type of wagons used in the early forms of transportation.

Porter, Florence, Manuscript Letter, Turlock, Oct. 13, 1931 [Early history of Turlock area].

Quinn, John R. Manuscript Letters, Los Angeles, December 19, 1931 and January 5, 1932. A son of the pioneer sheepman in the Delano area. Conveyed information secured from the elder Quinn.

Railsback, Sarah. Manuscript Letter, Berkeley, October 16, 1931. One of the original settlers in the Mussel Slough region.

Robertson, Dr. William. Manuscript Letter, Rochester, Minnesota, March 1, 1932. Head of the Section of Pathologic Anatomy, Mayo Clinic, and Professor of Pathology, University of Minnesota. Answer to a query concerning Joaquin Murrieta.

Schaedel, T. B., Manuscript Letter, Chicago, Illinois, October 20, 1933. Official of International Harvester Company of America.

Shafer, William H. Manuscript Letters, Selma, August 31 and September 29, 1930. Superintendent of the Consolidated Irrigation Company since 1898; has acquired an extensive knowledge of riparian rights and the fights between cattlemen and settlers.

Smith, A.A. Manuscript Letter, Oakland, September 3, 1930. Postmaster at Kingsburg from 1884-1888; now a lawyer at Oakland.

Sullivan, John L. Manuscript Letter, Hanford, September 3, October 30 1931; and January 28, 1932. A participant in the Mussel Slough fight.

Winchell, Lilbourne Alsip. Manuscript Letters, Fresno, September 21, 1930; September 5, 1931; and October 1, 1931. Settled at Millerton in the 1850s. Possesses much unpublished data concerning Fresno County.

B. Statements of Living Witnesses:

For more than twenty years it has been my hobby to collect data pertaining to the history and development of the San Joaquin Valley. Many of the older men residing in the valley possess a fund of information which is valuable to the searcher after truth. The men whose names are listed have been interviewed many times; the place of interview can be given, but not the dates. Each is recognized in his particular community as an authority on the subject upon which he was interrogated. Without their aid, this book could not have been written.

Adams, Sol G. [locomotive engineer]. Personal Interview, Calwa, November 26, 1933.

Crow, Clarence. Personal Interview, Hanford, November 16, 1934.

Draper, Lewis. Personal Interview, Burris Ranch, near Kingsburg.

Forney, John. Personal Interview, Kingsburg, December 31, 1931.

Landstrom, O. A., Personal Interview, Kingsburg, December 31, 1931. [Raisin-selling campaign of 1922.]

McCapes, Eugene L. Personal Interview, Reedley, October 15, 1933.

Porteous, James [developer of the Fresno scraper.] Personal Interview, Fresno, Sept. 26, 1933.

Rowe, William [veteran railroad section foreman]. Personal Interview, Fresno, November 11, 1933.

Shafer, William H. Personal Interview, Selma.

Sheridan, Elmer M.[developer of Orange Cove district], Personal Interview, Reedley, Sept. 20, 1933.

Smith, A. A. [see reference in above section]. Personal Interview, Oakland; July 30, 1931.

Swenson, Aaron W., Superintendent of Plant No. 25, California Packing Corporation. Personal Interview, Oakland, February 28, 1932.

Winchell, Lilbourne Alsip. Personal Interview, Fresno.

Index

847